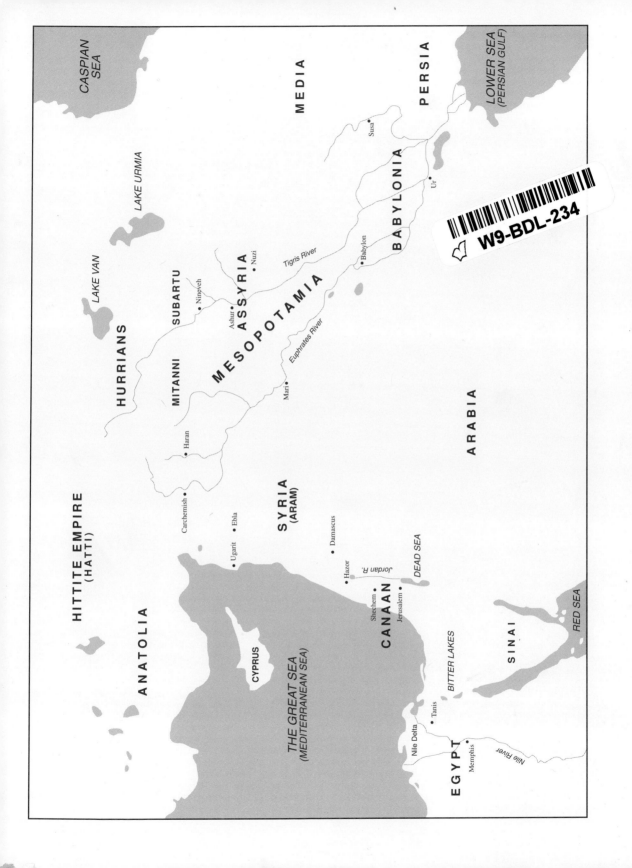

CASPIAN SEA

LAKE URMIA

LAKE VAN

MEDIA

PERSIA

LOWER SEA
(PERSIAN GULF)

Susa

BABYLONIA

Ur

W9-BDL-234

HURRIANS

SUBARTU

MITANNI

Nineveh

Ashur

ASSYRIA

Nuzi

Tigris River

Babylon

MESOPOTAMIA

Euphrates River

Mari

Haran

HITTITE EMPIRE
(HATTI)

Carchemish

Ebla

SYRIA
(ARAM)

Ugarit

Damascus

ARABIA

Hazor

Jordan R.

DEAD SEA

CANAAN

Shechem

Jerusalem

ANATOLIA

CYPRUS

THE GREAT SEA
(MEDITERRANEAN SEA)

BITTER LAKES

SINAI

RED SEA

Tanis

Nile Delta

EGYPT

Memphis

Nile River

www.wadsworth.com

wadsworth.com is the World Wide Web site for Wadsworth Publishing Company and is your direct source to dozens of online resources.

At wadsworth.com you can find out about supplements, demonstration software, and student resources. You can also send e-mail to many of our authors and preview new publications and exciting new technologies.

wadsworth.com
Changing the way the world learns®

READING THE OLD TESTAMENT

An Introduction to the Hebrew Bible

SECOND EDITION

BARRY L. BANDSTRA

HOPE COLLEGE

Wadsworth Publishing Company

I(T)P® An International Thomson Publishing Company

Belmont, CA • Albany, NY • Boston • Cincinnati • Johannesburg • London • Madrid • Melbourne
Mexico City • New York • Pacific Grove, CA • Scottsdale, AZ • Singapore • Tokyo • Toronto

Editor: Peter Adams
Assistant Editor: Kerri Abdinoor
Editorial Assistant: Mindy Newfarmer
Media Editor: Jennifer Burke
Marketing Manager: Dave Garrison
Project Editor: Cathy Linberg
Print Buyer: Barbara Britton
Permissions Editor: Susan Walters

Production: Thomas E. Dorsaneo
Designer: Lisa Berman
Copy Editor: Patti Picardi
Cover Design: Carolyn Deacy Design
Cover Photo: Israel Antiquities Authority
Compositor: Seventeenth Street Studios
Printer: RR Donnelly, Crawfordsville
Cover Printer: Phoenix Color

For permission to use copyrighted material, grateful acknowledgment is made to the copyright holders on pp. 560–561, which are hereby made part of this copyright page.

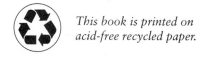

This book is printed on acid-free recycled paper.

For more information, contact Wadsworth Publishing Company, 10 Davis Drive, Belmont, CA 94002, or electronically at http://www.wadsworth.com

International Thomson Publishing Europe
Berkshire House
168-173 High Holborn
London, WC1V 7AA, United Kingdom

Nelson ITP, Australia
102 Dodds Street
South Melbourne
Victoria 3205 Australia

Nelson Canada
1120 Birchmount Road
Scarborough, Ontario
Canada M1K 5G4

International Thomson Publishing Southern Africa
Building 18, Constantia Square
138 Sixteenth Road, P.O. Box 2459
Halfway House, 1685 South Africa

International Thomson Editores
Seneca, 53
Colonia Polanco
11560 México D.F. México

International Thomson Publishing Asia
60 Albert Street
#15-01 Albert Complex
Singapore 189969

International Thomson Publishing Japan
Hirakawa-cho Kyowa Building, 3F
2-2-1 Hirakawa-cho, Chiyoda-ku
Tokyo 102 Japan

Library of Congress Cataloging-in-Publication Data

Bandstra, Barry L.
    Reading the Old Testament : an introduction to
the Hebrew Bible / Barry L. Bandstra — 2nd ed.
        p. cm.
    Includes bibliographical references and indexes.
    ISBN 0-534-52727-2
    1. Bible. O.T. — Introductions. I. Title.
BS1140.2.B32   1999
221.6'1—dc21
                              98–35207

To Debra, Adam, Jonathan, and Daniel

CONTENTS

PREFACE

The Old Testament, or in the Judaic tradition, the Hebrew Bible, is an antique book and we need help reading it. *Reading the Old Testament* introduces the kinds of help that are available, and teaches how to read the text by modeling the process. My goal for this second edition remains the same as for the first: to survey the content of the Old Testament and illustrate how modern discoveries can enrich our understanding of the biblical text. To achieve my goal I have shaped a book that follows these seven guiding principles.

1. *To read the biblical text, not just read about it.* Our focus is on reading the actual text of the Bible. To reinforce the centrality of the text I include sizeable portions of the Bible right in the book. These then become the starting point for interpretive comments that clarify and draw out the meaning of the text.

2. *To teach the story line of the Bible.* An important outcome of our study must be to know the story line and event sequence of the Old Testament. To that end each chapter begins with a section that summarizes the course of events. The chapter summary of each chapter's study guide also provides an overview. And the introductory chapter entitled "The Biblical Story" provides a quick survey of biblical history from earliest times to the common era.

3. *To illustrate the process of interpretation.* There are a variety of analytic and interpretive methods available to readers of the Bible. These include an analysis of biblical forms of speech and their origins in the life of the community, discovery of underlying oral and written sources of biblical books, explanation of the literary architecture of texts, and analysis of the editorial composition of books. Certainly not all of these methods can be applied to every text, but enough examples are given over the course of this book that the most widely used methods of biblical specialists are demonstrated in action.

4. *To present classical scholarship as well as current trends.* There are certain approaches, such as the documentary hypothesis of the Pentateuch, that are so widely practiced and referred to in scholarship that they have to be explained. Yet the field of biblical studies is dynamic and constantly changing. I acquaint readers with standard methods as well as new discoveries and emerging theories. Newer forms of literary analysis as well as

modern archaeological discoveries increasingly make the text more understandable. These insights are applied where appropriate, and the bibliographies to each chapter include both classical scholarship and up-to-date research.

5. *To respect the wholeness of the biblical text.* Many of the analytic tools at our disposal concentrate on small units of text. For example, source analysis sometimes demonstrates how the first half of a verse was written by a different author than the second half. If these were the only tools employed we might get the impression that authorities only dissect the text and leave it in pieces. There are other approaches that focus on the themes and literary structures that shape whole texts, and these too must be appreciated. I introduce and employ both analytic and synthetic methods of analysis. Each chapter has a section that gives an account of the wholeness of that book or section.

6. *To provide learning tools that enable the reader to master the Bible.* A variety of components, especially those available on the CD, provide reinforcement of the content of the biblical books. These include lists of key names and terms linked to the glossary, concept questions that review the content as well as stimulate further thinking, and comprehensive self-grading progress tests.

7. *To demonstrate how the Bible itself models the creative tension between tradition and change.* The composition process of the Old Testament as revealed by modern study displays how the books of the Hebrew Bible arose as a dynamic response to critical issues in the life of God's people. The writers were people of faith who were shaped by the traditions of the community and who reshaped those traditions to nurture and support the community of faith. These materials are more than just literature. They are writings of spiritual and religious significance that continue to be revered by people of faith within Judaism, Christianity, and Islam. And they continue to have the power to inspire and shape faith.

On the one hand, the Old Testament speaks clearly and directly to the reader's heart. Its cherished stories of heroes and villains need no scholar's interpretation. No one needs to explain the courage of a David downing Goliath in order for us to appreciate it. Without a scholar's commentary everyone immediately understands the fear of a Moses avoiding God's call to deliver the Hebrew slaves of Egypt.

But on the other hand, there are dimensions of the Bible that can only be understood after a closely researched reading. Why do there seem to be two creation stories in Genesis? Who exactly was the Satan of the book of Job? Why is Israel's history told twice, once in Kings and again in Chronicles? A close reading of the biblical text, informed by the best information gleaned from studying the ancient world and disciplined by the best methods of modern scholarship, cannot help but enrich our appreciation of the Old Testament. For this reason I wrote *Reading the Old Testament* and created its accompanying CD.

What's New in the Second Edition?

The basic plan of the second edition follows that of the first. The canonical order of books according to the Hebrew canon remains the organizing principle, and chapters still follow the threefold division of the Tanak into Torah, Prophets, and Writings. The only notable departure from this principle comes with the Book of the Twelve, also called the Minor Prophets, which are reordered and treated in groups according to their chronological order.

Certain material of the first edition was reorganized for purposes of clarity. The first three chapters covering the books of Genesis and Exodus were completely reshaped. Rather than following a source analysis agenda the chapters of these biblical books are treated in serial order from beginning to end. This brings these three chapters more in line with the way the other biblical books are treated. Coverage of Genesis and Exodus was also made more comprehensive. Another change: whereas the first edition had a prologue and an epilogue to each of the three sections, the second edition simplifies this into just an introduction to each.

The target audience of this edition remains the same as the first, a university student at the undergraduate level. It is a struggle to keep the text appropriately concise for such readers; the text all too easily takes on a life of its own and tries to inflate itself to encyclopedic dimensions. Such inflation is hard to resist because the most interesting features of the text are often drawn out only by detailed linguistic analysis and cultural history. The second edition tries to strike a compromise by marking commentary that goes beyond the essentials. These in-depth comments are identified by their indentation and a smaller typeface. Students should know that they can skip these more technical discussions and still get a general account of the biblical book at hand.

The biggest change in this edition is the inclusion of a CD that contains the entire textbook coordinated with and cross-referenced to the print edition. The print edition signals the presence of additional materials that can only be found on the CD. The CD contains a variety of tables, charts, and graphics that provide supplemental study material. Extensive bibliographies for each chapter are also now found on the CD. Each chapter has a study guide that includes a chapter summary, concept questions, and a self-graded progress test. In addition, the entire text of the New Revised Standard Version of the Bible is on the CD. It can be read off the CD, and it is linked to the textbook for ease of retrieval. This innovation marks a new departure from traditional textbooks, and I hope that it will prove to be an effective aid in studying the biblical text, which after all remains the focus of our interest and attention.

Acknowledgments

The completion of the second edition needed the gifts of time and place. I wish to thank Hope College for the gift of time that came by way of a sabbatical leave of absence. The Oxford Centre for Hebrew and Jewish Studies in Yarnton, England provided the gift of place. There I was able to carry on writing in a setting that jealously protects a scholar's peace. Special thanks to Bernard Wasserstein and Joan Sinclair for their hospitality.

Outside readers were very helpful in shaping the book and I owe them a debt of gratitude. Reading the first edition were Bernhard F. Batto, DePauw University; Rosalie Beck, Baylor University; Peter J. Haas, Vanderbilt University; Ralph Neall, Union College; John Priest, Florida State University; and Sharon Pace Jeansonne, Marquette University. Reading the second edition were John Barclay Burns, George Mason University; Marilyn Lundberg, University of Southern California; and John Modschiedler, College of DuPage.

The editorial staff at Wadsworth Publishing Company was entirely supportive. Peter Adams, senior editor, is not only a discerning critic and benevolent taskmaster, he is also a dear friend. Thank you, Peter, for many things but especially for encouraging me to develop the CD version. The project team of Jennifer Burke, Thomas E. Dorsaneo, Cathy Linberg, and Patti Picardi was outstanding.

Lastly comes the most pleasant task of all—thanking those who were closest to me from beginning to end. The work would never have been finished without the loving support and active contributions of Debra, Adam, Jonathan, and Daniel. Each of you helped in specific ways, but most importantly you loved me in spite of the project. For that you have my enduring gratitude, and to you I dedicate this book.

READING THE OLD TESTAMENT

An Introduction to the Hebrew Bible

INTRODUCTION

Key Terms

Ancient Middle East
Apocrypha
B.C.E. / C.E.
Canaan
Canon
Elohim
Fertile Crescent
Genre
Hebrew
Hebrew Bible
Israel
Israeli
Israelite
Jew
Ketuvim
LORD
Mesopotamia
Nevi'im
Old Testament
Palestine
Septuagint
Tanak
Tetragrammaton
Torah
Yahweh
YHWH

FIGURE 1   DAVID BY DONATELLO   David was one of the admirable heroes of the Old Testament. The stories of the Bible have inspired some of the great artistic works of Western culture.

The Bible is the single most important book in the history of the Western world, and it continues to be a perennial bestseller. The focus of our study is the first portion of the Bible, the Old Testament, also referred to as the Hebrew Bible. As sacred scripture for three of the world's great religions, Judaism, Christianity, and Islam, it is fundamental and continues to be revered. Full of rich tales, shining heroes, and even more colorful villains, it has inspired some of the world's greatest works of art, music, and literature. An informed acquaintance with the Old Testament befits every knowledgeable person, as it is intertwined with the course of culture in both East and West. But it is also a deeply religious book and can speak to one's heart, stirring the imagination and the soul.

WRITING AND READING RTOT

Reading the Old Testament (RTOT) is intended for students who wish to learn the Bible by reading the Bible. This may sound facetious, but it is not intended to be. After all, sometimes we find it easier to study a difficult text by reading about it rather than by reading the work itself. This is surely the case with Bible study, and multitudes of books are readily available that summarize and distill the biblical text down to easy morsels.

RTOT takes a different approach. It incorporates sizable chunks of the biblical text right within the textbook. Admittedly, portions of the biblical text are summarized because we cannot include them all, but significant passages are presented along with *close readings;* that is, interpretations that closely analyze the text.

RTOT takes the reader through the entire Hebrew Bible book by book, explaining the meaning of the text and making connections between yesterday and today. Along the way it draws from some of the best thinking of modern biblical scholarship in order to explain the literary shape of the text and the history in and behind it. After all, the Hebrew Bible is an ancient book, some portions are at least 3,000 years old, and we need help recovering the original meaning. Rest assured that historical and literary commentary will be specifically targeted to the text at hand. Always our goal is to increase comprehension and appreciation of the Bible, not to make a scholarly impression.

■ WHY WRITE RTOT?

Why write an introduction to the Hebrew Bible? Why write this particular one? An author might write such an introduction to the Hebrew Bible for any number of reasons, none of which this author will examine in any great depth. Reasons include its influence on religion, spirituality, church doctrine, culture, literature, and history. Suffice it to say the Hebrew Bible is such a significant book that it deserves all the attention it can get. But that attention needs to be disciplined and thoughtful and informed.

Actually the Bible gets a tremendous amount of attention in the contemporary world, but not all of it is right-headed. All too often the media connect current events to the Bible in a superficial or sensational manner—Noah's ark has been spotted! The Dead Sea Scrolls change everything! The ark of the covenant has been found!—or they disparagingly portray biblical religion as reactionary, authoritarian, and dangerous. Churches and synagogues sometimes use the Bible to support their own power rather than extend God's grace. Biblically based arguments often enter the debate on issues of public policy, such as gender and family issues, abortion and reproductive rights, gay rights, cosmology and science, and ecology. What is truth and what is fiction?

Perhaps today more than ever there is a need to understand the Bible. Not what others claim about the Bible, but what the Bible itself says and means. To be responsible world citizens we need to be able to analyze and critique how others draw upon biblical authority; and as we turn to the Bible we need to do it responsibly. This introduction teaches you to read the biblical text appropriately. Along the way it exposes you to the many and varied factors that affect interpretation, as well as methods to understand them.

Now, why was this particular introduction written? Maybe all textbook authors get started because they think they can do it better. Then they find out how difficult it is to get it right. This author wanted a textbook for his students that provided three things: the thread of the biblical story line, significant exposure to the biblical text itself, and serious practice in modern interpretive methods.

■ RTOT AND THE CD

This print edition of *Reading the Old Testament* is accompanied by a CD that augments the learning experience. The CD contains the entire print edition in a readable format. It includes a variety of components that would be impossible to include in the print edition, including an interactive study guide and the complete biblical text linked to references in RTOT. The CD also contains additional full-color graphics, explanatory notes, tables, and other enhancements. The print edition calls attention to these features throughout the chapters at relevant points.

■ NOTES TO READERS

All translations of the Hebrew Bible included in the body of the text are the author's, unless otherwise noted. Gender-inclusive language is used throughout the textbook, but not when referring God in the translations and discussions. The author acknowledges the ungendered nature of God and in principle endorses the use of inclusive language, but the translations here strictly follow the original text, which used male-gendered forms in reference to God. Let the reader make the transition to the God who transcends gender. Apart from references to the deity, inclusive language is elsewhere used where appropriate when translating the text. The spelling of personal and place names follows the NEW REVISED STANDARD VERSION of the Bible.

The following notes contain suggestions for how students and teachers can benefit from using RTOT and its accompanying CD.

To Students

RTOT was written for you. Inspired by my students, it has been informed by many years of teaching a college-level introductory course in biblical literature. Here are some suggestions for getting the most out of it.

This textbook examines the Hebrew Bible by quoting passages from the Bible and then interpreting them. Take the time to read these passages, and read them closely. The maps, historical explanations, illustrations, and textual commentaries are designed to help you comprehend specific texts of the Hebrew Bible, not substitute for reading the text itself. Each chapter incorporates the following components, all designed to aid you in studying the Hebrew Bible.

Key Terms. At the beginning of each chapter is a list of key names and terms for that chapter. Each term is in boldface where it is defined in the chapter. By looking over this list before you read the chapter you can alert yourself to the main characters and concepts you should end up knowing. The list can also be used to study before tests and quizzes. The glossary near the end of the textbook contains the names and terms from each chapter, along with their definitions.

In-Depth. Some explanatory notes have been set apart, and are indented and set in smaller type. These often include source analysis, or technical and archaeological detail. You can gloss over these paragraphs without missing any of the essentials of the story line. The content of these notes is not included in study guide questions or test items. They are provided to enrich your appreciation of the text.

Concept Questions. Each chapter includes questions to help you identify and review the main themes of that chapter. In addition, open-ended questions raise issues suitable for discussion.

For Further Study. At the end of each chapter is a short selection of books that can be used to study the material of that chapter in more depth. The resources included in these sections were chosen because they are especially understandable to students. The CD contains more complete bibliographies for each chapter, and you might want to check these if you have been asked to write an essay or interpretation paper.

To Teachers

RTOT was designed first and foremost to teach students how to read the biblical text. Although it treats literary issues throughout, it is not a "Bible as Literature" textbook. Although it utilizes historical research and reconstructs Israelite history, it is not a "History of Israelite Religion" textbook.

The overall approach of the textbook is this: beginning with actual biblical passages, it teaches how to draw out meaning by doing close readings of the text. Significant, sometimes lengthy, portions of the biblical text are included in the textbook for two reasons. First, by including biblical texts in the textbook, it is easier to follow the textual interpretations. Second, by including biblical texts right in the textbook, it is more likely that students will actually read those portions of primary material. Students often read a textbook but not the assigned biblical readings because it is more difficult to read the Bible itself, and the textbook summarizes the main points anyhow.

As RTOT develops the meaning of specific texts, it draws upon history, archaeology, and literature. It intends to do this not in isolation, but in order to explain something in the biblical text. It intends to show how the ancillary disciplines of history, archaeology, literary criticism, and linguistics can be used to inform a reading of the text. This approach teaches students *how* to interpret biblical texts properly by modeling the process. The long-term goal is to equip students to handle the Bible correctly, so that after the course they can evaluate how others read the text and can apply appropriate methods in their own reading.

RTOT also introduces modern critical methodologies in a practical way, by using them where appropriate to interpret texts. By the end of the course students will have practiced using source analysis, form-critical analysis, reader-response criticism, canonical interpretation, and more.

RTOT is appropriate for beginning students of the Hebrew Bible and is targeted at the freshman-sophomore university level. It can be used in Old Testament/Hebrew Bible courses whether they are organized by literature or history. If by literature, you would assign chapters as you cover specific books of the Bible. If by history, you would probably assign chapters as they correspond to the period of history you are covering.

RTOT is organized into three main sections, according to how the books of the Hebrew Bible have been grouped in the Jewish tradition. Each section has an introduction to draw attention to broad issues and matters that affect the collection as a whole. Special pedagogical components of the textbook are as follows:

Chapter Introductions. The introductions to each chapter establish functional and thematic parallels between the world of the biblical text and the present world. These parallels draw students into the material and suggest ways in which the ancient biblical text provides perspectives and articulates values that may be of service today.

The Biblical Story and the Story Line. If students get nothing else out of the course, at least they should know the main characters and the plot. This is encouraged in two ways. First, the chapter following this introduction summarizes the history of the Hebrew Bible, and in a general way relates the story line to the book traditions in which it is found. Then, for each chapter of Israel's primary history (Genesis through Kings) there is a summary of the story line of that biblical book.

Maps. Maps are generously distributed throughout, and are customized to illustrate specific moments in biblical history.

Time Lines. These, too, are frequently supplied because special efforts are needed to correlate literature, history, and text.

Concept Questions. The Questions for Review may be useful for testing your students' comprehension of the chapter, and are especially useful for review before tests. The Questions for Reflection and Discussion get students to think beyond the bounds of the chapter by suggesting ways the material may relate to issues with which they can identify. In addition to their use in a review or discussion setting, these questions make good topics for term papers.

Study Guide. Each chapter has a corresponding interactive study guide on the CD that contains a chapter summary; a list of the key terms with links to the glossary; the concept questions with answer links; and a battery of progress tests with true/false, multiple choice, matching, and identification components. Each component explains the correct answer after each test item. The progress test automatically scores students' performance and includes a printable score sheet. The study guides can be an effective means of student review, and score sheets could even be required as proof that students have worked through assigned chapters.

For Further Study. Appended to each chapter are suggestions of readings pertinent to topics within that chapter. The works are briefly described, and were deliberately chosen because they should be understandable to students at the beginning to intermediate level. The chapter bibliographies on the CD are more comprehensive, and many contain the table of contents of that book. These will be especially useful to students as they search for monographs to use in their term paper research.

Resources for Old Testament Study. The CD includes a classified bibliography of additional study resources. In addition to providing bibliographic information on individual books of the Old Testament, it can be used to introduce biblical research in general because it explains the various types of study tools available to students.

RTOT CD. The CD contains a number of resources that are useful in a classroom setting. Maps can be projected or printed to supplement lectures. Many of the tables contain summaries of textual data that might inspire reflection on the biblical text. A ready reference to the maps, tables, and other supplements are in the table of contents to each chapter on the CD under "Resource List."

WHAT IS THE OLD TESTAMENT?

This is a fairly basic question, but not an easy one to answer. The Old Testament could be any of a number of different things depending on who you are.

■ HEBREW BIBLE, OLD TESTAMENT, TANAK

If your frame of reference is the Jewish tradition, the Old Testament is the collection of sacred writings from ancient Israel and is called the **Hebrew Bible** or Hebrew Scriptures, or Written Torah (to distinguish it from the Oral Torah of the rabbis).

If your frame of reference is the Christian tradition, the Hebrew Bible is referred to as the **Old Testament**—*old* because Christians view it as the indispensable prologue to the New Testament. Recently some people have suggested the use of Older Testament or First Testament in order to avoid any suggestion that it is obsolete. The Hebrew Bible and the Old Testament may contain the same collection of books depending on which Christian Bible you are using, though the sequential order of individual books may differ. Though the title of this textbook refers to this collection of texts as the Old Testament (because this is the more recognizable term), the textbook more frequently refers to it as the Hebrew Bible. The latter term is increasingly being used in academic and religious circles because of its non-sectarian quality.

From another angle, the Old Testament could be many different things depending on why and how you are reading it. Viewed as literature, the Old Testament is a rich and varied collection of poetry, drama, story, and legal prose. Viewed linguistically, it is an ancient text written in foreign tongues, mostly Hebrew, but also with some Aramaic. Viewed as history, it provides a wealth of information about the culture and times of ancient Israel. Viewed as sacred text, it reveals Israel's concept of God and communicates spiritual truth. Although the Old Testament can be apprehended in a variety of ways, all make reference to the same collection of texts.

This next observation is potentially confusing. The Hebrew Bible is one book, judging by the fact that it is typically bound as a single volume. At the same time, it is an anthology of books—a virtual library of twenty-four originally separate works. In fact, the term Bible derives from the Greek *ta biblia* (itself from *biblion*, "papyrus") which means "the books." The individual books came from a variety of authors who wrote over a span of one thousand years or more. They were gathered together and included in a single work we call the Hebrew Bible. Early God-fearing Jews judged this particular collection of writings to contain an authoritative record of God's instruction for their community.

The Jewish community that gave rise to the Hebrew Bible divided the various books into three collections: the Law, the Prophets, and the Writings. The Hebrew names of these collections are **Torah, Nevi'im,** and **Ketuvim.** Taking the first letter of each of these three words, and inserting the vowel "a," the Jewish community gave the name **Tanak** (sometimes also spelled "Tanakh") to their Bible. RTOT takes its basic structure from these three main collections of the Hebrew Bible and uses the labels Torah, Prophets, and Writings.

■ CANONS

A final authoritative collection of books is called a **canon.** This implies that other books were available but were not chosen. The biblical canon institutionalizes the choices that were made. There were, in fact, many more Jewish writings, written in both Hebrew and Greek, circulating within the Jewish community before the common era. But the Jewish community came to accept only a certain number of books as the ones through which they believed God spoke. These they treated as divinely inspired books.

But not all Jews accepted the limits of this particular collection called the Hebrew Bible. There were many Jews living outside the territory of Palestine in what were largely Greek-speaking areas, called the Dispersion or the Diaspora. The Jewish communities of the Diaspora, especially the one in Alexandria, Egypt, were literarily productive, and had their own ideas of what should be included in the canon. They had come to revere other books in addition to those included in the canon recognized in Palestine.

The additional materials, some complete books, others just appendixes, are known as the **Apocrypha.** They are accepted as part of Scripture by the Roman Catholic and Orthodox churches. The Greek canon, which includes the Apocrypha, is called the **Septuagint** (often abbreviated by Roman numerals LXX, referring to the seventy-some Israelite elders who translated the Hebrew Bible into Greek). Protestant churches, along with the Jewish community, deny the authority of the apochryphal books and instead accept the more restricted Hebrew Bible of Palestinian Judaism.

Table 1 lists the differing canons of the major faith traditions.

Traditionally Jews and Christians have traced the origin of the Bible to God. The doctrine of biblical inspiration affirms that the very words of the biblical text in some significant way came directly from God. Using human agents, God "inscripturated" his word for humankind. Whatever one's view of the inspiration of the biblical text, all students of the text would agree that the text was also delivered through human agency.

Many groups and individuals were responsible for handing down the material contained in the Old Testament and for giving the individual books their final shape. Most remain nameless to this day. Even the books of identifiable prophets such as Isaiah and Amos were not entirely written by those men. The books are collections of their sayings, which anonymous editors gathered together and annotated.

Much of the material that eventually was included in the Hebrew Bible started out as folktales, songs, and religious liturgies. The common people inherited these stories and passed them on from one generation to the next by word of mouth. Oral tradition, as it is called, was the source of many of the stories that have survived about Israel's ancestors and early history. Priests and highly trained scribes, typically employed by the king, were virtually the only ones able to read and write. They were responsible for gathering materials from oral and written sources, organizing them, and compiling them into books. Probably the earliest that any books were written down was around 950 B.C.E. during the reign of Solomon, the king of Israel at its golden age.

The Hebrew Bible took centuries to shape. After individual books were completed, they were joined into collections of books. The earliest collection was the Torah. It was given its overall shape sometime during the Babylonian exile and was accepted as authoritative by 400 B.C.E. The Torah was followed by the Prophets, which was finalized around 200 B.C.E. After the Writings were added to these, the Tanak was completed around 100 C.E., as reflected in a conference of rabbis meeting at Jamnia. Though the process was in fact much more complicated than the above summary implies, the Hebrew Bible as we know it today became a fixed collection after a long period of growth and development.

INTERPRETING THE OLD TESTAMENT

Reading has never been as simple as it seems, especially when it comes to the Bible. The process of reading is always governed by a theory, conscious or unconscious, of how a text should be interpreted. When we approach a text we typically have a preliminary idea of its type, as in a bookstore where volumes are arranged in fiction, biography, travel, self-help, and other categories.

Categorizing the Bible is doubly difficult. Since it is a collection of books, it is like a bookstore that has a variety of types of books. But even when we think we know which type a particular biblical book is, we may not have it right. A book that appears to be history may be in fact be historicized fiction or myth, or a poetic text may tell us something important about history.

Consequently we need to develop a perceptual awareness of the literary, historical, and thematic qualities of all the texts we examine. We will apply a number of reading perspectives to the biblical text:

- a *literary* perspective, looking for style, repetition, and cross-text allusion;
- a *linguistic* perspective, to explain the meaning of names and terms;
- a perspective from *comparative literatures,* using parallel ancient Middle Eastern documents;
- an *archaeological* perspective, using artifacts that illuminate cultural and textual features;
- an *historical* perspective, placing biblical events within their broader setting, and gleaning the history of Israel from the texts.

■ LITERARY ANALYSIS

The literary material of the Hebrew Bible is some of the most ancient of the Western literary tradition, but this does not mean it is primitive or artless. Its writers were often masterful in utilizing a rich repertoire of literary techniques, including hyperbole, metaphor, symbolism, allegory, personification, irony, wordplay, and parallelism.

Conventions differ depending on the type of literature, so we will need to develop a sensitivity to different types and styles of writing. For example, writing styles and reader expectations for historical narrative differ considerably from those of poetic hymns, and these in turn are different from the conventions of apocalyptic literature. Each type of literature, such as those just mentioned, is called a **genre**. The major genres found in the Hebrew Bible include narrative, prophecy, law, hymn, proverb, chronicle, and genealogy. We have to become "literarily literate" and alert to the conventions of these genres.

■ HISTORICAL ANALYSIS

Because the origin of the Hebrew Bible is far distant from us, we will need to recover the original historical and geographical setting of the Hebrew Bible in order to understand and appreciate it. Insofar as we are able, we must try to see the world as David, Isaiah, and Ezra saw it. Though not an easy job, it is a rewarding one. To do so we will draw upon the discoveries of generations of historians, archaeologists, and biblical scholars.

The history of Israel is intertwined with the histories of many ancient nations. In Mesopotamia, the Sumerians pioneered civilization and were followed by Babylonians, Assyrians, Hurrians, Amorites, and Arameans. In addition, the Egyptians, Hittites, Phoenicians, and Philistines interacted with Israel and were significant factors in determining the directions Israel's history was to take. Historians, on the basis of ancient documents and archaeological discoveries, have been able to reconstruct the histories of these peoples, sometimes in remarkable detail.

Some of the most amazing discoveries have been textual ones. The Rosetta stone discovered in 1801 provided the key to deciphering hieroglyphics. This opened up for interpretation the vast library of inscriptions, letters, and texts from Egypt. The Ebla tablets from Syria, dating as early as the third millennium B.C.E., even now being translated and published, are increasing our knowledge of Semitic civilizations in western Mesopotamia and Syria. Other texts, artifacts, and building structures from Ugarit, Mari, Nuzi, Nippur, and many other sites enable us to reconstruct the context for the Hebrew Bible. Some of these discoveries will be described in more detail as they are relevant to the interpretation of specific texts.

The Hebrew Bible is itself the major source for the writing of Israelite history. It contains most of the information we have available concerning the kingdoms of Israel and Judah. It has virtually the only information available about the ancestors of Israel. But we have to remember that we cannot read the Hebrew Bible as a straight record of events. It is first and foremost a literary and theological creation that was profoundly shaped by the religious and social world of the writers. While it contains records of certain events, it is not first of all historiography. In other words, it was not intended to be a chronicle of events as they happened, such as modern scientifically researched works of history are. Consequently, it can provide some historical information, but it is not, strictly speaking, history.

■ TRADITION ANALYSIS

The text of the Hebrew Bible contains the record of Israel's faith journey and its application of tradition to life. As Israel faced new historical challenges it took the faith expressions of its ancestors and reapplied them anew. Its literature is the product of a God-fearing community. The people who wrote the books of the

Bible composed them as the expression of their faith and because they believed these writings might inspire faith, courage, and understanding.

Most of the books arose at important turning points in Israel's national life. The community grounded its experience of God in their history, and believed that His commitment to them provided a certain measure of security in a threatening world. But their world never stayed the same. Empires rose and empires fell, and Israel had to adapt to the changing political and social environment. Part of the adaptation was applying the traditional promises of God to an uncertain future. From Torah to Writings, the text reveals the community's record of how they heard God speaking to them.

The Hebrew Bible is the record of a creative tension between religious tradition and the need for change. Earlier forms of tradition were embodied in early documents and we can reconstruct and examine them. These earlier documents defined truth for the community that produced them. They provided the people with religious and ideological stability, a way to understand God and his ways. But as history moved on, new interpretations and applications were needed.

These texts encapsulate a long and lively dance of interpretation and reinterpretation, the written expression of a conversation which took place over a period of a thousand years. Political and social changes within the community inspired the need for new interpretations and applications of the older authoritative texts. The older texts provided the foundation for the life of the community, and allowed for stability in the midst of changed circumstances.

Part of what we mean by tradition analysis is reading the text as the record of the faith of a community that was defined by its theological traditions and took its traditions seriously. Those traditions were authoritative, and the community depended on them as they faced the future. Old and new, stability and change, tradition and innovation, text and reinterpretation—these are the parameters that will order our reading of the theology of the Hebrew Bible. We will be "tradition archaeologists" as we peel away the strata of this dialectic between tradition and change, and in the process perhaps learn how tradition can help us face the future.

KEY NOTIONS

■ TIME

B.C.E. refers to dates Before the Common Era, what used to be called B.C. (Before Christ). C.E. refers to dates of the Common Era, what used to be called A.D. (*anno domini*, Year of our Lord). This change in terminology has been developed to divest the dating scheme of sectarian religious associations.

Remember that year dates and century dates run in reverse in B.C.E. For example, the ninth century B.C.E. is the 800s, and 850 B.C.E. is earlier than 800 B.C.E. A millennium is a thousand-year period. When talking about large blocks of time, this term is sometimes used. There are many competing systems of dates for Old Testament events and the reigns of kings. We follow the widely used chronology of Bright (1981).

Judaism has a tradition of counting years from the day of creation as determined by biblical chronology. In this tradition creation happened on October 7,

3761 B.C.E. of the Gregorian calendar. Years are designated A.M. for *anno mundi*, year of the world. Islam dates years beginning with the *hijrah* (which is the year 622 of the Western calendar).

Archaeological Periods. The science of archaeology has developed a set of designations for the major spans of time; see Table 2.

PEOPLE

It is important to use terms appropriately when referring to biblical people. Before Israel became a nation its ancestors would not have been called Israelites. Properly speaking, the ancestors were **Hebrew**. The term **Israelite** should be reserved for the people of God from the time of Moses until the time of the exile. The term **Jew** should be reserved for the descendants of the Israelites beginning with the period after the Babylonian exile of the sixth century B.C.E. when Judaism emerged. The term derives from the name of the tribe of Judah, the only tribe to survive destruction, and still applies to the descendants of Judah today. The term **Israeli** should not be applied to any biblical people. It refers to citizens of the modern state of Israel, founded in 1948.

LAND

The terms that apply to the territory of Israel's existence are varied. The name **Canaan** occurs in Mesopotamian, Egyptian, and Phoenician writings beginning around the fifteenth century B.C.E. as well as in the Bible. It refers sometimes to an area encompassing all of Palestine and Syria, and sometimes includes the entire land west of the Jordan River. The term may derive from a Semitic word meaning "reddish purple," referring either to the rich dye produced in the area or to wool colored with the dye.

The name **Palestine** refers to the area from the Mediterranean coast to the Jordan valley and from the southern Negev to the Galilee lake region in the north. The term derives from the Hebrew word *peleshet*, the land of the Philistines. After the second Jewish revolt (132–135 C.E.) the Romans adopted the name *Palaestina* for this territory. The name Palestine was revived after World War I and applied to this territory under the British Mandate. Today it has been adopted as the name of the political entity of Arab people living in this region.

The name **Israel** comes from Hebrew Bible usage, and refers both to geographical territory (*erets yisrael*, the land of Israel) and the nation state that dwelled there. Its biblical origin is the name God gave to Jacob after they wrestled (see Genesis 32:28); *yisrael* means "strives with God" or "God strives." This land is also termed "the Promised Land" in the belief that Israel's possession of the land was a divine gift. Pilgrims and the devout also refer to it as "the Holy Land," in recognition of its associations with biblical saints and religious leaders.

Israel existed both historically and geographically within the context of a larger region. When authorities refer to the old world they call it the ancient Near East. When they refer to current events in that same region they call it the Middle East. RTOT calls it the **ancient Middle East** to reinforce the reality that the

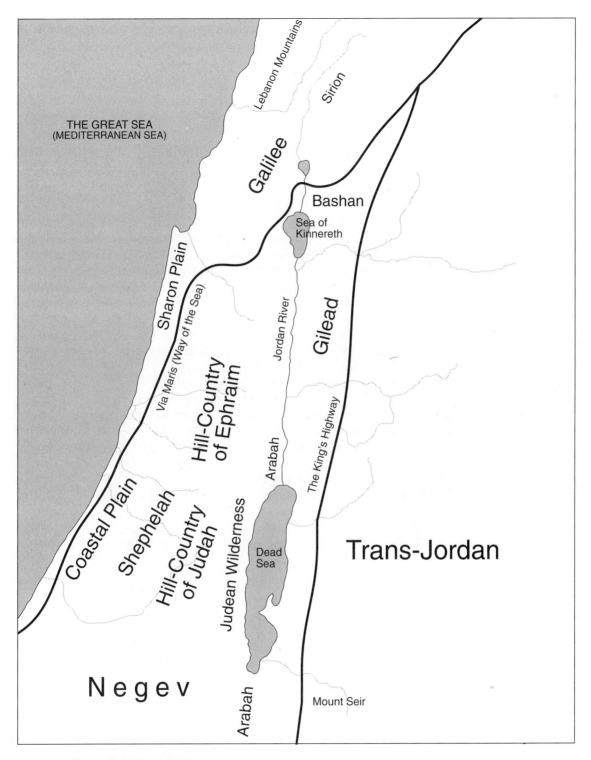

FIGURE 2 PALESTINE ROADS AND REGIONS Israel's history was in part shaped by geography. This map shows the major roads and geographical regions of Palestine.

ancient events of biblical history occurred in the same place we have come to know from our exposure to modern politics in the news.

Within the ancient Middle East there are other applicable terms. **Mesopotamia,** literally "between rivers," is the land between the Tigris River and the Euphrates River. It was home to the great Sumerian, Babylonian, and Assyrian civilizations, and is today roughly coterminous with Iraq.

The term **Fertile Crescent** refers to the half-moon-shaped inhabitable area of the ancient Middle East where civilizations thrived. This general area, in which Israel was located, has a rich and venerable history, and generated extensive literary and religious traditions.

■ DIVINE NAMES

The treatment of the divine name in English translations of the Hebrew Bible and in this textbook needs to be explained. The God of Israel was referred to in various ways. Sometimes God was just "God," or *elohim* in Hebrew. When you see "God" in the text, this typically translates **Elohim.** Other times God is referred to by his personal name, YHWH. It is rendered "Yahweh" in some versions, and "the LORD" in others. The letters "ORD" in LORD are in smaller-sized capital letters to distinguish it from the divine title "the Lord." Most modern translations of the Hebrew Bible employ this typographic convention to indicate when YHWH is the underlying Hebrew text.

The four-consonant divine name YHWH is referred to as the **tetragrammaton.** When the Hebrew text refers to **Yahweh** it uses the four consonants **YHWH** with a special configuration of vowels to signal that it should not be pronounced out loud to guard the sanctity of God's name. If the divine name is never spoken it can never be taken in vain. The name Yahweh, or Jehovah in its older pronunciation, is never spoken in Judaic contexts. In Jewish tradition the words "the LORD," *adonay* in Hebrew, are substituted for YHWH.

RTOT uses the convention of including YHWH in translated biblical quotations and the scholar's Yahweh in explanatory notes. In addition to the extensively employed terms *Elohim* and *Yahweh*, the Hebrew Bible uses other divine names such as *El Shaddai* and *El Elyon*. These will be explained in appropriate places.

THE BIBLICAL STORY

FIGURE 1 **ISHTAR GATE, BABYLON** Animals such as this lion made out of glazed bricks greeted Israelite prisoners when they entered the city of Babylon through the Ishtar gate. The Israelites suffered defeat and humiliation when they were conquered by the Babylonians in 587 B.C.E. and were forced into exile.

The biblical story moves from crisis to crisis. If it were graphed it would look like the valleys and peaks of a cardiogram. Valleys would be Israel in Egyptian and Babylonian bondage. Peaks would be the exodus from Egypt and the restoration of Judah.

The exodus and the exile are Israel's formative experiences. Both involved displacement from the Promised Land. The crisis in each case was precipitated by outside pressures from world-class empires. In fact, the whole of Israel's history is played out against the backdrop of international politics.

This chapter is a short course in the biblical story set against the history of surrounding empires. From creation to the rise of Judaism it tells the bare essentials so that our reading of Israel's literature might have a context.

When studying the Hebrew Bible, it is immensely beneficial first to get a sense of the scope and flow of history. Many of its historical books were written hundreds of years after the events they relate, so getting a sense of the historical context of composition provides helpful orientation. In addition to surveying the event history of the Bible we will place the written traditions of Israel within this event stream. The parenthetical references to chapters refer to this textbook.

The books in the Hebrew Bible are not arranged chronologically. Seeing the development of the books in relation to history will further our grasp of their meaning and intent. This introduction covers biblical history only with broad strokes. The details will come out later as we deal with individual books.

For convenience we divide history into four large-scale eras: pre-Israelite, early Israelite, monarchy, and early Judaism. There are texts in the Hebrew Bible that apply to each period. Extra-biblical documents and archaeological evidence will also enhance our understanding.

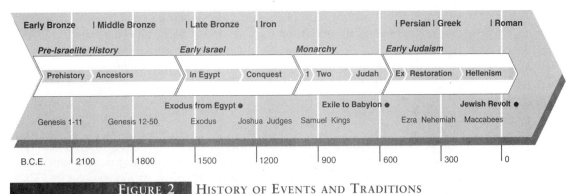

FIGURE 2   HISTORY OF EVENTS AND TRADITIONS

PRE-ISRAELITE HISTORY

The first eleven chapters of Genesis hint at the earliest ages of human life and civilization (see Chapter 1). While these chapters do not convey history in a scientific sense, they do show awareness of the momentous moves to civilization attested in anthropology and archaeology: the first construction of cities, the domestication of animals for human use, the conflict between agriculture and shepherding, the development of bronze and iron tools, and the invention of musical instruments and the fine arts.

■ PREHISTORY

Remains in caves on Mount Carmel near the Mediterranean Sea reveal the Paleolithic (Old Stone Age) presence of humans in Palestine of a type related to the Neanderthals of Europe. A later Mesolithic (Middle Stone Age) human culture of the Natufian variety has been identified at Jericho and 'Ain Mallaha.

Neolithic Period / New Stone Age (6000–4000 B.C.E.)
This period marks the transition from food gathering to food production. During this time humans gradually domesticated animals, cultivated grains, produced pottery, and built towns. Jericho developed into a sizable and fortified Palestinian settlement during this period.

Chalcolithic Period / Copper Age (40000–3200 B.C.E.)
Metal weapons and tools replaced stone implements during this period, and painted pottery became widely used. Beersheba in the Negev developed a copper-working industry, getting its ore from Sinai. The Dead Sea caves at Nahal Mishmar yielded a mass of copper ritual utensils, as well as baskets, leather, and ivory.

Early Bronze Age (32000–2000 B.C.E.)
The Bronze Age (early, middle, and late) in the ancient Middle East was a time of explosive human achievement. It also saw the development of empires. Outside

Palestine, great civilizations developed in Mesopotamia and Egypt. Both regions would have significant impact on the culture and politics of Palestine throughout Israelite history.

The Hebrew Bible retains strong memories of Mesopotamian connections. Abraham originated in Ur, one of the cities of Mesopotamia, and the twelve Hebrew clans spent many years in Egypt before the exodus. During the time of the Israelite monarchies there was much contact with the surrounding empires, mostly hostile.

Having come from the mountains of what is today Iran, the Sumerians settled in the Mesopotamian river valleys and instigated a wealth of cultural advances. They were the first to build cities and to practice irrigation agriculture. They invented writing and produced a literature that included proverbs and wisdom sayings, religious myths, heroic epics, hymns, and law codes.

Sumerian government took the form of city-states and an early form of democracy. Each was independent and controlled its surrounding countryside, each was governed by a council of elders, and all landholders had a say in decision making. But because this type of governing council was unable to cope effectively with military crises, it eventually gave way to dynastic kingship.

The Sumerians controlled the southern part of Mesopotamia, the land between the Tigris and Euphrates Rivers, until about 2400 B.C.E. After that time the Akkadians, led by Sargon of Akkad, established a Semitic empire, borrowing much of their culture from the Sumerians. Except for a resurgence of Sumerian rule for a hundred years beginning in 2050 B.C.E., the Semitic Akkadians, Babylonians, or Assyrians ruled Mesopotamia until Cyrus established the Medo-Persian empire in the sixth century B.C.E.

In Egypt, the time period corresponding to the Early Bronze Age is called the Early Dynastic period. The beginnings of the great Egyptian empire and the pyramids trace back to this time.

■ ANCESTRAL PERIOD (2000–1550 B.C.E.)

It is difficult to determine an exact date for the period of Israel's **ancestors**, the patriarchs and matriarchs. A widely held guess is that Abraham and Sarah, Isaac and Rebekah, and Jacob's family were of the Middle Bronze age, thus living sometime between 2000 and 1550 B.C.E. Historians have also placed them both earlier and later than this. Unfortunately, there is no external evidence that can confirm the existence of any of the ancestors. However, only the historical minimalists argue that they are completely fictitious.

Almost everything we know of Israel's ancestors comes from Genesis 12-50 (see Chapter 2), nothing from Mesopotamia or Egypt. From the biblical chapters they appear to have been a semi-nomadic people: Abraham traveled from lower Mesopotamia to upper Mesopotamia, then on to Canaan, and even as far as Egypt.

The God who was later identified as the God of Israel encountered Abraham and made a covenant with him that included promises of future well-being, including the inheritance of Canaan as a family homeland and the growth of the family into an international empire. The stories about Abraham and Sarah, Isaac and Rebekah, and Jacob and Rachel detail how those promises began to find fulfillment.

The Joseph story relates that the ancestral clan moved to Egypt because of a prolonged famine in Canaan. They were warmly received there because Joseph, the son of Jacob, held a high position within the Egyptian government. The family grew in number and ended up staying in Egypt for generations.

EARLY ISRAEL

The Jacob clan of Genesis becomes the nation of Israel in Exodus (see Chapter 3). The account of early Israel before the conquest of Canaan is found in Exodus, Leviticus, Numbers, and Deuteronomy. Joshua, Judges, and the early chapters of 1 Samuel provide accounts of Israel's initial efforts to secure possession of Canaan.

■ IN EGYPT AND THE EXODUS (1550–1280 B.C.E.)

After a change in Egyptian government, the attitude of the Egyptians toward the Hebrews turned sour and they enslaved them. God raised up Moses to lead the Hebrew people back to their ancestral homeland of Canaan. The Egyptians were at first reluctant to allow the Hebrews to leave but ultimately were convinced by a succession of devastating plagues sent by God. The escape from Egypt, called the **exodus**, is celebrated yearly in the Passover.

The Hebrews left Egypt around 1280 B.C.E. and were pursued by the Egyptian army. At one point it looked as if they were doomed, trapped between the chariots of Pharaoh and the deep Reed Sea. But God opened up a pathway through the sea for them to pass through, and then drowned the Egyptian army when it tried to follow. Some authorities believe the poem that celebrates this crossing (Exodus 15) is one of the oldest authentic compositions in the Hebrew Bible, though the exact nature of the crossing itself remains unclear.

The Hebrews traveled on to Mount Sinai, where God appeared to Moses and gave him the Ten Commandments. Termed the Mosaic covenant, God entered into an arrangement with them whereby he committed himself to them and they in turn agreed to obey these commandments. A variety of additional legislative codes are contained in the books of Exodus through Deuteronomy (see Chapters 3-5). They are all presented as having been revealed by God at Mount Sinai; however, close analysis reveals that they were edited and shaped by various groups at various later times in Israel's history. Some of the legal materials have significant parallels to official documents from Mesopotamia, such as the Code of Hammurabi.

Israel came into existence as a nation as a result of the events surrounding the exodus from Egypt and covenant-making on Mount Sinai. The people came together as a community, but they would still have to claim the Promised Land as their home.

■ CONQUEST AND SETTLEMENT (1280–1020 B.C.E.)

The Israelites remained in the Sinai wilderness for forty years, enough time for Moses and the original generation to die off after they disobeyed God and were denied entry into the Promised Land. Then, under the leadership of Moses' successor, Joshua, the twelve tribes penetrated Canaan in the **conquest** and began the long process of settling in (see Chapter 6). Loosely organized into a federation of tribes, there was no centralized government at this time and, after Joshua died, no overall leader. Each tribe was driven by its own interests.

Occasionally, certain gifted leaders came to the forefront, typically when there was a problem with other groups in the area. These leaders were called judges, and included Deborah, Gideon, and Samson (see Chapter 7). While certain judges did hear legal cases, typically they were military captains who organized and inspired Israelite tribal groups to defeat their enemies.

In addition to judges, priests directed the spiritual life of the people. Usually from the tribe of Levi, they managed various sacred sites throughout the land and presided over religious ceremonies, most of which involved animal sacrifices. There were rival priestly factions in Israel, and the tension among these factions gave rise to rival interpretations of Israel's history. These alternative perspectives are reflected in the different sources that underlie the Torah (see Part 1).

The most famous priest, who also happened to be a judge, was Samuel. Two books of the Old Testament are named after him. He was the most effective leader of his time. As a youth he lived in Shiloh, which was the major religious center of the twelve-tribe federation. There a tent shrine housed the ark of the covenant, the sacred chest which stored Israel's covenant documents.

The major national threat at the time of Samuel was the territorial expansion of neighboring Philistines. Around 1200 B.C.E. they settled on the coastal plain of Canaan. As they expanded westward toward the Jordan River they put pressure on the Israelites living there. Eventually, it became too much for tribal captains and regional judges to handle. The nation needed a centralized government and national leader capable of meeting the Philistine threat. Israel was on the verge of extinction until it found a king.

MONARCHY

Kingship arose in Israel as a defensive measure. It challenged traditional modes of leadership but was ultimately tolerated, if not wholly endorsed. The story of the rise of kingship is found in the books of Samuel (see Chapter 8). The books of Kings contain an account of the kings in Israel, during both the period of national unity under David and Solomon and the period of parallel monarchies in Israel and Judah after the separation (see Chapter 9). The account of kingship continues through the destruction of Israel and the conquest of Judah. A later revised account of national history comprises the books of Chronicles (see Chapter 18).

■ UNIFIED KINGDOM (1020–922 B.C.E.)

In the face of the Philistine crisis, the twelve tribes instituted a **monarchy**. Samuel, the most influential priest and prophet at that time, designated Saul from the tribe of Benjamin to be Israel's first king. Saul began his reign around 1020 B.C.E.

However, the decision to have a king was not altogether well received. There were many in Israel who felt that charismatic and *ad hoc* leadership was the godly way to go. The transition from a judge to a king came about only with great difficulty, and some people never did accept it.

Saul was, at first, an effective leader who could muster the troops to face Israel's enemies. But he lost the crucial support of Samuel when he offered an animal sacrifice before a battle, something only Israelite priests were allowed to do. For this faithless act Samuel disowned Saul and anointed young David to be king in his place.

Saul continued to reign until his death at the hands of the Philistines. After Saul died, his son Ishbosheth assumed the throne and the northern tribes accepted his authority. All the while, David was gathering support. He was acclaimed king by those who lived in the southern tribe of Judah, which was his home territory. After Ishbosheth was assassinated by men from his own court, David became king of all twelve tribes of Israel.

David was a remarkable leader and an astute politician. In order to appeal to the broadest constituency, he moved his headquarters from Hebron in Judah to the neutral site of Jerusalem. Previously belonging to the Canaanites, David captured it and made "the City of David" the administrative center of his kingdom. He also brought the ark of the covenant there, effectively transforming Jerusalem into the religious capital of the nation.

Hoping to unite the northern and southern components of his now **Unified Kingdom**, David appointed a chief priest from each region. Zadok became the chief priest from Judah, tracing his lineage back to Aaron, the brother of Moses. Abiathar became the chief priest from the north, a descendent from the priests of Shiloh where the ark of the covenant was once kept.

David effectively neutralized the enemies that had given Saul such resistance. He contained Philistia, and brought Syria, Ammon, Moab, and Edom under Israelite control. His empire stretched from the El-Arish wadi on the Sinai-Mediterranean coast to the Euphrates River in the north. During the reign of David, the territory and power of Israel was at its greatest extent ever.

But on the home front, David's sons were maneuvering to assume control, even before their father's death. A fight broke out over succession to the throne and Amnon and Absalom, two influential princes, died in the process. Then Adonijah, being one of the older remaining sons, made his move. He gained the support of David's general, Joab, and Abiathar, a chief priest.

However, Solomon was David's personal choice. Supported by Bathsheba (David's favorite wife and, not incidentally, Solomon's mother), Nathan the court prophet, and Zadok the other chief priest, Solomon won. Upon assuming the throne he had Adonijah and Joab executed and Abiathar exiled to a small town north of Jerusalem.

Solomon inherited an extensive empire and set about upgrading it to world-class standards through monumental building projects and international diplomacy. He constructed a finely adorned temple in Jerusalem for Yahweh and an even larger palace for himself. To protect his kingdom he built fortress cities around the country. In order to forge international diplomatic ties he married 700 foreign princesses.

To get the work done and pay the bills, he forced citizens of Israel to work as slaves and imposed a heavy burden of taxation on the country. This created considerable dissatisfaction among his constituency, especially those who lived in the north, who were already suspicious of the Davidic dynasty.

The stories of Saul and David can be found in the books of Samuel and an account of Solomon's reign in 1 Kings. The literature that by tradition is associated with this period includes the Psalms ascribed to David (see Chapter 14), the Proverbs of Solomon (see Chapter 15), and the Song of Songs (see Chapter 16). Many modern authorities associate the Yahwist stratum of the Torah with the period of the unified monarchy (see Part 1). The Unified Kingdom lasted through the rule of three kings: Saul, David, and Solomon. During this time the nation was magnificent, but Solomon had mortgaged its future in order to achieve greatness.

■ TWO KINGDOMS (922–721 B.C.E.)

Solomon may have died in peace but he left behind a precarious kingdom and a legacy of resentment. After his son Rehoboam took the throne, the northern leadership held a conference with him. They wanted to find out whether or not he would continue Solomon's oppressive policies. When Rehoboam refused to back down, they rebelled and opted out of the Davidic empire. Rehoboam was powerless to stop them.

In these events we see the old, fiercely independent spirit of the tribes reasserting itself. The kingdom reverted back to what it had been, a southern faction and a northern faction. Biblical historians may talk of a "United Kingdom," but while it lasted it was an unnatural alliance. It was only due to the military savvy and political genius of David that the two collections of tribes ever overcame their regional identities, put aside parochial differences, and became one kingdom.

The Northern Kingdom, now called **Israel**, chose Jeroboam to be its king. Jeroboam made Shechem his capital, the place of covenant renewal under Joshua and a city strongly associated with the tribal federation of the judges period. But Jeroboam had a serious problem: Israel, though politically independent of Judah, still worshiped Yahweh, the same god Judah worshiped. The religious practices of Yahwism were still associated with Jerusalem, the home base of the Davidic family. That was where the ark was housed, the temple was located, and the chief priest officiated. If the people had no choice but to go to Jerusalem to fulfill their religious duties, Jeroboam feared the people might develop divided loyalties.

To counter this threat he developed a version of Yahwism for Israel. He instituted alternate feast days, a new set of priests, and new religious centers. These religious centers, one at Bethel near the Judean border, and one at Dan near the northern border, housed golden bull statues which became the new symbols of divinity in Israel.

The powerful empire that once was David's no longer existed. In its place were two relatively small states, certainly insignificant compared to the empires of their day. They shared many of the same traditions and both still worshiped Yahweh, but they were different in other ways. The Elohist texts of the Torah, according to standard source analysis, come from the Northern Kingdom sometime in the ninth century (see Part 1).

Throughout its history, the Southern Kingdom of **Judah** was ruled by the Davidic family. It lasted as an independent nation until 587 B.C.E. Not so the Northern Kingdom, Israel, which never had a stable monarchy. Instead, one dynasty after another tried to establish itself, resulting in political instability. Israel only lasted as an independent nation for two hundred years. In 721 B.C.E.

it was conquered by the Assyrian empire. Much of its population was dispersed throughout Assyrian territory, but some Israelites escaped south to Judah.

The religious and civil politics of this period inspired the prophetic movement in its classical form (see Part 2). Prophets could be pro- or anti-monarchy, pro-Israelite or pro-Judean, but their unifying distinctive characteristic was the transcendent moral perspective they brought to bear on the realm of human affairs. Amos addressed issues of social justice in Israel, while Hosea exposed Israel's religious complacency (see Chapter 13).

■ JUDAH ALONE (721–587 B.C.E.)

After 721 B.C.E. Judah was the only kingdom of "Israelites" left; the territory north of Judah was now an Assyrian province. Ahaz, the Judean king at the time of Israel's demise, remained loyal to Assyria, but his son, Hezekiah, established alliances with Egypt and Babylon as a hedge against Assyria. This roused Sennacherib, king of Assyria, to mount an attack on Jerusalem in 701 B.C.E. Under mysterious circumstances Sennacherib withdrew his troops before achieving the surrender of the city. During this crisis Isaiah supported the Davidic dynasty in principle but criticized its particular rulers (see Chapter 10).

Manasseh, the next king of Judah, ruled for forty-five years, content to submit to the Assyrians and benefit from the international peace that came from the arrangement. Toward the end of his reign Assyria was on the decline, and Babylonia was gaining strength and territory. By the mid-seventh century B.C.E. things were astir in the ancient Middle East, and even Egypt was reasserting influence in Canaan.

Into this volatile situation Josiah assumed the throne in Judah. He was greeted as a David "reborn." He won back some territory in the north. He also backed a major religious reform in Judah, a reform that is intimately associated with the book of Deuteronomy. At this same time Jeremiah (see Chapter 11) and Zephaniah (see Chapter 13) challenged Judah to return to faith during its stand against mighty Babylonia.

In 622 B.C.E., during the reign of Josiah, a scroll was found in the Jerusalem temple in the course of cleaning up the sanctuary to return it to authentic Yahwistic worship. The scroll contained a collection of laws that originated in the Northern Kingdom. This scroll has been identified as the core of the present book of Deuteronomy (see Chapter 5). Called the "book of the covenant," it inspired serious Yahwistic revival in Judah, entailing sweeping political and religious changes.

Meanwhile, Nebuchadnezzar was extending Babylonian influence westward. Defeating the combined forces of Assyria and Egypt at Carchemish in 605 B.C.E., he now had access to Canaan, including Judah. Nahum gloated over the destruction of once-mighty Nineveh, the capital of Assyria (see Chapter 13).

Nebuchadnezzar captured Jerusalem in 597 B.C.E., deported its king Jehoiachin to Babylon, along with many of Jerusalem's influential citizens, and placed Zedekiah on the throne expecting him to be cooperative. When Zedekiah made an alliance with Egypt, Nebuchadnezzar returned to Jerusalem in 587 and destroyed Jerusalem, including its temple. Zedekiah was blinded and taken away captive. In a second deportation, Nebuchadnezzar took even more of Jerusalem's citizenry to Babylon, and rendered Judah incapable of challenging him again. Habakkuk agonized over a divine justice that could employ wicked Babylonia to punish God's chosen people (see Chapter 13).

EARLY JUDAISM

The destruction of Jerusalem in 587 B.C.E. initiated massive political, social, and religious changes among the survivors. The character of biblical faith and society changed markedly due to this crisis. Israel would not exist again as a sovereign state until the second century B.C.E. The disappearance of the temple from Jerusalem (and therefore the ability to offer sacrifices) initiated a reconsideration of what could constitute worship. The changes were so fundamental that the debacle of 587 marks the shift from a people called the Israelites to a people called the Jews and their faith **Judaism**.

This time also marks the beginning of a significant bifurcation within those of Israelite stock. The **exile** of thousands of Judahites to Babylonia was the start of an enduring population of Jews who live outside the Promised Land. Some would later return when given the opportunity, but many chose to remain expatriates indefinitely while retaining a Jewish identity. This amorphous group of Jews is called the Diaspora, and their lifestyle is called Diaspora Judaism. They lived in Babylonia, Persia, Syria, Anatolia, and Egypt; anywhere but in Palestine.

The Jews who continued to live in the Promised Land are called Palestinian Jews, and their lifestyle Palestinian Judaism. The character of Diaspora Judaism often differed markedly from that of Palestinian Judaism because it was more open to influences from non-Jewish culture. Palestinian Judaism was more conservative and traditional, as defined by the Hebrew Bible. There were no doubt many Jews who intermarried with non-Jews and assimilated to the local population, but they cease to be part of the mainstream biblical tradition.

■ BABYLONIAN EXILE (587–539 B.C.E.)

The demise of Jerusalem entailed major loss and massive disorientation among the Judeans. The people had lost everything which previously defined them.

1. *Independence.* Judea was now a backwater province of the Babylonian empire. It would not regain national sovereignty until the time of the Maccabees in the second century B.C.E.

2. *King.* The leader of the Davidic dynasty was unable to lead. Previously God had channeled national blessing through the house of David, but now the Davidic king was in a Babylonian prison.

3. *Temple.* The temple was the focus of their religious life, and now it, along with the royal palace and the entire city of Jerusalem, lay in ruins. The sacrifices that kept them right with God could not be offered.

4. *Land.* The Promised Land had been the preeminent evidence of God's favor, and now it was no longer in their hands. Many of those who survived the war of 587 B.C.E. had been taken captive to Babylonia, and those who remained had no resources or leadership.

But this tragedy was more than just a national defeat. According to the religious outlook of this period, each nation was protected by its patron god. Yahweh was the God of Israel, and was presumed to be the real power behind the nation. Nebuchadnezzar's victory could only imply that Marduk, the patron god of Babylon, was supreme. Israel's military defeat became a crisis of faith.

The prophetic tradition provided a frame of reference for understanding why the disaster had happened. Jeremiah in Judah (see Chapter 11) and Ezekiel in Babylonia (see Chapter 12) interpreted the events as divine judgment for the people's faithlessness to Yahweh.

The great miracle of the Babylonian exile was that faith in Yahweh did survive. Prophets such as Jeremiah and Ezekiel were instrumental in interpreting Yahweh's reason for allowing it to happen. The priestly tradition rekindled Israel's faith out of the ashes. The temple service and animal sacrifices that could not be performed in exile gave way to Sabbath worship and the study of the Torah as religious activities. A Davidic king no longer ruled, but a new sense of the kingship of Yahweh took hold. The land was lost, but circumcision became a symbol of transformed hearts whereby the faithful could enter a new spiritual kingdom.

This time of exceptional national crisis gave rise to some of the Hebrew Bible's most sublime and significant literature. The book of Lamentations (see Chapter 16) agonizes over the demise of Jerusalem. Second Isaiah (see Chapter 10) and Ezekiel (see Chapter 12) inspire hope with triumphant visions of a new glorious future. The Priestly document of the Torah (see Part 1) came out of the exile, as probably did the final form of the Torah itself. Also, sometime during the exile the final edition of the Deuteronomistic History, which consists of Joshua, Judges, Samuel, and Kings, was completed.

■ RETURN AND RESTORATION (539–333 B.C.E.)

After Nebuchadnezzar died, the Babylonian empire quickly disintegrated. In 539 B.C.E. Cyrus of Media captured Babylon without a fight. He then signed an edict allowing Judeans to go home if they wished and even supported the rebuilding of the temple in Jerusalem with royal funds. Many chose to return to Jerusalem.

The first group of refugees returned in 538 B.C.E. led by Sheshbazzar, and laid the foundations for a new temple. But life was hard and they soon abandoned the project. The second group returned in 520 B.C.E., led by Zerubbabel and the high priest Joshua. They managed to finish the temple by 515. Called the "Second Temple," this structure once again became the focus of religious devotion. The prophets Haggai and Zechariah motivated the people to complete the temple's construction (see Chapter 13). But the nature of religion had fundamentally changed from what it was before the exile.

The fifth century was a crucial time in the development of early Judaism. Nehemiah was a Jewish official of the Persian royal court. He asked the Persian king for permission to go to Jerusalem and direct its reconstruction. With two missions, in 445 and 432 B.C.E., he reestablished the viability of Jerusalem, still the holy city of faith. He managed to rebuild its walls and secure it against threats and attacks from its rivals in Samaria to the north—old Israel, the Northern Kingdom. Old feuds die hard. The regional rivalry of north and south surfaces again.

Ezra, too, was a Jewish official of the Persian court. He returned to Palestine around the same time as Nehemiah. He was perhaps even more important than Nehemiah because of the way in which he redefined the identity of God's people. Having the authority of the Persian crown, he dissolved any marriages involving Judeans and non-Judeans and sent them packing. He also applied the law of Moses as state law. Ezra was severe, but times were tough and the identity of the community was at stake. The books of Ezra and Nehemiah detail the efforts to restore faith in a renewed Jerusalem. Chronicles is associated with the perspective of these books in its retelling of Israel's history (see Chapter 18).

■ JUDAISM AND HELLENISM (333 B.C.E.–70 C.E.)

Judea remained a Persian province until Alexander the Great invaded the Middle East. With his victory at Issus in 333 B.C.E. he secured control of Asia and spread Greek culture, government, and language throughout his realm. The Hellenistic period had begun.

Alexander allowed the Jews to observe their own ritual laws and traditions and was generally kindly disposed to them. This lenient policy of "live and let live" continued through the period of Ptolemaic control of Judea. This changed when control of Palestine passed from the dynasty of Ptolemy to the dynasty of Seleucus in 198 B.C.E. The Seleucids, especially Antiochus IV Epiphanes, attempted to force Hellenism upon the Jews of Palestine, often with extreme cruelty.

Hellenism fundamentally challenged Jewish culture and religion. The Greek language displaced Aramaic as the language of the Middle East. Greek literature; philosophy; and institutions such as the gymnasium, polis (city), and theater, transformed traditional societies . . . and threatened Hebrew culture. Many Jews "modernized" and went along with the changes, but others resisted and refused to give up their Jewishness as traditionally defined. The book of Daniel tells of the struggles of Daniel and his friends to remain faithful to the Torah in a culture that sought to assimilate them (see Chapter 17).

The Maccabean uprising was one attempt to reverse the progress of Hellenization. Led by Judas the Maccabee, the Jews were able for a time to reestablish home rule. It was effective to the point that an independent Jewish state was created and ruled by the Hasmonean house for almost eighty years, from 142 to 63 B.C.E.

In 63 B.C.E. the Romans took control of the Middle East. Pompey captured Jerusalem, and the territories of Palestine were incorporated into the larger Roman empire. Local government was first entrusted to local princes, of whom Herod the Great (37–4 B.C.E.) was one. Herod was the ruler of greater Palestine at the time Jesus was born. Later, procurators appointed by Roman emperors were placed in charge of smaller Palestinian territories.

Jewish society was anything but homogeneous at this time. The Sadducees, a religious-political party, were not opposed to accommodating Greco-Roman forms. While they advocated an exclusively Torah-based form of religion and continued the ritual forms of the priesthood, they tended to cooperate with the occupiers of Palestine, thereby retaining a role in the administration of the province.

The Essenes, to whom many authorities attribute the Dead Sea Scrolls, were the most conservative Jewish group. They led an ascetic existence in the wilderness, withdrawn from the Jewish religious establishment in Jerusalem which they believed was corrupt. They devoted themselves to the Torah, and in this way prepared themselves for the eagerly expected messiah.

The militant Jewish group called the Zealots sought to rid Judea of Roman occupation. This form of Judaism, traceable to the Maccabees, campaigned for Jewish independence and a resurrection of the great Israelite monarchy. They precipitated a rebellion, called the First Jewish Revolt, which resulted in the destruction of Jerusalem in 70 C.E.

The Pharisees, the religious liberals of their day, practiced a dynamic faith which actively translated Mosaic and prophetic religion to life in their day. Of all the traditional Jewish groups, not surprisingly it was Pharisaic Judaism that survived the disasters of the first and second Jewish Revolts (66–73 C.E. and 132–135 C.E.), along, of course, with the early Christians. Christianity began as a Jewish religious phenomenon, shaped by the belief that the messianic age had been inaugurated through the life, death, and resurrection of their leader, Jesus of Nazareth. Only later was it altogether distinguished from Judaism.

FOR FURTHER STUDY

Hallo and Simpson (1971) for a concise yet authoritative history of the ancient Middle East, Hayes and Miller (1990) for biblical history.

 The Biblical Story Bibliography.

PART

1

TORAH

PROLOGUE TO THE TORAH

Key Terms

Anthropomorphism
Deuteronomy
Documentary Hypothesis
Elohim
Elohist Source
Pentateuch
Priestly Document
Tanak
Torah
Yahwist Narrative
Yahweh
YHWH

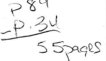

FIGURE 1   STUDYING TORAH   An observant Jew at the Western Wall in Jerusalem intently studies a Torah scroll. The Torah is the foundation document of Judaism and is the heart of the Old Testament.

The Hebrew Bible consists of three parts: the Torah, the Prophets, and the Writings. The **Torah** consists of five books: Genesis, Exodus, Leviticus, Numbers, and Deuteronomy. After explaining some terms, this chapter introduces general issues in the study of the Torah.

The term *Torah* has a variety of meanings and connotations. It can refer to the "T" section of the **Tanak** (the Jewish name for the Hebrew Bible, sometimes spelled "tanach" or "tanakh"), which consists of the first five books of the Bible. It also has a much broader meaning. In Jewish tradition, *torah* designates the instruction, revelation, or teaching of God, and as such it is another way to refer to the Bible. Torah was Israel's constitution and the foundation of its spiritual and communal life.

Although Torah is the traditional name for the set of books Genesis, Exodus, Leviticus, Numbers, and Deuteronomy, modern readers tend to call it the **Pentateuch,** a term derived from the Greek word for "five scroll jars." You will find the term Pentateuch most often used in academic settings and Torah most often in religious ones.

The Torah is the most intensely studied section of the Hebrew Bible both within Judaism and the academic community. Consequently, there is a wealth of scholarship which attempts to sort out where it came from and what it means. A good deal wrestles with issues of authorship and literary composition.

AUTHORSHIP

Ancient practices of authorship and text production differ significantly from those of today. In biblical culture writers did not sign their works, though some clay tablets do record the name of the scribe. The shaping of what we today call biblical "books" probably came about through the collaboration of many parties, and may have taken a lengthy period of time from the earliest oral stories to the final written product.

Every book of the Torah has ambiguous indications of authorship. Determinations of the authorship of these books, or parts of them, must be inferred from clues in the texts themselves. Scholars offer many proposals as to the dating and authorship of the books of the Torah but have reached no consensus.

■ MOSES

Jewish and Christian tradition holds Moses responsible for writing the Torah. Moses was the religious leader of the Hebrew people who led them out of slavery in Egypt and to the Promised Land of Canaan in the thirteenth century B.C.E. The books of the Torah are popularly referred to as the Five Books of Moses.

A number of texts attribute the Torah to Moses. Joshua built an altar using the specifications in "the book of the Torah of Moses" (Joshua 8:31). David charged Solomon to keep the commandments "as written in the Torah of Moses" (1 Kings 2:3). Ezra read from "the book of the Torah of Moses, which the Lord had given to Israel" (Nehemiah 8:1). About this same time the Chronicler referred to a passage from Deuteronomy as being from "the book of Moses" (2 Chronicles 25:4). The Jewish philosopher Philo, the Jewish historian Josephus, and New Testament writers (see Matthew 19:7-8 and Acts 15:1), all first-century C.E. sources, assumed the Torah's Mosaic authorship, as did the Babylonian Talmud (see Baba Bathra 14b).

A close study of the Torah reveals that the issue of authorship is more complex. Common sense informed scholars as early as the Middle Ages that Moses could not have written the account of his own death (Deuteronomy 34:5-12). Some suggested that Joshua, Moses' assistant and successor, might have appended it. Other features of the text suggest non-Mosaic authorship and a complex process of development. Often the text refers to Moses in the third person rather than the first person, suggesting someone other than Moses wrote those sections. In three distinct places Genesis contains the ploy of a patriarch lying about his wife's marital status to protect his own life—twice with Abraham and Sarah (12:10-20; 20:1-18) and once with Isaac and Rebekah (26:6-11)—possibly suggesting that one basic story circulated in variant forms in different documents, with all being included in the final text.

Some authorities affirm the Mosaic authorship of the Pentateuch, often out of a principled commitment to the veracity of the text as the inspired Word of God. Many others are convinced that the Torah was given its final shape much later than the lifetime of Moses. While differing considerably in how they reconstruct the underlying sources and the process of composition, most hold that the Torah was composed from a variety of materials assembled over a long period of time.

The following discussion summarizes the approach of source analysis, sometimes called the **documentary hypothesis.**

■ SOURCES

The study of ancient languages and literatures blossomed during the Renaissance and Reformation. This inspired a new look at the Hebrew Bible. The existence of similar stories in Genesis (such as the story of Abraham and Sarah just mentioned) prompted Richard Simon (1638–1712) to develop a theory that the Pentateuch was compiled from a number of sources, some of which may have derived from Moses. He claimed the final Pentateuch was produced by Ezra in the postexilic period (fifth century B.C.E.).

A variation in the way pentateuchal texts refer to God, either as **Elohim** (translated God) or **YHWH** (pronounced **Yahweh** or **Yahveh**, and rendered "the LORD" in most English translations), prompted Jean Astruc (1684–1766) to argue that Moses compiled the Pentateuch from two different written documents and other minor materials. Ironically, the approach he advocated gave birth to the documentary hypothesis, which ultimately took the Pentateuch out of Moses' hands.

Over the next two centuries the documentary hypothesis developed into the dominant explanation for the authorship and composition of the Pentateuch. Essentially, the hypothesis deconstructs the Pentateuch into four primary underlying documentary sources: a Yahwist narrative was dated to the tenth or ninth century B.C.E., an Elohist source to the ninth century, Deuteronomy to the seventh century, and a Priestly document to the sixth or fifth century. The documentary hypothesis goes by the acronym JEDP for the four sources in their presumed chronological order.

The classical documentary hypothesis uses five literary identifiers to distinguish the sources:

- duplication and repetition of material
- variation in the ways of referring to God
- contrasting author perspectives
- variation in vocabulary and literary style
- evidence of editorial activity

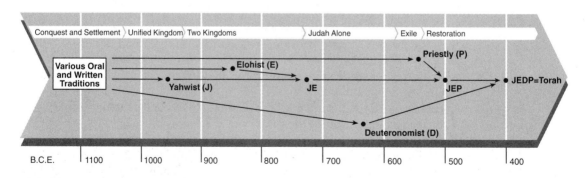

FIGURE 2 SOURCES AND COMPOSITION OF THE TORAH This time line illustrates the growth of the Torah through its various stages.

The editorial work of combining the various sources took place in stages. The editor (sometimes called a redactor) who joined the Yahwist (J) and Elohist (E) sources into JE put them together shortly after 721 B.C.E. The editor (a different one now) who added material from a Priestly Source (P) did so around 500 B.C.E., giving rise to JEP. When Deuteronomy was added around 400 B.C.E. the Torah as we now have it became complete.

None of the actual writers of the sources have been identified by name, but we can piece together some general features of the individuals and groups responsible. Each of the sources has a distinctive style, vocabulary, and theology; each came out of a particular period in Israel's history; and each reflects the attitude and perspective of a particular constituency within Israel.

Yahwist Narrative (J)

The earliest written source of the Torah is the Yahwist source. It got this name because it uses the divine name Yahweh to refer to God. Its story line formed the backbone of the Torah narrative, with the other sources building on it. The Yahwist is sometimes considered an epic because in rather sweeping and inclusive style it tells the story of how humankind developed and how one branch became the people of God. It frequently makes use of **anthropomorphism;** that is, it often describes God as having human characteristics, such as when he "walked" in the garden of Eden.

The Yahwist source is referred to as **J** in scholarly literature because German scholars first formulated this source analysis and *Yahweh* begins with a "J" in German. It appears to contain the first account of where the nation of Israel came from and why it was special to God. This national story provided a common identity for all the people united under the rule of the Davidic dynasty. The Yahwist composed his story sometime during the reign of Solomon (961–922 B.C.E.), though some scholars would date it as much as a century later. Remembering that it was written at the time of the early monarchy in Judah is one way to remember to associate the Yahwist, or J source, with Judah—both begin with "J."

The Yahwist source was written out of love for the royal house, providing a sense of history and destiny for the grand new kingdom of David. The Solomonic era was most conducive to such a historical project. This golden age had the resources and provided the opportunity to write a national epic. Royally sponsored scribal schools provided the training, royal income supported the work, and the increased international contact afforded by the new status of Israel stimulated historical reflection and perhaps even prompted the need for a national story.

The Yahwist was especially interested in those traditions that supported the legitimacy of Davidic rule and the centrality of the tribe of Judah. He (or she, if Bloom 1990 is correct) believed that God's plan was working itself out in the rule of David and Solomon. The Yahwist came from Judah, so he naturally thought highly of King David. David was originally from Bethlehem in Judah, and ruled from Hebron, a major city in Judah, for many years. The Judah connection is evident in the Yahwist's interest in Abraham. The bulk of the Abraham traditions are associated with locations in and around Judah. For example, several Yahwist stories of Abraham have him living in Hebron (Genesis 13:18; 23:2). On the other hand, the Jacob stories are generally located in the north or in Transjordan.

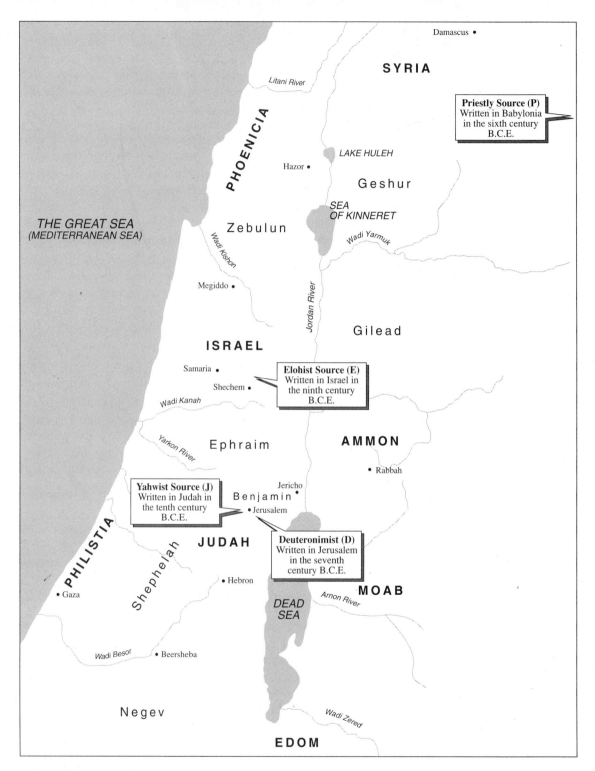

FIGURE 3 SOURCES OF THE TORAH BY GEOGRAPHICAL LOCATION

There are other obvious connections between the patriarch Abraham and the kingdom of David. The covenant God made with Abraham promised that his descendants would possess the land "from the river of Egypt to the river Euphrates" (Genesis 15:18-21). Not coincidentally, this turns out to be the extent of the nation under King David.

Thus the Yahwist epic provided supportive history and a theological foundation for David's new empire. Going back to its primeval stories, it first exposed the need for an enlightened empire by painting a picture of human sin and natural rebellion. Then, by unfolding the groundwork of the empire in Yahweh's promises to Abraham, it revealed the plan of Yahweh. David's empire was its culmination. The Yahwist is bold and honest in his portrayal of Israel's early history. He does not overly glorify the role of Yahweh's chosen ones, and has a keen eye for human failing. Yet his eye is always on the promises of Yahweh, which wend their way to fulfillment within the crucible of human history.

As you read the Pentateuch, watch for these features of the Yahwist source:

- divine promises, curse on disobedience
- sin as the impulse to be like God or the gods
- geographical locations in Judah
- use of anthropomorphic imagery
- use of the divine name YHWH

Table A Yahwist story line, style, and theology provide additional details and a list of Yahwist passages in the Pentateuch.

Elohist Texts (E)

The Elohist source was written after the Yahwist source and comes out of the Northern Kingdom in the ninth or eighth century B.C.E. The Elohist source gets its name from its use of the Hebrew word *Elohim,* to refer to God. Elohim is the general word for God, as opposed to the personal divine name Yahweh. The Elohist source has survived only as fragments which were inserted into the Yahwist epic. It is not nearly as extensive, at least in its recoverable form, as the other sources.

Fragments of the Elohist source are found in Genesis, Exodus, and Numbers, and maybe even in Joshua and Judges. The Elohist source appears for the first time at Genesis 20, where God appeared in a dream rather than directly to individuals as we tend to find in the Yahwist epic. The Elohist source favors a distant God who comes in dreams or in the form of an angel. In contrast to the Yahwist epic, the Elohist source refers to Sinai as Horeb and to the Canaanites as Amorites.

The Elohist author lived in the Northern Kingdom after the breakup of the Davidic kingdom, probably sometime in the ninth century B.C.E. The Northern Kingdom was ruled by a succession of dynasties. The largest tribal territory in the Northern Kingdom, called Israel after the breakup, was Ephraim. Because the tribe of Ephraim was immense and politically dominant, the whole northern territory was sometimes called Ephraim. An easy way to remember that this source is from the north is that both Elohist and Ephraim begin with "E."

The Elohist was a thinker, theologian, and probably a Levite. Based on his attitudes, he probably did not hold a position in the royal court, but authorities cannot be more precise than this. Whoever he was, his perspective was conditioned by the theological and political difficulties of Israel in the ninth century B.C.E.

While the Yahwist believed God would overcome the problem of sin and extend blessing to all the families of the earth through the Davidic empire, the Elohist lived at a time when the national mood was somber. Israel was struggling with its identity. God seemed distant; there was spiritual drifting as people were attracted to Canaanite Baal worship. The Levites had something to say about this, and drew upon stories which reinforced Israel's special relationship with God.

As you read the Pentateuch, watch for these features of the Elohist source:

- concern with moral and ethical issues
- the "fear of God" motif
- God revealing himself in dreams
- great heroes of faith portrayed as prophets
- importance of locations in Israel (Ephraim, the Northern Kingdom)
- use of the divine name Elohim

Table B Elohist story line, style, and theology provide additional details and a list of Elohist passages in the Pentateuch.

Combined Yahwist-Elohist Epic (JE)

The Elohist source eventually found its way south to Judah, where it merged with the Yahwist source. It is understandable that the two sources would be joined together. Both had the same basic scope, though the Elohist did not have any pre-ancestral stories, and both the Yahwist and Elohist sources shared the fundamental conviction that Yahweh is the God of the Israelites and that he must be worshiped by his people.

The joining of the two sources into JE, what some scholars call the "Old Epic" tradition and others the "Jehovistic source," took place shortly after the fall of Israel in 721 B.C.E. The northern Levite author of the Elohist source fled south to Judah after the Assyrian invasion, taking his writings with him. He ended up in Jerusalem, and king Hezekiah used both the Elohist and Yahwist materials as the manifesto for a national religious revival. Putting these two traditions together supported the legitimacy of the Davidic line, of which Hezekiah was a part, and also promoted the religious and moral devotion that was at the heart of the Elohist tradition.

Perhaps the combination of these two national stories, one from the north and one from the south, also promoted a sense of unity among the people. Those from the north who fled to the south and found a home there after 721 B.C.E. now had a voice in the national story.

Deuteronomy (D)

Deuteronomy follows the Yahwist, Elohist, and JE sources in composition order. It differs significantly in that it was not combined with the other sources into a larger work. While the Yahwist, Elohist, and Priestly sources were combined together to create Genesis, Exodus, Leviticus, and Numbers, the book of Deuteronomy stands apart from these four books. It does, however, continue the story line of the preceding books and provides the conclusion to the life of Moses. Deuteronomy also differs from the preceding four books of the Pentateuch in that it is not so much an account of events as it is a collection of Moses' sermons to the Israelites just before they entered the Promised Land. It has a style quite different from that of the preceding books. Most of it is addressed directly to the Israelites.

Deuteronomy contains traditions that can be traced all the way back to Israel's tribal origins. Levites living in the north are the ones who shaped the material and preserved it. It has certain affinities with the Elohist source. Details of the style and theology of Deuteronomy are dealt with in Chapter 5. It is not crucial at this point to go into detail because, unlike the other sources, we do not have to know about Deuteronomy in order to identify the sources of Genesis through Numbers.

Priestly Document (P)

The Priestly document is the last of the great pentateuchal documents. It comes out of the circle of priests who reassembled Israel, theologically speaking, after the tragedy of the Babylonian exile. Judah had been conquered by the Babylonians in the sixth century B.C.E. and many survivors of the disaster were taken to Babylonia as refugees. The trauma of this exile prompted the survivors to conclude that the tragedy happened because they had forsaken their covenant with God. In exile they were at risk of losing their social and religious identity. Priests took the initiative to sustain the faith of the refugees and rebuild their identity. In the absence of temple worship, these priests gave traditional religious practices new significance, particularly the observance of the Sabbath day and the covenant ritual of circumcision.

The Priestly source is usually dated to the period of the Babylonian exile (587–539 B.C.E.) or to the postexilic period immediately thereafter. The priests recovered and recorded religious traditions so that the identity of the community would not be lost. They sought to reinforce covenant practices in repentance for past neglect and to avert a subsequent and possibly worse tragedy.

The Priestly tradition also dealt with the problem of defining Judean faith in contrast to Babylonian religion. How do other nations and empires fit into our God's plan? How can we affirm the power of our God when we live in a world dominated by Babylonians, who trumpet the power of their god, Marduk? Why does our God seem to be silent as we suffer? Priestly theology sought to adapt Israelite faith to their circumstances in the sixth century B.C.E.

The writer of the Priestly source envisioned a world ordered and controlled by God. Israel's history was progressing according to God's predetermined plan. God was in total control, and the world was secure and stable. Israel's relationship with God was ordered by covenant. Even when Israel alienated itself from God, there were sacrifices and rituals that could atone for faithlessness. Indeed, Yahweh was a demanding God, but what he wanted was to bless Israel. These assurances inspired hope in the hearts of exiled Israelites struggling to keep hope alive.

As you read the Pentateuch, watch for these features of the Priestly source:

- blessing as fruitfulness and multiplying
- covenants with God that mark important moments
- genealogies that establish connections between people and events

- social and religious roles of priests
- Word of God as a driving force in history
- use of the divine name Elohim in the primeval era, El Shaddai in the ancestral era, and YHWH in the Mosaic era

Table C Priestly story line, style, and theology provide additional details and a list of Priestly passages in the Pentateuch.

■ CRITIQUE

Theories of pentateuchal sources continue to be revised in modern scholarship, with myriad refinements and counterproposals. Some scholars reject source analysis entirely, arguing that it compromises the literary integrity of the Pentateuch. Still others challenge critical analysis because it is perceived to be inconsistent with a theory of inspiration and a view that God spoke through Moses to deliver the Torah. It is fair to say the field of pentateuchal studies is more unsettled today than it ever was.

Table D is a list and discussion of some major revisions and alternatives to the documentary hypothesis, some rather technical.

Still, there seems to be a general consensus, apart from the most conservative readers, that the Torah is multilayered and that underlying sources of some kind did exist. Whether the sources were oral or written or a combination of both is not entirely clear. When they arose is not clear either. Still, for many students of the Torah, continuing to view it as having arisen out a combination of basic sources is a productive way to begin thinking about the shape of the literature and the theology of the writers. Reference to sources and their implied background permeates scholarship on the Torah and continues to be actively employed. One cannot join the conversation on the Pentateuch without a knowledge of source analysis.

The use of source analysis in RTOT does not imply an endorsement of it. It is used alongside other reading techniques, including literary and linguistic analysis, form criticism, and a canonical perspective. All these methods together constitute the toolkit of an informed readership. Our goal is to immerse readers in the text of the Hebrew Bible, and the use of these methods forces the reader into the minutiae. This is where the real fun of interpretation begins. If these methods help us attend closely to the text, then they are worth using.

WHOLENESS

Close attention to the minutiae of the text, especially with a view to source analysis, runs the risk of obscuring the proverbial forest for the trees. The Torah has remarkable wholeness, a unity in diversity, that must be noted before we dig into the texts. Keeping this wholeness in mind may serve to keep our close readings in perspective.

The Torah achieves unity in a number of ways. The story has a consistent unity of action as it moves in linear fashion from creation through the period of ancestors to the nation of Israel. In addition, the God who directs this history retains the same character and upholds the same promises throughout, even if he is known by different names at different times.

■ PRIESTLY COVENANTS

The Yahwist narrative may have been responsible for the backbone of the event line in Genesis involving the creation of humanity, their first rebellious impulses, and the turn to Abraham. This sequence set the parameters of God's challenge to create a people obedient to him. The Elohist source supplemented this story line, and the Priestly writers added continuity to the event line using genealogies.

In addition, the Priestly writer employed a series of covenants to add theological structure to Israel's relationship with God and an organization to history. In the biblical world a covenant was a basic structure, a legal metaphor, whereby two parties pledge their abiding commitment. The general schema of history developed by the Priestly writer is worked out in three covenants. Each covenant is marked by a distinctive sign (Hebrew 'ot) as evidence that it was in force.

Creation Covenant

God made the first covenant with all creation through Noah after the flood. The covenant contains the promise that God will never again destroy the earth by flood, and gave the rainbow as a natural sign of hope. This is the first recorded covenant in the Hebrew Bible. It established a binding relationship between God and the earth. In this covenant there is no reciprocity, no return pledge of loyalty from humankind or any other creature. All living things are the gracious recipient of God's promise to preserve life indefinitely. The rainbow signifies God's eternal commitment to this covenant (see Chapter 1).

Ancestral Covenant

The covenant through Abraham, recorded in Genesis 17, is more restricted, being nationalistic in scope. In this covenant God assures the ancestral family that it will become a nation under his care and protection. This covenant differs from the creation covenant in that it required the ancestral family to demonstrate commitment on its part: the circumcision of all males in the ancestral household (see Chapter 2).

| TABLE 1 | COVENANTS AND SIGNS |

Era	Party	Mediator	Sign	'OT Passage
1. Primeval	Creation	Noah	Rainbow	Genesis 9:12
2. Ancestral	Israel	Abraham	Circumcision	Genesis 17:11
3. Sinai	Israel	Moses	Sabbath	Exodus 31:13, 17

Sinai Covenant

The third great Priestly covenant was mediated by Moses, and marks the last. defining moment in the Priestly history of the divine-human bond. This covenant, made with the people of Israel, was regulated by an extensive set of laws and regulations contained in Exodus, Leviticus, Numbers, and Deuteronomy. The people express their solidarity with God in this covenant by observing the Sabbath day, called in Exodus 31:12-18 the "sign of the covenant," and by keeping the other laws.

Covenants and the Exile

Each of the three covenants marks a significant development in God's covenantal relationship with Israel. Each covenant has a specific sign attached to it whereby the continuation of the covenant would be evident. The special importance of the last two signs becomes clear in the context of the origin of the Priestly source in the Babylonian exile. All three are called eternal covenants (Genesis 9:16; 17:7; Exodus 31:16), and the signs of circumcision and Sabbath observance became the covenant community's primary identifying symbols of the exilic period and after. During those times when the religious identity of God's people was threatened, these rituals became primary identifiers because they could be practiced anywhere. Even though the people were not in Jerusalem, the only place temple rituals and sacrifices could be performed, they could still perform circumcision and observe the Sabbath.

■ DIVINE PROMISES

In addition to the series of covenants that structure history, the Torah views Israel's experience as the fulfillment of divine promises. It presents Israel's history as goal oriented and divinely guided. The promises specifically concerned posterity eventually leading to nationhood, a homeland, and continued divine presence. Clines (1978: 29) argues that promise is the heart of the Torah:

> *The theme of the Pentateuch is the partial fulfillment—which implies also the partial non-fulfillment—of the promise to or blessing of the patriarchs. The promise or blessing is both the divine initiative in a world where human initiatives always lead to disaster, and a re-affirmation of the primal divine intentions for man. The promise has three elements: posterity, divine-human relationship, and land. The posterity-element of the promise is dominant in Genesis 12-50, the relationship-element in Exodus and Leviticus, and the land-element in Numbers and Deuteronomy.*

If promise and fulfillment are the defining issues of the Torah, then the question must be asked why the Torah ends without fulfillment. Deuteronomy concludes with the death of Moses and the Israelites on the edge of the Promised Land without possession of it. This tension raises a rather large issue that bears on the overall meaning of the Torah and concerns how Deuteronomy relates to the preceding four books.

By the end of the fifth century B.C.E. there were two major collections of books. The first was Genesis through Numbers, a Tetrateuch, or set of four books. The second was Deuteronomy through Kings, the Deuteronomistic History. The first covered the early history of the nation, from creation to conquest. The second told the story of the rise and fall of Israel, from conquest to exile. Each collection has its own consistent voice and perspective.

But the compilers of the Hebrew Bible did not divide the material along those lines; the major break in the canon comes after Deuteronomy, not before it. Theologically speaking, a Tetrateuch would be more natural, since those books share the three sources J, E, and P. Why then did the early Jewish community of faith structure the early books of the Hebrew Bible as a Pentateuch and not a Tetrateuch? The answer has a great deal to do with when and where the Torah took shape.

The Torah was formed in an exilic setting to provide a theological framework for a postexilic Jewish community. Above all, the exilic community needed a narrative and legal tradition that could direct national life. The priests naturally turned to Moses as the great lawgiver. Since, in addition to Exodus through Numbers, Deuteronomy provided legal material attributed to Moses, it was included in this core community document, thus creating a Pentateuch.

More importantly, the Torah took shape as a document for a people "on the road," a people exiled and not yet home. In positing a Pentateuch, with a major break between Deuteronomy and Joshua, the community of faith affirmed this basic historical and theological fact; the people of God are continually moving from promise to fulfillment. The people of God have not "arrived." Like Moses, the exilic community viewed the Promised Land from a distance. By not including the conquest recorded in Joshua, the hope of the exilic people resonated with that of their forebearers. Like their forebearers, they too would gain possession of the land . . . someday. The structure of the Pentateuch affirms that the exilic community is essentially a community of hope.

HISTORICITY

The Torah begins at the beginning, with creation. The exact date of creation presumably could be calculated by following the genealogical notices of the Hebrew Bible—many genealogies provide lifespans—and working backwards. Bishop James Ussher (1581–1656) did just that and determined that the universe was born on 4004 B.C. Based on the priestly genealogies of Genesis 1-11, the span from creation to the flood was 1,656 years, and from the flood to Abram 290 years. Since these genealogies incorporate immense lifespans, as many as 969 years in the case of Methuselah, they are of questionable value in determining real dates. Yet Ussher's chronology was printed in the margins of many Bibles on into the twentieth century and was widely accepted.

Of course, determining the time line of the Hebrew Bible is not quite so simple, and contemporary science tells us that the universe is at least fifteen billion years old. Here is what we can say about Torah and time. The books of the Torah are in chronological order, with events moving in a linear fashion from creation, through the ancestors, and into the period of Moses and early Israel. But there is no Torah-internal dating scheme that positions events absolutely in reference to each other, nothing like years B.C.E. and C.E. that we use today.

Within the Hebrew Bible the exodus out of Egypt seems to be the pivotal point of history, and other events are dated in reference to it. For example, Aaron's death (Numbers 33:38) and the construction of the temple (1 Kings 6:1) are specified relative to the exodus. The internal evidence for the ancestral period enables us to determine that the time from Abram's migration to Canaan until Jacob and his family moved to Egypt was 215 years. And the length of time the Hebrews were in Egypt was 430 years (Exodus 12:40). After the exodus Israel remained in the wilderness between Egypt and Canaan for forty years.

The time indicator that can be correlated most effectively with absolute chronology is the 480 years from the exodus to the beginning of temple construction in Solomon's fourth year, as stated in 1 Kings 6:1. Because the fourth year of Solomon's reign can be dated to 964 B.C.E. it places the exodus in 1444 B.C.E. Unfortunately, this conflicts with the evidence of Exodus 1:11, which mentions the Hebrews were engaged as slaves to build the Egyptian cities Pithom and Rameses. These in turn have been associated with the reign of the pharaoh Ramses II (1290–1224 B.C.E.). The result is a discrepancy of around two centuries. Based on the confluence of archaeological, historical, and textual evidence, the generally accepted date of the Hebrews' exodus from Egypt is around 1280 B.C.E.

There is no firm way to locate the ancestors within absolute chronology. There is no external Egyptian or Mesopotamian evidence that can verify when or even if the patriarchs and matriarchs existed. About all that authorities are left with is to infer from circumstantial evidence when Abraham, Sarah, and the other ancestors best fit. Some interpreters place them in the Middle Bronze I Age (2000–1800 B.C.E.). This is based primarily on the description of the ancestors as semi-nomadic clans similar to the Amorites who moved through the Old Babylonian empire, as described in documents from Mari. Other interpreters place them in the Late Bronze Age (1550–1200 B.C.E.) based on certain social practices that are attested at Nuzi.

Historical minimalists argue that the ancestral stories were written very late, and that we should not infer that the events really happened, or even that the ancestors ever existed (see Thompson 1974, 1992; Van Seters 1975). Others argue that the stories, while admittedly written well after the fact, retain a valid remembrance of historical figures and fit what we know of the second millennium based on other sources (see Millard and Wiseman 1980; Bright 1981). With Moses and early Israel the situation is only slightly better. Though Moses is not attested outside the Bible, there are some clues in Exodus that may provide connections to Egyptian and Palestinian history. The relevant data will be treated in the appropriate chapters.

The uncertainties concerning the chronology and the very reality of the early figures of biblical history inevitably raise the question of the Bible's historicity. Readers will want to know if the events described in the Torah—and elsewhere in the Hebrew Bible for that matter—are fictional or true. And if they happened, was it in the way described? Our discussion of the written traditions of the Torah suggests this is not an easy issue. The biblical text we have before us is surely not a first-hand travelogue, nor can it be in its entirety an eyewitness record of what happened. It has been deliberately shaped and molded so as to present Israel's historical experience in a way relevant to the concerns at that time.

This is not to suggest that subversive or misleading intentions lurk behind the process. Rather, the contemporary framing of past experience is inevitable, and is a good and necessary thing. All history writing is a selective and intentional appropriation of the past. All history writing is done inevitably from a certain point of view that incorporates the writer's individual personality and larger cultural setting. Source analysis in all its forms and permutations attempts to identify just such factors.

Though there is a necessary subjectivity to history writing, this does not imply that all history writing is equally subjective. Some writing may be more or less faithful to the events themselves, and personal or political agendas may distort that writer's account of events. That is why critical study of the biblical text, indeed of all writing, is essential. Understanding a text involves more than just understanding what the words mean. It also involves grasping the reasons why it was written, in light of who wrote it and when. This is an imperfect science, an impossible achievement, yet a necessary goal.

A fascinating one, too, especially where the biblical text is concerned. The Hebrew Bible presents us with an account of Israel's history and ancestors. By reading between the lines it also presents us with how Israel's thinkers interpreted these events, and how they related these events to their concept of God. By doing our historical and literary research we are able to reconstruct their worldview—for them, their human experience in the context of divine realities.

With all serious study there can be a range of positions on the basic issues. When it comes to the study of Israel's historical works this is especially true. On one side are those who accept every historical statement in the Hebrew Bible as fact, pure and simple. Often such readers are predisposed to the Bible's accuracy out of their understanding of what it must be as the Word of God. On the other side are those who are suspicious of every biblical statement and tend to consider the text historically unreliable. Such readers are sometimes called historical minimalists and tend to view all Torah sources as late.

This book is somewhere in the middle. It values the contributions of modern study of the Pentateuch and advocates their use as a means to enter the mind and worldview of the ancient writers. While it takes a studied approach to the text, RTOT also respects the Hebrew Bible. Of course, this will be challenged by parties on the poles, with precritical readers charging that it tears apart the Bible and hypercritical readers charging that a moderate position is historically naive. No doubt the debate will continue long after this book is out of print.

FOR FURTHER STUDY

Fox (1995) has translated the Torah in such a way as to recover the rhythm and power of the original language more effectively than other renditions. For close study of the source documents, Campbell and O'Brien (1993) is indispensable by providing the documents in continuous form, along with detailed notes. Mann (1988) works through the Torah with an insightful literary and thematic retelling.

Part 1 Bibliography lists works that apply to the Torah generally. Each RTOT chapter covering the books of the Torah also has its own bibliography.

[handwritten: X ? do we need to know ~~all~~ all of the characteristics for each or just the general list on p. 36]

QUESTIONS FOR REVIEW

1. What are the arguments for and against Mosaic authorship of the Torah?

2. According to the documentary hypothesis, what are the four literary sources of the Pentateuch? *[handwritten: p. 36]*

3. Why was the source theory of the documentary hypothesis developed in the modern study of the Pentateuch? Why has the source theory been questioned in recent scholarship?

[handwritten: b/c there is argument that the theory compromises the literary integrity of the Pentateuch & that it is inconsistent with the theory as being the inspired word of God]

4. What are the distinguishing characteristics of the major pentateuchal sources?

5. What are the unifying themes of the Torah?

6. What is the likeliest historical chronology *[handwritten: p. 45]* for the time of Moses? What problems arise in *[handwritten: p. 46]* trying to establish dates for the early figures of Israel's history? *[handwritten: (?) It raises the question of the Bible's historicity]*

QUESTIONS FOR REFLECTION AND DISCUSSION

1. How might the compositional issues in the study of the Torah affect a reader's attitude toward the text and its authority?

2. Is it important to prove that Israel's ancestors and Moses actually existed?

Part 1 Study Guide
- *Chapter summary*
- *Key terms linked to the glossary*
- *Concept questions with answer links*
- *Progress tests: true/false, multiple choice, matching, and identification*

[handwritten: (?) #5. The ~~Story~~ It has a consistent unity of action as it moves in linear fashion & God upholds the same character & promises throughout.]

[handwritten: #1. A # of texts attribute the Torah to Moses & there is a principled commitment to the text being the inspired word of God. The arguments against Mosaic authorship is that often the text refers to Moses in third person rather than 1st & that common sense shows that Moses could not have written the accounts of his own death.]

GENESIS 1–11: THE PRIMEVAL STORY

FIGURE 1.1 EA IN THE APSU   The Mesopotamian god Ea, residing in the fresh water ocean Apsu on this seal impression, receives another god. Mesopotamian mythology imagined that the world was created by the mingling of two oceans, Apsu and Tiamat. Hebrew creation, in contrast, was by the one god Elohim who controls the deep waters and brings forth life.

We call the origin stories of Genesis 1–11 the **Primeval Story,** referring to the earliest ages of cultural development. The Primeval Story is a sweeping account of the earliest events, from the **creation** of the world to the spread of humanity over the face of the earth. But the writer only mentions those seminal events that fit his purpose.

The Primeval Story is not history as we ordinarily use the term. The earliest events of creation, for example, had no human eyewitnesses. Stories such as we find in the early chapters of Genesis are mostly myths and sagas. A literalistic approach to Genesis 1–11 would confuse history with myth and reality with symbol. Applying such terms as "myth" to Genesis in no way devalues or demeans the stories. They may not provide the earliest history exactly as it happened, but they do communicate Israel's deepest truths about the world in its relationship to God.

Source Analysis. One of the ways we will probe the Primeval Story is by isolating its early literary sources (see Part 1). The Primeval Story was constructed out of originally separate stories and genealogies. Of the two literary sources found in Genesis 1–11, the Yahwist source seems especially fascinated with the primeval period. Yahwist stories shape the plot of the Primeval Story. According to classical source analysis, the Yahwist narrative was written during the time of the Davidic monarchy or shortly thereafter. The growth of the Davidic kingdom and the development of cultural contacts with other nations inspired Israel's interest in stories with global connections. Israel was striving to understand its place in the larger world, including its God's relationship to other nations. The other literary source found in the Primeval Story is the Priestly source. It contributed its own versions of the creation and flood, along with some other, mostly genealogical, material. The Elohist source is not present at all.

Story Line

God created the universe of stars, earth, and animal life in six days and rested on the seventh (Genesis 1). The first humans were placed in the perfect world of Eden (2) but were expelled after they disobeyed a divine command (3). Out of Eden the first couple had offspring who typified the worst of sin and the best of culture (4). But sin ran rampant, prompting God to cleanse the earth with a flood (6). Only Noah, his immediate family, and a representative sample of animal life survived in a boat of God's design (7). After the waters subsided (8) God made a covenant with Noah, but Noah's episode of insobriety marked the return of wrongdoing (9). Still, humanity grew in number (10). They began building a massive tower ascending heavenward in order to make a name for themselves, but God frustrated their plan and scattered them abroad (11). The Primeval Story ends with the genealogy of Shem from whose line comes Abraham. Through him God would reestablish fellowship with humanity (see Chapter 2).

CREATION TO THE FLOOD (1–7)

The first half of the Primeval Story contains two versions of creation. The first version is comprehensive in scope, giving account of the big moments of world creation, yet also treating the creation of humans in God's image. The second version makes only passing reference to the grand environment and dwells on human origination.

After God created Adam and Eve they disregarded their maker's explicit command not to eat the fruit from the tree of knowledge and were expelled from the garden. They became the first family with the birth of Cain and Abel . . . and the first dysfunctional family after Cain killed Abel.

The remainder of these chapters contains two parallel, sometimes interwoven, threads. One traces the growth of the human race and its developing culture. Cain's offspring pioneered the building of cities, the domestication of animals for human service, and the arts. The other thread dwells on the problems that human willfulness created. Sin grew horribly, as told in episodes following the first murder. Lamech broke out with wanton violence, the sons of God sired monstrous creatures, and general human wickedness prompted God to send the flood. Overall, this section is enclosed in a creation-destruction, goodness-sin envelope.

■ CREATION (1–3)

The deepest human questions give rise to creation **myth:** Who are we? How did we get here? What is the purpose of life? It is no surprise that virtually every people has given thought to ultimate origins and every culture has shaped creation myths (see Sproul 1979 for a collection of creation myths from around the world).

> **Myth.** Modern authorities do not use the term *myth* to denote something that is false. Rather, myth is a culture's way of coming to grips with fundamental realities, and a culture's myth reflects its worldview. A myth is a traditional story of supposedly real events that is told in order to explain a culture's beliefs, practices, institutions, or something in nature. Myths are often associated with religious rituals and doctrines (see Kirk 1971). Both early cultures and modern ones have their particular myths. The cosmology of the "Big Bang" is a contemporary myth that strives to account for the universe. It remains a construct under frequent revision, even though it is backed by scientific evidence and reasoning.

The Hebrew Bible contains reflections on creation in various places, including the Psalms (Psalm 33), wisdom literature (Proverbs 8:22–31; Job 38–41), and prophecy (Isaiah 40:12–31). But the most well-known statements come out of Genesis. The book of Genesis contains two accounts of the creation. The first account comes out of the Priestly document of the exilic period. The second account is earlier and comes from the Yahwist narrative. While the Yahwist creation and flood stories deal primarily with the problem of sin, the Priestly writer was intensely concerned with the gift of divine blessing expressed as the structure and ground of all life. They were expertly combined with the big picture of world beginnings flowing smoothly into the story of the first human couple.

Priestly Creation Story (1:1–2:4a)

The Priestly creation story opens with an earth that was "shapeless and void." This world was dominated by vast depths of ominous and unruly water. Into the watery wilderness God injected his voice and created life, along with the means to sustain it. First came light, then the firmament to control the waters, then land and vegetation to sustain life. In succession God created birds, fish, terrestrial animals, and human beings.

The individual creative acts are spread out over six days and culminate with the creation of human beings as the image of God. God gave them charge of his entire realm, both to care for and utilize it. On the seventh day, later termed the Sabbath, God ceased creating and reflected with satisfaction that everything was very good.

> **Priestly Source.** As the term *priestly* indicates, the authors responsible for this account were priests. In addition to being spiritual leaders they were concerned with ritual matters, including Sabbath rules and food laws. These concerns are implicit in the creation story, with its seven-day structure and clear distinctions of types of animals. The cadence is so repetitive that some have classified Genesis 1 a liturgy, that is, a text used in formal temple worship.

TABLE 1.1	**BILATERAL SYMMETRY OF GENESIS 1**		

Day	Environment	Day	Inhabitant
1	Light	4	Sun, Moon, Stars
2	Sky and Sea	5	Birds and Fish
3a	Dry Land	6a	Land animals
3b	Vegetation	6b	Humanity

The account of creation in the Priestly document is structured symmetrically. The distribution of the separate creative acts into six 24-hour days was a deliberate scheme utilized by the Priestly writer. Organizing the activities in this way implies that God's design had rhythm and intentionality. The world that humanity inherited was well-formed. A hint of artificiality is evident in that there are eight discrete creating acts, yet they are contained within a six day structure. Additionally, this six-day structure is symmetrically bracketed by day zero representing primeval chaos and day seven representing cosmic order.

Table 1.1 clarifies the structure. Notice especially the obvious connection between the environments created on the first three days and the creatures made to inhabit them on the last three days. Each living being has its place within the structure. Also noteworthy is that humanity stands as the culmination of all God's acts, and in some sense as their goal. God ceased making new things after he made man and woman.

The Priestly creation story uses repetitious phrases to order the events of creation into six days. For a list of the repeated words and phrases that provide the structure of Genesis 1:1–2:3 see Table 1.A: Repetitions in the Priestly creation account.

Day 0: Waters of Chaos

The first two verses of the Priestly creation story describe the world before God shaped it into a life-sustaining cosmos. Then come the six days in which God created the elements of this new world. Lastly, the seventh day marks the grand conclusion of the process by the absence of creating activity.

> *1 When Elohim began to create heaven and earth, the earth was untamed and shapeless, and darkness was on the surface of the deep water. 2 And the wind/spirit of Elohim hovered over the surface of the water. (1:1–2)*

The book of Genesis received its Hebrew title *bereshit* from the first phrase of its first line, in some versions translated "in the beginning." Indeed, Genesis begins at the very beginning. While the text describes how the world came into being, it simply assumes the existence of God with no explanation of where he came from. The reference to God used in this account of creation is **Elohim.** It is Israel's most neutral and general way of referring to God, and suggests a powerful and kingly divine being.

Ancient texts can be difficult to interpret, either for linguistic or cultural reasons. This is evident, for example, when we try to understand this first verse of Genesis. It can be translated in two ways, both of which are linguistically correct. The first option, "In the beginning God created heaven and earth," implies that the writer was interested in positing an absolute beginning to the world. The second option, "When God began to create heaven and earth, the earth was untamed and shapeless," suggests that the writer was more interested in the condition of the world when God started his creating work, rather than in absolute beginnings.

The issue might seem of little significance, but it bears directly on the question of whether God created the world out of nothing, *creatio ex nihilo,* or whether there was an already-existing substance that God shaped into a structured world. The doctrine of creation from nothing, if not found here, is found for the first time in 2 Maccabees 7:28, which postdates the Hebrew Bible. The second option seems more consistent with the rest of the account and is the one we follow here.

The introduction contains a description of the universe before God started ordering and creating. While there seems to have been some sort of preexisting material, probably imagined as masses of murky water, it did not constitute a life-sustaining world. Thus, God did not start with a clean slate, with nothingness. Instead, the world at the beginning was dark and brooding. Everything was just a mass of water, the **waters of chaos** residing in deepest darkness.

> **Primeval Chaos.** The phrase "deep water" (1:2) signifies not just bottomless oceans, but the threatening waters of Mesopotamian lore that ancient peoples always feared would be their undoing. The Hebrew word behind "deep water" is equivalent to the Akkadian word *tiamat* which names the ocean goddess in the Mesopotamian creation story, called the Enuma Elish (see below). A variety of ancient myths describe a cosmic battle at the beginning of time. The sea monster is variously called Sea (Yamm), River (Nahar), Serpent (Lotan/Leviathan), Dragon (Tannin), or Arrogance (Rahab). After a battle, the high god subdues and restrains the villain of primeval chaos and so achieves victory. The description of the move from chaos to cosmos in Genesis 1 is not described as battle, but many authorities find tell-tale remnants of the cosmic myth here and elsewhere in biblical literature (see McCurley 1983 and Batto 1992).

Day 1: Light

> *3 Elohim said, "Let there be light!" And there was light. 4 Elohim saw that the light was good, and he separated the light from the darkness. 5 Elohim called the light day and the darkness he called night. Evening and morning of the first day came about. (1:3–5)*

God's work of creating things begins at verse three, and the means turns out not to be manual labor but speech. When God speaks, things happen. This suggests that God was intentionally pictured here as a royal figure—kings are the only human beings whose word is law and at whose mere uttering things happen.

The first element God created was light. It is the physical and spiritual precondition of all life. It also has connotations of goodness, warmth, and safety, especially when contrasted with the darkness of chaos.

> **Sun and Light.** The creating activity of this day is curious, at least from a modern perspective. First God created light. Only later did he create the sun. We would think that the order should be reversed or that the two events should be simultaneous. Light comes from a sun, it does not exist by itself, so how can there be a first day and night without the sun? This is evidence that the creation story was not designed to be a science textbook. The writer had other intentions. He created a somewhat artificial sequence that highlights the order of God at the expense of technical precision.

The first portion of the Priestly creation account of Genesis 1:1–5 can be heard as it is read in Hebrew.

Day 2: Water Barrier / Dome

> *6 Elohim said, "Let there be a barrier in the middle of the water, a separator between water and water." 7 Elohim made the barrier and separated the water under the barrier from the water above the barrier. And it happened. 8 Elohim called the barrier heavens. So evening and morning of the second day came about. (1:6–8)*

On the second day God created a solid barrier to separate the original waters of chaos into two massive bodies of water. This barrier is called a "firmament" or "dome," depending on the translation.

To understand what God accomplished, it helps to visualize biblical **cosmology,** that is, the Bible's picture of the universe (see Figure 1.2). Ancient people in the Middle East, including the Israelites, believed that the inhabited earth existed as an island of sorts, surrounded completely by water. Its existence was precarious at best, because the waters that surround the inhabited earth always threatened to break the dams and come flooding down on top of it. God actively kept the waters at bay. There were two great bodies of water. One above the sky, the source of rain and snow, and one below the sky, the source of oceans, lakes, rivers, and wells. While strange to us, this design made perfect sense to pre-scientific Mesopotamian minds. It is not difficult to see why. Beyond the sky on a clear day there is a vast blueness, in hue very close to that of the ocean. Looking over the horizon of the Persian Gulf or the Mediterranean Sea, water blended into sky, suggesting that they were made out of the same material. It is not surprising that they might have thought water lay beyond the sky in the heavens. And they may have asked, "Where do rain and snow come from?" Well, God opens the windows of heaven and releases them in measured amounts. This they could understand, though they knew nothing about the cycle of evaporation, condensation, and precipitation.

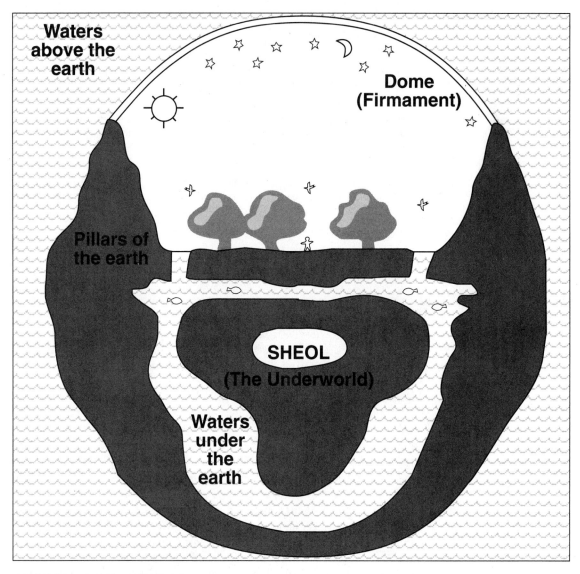

FIGURE 1.2 ANCIENT COSMOLOGY

Day 3: Dry Land and Vegetation

    9 Elohim said, "Let the water under the heavens be gathered to one place and let dry land appear." And it happened. 10 Elohim called the dry ground earth and the waters gathered to one place he called seas. Elohim saw that it was good. 11 Elohim said, "Let the earth sprout greenery on the earth, seed-producing plants, fruit trees producing fruit according to their type. And it happened. 12 The earth brought forth greenery, seed-producing plants according to their type, and trees producing fruit which have their seed in it. Elohim saw that it was good. 13 So evening and morning of the third day came about. (1:9–13)

At the end of the second day the water under the barrier was still mixed with what was to become dry land. These two elements were separated on the third day. The dry land was called earth and the water was called sea. As a second act the ground sprouted with plants that could propagate themselves. The work of creation took the shape of separating, gathering, and growing. Thus, by the end of three days God had created a basic environment with light, the heavens, the seas, and the earth.

Day 4: Heavenly Lights

14 Elohim said, "Let there be lights in the barrier of the heavens to sepa-rate day and night, and let them be used for signs, seasons, days, and years. 15 Let there be lights in the barrier of the heavens to light the earth." And it happened. 16 Elohim made the two great lights, the great light to govern day and the small light to govern night, and the stars. 17 Elohim put them in the barrier of the heavens to light the earth, 18 to govern day and night, and to separate light and darkness. Elohim saw that it was good. 19 So evening and morning of the fourth day came about. (1:14–19)

The work of creation continued through separating and dividing. On the fourth day the lights in the sky separated day from night and distinguished times and seasons. In the overall structure of creation, the fourth day is related to the first day. Light in general was created, and then on the fourth day this light was embodied in light-giving entities.

The language of ruling is introduced into the account at this point and becomes a prominent factor in days four and six. The bodies of light have a ruling and reg-ulating function. They determine the calendar and the seasons. Here we see the Priestly writer affirming the orderliness of the created world; religious life was organized around a cyclic series of holy days and festivals, all determined by the course of the sun and moon. Priests were the caretakers of religious life, and it was important for them to point out that the regularity of life was established by God at creation.

Day 5: Birds and Fish

20 Elohim said, "Let the waters swarm with swarms of living creatures, and let birds fly over the earth up against the barrier of the heavens." 21 Elo-him created the great sea monsters and every teeming living creature which swarms the waters according to their type, and every flying bird according to its type. Elohim saw that it was good. 22 Elohim blessed them by say-ing, "Be fruitful and increase in number and fill the waters in the seas, and birds, increase in number on the earth. 23 So evening and morning of the fifth day came about. (1:20–23)

On this day the sky and the sea became home to swimming and soaring crea-tures. The literary scheme the writer used to structure the account becomes clearer. The fifth day corresponds to the second day. The arenas for life that appeared as a result of the water barrier being created, the sky and sea, are now filled with resident creatures.

A new element is added when these living creatures are given God's verbal blessing to be fruitful and increase. Such a word of **blessing** expresses God's intention for the future welfare of these creatures. This becomes a very important theme in Genesis. Growth and living space are blessings from God, and express his desire for the welfare of all beings he has created, including humanity.

Day 6: Animals and Humanity

24 Elohim said, "Let the earth produce living creatures according to their type: beast and swarmer and land animal according to its type. And it happened. 25 Elohim made the land animal according to its type, and the beast according to its type, and the swarmer of the ground according to its type. Elohim saw that it was good. 26 Elohim said, "Let us make humanity as our image, according to our likeness. And let them rule over the fish of the sea, the bird of the heavens, the beast, the whole earth, and all the swarmers which swarm on the earth. 27 And God created humanity as his image: as the image of God he created him, male and female he created them. 28 And God blessed them and God said to them, "Be fruitful and increase in number and fill the earth and dominate it and rule the fish of the sea, birds of the heavens, and every swarming creature on the earth." (1:24–28)

As with the third day, there were two distinct creative acts on the sixth day. First, God created the animals to live on land. Then, in a separate act, God created humanity. This last act of creation is set off from the others in two ways. Instead of saying, "Let there be humanity" God said, "Let us make humanity." And humanity is the only entity whose creation is related to the **image of God.**

> **"Let us make . . . "** The description of this last act differs from all the preceding acts. Instead of "Let there be . . ." God said, "Let us make . . . ." A similar reference to the divine "us" is found in 3:22 and 11:7. To whom was God speaking? There are three possibilities.
>
> 1. *Royal Plural.* God was simply thinking out loud, talking to himself. Supporters of this position point to the fact that *Elohim*, the word for God, is grammatically plural. This might account for the plural "us." A variation is to call this the "plural of majesty," which royal officials preferred others use when addressing them, something like "your Highness."
>
> 2. *Holy Trinity.* Those trained in Christian theology see a reflection of the Trinity here. God the Father was conferring with God the Son and God the Holy Spirit. This option is remote, however. Certainly the early writer of this passage had no conception of a Trinity. That doctrine is only a much later theological development. The first control on our interpretation is, What could the original writer have meant?
>
> 3. *Divine Council.* Based on an analysis of similar notions in the Hebrew Bible, the most likely reading is that "us" refers to the Divine Council. The Divine Council was thought to be the governing assembly of angelic divine beings that supervised the world with God. The angels, called "sons of God" in other texts, were the parliament of heaven. A good example of this notion is in Job 1-2, where the "sons of God" met in session with Yahweh and the accuser (the satan) to evaluate the sincerity of Job's piety.

God said, "Let *us* make humanity in *our* image." The act of creating humanity was so momentous that God sought the approval and cooperation of the **Divine Council,** the heavenly court that attends the Most High. This underscores the importance of humanity. In addition, it implies that the image of God, to which humanity was to be related, was something common to God and angels.

See Table 1.B for evidence of the Divine Council in biblical literature.

A couple of important points should be noted with regard to the image of God. Whatever it is, male and female alike are related to it. Furthermore, God's blessing is somehow associated with being created in God's image. This blessing is to be realized as growth and fruitfulness, as well as power and rulership. Verses 29–31 detail all the created elements that God places under human dominion. And at the conclusion of the sixth day God declares that everything was "very good" using the qualifier "very" for the first time.

The image of God notion is central to a biblical and theological understanding of the nature of humanity. At the very least it posits that we have something in common with God. Furthermore, it defines who we are and what we should do. Humanity was created as the image of God on earth to represent and implement God's rule. Done rightly, this would lead to blessing and benefit for all of God's world.

Image of God. What exactly is meant by the phrase "image of God"? Many theologians have made suggestions (see Clines 1968 for a review of the proposals). Some suggest the image of God has to do with the spiritual qualities of God that humans originally shared with him, qualities such as wisdom and righteousness. Others suggest that the image of God has to do in some way with a physical shape or form that we have in common with God. This view, which implies that God has arms and legs, is usually rejected. Still others, including theologian Karl Barth, note how being made in the image of God is followed immediately by the words, "male and female he created them." This, they say, means that in God, as in humanity, there is relationship within unity. Being made in the image of God, therefore, means that interpersonal relationship is the essential characteristic of personhood. Giving it another twist, others suggest the mention of male and female makes explicit that both males and females image, or reflect, God, that God has both male and female components. Being so concise and without elaboration, the text can only be suggestive. So how can we decide what it means?

As always, the text itself provides the essential clues. The image of God specified in verses 26–27 is immediately followed by the mandate to rule and have dominion. This in itself suggests that the image of God is not something we *have*, but it is something we *do*. Humanity was created to model God's (and the Divine Council's) ruling function on the new earth God had created. Humanity was created *as* God's image rather than in it. As such the image of God notion is a royal concept.

In Egypt and Mesopotamia a ruling king could be described as the image or the likeness of a god. A conquering monarch in Mesopotamia would install statues of himself in the territories subject to his rule. These statues would be visible evidence of his claim to authority. It would remind citizens that he was in charge. In a similar way, according to Genesis 1, humanity was to represent the rule of God on earth, and put that rule into effect. Humans are to function as walking, talking images of God, created by God's authority, and designed to rule the earth on his behalf. Curtis (1990) defines the role of the divine statue in the religion and society of ancient Mesopotamia as "a local representation of the deity." We are not to infer anything about the physical shape of God from the fact that humanity is God's "statue." Rather, the text is saying that humanity was created to perform a unique function, to be a reminder of God's rule and to rule the earth as God's agents.

Day 7: Sabbath

> 1 The heavens and the earth and all their host were complete. 2 Elohim finished the work he had done on the seventh day, and he ceased on the seventh day from all the work he had done. 3 Elohim blessed the seventh day and made it holy, because on it he ceased from all his work of creating he had done. (2:1–3)

These last verses complete the week of creation. God had finished and he pronounced the whole "very good." This implies that creation was perfect, no more work was needed, no tinkering necessary to fine-tune the product, so God could cease working. The Hebrew verb for "cease" is *shabbat,* from which comes the word for the Jewish weekly holy day, **Sabbath.**

The seventh day was given special status. It was the only day God blessed. A priestly concern surfaces here. In the very story of creation the writers find hard and fast warrant for the holiness of the Sabbath day, and the week as the structure of life before God. The Sabbath commandment in Exodus 20:8–11 cites the divine week of creation as the reason for keeping the Sabbath day holy.

The Toledot of Heaven and Earth

> 4 This is what became of the heavens and the earth after they were created. (2:4a)

This half verse provides the transition between the Priestly creation story and the Yahwist creation story. It was provided by the Priestly editor of the final form of Genesis. This verse contains the Hebrew word *toledot,* which is often translated "generations." The phrase "these are the generations of" or, as we translate it, "this is what became of," introduces outcomes. Here it introduces the story of Adam and Eve as a continuation of the broad-scale creation story.

Toledot. Verse 2:4a is the closing bracket matched to 1:1, a technique literary analysts call inclusion. Verse 2:4a contains the first of eleven *toledot* formulas in Genesis (see Chapter 2). *Toledot* formulas are usually attributed to the Priestly editor who used them to organize the large blocks of Genesis. The Hebrew term *toledot* is derived from the verb "give birth," and can be translated "generations," "story," "history," or "developments." A narrative section introduced by a *toledot* formula typically elaborates the outgrowth of the specified figure, in this case, heaven and earth. Thus, the following Yahwist creation story relates what became of heaven and earth.

Yahwist Creation Story (2:4b–3:24)

According to the Yahwist creation story, the LORD God, *YHWH Elohim* in Hebrew, created the shape of a man out of clay and breathed life into him. This man cared for the garden of Eden and was allowed to eat from any tree except the tree of knowledge. When the man did not find fit companionship among the animals, God anaesthetized him and fashioned a woman out of one of his ribs. The man and woman were thus made companions matched to each other.

The perfect harmony of the garden was shattered when the serpent appeared. This creature instigated Eve and Adam to disregard God's command not to eat from the tree of good and bad knowledge. Realizing their transgression Adam and Eve tried to hide their shame from God, but with no success. God placed curses on all of them, including the serpent, and then expelled Adam and Eve from Eden. The Yahwist creation story thus shapes an enduring morality tale of human craving, personal responsibility, and divine punishment for wrongdoing.

Source Analysis. The Yahwist story of creation is the first episode of the Yahwist narrative. Its stories of Genesis 1–11 establish the basic plot of the Primeval Story. They primarily focus on the growth of the human race, and they demonstrate how sin dogged that development. They are told by learned court scribes who wanted to account for the big issues: Where did we come from? To whom are we accountable? Where did sin come from? Why do we have to die?

In the Yahwist creation account God is referred to as *YHWH Elohim,* translated "the LORD God." This designation is perhaps a deliberate literary and theological way of combining the name for God used by the Priestly source (Elohim), with its connotations of power, and the personal name of God used throughout the Yahwist source (YHWH).

In Genesis the older Yahwist creation story follows the younger Priestly one, but the order makes sense if the ruling logic was to move from a comprehensive world picture to an intimate tale of the earliest humans living in a God-created world. The Yahwist account focuses on the first human couple.

When comparing the two accounts one might notice that there are seeming inconsistencies, as when the creation of animals precedes the creation of humans in the first account, but follows the creation of the male in the second. Still, such tensions do not get in the way, and the Yahwist story effectively communicates the humanity of the earliest people: their desires, needs, aspirations, and transgressions.

Garden of Eden Gallery. The garden of Eden, especially Adam and Eve's disobedience, is the subject of many artistic renditions.

The Yahwist creation story includes the separate creation of the man and the woman. The account of the first sin in the garden of Eden (chapter 3) is an integral part of this creation tale.

Creation of Adam and Eve (2:4b–25)

> *4b On the day YHWH Elohim made the earth and the heavens, 5 no vege-*
> *tation yet being on the earth, no plant yet springing up (for YHWH Elohim*
> *had not caused it to rain on the earth and there was no man to till the*
> *ground; 6 only a mist rose from the earth and watered the surface of the*
> *ground), 7 then YHWH Elohim fashioned some dust of the ground into a*
> *man (Hebrew adam). He breathed the breath of life into his nostrils and he*
> *became a living being. (2:4b–7)*

Yahweh God is portrayed as a potter using earth to fashion a man, called **adam**
in Hebrew. One can almost picture God on his knees in the clay, working over the
body, manually shaping the man's physical form. This picture of God as crafts-
man is a good example of the Yahwist's use of anthropomorphic language; that
is, he describes God in human terms. Note also how life resulted only after God
infused the body with his own breath. These details imply that a human person
consists of both physical body and divine life-breath.

> **Adam.** The term *adam* as used in Genesis is ambiguous. It can variously des-
> ignate humanity collectively (as in 1:24, 27), the first man (when used with the
> definite article *the*, as in chapters 2–3), or the personal name Adam (when used
> without the definite article, as in 5:3). His mate is referred to in general terms
> as "the woman" or "his woman" until 3:20 when she is named *chavvah*, Eve,
> which means "life." The Adam and Eve described in the Yahwist creation
> story are the first individuals, yet at the same time they are archetypal humans,
> "everyman" and "everywoman."
>
> Notice how many times the words "earth" and "ground" are used. The
> "earthiness" of the story suggests it comes out of an agricultural setting. The
> story reinforces a connection between earth and humanness by a linguistic pun
> in the Hebrew text: "ground" is *adamah* and "man" is *adam*. Word-play occurs
> frequently in the Hebrew Bible and was often used to make a serious point. We
> could duplicate the pun with *humus* and *human*; that is, if our culture did not
> think puns were silly.

> *8 YHWH Elohim planted a garden in Eden in the east and there put the man*
> *he had fashioned. 9 YHWH Elohim caused to grow from the ground every*
> *tree that was pleasant to view and good to eat, including the tree of life in*
> *the middle of the garden, and the tree of good and bad knowledge. (2:8–9)*

These few verses describe a place called **Eden,** a garden of lush plantings that
included the tree of life. Verses 10–15 locate this garden somewhere in relation to
the two rivers that define Mesopotamia, the Tigris and Euphrates (see Figure 1.3).
This place was the locale of all good things, including intimate fellowship with God.

> **Eden.** The term is related to the Sumerian word *edin*, which refers to the fer-
> tile steppe region in the Mesopotamian basin, later to become barren. The
> Babylonian word *edinu* then came to mean "plain, desert." This derivation
> may be superseded by evidence from the bilingual Tell-Fekheriyeh statue of
> Adad-iti, which uses the word *'dn* in the sense of "enrich" when describing

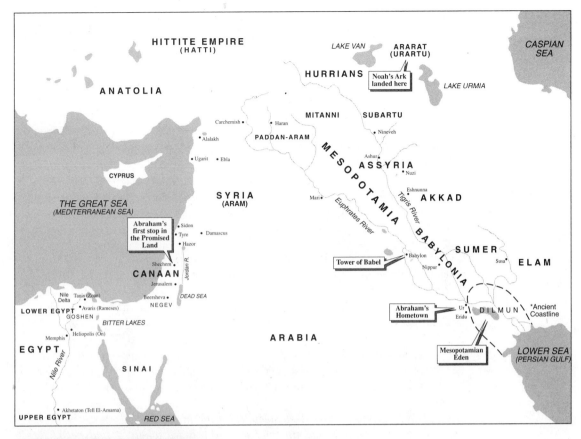

FIGURE 1.3   THE ANCIENT MIDDLE EAST

a god who provides all things necessary to produce food. Consequently *eden* may mean "place of luxuriance" rather than "steppe" (see Millard and Bordreuil 1982: 140). It was translated *paradeisos* in the Septuagint, which in turn became "paradise" in English. By locating Eden in proximity to the Tigris, Euphrates, Pishon, and Gihon rivers the text seems to imply that it lay somewhere in Mesopotamia. Eden has never been located, nor should we expect to find it. Sauer (1996) speculates that the Kuwait River may be the ancient Pishon.

Enki and Ninhursag. The ancient Sumerians of Mesopotamia had their own story of origins in a primeval wonderland. Enki and Ninhursag were two gods, as well as husband and wife, who enjoyed goodness as long as they stayed near the tree of life (see Pritchard 1969: 37–41). They lived in a place called Dilmun.

15 YHWH Elohim took the man and placed him in the garden of Eden to till it and oversee it. 16 YHWH Elohim commanded the man, "You may eat from any tree of the garden; 17 except you shall not eat from the tree of good and bad knowledge. On the day you eat from it you shall die." (2:15–17)

The man was placed in Eden to tend it, not simply to enjoy it. Perhaps we can extrapolate a lesson that even from the beginning humanity's task was to be the caretaker of the world. Of all the good things in the garden, God only prohibited the man from sampling the tree of knowledge. The punishment for disobedience was death. The tree of knowledge plays a crucial role in Genesis 3, and eating from it becomes the quintessential symbol of human defiance.

> *18 Then YHWH Elohim said, "It is not good that the man should be alone. I will make him a helper matched to him." 19 So out of the ground YHWH Elohim formed every beast of the field and every bird of the air, and brought them to the man to see what he would name them. Whatever the man named each living creature, that became its name. 20 The man named all the beasts, birds, and living things. But Adam had no helper matched to him. (2:18–20)*

God was concerned that he might get lonely. So animals were fashioned to provide companionship. The man named the animals, but still he found no fit friend. The animals, not being his equal, failed to satisfy his deeper longing. Note that verse 20b is the first time the Hebrew text uses the word *adam* as a personal name.

> **Names.** In the ancient world, having authority to give names implied mastery (see Marks 1995). Some see in the man's naming the animals an early form of scientific classification and an attempt to order the world in which he lived.

> *21 YHWH Elohim cast a deep sleep upon the man. While he slept he took one of his ribs and closed up with flesh the place where it had been. 22 YHWH Elohim built a woman from the rib he had taken out of the man. He brought her to the man. 23 Then the man said, "Finally this is bone of my bones, flesh of my flesh. Let her be called woman because she was taken out of man." (2:21–23)*

Yahweh, as is typical of this epic, was sensitive to innate human needs and wanted to provide genuine fulfillment for the man he had fashioned. He crafted a woman out of the man's body so that they would be of the same substance. Later (3:20) Adam gave her the name **Eve,** which means "mother of all life."

The choice of the rib, being so specific and unusual, seems deliberate. The Hebrew word for "rib" can also mean "side." Perhaps the choice of this word implies that the man and the woman were meant to be side-by-side, or in other words, to complement each other.

The woman is now the one who is "a helper matched to him," according to the Hebrew text (see Clines 1990). The term "helper" does not imply inferiority. In support we need only cite Exodus 18:4, where God is described as a helper to Moses using the same term *ezer.* The original text uses a pun on the word *man,* which can be mirrored by the pun in English: "man" is *ish* and "woman" is *ishah.* This is yet another way of affirming the essential relatedness of man and woman.

24 Therefore a man leaves his father and his mother and adheres to his wife, and they become one flesh. 25 And the man and the woman were both naked, but they were not ashamed. (2:24–25)

These words are comments of the narrator from a time when marriage had become an established social practice—obviously from a much later time than the implied setting of creation. They comment on the oneness of a man and a woman in marriage. The primary allegiance will be to the marriage partner, rather than to one's parents.

Becoming "one flesh" denotes the spiritual, emotional, and sexual union that characterizes marriage. Though without clothes, the original couple were unabashed at their nakedness, and felt no need to shield themselves from the other's gaze. Their relationship was characterized by an almost childlike innocence and naiveté.

Overall, this account stresses God's involvement with the newly fashioned creatures. Deity lived in intimate association with humanity in the garden of Eden. What happens next in the story explains why humanity no longer lives in the immediate presence of God in a perfect world.

> **Naked and Crafty.** The Hebrew text makes a subtle connection between Genesis 2 and 3. Whereas the primeval couple was "naked" (Hebrew *arom*), the serpent was "crafty" (Hebrew *arum*). This is a literary signal that these two chapters form a unified story. Another signal is the continuation of the name YHWH Elohim to refer to God. This is a relatively rare designation, and is found only in the Yahwist source.

Disobedience and Expulsion from Eden (3:1–24)

1 The serpent was craftier than any other wild creature that YHWH Elohim had made. It said to the woman, "Did Elohim say, 'You shall not eat of any tree of the garden'?" 2 And the woman said to the serpent, "We may eat of the fruit of the trees of the garden, 3 but Elohim did say, 'You cannot eat of the fruit of the tree which is in the middle of the garden, nor can you touch it, or you will die.'" 4 But the serpent said to the woman, "You would not die. 5 Elohim said this because he knows that when you eat from it your eyes will be opened, and you will be like Elohim (gods/God), knowing good and evil." (3:1–5)

Genesis 3 is a continuation of the Yahwist creation story. Theologians call this episode the **fall.** The man and woman intentionally disregarded God's instruction not to eat from the tree of knowledge. This marks the first occasion when humans rejected the authority of Yahweh. The essential temptation to the woman and man was to become like gods (or like God, *elohim* can be translated either way, though the verb "knowing" in verse 5 is plural, so the translation "gods" may be preferable). The urge to achieve divinity becomes the persistent impulse of humanity in these early chapters of Genesis, surfacing again in chapters 6 and 11.

The Fall. Although the notion of a "once for all fall" is not found in the Hebrew Bible, this story became the basis for the Christian notion of original sin. It appears first in 2 Esdras 7:118, and was developed by Paul in the New Testament, who said, "sin came into the world through one man," and "one man's trespass led to condemnation for all" (Romans 5:12, 18). Judaism does not accept the notion of original sin. Instead, it holds that one is subject to the evil impulse (*yetser hara*) that must be controlled by the good impulse (*yetser hatov*). This good impulse is cultivated by doing godly deeds and observing the commandments.

The serpent planted doubt in the woman's mind about God's motivation as they conversed about the trees. It was able to entice the woman by suggesting that God did not have their best interests in mind, that maybe God was trying to keep something from them in order to protect his power. The serpent never actually lied, it simply sowed the seeds of distrust by suggesting that God might be withholding something very desirable from them.

Serpent. Who/What was the serpent and where did it come from? Apparently, it was one of the creatures God had made. Only in later interpretations is the serpent identified with Satan and the Devil (for example, Revelation 12:9 in the New Testament; see Pagels 1995). Ancient mythological texts, however, suggest that more is involved than just snakes. The serpent is akin to the dragons and monsters of ancient creation myths, creatures such as Lotan (Leviathan) in the Baal texts from Ugarit and the water god Apsu in the Enuma Elish from Mesopotamia (see the note on Primeval Chaos, p. 54).

6 So when the woman saw that the tree was a good food source and that it was pleasant to look at and desirable for gaining wisdom, she took some of its fruit and ate. She also gave some to her husband and he ate. 7 The eyes of both of them were opened and they knew that they were naked. They sewed fig leaves together and made themselves loin cloths. (3:6–7)

Since the tree's fruit was appealing, and she wanted to gain wisdom and knowledge, Eve ate the fruit and passed it on to Adam. Immediately they recognized that something had gone wrong. They felt vulnerable with each other and defensive toward God.

Adam's Apple. Common lore has it that the fruit the original couple ate was an apple. The text says nothing about apples. The fruit was probably something native to the ancient Mesopotamian world, perhaps a pomegranate, date, or fig.

8 They heard the sound of YHWH Elohim walking in the garden in the cool of the day. The man and his wife hid from YHWH Elohim among the trees of the garden. 9 YHWH Elohim called to the man and said to him, "Where are you?" 10 He said, "I heard you in the garden and I became afraid, because I am naked. So I hid." 11 He said, "Who told you that you were

naked? Did you eat from the tree from which I commanded you not to eat?"
12 The man said, "The woman you gave me, she gave me something from
the tree and I ate." 13 Then YHWH Elohim said to the woman, "What did
you do?" And the woman said, "The serpent tricked me and I ate." (3:8–13)

Adam and Eve now felt estranged from God and became fearful. They sought
to distance themselves from God, so they hid in the garden, of course to no avail.
When God confronted them, both tried to disown responsibility for their actions.
The man blamed the woman and she blamed the serpent. The text suggests that
denying personal responsibility for one's actions is the primal human reaction to
guilt. Their choice to disregard God's instruction not to eat from the tree of
knowledge epitomizes the human tendency to assert its independence and autonomy and deny subordination to God.

Contrary to what God seemed to mean in his warning "on the day you eat of
it you shall die," they did not die on the spot. The death predicted in Genesis 2
apparently implied much more than just the cessation of physical life. Death sig-
nified alienation from God, which first became evident as interpersonal dishar-
mony and shame, and later as biological death.

14 Then YHWH Elohim said to the serpent, "Because you did this, cursed
are you more than any beast or creature of the field. On your belly you will
go, and dust you will eat all the days of your life. 15 Enmity I will create
between you and the woman, and between your offspring and her off-
spring. He will bruise your head and you will bruise his heel." (3:14–15)

God cursed them and expelled them from the garden. Each of the three received
a suitable punishment through a curse. God's curse is the opposite of his blessing.
In the serpent's case God made it the lowest of all creatures, forced now to crawl
on its belly. The curse on the serpent is somewhat cryptic, but God seems to be
saying that the temptation to do evil, as represented by the serpent, will not dominate humanity. The couple's offspring will be bruised by the serpent's evil but not
overcome by it. Perhaps this suggests that, at the very least, there is hope for
humanity.

16 To the woman he said, "I will greatly increase your pregnancy pain: in
pain you will bear children. Yet you will long for your husband and he will
dominate you." 17 And to the man he said, "Because you heeded your wife
and ate from the tree I commanded you not to, cursed is the ground on
account of you: you will eat with pain all the days of your life. 18 Thorn and
thistle will sprout for you when you want to eat the plants of the field: 19
by the sweat of your forehead you will eat bread until you return to the
ground (for from it you were taken)—dust you are and to dust you will
return." (3:16–19)

The curses were targeted to the created roles of the man and woman. The
woman was cursed in her relationship to her husband and in her essential role
of continuing the race. They had been created for a relationship of mutuality, but

now the husband would dominate. The text states unambiguously that woman's subordination to man follows the break with God, and is a result of the curse; it was not part of the created order. In addition to interpersonal dysfunction, the woman would have great pain in the course of child birthing and child rearing.

The man was created to care for and till the ground. His curse related to his essential function of caring for creation. From now on food production would be accomplished only with great difficulty. Although he was inextricably tied to the ground (remember the pun on his name), it would resist him as he tried to live off it. Furthermore, when he died, he would return to the soil out of which he came.

As a whole, these curses set the stage for the blessing that would be voiced by God in Genesis 12. God's blessing of Abram marked the beginning of his program to overcome the relationships broken in the garden. In the meantime he clothed the couple. Then they were expelled from the garden, according to God, because "the man has become like one of us, knowing good and evil" (3:22). Cherubim guards were placed at the entrance to the garden to keep the man away from the tree of life.

The break between humanity and deity is decisive for the course of events that follows. God was deeply offended by human disobedience. What exactly was the offense (in identifying the nature of the offense reconciliation becomes possible)? Was the sin a moral failing, or intellectual craving, or sexual transgression?

Primeval Sin. The significance of the tree of knowledge and the prohibition of eating its fruit is much debated (see Barr 1993). Here we outline three basic interpretations of the nature of the transgression.

1. *Morality.* By eating from the tree of knowledge, humanity chose to discriminate between what is good and what is bad on the basis of their own judgment, rather than by automatically accepting God's definition. By acting on their own, the couple irrevocably separated themselves from God, and their relationship to God was forever changed.

2. *Knowledge.* The Hebrew phrase "good and evil" can sometimes designate the totality of knowledge (see Deuteronomy 1:39 and 2 Samuel 19:35). Eating the fruit of that tree was an act of human pride, an attempt to know everything God knows. God would not tolerate any such challenge to his preeminence, and expelled the original couple from the garden lest they also eat from the tree of life and become invulnerable.

3. *Sexuality.* The story in Genesis 2–3 deals quite a bit with sexual matters. The couple is naked and not ashamed. Later they experience shame because of their nakedness. Even the serpent has been interpreted by psychoanalysts as a sexual symbol. The Hebrew term for "knowledge" can have sexual associations, as in Genesis 4:1, where "Adam knew Eve," which is clearly a euphemism for sexual intercourse. The sexual interpretation suggests that coming to knowledge, symbolized by eating the forbidden fruit, signifies the passage from childhood through puberty to adulthood. Sexual experience involves the pain and alienation of coming to know oneself and the other in new ways. Discovering the sexual impulse means one cannot go back to the state of innocence ever again.

All three interpretations have hints of truth in them. Yet the big affront to Yahweh seems to be humanity's desire to become like gods, to be independent, self-sufficient entities. By focusing on this dimension, perhaps the first interpretation contains the most truth. By their act of self-determination, the original couple expressed their intent to live by their own authority, not by God's. They tried to seize what could only be divinely granted. God would not abide this direct challenge. He expelled them and denied them access to perpetual life, symbolized by the tree of life.

This concern with self-determination versus divine-determination appears to be the key to the Yahwist's interest in this story. Would the prosperity of the Davidic empire lead the Israelites into an attitude of self-sufficiency? Would they forget about Yahweh? Would they try to grasp greatness on their own or wait for God's blessing? The Yahwist recalls the story of the first ancestors as a warning against self-determination.

The two creation accounts of Genesis taken together establish fundamental Hebrew truths about God in relation to the universe and humanity. God is sovereign and powerful, yet approachable and concerned. God established certain boundaries for proper human behavior, yet granted humans tremendous freedom. The world is wonderfully ordered and internally consistent, indeed very good, yet it is distorted by human willfulness.

These features of the Hebrew worldview were not held universally throughout the ancient Middle East. While the biblical creation narratives share certain similarities of detail with the creation stories of the ancient Middle East, their understandings of deity and humanity significantly differ. By comparing the stories we can identify commonly held mythic motifs, but also grasp the Bible's distinct perspective.

Ancient Middle Eastern Creation Stories

The biblical writers drew from legends, stories, and literary materials that were part of the larger ancient Middle Eastern cultural environment when they constructed the Israelite accounts of creation. Some of the surviving creation material includes the Egyptian creation theology, the Atrahasis Epic, and the Enuma Elish.

Creation Theology from Egypt

In the earliest Egyptian creation story, the world began as a formless watery void, entombed in darkness. When this primeval "water-stuff" subsided, the first mound of earth appeared. On this first island the creator-god Atum brought into being all other creatures and things. How he did this varies in the versions. According to one account, he masturbated (since he was male and had no mate) and brought the lesser male and female deities into existence. From their mating came the populated earth. According to another version, Atum named his own body parts and, as it were, out of himself came other separate beings.

Another creation story later emerged, called the Memphis theology of creation. Dating to the earliest dynastic period in Egypt (third millennium B.C.E.), this story supported the superiority of Memphis and its patron god Ptah over the previous capital. It states that Ptah was the heart and tongue, which is to say he was divine mind and speech. Ptah conceived the idea of the universe, ordered it, and called it into being with a command. Because of this Ptah existed prior to Atum as the principle and mechanism through which the world came into being. In positing the priority of the divine word, this theology of creation has a notable similarity to the Priestly account of creation in Genesis.

> For a full account of Egyptian creation theology see Wilson (1951). For the text of the Memphis theology of creation see Pritchard (1969: 4–6) or Simpson (1972). The Instructions for Merikare', written shortly after 2000 B.C.E., contains a creation account with similarities to the biblical story of creation.

Atrahasis Epic

The Atrahasis Epic, named after its human hero, is a story from Mesopotamia that includes both a creation and a flood account. It was composed as early as the nineteenth century B.C.E. In its cosmology, heaven is ruled by the god Anu, earth by Enlil, and the freshwater ocean by Enki. Enlil set the lesser gods to work farming the land and maintaining the irrigation canals. After forty years they refused to work any longer. Enki, also the wise counselor to the gods, proposed that humans be created to assume the work. The goddess Mami made humans by shaping clay mixed with saliva and the blood of the under-god We, who was slain for this purpose.

The human population worked and grew, but so did the noise they made. Because it disturbed Enlil's sleep, he decided to destroy the human race. First he sent a plague, then a famine followed by a drought, and lastly a flood. Each time Enki forewarned Atrahasis, enabling him to survive the disaster. He gave Atrahasis seven days warning of the flood and told him to build a boat. Atrahasis loaded it with animals and birds and his own possessions. Though the rest of humanity perished, he survived. When the gods realized they had destroyed the labor force that had produced food for their offerings they regretted their actions. The story breaks off at this point, so we learn nothing of the boat's landing or the later Atrahasis.

> The account has similarities to the Primeval History, including the creation of humans out of clay (see Genesis 2:7), a flood, and boat-building hero. For the text of the Atrahasis Epic see Pritchard (1969: 104–106). For a detailed study see Lambert (1969).

Enuma Elish

The Enuma Elish is the best-known Babylonian creation account. It existed in various versions and copies, the oldest dating to at least 1700 B.C.E. According to this account, before heaven and earth were formed there were two vast bodies of water. The male freshwater ocean was called Apsu and the female saltwater ocean was called Tiamat. Through the fusion of their waters successive generations of gods came into being. As in the Genesis 1 story, water is the primeval element, but here it is identified with the gods, who have unmistakable gender.

Younger gods were created through sexual union. These younger, noisy gods disturbed the tranquillity of Apsu, so Apsu devised a plan to dispose of them. The wisest younger god, Ea, found out about the plan and killed Apsu. To avenge her husband Tiamat decided to do away with the younger gods with the help of her henchman Kingu.

When the younger gods heard about this, they found a champion in the god Marduk. He agreed to defend them only if they would make him king. After they tested his powers, they enthroned him. When finally they met on the field of battle, Tiamat opened her considerable mouth as if to swallow Marduk and plunge him into the immeasurable deeps. Marduk rallied by casting one of the winds into her body, expanding her like a balloon. He then took his bow and shot an arrow into her belly, splitting her in half. Marduk cut her in two like a clam, and out of her carcass he made the heavens. The "clamshell" of heaven became a barrier to keep the waters from escaping, a parallel to the Genesis notion of a barrier or firmament. Marduk also fixed the constellations in the heavens. They, along with the moon, established the course of day and night as well as the seasons.

Then Marduk devised a plan to relieve the drudgery of the gods. They were tired of laboring to meet their daily needs, so he created humanity out of the blood of Kingu to be the servants of the gods. In appreciation for their deliverance, the gods built Marduk a palace in Babylon, called Esagila, meaning "house with its head in heaven." There Marduk sat enthroned.

The similarities and differences between Genesis 1 and the Enuma Elish are intriguing (see Heidel 1963). One of the most striking features of Genesis that the Enuma Elish helps bring to light is the struggle between order and chaos that lies just under the surface of the Genesis text. Marduk's battle with Tiamat reveals that the effort to create the world took the form of a battle. The victory secured Marduk's position as king of the world. The comparison may help to explain the claims of Yahweh's kingship over creation in such places as Psalms 29 and 93, where he is pictured as sitting enthroned over the floods.

■ PRE-FLOOD GENERATIONS (4:1–6:4)

Genesis 4:1–6:4 fills the gap between the first couple, Adam and Eve, and the story of Noah. These chapters tell two stories: one of the growth of population and culture, and the other of the growth and development of sin. The narratives of the pre-flood heroes and villains come from the Yahwist narrative. Taken with the story of Adam and Eve they explain why God sent the flood. Yet, at the same time these aberrations were occurring human culture was developing, including the construction of cities, the domestication of animals, and the rise of the fine arts.

There are two genealogies in these chapters, one in chapter 4 and one in chapter 5. The genealogy in Genesis 4 comes from the Yahwist narrative and tracks the growth of humanity through Cain. The one in Genesis 5 comes from the Priestly source and extends from Adam to Noah. A **genealogy** is a record or table of the descent of a person, family, or group from an ancestor or ancestors; in other words it is a family tree. Most readers would probably rather ignore genealogies completely. On the surface they appear boring, but they are rather important to the overall scheme of Genesis.

The genealogies of Genesis 1–11 accomplish at least two things. First, they give evidence that humanity did in fact multiply and fill the earth, as God mandated. This is evidence of blessing. Second, they establish the connection between Adam and

Abraham so that the line of continuity between Israel and its origin can be traced all the way back to creation (see Wilson 1977 for the social functions of genealogies).

Cain, Abel, and After (4)

Once expelled from the garden, Adam and Eve had sexual relations and their first son **Cain** was born. He was followed shortly afterward by **Abel**. Cain was a farmer and Abel a shepherd. Each offered a gift to God from his respective produce. Abel's offering was accepted by God but Cain's was not. Out of envy Cain killed Abel. God punished him by cursing his relationship to the ground, which would no longer bear fruit for him. So Cain was forced to become a wanderer.

The first murder is a continuation of the series of human perversions begun in Eden. Its immediate effect is to demonstrate the snowball effect of sin. Adam and Eve sinned against God and were cursed. The curse was passed on to their children. With the second generation death was no longer just a spiritual condition of alienation from God, but also a physical reality.

> **Dumuzi and Enkimdu.** A conflict story similar to Cain and Abel is found in Sumerian literature. In this tale the shepherd-god Dumuzi vies with the farmer-god Enkimdu for the favors of the goddess Inanna. Dumuzi quarrels with Enkimdu and wins the prize of Inanna's attention (see Pritchard 1969: 41–42). Both the biblical and Sumerian stories reflect the early conflict between shepherds and farmers over use of the precious arable land.

The escalation of violence continued. Cain's offspring included Lamech, who was the prototype of violent attackers (4:17–24). He boasted to his two wives that he took revenge on a man by killing him, although he himself had only been slightly wounded.

But even while violence was increasing, there was a parallel development. Culture and technology rapidly developed. Cain's son Enoch built the first city. Lamech's three sons were credited with various first-time achievements: Jabal for domestication of animals, Jubal for music, and Tubal-cain for copper and iron industries. By associating these developments with the notoriously sinful line of Cain was the writer making a negative judgment on these so-called advances? There was a tradition in Israel that a patriarchal, semi-nomadic, and unurbanized lifestyle kept one closest to God. The Yahwist writer may have been implicitly criticizing the cultural advancements of the Davidic monarchy by associating them with the line of Cain and Lamech.

Certainly such momentous human achievements were not the work of single men from the same family. The text telescopes into a brief span developments that took many, many generations. But interestingly, the text does evidence the importance of these developments and places them in early prehistory. Archaeologists and anthropologists have confirmed the importance of these developments for the progress of civilization, saying that these developments occurred first in the Middle East.

> **Apkallu.** Mesopotamian tradition likewise traces the arts and accomplishments of civilization back to primeval times. It recalls a line of seven *apkallu* figures, wise men who lived before the flood, and taught humanity the arts and

crafts of civilization. Genesis 4, which also contains seven generations in the Cain genealogy, may retain a reflection of this tradition. For the pre-flood Mesopotamian tradition see the Sumerian King List (Pritchard 1969: 265–66). The seventh pre-flood king, Enmeduranki, who was taken to sit before the gods and given special wisdom, may be the model for Enoch in Genesis 5, who is the seventh in the Priestly genealogy.

Chapter 4 ends with the mention of the birth of Seth, Adam and Eve's third son. The Yahwist tells us that at this time people began to call on the name of Yahweh.

Genealogy: Adam to Noah (5)

The Priestly source contributed the genealogies of chapters 5 and 11 to the Primeval Story. The genealogy of Genesis 5 contains ten generations between Adam and Noah, and the genealogy of Genesis 11:10–27 contains ten generations between Shem and Abraham. These two genealogies are essentially alike in that they are linear, going directly from one generation to a single offspring in the next. Both genealogies have a similar pattern (though chapter 11:10–27 omits the last sentence, "He died"):

> *After X had lived M years he sired Y. X lived N years after he had sired him and he sired other sons and daughters. All the days of X were P years. He died.*

Two descendants are of special interest in chapter 5, Enoch and Methuselah. Enoch is said to have "walked with the gods" and then mysteriously "was no more because God took him" (5:24). Because he did not die, Enoch became associated with a large body of post-biblical apocalyptic literature that supposedly was revealed to him in heaven. Methuselah lived longer than any other person, reputedly 969 years.

The Priestly genealogies of Genesis 5 and 11 provide the framework for the Primeval Story; see Table 1.C. The Priestly genealogy of chapter 5 has notable similarities to the Yahwist genealogy of chapter 4, as if they were different versions of the same underlying tradition; see Table 1.D for a comparison of the Genesis 4 and 5 genealogies.

Divine-Human Intermarriage (6:1–4)

The Yahwist exposed the limitless human capacity for wickedness. Sin grew in extent and intensity, from sibling murder to the blood feud of Lamech (4:23–24). The growth of sin culminated in the encounter between the sons of God and the daughters of men.

> *1 When humanity began to multiply on the face of the ground, and daughters were born to them, 2 the sons of Elohim saw that the daughters of humanity were good. They took wives for themselves from them as they chose. 3 And YHWH said, "My spirit shall no longer remain with humanity forever, because they are flesh. His life span will be 120 years. 4 The fallen*

ones were on the earth in those days (and also afterward) when the sons of Elohim had intercourse with human daughters and bore offspring for them. They are the warriors, from eternity called the men of a name. (6:1–4)

Certainly one question that jumps out of this text is, Who are the sons of God? Some interpreters have suggested they are the offspring of Cain, and that this story records the interbreeding of the lines of Cain and Seth. This would represent a mixture of the good and the bad lineages. This view is probably mistaken. Parallels to the phrase "sons of Elohim" in biblical and extra-biblical literature strongly suggest that they are divine creatures, commonly identified as angels (for example, see Job 1:6; 2:1; 38:7). They appear to have been errant members of the **Divine Council**, the body of angels who rule the universe with God. According to 6:1–4 certain of these angels were sexually attracted to human women and sired a race of giants.

The possibility of such interbreeding defies human conceiving (pun intended). Were it possible, presumably such interbreeding would have resulted in humans acquiring the immortality of divine creatures. Probably for this reason God took steps to limit the longevity of humans to a maximum of 120 years.

Fantastic and strange as the incident may seem, it plays an important role in the narrative scheme. The Yahwist used the incident to explain why God was finally moved to action. Sin had evolved so far as to infect the relationship between the divine and the human realms. The proper distinction between heaven and earth was no longer being maintained.

> **Myth.** Many authorities see the survival of an early myth about the gods and humanity in this story. Kilmer (1987) notes the parallels between the "fallen ones" and the pre-flood *apkallu* sages of Mesopotamian tradition. The biblical tale also recalls those notorious incidents of divine-human intercourse in Greek mythology, as when Zeus bedded Io and Europa.

■ THE FLOOD (6:5–7:24)

The episode of divine-human intercourse exceeded the limit of God's tolerance, so he decided to destroy what he had made and start again with righteous **Noah**. God chose the flood as the instrument of destruction and cleansing. The **flood** was no ordinary overflow. It is portrayed as a veritable reversal of creation. The language and imagery of the flood narrative echo the Priestly creation story at too many strategic points to be coincidental. The parallels indicate that God intended to return the universe back to its pre-creation state of watery chaos and then remake it using the microcosm of Noah's ark. The story of the flood is the pivotal point of Genesis 1–11.

> **Sumerian King List.** An ancient list of kings from the early Mesopotamian civilization of Sumer uses the flood to divide history into pre-flood and post-flood periods, much as the biblical account does. The pre-flood kings had enormous life spans, whereas those after the flood were much reduced. Like-

wise, the pre-flood heroes of the biblical story had tremendous life spans, while those after are closer to what we would consider normal. See Pritchard (1969: 265–66) and Jacobsen (1939).

See Table 1.E for parallels between the creation and the flood.

Prologue to the Flood (6:5–13)

The immediately preceding Yahwist story of the sons of God and the daughters of men in Genesis 6:1–4 provides the premier instance of moral erosion. Following this episode, both Yahwist and Priestly writers analyze the state of the world and why God decided to "uncreate" it.

Yahwist version

> *5 And YHWH saw that the evil of humanity on the earth was great; every willful plan of its mind was only evil every day. 6 YHWH regretted that he had made humanity on the earth, and he was pained to his heart. 7 YHWH said, "I will wipe out humanity which I had created from the face of the ground, from humanity to beast to reptile to bird of the sky. For I regret that I had made them. 8 And Noah found favor in the eyes of YHWH. (6:5–8)*

Priestly Version

> *9 This is the account (Hebrew toledot) of Noah: Noah was a righteous man, upright was he in his generation. Noah walked with the gods. 10 Noah sired three sons: Shem, Ham, and Japheth. 11 And the earth was corrupt before Elohim, and the earth was full of violence. 12 And Elohim saw the earth: it was corrupt. For all flesh corrupted his way on the earth. 13 And Elohim said to Noah, "The end of all flesh before me is coming. For the earth is full of their violence. I am destroying them with the earth." (6:9–13)*

These two versions are not contradictory; they just use different vocabulary to get the point across. In the Yahwist version, humanity is at fault and humanity along with all other living things becomes the focus of Yahweh's wrath. In the Priestly version, the earth and how flesh had corrupted it is the focus.

> **Source Analysis.** This difference in outlook of the two sources is consistent with what we saw in the creation accounts. The Priestly account in Genesis 1 is world-focused compared to the Yahwist account in Genesis 2 which is humanity-focused. Also note that the Priestly version here is introduced by this version's characteristic *toledot* notice, "these are the generations of . . ." (for an explanation of *toledot* see Chapter 2).

Undoing Creation (6:14–7:24)

Noah was given instructions for constructing a waterproof vessel in which to house his immediate family, along with a sample of animal life. After they entered the ark the springs of the deep burst open and the floodgates of heaven broke wide. This is the reverse of the separation of the waters in chapter 1. The flood rose over the earth killing everything that was not in the ark.

The waters rose so high they covered even the loftiest mountain by fifteen cubits (about forty-five feet). A number of Mesopotamian cities give evidence of ancient flooding caused by the overflow of the Tigris and Euphrates rivers. But there is no archaeological evidence for a worldwide flood. The biblical flood account probably derives from the memory of a local disaster.

> **Flood Archaeology.** There is no evidence of a widespread flood in Palestine, but that does not pose a problem. The flood account locates itself in Mesopotamia with the resting place of Noah's ark in the Urartu mountain range. Ancient Shuruppak, where Utnapishtim lived (the survivor of the Gilgamesh Epic flood), as well as Ur, Kish, Uruk, Lagash, and Nineveh all present evidence of flooding. But the evidence comes from different times. See Parrot (1955).

Mesopotamian Flood Stories

As with the creation stories, there are notable ancient Middle Eastern tales of a flood that, in some cases, display close parallels to the biblical account. In the Deluge Tablet, Ziusudra survived a flood sent by the gods by building a boat. In the Gilgamesh Epic, Utnapishtim survived a flood and was granted eternal life. The Atrahasis Epic also has a flood component (see above, p. 70).

Deluge Tablet

The hero is Ziusudra, the counterpart of the biblical Noah. Ziusudra heard the decision of the Divine Council to destroy humanity. He was able to survive the flood by building a boat. The mention of the great waters, the boat, and the window on the boat all have biblical parallels.

> All the windstorms, exceedingly powerful, attacked as one,
> At the same time, the flood sweeps over the cult-centers.
> After, for seven days (and) seven nights,
> The flood had swept over the land,
> (And) the huge boat had been tossed about by the windstorms on the great
>   waters,
> Utu [the sun-god] came forth, who sheds light on heaven (and) earth.
> Ziusudra opened a window of the huge boat,
> The hero Utu brought his rays into the giant boat. (Pritchard 1969: 44)

The Gilgamesh Epic

The **Gilgamesh Epic** was a widely known and often copied epic about Gilgamesh, the king of Uruk. One episode of this lengthy epic contains an account of a flood. After losing his best friend and thereby confronting the issue of human mortality, Gilgamesh went to Utnapishtim to learn the secret of eternal life. Utnapishtim was a pre-flood hero who survived the flood and was granted eternal life by the gods. The following is Utnapishtim's recollection of what the gods advised him to do to survive the coming flood:

> *Tear down (this) house, build a ship!*
> *Give up possessions, seek thou life.*
> *Forswear (worldly) goods and keep the soul alive!*
> *Aboard the ship take thou the seed of all living things. Six days and [six] nights*
> *Blows the flood wind, as the south-storm sweeps the land.*
> *When the seventh day arrived,*
> *The flood(-carrying) south-storm subsided in the battle,*
> *Which it had fought like an army.*
> *The sea grew quiet, the tempest was still, the flood ceased. When the seventh day arrived,*
> *I sent forth and set free a dove.*
> *The dove went forth, but came back; Then I sent forth and set free a raven.*
> *The raven went forth and, seeing that the waters had diminished,*
> *He eats, circles, caws, and turns not round.*
> *Then I let out (all) to the four winds and offered a sacrifice. The gods smelled the sweet savor,*
> *The gods crowded like flies about the sacrificer.* (Pritchard 1969: 93–95, selections)

Biblical parallels. The Gilgamesh Epic has notable parallels to the biblical flood story, from the waters that come, to the boat, to the birds Utnapishtim sent out the window to look for dry land. And as with Noah, Utnapishtim sacrificed to the deity after he abandoned the boat. The Gilgamesh Epic may be based on the flood story found in the Atrahasis Epic (see Lambert 1969). The version quoted here dates to around 650 B.C.E. The Gilgamesh Epic has a long literary history going back as early as 2000 B.C.E. (see Tigay 1982). After closely examining its tradition history, Tigay says this in defense of the plausibility of pentateuchal source analysis: "The stages and processes through which this epic demonstrably passed are similar to some of those through which the pentateuchal narratives are presumed to have passed. What is known about the evolution of the Gilgamesh Epic shows that some of the results of biblical criticism are at least realistic" (Tigay 1985: 27).

Gilgamesh Epic. The Gilgamesh epic is the single most important work of ancient Mesopotamia; see the extensive bibliography.

RE-CREATION TO ABRAM (8–11)

The second half of the Primeval Story parallels the first half in its broad developments and details. Noah patterns after Adam in overseeing the earth coming to life. Both receive the divine injunction to "be fruitful, multiply, and fill the earth." Both also were implicated in wrongdoing, though curiously, to a degree passively: Adam followed Eve's initiative and Noah's stupor became the occasion for Ham's indiscretion. In both phases the human population increased, as the genealogical witness attests, but sin also increased and prompted a divine reaction.

So they seem to tell, in many ways, the same story: creation, transgression, crisis. The critical issue is this: What shall now become of God's bold human project? In the first phase, except for Noah and the boatload, all life perished because of disobedience. Will God respond in a similar manner now that humans again revealed a propensity toward perverse behavior?

■ RE-CREATION (8–9)

The devastation of the flood eliminated all life from the earth. We are told that the waters rose even higher than the highest peak, essentially removing the earth itself. The narrative in effect takes us back to the pre-creation state of the world, and it would have been a totally formless, watery void except for the preservation of Noah and those with him in the boat.

The remaking phase of the Primeval Story establishes important thematic points. Noah is pictured as a second Adam and the earth is recreated. God brings the divine relationship with humans to a new level and, in an episode of suspicious sexuality, we see the return of wrongdoing.

Return of Earth and Life (8)

The tragedy of the flood was reversed when "Elohim remembered Noah" (8:1). God had a wind blow over the earth so that the waters would begin to recede, similar to God's wind blowing over the deeps in Genesis 1:2. Eventually the ark came to rest on one of the peaks of the Ararat mountain range, called Urartu in Mesopotamian sources.

> **Noah's Ark.** The traditional identification of Mount Ararat is 17,000-foot-high Agri Dagi, northwest of Lake Van in Turkey. Various expeditions have claimed to recover remains of Noah's ark, but none of the reports have been substantiated. See Bailey (1989).

Noah first sent a raven out the window of the boat and then a dove three times to see if there was any dry land. The first time the dove returned with nothing, then it came back with an olive twig in its beak, and finally it did not return. Knowing that the ground was dry, Noah, his family, and the survivors of the animal kingdom disembarked. The list of creatures that left the ark (8:17–19) mirrors that in the Priestly creation story.

The Yahwist tells us that Noah immediately built an altar to Yahweh and presented sacrifices from every ritually clean animal and bird as an offering to Yahweh (8:20–22). God accepted his sacrifice, indicating that now deity and humanity were reconciled. Yahweh vowed never again to curse the ground or destroy all life as punishment, knowing now that evil is ingrained in humanity. The short poetic conclusion to the divine musing signals a blessed return to order:

As long as earth lasts,
sowing and harvest,
cold and heat,
summer and winter,
day and night
will not end. (8:22)

Source Analysis. With creation, the Priestly and Yahwist versions were separate. With the flood, the Priestly rendition is artfully woven into the earlier Yahwist version. But the vocabulary of each is so distinctive that, for the most part, the two sources can be easily distinguished. Read separately, we would notice the following contrasts. The Yahwist version tells nothing of the building of the ark, though perhaps it was eliminated in favor of the Priestly description. In the Yahwist version the flood waters are the result of a torrential downpour lasting forty days, later receding in seven-day periods. In the Priestly version the flood is supernatural, inundating the earth from above the firmament (the windows of heaven) and from below the surface of the ground (the sources of the great deep). It prevails for 150 days, and takes 220 days to finally disappear.

In the Yahwist version the animals are gathered in sevens for the clean and only by twos for the unclean. The excess clean animals were presumably the ones used for Noah's sacrifice after leaving the ark. Only clean animals would be accepted by YHWH. The Priestly writer is content with one pair of each species of animal, and Noah does not offer a sacrifice, presumably because the proper rules for sacrifice have not yet been established. Proper sacrifices could only be offered beginning with the time of Moses.

Newer literary analysts have sought to move beyond classical source analysis in demonstrating the literary wholeness of the flood narrative. Some have discerned a comprehensive literary symmetry that is evidence of unitary composition (see Wenham 1978). Nonetheless, the fact that the final text shows symmetry does not disallow that the final compiler may have used a variety of separate sources.

Text of the flood account by sources. The story of the flood can be separated into its two versions for easy comparison. It is a superb case study of a story in double tradition. Read the two versions separately, being attentive to the differences as well as the similarities, then study the combined account.

Table 1.F: Yahwist version of the flood account

Table 1.G: Priestly version of the flood account

Table 1.H: Combined Yahwist-Priestly version of the flood

Table 1.I contrasts the vocabulary of the Yahwist and Priestly versions

Table 1.J explains the complex chronology of the flood

Table 1.K displays the palistrophic structure of the flood narrative according to the new literary analysis of Wenham (1978)

God's Covenant with Noah (9:1–17)

Both Yahwist and Priestly writers record God making a pledge of commitment to Noah. The version in chapter 9 takes the form of a **covenant**. Covenants in the ancient world were formalized relationships regulated by terms and conditions.

> 11 I establish my covenant with you, that never again shall all flesh be cut off by the waters of a flood, and never again shall there be a flood to destroy the earth." (9:11)

This is the first explicit act of covenant in the Hebrew Bible, and for that reason it is highly significant. In fact, the term covenant is used a total of seven times in this episode. Through this act of relationship God commits to continue life, both human and animal. As the following episode demonstrates, perversity still characterizes human behaviors, but because of the covenant God refrains from initiating a second deluge. The rainbow in the sky, the return of brilliance after the dark of storm, is the sign and reminder of this covenant.

Notable elements of this covenant episode echo the language of the Priestly creation story. God blesses Noah and his sons using the same language as Genesis 1:28: "Be fruitful and increase and fill the earth." As in the creation story humans here are given charge of the created world with the added provision that animals may be eaten as food—if the blood is first removed. Human life receives special divine sanction because humanity is made in the "image of Elohim" (9:6; see also 1:27).

Noah's Insobriety (9:20–27)

Noah and his three sons set about repopulating the earth. Noah settled down and became a farmer, much in the tradition of Adam and Cain. In the process, Noah, although "a righteous man, upright in his generation" (6:9), fell prey to what appears to be unseemly behavior—he gets drunk. God's judgment on humanity in the flood obviously had not improved human nature.

> 20 Noah became a man of the ground. He planted a vineyard, 21 drank wine and got drunk. He was uncovered in his tent. 22 Ham, the father of Canaan, saw the nakedness of his father and told his two brothers outside. 23 Shem and Japheth took a cloak, placed it on their shoulders, walked backwards, and covered the nakedness of their father. Their faces were turned away so they did not see the nakedness of their father. (9:20–23)

The text is not direct in its negative judgment on Noah's insobriety, but from other biblical passages we might assume this.

Ham's Indiscretion. We cannot be sure exactly what made Noah so distraught. Bassett (1971) suggests that Ham committed incest with Noah's wife, arguing that uncovered nakedness is equated with sexual intercourse. Cohen (1974) suggests that Ham acquired Noah's sexual potency by the act of seeing him naked. Such interpretations go beyond what is given in the text, which is not specific enough to determine exactly what Ham's offense was, beyond the fact that he dishonored his father.

24 When Noah awoke from his insobriety, he knew what his youngest son had done to him. 25 He said, "Cursed is Canaan! The most lowly servant will he be for his brothers." 26 He also said, "Blessed is YHWH, the Elohim of Shem. May Canaan be his servant. 27 May Elohim enlarge Japheth. He will dwell in the tents of Shem. May Canaan be his servant." (9:24–27)

Note the special interest in Canaan. Noah's curse of Ham's son, Canaan, is especially difficult to justify. Why does not Ham himself suffer the consequences of his actions? Perhaps the "Ham to Canaan" direction of cursing reinforces the biblical rule that later generations suffer the consequences of the sins of previous generations. Furthermore, this story is here to prove that sin was still around after the flood. Not even Noah was perfectly righteous.

> **Yahwist and Other Nations.** There also may have been a political agenda in this story. Living in the tenth century and connected to the royal court, the Yahwist was interested in justifying the elimination of the Canaanite inhabitants of Palestine who were Israel's enemies. This story gives Israel religious warrant for dispossessing the Canaanites and possessing the land. Other places where the Yahwist shows special interest in neighboring peoples include Genesis 26 on the Philistines (this is especially anachronistic, since the Philistines did not establish a presence in Palestine until the thirteenth century B.C.E.; presumably, Abraham is much before that); Genesis 29–31 on the Arameans; and Numbers 20–25 on the wilderness stories on Ammon, Moab, and Edom.

■ POST-FLOOD GENERATIONS (10:1–11:9)

After the flood and the death of Noah humanity began to repopulate the earth. Chapter 10, called the Table of Nations, is entirely devoted to Noah's sons Shem, Ham, and Japheth and their descendants. This genealogy comes from the Priestly source, but it differs structurally from the genealogies in chapters 5 and 11. It has a segmented or tree-like structure, going from one father to many offspring. The account details three broad groups of people, one from each of the three sons. Many of the offspring bear the names of geographical areas or cities. For example, the descendants of Ham include Egypt and Canaan. Nimrod, "a mighty hunter before Yahweh," is singled out for special attention and is credited with building Nineveh, the great capital city of Assyria.

The Tower of Babel account (11:1–9) follows the Table of Nations. These two accounts seem strangely out of order. The Tower of Babel story presumes a unitary human population that disperses after God confused their language. But the Table of Nations precedes it and locates peoples in their places around the world.

In spite of the logistic tension between the Table of Nations and the Tower of Babel, the two accounts tell somewhat the same story of tremendous post-flood human growth ("be fruitful and multiply"). At the same time the narrative reveals that human nature has not changed a bit, even after the cleansing effort of the flood. Humans still want to be like God, to reach heaven, the realm of the divine. And God is not going to allow it. The question that must nag the reader at this point, remembering how God earlier responded to human presumption, is this: What will God do now? Will he destroy humans again? Yet that option is not available because of the covenant God made with Noah. So then, how will God respond?

Table of Nations (10)

The genealogy of Genesis 10, called the Table of Nations, is different from the other main genealogies of the Primeval Story in chapters 5 and 11. The Table of Nations is a lateral rather than linear genealogy. It follows this general pattern: the sons of A were B and C and D . . . . The sons of B were X and Y and Z . . . . Its primary purpose was to identify connections among population groups based on their common paternity. Repeatedly we are told that "these are the sons of X, by their families, their languages, their lands, and their nations" (10:5, 20, 31).

The narrative placement of this material is logical in that it fills out the lines of descent of the three sons of Noah. From Shem, Ham, and Japheth "the nations spread abroad on the earth after the flood" (10:32). But the placement is also illogical in that it comes before the Tower of Babel incident (11:1–9), which pre-supposes that humanity is one entity, linguistic and otherwise.

Additional genealogies follow the Tower of Babel story in chapter 11. The genealogy of Shem (11:10–32) concludes the Primeval Story on a positive note—positive because God did not destroy humanity even though it offended him yet again, and because Shem became an ancestor to Abram, who would become the father of Israel.

Tower of Babel (11:1–9)

The Yahwist narrative contributes the plot line of humanity's reach for deity. The **Tower of Babel** episode continues the story of rebellion against God and depicts the overreach of human aspirations. A united humanity initiates an enormous project to build a turret that would reach heaven.

> *1 The whole earth had one language and the same vocabulary. 2 When they left the east they found a valley in the land of Shinar and settled there. 3 They said to each other, "Let us make bricks and bake them thoroughly." So they had bricks for building blocks and tar for mortar. 4 Then they said, "Let us build a city, and a tower with its top in the heavens. Let us make a name for ourselves so we will not be scattered around the earth." (11:1–4)*

The locale of this story is the broad plain of lower Mesopotamia called Shinar. In this episode humanity is still a unified community. The people had plans to secure their own greatness, "to make a name for themselves." They were intent on creating their own city and culture. Building a tower that would reach heaven itself was their goal. Yahweh, however, took considerable offense at this.

> *5 YHWH came down to see the city and the tower which the men had built. 6 YHWH said, "If as one people with one language this is the beginning of what they can do, then nothing they plan will be impossible for them. 7 Let us go down and confuse their language there so no one can understand the other's language." (11:5–7)*

Divine Name. Notice how the name of God in this episode is now simply YHWH, and not YHWH Elohim as in some earlier Yahwist stories. And who is the "us" in "Let us go down"? Possibly the Divine Council again (see the notes to Genesis 1:26, p. 58–9).

Why should Yahweh get so upset? Surely these ancient people were not capable of building a skyscraper that could physically reach heaven and thereby challenge God. Whether or not they could actually do it, God took their activity as yet another attempt to grasp greatness, rather than waiting for God's blessing. God took offense at their plan because it seemed as if they were trying to become gods unto themselves by reaching heaven on their own.

> *8 And YHWH scattered them from there around the earth. They quit building the city. 9 For that reason he called its name Babel because there YHWH confused the language of the entire earth, and from there YHWH scattered them around the earth. (11:8–9)*

God confounded their ability to communicate effectively. They could no longer cooperate, so their building plans had to be scrapped. The result was human disunity. The word "confuse" used here is the seed of another pun in the original text; the Hebrew *balal* contains a word-play on Babel.

Perhaps there is an additional level of meaning in the text. *Babel* is also the way the Hebrew language writes "Babylon." With this story we may be learning how and why Israel's great nemesis later in history, the Babylonian Empire, got its name. This story characterizes the great Babylon, even at the very beginning of history, as an evil city that by its primeval activities demonstrated its defiance of God.

The Tower of Babel story is a good example of how thematic analysis can be supported by literary analysis. New literary criticism, to be distinguished from classical source criticism, focuses on the structure and plot development of stories. Fokkelmann intensively studied the literary shape of the Babel episode. He shows it to have interweaving symmetrical structures, defined by repeated words and phrases. One such structure contains parallel action sets (see Table 1.2).

This is the effect of the literary structure. Humanity's attempt to go up is placed alongside God's going down. The language of the text highlights how God's actions are a response in kind to human efforts. For everything that humanity tried to do,

TABLE 1.2 LITERARY PARALLELS IN THE TOWER OF BABEL STORY

Human Plans (verses 1–4)	*Divine Actions (verses 5–9)*
One language, same vocabulary (1)	One people, one language (6)
Settled there (2)	Confuse language there (7)
Let us make bricks (3)	Let us go down (7)
Let us build a city (4)	Quit building the city (8)
Make a name (4)	Called its name (9)
Lest we be scattered around the earth (4)	YHWH scattered them around the earth (9)

God had a countermeasure. This reactive nature of God seems to characterize the Yahwist epic. It portrays God as ready to respond to the problem of human sin, both negatively (curses) and positively (blessings).

In addition to thematic and literary analysis, archaeology and cultural analysis can further increase our understanding of the text. The "tower with its top in the heavens," was a **ziggurat,** a stepped, pyramid-shaped structure that typically had a temple at the top. Remains of ziggurats have been found at the sites of ancient Mesopotamian cities, including Ur and Babylon (see Figure 1.4).

> **Ziggurat.** The term *ziggurat* comes from the Akkadian word *ziqquratu* meaning mountain peak. The reason ancient Mesopotamians built ziggurats derives from their understanding of religion and the gods. In ancient times mountains were often considered to be holy places where gods were thought to dwell. For example, Zeus dwelt on Mount Olympus, Baal on Mount Saphon, and Yahweh on Mount Sinai. Such mountains were thought to be contact points between heaven and earth. On the Mesopotamian plain there were no mountains. To remedy this, the inhabitants constructed artificial ones, ziggurats. One of the most famous ancient ziggurats was Etemenanki in Babylon, completed by Nebuchadnezzar around 600 B.C.E. According to Babylonian religion, Babylon was built by the gods and was the dwelling of Marduk. From there people could meet the gods. This is reflected in the authentic Akkadian name for Babylon. Derived from the Babylonian phrase *bab-ilu,* it literally means "gate of the gods." The Hebrew folk derivation of the name from "confuse" does not correctly reflect this true native meaning of the name Babylon. The Babylonians believed their capital city, through its ziggurat, gave them access to the heavens, as the meaning of the name Babylon suggests. The ziggurat itself embodied the concepts of pagan polytheism

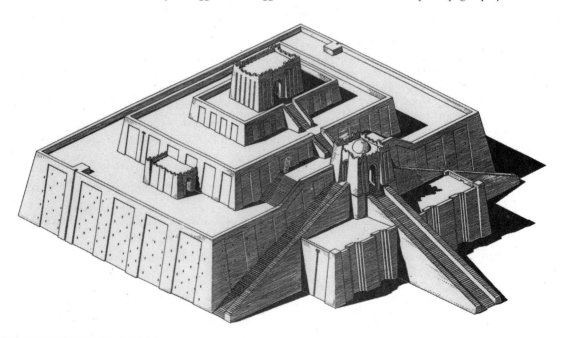

FIGURE 1.4 ZIGGURAT

to the Israelites, as it developed in the early stages of city development in Mesopotamia (see Walton 1995). The ziggurat represented this affront to the true God and lies somewhere behind Israel's Tower of Babel story.

The Tower of Babel story closes the Yahwist Primeval Story on a sad note. As a collection, the Primeval Story of the Yahwist deals with the relationship between God and humanity. Originally the relationship was close and pure. Then humans wanted to be gods themselves. This destroyed the intimacy of the divine-human relationship and had destructive effects on humanity and the larger created world. The episodes of the Yahwist core of the Primeval Story demonstrate the disastrous effects of human sin.

Tower of Babel Gallery, a collection of excavation photographs, reconstructions, and site diagrams of Mesopotamian ziggurats, including artistic renditions of the Tower of Babel.

■ GENERATIONS TO ABRAM (11:10–32)

The genealogy of Shem, to the exclusion of Japheth and Ham, indicates that he will now carry on the line of promise. The genealogy of Terah that follows it enables us to place the origin of Abraham's clan in Ur. Both connect the Primeval Story to the family of Abraham.

> **Terah Toledot.** The ten-level genealogy from Shem to Terah completes the genealogical material of the Primeval Story and draws it to a conclusion by accounting for the origin of Abram. In fact, the genealogy consists of two tole-dot: the toledot of Shem (11:10) and the toledot of Terah (11:27). In so far as the toledot of Terah is really the story of Abram, this is the real beginning of the Abraham cycle (see Chapter 2). The editors who drew up chapter and verse divisions should have made the major break here. The Terah genealogy locates the family originally in Ur of the Chaldeans and establishes a number of important facts and connections. First, the family left Ur and headed west, perhaps as part of the historically attested movement of the Amorites, called Amurru in Mesopotamian sources. When Terah's family came to Haran on the Euphrates they settled there. The story of Abram develops beginning in Genesis 12. Presumably, when Yahweh commanded Abram to leave, he would have left Haran, not Ur, as later tradition has it (for example, see Acts 7:2–5). Second, Terah's family evidently had put down roots in Haran. This explains why Abram and Sarai later got a wife for Isaac from there, to keep it all in the family. Also, when Jacob fled Canaan, he went to this area, located his uncle Laban, and eventually married his daughters.

GENESIS 1–11 AS A WHOLE

When we focus on the account as a whole we see that there are themes and structures that unite the variety of materials in Genesis 1–11 and, indeed, extend through the whole of Genesis. In addition, the final composition has a remarkable parallel development. Chapters 1–7 tell a story of creation to destruction, and chapters 8–11 tell a story of divine grace in spite of continued human willfulness. The startling conclusion of the Primeval Story is that in the face of the post-flood return of sin, humanity does not meet the same fate as before the flood, but instead God singles out Shem, blesses his line, and creates a nation through it.

■ LITERARY UNITY

Table 1.3 displays that the Yahwist supplies the bulk of the Primeval Story—almost everything except for the first creation story, parts of the flood story, and the covenant with Noah. For these, the Priestly writer had his own traditions, which supplement the Yahwist core narrative.

Table 1.L is a detailed content outline of Genesis 1–11. For a comprehensive literary source analysis see Table 1.M, the sources of the Primeval Story.

The Yahwist source contributed the core of the Primeval Story, which details human failings. The Priestly source contributed its own versions of the creation

TABLE 1.3 LITERARY SOURCES OF THE PRIMEVAL STORY

Genesis 1–11	Yahwist (J)	Priestly (P)
1:1–2:4a		World creation
2:4b–25	Creation of humanity	
3:1–24	Garden of Eden	
4:1–16	Cain and Abel	
4:17–26	Cain's generations	
5		Adam's genealogy
6:1–4	Sons of God	
6:5–8	Reason for flood–1	
6:9–13		Reason for flood–2
6:14–7:24	Flood (J+P)	Flood (J+P)
8	Re-Creation (J+P)	Re-Creation (J+P)
9:1–17		God's covenant with Noah
9:18–27	Noah's insobriety	
10	Table of Nations (J+P)	Table of Nations (J+P)
11:1–9	Tower of Babel	
11:10–26		Shem's genealogy
11:27–32		Terah's genealogy

and flood stories, as well as most of the genealogical material, but had a different agenda in his primeval stories. His creation and flood stories do not deal with the problem of sin but present the gift of divine blessing. The Elohist source, found elsewhere in Genesis through Numbers, is not present here at all. An exilic Priestly editor skillfully combined the Yahwist and Priestly sources and used genealogical material to give the chain of stories historical connectedness, inserting a variety of transitional phrases and sentences.

■ THEMATIC UNITY

What is the overall intent of these stories when seen together as a whole? The Primeval Story as a whole tells the following tale.

God created the world a perfect place. The creation, however, was distorted and corrupted by humanity's efforts to achieve autonomy from God. God's first response to the growing problem of sin was to wipe the slate clean with a flood and begin again with righteous Noah.

Even after the earth was un-created and then re-created, sin was still present. Noah's drunkenness, perhaps a sin in itself, brought out the worst in his son Ham. Just as before the flood, sin continued to spread and increase in perversity. The immensity of sin was evident in the monstrous city and tower building project conceived by humanity. God was outraged by this project. But he did not repeat his prior attempted solution by sending another flood. Indeed, he could not. He had made a covenant through Noah that he would never again eliminate the life he had created just because of sin. Instead, at that point, he narrowed the focus of his attention and concentrated on the line of Shem. Out of that line he took Abram and created a people called Israel.

The true nature of sin, from first to last, was trying to become like God: by knowing good and evil (Adam and Eve), or through divine marriage (Sons of God and human women), or by ascending to heaven (Tower of Babel). Humanity was created as the image of God. But there is a vital distinction between being the image of God and being God. Humanity persistently tried to blur this distinction.

Table 1.4 summarizes the parallel thematic development of the Primeval Story. Specific parallels and similarities between equivalent stories are suggested by the arrangement of elements in the table. Some of the correspondences are remarkable. In part one Eve and Adam eat the forbidden fruit and thereby sin; in part two Noah drinks from the fruit and thereby occasions sin. In part one Cain sins and is cursed; in part two Ham sins and Canaan (which in Hebrew, as in English, sounds much like Cain) is cursed. Genealogies stand in parallel positions across the columns.

The Hebrew word *shem,* meaning "name," appears to have some significance as a signal of structure. Humanity's essential failure was in trying to make a name for itself. In each parallel series of events, the culminating sin was humanity's attempt to become like God, rather than implicitly trusting God. Be it marriage with divine beings or a building project that gives access to heaven, they were self-deluded and were ultimately frustrated by God.

The first attempt resulted in the flood, a destructive cleansing of the world that had become corrupted. After the second attempt, the Tower of Babel, God turned his attention to Shem, whose name in Hebrew means "name." From his line God

TABLE 1.4   PARALLEL STRUCTURE OF GENESIS

Creation to Noah (10 Generations)	Flood to Abram (10 Generations)
A. Creation (1–2)	A. Re-Creation (8:1–9:17)
1. Deeps (1:2)	1. Deeps (8:2)
2. Blessing (1:22)	2. Blessing (8:17)
3. Mandate (1:28)	3. Mandate (9:1–2, 7)
4. Food (1:29–30)	4. Food (9:3)
5. Adam worked the ground (2:15)	5. Noah worked the ground (9:20)
B. Adam and Eve ate fruit of the tree (3)	B. Noah drank fruit of the vine (9:18–28)
1. Fruit of the tree (3:1–7)	1. Wine (9:20–21)
2. Nakedness exposed (3:7)	2. Nakedness viewed (9:21–23)
C. Cain sinned and was cursed (4)	·C. Ham sinned and Canaan was cursed (9:25–27)
D. Genealogy: Adam to Noah (5)	D. Genealogy: Sons of Noah (10)
E. Sons of God (6:1–4)	E. Tower of Babel (11:1–9)
1. Divine-human mix (6:1–2)	1. Reach heaven (11:4)
2. Men of a name [Heb. *shem*] (6:4)	2. Make a name [Heb. *shem*] (11:4)
F. Flood (6:5–7:24)	F. Genealogy of Shem (11:10–26)
Result: Undoing creation	Result: God focuses on Abram and makes his name [Heb. *shem*] great (12:2)

took Abram and made a special covenant with him. God promised to make his name great and to make him into a great nation. The lesson was this: The human race would achieve blessing and distinction only through God's initiative, and not through its own engineering and scheming.

The ancestral story comes next in chapter 2 and continues the story line of the Primeval Story. It shows how God developed a plan to bless humanity.

FOR FURTHER STUDY

Alter (1996) is a literary translation of Genesis, Levenson (1988) plumbs the theological depths of chaos, and Miller (1978) synthesizes the themes of Genesis 1–11.

Chapter 1 Bibliography; see Chapter 2 Bibliography for works treating the themes of Genesis as a whole.

QUESTIONS FOR REVIEW

It continues the story of rebellion against God & depicts the overreach of human aspirations.

? 1. Compare and contrast the Israelite understanding of God as implied in Genesis 1:1–2:4a with the understanding of God implied in 2:4b–25. *p. 52, p. 69*

p. 67 2. What does the story of disobedience in the garden of Eden (Genesis 3) tell us about the Israelite understanding of basic human sin?

3. What are the similarities and differences between the Enuma Elish and the biblical stories of creation? *p. 71 (?)*

4. What is the theological and thematic importance of the biblical flood story in relation to the entire Primeval Story?

5. How is the Tower of Babel story related to previous stories of sin in Genesis 3–10? Why is it a fitting conclusion to the overall tale of disobedience told in the Primeval Story?

That they understand it as being the human tendency to assert its independence & autonomy & deny the subordination to God.

b/w they both show the struggles order & chaos. The Enuma Elish shows creation through battle & the biblical stories of creation shows of creation through both God Speaking & God delegating responsibility.

QUESTIONS FOR REFLECTION AND DISCUSSION

1. We have seen that the Primeval Story is a composite literary product with identifiable original sources, including the Yahwist epic core and later Priestly additions. In what way does the epic core of the Primeval Story reflect the historical context of its writer? Likewise, how do the Priestly additions reflect their exilic context? Our modern origin stories, of cosmology (the "Big Bang") or national origin, reflect to a certain degree our understanding of ourselves (or how we would like to be). What are the similarities and the differences between our story and the Primeval Story?

2. Compare and contrast the various creation stories described in this chapter: the Yahwist account in Genesis 2–3, the Priestly account in Genesis 1, and the Mesopotamian account of the Enuma Elish. What does each account say about the nature of the divine realm? What does each imply about the nature of humanity? In much the same way, our modern world tries to account for origins, and these accounts imply something about values. What does a modern scientific account of human origin, such as that found in physical anthropology and modern medicine, imply about human nature?

3. Compare the following quotation from Josephus (first century C.E.) with your reading of the Primeval Story and its narrative of the creation of woman:

> *Woman, says the Law, is in all things inferior to man. Let her accordingly be submissive, not for humiliation, but that she may be directed; for authority has been given by God to man. (Against Apion, ii. 24)*

4. The Primeval Story as a whole implies that God created the world by subduing and shaping the waters of chaos. Later, humanity rebelled against God and contaminated the world. After an attempt to start over, even the "reborn" world of Noah was sinful. What does it say about God that he started over and never gave up trying to fashion a perfect world? What does it imply about humanity?

Chapter 1 Study Guide
- *Chapter summary*
- *Key terms linked to the glossary*
- *Concept questions with answer links*
- *Progress tests: true/false, multiple choice, matching, and identification*

GENESIS 12–50: THE ANCESTRAL STORY

2

FIGURE 2.1 ASIATIC SEMITES ARRIVE IN EGYPT This painting on the wall of a tomb at Beni Hasan depicts people from Asia arriving in Egypt. In a similar manner the clan of Jacob traveled from Canaan and settled in the Goshen region of the Nile Delta.

Genetic engineering is changing personal destiny by reading, and sometimes altering, human DNA. The traits of children can be determined at conception, and inherited disease can be treated at the source. Genetic programming modifies what nature has dealt us.

Still, we are inescapably shaped by our genetic inheritance, the DNA of our parents. Additionally, the environment into which we are born, including family, community, and country, shapes what we can and will become.

How much we are a product of our environment versus our parentage is the perennial nature-nurture debate, and is for philosophers, psychologists, and now also geneticists to work out. Almost everyone would agree that we tend to mirror our mothers and fathers. Knowing who they are and how they came to be tells us a lot about ourselves. The writers of Israel knew this, too.

The **Ancestral Story** is the Genesis account of Israel's forebears. The great Hebrew storytellers instinctively knew that Israel's parentage could teach a great deal about the nation's character. The Ancestral Story is the pre-history of Israel, the cultural genetics of the nation.

The Ancestral Story is dominated by sibling rivalry and family infighting. Yet the tales also have international significance. The names of many of the characters are eponyms, hence they are eponymous ancestors. An **eponym** is one who gives his name to a people, place, or institution. For example, Jacob's name was changed to Israel, and his sons bore the names of Israel's tribes.

The main protagonists of the Ancestral Story are Abraham, Isaac, and Jacob. They are often referred to as the patriarchs, or first fathers, of Israel. Male family and clan heads dominated social structures in Israel, although the powerful role of matriarchs, or first mothers, is evident throughout the biblical story. Calling Israel a patriarchal society would oversimplify its complex social organization.

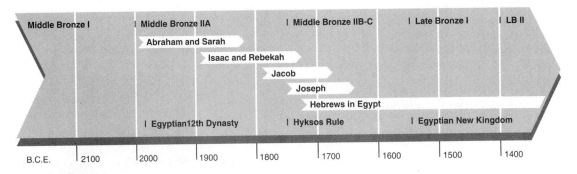

FIGURE 2.2 THE ANCESTORS Many interpreters place the ancestors in the Middle Bronze period, but this cannot be established conclusively.

The ancestral story gives ample witness to the essential functions of women in shaping national destiny. Most of the episodes of the Ancestral Story are tales of family life with a domestic orientation, and the matriarchs are dominant players in this realm.

The primary literary form of the Ancestral Story is the **saga**. A saga is a legendary narrative about an ancestor or community figure, though not usually the king. The plot of a saga is simple and recounts the leader's success in weathering threats or overcoming obstacles. Sagas explore human experiences and may have been intended to support the leader through life's problems.

Overall, the Ancestral Story does not have the same architecture as the Primeval Story, which was organized into two series of parallel developments (see Chapter 1). The Ancestral Story is organized into three major saga collections. Each collection is called a **cycle** because the stories revolve around a major ancestral figure, respectively Abraham, Jacob, and Joseph. These three cycles are separated from each other by brief genealogical notices of the two ancestral offspring who branched off from the trajectory of Israel, namely Ishmael and Esau.

The Abraham and Jacob cycles could be called albums, the stories being similar to snapshots. The individual tales within each cycle are not altogether tightly connected nor are they ordered by a linear plot structure. Nonetheless, threads and themes unite the collections. In contrast, the stories of the Joseph cycle are dramatically unified in what may be the world's earliest novella. It is replete with consistent characterization, theatrical tension, and narrative suspense—befitting any good tale.

The literary shape of the Ancestral Story is much easier to establish than the ancestors' relationship to history. No outside source makes reference to the ancestors of Israel, and Genesis makes no unambiguous references to otherwise known historical figures. Authorities have attempted to establish the time frame of the ancestors using biblical parallels to the known social customs (see Millard and Wiseman 1980, Kitchen 1995). On this basis the ancestors have been positioned in the Middle Bronze period (2000–1550 B.C.E.; see Figure 2.2).

Other authorities have challenged the social and historical parallels and have built a case that the Ancestral Story is largely a fictional account written after Judah's exile in Babylonia (see Van Seters 1975 and Thompson 1987, 1992). According to this view, the story reflects the later community's understanding of its identity, and as such is not an historically reliable chronicle of actual events. This view is supported by anachronisms in the narrative. For example, the city of Abraham's origin is called Ur of the Chaldeans, but the term *Chaldean* could only apply to southern Mesopotamia from the tenth to eighth centuries B.C.E. at the earliest.

The chronology of the ancestral period is problematic. Table 2.A provides relevant data.

As you read the Ancestral Story pay special attention to the following concerns that are common to the three cycles. Each is concerned with how God extends blessing to the ancestral family and from them to others, but each cycle has its own variation on the theme. Each employs a journey motif that mirrors in some way the movement from barrenness to blessing. From the perspective of text composition, the first episode of each cycle also contains in embryonic form the dynamics of the blessing theme, especially as it relates to offspring and land.

ABRAHAM CYCLE (11:27–25:11)

The **Abraham cycle** both continues the primeval theme of blessing and begins the history of Israel. The new beginning notably coincides with its hero, **Abraham**, departing for a new land. Reflecting universal epic patterns, the hero's journey (see Campbell 1968) is played out in Abraham's story. He leaves his comfortable surroundings with an eager but simple faith, faces many dangers, and occasionally stumbles. Through these challenges his faith matures and his relationship with God deepens. When God commands Abraham to sacrifice his son he faces his most difficult challenge—and is forever changed.

Story Line

When God held out the promise of a homeland and a large family, Abram migrated from Ur in southern Mesopotamia (see Figure 2.3) to Palestine (Genesis 12). Because of a famine, he and his wife Sarai sought refuge in Egypt. Abram and Lot had competing claims to Canaan and finally separated (13). God made a covenant with Abram as an assurance that he would fulfill his promise of offspring (15). When many years had passed and yet they had no son, Abram and Sarai arranged to have a surrogate son by Sarai's servant, Hagar, and Ishmael was born (16). God reaffirmed the covenant promise of offspring, founded the ritual of circumcision, and gave new names to Abram and Sarai (17).

When Abraham was almost one hundred and Sarah almost ninety, God announced that they would have their own son (18–19). After the promised son, Isaac, was born, Ishmael and Hagar came into conflict with Sarah and were driven away (21). Then God tested Abraham's faith by commanding him to slaughter and sacrifice Isaac. At the last moment God stopped Abraham from killing Isaac (22). Sarah died shortly thereafter and was buried in a plot purchased by Abraham (23). Abraham arranged a wife for Isaac, Rebekah from the Terah clan back in Aram (24). So Abraham passed away knowing his line would continue (25).

Abram and Sarai. There may be confusion over the names Abram and Sarai. Genesis refers to the first patriarch as Abram and the first matriarch as Sarai from the time of their departure from Ur until the covenant of circumcision is given. At this point God changed their names to Abraham (17:5) and Sarah (17:15). Where a distinction is not relevant, discussions will use the names Abraham and Sarah.

The Abraham cycle of stories formally begins with the *toledot* or genealogy, of Terah (11:27–32; for an explanation of *toledot* see Chapter 2). This genealogical notice mentions two essential details: Abram married Sarai, who was barren, and Abram's clan left Ur for Canaan but stopped short and settled in Haran. These facts set the stage for the two itineraries that drive the cycle. The first is the metaphorical journey from barrenness to fertility. If there is any unifying motif to the cycle it is the concern for a son. The second itinerary is the geographical journey from Mesopotamia to the Promised Land (see Figure 2.3). The cycle tracks the physical movement of Abraham closely, and Abraham's position with respect to the Promised Land of Canaan is a measure of his faith and the fulfillment of God's promises.

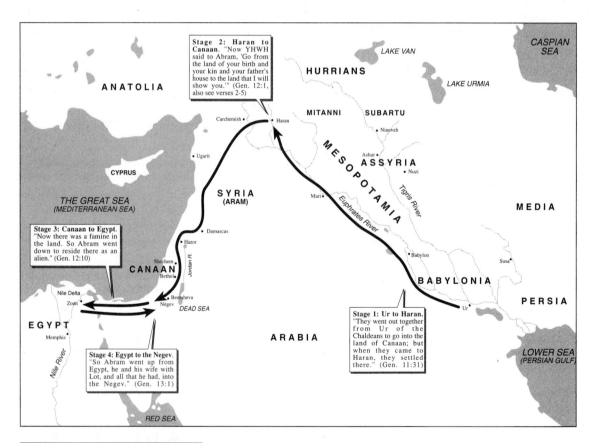

FIGURE 2.3 ABRAHAM'S JOURNEY Abraham's clan originally came from southern Mesopotamia, then settled in western Mesopotamia. Abraham, Sarah, and Lot traveled from Haran to Canaan. Abraham's principle sphere of activity is the territory of Judah.

Abraham's wide-ranging travels through the Middle East may be related to the well-known movements of the Amorites of the second millennium B.C.E. Also, the type of names held by Israelite ancestors fits the pattern of Amorite personal names. Abraham was not an Amorite, but the biblical portrait of him correlates generally with Bronze Age western Mesopotamia.

> **Amorites and Amurru.** The term "Amorite" comes from *amurru,* an Old Akkadian word meaning "west." It refers to the population of the western territories of Mesopotamia. Sumerian and Akkadian traditions described the Amorites as uncivilized. They ate their meat raw and did not bury their dead. Amorite culture might better be characterized as village agricultural, which explains why the Mesopotamian urban mainstream disparaged the Amorites. The Abraham narrative fits the picture of Bronze Age Amorite culture, and Abraham's movements are consistent with what is known of Amorite migrations (see Haldar 1971 and Mendenhall 1992).

■ CALL AND COVENANT (12–17)

The first episode of the Abraham cycle articulates what God intended to do with Abraham. The divine charge in 12:1–3 contains the program of the cycle. In it Yahweh makes some rather bold promises to Abraham, perhaps as incentive to get him moving. Having given up everything to follow Yahweh's lead, Abraham awaits fulfillment of the promises . . . but as years turn into decades Abraham verges on disillusionment. Still no children, still no land. Through various means, including the device of covenant, God maintains Abraham's hope.

To and From Canaan (12–14)

The divine promise speech in 12:1–3 is crucial for understanding the theological intention of the Yahwist source. Abraham was commanded to leave home and family to follow Yahweh's leading to a new land.

> *1 Now YHWH said to Abram, "Go from the land of your birth and your kin and your father's house to the land that I will show you. 2 And I will make you into a great nation, and I will bless you, and make your name great, so that you will be a blessing. 3 I will bless those who bless you, and him who curses you I will curse; and through you all the families of the earth shall bless themselves/be blessed." (12:1–3)*

God essentially promised Abraham three things: a homeland, offspring, and, less tangible than these two, that he would be a blessing. Take note of the phrases "great nation" and "make your name great" in Yahweh's speech. God is the one who will secure Abraham's future greatness. This language recalls the earlier significance of "name" in Genesis 6:4 ("men of a name") and 11:4 ("make a name for ourselves"). The name (Hebrew *shem*) God will make for Abraham will reverse humanity's previous misguided aspirations.

The prominence of the word *blessing* in this text suggests that God had something special in store for Abraham. But not only for him; through Abraham, all humanity would be blessed and move out from under Yahweh's curse. This is as close as we come to an overall theological theme of the Yahwist narrative. Perhaps the Yahwist writer, presumably connected to the Davidic or Solomonic court, believed that God's blessings had been given to David, especially through the gift of an empire, and he saw this as the beginning of the renewal of society—perhaps even a new world order.

Abraham followed Yahweh's command and traveled from Haran to Canaan. He stopped at two places, Shechem and the region of Bethel, before arriving in the Negev. At both Shechem and Bethel he built an altar to Yahweh, demonstrating his devotion to God, and perhaps also, at least in the eyes of later Israelites, founding these sites as authentic worship centers.

No sooner had Abraham journeyed to Canaan under Yahweh's promise than a famine forced him and Sarah to go elsewhere in search of sustenance. Arriving in Egypt, Abraham feared for his life, believing that the Egyptians would dispose of him to gain his beautiful Sarah. He and Sarah agreed to keep their spousal relationship a secret so that he would be spared. Pharaoh did take Sarah to his court, but as a consequence Yahweh afflicted the royal house with plagues. When confronted by Pharaoh, Abraham admitted his deception and was summarily expelled.

This story is notable for a number of reasons. First, Abraham is pictured in a less than flattering way. The story reveals his striking lack of faith—even after having just received Yahweh's remarkable promises. The episode is strategic for the theological plot development of the cycle. It benchmarks Abraham's insecurity and sets the story up for Abraham to grow in trust and confidence in Yahweh's promises as the narrative progresses. Second, the famine, the routing from Canaan to Egypt and back, and Pharaoh and plagues foreshadow the large-scale confrontation between the Hebrews and Egyptians told in the book of Exodus (see Chapter 3).

After the famine, another threat to the promise of land came by way of Abraham's nephew **Lot.** Both of their flocks had grown so large that they started competing for pasturage. In a fit of generosity, and evidently also a show of faith, Abraham allowed Lot to choose where he wished to be. Lot chose the well-watered Jordan valley. In response God reiterated to Abraham his promises of land and offspring (13:14–17), and Abraham moved to the Hebron area.

In the meantime Lot drifted toward Sodom and Gomorrah. A coalition of Middle Eastern kings ransacked these cities and carried off Lot. Abraham mustered a fighting force of 318 men out of his own estate and gave chase. His troops recovered the goods and people stolen from the cities of the plain. On his journey back to Hebron, Melchizedek, the king of Salem (possibly Jerusalem), blessed Abraham in the name of "El Elyon, Creator of heaven and earth" (14:19). This episode illustrates how powerful Abraham had become, displays concretely how the nations were blessed through him, and confirms that he was blessed by God.

> **El Elyon.** This divine name is found only in Genesis 14 and Psalm 78:35. It is composed of two elements. *El* is the common Semitic term for "god," and is widely found in personal and place names (Elijah, Samuel, Bethel). Elyon is attested as an epithet of Baal, meaning "the exalted one" in Ugaritic texts. In other texts El and Elyon appear to be two different deities. See Cross (1973) for a study of divine names.

Heir to the Promise (15–16)

Although Yahweh had promised that Abraham would become a great nation, by advanced old age he and Sarah still did not have children. In chapter 15, a highly significant passage, Yahweh approaches Abraham and confirms his promises with a covenant. A **covenant** is an oath-bound relationship with defined expectations and obligations. Covenants originated in politics and international law, and have conventional forms. We have many surviving examples of ancient Middle Eastern covenants (see McCarthy 1978). Treaty and charter covenants were the two main types of covenants in the ancient Middle East.

A treaty covenant defined and regulated a relationship between nations. The parties to the covenant could be of equal power and status (a parity covenant) or of unequal status (a suzerain-vassal covenant). The covenant God made with Israel through Moses at Mount Sinai was a suzerain-vassal covenant (see Chapters 3 and 5). Ancient treaty covenants are analogous to the formal international alliances and trade agreements modern countries still negotiate.

A charter covenant consisted of a grant of property (see Weinfeld 1970). The grant was usually made to reward faithfulness or loyal service. For example, kings would bestow land on loyal military officers after a campaign, hence it is sometimes called a royal grant covenant. This type of covenant is perhaps analogous to modern property titles and deeds.

> **Source Analysis.** Chapter 15 is the Yahwist's record of God's charter covenant given to Abraham, and concerns the issue of an heir. It is assigned to the Yahwist source because of its style and theme, but we should note that it contains some inconsistencies that suggest it has elements from elsewhere, perhaps the Elohist source. Verses 3, 5, and 13–16 are usually assigned to the Elohist source because revelations in visionary form are typically an Elohist characteristic. Rendtorff (1985) argues chapter 15 is Deuteronomic. The Abraham charter covenant is similar in structure to the David charter covenant in 2 Samuel 7 (see Chapter 8). Clements (1967) argues that they come from the same source.

In this passage the Yahwist uses the charter form of covenant to give shape to God's commitment to Abraham. It is a unilateral divine promise in which God binds himself by an oath to provide offspring for Abraham.

> *1 After these events, the word of YHWH came to Abram in a vision, "Don't be afraid, Abram. . . ." (15:1a)*

God came to Abraham in a vision, indicating Abraham's special relationship with God. The phrase "The word of YHWH came" typically introduces prophetic revelation (see 1 Samuel 15:10 and Hosea 1:1). Fear is a natural reaction when someone is in the presence of God, and therefore "Don't be afraid" is a phrase that frequently introduces announcements of salvation (see 21:17; 26:24; 35:17; as well as Isaiah 10:24).

> *". . . I am your shield. Your reward will be very great." (15:1b)*

God declared himself to be Abraham's shield, that is, his protector. The reward will not be an earned prize but a gift of special recognition for a faithful servant of the king.

> *2 Abram said, "My Lord YHWH, what of lasting significance can you give me since I continue to be childless, with Eliezer of Damascus, a servant, standing to inherit my estate?" 3 Abram further stated, "You have not given me offspring. One of my servants stands as my heir." 4 Then there was a word of YHWH for him, "That one shall not be your heir! One who comes from your own loins—he will be your heir." 5 He took him outside and said, "Look at the heavens and count the stars if you can. So will your offspring be." 6 He placed his trust in YHWH, and he (YHWH) considered that a righteous act. (15:2–6)*

Since Abraham had no natural-born son, his inheritance was due to go to his servant, Eliezer of Damascus. This story demonstrates that concern over descendants is central to the plot line. This will be a continuing interest of the Yahwist within the Ancestral Story. Lacking a son, Abraham was not sure that God's promise would ever be realized. After God reassured him that he would have numerous offspring—even more than the stars—Abraham committed his future to God, even though he saw no evidence of impending fulfillment. God took Abraham's faith as an indication that he wanted to stand in a relationship of living trust with him.

The word *righteous* is significant. Righteousness in the Torah applies to human activity. Righteous acts are God-approved ones, whereby the doer demonstrates he or she intends to stand in a relationship of dependence on God. Here Abraham's faith is reckoned as a righteous act.

The next part of the story (verses 7–12, not given here) describes a rather strange ceremony. Abraham slaughtered a heifer, goat, ram, turtledove, and pigeon, and he placed the animal halves in two rows. Then Abraham was cast into a deep sleep, and Yahweh appeared to him and symbolically passed between the animal halves.

> *17 When the sun set and it was dark, a smoking oven and a flaming torch passed between these pieces. (15:17)*

This ceremony drew Abraham into a formal relationship with God. In the ritual God demonstrated to Abraham the depth of his commitment to him. The narrative says that God took the form of a smoking oven pot and torch for the purposes of the ceremony. According to the Hebrew Bible, God has no physical form, but when he does appear, typically he is represented by smoke and fire. Such a symbolic appearance of God is called a **theophany.** The most notable appearance was his descent onto Mount Sinai in Exodus 19, when he appeared to the Israelites and delivered the Ten Commandments.

The ceremony took the form of a ritual of self-condemnation. By passing between the bisected animals, God was ritually calling down upon himself the same fate that the animals suffered, should he be unfaithful to the covenant promise. In this ceremonial way God staked his life on the promise of offspring.

18 On that day YHWH cut a covenant with Abram: "To your offspring I give this land: from the River of Egypt to the Great River, the Euphrates." (15:18)

The entire encounter between Abraham and Yahweh in this passage is summarized in the statement, "Yahweh cut a covenant with Abram." In biblical language, "to cut a covenant" refers to the animals that were ceremonially cut in half. Cutting animals in a covenant ceremony may have been a traditional practice. Cutting an ass in half was part of a ritual of covenant ratification attested in Mari. The cutting of the animals and passing between the pieces is ritualized self-condemnation, invoking mutilation and death on oneself if one is disloyal to the covenant.

Here the cutting ritual was used to assure Yahweh's grant of offspring and land. Land boundaries were typically specified in charter covenants. Such is the case here. Yahweh gave Abraham a grant of land and finalized it with a charter covenant because Abraham had demonstrated his faith. Not accidentally, these borders correspond with the limits of the Davidic-Solomonic kingdom (see 1 Kings 4:21). The point is that Israel's claim to the land, even to the definition of the borders, was traced back to the covenant promise Yahweh made to Abraham.

In spite of the covenant and the promises, Abraham and Sarah were unable to have children for a long time. They grew impatient and Sarah arranged for a surrogate wife for Abraham, **Hagar**, who bore a son, **Ishmael** (chapter 16). Hagar then refused to take second place behind Sarah. Sarah made life so difficult for Hagar that she fled into the wilderness, only later to return to Sarah and Abraham.

These stories clearly reflect the concern for an heir, which was the ancestors' great hope for the future. They also reveal the uncertain nature of the inheritance, given the constant threat of infertility. Perhaps the fixation on such matters reflects the monarchic setting of the Yahwist narrative and its consuming interest in heirs and succession within the royal house of David.

Covenant of Circumcision (17)

As Genesis 12:1–3 is central to the Yahwist's theology of promise, so Genesis 17 is foundational to the Priestly theology of covenant.

1 Abram was ninety-nine years old. YHWH appeared to Abram and said to him, "I am El Shaddai. Live in my presence and be perfect. 2 So I will put my covenant between me and you: I will multiply you greatly. 3 Abram fell on his face. Then Elohim spoke with him: 4 My covenant now is with you; you will be the father of a multitude of nations. 5 And your name will no longer be Abram, but your name shall be Abraham, for I will make you the father of a multitude of nations. 6 I will make you very prolific, and I will make you nations, and kings will come from you. 7 I will solidify my covenant between me and you and your offspring after you for generations, as a long-lasting covenant as your Elohim and your offspring's Elohim after you. 8 And I will make the land of your sojournings, the land of Canaan, your and your offspring's long-lasting possession. And I will be their Elohim. 9 Elohim said to Abraham, "You will keep my covenant, you and your offspring after you. 10 This is the covenant you will keep, the one between me and you and your offspring after you: Circumcise every male." (17:1–10)

The language of multitudes and multiplying recalls the blessing placed on humanity in Genesis 1:28. The Priestly writer viewed Abraham as the fulfiller of the promise given at creation. "Father of a multitude of nations" is the Priestly equivalent to the Yahwistic promise of becoming a great nation, spoken by God to Abraham in 12:2.

> **God of Abraham.** Notice how three different designations of God (YHWH, El Shaddai, and Elohim) are used in this passage. From creation until Abraham the deity was Elohim. Then he revealed himself to Abraham and the other ancestors as El Shaddai. The ancestors never knew his name to be Yahweh. Here, in one of its rare uses of the name Yahweh, the Priestly tradition makes the identification between Yahweh and El Shaddai explicit so readers will not be confused. In the Priestly historical record, God did not clarify that he was both Yahweh and El Shaddai until he spoke to Moses (Exodus 6:3). In 17:3 the Priestly writer reverts to Elohim, which is his normal pre-Exodus designation for God.

The imminent fulfillment of the promise of offspring was signaled by a name change. Abram, meaning "Exalted Father," was changed to Abraham, "Father of a Multitude," affirming that the promise of offspring was still intact.

Immediately after God's reaffirmation of the promises, **circumcision** was introduced as the ceremony and perpetual sign of the commitment of Abraham and his offspring to God (see Figure 2.4). Circumcision is the surgical removal of the foreskin of the penis, and is still practiced today in many communities. For parents

FIGURE 2.4 EGYPTIAN CIRCUMCISION   Circumcision was not unique to the Israelites, as this Egyptian tomb painting from sixth dynasty (2350–2000 B.C.E.) Saqqara demonstrates, but the Israelites invested it with unique significance by using it as the mark of the covenant.

who choose to have their sons circumcised, it usually takes place a day or two after birth in the hospital. In the Jewish community it happens with great ceremony in the synagogue or the home eight days after a son is born. For a comprehensive account of circumcision see Hoffman (1996).

Chapter 17 on circumcision is theologically important because God requires Abraham to do something to demonstrate his good faith as part of the covenant arrangement. This covenant assumes the structure of a treaty covenant, with mutual rights and obligations rather than a grant covenant. In this case, Abraham had to perform the ritual of circumcision on himself, Ishmael, and all the males in his household. Abraham vowed to live in such a way that he would please God—live "perfectly," the text says.

Circumcision established itself within Judaism as the premiere mark of covenant commitment. Sealing the covenant by circumcising the organ of procreation with a knife, with its obvious threat of infertility, has the effect of symbolically handing over the possibility of offspring to the grace of God. By practicing the rite from generation to generation, the Israelites almost literally placed their future into the

EXPERTS DIVIDED OVER CIRCUMCISION

Dear Ann Landers: My wife and I were both in our mid-30s when we married four years ago. We did not plan on having a family, but when she discovered she was pregnant at the age of 40, we were thrilled.

We learned through amniocentesis that the baby she is carrying is a boy. We are terribly excited. Now comes the problem:

Should the baby be circumcised? I say yes. My wife says no. According to what she has read, the practice is no longer necessary, and she sees no reason to put the infant through all that pain.

Our family physician and my wife's obstetrician are both in favor of circumcision, but they say the decision must be made by the parents. Since my wife and I hold opposite views, we'd like yours.
—**Mr. Pro and Mrs. Con in Baltimore**

Dear P. and C.: Some highly respected physicians can be found on both sides of this issue.

Circumcision of newborns was considered a routine procedure until 1971 when the American Academy of Pediatrics said there might be religious reasons for circumcision, but it had no medical benefits whatsoever.

Years later, after a survey was taken at several hospitals, it was discovered that the babies who were NOT circumcised were 10 times more likely to suffer from urinary tract problems and kidney infections than those who had gone through the procedure.

Dr. Thomas E. Wiswell, chief of neonatology at Walter Reed Army Medical Center, who previously had opposed circumcision, changed his mind when he read studies that indicated circumcision affords a high degree of protection against cancer of the penis. Of the 50,000 cases of penile cancer reviewed, only 10 occurred in men who were circumcised.

Have I told you more than you wanted to know? Perhaps, but the statistics make a strong case for circumcision. (February 21, 1993) hands of the God of covenant. Contrast the Yahwist perspective, in which covenant was primarily a convention whereby Yahweh granted blessing in perpetuity. For the Yahwist, covenant took the form of a charter covenant given to Abraham with no required action in return, only a commitment of faith. By retaining both notions of covenant within the Abrahamic narrative, the final edition affirms that the two covenants complement each other.

 Genesis contains restatements of the Priestly version of the covenant with Abraham; see Table 2.A. Table 2.B contains a comprehensive list of the use of the term "covenant," berit, in Genesis and Exodus.

■ ABRAHAM AND ISAAC (18–22)

The decisive action of the Abraham cycle takes place surrounding the birth of the son of promise. Surrogate son Ishmael and dependent nephew Lot were marginalized and made satellites of the ancestral orbit, while true son Isaac emerged from the matriarchal womb to take his destined position. But all threats to the promise did not automatically vanish. Indeed, the promise faced its greatest challenge just at the point that fulfillment seemed sure.

Birth Announcement (18–19)

One day three men appeared at Abraham's door. As the account develops we learn that one is Yahweh and the other two apparently the angels that rescue Lot. Abraham prepared a bedouin banquet for these visitors, and the disguised Yahweh in return promised that Abraham and Sarah would have a son by the same time next year. When Sarah overheard this prediction she could not suppress a loud guffaw because she was so old.

After the meal Abraham and "the men" gazed down on Sodom, and Yahweh revealed that he intended to destroy Sodom and Gomorrah for their wickedness. Because Lot lived there Abraham bargained with God to save Sodom if even ten righteous people could be found. But there were not even ten righteous ones to merit saving the city.

The two angels entered Sodom to rescue Lot. To demonstrate the depravity of Sodom we are told that the men of the city demanded that Lot throw out his visitors so they could "sodomize" them. The angels urged Lot to leave, and he took his wife and two daughters with him. After they reached safety "YHWH rained brimstone and fire from YHWH out of heaven on Sodom and Gomorrah" (19:24). But when Lot's wife cast a longing glance back toward Sodom she was converted into a salt pillar. Lot's daughters despaired of finding husbands, so they got their father drunk enough to sleep with them. Their children of incest became the Moabites and Ammonites; the Israelites had quite an engaging way of casting aspersions on their neighbors.

> **Sodom and Gomorrah.** The ruins of Sodom and Gomorrah have not been located. The only possible candidates are Bab edh-Dhra and some related towns near the eastern shore of the Dead Sea, for they are the only sites in the

area that were occupied before the Roman period (see Harland 1980 and van Hatten 1981). British geologists Harris and Beardow (1995) argue that Sodom and Gomorrah were destroyed when an earthquake liquefied the ground on which they stood. This leveled the cities, then caused them to sink beneath the waters of the Dead Sea. They theorize that the earthquake also ignited bitumen deposits, which are common to the area, resulting in the "fire and brimstone" description (19:24).

Threat (20–21)

The Primeval Story contains no material from the Elohist source. The first Elohist stories we can find in Genesis have to do with the ancestors. Genesis 15 seems to bear some of the characteristics of the Elohist source, but chapter 20 is the first full-scale Elohist episode.

In chapter 20 Abraham and Sarah encounter Abimelech, and Abraham again seems threatened. It is an instructive as well as interesting story because it contains many of the central themes of the Elohist.

> *1 Abraham traveled from there to the area of the Negev and made his home between Kadesh and Shur. When he was staying in Gerar 2 Abraham claimed about his wife Sarah, "She is my sister." So Abimelech, king of Gerar, had someone get Sarah. (20:1–2)*

It is not clear where "there" was. It probably refers to Mamre-Hebron, the last known home of Abraham. From "there," Abraham and Sarah moved to the area around Gerar. Its powerful king, Abimelech, took Sarah for his wife.

Abimelech desired Sarah—strange, since according to Genesis 17:17 she was ninety years old. Remember, though, these seemingly contradictory points arise because of the combination of stories from different sources, and we may just have to accept the fact that certain inconsistencies like this remain unresolved in the final text.

> *3 Elohim came to Abimelech in a dream at night and said to him, "You are a dead man on account of the woman you have taken. She is married." 4 Now, Abimelech had not made any sexual advances. He said, "My Lord, would you kill people even though they were innocent?" 5 Did he not say to me, 'She is my sister'? And she is the one who said, 'He is my brother.' With a pure heart and clean hands I did this." (20:3–5)*

Characteristic of the Elohist, God does not appear directly, but communicates in dreams or visions. Also, this story contains a first for Genesis: in a dream God comes to Abimelech, a foreigner. This opens up an intriguing possibility that Israel's God could be in relationship with a foreigner, and that a righteous Gentile could exist.

The question of Abimelech's guilt is thorny. He is guilty of wrong because he took someone else's wife, but he is innocent insofar as he was deceived by Abraham. On top of it, Abimelech never even touched Sarah. So why should he be found guilty?

6 Elohim said to him in the dream, "I, too, know that you did this with a pure heart. It was I that kept you from sinning against me; for that reason I did not let you touch her. 7 Now then, return the man's wife. He is a prophet, he will pray for you, and you will live. But if you do not return her, you should know that you will die, you, and everything that belongs to you." (20:6–7)

God came to Abimelech a second time in a dream and revealed that he had been working in Abimelech's life to prevent him from doing anything wrong. Is the Elohist telling us God providentially attends to the behavior even of non-Israelites?

Note also the language used to describe Abraham. God calls him a prophet. This is the first time the label of "prophet" is used in the Hebrew Bible. The term here refers to someone who is able to intercede between God and other people. The Elohist source as a whole appears to be intimately associated with prophetic circles in the North, and so would naturally be interested in prophetic models and in tracing the prophetic calling to Israel's earliest history.

8 So Abimelech rose early in the morning, and called all his servants, and told them everything; and the men were very afraid. 9 Then Abimelech called Abraham, and said to him, "What did you do to us? What did I do to you, that you should bring on me and my kingdom this problem? You did things to me that should not have been done." 10 Abimelech also said to Abraham, "What were you thinking when you did this thing?" (20:8–10)

Abimelech took the whole matter very seriously. He called together his servants and they talked about it. Then he turned the tables and blamed the situation on Abraham. Abraham really was the guilty one because he led Abimelech into trouble with his deception.

11 Abraham said, "I did it because I thought, 'There is no fear of Elohim at all in this place. They will kill me because of my wife. 12 Besides, she is my sister anyway, the daughter of my father (though not the daughter of my mother), and she became my wife.' 13 When Elohim made me leave my father's house, I said to her, 'This is how you should show your loyalty to me: everywhere we go, say of me, He is my brother.'" (20:11–13)

The reason Abraham acted the way he did is now made clear. He was concerned that there was no "fear of God" in Gerar. In fact, Abimelech and his men seemed to have had a very healthy respect for God, confirmed by the way in which God came to Abimelech directly, warned him, and saved him from disaster. The story seems to suggest that Abraham had underestimated the moral character of these foreigners. Apparently, "fear of God," a big interest of the Elohist, was not found exclusively in Israel.

14 Then Abimelech took sheep and oxen, and male and female slaves, and gave them to Abraham, and returned his wife Sarah to him. 15 And Abimelech said, "Now, my land is open to you; live where you want to." 16 To

Sarah he said, "See, I have given your brother a thousand pieces of silver; it is your vindication in the eyes of all who are with you; and it proves to everyone that you are in the right." 17 Then Abraham prayed to Elohim; and Elohim healed Abimelech, and also healed his wife and female slaves so that they could bear children. 18 For YHWH had closed all the wombs of the house of Abimelech because of Sarah, Abraham's wife. (20:14–18)

Abimelech graciously gave gifts to Abraham to make a public acknowledgement of responsibility. Furthermore, he gave an open invitation to Abraham to settle anywhere he wanted to. Then Abraham interceded prophetically and Abimelech and his people were made whole again. Even though Abraham was the one at fault, curiously he is also the one who can remedy the situation. He is a prophet and hence is capable of mediating healing to Abimelech and his people.

> **Sister=Wife.** The motif of the patriarch claiming that his wife is his sister is also found in Genesis 12:10–20 and 26:6–11, both by the Yahwist. Having this particular motif in three separate stories is one of the supporting reasons for a multiple literary source theory of the Pentateuch.

The account of the birth of **Isaac** (21:1–7) is amazingly brief given the tremendous buildup. We learn that Abraham was one hundred years old at his birth and Sarah was ninety. The child was named Isaac, "he laughs," to memorialize Sarah's incredulous response upon hearing that she would become pregnant in her old age. Conforming to covenant, Isaac was circumcised on the eighth day.

Testing (22)

The story of the near sacrifice of Isaac is one of the most profound tales of the Torah. It conveys a deep lesson in testing and faith. Not only is it one of the most poignant tales in the Hebrew Bible, it is also well told.

In the larger thematic and theological development of the Abraham cycle, the stage is set for this Elohist account of Isaac's near sacrifice by the birth narrative of Isaac and the subsequent expulsion of Ishmael in chapter 21. Now that Isaac is the ONLY one, God tests Abraham to expose the authenticity and the object of his faith.

Applying the perspective of the newer literary criticism that looks for structure, we see that the account is segmented into three units on the basis of repeated phrases. Each of the three units is introduced with a summons addressed to Abraham. In each unit Abraham responds the same way.

1. God summons Abraham (1–2)
   God: "Abraham!"
   Abraham: "I am right here."
   Command: "Take your son"
2. Isaac summons Abraham (7–8)
   Isaac: "Father!"
   Abraham: "I am right here."
   Question: "Where is the lamb?"

Abraham: "God will provide."
3. Angel summons Abraham (11–12)
   Angel: "Abraham, Abraham!"
   Abraham: "I am right here."
   Command: "Do not harm the boy."

The following discussion of Genesis 22 examines the account by units. The words in boldface are the elements of the outline that reveal the structure.

1. *God summons Abraham*
   *1 After these events, Elohim tested Abraham. He said to him, "**Abraham!**" He answered, "**I am right here.**" 2 He said, "**Take your son,** your only one, he whom you love, Isaac, and go to the land of Moriah, and sacrifice him there as a whole burnt offering on one of the mountains, the one I will tell you." (22:1–2)*

The first sentence of this unit is a theme statement. "Elohim tested Abraham" gives us the purpose of the story right at the beginning. God was testing Abraham's faith. Many Elohist stories have to do with faith and faithfulness. Interest in this theme can be partially explained by conditions at the time the Elohist source was written. It was a time of severe testing in Israel, and a story like this assured the people that God could be behind such testing, and that it could serve a purpose.

Unit 1 contains God's command to sacrifice Isaac. Moriah is impossible to locate geographically. The later tradition of 2 Chronicles 3:1 identifies Mount Moriah with the site of Solomon's temple. The connection this story draws between Abraham and Solomon's temple through the interpretation of the Chronicles tradition gives the site of the temple an ancestral connection, hence the site acquires greater venerability.

3 Abraham got up early in the morning and saddled his donkey and took two of his servants with him, and Isaac his son. He cut offering wood and journeyed to the place Elohim told him. 4 On the third day Abraham glanced up and saw the place in the distance. 5 Abraham said to his servants, "Stay here with the donkey. I and the boy will go there. We will worship and we will return to you." 6 Abraham took the offering wood and put it on his son Isaac. He took in his own hand the fire and the knife. And the two of them walked together. (22:3–6)

Unit 1 contains emotionally charged narrative. Abraham and his dear son together traveled to the mountain. They ascended the mountain, Isaac carrying in his own arms the wood that was intended to ignite him as a burnt offering to God. The notice that "the two of them walked together" is touching in its simplicity.

2. *Isaac summons Abraham*
   *7 Isaac said to Abraham his father, "**Father!**" And he said, "**I am right here,** my son." And he said, "The fire is here, and the wood. **Where is the**

sacrificial lamb? " *8 Abraham said, "Elohim himself will provide a lamb for the offering, my son." And the two of them walked together. 9 They came to the place Elohim told him and Abraham built there the altar and arranged the wood and bound Isaac, his son, and put him on top of the wood. 10 Abraham reached out his hand and took the knife to slaughter his son. (22:7–10)*

Unit 2 is distinctive among the three units. Only here Abraham replies a second time. He says, "God himself will provide a lamb for the offering, my son." By the way, catch the double-entendre in the phrase "God will provide a lamb, my son." "My son" is both the one addressed and the lamb. At this point Abraham makes his most profound statement of faith: "God will provide." Note how the story centralizes Abraham's profession of faith by placing it in the middle of the three-unit literary structure.

Note also how Abraham went all the way and bound Isaac on the altar. This story is called the *akedah* in the Jewish tradition, the word for "binding" in the original Hebrew text of verse 9.

3. Angel summons Abraham

11 The Angel of YHWH called to him from heaven, "Abraham, Abraham!" And he said, "I am right here." 12 And he said, "Do not reach out your hand to the boy and do not do anything to him. For now I know that you fear Elohim. You have not held back your son, your only one, from me." 13 Abraham raised his eyes and saw a ram right there, with one of its horns caught in a thicket. Abraham went and took the ram and sacrificed it as a whole burnt offering in place of his son. (22:11–13)

In the nick of time the angel of Yahweh stopped Abraham. The sacrifice was halted because God felt assured that Abraham truly feared him, and a ram was sacrificed in his place.

Note the introduction of the name of God "YHWH" at this point in the story. Verses 11–18 have certain characteristics of the Yahwist, especially the mention of blessing. Perhaps this indicates that the Elohist used an earlier form of the story from the Yahwist source, which he reshaped to develop his own version.

Units 1 and 3 are tightly linked. Verses 2 and 12 are linked by the phrase "your son, your only one." Verse 2 establishes the test: take your son. Verse 12 records passing the test: you have not withheld your son. Moberly (1992) notes that only in Exodus 20:20 and Genesis 22 are the concepts of "testing" (22:1) and "the fear of God" (22:12) found in proximity. Perhaps we are to infer that Abraham is presented as a model for Israel by the way he demonstrates full and immediate obedience to God's word.

14 Abraham called the name of that place "YHWH provides." To this day it is said, "On YHWH's mountain it will be provided." (22:14)

Tradition apparently invested this place with great significance, even though today we do not know exactly what place is being referred to. In the editor's own day it was still an important place of worship. It gets its name from the ram God provided as a substitute for Isaac. The place name "Yahweh provides" echoes Abraham's answer to Isaac in verse 8, "Elohim himself will provide a lamb."

> *15 The Angel of YHWH called to Abraham a second time from heaven 16 and said, "I swear by myself (YHWH's oracle) that because you did this, you did not withhold your son, your only one, 17 I will richly bless you and greatly increase your offspring, like the stars of heaven and the sand of the sea shore. And your offspring will inherit the gate of their enemies. 18 All the nations of the earth will bless themselves through your offspring, because you obeyed my voice." (22:15–18)*

Having passed the test of faith, God repeated the promise of blessing. Abraham's offspring would increase and he would be richly blessed. This reaffirms the Yahwist principle that blessing follows obedience. The analogies of sand and stars recall the covenant promises found in Genesis 13:16 and 15:5, respectively. The phrase "sand of the seashore" also creates a link to 1 Kings 4:20, where this promise was seen to be fulfilled in the Solomonic kingdom. This further reinforces the theological understanding that the blessings of the later monarchy were founded on the promises to the ancestors.

> *19 And Abraham returned to the servants and they journeyed to Beersheba together. And Abraham lived in Beersheba. (22:19)*

Abraham traveled to the southern part of Palestine, called the Negev, where he established himself in Beersheba.

Curiously, no mention is made of Isaac in the conclusion, only of Abraham and the servants. Having survived a close encounter with the knife, one might think Isaac would be explicitly mentioned. Yet the focus of the entire episode is on Abraham. In this remarkable story we see a changed man, one radically different from the early Abraham of chapter 12. Then, he was afraid of losing his own life, he was insecure, and he deceived the Pharaoh of Egypt to save his own skin. He did not trust God to protect him, even though God had promised to.

The later Abraham of this episode declined to cling to what, humanly speaking, must have been his last hope for a future. He did not take Isaac and run from God. Instead, willing to sacrifice Isaac, he obeyed God. In so doing he demonstrated his deep and secure faith in the promises of God. The testing of Abraham episode within the Abraham cycle displays his maturation in the faith.

There are structural indications in the overall account of Abraham that we should see the Abraham of chapter 22, the "late" Abraham, in relation to the "early" Abraham. There is point-counterpoint between Genesis 12 and 22 drawn by verbal and thematic parallels. Table 2.1 is a list of explicit parallels between them.

These correspondences suggest that these two stories are to be seen in juxtaposition, as a kind of framework perhaps, around the Abraham collection of stories. What is the point of these connections? The editor who brought J and E together urges us to see the testing of Abraham as a major step toward the realization of the promises stated in 12:1–7. As a result of his willingness to sacrifice

TABLE 2.1   CALL AND TESTING OF ABRAHAM PARALLELS

Genesis 12	Call of Abraham	Genesis 22	Testing of Abraham
12:1	Go (Heb. *lek-leka*) from your land	22:2	Go (Heb. *lek-leka*) to the land
12:6	Moreh	22:2	Moriah
12:3	All peoples on earth will be blessed/bless themselves through you	22:18	Through your offspring all the nations on earth will bless themselves

his son Isaac, Abraham finally demonstrated that he relied implicitly on the promises of God. He staked his future on God, not on the life of his son. So, the account of Abraham finds satisfying resolution.

> **Child Sacrifice.** Maybe this story had a different meaning before it found its way into the Ancestral Story. It is probable that this Abraham-Isaac story originally existed independently, before the Elohist or any other source existed. Using the procedures of form criticism to recover the original setting of the isolated tale, some scholars have suggested that the original intent of this story was to displace child sacrifice as a form of worship and replace it with animal sacrifice. Perhaps this is the story the Elohist found.
>
> Reconstructing the course of its inclusion into the book of Genesis, the Elohist took the core story and supplemented it with the promise of blessing and other details from the Yahwist source. He was interested in the story for his own reasons and reshaped it to show how God may test one's faith, yet ultimately provide. This story is a likely example of an early tale which meant one thing, then was taken up by a later writer and given new meaning in connection with his themes and interests.

Sacrifice of Isaac Gallery. The near sacrifice of Isaac has given rise to a variety of interpretations and artistic depictions. The gallery includes works from ancient mosaics to modern art.

■ LAST DAYS (23:1–25:11)

After the Testing of Abraham, the cycle seems to end quickly. First, Sarah died. Abraham approached Ephron, a Hittite who owned property near Hebron, and bought from him a field that contained a cave, called the Cave of Machpelah, where he buried Sarah.

Next Abraham took steps to insure family continuity by securing a wife for Isaac. However, a wife from among the Canaanites would not do. Abraham sent his servant to Aram where his clan had settled after leaving Ur (see 11:31 and Figure 2.3). The servant brought back **Rebekah,** who then became the mother of Esau and Jacob, and the generations continued.

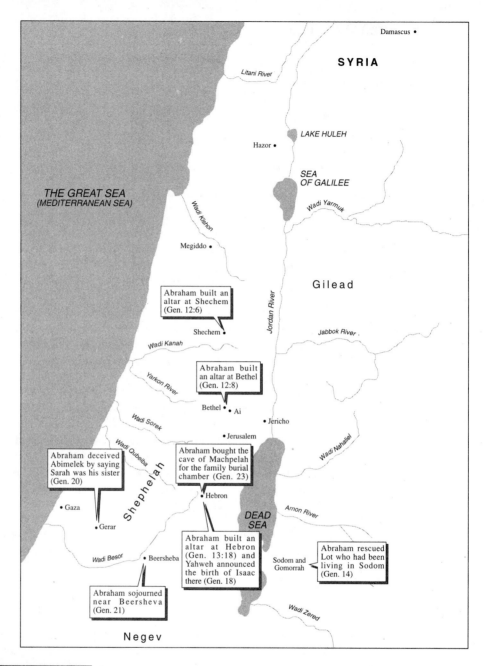

FIGURE 2.5 ABRAHAM IN CANAAN   The Abraham traditions are mostly associated with locations in southern Palestine, especially Judah and the Negev.

Interlude: The Ishmael Toledot (25:12–18)

While not the son of the covenant, Ishmael nonetheless was blessed and would become a great nation in his own right (17:19–22). The offspring of Ishmael were twelve tribes which, according to tradition, developed into the Arabic peoples.

JACOB CYCLE (25:19–35:29)

The **Jacob cycle** continues the themes of the Abraham cycle, including blessing, offspring, and land, but it gives each theme a new twist. The Abraham cycle dealt with fertility and offspring via the father-to-son relationship. The Jacob cycle analyzes the brother-to-brother relationship within the promise. If there is more than one son, who should inherit the promise? Is there an iron-clad law that the first-born gets it? The action of these stories is driven by sibling rivalry.

Jacob, impelled by his own (and sometimes his mother's) scheming and trickiness, connived to possess the blessing. Do we see here a reprise of primeval sin, trying to steal rather than await God's favor? The Jacob cycle proceeds in a threefold series of struggles. First, Jacob outwits his twin brother, **Esau,** to gain possession of the family birthright. Second, Jacob outmaneuvers his uncle **Laban** and acquires substantial wealth. Third, Jacob outlasts God in a wrestling match, determined to receive divine blessing.

Story Line

Twin sons, Esau and Jacob, were born to Isaac and Rebekah. Esau, the firstborn, sold his birthright to Jacob (Genesis 25). Residing in Gerar, Isaac felt threatened and deceived Abimelech saying Rebekah was his sister (26). Later Jacob and Rebekah deceived Isaac and stole the family blessing from Esau (27). Jacob fled from his brother (28) and lived for an extended period of time with his uncle Laban in Haran. Jacob eventually married **Rachel** and **Leah,** the daughters of Laban, and had many children (29–31). Rachel became the dominant wife. Laban grew jealous of Jacob because his flocks increased at Laban's expense. So Jacob felt compelled to leave Paddan-aram with his family and considerable belongings. Returning to Palestine he wrestled with God (32), then he met up with Esau (33). He and his family settled in Palestine, but tried to remain separate and distinct from the Canaanites who lived in the land, as the story of Shechem illustrates (34). Jacob journeyed to Bethel and settled there (35).

■ JACOB VERSUS ESAU: STEALING THE BLESSING (25:19–28:22)

The birth narrative of Jacob and Esau establishes points of contact with the Abraham cycle. Rebekah was barren. Like Sarah before her she had children only after Yahweh intervened. The pregnancy proved painful as the babies jostled each other in the womb. Yahweh revealed this was happening because the twins would be rivals.

Two nations are in your womb, and two peoples born of you will be divided; the one will be stronger than the other, the elder will serve the younger. (25:23)

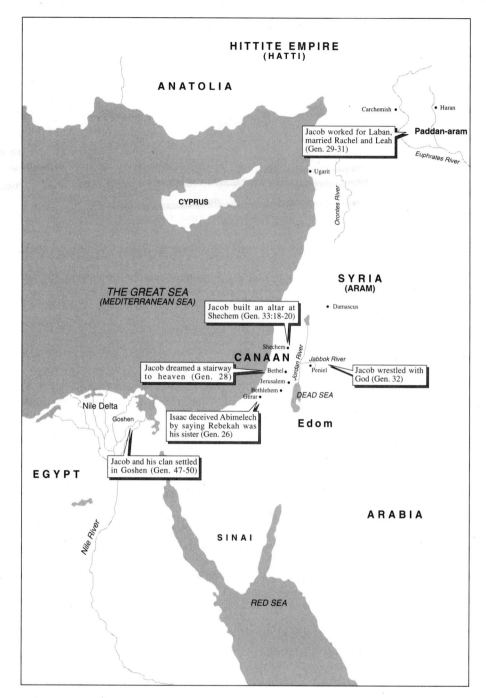

Within the map:

HITTITE EMPIRE
(HATTI)

ANATOLIA

Carchemish •   • Haran

Jacob worked for Laban,
married Rachel and Leah
(Gen. 29-31)   **Paddan-aram**

Euphrates River

• Ugarit

CYPRUS

Orontes River

SYRIA
(ARAM)

THE GREAT SEA
(MEDITERRANEAN SEA)

Jacob built an altar at
Shechem (Gen. 33:18-20)

• Damascus

Shechem •

CANAAN   Jabbok River

Jacob dreamed a stairway   Bethel •   Peniel •   Jacob wrestled with
to heaven (Gen. 28)   God (Gen. 32)

Jerusalem •
Jordan River

Bethlehem •
Gerar •   DEAD SEA

Nile Delta

Goshen

Isaac deceived Abimelech
by saying Rebekah was   Edom
his sister (Gen. 26)

Jacob and his clan settled
in Goshen (Gen. 47-50)

EGYPT   ARABIA

Nile River

SINAI

RED SEA

FIGURE 2.6 JACOB'S TRAVELS   Most of the sites associated with Jacob are located in northern Palestine and Transjordan, especially the tribal territories of Ephraim and Manasseh. With its interest in this region, especially Bethel and Penuel (for a time the capital of Jeroboam's kingdom, see 1 Kings 12:25), the Jacob cycle seems to legitimate the beginnings of the Northern Kingdom's religious institutions.

The brothers would struggle with each other, but the outcome was foreordained. The younger would win. The Jacob cycle finds affinity with the Abraham cycle in the rivalry of the favored sons Ishmael and Isaac, though the earlier rivalry was played out by the mothers. In the present case the cycle is driven by Jacob's determination not to let Esau inherit. First, Jacob bought the birthright (25:27–34) from Esau, who was willing to sell it for a pittance. The birthright is the right of the firstborn to inherit the family estate. Then Jacob deceived his father, Isaac, into giving him the blessing that was intended for Esau (27). The irony of the cycle is that Jacob did not know he had been foreordained to prevail. He schemed to get what God had already granted him at birth.

There is also a transparently deeper level to the sibling conflict. The divine oracle to Rebekah reveals that these stories are about more than just brothers at war. "Two nations are in your womb"—they are stories of national conflict. These tales prefigure the later antagonism of Israel and Edom.

> **Israel and Edom.** Jacob and Esau are respectively the eponymous ancestors of Israel and Edom. Throughout their history Israel and Edom were bitter rivals. The Edomites refused the Israelites passage during the wilderness sojourn (Numbers 20:14–21). David defeated the Edomites (2 Samuel 8:13–14) in the process of establishing his kingdom. On many occasions Israel's prophets condemned the Edomites. The Jacob-Esau conflict is, among other things, a story of the origin of Israelite-Edomite animosity.
>
> The birth account and the birthright episode relate Esau to Edom. Esau's red and hairy appearance provide opportunity to pun on the place names Edom (from the word *red*) and Seir (sounds like *hairy*). The land of Seir was the homeland of the Edomites. Jacob sounds like *heel*, and he had a hold on Esau's heel coming out of the womb. A more precise linguistic derivation of the name Jacob relates it to the word for "protect," so that Jacob (probably originally Jacob-el) means "May God protect." Later in the cycle God will change Jacob's name to Israel (32:28). For Edom and the Edomites in biblical tradition see Dicou (1994) and Edelman (1995).

The blessings intended for the firstborn go to the younger. Whether intended or not, this reversal of tradition, as well as the unity of birthright and blessing, seem to be reinforced by clever word choice. *Firstborn* and *birthright* derive from the same root, and *blessing* has the same consonants, with the second and third reversed. Rebekah, who loves Jacob over Esau, has a name suspiciously close to these central terms (see Table 2.2).

Throughout the Ancestral Story threats to the promise come both from inside, in the form of barrenness, and outside, in the form of enemies. Sandwiched between Jacob buying the birthright and stealing the blessing is the tale of Isaac and Rebekah's sojourn in Philistia where they found themselves in danger (26:1–11). Isaac deceived the local population into thinking Rebekah was his sister so that he would not be killed for her. This incident recalls similar situations with Abraham and Sarah (12:10–20 with Pharaoh in Egypt and 20:1–18 with an Abimelech in Gerar). Later, as Isaac's holdings increased, he came into conflict with the Philistines over water rights and wells. The conflict was settled amicably when both parties agreed to a non-aggression treaty.

TABLE 2.2   BIRTHRIGHT AND BLESSING COMPLEX

Translation	Hebrew Word	Hebrew Root Consonants
Firstborn	*bekor*	b-k-r
Birthright	*bekorah*	b-k-r
Blessing	*berakah*	b-r-k
Rebekah	*rivkah*	r-b-q

Type-Scene. The Ancestral Story contains a number of episodes that have similar features and motifs. An example is the ancestor who says his wife is his sister (see above). It is possible that the writers drew upon conventional settings, situations, and action sequences to wrap their stories. Such scenarios have been called type-scenes (see Alter 1981: 47–62). Other biblical type-scenes include the birth of the heir to a previously barren mother (Isaac to Sarah, Esau and Jacob to Rebekah, Joseph to Rachel) and meeting one's future wife at a well (Rebekah, Genesis 24; Rachel, Genesis 29; Zipporah, Exodus 3).

The culminating episode of Jacob's early life is his flight from the Promised Land to Mesopotamia. Fearing Esau he fled for his life and headed to the territory of Laban, Rebekah's brother. Leaving parents behind and traveling alone, Jacob stopped for the night in a remote place. Jacob is now on his own. Or is he?

Genesis 28:10–22 is one of two passages in the Jacob cycle where the patriarch has a direct encounter with God. The two places are marked by complementary names. In this passage the place comes to be called Bethel; the other place was Penuel.

10 Jacob left Beersheba and walked toward Haran. 11 When he reached the place, he spent the night there, because the sun had set. Taking one of the stones of the place, he put it under his head and lay down to sleep in that place. 12 He had a dream. There was a stairway set on the ground with its top reaching to heaven. Angels of Elohim were going up and down it. 13 YHWH stood above him/it and said, "I am YHWH, the Elohim of Abraham your father and the Elohim of Isaac. The land on which you sleep, to you I will give it and to your descendants. 14 Your descendants will be like the dust of the earth. You will spread out to the west and to the east and to the north and to the south. By you and your descendants will all the families of the earth bless themselves/be blessed. 15 I am with you and will protect you wherever you go, and will return you to this land. I will not leave you until I have done what I have spoken to you." 16 Jacob woke from his sleep and said, "Surely YHWH is in this place, and I did not know it." 17 He was afraid, and said, "How awesome is this place! This is none other than the house of Elohim, and this is the gate of heaven." (28:10–17)

In this dream God spoke to Jacob and personally confirmed the promises of descendants and land that had been transferred to him by his father Isaac. Many phrases echo earlier promise statements, including "all the families of the earth bless themselves/be blessed" (12:3) and "dust of the earth" (13:16).

God's promises to the ancestors often incorporated an "international" component. See Table 2.C for a list of the "bless themselves" passages.

> **Source Analysis.** This episode appears to have elements of both Yahwist and Elohist writing. The shell of the story is the dream setting in which angels of Elohim appear on a stairway (11b–12, 17–18, 20–22). This bears the marks of the Elohist, for whom theophanies typically occur in dreams. The Yahwist contributed the content of the divine oracle (13–16) and the location references (10–11a, 19). The Yahwist also contributed the Abraham promise statements in Genesis 12 and 13, which are similar to this passage.

In his dream Jacob sees a stairway reaching to heaven. This component of the incident may be intended to provide counterpoint to the notorious primeval tower project (Genesis 11:1–9; see Chapter 1). In that episode humanity tried to build a tower with its top in heaven. Babel was to be the gate to heaven. In this episode Jacob happens upon the authentic heavenly access point, Bethel. The similarity of the names Babel and Bethel may be more than just coincidence.

> *18 Jacob rose early in the morning and took the stone that he had put under his head and set it up as a pillar and poured oil on the top of it. 19 He called the name of that place Bethel (previously the name of the city was Luz). 20 Then Jacob vowed a vow, "If Elohim stays with me, and protects me on this path I go, and will give me bread to eat and clothes to wear, 21 and I return to my father's house in shalom, then YHWH shall be my Elohim. 22 This stone that I have set up as a pillar shall be the house of Elohim. Of all that you give me I will give a tenth back to you." (28:18–22)*

Jacob set up his stone pillow as a pillar, called a *matsevah* in Hebrew. A standing stone could be used for a variety of functions in the ancient world. It could memorialize a dead person (35:20), commemorate a covenant (31:45; Exodus 24:4), or represent a deity in a holy place. Standing stones at worship centers have been found at Arad, Megiddo, Hazor, Gezer, and Beersheba (see Graesser 1972). Later, standing stones were condemned because of their association with the cult of Asherah (see Exodus 34:13; Leviticus 26:1; 1 Kings 14:23; 2 Kings 17:10).

Jacob named this place Bethel, literally "house of El/god." Excavations have suggested that Bethel (if it is to be identified with modern Beitin) may have been a Canaanite religious center. It certainly became a major worship center in Israel's history. It housed the ark of the covenant at the time of the judges. After the breakaway of Israel, Jeroboam chose Bethel as one of two national sanctuary cities. This story provides the initial holiness experience on which its later

Israelite significance is grounded. When Jacob returned to Bethel after his journey he erected an altar and God appeared to him again (35:1–15).

Jacob took a solemn vow pledging the adoption of Yahweh as his God if his journey was successful. The conditional character of the vow seems characteristic of the Jacob who was ever ready to negotiate to his own advantage. Though the word *covenant* is not used explicitly here, making a covenant may have been the intent of setting up and anointing the pillar. Joshua set up a pillar as a witness to God's covenant with Israel (Joshua 24:27), and this practice is also attested in Aramean treaties from Sfire. Jacob's obligation in covenant was to return a tithe or tenth of his wealth to God. Perhaps this pledge grounded a later Israelite practice of bringing a tithe to the priests at the Bethel sanctuary.

■ JACOB VERSUS LABAN: BUILDING A FAMILY (29–31)

Jacob arrived in Haran and soon met Rachel at the local watering hole. He was warmly welcomed by Rachel and Laban after he revealed he was Rebekah's son. Jacob stayed with Laban and agreed to work seven years for the right to marry Rachel. On the wedding night he slept with his bride, only to wake up in the morning to find he had consummated the marriage with Leah, Rachel's older sister!

Indignant, Jacob confronted his uncle with the deception. Filled with irony Laban replied, "It is not done so in our place, to give the younger before the firstborn" (29:26). The motif of birthrights returns. Laban also agreed to allow Jacob to marry Rachel in return for another seven years of labor. It appears that Jacob, the consummate trickster, had himself been tricked.

Though in exile, Jacob prospered. He sired a large family by his two wives and their handmaids, Zilpah and Bilhah. Leah bore him six sons, and when she was past childbearing her maid, Zilpah, served as surrogate mother (remember the surrogacy of Hagar in the Abraham cycle) bearing another two. Rachel was at first barren (remember the barrenness motif of the Abraham cycle), so Bilhah became a surrogate bearing another two sons. Finally, Rachel became pregnant and bore Joseph. Later she had another son, Benjamin, and died in childbirth.

Jacob wished to return to Canaan with his family. But Laban sought to retain him because he realized he was being blessed through Jacob (remember the ancestral blessing: "through you all the families of the earth will be blessed"). Jacob bargained with Laban to acquire his own holdings of sheep and goats. By a devious breeding method Jacob increased his flocks to the detriment of Laban's. Tensions mounted until Jacob thought it prudent to leave. Jacob took his family and flocks—and Rachel plundered Laban's household gods.

They departed in the middle of the night. When Laban found out his daughters had left with Jacob he pursued and confronted this Jacob who had "deceived" him (31:20, 26). Jacob and Laban parted ways after making a covenant and setting up a pillar. The covenant included a pledge that Laban would stop pursuing Jacob and Jacob would not return to Mesopotamia.

Jacob now found himself between a rock and an angry brother. However, he had no choice but to continue on toward Canaan, where he knew Esau would be waiting to greet him.

The final sequence of the Jacob cycle finds Jacob returning to Canaan.

1 Jacob went on his way and angels of Elohim met him. 2 Jacob said when he saw them, "This is the camp of Elohim." (32:1–2)

A greeting party was waiting for Jacob at the border, presumably ready to welcome and protect him. He might need them, for back in Canaan the great issues of his life and destiny would seek resolution, and resolution would come only after more conflict.

Jacob expected to meet Esau shortly after entering Canaan, still enraged about having been deceived. Jacob took great pains to soften Esau's anger by sending ahead wave upon wave of gifts. He also made contingency plans to escape if Esau met his entourage with force.

However, a more trying confrontation would come before he had the chance to meet his brother. All alone and completely vulnerable he met a fighting deity face to face.

The story of Jacob's wrestling with God, Genesis 32:22–32, demonstrates the patriarch persistently taking advantage of every situation to secure a blessing.

22 That same night he got up and took his two wives, his two maids, and his eleven children, and crossed the ford of the Jabbok. 23 He took them and sent them across the wadi, along with everything he owned. 24 Jacob was left alone; and a man wrestled with him until the break of the day. (32:22–24)

Jacob separated himself from his flocks and family and remained on the far side of the Jabbok river. Should Jacob's behavior be construed as an act of cowardice, or did he just need time to contemplate his future? This may have been part of a scheme to distance himself from Esau, using his dependents and estate as buffers. Perhaps he sought again to call on God for help (see 32:9–12). It may have been both. In any case, the aloneness of Jacob here at Penuel matches his aloneness at Bethel at the beginning of his journey. Both leaving and returning, Jacob met his God alone.

> **Source Analysis.** These introductory verses (22–24) meld the wrestling into the larger Jacob narrative by giving it a context. They are part of the Yahwist's account of Jacob's trip back to Canaan. The story of the wrestling (25–32) is itself actually quite self-contained and comes from the Elohist source. After the Testing of Abraham story of chapter 22 the Elohist contributed no other episode to the Abraham cycle. In fact, the Elohist seems to be more interested in Jacob than Abraham or Isaac. This is not surprising because many of the Jacob stories have Ephraimite or Transjordan locations, precisely the places dear to the Elohist tradition.

Instead of being alone, Jacob found himself wrestling with "a man."

25 When the man saw that he could not gain the advantage over Jacob, he touched his hip socket; that put Jacob's hip out of joint as he wrestled with him. 26 Then he said, "Let me go, for day is breaking." But Jacob said, "I will not let you go, unless you bless me." 27 And he said to him, "What is your name?" And he said, "Jacob." 28 Then he said, "Your name will no longer be called Jacob, but instead Israel, for you have wrestled with Elohim and with men, and have prevailed." (32:25–28)

The assailant is called a man, but as the story develops it becomes clear that it is Elohim himself. Jacob, whose name means "heel-grabber," hence "trickster," undergoes a name change to Israel, which means "wrestles with God." By giving an account of his dual name Jacob/Israel, the Elohist identifies Jacob as the patriarch of the nation of Israel. Again, the story is both personal and national.

29 Then Jacob asked him, "Please tell me your name." But he said, "Why are you asking for my name?" And there he blessed him. 30 So Jacob called the name of the place Peniel, saying, "I have seen Elohim face to face, and I am still alive." 31 The sun rose upon him as he passed Penuel; he was limping because of his thigh. 32 Therefore to this day the Israelites do not eat the muscle of the hip which is part of the hip socket, because he touched Jacob's hip socket on the muscle of the hip. (32:29–32)

Penuel (with an alternate spelling *Peniel*) literally means "face of God," because there Jacob saw God directly. A recurring theme in the Elohist is that one cannot look at God and live (see also Moses at the burning bush in Exodus 3). This reinforces the utter powerfulness of Elohim. Yet Jacob saw the face of God and lived—a sign that indeed he was blessed.

The final note in verse 32 is introduced by "Therefore to this day," indicating that this version of the story was written down later than the event itself, namely, when Israelites were around. Apparently this story, however old the core of it may have been, was appropriated at a later time and was used to explain the Jewish avoidance of eating the thigh muscle, identified in Jewish tradition with the sciatic nerve. Determining earlier meanings of the episode is more difficult.

> **River Demon.** Working with the methodology of form criticism, some authorities have reasoned that this story contains the remains of a very early mythic tale of a river-spirit or demon. In many cultures rivers were thought to possess a power that tried to thwart a crossing unless the river-spirit was appeased. This element may have been present at a very early stage. Although a primitive motif may have been behind this story at one time, those notions of demonic spirits have been sublimated in this version. The one trying to stop Jacob is identified with Elohim. See Barthes (1974) for a structural analysis of Genesis 32:22–32 and Miller (1984) for a history of its interpretation.

The meaning of the story is elusive. Yet at the very least it serves to characterize Jacob as persistent, even relentless, in his pursuit of blessing. Taken together with the other Jacob stories, this story says Jacob would stop at nothing to secure a personal advantage. Jacob never waited for his destiny. He made it happen. Singlemindedly and often deviously he pursued the divine blessing. Divine destiny and human response are united in one action sequence in the Jacob cycle.

Recognizing that Jacob stands for all Israel, one might expect the story also to be saying something about the nation. Is it saying that Israel also worked hard to secure a blessing, sometimes too aggressively? Is it saying that all along, when Israel fought others, it was wrestling with God? Is the story suggesting that persistence pays off, and that in spite of sometimes questionable tactics, tenacity gains the blessing? Perhaps not in spite of but because of dubious methods?

After Jacob wrestled with God, he met Esau. It was a tense but non-violent encounter, with an uneasy parting of ways. In the gracious way Esau received his brother we see that time had changed the ruddy one as much as the trickster. Jacob saw in Esau's warm embrace the evidence of God's protection and said to Esau, "Seeing your face is like seeing the face of Elohim" (33:10)—a remark with obvious double meaning in light of Jacob's recent encounter with God at Penuel, "face of God."

After leaving Esau Jacob headed to Shechem, where one of the strangest biblical stories is set (Genesis 34). The ruler of Shechem ravished Jacob's daughter Dinah and sought to marry her, offering anything for the marriage rights. Jacob's sons set one condition, that all Canaanite males in the area be circumcised. The Shechemites agreed, and on the third day when they were in debilitating pain, Simeon and Levi entered the town and slaughtered all the males. They defended their actions to Jacob by claiming they were only avenging their sister's honor. The story reinforces the separation of Canaanites and Israelites and attests the zeal of Simeon and Levi. After this Jacob returned to Bethel with his family (Genesis 35). There he built an altar and set up a pillar to commemorate the fulfillment of God's promises given there earlier when he was alone and a refugee.

The Jacob cycle reveals an interesting quality about our storytellers. As much as they revered their patriarchs and matriarchs, the biblical writers harbored no illusions. They knew that Abraham, Isaac, and Jacob—indeed the whole lot—had serious character flaws. Certainly the stories about Jacob's ill treatment of Esau, the heinous behavior of Simeon and Levi, and the incest of Reuben (35:22) are at the top of the list. Israel's stories about its forerunners are remarkably honest, especially in this cycle. Insofar as the nation identified itself with its forebears (remember, Jacob IS Israel), the chosen people had an amazing capacity for self-criticism. The Israelites saw themselves in their parentage, and it was not always a flattering picture.

As we have seen, the Jacob cycle has a decided thematic unity based on the promises. In addition, it evidences a literary symmetry. The following outline displays the broad narrative scheme that takes its shape from corresponding notions.

A —Birth of Jacob and Esau: Jacob gets the birthright (25)
  B —Isaac and Abimelech: conflict over land (26)
    C —Jacob flees from Esau with the blessing (27)
      D —Jacob at Bethel: "house of God" (28)
        E —Jacob stays with Laban (29–31)
      D'—Jacob at Penuel: "face of God" (32)
    C'—Jacob and Esau reconciled (33)
  B'—Jacob and Shechem: conflict over marriage (34)
A'—Return to Canaan and death of Isaac (35)

As the outline illustrates, the stories have a recursive structure, with A returning to A', B to B', and so on. Chapters 26 and 34 often seemed out of place to interpreters because they seemed to break the flow of Jacob-centered events. Yet in this general scheme these otherwise isolated and incongruous B episodes have a place. In literary, thematic, and structural ways, the Jacob cycle displays a remarkable wholeness.

Interlude: The Esau Toledot (36)

An entire chapter is devoted to Esau's descendants by his three wives. Esau, like Jacob, had received the promise that he would become a nation (25:23). The fulfillment of this promise is thus attested here. A supplement contains a list of kings who ruled Edom before the Israelite monarchy.

JOSEPH CYCLE (37:1–50:26)

The **Joseph cycle**, Genesis 37–50, is one of the most artfully crafted works of Hebrew literature. Some call it a short story, others a novella. Whereas most other Hebrew stories are only a few paragraphs long, the Joseph narrative sustains a story line over many chapters. In spite of the variety of its sources, the Joseph cycle is a cohesive tale of sibling rivalry and providential deliverance.

> **Source Analysis.** In a sense it is curious that Joseph should get so much attention. Judged on the basis of later tribal history, Joseph is not the most significant of Jacob/Israel's sons. Instead, Judah would be the expected focus. His tribe is the source of so much later history and the home of the Davidic monarchy. Still, Ephraim was the core of the Northern Kingdom, and Joseph was the father of Ephraim and Manasseh, the two largest tribes of the ten northern tribes. Certainly this is one reason the Elohist writer, who contributed a sizable proportion of the cycle, was interested. In the Yahwist version Judah tried to save his brother Joseph, but in the Elohist version it was Reuben, the firstborn of Leah.

The Joseph cycle is a mixture of elements from three pentateuchal sources, the Yahwist, Elohist, and Priestly. See Table 2.D for the distribution of sources in the Joseph cycle.

The Joseph cycle continues the theme of birth order and birthrights found in both the Abraham and Jacob cycles. **Joseph** is the son who receives the greatest attention, though as the firstborn of Rachel, he was not the firstborn overall. Reuben, the firstborn overall, was denied preeminence because he slept with one of Jacob's wives. **Judah** was one of the youngest sons of Jacob and Leah, yet he became one of the premier tribes of Israel. This theme is reinforced by Jacob switching the blessing on Manasseh and Ephraim.

The birthright details may have been included in Israel's epic to explain later geographical and social realities. The tribes of Judah and Ephraim rose to preeminence, even though they did not descend from firstborn sons. There may have been an additional interest in the issue of birth order to support the legitimacy of David, Israel's greatest king. He was the youngest son of Jesse, not the oldest. Likewise Solomon, David's son, was not first in line for the throne by birth order.

Story Line

Joseph was Jacob's favored son, and for this as well as Joseph's arrogance his brothers despised him and eventually sold him into Egyptian slavery. He became a servant to Potiphar, an Egyptian official (Genesis 37). An interlude describes Judah and Tamar's conflict over marriage rights and offspring (38). Back on the main story line, Joseph faithfully served Potiphar, but was sent to jail after Potiphar's wife tried to seduce him and was rebuffed. While in jail Joseph distinguished himself by his trustworthiness and his ability to interpret dreams (39–40). When **Pharaoh** had a series of dreams he could not comprehend, Joseph was called upon to interpret the dreams and came to a high government post (41). Under his leadership Egypt prepared for a famine, thus providing the occasion for a reunion with his brothers. When they came to buy grain he accused them of espionage and imprisoned one of his brothers, inflicting on Simeon the ordeal he himself had suffered because of them (42). Eventually he revealed his identity to them and forgave them (43–45).

Joseph brought the entire family to live in the Goshen region of Egypt, a fertile area in the eastern Nile delta. They grew into a sizable clan under the care of Jacob. In his old age he passed on the family blessing to his grandchildren, Ephraim and Manasseh (48) and his sons (49). Shortly afterward he died and was taken back to Canaan for burial. Before he died in Egypt Joseph extracted a promise from his family that they would not bury him there but would carry his bones back to Canaan (50).

■ JOSEPH AND HIS BROTHERS (37–45)

The Joseph cycle continues the theme of sibling rivalry from the Jacob cycle. Joseph and Benjamin, sons of Rachel, receive Jacob's special affection, and this drives the plot. But the linkage between favored son and line of promise is not as obvious in this cycle as in the preceding one. While Joseph is the focus of narrative attention, by the end of the cycle all Jacob's sons receive paternal blessing before he dies.

Judah's character development is a lesser thread running through the cycle. He is certainly secondary to Joseph, but he is significant nonetheless. He convinced his brothers not to kill Joseph but instead to sell him into slavery. He briefly takes center stage in his dealings with Tamar, then he returns to the drama at the climax of the story when Benjamin was threatened and Judah offered to take his place. His willingness to sacrifice himself stands in stark contrast to his failure to take a risk for Tamar.

Joseph the Dreamer (37)

Joseph was the firstborn son of Jacob's most-loved wife Rachel, and Jacob made no secret of favoring him. The motif of preferential parental treatment continues (remember, Isaac loved Esau, but Rebekah loved Jacob) and continues to be the source of family discontent.

The first episode of the cycle effectively foreshadows later events. Joseph has two dreams in both of which his family bows down to him—and Joseph expends no effort in trying to hide this. The dreams and Joseph's skill at interpreting them also portend his use of his gift at Pharaoh's court.

Understandably, his brothers became jealous of the favoritism Joseph gets, and perhaps they are equally put off by his superior airs. One day when he was far from his father making a delivery to his working brothers they seized him with the intention of killing him. The narrative turns a bit murky here as both Reuben and Judah seek to save his life. In the end Judah convinced his siblings to sell Joseph to traders (sometimes called Ishmaelites, other times Midianites). They returned Joseph's trademark colored tunic to Jacob all bloody and torn so that Jacob would believe he had been killed by an animal.

Judah and Tamar (38)

With minimal transition the cycle introduces a story of Judah's family. Judah married a Canaanite woman who bore him three sons. His firstborn son, Er, married Tamar, but he died before having any children. According to the Israelite law of levirate marriage (from the Latin *levir,* meaning "a husband's brother"), the brother of a childless dead man is required to raise children in his dead brother's name by marrying the widow (see Deuteronomy 25:5–10). Judah's second son failed in his responsibility and died for it, and Judah out of fear intentionally withheld his third son.

Once Tamar realized that Judah would not provide her with a husband surrogate, she devised her own plan. She dressed as a prostitute, perhaps of the type associated with the Canaanite fertility cults of Baal and Asherah. Judah engaged her services one day not knowing he had slept with his daughter-in-law. He left his seal and staff with her in place of the payment he would send later. When he attempted to make payment, the prostitute was nowhere to be found.

Three months later Judah learned that Tamar was pregnant and thought it could only be because she had played the harlot, since he had not provided her a proper husband. Judah decreed that she be burned to death. When Tamar appeared for the execution she produced Judah's seal and staff and said, "Do you recognize these?" Immediately he owned the items along with his responsibility and said, "She is more righteous than I am." Her righteousness was to be found in the duty she performed for her dead husband, to raise up offspring to perpetuate his name, something Judah had failed to accomplish. Tamar gave birth to twins, the younger of whom went on to become an ancestor of David (see Ruth 4:18–21).

The reason for including this story is difficult to discern. It intersects the encompassing Joseph plot but does not obviously connect. Perhaps because it centers on Judah, later the tribe to become the core of the Davidic kingdom, there was reason enough to retain it. Some authorities have argued for its fittingness in this place on the basis of subtle literary allusions (see Alter 1981). Judah may serve as a foil for Joseph. Judah failed in his responsibility to his son and was exposed because of his sexual desire. Joseph upheld his responsibility to his master, Potiphar, by refusing to give in to the sexual advances of Potiphar's wife.

The literary and linguistic allusions that connect the Judah–Tamar story to the Joseph cycle are in Table 2.E.

Joseph's Rise to Power (39–41)

Joseph distinguished himself while serving Potiphar, an Egyptian military official. Not only was he a faithful servant, he was handsome; so much that Potiphar's wife made sexual advances. One day Joseph rebuffed her seductions and fled the house. Out of spite she accused him of rape and he was thrown in prison. While in prison he again distinguished himself by his administrative ability and trustworthiness, and when two inmates had dreams he was able to convincingly interpret them.

Later, when Pharaoh had dreams he could not comprehend, Joseph was brought to court and interpreted the dreams as portents of seven coming years of agricultural abundance, to be followed by seven years of famine. The Pharaoh immediately put him in charge of food production and management, so that the people could prepare for the coming crisis.

> **Egyptian Parallels.** Egyptian literary tradition provides documents with similarities to the Joseph story. "The Story of Two Brothers" (Pritchard 1969: 23–25) has a scene similar to the seduction of Joseph. "The Tradition of Seven Lean Years in Egypt" (Pritchard 1969: 31–32) parallels the famine portion of Pharaoh's dream.

Joseph versus His Brothers (42–45)

The famine affected Canaan as well as Egypt. Jacob sent his sons to Egypt to buy grain. When they requested grain from Joseph the governor, whom they did not recognize, he accused them of being spies and proceeded to interrogate them. In the process of detailing their background they alluded to their youngest brother Benjamin. Joseph agreed to sell them grain on condition that one of them remain in Egypt as pledge. They were required to return with their youngest brother in order to prove the truth of their story.

Once home they told Jacob that they would have to take Benjamin to Egypt if they expected to buy more grain. Jacob reluctantly agreed, and they traveled back to Egypt, this time with gifts to appease the harsh governor. Joseph was overcome at the sight of Benjamin, but hid his feelings. Still not revealing his identity, Joseph threw a banquet for his brothers, seating them all in order of their age. The brothers were amazed, but still did not recognize Joseph.

Joseph sent his brothers away heavily laden with grain, along with one of his own religious implements hidden in Benjamin's sack. Then he sent soldiers after them to accuse the brothers of stealing. The cup was found in Benjamin's possession and Joseph demanded that he become a slave and remain in Egypt. At this point Judah came forward and pleaded with Joseph to reconsider, even going so far as to offer to take Benjamin's place.

Joseph could no longer hold back. He cried out, "I am Joseph. Is my father still alive?" His brothers understandably were terrified at this revelation, but Joseph proceeded to explain how he had come to understand all of the past events as the work of God.

> 5 Do not be agitated or angry with yourselves because you sold me here. Elohim sent me ahead of you to preserve life. 6 The famine has been in the land for two years, and five more years of no plowing or harvest are coming. 7 Elohim sent me ahead of you to preserve a remnant on earth for you and to keep survivors alive for you. 8 It was not you who sent me here, but Elohim. (45:5–8)

The Joseph cycle is notable for its lack of God-talk, and clearly differs in this respect from the other two cycles. There are no theophanies, no divine oracles to Joseph, no angels or visions. The only explicit religious dimension to the tale is these words, Joseph's theological interpretation of events. With them Joseph presents a remarkably comprehensive theology of historical experience and divine providence. After these words and a tearful reunion Jacob sent his brothers home with instructions to come back as soon as possible with everything, including their father Jacob.

> **Joseph and Wisdom.** The Joseph cycle has affinities with the wisdom tradition of the ancient Middle East (see Part 3). Absence of theophany, oracle, and overt God-talk is characteristic of the wisdom approach, as is a more studied approach to divine providence. See Crenshaw (1981).

■ ISRAEL IN EGYPT (46–50)

When Jacob heard the news about Joseph he eagerly packed up the family's belongings and traveled to Egypt. The family received royal permission to settle in Goshen.

The themes of blessing and growth are most obvious in these chapters. The family of Jacob prospered in Egypt, and he lavished the patriarchal blessing on each of his sons (Genesis 49), as well as on his favored grandsons (Genesis 48), before he died. This latter episode, the account of Jacob blessing Joseph's sons Manasseh and Ephraim, demonstrates that Jacob had lost none of his trickery. Joseph had positioned his sons before Jacob in such a way that the preferred right hand of blessing would fall on Manasseh's head, the firstborn. But true to form, Jacob defied expectations, crossed his arms, and gave the younger Ephraim the better blessing.

Yet the richness of blessing was tempered by Israel's family being in Egypt. Even as the blessings of fertility and benefit were coming to fruition, the promise of land was still elusive. While the family was fruitful and multiplied, they were exiles from the land of promise because of the famine there.

Lastly, we should note that the Joseph cycle is important because it gave the explanation of how and why the Israelites ended up in Egypt. Looking ahead to the book of Exodus, where the Israelites are in bondage, we need to know how they got there. The Joseph cycle explains this, and points ahead in anticipation of how God will rescue his people in the great exodus from Egypt.

GENESIS AS A WHOLE

The book of Genesis displays a remarkable unity of structure and purpose. Its structure is provided by a coherent and comprehensive plot line, as well as by the deliberate device of *toledot* introductory statements. The spiritual and moral themes of the book also engage the reader at a deeper level. It is no wonder that Genesis has fired the imagination of artists, writers, and theologians more than any other book of the Hebrew Bible.

The three literary sources of the Torah—the Yahwist narrative, the Elohist source, and the Priestly document—interweave to create the Ancestral Story. All three sources are well attested in Genesis 12–50 and make significant contributions. Elohist passages appear here in the Pentateuch for the first time.

For the literary sources of the Ancestral Story see Table 2.D. Table 2.E is a detailed content outline of the book of Genesis.

■ TOLEDOT OF GENESIS

The overall structure of the Ancestral Story is provided by the repeated use of the Hebrew term **toledot**. *Toledot,* sometimes spelled "toledoth," means "generations," and comes from the Hebrew word for giving birth. It is rendered in various ways by different English translations, as you can see from the options available for handling Genesis 2:4.

> NEW REVISED STANDARD VERSION:
> *"These are the **generations** of the heavens and the earth when they were created."*

> NEW INTERNATIONAL VERSION:
> *"This is the **account** of the heavens and the earth when they were created."*

> NEW JEWISH PUBLICATION SOCIETY VERSION:
> *"Such is the **story** of heaven and earth when they were created."*

The term *toledot* has to do with developments, outcomes, begettings. When found in the phrase "These are the generations of X" it introduces an account of what happens next to the offspring named in the *toledot* expression. Virtually every time it is found it has a transitional function. It draws the preceding section to a conclusion and at the same time introduces the next section.

The term is found twelve times in Genesis. Ten of those times it is found at important break points in the narrative (the *toledot* in 10:32 is not in a formula, and the *toledot* in 36:9 is a repetition of the one in 36:1). These ten *toledot* units divide cleanly into two collections of five each according to their subject matter; the Primeval Story and the Ancestral Story.

The Primeval Story consists of five *toledot* units in a straight linear fashion. The Ancestral Story consists of five *toledot* units of alternating interest: three major ones (6, 8, and 10) and two minor ones (7 and 9). The three major units contain cycles of stories and the two minor ones consist merely of descendant lists. Table

TABLE 2.3   THE *TOLEDOT* OF GENESIS

Primeval Story Toledot	*Ancestral Story Toledot*
1. Heavens and Earth (2:4) = Creation and Expulsion (2:4b–4:26)	6. Terah (11:27) = Abraham cycle (11:27–25:11)
2. Adam (5:1) = Adam to Noah Genealogy (5:1–32) and Sons of God (6:1–4)	7. Ishmael (25:12) = Ishmael Genealogy (25:12–18)
3. Noah (6:9) = Flood and Re-Creation (6:9–9:29)	8. Isaac (25:19) = Jacob cycle (25:19–35:29)
4. Shem, Ham, Japheth (10:1) = Table of Nations (10) and Tower of Babel (11:1–9)	9. Esau (36:1, 9) = Esau Genealogy (36:1–43)
5. Shem (11:10) = Shem to Terah Genealogy (11:10–26)	10. Jacob (37:2) = Joseph cycle (37–50)

2.3 displays the *toledot* series of the Primeval and Ancestral stories along with the narrative units they introduce.

The ten *toledot* of Genesis evidence a unity of direction. The book begins with the widest possible scope, the cosmos, and gradually constricts its attention to Israel as it ends with the *toledot* of Jacob, the eponymous ancestor of the nation of Israel.

■ THEMES OF GENESIS

Each narrative cycle has its own literary integrity. Yet there are common themes, motifs, and concerns that serve to give the Ancestral Story a wholeness that is greater than the sum of its parts.

1. *Divine-Human Relationship.* These stories take for granted the existence of an intimate relationship between the ancestors and their patron God. The deity promises, protects, and directs the lives of the ancestors. He treats them differently than the people with whom they are in contact (and conflict). Still, these other people, be they Egyptian or Philistine, Edomite or Aramean, would find benefit in being associated with the ancestral family.

a. *Promise.* God determined and guided the ancestors' future, and he pledged that future through promises. The consistent way in which the divine promises were transferred from one generation to the next signals their programmatic character. The promises assured longevity through their offspring who would become a nation, and assured possession of the land of Canaan. In their Priestly form the promises entailed fruitfulness and multiplication.

b. *Covenant*. The relationship between God and the ancestors was formalized by covenants. God bound himself by oath to fulfill his promises. In its Priestly form the covenant was termed everlasting. There is a succession of covenants beginning with Noah, to Abraham, and then to Moses at Mount Sinai that progressively builds and defines the relationship of God with his world.

c. *God of the Fathers*. The patriarchs developed an intimate relationship with the deity such that Abraham could be found in conversation with God near his tent. God also came to Abraham and Jacob in visions. The deity came to be personally associated with the patriarchs and was termed "the Elohim of Abraham, Isaac, and Jacob." God was not immediately present to Joseph in the same way, and appears only as the force of history in Joseph's lecture to his brothers. In Israel's developing history God seems to continue receding from personal contact (see Friedman 1995).

2. *Offspring*. Israel understood itself as having descended from Abraham in a line of succession miraculously engineered by God. Many of the stories touch on the question of family succession: conceiving, having children, determining the line of inheritance. The frequent genealogies and the *toledot* structure of Genesis reinforce this overall theme.

a. *Firstborn*. Consistently the oldest son does not end up being the favored son. Perhaps one of the lessons intended by all three cycles is that God does not follow human convention when he decides whom he will bless. He is unpredictable, and likely as not will choose the younger over the older. Yet it must also be observed that each of the firstborn sons had some flaw that may have been the reason for their disqualification. Ishmael was the son of a concubine; Esau cheaply bartered away his status; Reuben slept with Bilhah, his father's concubine. However, one could ask if their failings were inherently more heinous than some of the actions of Jacob or Judah.

b. *Barrenness*. As a further indication of the sovereignty of God, the younger son predestined for greatness was in almost every case conceived through the help of God after an extended period of barrenness: Isaac to Sarah, Jacob and Esau to Rebekah, Joseph to Rachel, Perez to Tamar (though more through Tamar's initiative than God's help). Divinely enabled conception of the gifted son is a pattern repeated later with Samson, Hannah and Samuel, and Jesus of Nazareth in the New Testament.

c. *Matriarchs* (see Jeansonne 1990). Women were marginalized within the patriarchal social system of the ancient Middle East. Although they may not have had institutionalized power, they were not powerless. Within the family they exercised considerable control. Israel's matriarchs—strong-willed, often employing trickery and deceit—were directly responsible for determining lines of descent and inheritance. Abraham deferred to Sarah, who expelled Hagar and her son Ishmael. Sarah and Rebekah agreed to play sister instead of spouse to save their husbands and the promise of offspring. Rebekah conspired against her husband with Jacob to steal the blessing from Isaac's favorite son Esau. Rachel and Leah were rivals to Jacob's sexual attention, and presumably also rivals to inherit the promise. Rachel stole her father's household gods and cleverly hid them from him. Tamar entrapped Judah into siring a child by her, and was judged more righteous for it. Quite possibly some of these women may have been models for the likes of Bathsheba who deftly secured the throne for her son Solomon over his rivals (see Chapter 9).

3. *Land.* Israel was vitally invested in the claim that Canaan was its heritage and homeland. The people found justification for that claim in the promise made first to Abraham, and in the fact that he actually lived in Canaan for many years. Each of the cycles contains the notice that at least an earnest of land had been purchased; Abraham bought Ephron's field near Hebron (23) and Jacob bought a plot near Shechem (33:18–20). The family of Jacob even purchased property in Egypt (47:27). The divine land promise is the foundation for Israel's claim to the land, and justifies their conquest of Canaan under Joshua in the thirteenth century B.C.E. All three ancestral cycles are shaped around geographical itineraries, and always in respect to Canaan. Abraham left Mesopotamia and journeyed to Canaan with a sojourn in Egypt; Jacob left Canaan for Haran and returned to Canaan with huge wealth and family. Joseph was deported to Egypt but eventually brought the entire family there to survive another famine. All these peregrinations suggest Israel's hold on the land was tenuous, and separation from the land a periodic reality. Perhaps these ancestral periods of exile and return shaped the hope of the Israelites who experienced their greatest trial in the Babylonian exile. Certainly the ending of Genesis, as it leaves Jacob's family in Egypt awaiting return to the Promised Land for the burial of Joseph's bones, thrusts the reader onward to the book of Exodus in expectation, looking for return and rest. (For the narrative and theological significance of land see Brueggemann 1977 and Weinfeld 1993.)

FOR FURTHER STUDY

Genesis, for all its colorful stories and human interest, has inspired an explosion of provocative and exploratory treatments; see Bloom (1990), Rosenblatt and Horwitz (1995), Armstrong (1996), Visotzky (1996), Moyers (1996). Westermann's commentaries are comprehensive and at times technical, but they are the best; his three-volume commentary series on Genesis is distilled down to one paperback (1992). Brueggemann's commentary on Genesis is theologically insightful (1982).

Chapter 2 Bibliography. For translations and commentaries on the book of Genesis see Chapter 1 Bibliography.

QUESTIONS FOR REVIEW

1. Compare the accounts of God's covenant with Abraham in 13:14–17, 15:17–21, and 17:1–21. How are they alike and how are they different?

2. Define the term *theophany*. List the episodes where God appeared to people in the Ancestral Story. List the ways in which God appeared. Identify the typical ways God appeared to people in each of the three literary sources.

3. What changes did Abraham and Sarah undergo from the beginning of the Abraham cycle to the end? To what did Jacob's name change? Did Joseph's name change?

4. Trace the theme of blessing and curse through the Jacob cycle. What is the significance of blessing in the Ancestral Story as a whole?

5. What are the similarities among the stories about Sarah and the Pharaoh (Genesis 12:14–20), Sarah and Abimelech (Genesis 20:10–20), and Rebekah and Abimelech (Genesis 26:6–11). How can we account for them?

6. How does the Joseph cycle differ from the preceding two cycles? How is it similar?

7. Which firstborn sons fail to inherit the richer divine promises, and which sons get them instead? Does the narrative provide a reason why they fail to inherit, or is the reason divine and/or patriarchal whim?

QUESTIONS FOR REFLECTION AND DISCUSSION

1. Abraham, Isaac, and Jacob are considered the fathers of the nation of Israel. In a way, telling their stories is telling the story of the Israelites. What episodes in the Ancestral Story reveal especially clearly the character of Israel? What episodes may have reinforced a northern Israelite identity? What episodes may have reinforced a southern Judean identity? How do we use stories to clarify our personal identities? Our national identities?

2. Which ancestral stories relate to the issue of faith in God? List some specific episodes that stand out in your mind that have to do with issues of belief, trust, and faith. What developments can you trace in the growth and quality of the ancestors' faith? What may the Ancestral Story as a whole say about the nature of faith and relationship to God?

3. What do the stories of the matriarchs reveal about the social roles of women in the ancestral period? How does the sociology of women in that time, insofar as you have been able to glean it from the texts, compare with your understanding of the role of women in society today?

4. Was Joseph malicious or justified in the way he treated his brothers in Egypt?

5. The main characters of the Ancestral Story, both male and female, are all strong and determined. How do you see the patriarchs and matriarchs as history creators in relation to the promises of God and his role in directing history?

Chapter 2 Study Guide

- *Chapter summary*
- *Key terms linked to the glossary*
- *Concept questions with answer links*
- *Progress tests: true/false, multiple choice, matching, and identification*

EXODUS: DELIVERANCE AND COVENANT

3

Key Terms

Aaron
Absolute law
Book of the Covenant
Burning bush
Case law
Code of Hammurabi
Covenant
Ethical Decalogue
Exodus
Golden calf
Horeb
Hyksos
Miriam
Moses
Mount Sinai
Passover
Plagues
Pharaoh
Ramses
Ritual Decalogue
Reed Sea / Red Sea
Tabernacle
Theophany

FIGURE 3.1 **THE SINAI PENINSULA** The Sinai Peninsula is the triangular area in the middle. It is defined by the Mediterranean Sea on the left and the two gulfs extending from the Red Sea on the right. Led by Moses, the Israelites escaped slavery in Egypt and traveled through the Sinai wilderness to Mount Sinai.

The book of Exodus is the bedrock book of Israel's faith. It is Israel's Magna Carta, Declaration of Independence, and national constitution rolled into one. The nation's two root experiences are contained in this book: the miraculous flight from Egypt, called the exodus, and the covenant of Mount Sinai.

The **exodus** declared that Israel exists by the powerful delivering action of Yahweh. The **covenant** shaped Israel's relationship with Yahweh. This relationship has clear expectations of both parties and holds the promise of a glorious future. Taken together these events establish Israel's elemental identity as a delivered people in covenant with God.

Moreover, the exodus is basic to Judaism and Christianity. It is celebrated in Judaism as *pesach*, the Passover, and is the premier festival of freedom and liberty. In Christianity it has been transformed into Easter, with Jesus of Nazareth being the Passover lamb.

The book of Exodus gets its name from the central event recounted therein: Israel's miraculous departure from Egypt. In serial order the book of Exodus follows the book of Genesis, but in terms of its religious and national significance it is number one. It can be divided into two main parts: traditions centering on the exit from Egypt (chapters 1–18) and traditions centering on the Mount Sinai revelation of Yahweh (chapters 19–40).

Story Line

The opening (Exodus 1) describes how the Egyptians oppressed the descendants of Jacob, subjecting them to forced labor. Because this failed to curtail their growth, all male Hebrew infants were to be killed. When Moses was born (2) his parents hid him temporarily and then put him into a basket and set him afloat on the Nile River. Pharaoh's daughter found Moses, had compassion on him, and raised him as her own in the royal court.

When Moses became a man he rashly attempted to rescue some fellow Hebrews by killing their Egyptian task master. He fled Egypt and took refuge in the Sinai wilderness. There he married Zipporah and raised a family. While shepherding the flocks of his father-in-law, Jethro, he met Yahweh at a burning bush (3–4). God told Moses to return to Egypt, which was not what he wanted to hear. However, back in Egypt he mediated Israel's deliverance from slavery and oppression. With a series of natural and supernatural disasters (5–11), Yahweh demonstrated his superior power. After celebrating the first Passover the Hebrews escaped into the Sinai wilderness (12–13). The Egyptian army pursued them and, just when it looked like the Hebrews were doomed, God miraculously opened a pathway through the Reed Sea. The Hebrews passed through safely, but the Egyptians were drowned when they tried to follow (14–15). Then Moses led the people to **Mount Sinai** (16–18) where earlier he had met Yahweh at the burning bush.

At Mount Sinai Yahweh revealed the Law to the Hebrews and established an abiding covenant relationship with them (19–24). In addition to making this covenant he gave them instructions for building worship items and a portable shrine (25–31). Soon after the people agreed to the terms of the covenant they broke it by worshiping the golden calf instead of Yahweh (32–34). Though they deserved to be annihilated, God reestablished his covenant with them. Then, while still encamped at Mount Sinai, the Hebrews built a tabernacle as the residence for their God (35–40).

EXODUS: DELIVERANCE TRADITIONS (1–18)

The first half of Exodus is a narrative account of the Israelites' escape from Egyptian bondage and their journey to Mount Sinai. This deliverance account includes the story of Moses, Yahweh's chosen leader. Moses mediated a series of disasters that culminated in the Israelites' release. Overcoming all obstacles, including a great expanse of sea, the Israelites made their way through the wilderness until they came to the mountain of God, where the terms of the covenant were revealed to them through Moses.

■ ISRAEL IN EGYPT (1)

The first verse of the book of Exodus connects the Joseph cycle of Genesis (see Chapter 2) to the exodus story by showing how the Hebrew people came to Egypt.

1 These are the names of the sons of Israel who entered Egypt with Jacob, each with his family. (1:1)

After naming all the sons the writer remarks that the Israelites were fruitful and prolific, so much so that Egypt was teeming with them. The language of multiplication echoes the ancestral covenant blessing (Genesis 17:2; 28:3; 35:11), and goes back even further to the priestly creation blessing (Genesis 1:28; 9:1).

> **Shemot.** In Jewish tradition the book of Exodus is named *shemot,* "names," from the first sentence of the book. Could the use of *shemot* here be an allusion to the importance of name in the primeval story and in Genesis 12:2, "I will make your name great"? Blessing is a prominent theme of the Priestly source (see Chapter 1). Using the phrase "sons of Israel" for the Israelites is deliberate because Jacob's name had been changed to Israel. He is the eponymous ancestor of the nation, that is, the nation takes its name from him.

Beginning with Jacob's clan the Hebrews lived in Egypt for many generations. After a time the government changed hands and the Egyptian **Pharaoh,** or king of Egypt, enslaved the Hebrews. The term *pharaoh* is derived from the Egyptian phrase "the great house." It designates the highest office of Egypt and is not a personal name. Notice how their covenant blessing became their curse; they had become so numerous that the new ruler considered them a threat.

8 A new king rose to power over Egypt, who did not know about Joseph. 9 He said to his people, "Now, the Israelites are more numerous and powerful than we are. 10 Come on, let us deal shrewdly with them, or they will become even more numerous. If war breaks out they would join our enemies, fight against us, and leave the land." 11 They put slave masters over them to inflict hard labor on them. They built the store cities Pithom and Rameses for Pharaoh. (1:8–11)

Unfortunately, there are no direct references to Moses or the Israelite exodus outside the Hebrew Bible. Still, extra-biblical sources have helped to build a plausible setting for Israel's experience within Egyptian history.

Egyptian history provides a context for understanding the Egyptians' change of heart toward the Hebrews, implied by the reference in verse 8 to the "new king" who rose to power. Prior to this time, from 1750 to 1550 B.C.E., a group of non-Egyptians had ruled northern Egypt. This foreign rule, which historians call the Second Intermediate Period, was a break in the flow of native Egyptian government. The invaders were the **Hyksos,** an Egyptian term that means "rulers of foreign lands." Most of them were Semites from Syria and Palestine, the same general area the ancestors of the Hebrews called home. If Joseph was part of the influx of the foreign Hyksos, this might explain how he could come to such prominence and power in Egypt.

Under Pharaoh Ahmose I (1552–1527 B.C.E.) of the eighteenth dynasty, native Egyptian rule resumed and Egyptians began to subjugate foreigners. According to Exodus 12:40, the Israelites were in Egypt for 430 years, and perhaps as many as 300 years of that were spent in subservience. If the traditional date of the exodus

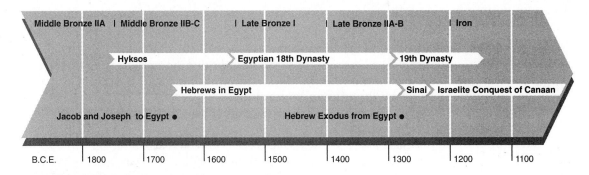

Middle Bronze IIA | Middle Bronze IIB-C | Late Bronze I | Late Bronze IIA-B | Iron

Hyksos | Egyptian 18th Dynasty | 19th Dynasty

Hebrews in Egypt | Sinai | Israelite Conquest of Canaan

Jacob and Joseph to Egypt ● | Hebrew Exodus from Egypt ●

B.C.E. | 1800 | 1700 | 1600 | 1500 | 1400 | 1300 | 1200 | 1100

FIGURE 3.2 EARLY ISRAEL AND EGYPT

early in the thirteenth century B.C.E. is accepted, the Pharaoh at the time of the exodus was **Ramses II** (1290–1224 B.C.E.), the great empire builder of the nineteenth dynasty. He moved Egypt's center of government to the eastern Nile delta and initiated sizable building projects there.

> **Dating the Exodus.** This is a complex issue, dependent on chronological hints in the biblical text as well as evidence from history and archaeology. There are two recognized candidates, 1440 B.C.E. and 1280 B.C.E. The early date is calculated by counting back from the known date of Solomon's temple building using the 480 years of 1 Kings 6:1. The late date depends heavily on the date of the conquest of Canaan as determined by archaeology and then working back from the forty years of the wilderness wandering to the exodus. See Bimson (1978).

The Israelites were set to work building Pithom and Rameses (1:11), two Egyptian fortress cities in the eastern Nile delta region. The cities were strategic in defending Egypt from Asian attack, and served as bases for extending Egyptian power into Palestine and Syria.

The Hebrews were forced to manufacture the mud bricks (see Figure 3.3) and construct the fortresses. The hard work of city building did not diminish the Hebrew population, however, so the Egyptians initiated a policy of male infanticide. The midwives who serviced the Hebrews (it is not clear whether the midwives themselves were Hebrew) secretly refused to cooperate. The desperate Pharaoh then commanded that all Hebrew infant sons be drowned in the Nile. The stage is set for the birth and early life of Moses.

> **Hebrew and Israelite.** Israelites are sometimes referred to as Hebrews in the early chapters of Exodus. The term *Hebrew* is used only about thirty times in the entire Hebrew Bible. Its pattern of usage indicates that it refers to Israelites in contrast to other ethnic groups. Interestingly, it is used mostly of early Israelites when people of other ethnic groups refer to them, rather than by Israelites themselves.

Table 3.A shows the distribution and usage of the term Hebrew.

MAKING BRICKS IN EGYPT   This depiction of the brick-making process is from the tomb of Thut-mose III of the 18th Egyptian dynasty, c. 1460 B.C.E. Laborers are shown processing the raw mud and forming the bricks used to construct walls and buildings.

Hebrew and Habiru. Documents from Mesopotamia and Egypt from the second millennium to the twelfth century B.C.E. make frequent reference to groups of people associated with the term *habiru*. These *habiru* were evidently not a homogenous ethnic group but a class of social misfits and troublemakers. The term may be linguistically related to the biblical term for a Hebrew, *'ivri*. The question has been raised whether the Israelites were originally such people. If so, this would have implications for the origin of the Israelites, their social formation, and their ethnic constitution or lack thereof (see Na'aman 1986).

■ THE EARLY MOSES (2–4)

Moses was born to Amram and Jochebed from the tribe of Levi (6:20). After they were no longer able to conceal Moses, they placed him in a reed basket waterproofed with tar and set him afloat in the Nile. This was a deliberate ploy to win the compassion of Pharaoh's daughter who frequented the river to bathe. When she discovered Moses she took him to court and raised him there as a virtual grandson of the Pharaoh.

> **The name Moses.** Pharaoh's daughter gave him the name Moses, *moshe* in Hebrew. The Hebrew Bible attaches a folk etymology to the name (2:10); the Hebrew verb "draw out" puns with Moshe. In reality Moshe is a name derived from the Egyptian verb *msy*, meaning "be born," and the noun *ms* meaning "child or son."

Though raised as an Egyptian, apparently it was through his birth-mother, hired as his wet-nurse, that he came to realize his Hebrew identity. Clearly Moses had a mixed Hebrew and Egyptian identity. This explains how he could on the one hand be knowledgeable of the royal court to negotiate the departure of the Israelites and on the other hand sympathize with the plight of the Israelites.

Sargon Birth Legend. The Mesopotamian birth story of Sargon of Akkad contains similarities to the Moses birth story. Sargon was the illegitimate son of a high priestess. To keep her position she needed to conceal the birth, so she placed Sargon in a basket of reeds caulked with tar and set him afloat on the Euphrates River. He was discovered downstream by Akki the water drawer, who adopted and raised him. Sargon rose to become the architect of the empire of Akkad (see Pritchard 1969: 119; Longman 1991).

One day as Moses was surveying the royal projects, he rescued a Hebrew slave by killing his abusive Egyptian master. In danger of being exposed, Moses fled to Midian where he found refuge with Jethro, the priest of Midian. Moses eventually married one of his daughters and served as shepherd of his father-in-law's flocks.

Tale of Sinuhe. This Egyptian tale relates the adventures of an Egyptian court official who fled Egypt to live in Syria-Palestine (see Pritchard 1969). Sinuhe has some similarities to Moses, and the tale provides an interesting glimpse of Syria-Palestine, especially of its fruitfulness and desirability.

Moses' encounter with Yahweh at the **burning bush** in Exodus 3:1–15 marks a turning point in Israel's history. Here Moses learned the identity of the God who would deliver the Israelites from bondage. Moses would be his mediator. The full account is a mixture of Yahwist (J) and Elohist (E) material, with the Elohist predominating.

Moses at the Mountain (E)

1 Moses was tending the flock of his father-in-law, Jethro, the priest of Midian; and he led his flock to the west side of the wilderness, and came to Horeb, the mountain of Elohim. (3:1)

Jethro is the name of Moses' father-in-law in the Elohist source, Reuel in the Yahwist source. Horeb is the name the Elohist (and Deuteronomist) applies to the mountain of God, whereas the Yahwist and Priestly sources call it Mount Sinai. Some authorities have suggested that Horeb and Mount Sinai are not the same place. According to such a view, Mount Sinai would be located in the Sinai peninsula and Horeb somewhere in Midian. Midian is notoriously difficult to pin down, too.

The Burning Bush (J)

2 The angel of YHWH appeared to him in a flaming fire out of the middle of a bush. As Moses watched, the bush burned but it did not burn up. 3 Moses said to himself, "I am going to stop and observe this amazing thing! Why does the bush not burn up?" 4 When YHWH saw that Moses stopped to observe . . . (3:2–4a)

Verse 2a summarizes the story. Probably added later, it gives the story an explanatory framework so we will understand that Yahweh did not appear directly to

Moses (as the story implies), but indirectly in the form of an angel or messenger. The word here translated "angel" can also mean "messenger."

The "flaming fire" that is such a prominent part of this story is typical of a biblical **theophany,** or appearance of God. In Genesis 15 God appeared to Abraham in a smoking fire pot. Here he appears to Moses in a flaming bush. On Mount Sinai he appears in lightning, smoke, and cloud. In the wilderness he appears in pillars of cloud and fire.

*Start
9/12*

The God of the Fathers (E)

. . . Elohim called to him out of the middle of the bush and said, "Moses! Moses!" He replied, "Yes, I am here." 5 He said, "Do not get any closer. Take your sandals off your feet. The place where you are standing is holy ground. 6 He said, "I am the Elohim of your father, the Elohim of Abraham, the Elohim of Isaac, and the Elohim of Jacob." Then Moses hid his face, because he was afraid to look at Elohim. (3:4b–6)

Whereas the deity is referred to as Yahweh in verse 4a, in 4b the reference changes to Elohim, indicating the return to the Elohist form. Note the similarity between this story and Genesis 22 (also an Elohist account) in the way God initiates the encounter, saying Moses' name twice and him answering, "Here I am."

*Midian
burning bush
on Mt.
Sinai .*

Verse 6 explicitly associates the God of the exodus with the God of the ancestors, thus connecting Israel's deliverance with the history of and promises to the ancestors. The phrase "God of my/your/his father" is often found in Genesis and in Mesopotamian literature of a personal patron god and protector. It suggests a special relationship between the individual and his deity. Beginning with Moses the phrase becomes "God of our/your/their fathers," with the plural referring to the Israelites as a people.

We are no longer dealing with the angel of Yahweh. Note also how the Elohist protects Moses from looking directly at God. Facing God directly is not allowed in Elohist theology; the fear of God is a prominent motif in the Elohist source.

Land of Milk and Honey (J)

7 YHWH said, "I have seen the hardship of my people in Egypt. I have heard their cry for relief from their oppressors. I know of their suffering. 8 I have come down to deliver them from the grip of Egypt and bring them up out of that land to a good and spacious land, a land flowing with milk and honey, to the place of the Canaanites, the Hittites, the Amorites, the Perizzites, the Hivites and the Jebusites." (3:7–8)

As always in this source, Yahweh is a caring and compassionate God. He hates to see his people suffer and acts out of compassion. Not only will he relieve their suffering, he will bring them to the land promised to the ancestors. The land is described as "flowing with milk and honey." Obviously milk did not flow through the streams and honey did not ooze down the wadis; these images depict the wealth of the land. It supports cattle and all the flowering plants that support life. The six nations listed here are often cited as inhabiting Palestine (for example, see Genesis 15:18–21, where these and more are listed).

Moses the Mediator (E)

9 "The cry of the people of Israel has now reached me. I have seen the oppression with which the Egyptians mistreat them. 10 Go, I will send you to Pharaoh so that you can bring my people, the sons of Israel, out of Egypt." 11 But Moses said to Elohim, "Who am I that I should go to Pharaoh and bring the sons of Israel out of Egypt?" 12 He said, "But I will be with you. This shall be the sign for you to know that I have sent you: when you have brought the people out of Egypt, you shall worship Elohim on this mountain." (3:9–12)

In contrast to the Yahwist above, here the focus is on the Egyptians' wrongdoing rather than on the Israelites' suffering. Characteristic of the Elohist, God acted through an intermediary, Moses in this case. He revealed his deep-seated feelings of inadequacy as mediator, humility being a sign of genuine godliness in God's prophets. The Yahwist source, which is not quite so adoring of Moses as the Elohist, later portrays him as putting up more resistance.

The sign God gave him was not something that could give him assurance right then and there, but would be a later confirmation of his calling.

13 Then Moses said to Elohim, "If I come to the people of Israel and say to them, 'The Elohim of your fathers has sent me to you,' and they ask me, 'What is his name?' what shall I say to them?" 14 Elohim said to Moses, "Ehyeh-asher-ehyeh." And he said, "Say this to the people of Israel, 'Ehyeh has sent me to you.'" 15 Elohim also said to Moses, "Say this to the people of Israel, 'YHWH, the Elohim of your fathers, the Elohim of Abraham, the Elohim of Isaac, and the Elohim of Jacob, has sent me to you': this is my name for ever, and thus I am to be remembered throughout all generations." (3:13–15)

Moses impertinently asked God for identification: Who are you? How can I identify you to the Israelite elders? In response God identified himself as the God of the fathers, later specified as the patriarchs Abraham, Isaac, and Jacob. Then God in a cryptic manner said, "Ehyeh-asher-ehyeh" is my name, enigmatically translatable as "I am who I am."

The Divine Name. This revelation of the divine name has given rise to reams of research and speculation. Most authorities acknowledge that *ehyeh* is a Hebrew verbal form meaning "I am." The whole phrase means "I am who I am," or "I will be who I will be." When the first-person verbal form *ehyeh* is transformed into the third-person form it becomes *yahweh*, which can be translated "he is." It has also been translated "he causes to be." However, what this name really signifies remains a mystery, and probably deliberately so. At the same time God revealed his name he also concealed its precise meaning. We can only speculate what "I am" means. Perhaps God was suggesting he was the only self-existing one. Others, relating the name to the verb "to be" in a causal sense, have said it is a statement about God's creative power: "I am the one who calls into being."

Whatever the deeper meaning of the divine name Yahweh, it is the name by which all the textual sources identify the God of Israel from now on. It is the name of Israel's patron deity, a name which is specifically associated with the covenant. From this point on, even the Elohist uses YHWH for the divine name, though not to the exclusion of the designation Elohim. The change of divine name is also noted in the Priestly source at Exodus 6:2–5. This account adds that the ancestors knew God as El Shaddai (probably meaning "God Almighty"), but through Moses and the exodus he made himself known as Yahweh.

Each of the three Pentateuchal sources has a specific point at which it begins to use the divine name Yahweh. See Table 3.B, the first use of the divine name Yahweh in the sources.

Moses raised excuses about why he should not go back to Egypt. In response God gave him signs to authenticate his calling, including a staff that could transform itself into a snake. When Moses claimed he was not eloquent enough to speak before Pharaoh God appointed **Aaron,** Moses' brother, to be his spokesman.

21 YHWH said to Moses, "When you return to Egypt, make sure you perform before Pharaoh all the miracles I have given you the ability to do. Yet, I will harden his heart so that he will not allow the people to leave. 22 You must say to Pharaoh: 'This is what YHWH says: Israel is my firstborn son. 23 I command you, "Let my son leave so that he may worship me." If you refuse to let him leave, I will slay your firstborn son.'" (4:21–23)

Having received the revelation of the divine name, as well as his mission, Moses went back to Egypt and presented Yahweh's demand to Pharaoh. "Let my people go!" Pharaoh refused to budge. Only after a devastating series of disasters did he allow them, indeed urge them, to leave Egypt.

> **Moses and Monotheism.** Moses stands at the heart of a religious revolution. He championed a religion focused on one God over against the polytheistic notions of the surrounding peoples. Is it possible that he was influenced in this monotheistic direction by the Egyptian king Akhenaton (1360–1340 B.C.E.), who tried to simplify Egypt's religious system by declaring that the sun god, Aton, was the only deity? See Redford (1984) and Assmann (1997).

■ PLAGUES (5–11)

Because Pharaoh refused to grant permission to leave, God sent the **plagues.** The description of disasters is an example of graphic storytelling. The Nile turned to blood, making the water undrinkable. Then frogs invaded the land, and after they died there was an infestation of gnats, then flies. Soon the livestock became diseased, and later animals and humans suffered from boils. Crops were devastated, first by a hail storm and then by locusts. After all this an impenetrable darkness descended on the land. Though the Egyptian population reeled, Pharaoh still refused to let the Israelites go.

The story of the plagues has given rise to a variety of interpretations deriving from different perspectives. The varying readings are not mutually exclusive, and, in fact, taken together they can demonstrate the multifaceted character of the text's meaning.

From the perspective of biblical history the plagues were intended to reveal Yahweh's power to break Egyptian resistance. They are called God's great acts of judgment and were said to come from the finger of God (8:19). From a naturalist perspective many of the plagues can be explained by identifiable phenomena attested in the Nile valley. Hort (1957) developed a theory that the majority of the plagues have direct natural causes. From a history of religions perspective the plagues may represent Yahweh's judgment on the gods of Egypt, including Re the sun god who was attacked in the ninth plague. From a literary perspective the plagues are arranged in three series of three disasters, with the tenth plague as the climax. From the perspective of source analysis there were two different traditions of the plagues, a Yahwist and a Priestly version. The core plague narrative comes from the Yahwist source. It attests eight plagues and focuses on the role of Moses. The Priestly source added two plagues and highlights the role of Aaron.

The following tables present the data along with further explanations of these interpretive perspectives on the plagues:

- *Table 3.C, descriptions of the plagues as the work of God*
- *Table 3.D, the plagues as judgment on the gods of Egypt*
- *Table 3.E, the literary structure of the plagues narrative*
- *Table 3.F, the Yahwist and Priestly versions of the plagues*

After each plague Pharaoh's heart became hard and he refused to allow the Israelites to leave. Pharaoh's response is variously attributed to his hardening of his own heart and to God hardening Pharaoh's heart (see Wilson 1979). Thus Exodus both lays responsibility on Pharaoh and indicates that his stubbornness was part of a higher purpose.

The last plague was the death of Egypt's firstborn humans and animals. It was the last straw. It compelled Pharaoh to let the Israelites go.

Exodus attributes Pharaoh's resolve both to his own stubbornness and to God's initiative. The textual evidence is displayed in Table 3.G on Pharaoh's hard heart.

■ PASSOVER (12:1–13:16)

The Israelites avoided the devastating tenth plague because each family slaughtered a lamb as a substitute for its firstborn. They painted blood from the lamb on the door frames of their homes, and when God saw this evidence of the sacrifice on a house, he "passed over" that house, sparing the firstborn son. Beginning with the exodus God laid claim to all firstborn sons, and provided for their redemption, or buying back, with a substitutionary sacrifice (13:11–16). On the significance of the firstborn in biblical literature see Greenspahn (1994).

The avoidance ritual of the tenth plague developed into a ceremonial meal called the **Passover**, or *pesach* in Hebrew. During this meal a roasted lamb was eaten along with bitter herbs and unleavened bread (bread made without yeast) called *matsot*. Eating *matsot* symbolized the hurriedness of Israel's departure; the bread simply had no time to rise. In pre-Israelite times the Passover sacrifice and the feast of unleavened bread may have been two separate occasions, one pastorally based and the other agriculturally based. They were combined in biblical tradition and stand as a memorial and eternal ordinance of the exodus (12:14). The Passover ritual is defined not just in Exodus but also in a variety of Torah texts (see Leviticus 23:4–8; Numbers 9:1–14; 28:16–25; Deuteronomy 16:1–8).

The exodus story became so important to Israel's identity that the prescription for remembering it came to be contained within the tradition of the event itself. The yearly Passover celebration developed into one of Israel's most important festivals. Observing it or failing to observe it became a measure of the faithfulness of Israel in the Hebrew Bible. It is still widely celebrated today and serves as an enduring memorial to human freedom and divine compassion.

■ EXODUS FROM EGYPT (13:17–15:21)

After leaving Egypt the Israelites fled into the Sinai peninsula (see Figure 3.1). Pharaoh had second thoughts about allowing them to depart so he mustered his chariotry and gave chase. The Israelites took a jagged route, avoiding the main road controlled by Egyptian troops before heading south into the wilderness (see Figure 3.6).

After a short time the Israelites were pinched between Pharaoh's army and the **Reed Sea.** The Israelites, as was their tendency, blamed Moses for their predicament.

> **Reed Sea or Red Sea?** "God led the people by the roundabout way of the wilderness toward the Red Sea" (13:18, NRSV). Most English Bible versions locate Israel's miraculous escape at the Red Sea, but the underlying Hebrew phrase *yam suf* might better be rendered Reed Sea. *Suf* is derived from the Egyptian word for the papyrus reed, which only grows in fresh water. This would place the crossing at one of the lagoons or inland lakes in the northeast of Egypt near the shore of the Mediterranean Sea (see Batto 1984, who presents the evidence but opts for a mythological interpretation of *yam suf*).

When all hope seemed lost, by a divine act the Israelites escaped through the sea on dry ground and the army of Pharaoh drowned when they tried to follow. This escape is the most important event in Israel's history. It is the culmination of God's great work in delivering the Israelites from oppression and bondage and providing salvation. It would forever be remembered as the event that revealed both the compassion and power of Israel's God. Its significance to the religious faith of Israel cannot be overestimated.

> **What happened at the Reed Sea?** Authorities continue to speculate about precisely what happened at the Reed Sea. Granting that the account retains memories of a miraculous event (and is more than just a historicizing of the creation myth), some have developed scientific scenarios. Goedicke argues that the eruption of a volcano on Thera and the resulting tidal wave swept Pharaoh's army away, while Israel occupied the high ground (see Shanks 1981). Nof and Paldor (1992) attribute the drying of the sea to identifiable oceanographic patterns.

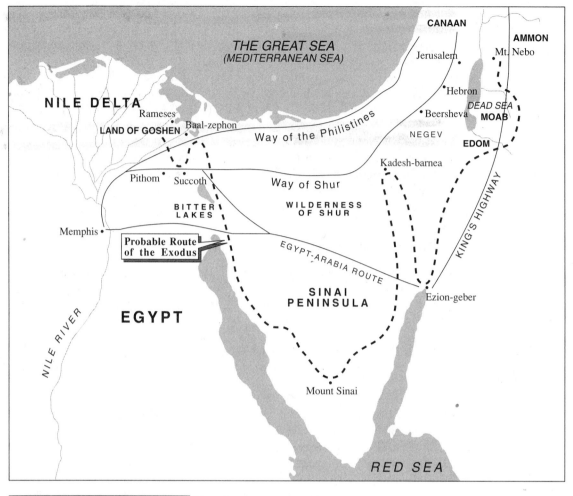

FIGURE 3.4 THE ROUTE OF THE EXODUS   See Beit-Arieh (1988) and Krahmalkov (1994) for evidence relating to the route of the exodus.

The exit from Egypt and deliverance at the Reed Sea is the salvation high point of Israel's history. In this event Yahweh revealed his deep love and care for Israel. In biblical literature it became the prototype saving event. When at a later time the Israelites were alienated from the Promised Land and oppressed by foreign overlords, especially during the Babylonian exile, they recalled the great exodus from Egypt and were encouraged.

Comparing the Yahwist and Priestly accounts reveals notable differences in narrative emphasis. Each seems to portray the miracle and the role of Moses somewhat differently.

Yahwist version: *YHWH drove the sea back with a strong east wind all night and turned the sea into dry land* (14:21b). According to this version the people were saved when God sent a wind to drive back the sea. In this version God acted directly. Overall, the Yahwist places primary focus on Yahweh and his activity. He was present in the cloud. He was the one that saved Israel. Moses' only role was to reassure the people that they would be saved. The Yahwist strand concentrates less on the details of the miracle and more on the faith response of the people. The Israelites moved from fear to faith as they stood back and observed what Yahweh had done.

Priestly version: *Moses stretched out his hand over the sea. . . . And the waters were divided. The Israelites went into the sea on dry ground. The waters formed a wall on their right and on their left* (14:21a, 21c–22). In this version the miracle is more spectacular, with the water rising up on either side of the traveling Israelites. God acts indirectly through the agency of Moses rather than directly.

Old Epic version: *You blew with your wind, the sea covered them. They sank as lead into the mighty waters* (15:10). In addition to the Yahwist and Priestly versions there is a third witness. The victory hymn in Exodus 15 contains an independent description that concentrates on the destruction of Pharaoh's army. There is no mention of God splitting the sea or the Israelites crossing on dry ground.

The Exodus text of each source is available separately, as well as in a combined form. Pay special attention to the Yahwist and Priestly versions. You will see how each tells a clear and coherent story when read on its own.

- *Table 3.H, Yahwist exodus account*
- *Table 3.I, Elohist exodus account*
- *Table 3.J, Priestly exodus account*
- *Table 3.K, combined exodus account*

Exodus 15 celebrates the victory over Pharaoh in a poetic song of triumph. Moses and his sister **Miriam** led the people in a victory hymn to Yahweh: "I will sing to YHWH, for he has triumphed gloriously; horse and rider he has thrown into the sea." The style and vocabulary of this hymn date it as one of the oldest Hebrew compositions in the Bible and tend to place it quite close to the time of the event itself.

The history of the Reed Sea crossing seems to have been combined with the divine warrior myth of the ancient Middle East (see Dozeman 1996). In this common myth the high god slays the monster of chaos, personified as the sea or the great river. In Canaan, for example, Baal subdued Yamm, the sea god. This myth finds expression in Israel's poetry (see Psalms 29 and 74:12–15) and in prophetic literature (Isaiah 51:9–11). In an evocative way, the exodus deliverance myth combines with the priestly creation myth in the triumph of life over death, symbolized in both by the threatening waters. At creation God divided the waters of chaos and created a world. At the exodus God divided the sea and created a people.

■ WILDERNESS JOURNEY (15:22–18:27)

After the escape from Egypt, Moses led the Israelites toward the burning bush locale so that they too could meet Yahweh. Moving on from the shore of the Reed Sea, they traveled toward Mount Sinai where Yahweh would make a covenant with them. Along the way they had numerous difficulties that tried Moses' leadership ability and patience, and tested the faith of the people. These troubles also served to test the resourcefulness of God and to reveal the character of the Israelites.

When they arrived at an oasis the water was undrinkable, so the people complained to Moses, who changed the bitter water to sweet. When they lacked food, God rained down manna and quail.

> **Manna.** Manna is called the "bread of heaven." It is described as thin flakes, white like coriander seed that taste like wafers made of honey. The term *manna* is given a folk etymology in 16:15, 31 based on the people's exclamation when they first saw it: *man hu'*, "what is it?" Some seek a naturalist explanation for manna. Bodenheimer (1947) relates it to the honey-like secretion of a scale insect on tamarisk trees that are common to the Sinai.

When they came to Rephidim expecting to find water, they found none. The people again turned on Moses and blamed him for their predicament. God instructed Moses to strike a rock and water flowed.

Then the Amalekites fought the Israelites. Joshua led the counterattack, and the Israelites prevailed as long as Moses' arms were raised to God. This episode is notable because it introduces the Amalekites, who are a persistent Israelite enemy. The Amalekites receive the honor of being the archetypal Israelite enemy because they were the first to attack this new nation. Always attentive to the worship dimension of Israel's experience, the Elohist notes that Moses built an altar there to commemorate the event and called it "Yahweh is my banner."

Jethro, Moses' father-in-law, met the Israelites in the wilderness. Observing that Moses was exhausting himself by single-handedly administering the entire community, he convinced Moses to delegate all but the most difficult cases to subordinates. Jethro, called the priest of Midian, also made a most remarkable confession. He professed that Yahweh was greater than any other god because he delivered the people from Egyptian oppression. Then Jethro offered sacrifices to God. The Elohist is showing how outsiders, too, can perceive the greatness of Israel's God and worship him.

The wilderness experiences of Israel related in these pre-Sinai stories, getting water from the rock at Meribah, manna and quails, and meeting Moses' father-in-law, are similar to Israel's post-Sinai wilderness experiences. The repetitions form brackets, or what literary analysts call *inclusions,* around Israel's Mount Sinai experiences.

For Israel's wilderness itinerary see Table 3.L. For a comparison of Israel's pre-Sinai and post-Sinai wilderness experiences see Table 3.M on Israel's wilderness experiences.

SINAI: COVENANT TRADITIONS (19–40)

Mount Sinai is the geographical setting of the second half of Exodus, as well as the entire book of Leviticus and a portion of Numbers. At Mount Sinai the Hebrews received the definitive revelation of covenant from Yahweh. The covenant traditions in Exodus lay out crucial dimensions of the relationship between Yahweh and Israel.

All three Pentateuchal sources contribute components of law giving in the book of Exodus. To view the sources separately see:

- *Table 3.N, law giving in the Yahwist narrative*
- *Table 3.O, law giving in the Elohist source*
- *Table 3.P, law giving in the Priestly document*

The sources are combined and distinguished by color in Table 3.Q, law giving in the combined sources.

■ THEOPHANY ON THE MOUNTAIN (19)

Moses brought the Israelites to the mountain in the wilderness where earlier he had met God. This very important chapter marks the moment the Israelites arrived at Mount Sinai. They witnessed God's appearing on the mountain in the typical symbolic forms of the storm, including dark cloud, thunder, and lightning. Through Moses God revealed what Israel would become if only they kept their side of the covenant.

Upon arrival God first met with Moses individually, then he appeared to all the people. In our close reading of chapter 19 we segment the text into paragraphs distinguished by literary source.

Introduction (P)

1 On the third new moon after the people of Israel had gone forth out of the land of Egypt, on that day they came into the wilderness of Sinai. 2 And when they set out from Rephidim and came into the wilderness of Sinai, they encamped in the wilderness . . . (19:1–2a)

Verses 1–2a are attributed to the Priestly source, which typically tracks the itinerary of the Israelites as they travel from Egypt to the Promised Land. This passage builds a bridge between the exodus event and the giving of the covenant at Mount Sinai.

God to Moses (E)

. . . and there Israel encamped before the mountain. 3 And Moses went up to Elohim, and YHWH called to him out of the mountain, saying, "Thus you shall say to the house of Jacob, and tell the people of Israel: 4 'You have seen what I did to the Egyptians, and how I bore you on eagles' wings and brought you to myself. 5 Now then, if you will obey my voice and keep my covenant, you shall be my own possession among all peoples (though all the earth is mine), 6 and you shall be my kingdom of priests and holy nation.' These are the words which you shall speak to the children of Israel." (19:2b–6)

Verses 2b–9 are exclusively the work of the Elohist. The destination of the people was the mountain of God, as the Elohist refers to it; here, mountain for short. God's statement is a well-formed literary unit with an introduction ("Thus you shall say") and a conclusion ("These are the words which you shall speak"). Israel is called the house of Jacob. You may recall that Jacob was most closely associated with the northern territories, especially the city Bethel. You may also recall that the Elohist hails from the north.

The Elohist stresses the conditional character of covenant. The people will remain God's adopted people if they demonstrate obedience as defined in the covenant. They were separated from the rest of the nations to become God's special possession. Yet the Elohist also knows of Israel's broader responsibilities. They will minister to the remainder of humanity as a kingdom of priests.

Moses to the Elders (E)

7 So Moses came and called the elders of the people, and set before them all these words which YHWH had commanded him. 8 And all the people answered together and said, "All that YHWH has spoken we will do." And Moses reported the words of the people to YHWH. 9 And YHWH said to Moses, "Now I am coming to you in a thick cloud, so that the people may hear when I speak with you, and may also believe you for ever." Then Moses told the words of the people to YHWH. (19:7–9)

Moses presented God's program to Israel's leadership and they agreed to covenant in principle. Throughout the process Moses functions as the intermediary between God and the people. The Elohist portrays Moses as the prototypical prophet, standing between God and Israel to mediate the covenant. The people could not view God directly, but when they saw the luminescent cloud they were assured of God's presence, and knew he was conferring with Moses. Here, as throughout Israel's history, a glowing cloud is evidence of God's presence. In the Priestly tradition this visible aura is called the glory of Yahweh.

In the next section, largely attributable to the Yahwist, God tells Moses how to prepare the people for their meeting.

Yahweh to Moses (J)

10 And YHWH said to Moses, "Go to the people and consecrate them today and tomorrow, and let them wash their garments, 11 and be ready by the third day; for on the third day YHWH will come down upon Mount Sinai in the sight of all the people. 12 And you shall set bounds for the people round about, saying, 'Take heed that you do not go up into the mountain or touch the border of it; whoever touches the mountain shall be put to death; 13 no hand shall touch him, but he shall be stoned or shot; whether beast or man, he shall not live.' When the trumpet sounds a long blast, they shall come up to the mountain." 14 So Moses went down from the mountain to the people, and consecrated the people; and they washed their garments. 15 And he said to the people, "Be ready by the third day; do not have intercourse with a woman." (19:10–15)

This version implies that God will appear personally. Consequently, the people had to prepare themselves ritually in order to be qualified to meet Yahweh. Here in the Yahwist version the people meet God directly, contrasting with the Elohist version where Moses is the intermediary between God and the people.

The people made themselves ritually clean through a process called consecration. The instructions in verse 15 were obviously directed at the male population. Note the directive: Do not have intercourse with a woman. Laws of ritual purity demanded refraining from sexual intercourse.

The Theophany (J and E)

16 On the morning of the third day there were thunders and lightnings, and a thick cloud upon the mountain, and a very loud trumpet blast. All the people in the camp trembled. 17 Then Moses brought the people out of the camp to meet Elohim; and they took their stand at the foot of the mountain. 18 Mount Sinai was wrapped in smoke, because YHWH descended upon it in fire; and the smoke of it went up like the smoke of a kiln, and the whole mountain quaked greatly. 19 And as the sound of the trumpet grew louder and louder, Moses spoke, and Elohim answered him in thunder. 20 YHWH came down onto Mount Sinai, on the top of the mountain. YHWH called Moses to the top of the mountain and Moses went up. (19:16–20)

Verses 16a, 18, and 20 belong to the Yahwist source; 16b–17 and 19 belong to the Elohist source (underlined). In the Elohist source God reveals himself in meteorological phenomena: thunder and lightning and a thick cloud. These signs are all associated with the thunderstorm. In such a portrayal Yahweh is manifest as a storm God. Baal of Canaanite religion was also associated with such phenomena. The people were fearful of God and trembled (the "fear of God" is one of the characteristic themes of the Elohist).

In verse 18, which bears the marks of the Yahwist source, the appearance of Yahweh is more like a volcanic eruption than a thunderstorm. Smoke ascended in a column, and there was an earthquake. This is evidence that we might have two different theophany traditions in Exodus 19, an Elohist-Horeb one and a Yahwist-Mount Sinai one.

Verse 20 returns us to the Yahwist version. God came down upon the mountain, and Moses went up—yet another time. Moses is in communication with God but, according to the Yahwist, it must take place on the mountain. The Elohist makes things easier. A meeting tent would be constructed, which would be a place Moses could go to confer with God.

The theophany passages of Exodus 19 establish a model of divine communication. It was on the mountain of God, called Mount Sinai by the Yahwist and Horeb by the Elohist, that direct revelation from God was delivered. This narrative lays down the foundation of all the laws that follow in Exodus, Leviticus, and Numbers. All of the moral and ritual legislation specified in those books is presented as having been delivered to the people by God through Moses.

■ LAW AND COVENANT (20–24)

Although the Elohist source contained some of the ancestral material of the book of Genesis, the heart of the Elohist source is the exodus from Egypt and the law giving on the mountain. The Elohist contains one of the fullest records of the nature of the covenant relationship God established with his people.

Elohist Covenant Tradition. Covenant traditions were stronger in the northern territories of Israel than in Judah to the south. The covenant accounts of the Elohist provide a direct link to these covenant traditions going all the way back to the time before the monarchy. Before becoming a nation, the tribes had formed a federation headquartered at Shechem. There they periodically engaged in covenant renewal ceremonies that affirmed their solidarity and confirmed their faith in Yahweh. The ceremony led by Joshua in chapter 24 is the most elaborately described of these ceremonies. It is probable that the Elohist was associated in some way with prophetic circles in Israel, most likely with an Elijah group. Moses' activities on the mountain of God are very much like those of the northern prophet Elijah who came after him. Points of similarity include the following. Moses, like Elijah, was the champion of God confronting a difficult and contentious Israelite people. Each had a loyal disciple, Joshua and Elisha, respectively. And both Moses and Elijah traveled to Horeb (for an account of Elijah see Chapter 9).

The covenant making that takes place in Exodus was a response to the miraculous escape from Egypt that God had arranged. In this covenant God formalized his relationship with the Hebrews by, in effect, putting it down in a contract, what governments would call a treaty.

Ethical Decalogue (20:1–17)

God devised a set of ten basic moral mandates that defined the relationship of Israel with Yahweh and people with one other. They were delivered to the Israelites through Moses. Commonly referred to as the Ten Commandments ("ten words" in Deuteronomy 4:13), they are the **Ethical Decalogue** of religious and moral commands. The core stipulations appear to come from the Elohist, with elaboration to some of them coming from later Priestly additions. Deuteronomy 5 contains a duplicate of the Ten Commandments of Exodus 20, with some subtle but interesting variations (see Chapter 5).

The commands are framed in the second-person singular form of address, as if to target each individual person in Israel while at the same time addressing Israel as a collective unit. The ambiguity of "you" in English (is it singular or plural?) is not present in the Hebrew text. In the discussion that follows we will not refer to the commandments by number because Judaic and Christian traditions enumerate the commandments differently.

Table 3.R offers a comparison of Exodus 20 and Deuteronomy 5. Table 3.S lists the commandments in different post-biblical traditions.

The commandments begin with God's self-identification and also evoke the exodus.

1 And Elohim spoke all these words, saying, 2 "I am YHWH your Elohim, who brought you out of the land of Egypt, out of the house of enslavement. (20:1–2)

This prologue to the commandments emphasizes the loving character and concern of God in rescuing the Israelites from slavery. First he delivered them from slavery, then he came to them with a covenant. The implication of this prologue is that obedience to these commands would be Israel's expression of appreciation, and not an onerous imposition from a distant and demanding God.

> 3 *"You may not have any other Elohim (translated as either "gods" or "God") except me." (20:3)*

This command prohibits devotion to any deity but Yahweh. Perhaps to your surprise, it does not categorically deny the reality of other gods.

> 4 *"You may not make for yourself a sculpted image, or any representation of anything that is in heaven above, or on the earth below, or in the water under the earth. 5 You may not bow down to them or serve them; for I YHWH your Elohim am a possessive god, visiting the guilt of the fathers upon the children, upon the third and the fourth generation of those who disown me, 6 but showing loyalty to the thousandth generation of those who love me and keep my commandments." (20:4–6)*

This command prohibits using any physical form to represent Yahweh. Nothing that God has created could ever adequately represent him. The only thing that bears a likeness to God is humankind, which was created in his image, "after his likeness," according to Genesis 1. This command to appropriately honor God stresses the seriousness with which God treats loyalty and disloyalty. The reference to heaven above, earth below, and water under the earth in the formulation of this command is evidence that the Israelites had a tri-level concept of the cosmos. This is also evident in the creation narrative of the Priestly source (see Chapter 1).

> 7 *"You may not take the name of YHWH your Elohim in vain; for YHWH will not hold him guiltless who takes his name in vain." (20:7)*

This command originally intended to prohibit taking false oaths. More than that, it also forbade disrespect shown to God by using his name wrongly or frivolously. God's name was special. It was the nearest the Israelites came to possessing any part of God, and had to be treated with the utmost care. Later Jewish practice takes this prohibition so seriously that the name of God, and even the word God, was never spoken, with phrases such as "the Lord" and "the Name" used in its place, and G_d used in print.

> 8 *"Remember to keep the Sabbath day holy. 9 Six days you may work, and do all your jobs; 10 but the seventh day is a Sabbath to YHWH your Elohim; in it you shall not do any work, you, or your son, or your daughter, your male servant, or your female servant, or your cattle, or the resident alien who lives with you; 11 for in six days YHWH made heaven and earth, the sea, and*

everything in them, and ceased from work on the seventh day; by doing this YHWH blessed the Sabbath day and made it a holy day." (20:8–11)

The Sabbath command institutionalizes a periodic cessation of typical daily work. The Hebrew term *shabbat* literally means "cease, stop, rest." The warrant for such a time of inactivity is the pattern of creation in which God completed his efforts in six days and ceased work by the seventh. The explanation from creation was added by the Priestly writer to provide the reason for Sabbath observance. The Deuteronomy 5 restatement of this command warrants Sabbath rest by recalling Israel's period of slavery in Egypt and God's deliverance from it. In this light, Sabbath rest commemorates Israel's freedom rather than God's creation.

12 "Honor your father and your mother, so that your days in the land which YHWH your Elohim gives you may be numerous." (20:12)

Respect must be shown to ancestors and especially parents. A high social value was placed on children's duty to care for parents, and veneration of ancestors, even dead ones, was broadly practiced in the ancient Middle East. Note that this is the only command that is future oriented and holds the promise of blessing attached to its observance. The blessing is evidently one of communal more than individual application, assuring lasting possession of the Promised Land.

13 "You must not murder." (20:13)

This is a prohibition of murder, and not of killing generally. Capital punishment was mandated for a variety of offenses in the Hebrew Bible (for example, see 21:12–17).

14 "You must not commit adultery." (20:14)

In its original setting this command primarily prohibited sexual relations with another man's wife. This prohibition against the sexual promiscuity of married persons is aimed to protect the blood line of offspring. This was a crucial issue in matters of inheritance where a father wants to be sure he and not someone else has sired his heir.

15 "You must not steal." (20:15)

Stealing in the first instance probably applied to persons rather than property in the biblical world. Kidnapping was a common ancient practice (see 21:16 where the same Hebrew verb is used) and this commandment was intended to provide for personal security. Later it was extended to material property.

16 "You must not bear false witness against your neighbor." (20:16)

Here deceitfulness and perjury are in view, perhaps first of all in a judicial setting. However, the commandment extends to a general protection of personal reputation, which is crucial for maintaining social order.

17 "You must not covet your neighbor's estate: that is, you must not covet your neighbor's wife, or his male servant, or his female servant, or his ox, or his ass, or anything that belongs to your neighbor." (20:17)

This is the only command that was intended to regulate attitude rather than behavior. The reason is clear: coveting, or deeply desiring what is not one's own, is a state of mind that often leads to other prohibited behaviors. Contentment with what God has already provided is implicitly enjoined.

The commands naturally divide into two general categories. The first commands define behaviors that apply to the people's relationship with God. This relationship is an exclusive one that demands total loyalty. The latter commands define behaviors which apply to relationships within the community. Both categories of behavior together constitute the essence of covenant. Put positively they command this: Love God and your neighbor as yourself (see Deuteronomy 6:5 and Leviticus 19:18).

Most of the Ten Commandments take the form of **absolute law,** also termed apodictic law. The commands, in other words, are unconditional. They apply with no "ifs, ands, or buts." Even though most of these commands are negative in form ("do not do this"), this does not imply that God's requirements were oppressively restrictive. In fact, they merely placed certain general types of actions and attitudes out of-bounds. Beyond that they leave a rather wide latitude for freedom of action. They were certainly not perceived as oppressive by the Israelites, who found delight in God's law (for example, see Psalms 1 and 119). Although cast in the negative, they can be considered general policy statements which were intended to shape the broader religious and moral character of the nation.

Book of the Covenant (20:18–23:33)

The **Book of the Covenant** (Exodus 20:22–23:19), also called the Covenant Code, is the earliest biblical collection of covenant laws. Probably going back to premonarchic traditions, it seems to have been an independent collection predating the Elohist, but preserved by the Elohist. The observation that the setting of this law code reflects a livestock economy rather than a settled agricultural or urbanized economy supports a premonarchic setting.

The Book of the Covenant is introduced with a narrative describing the theophany and the people's reaction to it.

18 Now when all the people witnessed the thunder and the lightning and the sound of the trumpet and the mountain smoking, the people were afraid and trembled; and they stood far away. 19 They said to Moses, "You speak to us, and we will listen; but do not let Elohim speak to us, otherwise we will die." 20 Moses said to the people, "Do not be afraid. Elohim has come to test you, and so that you may be aware of his fearfulness. Then maybe you will not sin." (20:18–20)

Following the giving of the Ten Commandments God again appeared in a storm theophany heralded by a trumpet. The people were terrified of God's appearing. Fear of Elohim is very important in this narrative, as in the Elohist source as a whole. Out of fear of getting too close to God the people enlisted Moses as their intermediary. Moses assumed the role of the prophet and explained that God was putting them through this experience so that they would be impressed with his power and think twice before sinning.

> *21 The people stood far away, while Moses drew near to the thick cloud where Elohim was. 22 And YHWH said to Moses, "This is what you should tell the people of Israel: 'You have seen for yourselves that I have spoken with all of you from heaven. 23 You must not make me into a god of silver, and you must not make for yourselves gods of gold.'" (20:21–23)*

Moses approached God who was in the form of a thick dark cloud. The cloud was the visible evidence of God's presence. The Book of the Covenant proper begins with verse 22. Note that a change from the preceding verse is evident; the divine name changes from Elohim to Yahweh.

Yahweh impressed upon them that they were encountering the God of heaven. Their prime directive was the absolute prohibition of making statuary representations of God. The Israelites must not represent the God of heaven with metal images, as the Canaanites did of their gods.

This general prohibition of idols and the prescription concerning the type of altar they could use (20:23–26) precedes the main body of laws which is introduced with the preface: "These are the ordinances which you must place in front of them" (21:1). The typical form of these ordinances in the Book of the Covenant differs from the form of the Ethical Decalogue. The Book of the Covenant contains case law, also called casuistic law. This type of law takes the form "If . . . then." An example of case law is the law of the goring ox.

> *28 "If an ox gores a man or a woman to death, the ox must be stoned, and its flesh may not be eaten; but the owner of the ox will not be liable. 29 But if the ox has had the habit of goring in the past, and its owner had been warned but had not kept it restricted, and it kills a man or a woman, then the ox must be stoned, and its owner also must be put to death." (21:28–29)*

Typical of case law, first a condition is specified, in this case an ox which gores a person. The consequence is then specified: the ox must be killed, but the owner may not benefit from it by eating the meat. In this instance the owner is not held responsible. This particular statute specifies a subcategory that results in a much harsher punishment. If the ox had been in the habit of terrorizing the community and the owner had done nothing to prevent it, and then it kills someone, the owner will be held directly responsible and must be put to death along with the animal. Biblical law obviously distinguished degrees of responsibility.

In addition to injury laws, the Book of the Covenant also contains laws regarding slaves, death sentences, bodily injuries, a calendar of feasts, and other religious duties.

For a summary of the contents of the Book of the Covenant see Table 3.T.

FIGURE 3.5 HAMMURABI MONUMENT   The Code of Hammurabi contains 282 laws chiseled onto a pillar of basalt rock. The upper register is a picture of Hammurabi standing before the sun god Shamash, the patron god of justice. The bottom register contains the Code of Hammurabi in cuneiform. This standing stone was a monument to justice and did not first of all function as a reference manual for the use of judges at court, but gave public testimony to the character of Hammurabi as a promoter of righteousness.

Law Collections from Mesopotamia

Many ancient Middle Eastern cities have yielded documents through the work of archaeologists. At least seven law codes have been found. The earliest one is the Sumerian Code of Ur–Nammu, dating to the twenty-second century B.C.E. Others include the Code of Lipit-Ishtar, the Code of Eshnunna, Middle Assyrian laws,

Hittite laws, and Neo-Babylonian laws (see Pritchard 1969: 159–98). Thus, the legal traditions of Israel stand within a well-developed context of legally ordered societies in the ancient Middle East. Israel's law codes have many points of contact with ancient extra-biblical law codes.

The most famous collection is the **Code of Hammurabi** (see Figure 3.5). Hammurabi was a Babylonian ruler from the eighteenth century B.C.E. The code begins with Hammurabi's call

> "…to promote the welfare of the people . . . to cause justice to prevail in the land, to destroy the wicked and the evil that the strong might not oppress the weak." (Pritchard 1969: 164)

There are notable similarities between the Code of Hammurabi and certain Israelite legal materials, especially the Book of the Covenant. For instance, as in Israelite law, the Code of Hammurabi contains the law of retribution in kind (*lex talionis*), which prescribes proportional punishment: an eye for an eye, a tooth for a tooth.

Code of Hammurabi

> If a man has destroyed the eye of another man, they shall destroy his eye. If he has broken another man's bone, they shall break his bone. (§§196–97)

Book of the Covenant

> If any injury occurs, you shall take life for life, eye for eye, tooth for tooth, hand for hand, foot for foot, burn for burn, wound for wound, beating for beating. (21:23–25)

While such physical retaliation may seem brutal, in fact, it was humane in its day. Specifying restitution in kind prevented resort to harsher punishments for such offenses, typically the death penalty. The existence of this code and others like it demonstrate that Israel shared with her neighbors an ideal of justice that would be administered by a righteous king. In Israel, David and Solomon were thought to epitomize this ideal.

■ COVENANT CONFIRMATION (24:1–15)

After the content of the covenant had been revealed, the covenant relationship was ceremonially initiated. Chapter 24 contains two different traditions relating to the covenant ratification ceremony. In the first tradition, only representatives of the people approach God.

> 1 And he said to Moses, "Come up to YHWH, you and Aaron, Nadab and Abihu, and the seventy elders of Israel, and worship at a distance. 2 Moses alone shall come near to YHWH; but the others shall not come near, and the people shall not come up with him." (24:1–2)

This tradition is continued in verses 9–11, which describe a meal Moses, Aaron, Nadab, Abihu, and the elders ate with God in a covenant confirmation (or ratification) ceremony. In this version the Israelites as a whole take part in the covenant ceremony only indirectly through their leaders.

> **God's Appearing.** The traditions of Yahweh's appearing are complex. In 24:9–11 Moses, Aaron, Nadab, Abihu, and the seventy elders all saw God. In the tent of meeting Yahweh appeared to Moses "face to face, as one speaks to a friend" (33:11). In 33:18–23, an Elohist text, Moses would see only the divine backside. In 34:5–8, a Yahwist text, Yahweh descends in a cloud and stands with Moses. On the one hand, no one can see God and live (33:20), but on the other hand, many do see God.

9 Then Moses and Aaron, Nadab and Abihu, and the seventy elders of Israel went up, 10 and they saw the Elohim of Israel; and there was under his feet what looked like a sapphire stone street, like the heavens itself for clarity. 11 And he did not lay his hand on the leaders of the people of Israel; they saw Elohim, and ate and drank. (24:9–11)

All in all this is a remarkable story and quite uncharacteristic of Elohist theology, which guards people from seeing God. Perhaps this is a story from a different source. Here Israel's leaders actually saw God and ate with him, but even though they gazed on him, they did not die.

> **Covenant Banquet.** Eating a meal at the conclusion of covenant making also is found in Genesis 26:30 and 31:46, 54. Eating a ceremonial meal in the presence of God is an important component in later sacramental meals such as the Eucharist.

In the second version the people gathered together for sacrifices and directly took part in the covenant ceremony.

3 Moses came and told the people all the words of YHWH and all the ordinances; and all the people answered with one voice, and said, "All the words which YHWH has spoken we will do." 4 And Moses wrote down all the words of YHWH. And he got up early in the morning, and built an altar at the foot of the mountain, along with twelve pillars, matching the twelve tribes of Israel. 5 And he sent young men of the people of Israel, who offered burnt offerings and sacrificed peace offerings of oxen to YHWH. 6 And Moses took half of the blood and put it in basins, and half of the blood he threw against the altar. 7 Then he took the book of the covenant, and read it in the hearing of the people; and they said, "All that YHWH has spoken we will do, and we will be obedient." 8 And Moses took the blood and threw it upon the people, and said, "Here is the blood of the covenant which YHWH has made with you, in agreement with all these words." (24:3–8)

In this ceremony the altar represents God. When Moses took blood from the sacrifices and sprinkled it on the altar and on the people, the two parties were bound together in the covenant. Blood represents life in the Hebrew Bible. This ceremony symbolically states that both parties were pledging their lives to the endurance of the covenant relationship.

Note how the people agreed to the covenant with full knowledge of its requirements. The Book of the Covenant was read directly to them and the people knowingly accepted the covenant requirements. The covenant would remain in effect as long as they were obedient. As with Exodus 19:3b–6, here too the Elohist covenant has the condition of the people's obedience attached to it.

After the covenant ratification ceremonies, God called Moses up to the mountain to receive copies of the law.

> 12 YHWH said to Moses, "Come up to me on the mountain, and wait there. I will give you the stone tablets containing the law and the commandment, which I have written for their instruction." 13 So Moses got up with his servant Joshua, and Moses went up into the mountain of Elohim. 14 And he said to the leaders, "Wait here for us, until we return. For now, Aaron and Hur are with you; whoever has a problem, let him go to them." 15 Then Moses went up onto the mountain, and the cloud covered the mountain. (24:12–15)

These verses record yet another trip up the mountain, and seem to contain yet another tradition of meeting God. Joshua and Hur are introduced in this account, while Nadab and Abihu are absent.

Moses received the stone tablets containing "the law and the commandments." This seems to be a reference to the Ethical Decalogue, but one cannot be sure. Moses presumably already had something written down according to 24:7, which refers to the Book of the Covenant. In any case, these two stone tablets are the ones Moses smashes in Exodus 32.

> **Two Tablets.** Exodus 31:18; 32:15; and 34:1, 4, 29 specify two tablets (or tables) of stone. Traditionally it has been imagined that five commandments were written on each tablet. Studies of ancient Middle Eastern covenant conventions clarify that the two tablets represent two complete copies of the covenant document, one for each party to the covenant.

Reading through these chapters we might get exhausted for Moses—he has been going up and down, up and down. It is really difficult to sort out how many trips he actually takes. Apparently, these chapters have a very complicated editorial history. Each tradition has Moses going up the mountain, and they were all retained in the final version.

For the traditions concerning the written form of the covenant see Table 3.U, scribing the covenant. For the collection of texts that tracks Moses' trips up Mount Sinai to meet God see Table 3.V, Moses up and down the mountain.

■ COVENANT BREAKING AND REMAKING (32–34)

The section between chapter 24 (covenant confirmation) and chapter 32 (covenant breaking) is a collection of Priestly documentation on the tabernacle, the ark, and the priesthood (see below). When the narration of events resumes following this interlude we come to the dramatic and sad affair of Israel's worshipping an idol. This episode demonstrates that almost immediately after the covenant was ratified the Israelites were willing, even eager, to break it.

Golden Calf (32–33)

Moses spent a longer time on the mountain receiving the covenant from God than the people had expected. Thinking that they had lost Moses and thus their contact with the deity, they demanded that Aaron the high priest provide a substitute. Responding to their urging, Aaron solicited gifts from the people and proceeded to make a **golden calf.**

> 4 He took the gold from them, cast it in a mold, and made a calf image. They said, "These are your gods, Israel, who brought you up out of the land of Egypt." 5 When Aaron saw it, he built an altar before it and made a proclamation, "Tomorrow there will be a feast to YHWH." (32:4–5)

Thus the Israelites committed idolatry. This idol is reminiscent of the bull of Canaanite religion that was associated with the high god Baal. This episode stands as a warning against worshiping the gods of the Canaanites who inhabit the Promised Land.

Jeroboam's Golden Calves. Also, the golden calf unmistakably echoes the golden calves that Jeroboam, the first king of Israel after the civil dispute, erected in Dan and Bethel when he established religious centers in the Northern Kingdom of Israel in the tenth century B.C.E. (see Chapter 9). The negative way in which the golden calf is viewed in Exodus is a veiled prophetic condemnation of Jeroboam's golden calf worship centers. The statement, "These are your gods," in the plural, when only one calf was molded, evokes the multiple calves of Jeroboam. In fact, these words are the same as the words of Jeroboam in 1 Kings 12:28.

In response God became extremely angry and resolved to destroy the people and begin building a nation from Moses. Moses argued with God, suggesting that if all the Israelites died, the Egyptians will have triumphed. He urged God saying, "Turn from your fierce anger, change your mind, and do not bring catastrophe on your people." Remarkably, God responded to Moses' plea and voided his threatened punishment.

God instructed Moses to return. Going down the mountain he saw the pagan revelry of the people. Partly out of anger he smashed the two tablets containing the record and testimony of the covenant. It also effectively signaled that the covenant had been broken because the people had compromised their loyalty by worshiping another god.

The people had gone wild in celebration, and Aaron was held to blame.

25 When Moses saw that the people were out of control (for Aaron had let them get out of control, to the point that they were a menace to anyone opposed to them), 26 Moses stood at the entrance to the camp and said, "Who is on YHWH's side? Come over to me!" 27 He said to them, "This is what YHWH, the Elohim of Israel, says, 'Each of you, strap your sword to your side. Go back and forth through the camp, from gate to gate. Each of you kill your brother, your friend, and your neighbor.'" 28 The Levites did what Moses commanded, and about three thousand people fell on that day. 29 Moses said, "Today you have dedicated yourselves to YHWH, each at the cost of a son or a brother. You have earned a blessing today." (32:25–29)

This incident demonstrated the loyalty of the Levites to the cause of Yahweh. They were the only ones who had not succumbed to the lawlessness of golden calf worship. The story, again, pictures the Levites in a very favorable light; not surprisingly, for the Elohist was a Levite.

> **Aaron and the Elohist.** Though he was an advocate for the Levites generally, the Elohist did not admire Aaron. He directly implicates Aaron in the golden calf incident. Why would he want to put Aaron in such a bad light? Perhaps because the Elohist and his group had migrated to Jerusalem after the fall of Israel in 721 B.C.E. They were unable to practice their livelihood in Jerusalem even though they were Levites, because the family of Aaron, also of the tribe of Levi, had locked the priestly craft up tight. The privilege of serving as a priest was inherited, and one had to be from the family of Aaron of the tribe of Levi to qualify. Aaron, understandably, came under their severest criticism.

Yahweh then told Moses to take the people and head on to the Promised Land without him. Distressed at this change of plan Moses met with Yahweh in the tent of meeting and urged him to reconsider. Again Yahweh changed his mind and decided to continue on with the Israelites. As proof of his commitment, the glory of Yahweh passed by Moses, and Moses caught a glimpse of the backside of Yahweh.

> **Tent of Meeting.** The tent of meeting is the symbol of Yahweh's dwelling among the Israelites in the Elohist tradition. It never mentions the ark of the covenant, only the tent of meeting. Perhaps this is because the Elohist was from the north, where Shiloh was situated. Shiloh was the home of the tent shrine during the days of the tribal federation (see Chapter 8). The Yahwist never mentions the tent of meeting. The ark ended up in Jerusalem, and that was the focus of worship there. That was of interest to the Yahwist, who was from Judah, but the Elohist ignored it, because northern priests were not allowed to minister in the temple.

Covenant Remaking (34)

Having destroyed the first copy of the covenant tablets Moses was instructed to ascend Mount Sinai and receive another copy. However, the conditions of this version of the covenant differ from the more famous ones of Exodus 20. While

still containing ten commandments, Exodus 34 consis~
worship practices and is called the **Ritual Decalogue.** V~
devised to come up with the exact ten suggested bv
enumeration.

1. You may not worship another other god, beca~
   is Jealous One, is a jealous God. (14a)
2. You may not make molten gods for yourselves. (1~,
3. Every firstborn human or animal belongs to God. (1~.
4. No one may appear before God without an offering. (2~
5. You can work six days, but on the seventh day you may no~
6. You must observe the feast of weeks, the first fruits of the whe~
   and the feast of ingathering. (23)
7. You may not offer the blood of my sacrifice with anything leavened. ~
8. The Passover sacrifice must not remain until the morning. (25b)
9. You must bring the best of the first fruits of the soil to the house of Yahweh your God. (26a)
10. You may not boil a kid in its mother's milk. (26b; also 23:19 and
    Deuteronomy 14:21)

> **Kashrut.** The practice of boiling a kid in its mother's milk may derive from
> Canaanite fertility rituals. The prohibition of eating milk and meat together is
> part of the elaborate Kashrut system of Jewish laws that regulates food and
> cleanliness.

Moses descended Mount Sinai with the two tablets of the covenant. Because
he had been talking directly with God his face was aglow with the glory of
Yahweh.

> *The people of Israel saw the face of Moses, that the skin of Moses' face shone;
> and Moses would put the veil upon his face again, until he went in to speak
> with him (34:35).*

■ TABERNACLE (25–31, 35–40)

The covenant established with Israel from Mount Sinai was foundational. And for
the Priestly writer, the most important aspect of the Mount Sinai experience was
receiving the gift of the **tabernacle,** a portable tent shrine that served as God's
place of residence among his people throughout their wilderness travels and on
into the Promised Land. The Priestly source in Exodus devotes two extended passages to the tabernacle because the main duty of the priesthood was to facilitate
the fellowship of Yahweh and his people. The tabernacle assured the Israelites that
God would be present to them throughout their history.

The first tabernacle passage details the design of the worship center (Exodus 25–
31) and the second narrates its construction (Exodus 35–40). The narrative itself
is ordered as seven divine speeches each introduced with the formula "YHWH said
to Moses." The seventh features the Sabbath, suggesting a parallel with the Priestly

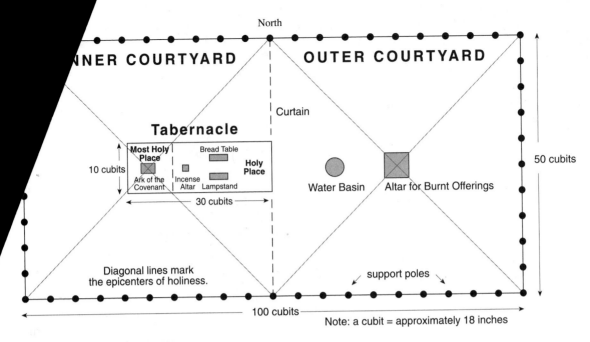

North

INNER COURTYARD | OUTER COURTYARD

Curtain

Tabernacle

Most Holy Place | Bread Table

10 cubits | Holy Place

Ark of the Covenant | Incense Altar | Lampstand

Water Basin | Altar for Burnt Offerings

30 cubits

50 cubits

Diagonal lines mark the epicenters of holiness.

support poles

100 cubits

Note: a cubit = approximately 18 inches

FIGURE 3.6 THE TABERNACLE COMPLEX

creation narrative of Genesis 1 (see Kearney 1977). The design is presented as a divine blueprint, a notion attested as early as 2200 B.C.E. when Gudea of Lagash was given divine instructions to build a sanctuary (see Hurowitz 1985).

Creation and Tabernacle. Parallels between the creation and the priesthood-sanctuary complex of the Priestly source suggest that worship derives from the order of creation and is designed to bring humanity into conformity with it. The construction of the tabernacle sanctuary and its management by the priesthood is the completion of the work of God in creation. See CD Table 3.W for parallels between the Priestly creation story and the construction of the tabernacle.

The tabernacle complex (Figure 3.6) was divided into three distinct zones of increasing holiness: the outer courtyard, the holy place of the tabernacle, and the most holy place. Note the symmetry of the overall layout and the placement of the ark of the covenant within the most holy place at the precise point of intersection. The most holy place is itself perfectly symmetrical, a cube of 10 cubits by 10 by 10. For a complete description of the tabernacle and its symbolism, including the way the temple of Solomon mirrors the tabernacle, see Haran (1978).

In addition to the portable tent shrine, the Israelites constructed the many implements, utensils, and articles of ceremonial clothing they would need to perform their ritual service. Included in the list are the ark of the covenant to store the covenant documents, the table for the bread of the presence, the lampstand (*menorah* in Hebrew), and the altars of incense and burnt offering.

Tabernacle Symbolism. Specifically Yahweh sat enthroned between the cherubim (Psalm 80:1; Isaiah 37:16), who represent the Divine Council (see Chapter 1). The symmetry and symbolism of the tabernacle reflect the perfection of God and his relationship to creation. The most holy place represents heaven, and the holy place represents the earth. The outer courtyard with its massive water basin may symbolize the waters of chaos, where one is most distant from God.

The climax of the Priestly tabernacle narrative comes in 40:34–38 when the cloud of God's presence descends on the tabernacle and the glory of Yahweh fills it. The reality of God which once resided on Mount Sinai now enters the sanctuary. God's presence would accompany the Israelites throughout their travels, and would eventually take up residence in the temple built in Jerusalem during the time of Solomon.

EXODUS AS A WHOLE

The deliverance and covenant traditions have been combined in the book of Exodus to tell a profound story. The final form of Exodus, in particular the way the story of the exodus was placed before the Sinai traditions, conveys a deep truth about the relationship between God's care and Israel's life. The flow of the story communicates that God gave special treatment to the Israelites because of his love for them and out of his faithfulness to the ancestral promises. Only after delivering them from slavery did God formalize their relationship with a national covenant. In other words, obedience to Torah, as defined by the Sinai covenant, was expected, but only as a response to the deliverance of the exodus. It was not a precondition of experiencing God's care and salvation. In fact, going all the way back to the ancestral story, God had made the first move by choosing them as his special people through Abraham.

Exodus Traditions. As with Genesis, the book of Exodus contains material from the Yahwist, Elohist, and Priestly sources. However, in contrast to Genesis where the Elohist had a small role, in Exodus the Elohist makes a substantial contribution. In addition, the final form of Exodus included independent traditions such as the Song of the Sea in Exodus 15 and the Book of the Covenant.

For a content outline of the book of Exodus see Table 3.X. For a complete source analysis of the book of Exodus see Table 3.Y, the literary sources of the book of Exodus.

Furthermore, the book of Exodus places the phenomenon of biblical law in perspective. When we examine Exodus, Leviticus, Numbers, and Deuteronomy we see that these books contain many collections of legislation, including

- the Ethical Decalogue (in two versions, Exodus 20 and Deuteronomy 5)
- the Book of the Covenant (Exodus 20:22–23:33)
- the Ritual Decalogue (Exodus 34)

- Ritual Laws (Leviticus 1–16 and Numbers 1–10)
- the Holiness Code (Leviticus 17–26)
- and the Deuteronomic Code (Deuteronomy 12–26).

Viewed with an eye to each collection's source and historical context, we see that they come from different settings, many of them no doubt later than the lifetime of Moses. Yet all of them are attached to Israel's historical experience at Mount Sinai and are associated in the present books with the figure of Moses. This association was deliberate, as Moses was regarded as the prime lawgiver of Israel; for any legal tradition to have full legitimacy it would have to be associated with him.

Rather than being presented in catalog fashion (such as the Code of Hammurabi), all this technical legal and ritual material is embedded within historical narrative. Biblical law does not stand in isolation but is associated with the life story of Israel. This provides law and covenant with a grounding in Israel's experience with Yahweh, especially his acts of deliverance. Torah comes with divine authority; though Moses transmitted the laws, they originated with Yahweh.

This helps us understand the overall purpose of Torah in its setting within the Hebrew Bible. Law was not given as a set of conditions to be met in order to establish a relationship with God; the narrative demonstrates that the relationship, by the time of the exodus, was already a long-standing one. The purpose of covenant law was to preserve and perpetuate an already functioning bond between God and his people. In this perspective, law defined the shape that Israel's obedience would need to take in order to sustain that already initiated relationship.

FOR FURTHER STUDY

Sarna (1986) is a readable interpretation of the book of Exodus that relates it to historical and cultural factors, Hillers (1969) is a comprehensive treatment of covenant, Harrelson (1980) relates the Ethical Decalogue to human moral universals, and Redford (1992) is a detailed study of the historical relationships between Egypt and Israel.

 Chapter 3 Bibliography

QUESTIONS FOR REVIEW

1. Summarize the Egyptian historical context for the exodus.
2. Where and when did God reveal his name to Moses and how was this related to the exodus?
3. What is the Passover and how is it related to the exodus from Egypt?

4. What different collections of biblical law are found in the book of Exodus and how do they differ?
5. What was the Tabernacle and what was its function?

QUESTIONS FOR REFLECTION AND DISCUSSION

1. The book of Exodus brings together two great human themes, namely, freedom from oppression and rule by law. What is the relationship between these two themes? Why was it important and what effect did it have that both were associated with Israel's supreme deity, and, in fact, came about through his initiative?

2. Why was it important for Israel to associate its primary legal and covenantal tradition with Moses and with God's appearing on Mount Sinai? What effect did this have on the authority of law and the nature of the covenant in Israel? How does this compare with the foundation of law and the grounding of authority in modern nation-states?

3. Describe the various ways God revealed his presence and made himself known in Exodus. In what ways was God visible and in what ways invisible? What does this imply about Israel's understanding of the nature of its God and life in his presence?

4. Exodus addresses the identity of God in major ways. What moments in the story bear on God's identity? How is God's identity revealed progressively? Is it also in some ways intentionally concealed? In what way is the identity of Israel dependent on the identity of God?

Chapter 3 Study Guide

- *Chapter summary*
- *Key terms linked to the glossary*
- *Concept questions with answer links*
- *Progress tests: true/false, multiple choice, matching, and identification*

LEVITICUS AND NUMBERS: IN THE WILDERNESS

4

FIGURE 4.1 MOUNT SINAI RANGE The traditional identification of Mount Sinai is Jebel Musa in the south of the Sinai peninsula. The Israelites spent a year at Mount Sinai receiving laws and ritual legislation. This picture, taken from the summit of Mount Sinai, displays the rugged nature of the terrain.

We are all creatures of habit, and we all observe rituals; daily rituals of meeting and greeting, and special public rituals for occasions such as graduations, weddings, and funerals.

Ritual and convention provide standard formatting for human interaction. As accepted scripts for social intercourse they spare us from having to decide each time what we are going to say and do. Ritual greases the gears of social life.

Israel had rituals and procedures, as Leviticus and Numbers explain. They defined the steps Israelites were to follow when they met Yahweh. It all came down to how Israel was to maintain a sound and respectful relationship with their God.

This chapter combines the books of Leviticus and Numbers because they are similar in several ways. Both contain a good deal of religious legislation, which God revealed to Moses at Mount Sinai. Both are predominantly concerned with matters of ritual, sacrifice, and priesthood. Both also are set in the Sinai wilderness between Egypt and the Promised Land. The complete Mount Sinai revelation actually begins at Exodus 19:1, runs through the entire book of Leviticus, and continues until Numbers 10:10. This collection of moral and ritual laws can be referred to as the **Priestly Code.** It constitutes the bulk of the Priestly source of the Pentateuch.

The style of these books differs from that of Genesis and Exodus. There is no drama to relate because nothing really "happens" to the Hebrews in Leviticus and the first part of Numbers. For the most part, the material is a record of religious laws. The story about their journey to the Promised Land resumes only in the latter half of Numbers. We turn first to the book of Leviticus.

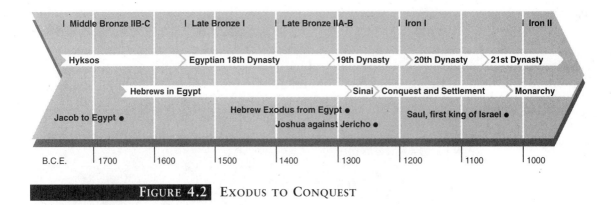

Middle Bronze IIB-C		Late Bronze I		Late Bronze IIA-B		Iron I		Iron II

Hyksos — Egyptian 18th Dynasty — 19th Dynasty — 20th Dynasty — 21st Dynasty

Hebrews in Egypt — Sinai — Conquest and Settlement — Monarchy

Hebrew Exodus from Egypt ●
Joshua against Jericho ●

Jacob to Egypt ●

Saul, first king of Israel ●

B.C.E. 1700 1600 1500 1400 1300 1200 1100 1000

FIGURE 4.2 EXODUS TO CONQUEST

LEVITICUS

Leviticus immediately follows Exodus in the Hebrew Bible and continues the account of the Israelites in the Sinai wilderness. Most of Leviticus is devoted to ritual legislation and cultic rules. Its rabbinic name is *torat kohanim,* which means "instruction of priests." Since priests came from the tribe of Levi, the **Levites,** the book came to be called Leviticus.

Story Line

Leviticus is presented almost entirely as the speeches of Yahweh to Moses at the tent of meeting, a shrine used solely as the meeting place of Moses and God. There are a few chapters of narration but no continuous story line. After divine descriptions of the types of sacrifices (Leviticus 1–7) Moses ordained and consecrated **Aaron** and his sons to serve as priests (8). At the conclusion of the eight-day ceremony Aaron blessed the people and the fire of Yahweh consumed their offerings (9). When Aaron's sons Nadab and Abihu burned incense with illicit fire (it is not clear what that was) they were destroyed by the fire of Yahweh (10). Then follows the laws concerning what is clean and unclean (11–15), the Day of Atonement (16), and the Holiness Code (17–26). Within the latter is found the only remaining narrative, a description of a situation when someone blasphemed the name of Yahweh. At Yahweh's instructions he was taken outside the camp and stoned (24). The book concludes with a discourse on religious vows (27).

■ PRIESTLY WORLDVIEW

At this point the author of a Hebrew Bible textbook typically apologizes for having to deal with the book of Leviticus. Most readers think it is boring; after all, it deals with rules for sacrifices, worship, priests, and purity. Since most of these rules are not followed today by any religious community, Jewish or Christian, what could be less interesting or relevant?

Well, maybe the text and its subject matter are not all that gripping at first, but they do convey the vision of Israel's ideal relationship with God. Leviticus deals with a fundamental human question: How can rebellious people meet God and exist in his presence?

Given the highly detailed and monotonous nature of the priestly legislation, it is easy to get lost in minutiae. An overall framework is needed to understand the meaning of the purity and holiness laws. There are three general approaches to the biblical system of clean and unclean things.

The hygiene theory claims that the laws were intended to keep Israelites from things that had a high likelihood of doing bodily harm, such as pork and contagious skin diseases. The cultic theory argues that objects and actions that were associated with forbidden pagan cults were forbidden to Israelites, and so were declared unclean. Anthropologists Douglas (1966) and Turner (1969) pioneered the structuralist perspective which analyzes ritual as components of worldview, and argue that Israel's ritual system discerns an ordered world in which everything exists either as normal or abnormal (see Wenham 1979, Gorman 1990, Jenson 1992). Deviations from normalcy were classified as unclean. Rituals provided the means to move from abnormality to normality.

Leviticus, along with the rest of the Priestly Code, employs a distinctive way of looking at the world in relation to God. Everything in the world is graded in holiness, to use Jenson's terminology, in relation to Yahweh. The result is that everything has a set place in the divine order, and everything derives its meaning from its relationship to God.

The major religious dilemma facing the Israelites was how a perfectly holy and righteous God could be in direct contact with sinful people? The rituals and regulations of Leviticus explain how. In essence it means the Israelites must become a holy people, sometimes also called a holy nation. "You must be holy, for I am holy" is a constant refrain throughout Leviticus.

The terms that are critical to this worldview and that need explanation are *holy* and *clean,* and their opposites, *profane* and *unclean.* According to Leviticus 10:10, the Aaronic priesthood was "to distinguish between the holy and the profane, and between the unclean and the clean."

Holiness is a difficult notion to grasp. It has to do with the infinite and qualitative difference between humanity and God, in other words the total otherness of God. God is of a fundamentally different category than human beings. Because he is totally different from humanity, especially in regard to his absolute power and perfection, humans need to respect his total otherness and live in awe of him. Though the analogy is woefully inadequate, the awesomeness of God is like the awe ordinary citizens might feel when they are in the presence of a president or prime minister, or better yet, a sports superstar, renowned actor, or famous rock musician.

The **Holiness Code,** found in chapters 17–26, is the most distinctive subcollection of the Priestly Code. While the issue of dating for the Priestly writings as a whole is debated, it is quite likely that the Holiness Code comes from the period of the late Israelite monarchy. It appears to have been composed in Jerusalem not long before the Babylonian exile. As its name suggests, it is preoccupied with matters of holiness.

The priestly rituals of Leviticus were intended to distance humans from their imperfect world so they could assume a measure of God's holiness. In order for the Israelites to become holy they must refrain from sin and stay away from uncleanness. In the priestly worldview, sin was closely associated with uncleanness. Leviticus categorizes the world into clean and unclean things, and describes procedures that can move one from the state of uncleanness to cleanness. Some of the most important rituals involve animal sacrifices to reconcile penitent Israelites to God if sin and uncleanness have separated them. In short, Leviticus defines the procedural means by which God and humanity can dwell together harmoniously.

The normal or natural state of objects and persons is to be clean, and a clean thing could be elevated to the status of holiness through the process of sanctification (literally, making holy). Clean things could become unclean through contact with other unclean things, such as dead bodies. In order for an unclean person or thing to get back to the state of cleanness, it had to be purified. Once clean, it could then be sanctified through an additional procedure. Once made holy, it was devoted exclusively to divine service.

Holy persons and things could be rendered profane, or unholy, through ritual procedures of decommissioning or by contact with something unclean. A profane thing could be clean or unclean, but in either case, it could not be in direct contact with Yahweh.

The notions of clean and unclean are related to the way the priestly group understood the created world and expressed a comprehensive worldview in which everything had its proper place. The process of putting things in their place began with creation, as told in the Priestly version (Genesis 1). On the second and third days of creation the three elements of sky, earth, and sea were delimited through a process of separation. Then, God fashioned living creatures for each environment, and each environment's creatures received standard habits and means of locomotion which defined them. In particular, the sky was populated by noncarnivorous winged creatures. The earth was inhabited by four-legged creatures that chewed the cud and had cloven hooves. The sea was inhabited by creatures with scales and fins.

Creatures that did not fit the standard profile were considered unclean, for example, crabs and lobsters. Although they live in the sea, they have legs rather than fins. Thus, cleanness was related to a notion of "normalness," and cleanness was protected by keeping things separate and in their proper environment. Food sources that did not meet the priestly definitions of normalcy were unclean and therefore not fit for human consumption. The definitions of what was clean and unclean are also called **kashrut,** the rules of **kosher.**

Definitions of normalcy and laws for maintaining separations applied to many things besides food. For example, they dictated which kinds of thread could be woven together to make fabric, and which kinds of people could marry. Priestly legislation defined a total lifestyle that regulated diet, hygiene, social activity, and the calendar.

Table 4.1 is a synthesis of the priestly worldview. It relates the basic areas of life to the notions of holiness and cleanness. The following discussion is a survey of the particular areas of existence and reality (derived from the left vertical column of Table 4.1) as they are defined by the range of holiness (the top horizontal row).

Table 4.A presents the evidence and diagrams the process for moving among the states of uncleanness, cleanness, and holiness.

TABLE 4.1 **HOLINESS CONTINUUM** Jenson (1992) develops the notion of "a holiness spectrum" upon which this table is based. He devotes a separate chapter to each dimension: spatial, personal, ritual, and temporal.

	Very Holy	*Holy*	*Clean*	*Unclean*	*Very Unclean*
Place	holy of holies	holy place	court	camp	outside the camp
People	high priest	priest	Levites, clean Israelites	minor impurities	major impurities, the dead
Rituals	sacrifice (not eaten)	sacrifice (priests eat)	sacrifice (non-priests eat)	purification (1 day)	purification (7 days)
Times	Day of Atonement	festivals, Sabbath	common days		

Holy Places

A fundamental concern of the Priestly Code was the creation of a place where Israel could dwell in the presence of God. Throughout the Hebrew Bible a key to Israel's welfare is living in proximity to the presence of God.

The place where Yahweh lived was the holiest place imaginable. The tabernacle complex, whose structure, service, and construction is described in Exodus 25–31 and 35–40, was the portable temple of the Israelites (see Chapter 3). Leviticus and Numbers contain many references to the structure and implements of the tabernacle.

Haran (1978) and Jenson (1992) explain the significance of the structural details. The tabernacle complex, as with the other symbols of Israel's ritual system, had zones of holiness. The direction of holiness moved from outside the camp to the holy of holies. For each zone the Priestly Code defined who is allowed to be there, ending up with only the high priest in the holy of holies, and that on only one day each year. Gradations of holiness are evident also in the construction materials of the tabernacle complex, with fabrics and metals increasing in value moving up each level of holiness.

The symbolism of the tabernacle expresses two important themes of priestly theology: continuity of life and the presence of God. The floral designs on the walls of the tabernacle and implements suggest the "tree of life" artistic motif. The untarnishable gold of the implements and holiest room suggest the unchangeableness of God. The daily lamp-lighting ceremony symbolizes the light of God that never ceases. Regarding the presence of God, the tabernacle was considered God's dwelling place, so the structure and all the rituals allow for God to be present among his people.

The portability of the tent of dwelling indicates that God was not sedentary but was with his people wherever they went. This notion may have been especially important to the priests of the exilic period who shaped these texts, giving expression to their conviction, similar to Ezekiel's, that God was present with them even outside the Promised Land.

Holy People

The Priestly Code defined the social and ritual roles of all people within Israel, and an examination of these roles reveals a hierarchy of holiness. Membership in social groups was based on family lineage, and roles were assigned accordingly. The tribe of Levi provided the officials who were authorized to perform religious functions. Both Moses and his brother Aaron were from this tribe.

Only direct descendants of Aaron could function as priests or become the high priest. Priests were the only ones allowed to offer sacrifices and enter the sanctuary. The high priest could consult with God directly in the cloud and by means of divination dice called the Urim and Thummim. Other members of the tribe of Levi, those not of the family of Aaron, had duties outside the sanctuary itself, and in general assisted the Aaronic priests. This included guarding the sanctuary and dismantling and erecting in when it was moved. Israelites belonging to the other eleven tribes could not perform religious rituals but had them done by priests.

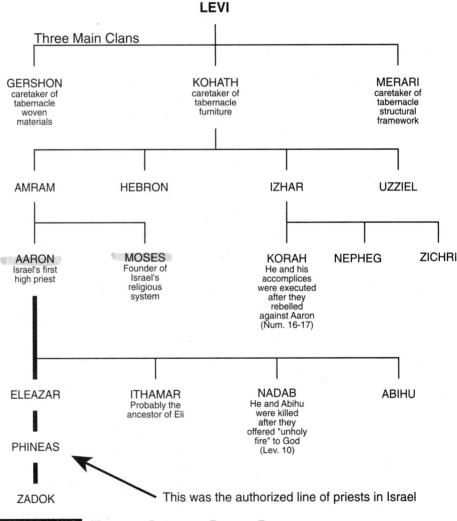

FIGURE 4.3 **TRIBE OF LEVI AND RITUAL ROLES**

Figure 4.B The tribe of Levi and ritual roles illustrates the structure of the tribe of Levi in relation to the roles assigned to particular members and families.

A number of ritual descriptions and camp narratives define the status and role of the tribe of Levi and of groups within it. Leviticus 8–9 describes the process of the ordination of Aaron and his sons. The fact that the ordination rituals lasted seven days aligns the priesthood with the created order of seven days (Genesis 1:1– 2:3). Leviticus 10 recounts the deaths of Nadab and Abihu, two sons of Aaron, who illegally performed certain rituals and died for it. Numbers 8 describes the process of the ordination of the Levites. Numbers 16–17 narrates the rebellion of Korah and his followers, Levites but not from the family of Aaron, who presumed to perform priestly rituals and were executed by God for it. This narrative also contains the story of the blossoming of Aaron's rod, which demonstrated the God-given authority of the tribe of Levi over the other eleven tribes. Numbers 18 defines the responsibilities of Aaronic priests and other Levites.

Sacrifices

The primary religious rituals of Israelite religion involved sacrifices and offerings. The priestly ritual system was complex, and the meaning of procedures was rarely explained. In most respects it is quite foreign to our way of thinking. Consequently, the precise theological significance of sacrifice is still open to debate.

The rules of the priestly sacrificial system are laid out in Leviticus 1–7. There are five main types of **sacrifice**: whole burnt offering, grain offering, peace offering, purification offering, and reparation offering. Any given priestly ritual usually incorporated several different types of sacrifice (see Table 4.2).

The whole burnt offering may be considered the preeminent sacrifice. Its name refers to the fact that the entire animal was consumed by the fire on the altar. Such a sacrifice was made daily to Yahweh. The purpose of the sacrifice was to give something pleasing to God, not to atone for sin. Levine (1989: 6–7) argues it offered protection from God's wrath rather than expiation from sin.

Not all sacrifices were bloody sacrifices of animals. Offerings of grain and other agricultural produce were given as gifts to God, and a portion of such sacrifices was used to support the priests.

With the peace offering, a portion of the meat of the sacrificed animal was retained and eaten by the person making the offering. This offering, sometimes also called the fellowship sacrifice, drew the parties together, including God, in a festive meal. Meat was not often eaten in biblical times, so when it was, it was a time of celebration and was done in the presence of God.

The purification offering, sometimes called the sin offering, was to purify a person after he or she had incurred an impurity of some kind, such as through childbirth, a skin disease, or contact with something dead. This offering was also used to secure forgiveness after a deliberate sin.

The reparation offering involved an offering of restitution; that is, if an action involved economic loss to someone else, reparation must be made to cover the loss, with an additional portion as punitive damages.

TABLE 4.2 **SACRIFICES** The first three types of sacrifice are optional, the last two are mandatory after applicable types of disruption.

Offering	Hebrew	Item	Purpose	Leviticus
whole burnt	'olah	whole animal	gift to God	1:3-17
grain	minchah	flour and oil	gift to God	2:1-16
peace	shelamim	unblemished animal	fellowship	3:1-17
purification	chatta't	bull, goat, lamb, doves, pigeons	purification after involuntary impurity	4:1-5:13
reparation	'asham	ram	restitution for deliberate acts	5:14-26

The overall significance of sacrificial rituals may have been this. Various types of impurities and deliberate sins disturbed God's ordered universe. Sacrificial rituals were the mechanism by which disruptions within God's world were acknowledged and made right. The various rituals of purification brought one closer to the state of holiness so that one could live in proximity to God. This is the purification model of sacrifice that is argued by Milgrom (1983) and Jenson (1992).

Within this system sacrifice seems to play a significant role in the process of **atonement**. Atonement, reconciliation or "making at one," brings a person back into fellowship with God after a disruption in the relationship. In the priestly system, this could only be achieved through a blood sacrifice. Leviticus 17:11 is often taken as a key to priestly atonement theology.

11 For the life of the flesh is in the blood; and I have given it to you for making atonement for your lives on the altar; for, as life, it is the blood that makes atonement. (17:11 NRSV)

Blood was held in particular reverence because it was considered the substance of life. The blood of the sacrificed animal substituted for the life of the offending person, and functioned to return that person to fellowship with God.

Holy Times

Just as space was sacred or profane, so was time. The year defined the basic cycle of larger events and organized the cultic calendar. The year was defined by the solar calendar, but because months were defined by the cycle of the moon, there was a need to adjust the shorter twelve-month lunar year (354 days) to the solar year (365 days) by occasionally adding a thirteenth month.

There were longer periods of time, including the sabbatical year cycle (every seventh year was sacred), and the year of Jubilee (the year after seven sabbatical year cycles; that is, the fiftieth year). But the most important units of repeated time were the day, the week, and the month (which was defined by the moon). Months were labeled by number, with the year beginning in the spring.

The Sabbath, the seventh day of the week, was a day set apart from the others. Special rules governed activity on that day, mainly restricting what could be done. Hallo (1977) shows the extent to which the Sabbath and the sabbatical idea shaped the worship calendar of Israel, and distinguished it from the worship patterns of Egypt and Mesopotamia.

Special yearly sacred days were also defined. There were five primary sacred times, all of which are still observed within Jewish communities (see Table 4.3), and some of these correspond to calendaric moments in the Western world. For example, the Spring equinox, Passover, and Easter all converge, and not by accident.

Israelites were required to observe these festivals in Jerusalem. They were worship occasions, and in the rabbinic period were marked by the reading of books from the Five Scrolls of the Hebrew Bible. For example, the Song of Songs was read on Passover and the book of Ruth during the Feast of Weeks.

In addition to these festivals, other feasts and fasts were instituted later during the postexilic periods. Purim celebrates the deliverance of the Jews during the Persian period, as told in the book of Esther (see Chapter 16). The story of the rededication of the temple during the Greek period is told in the book of 1 Maccabees, and is celebrated as Hanukkah, the Festival of Lights, which comes at the Winter solstice. Fasts were instituted to memorialize tragic historical events. The fall of Jerusalem and the destruction of the temple in 587 B.C.E. is marked as Tisha b'Av and the book of Lamentations is read (see Chapter 16).

Features of holy place, holy people, holy time, and sacred ritual all come together in Leviticus 16, where the **Day of Atonement** ritual is described, in Hebrew called *yom kippur*. Of all the sacred times, the Day of Atonement was considered the holiest. It was only on this day that anyone entered the Holy of Holies of the tabernacle, and later, the temple.

> *6 Aaron will offer the bull as a sin offering for himself and make atonement for himself and his household. 7 Then he will take the two goats, and stand them before YHWH at the door of the tent of meeting. 8 Aaron will cast lots for the two goats, marking one for YHWH and marking the other for Azazel. 9 Aaron will present the goat on which the lot fell for YHWH and offer it as a sin offering. 10 The goat on which the lot fell for Azazel will be presented alive before YHWH to make atonement with it. It will be sent away into the wilderness to Azazel. (16:6–10)*

On the Day of Atonement the High Priest, here Aaron, offers a bull as a purification offering. Then he takes two goats. He slaughters one of them, collects its blood, and sprinkles it on the mercy seat, a term designating the lid of the ark of the covenant. After exiting the tabernacle, he places his hands on the head of the other goat, thereby transferring the sins of the people to this animal. Called the goat for Azazel in Hebrew (where Azazel may designate the underworld), this goat has come to be called the scapegoat. It was sent away into the wilderness to disappear, symbolically taking with it the sins of the people.

TABLE 4.3   FEASTS AND HOLY TIMES

Sacred Time	Hebrew Name	Agricultural Occasion	Historical Association	Biblical References	Festival Scroll
Feast of Passover (Feast of Unleavened Bread)	*pesach*	Spring barley harvest	The Exodus: deliverance from bondage and freedom	Exod. 12:8; Lev. 12:1-28, 13:1-16, 23:5–8; Num. 28:16–25; Deut. 16:1–8	Song of Songs
Feast of Weeks (first fruits, Pentecost)	*shavuot*	Summer wheat harvest		Exod. 34:26; Lev. 23:9–21; Num. 28:26–31; Deut. 26:1-11	Ruth
Trumpets	*teruah*		God's revelation at Sinai (?)	Lev. 23:23–25; Num. 29:1–6	
Day of Atonement	*yom kippur*			Lev. 16; 23:26–32; Num.29:7–11	
Feast of Booths (Feast of Ingathering)	*sukkot*	Autumn harvest	Wilderness wandering	Exod. 23:16; Lev. 23:33–36; Deut. 16:13–15	Ecclesiastes

LEVITICUS AS A WHOLE

Leviticus in its entirety belongs to the Priestly tradition of the Pentateuch. In practice the book functioned as a manual of priestly practice. The last verse of the book (27:34) gives Leviticus a historical and geographical setting at Sinai during Israel's sojourn in the wilderness. Thus as it stands the book is a continuation of the story of God's revelation to Moses. Even though Leviticus is a virtual catalog of rules and regulations it is framed as part of a Sinai narrative. The phrase "YHWH said to Moses" (34 times) contextualizes the laws as narrative events rather than list items.

The book of Leviticus consists of various collections of religious laws, all of them *torat kohanim*, "instruction of priests"—the *of* can be understood in two ways (linguistically the objective and the subjective genitive). Levine (1989) observes that chapters 1–16 are instructions *for* the priests in the performance of their duties, and chapters 17–26 are instructions *by* the priests addressed to the people to remain holy. This effectively creates two main units in Leviticus. The main sections of Leviticus are displayed in Table 4.4.

> **Structural Clues.** Internal clues signal that these sections were identifiable units before they came together in Leviticus. The Laws of Sacrifices has a clear introduction (1:1) and formulaic conclusion ("this is the teaching (*torah*) on . . . "; 7:37–38), which is also used in the Laws of Purity (11:46–47, 12:7b, 13:59, 14:32, 14:54–57, 15:32–33). This suggests that the ordination materi-

TABLE 4.4   STRUCTURE OF LEVITICUS

Text	Content
1–7	Laws of Sacrifices
8–10	Ordination Rites of the Priests
11–15	Laws of Purity
16	Day of Atonement
17–26	Holiness Code
27	Appendix on Religious Vows

als of 8–10 are an insertion. The Day of Atonement is the positional and theological center piece of Leviticus. It describes the premiere procedure for removing sin and impurity. The Holiness Code is marked by the use of summary formulas that conclude each subsection (18:24–30, 20:22–26, 22:31–33, 25:18–24, 26:3–45).

A close examination of the language, style, and presumed sociological setting of the laws suggests that in their present form they have come from the exilic period or later. Other books of the Hebrew Bible—Ezekiel, Ezra, and Chronicles—have a close affinity with the Priestly Code, and they are all postexilic, but the traditions behind many of the Levitical laws go back as early as the premonarchic period. Some of the laws even have analogies to early Mesopotamian legal material (see Pritchard 1969: 325–26, 331–53). Though some of the individual laws and collections were preexilic, they were given their final shape by a priestly group in the exilic period.

Table 4.C is a detailed content outline of the book of Leviticus.

NUMBERS

The book of Numbers, which follows Leviticus, also contains some ritual law, but overall it is more diverse in style and content than Leviticus.

Story Line
The early chapters detail the organization of the Israelite encampment. A census of the tribes was taken (Numbers 1), the tribes were arrayed around the tent of meeting (2), then the Levites were counted (3–4). A test for female marital faithfulness was established (5) and regulations for Nazirite vows given (6). The tabernacle was dedicated (7), the Levites were purified for tabernacle duty (8), and the Passover was celebrated (9).

The Israelites packed up and left Mount Sinai and resumed their travels (10). When they complained about their diet, God sent quail (11). When Miriam complained about Moses, she was infected with leprosy (12). Twelve spies investigated the fortifications of Canaan, but the Israelites refused to attack (13–14). After more laws of sacrifice (15) Korah, Dathan, and Abiram rebelled and were destroyed (16). Aaron's budding staff proved to the people that he was God's choice (17). More technical instructions were given (18–19), and then Moses got water from a rock by striking it, thereby incurring God's wrath (20).

Israel resumed its journey by avoiding Edom but destroyed many other opponents (21). Moab feared Israel and tried to curse them using Balaam, but this failed (22–24). Then some Israelites slept with cult prostitutes (25), and this was not a good thing. More technicalities, lists, and laws (26–36).

■ FROM MOUNT SINAI TO MOAB

The book of Numbers contains another block of the Priestly Code. The book begins with Israel still situated near Mount Sinai. Later the Israelites' journey continues through a variety of perilous encounters until they reach Transjordan and the border of the Promised Land.

Priestly Code Continued (1:1–10:10)

Numbers 1:1–10:10 is the final section of the Sinai legal tradition complex. which extends all the way back to Exodus 19. Chapters 1–4 describe the organization of the Levites and the arrangement of the camp. At the center stood the tabernacle. Closest to it were the Levites, and then came the other tribes. This layout is a component of the holiness continuum, where priests and Levites were the holiest class of people.

Figure 4.D Layout of the Israelite camp. The configuration of the Israelite camp shows how the clans and tribes were arrayed around the tabernacle in concentric regions of holiness.

The Priestly Code defined a social hierarchy within Israel, not surprisingly putting the priests of Aaron's family at the top of the scale. Next came the other families of the tribe of Levi. Of the remaining tribes, Judah was placed in a position of preeminence directly to the east, right near the entrance of the tabernacle compound. Lowest on the scale were resident aliens; that is, people not belonging to any tribe but living among the Hebrews. Farthest out were the foreign nations, by implication also furthest from God.

Additional laws of cleanness are given in subsequent chapters, as well as regulations concerning the firstborn and the Nazirite vow. The common thread uniting all this material is a concern with the holiness of the people. They must be holy for Yahweh to remain in their midst.

The Journey Continues (10:11–22:1)

With Numbers 10:11–22:1 we are back to material deriving from all three Pentateuchal sources, the Yahwist, Elohist, and Priestly. This block of material is mostly historical narrative and describes the journey from Sinai to Kadesh, the long stay at Kadesh, and the journey to Moab.

About a year after they had arrived in the Sinai wilderness, the cloud of God's presence lifted and signaled that Israel must move on to the Promised Land. The Israelites had a number of experiences in the wilderness, many at Kadesh, before they reached the edge of Canaan.

The people complained about the monotony of daily manna meals. **Manna** was the substance the people had been gathering as food, perhaps the sweet secretion of certain insects that feed on the sap of tamarisk bushes in the Sinai region (Bodenheimer 1947). The people demanded meat, and the strain of handling the complaints and demands of the people wearied Moses. In response, Yahweh instructed Moses to appoint seventy elders to assist him. Similar to Exodus 18, Moses commissioned officers of tens, fifties, hundreds, and thousands at Jethro's advice. He arranged the seventy men around the tent of meeting to receive their commission (11:25). Then YHWH came down in the cloud and spoke to him, and took some of the spirit that was on him and placed it on the seventy elders. When the spirit took possession of them they prophesied, but did not keep doing it.

Two men who had been designated for leadership, Eldad and Medad, were not present at the tent. Nonetheless, they too received the spirit and prophesied in the middle of the camp. Joshua was upset over this, but Moses said, "Why are you upset? It would be good if all Yahweh's people prophesied." Yahweh had put his spirit on all of them. Here the Elohist expresses his ideal of prophecy, that all the people would be inspired by God as were Moses and the other leaders. Moses is portrayed as the good and enlightened leader who is not trying to exalt himself. Rather, he wishes all the people would be close to God.

The special position of Moses is nonetheless reinforced in Numbers 12. Aaron and Miriam (Moses' brother and sister) challenged Moses after he married a foreigner. They claimed that Yahweh could also speak through them. The three of them went to the tent of meeting, where Yahweh appeared in the pillar of cloud and spoke to Aaron and Miriam.

> 6 Hear my words: If you have a prophet among you, I, YHWH, reveal myself to him in a vision, I speak with him in a dream. 7 With my servant Moses it is different. He is entrusted with my entire estate. 8 I talk with him mouth to mouth, plainly and not in riddles. He beholds the shape of YHWH. 9 Why are you not afraid to challenge my servant Moses?" (12:6-9)

Miriam was afflicted with a skin disease for seven days and remained outside of camp. Aaron was spared, but probably only because he was the high priest. This story tells us many things. It reflects once again the disdain the Elohist had for Aaron because he had the audacity to challenge Moses. The Elohist had a special contempt for the Aaronid priesthood in Jerusalem. The story also demonstrates the high regard the Elohist had for Moses. Throughout the Elohist source, Moses is pictured as central to the purposes of God. Here we learn why. Moses was closest to God. He was not an ordinary leader but a prophet, and even more than just a prophet, God had put him in charge of the entire project.

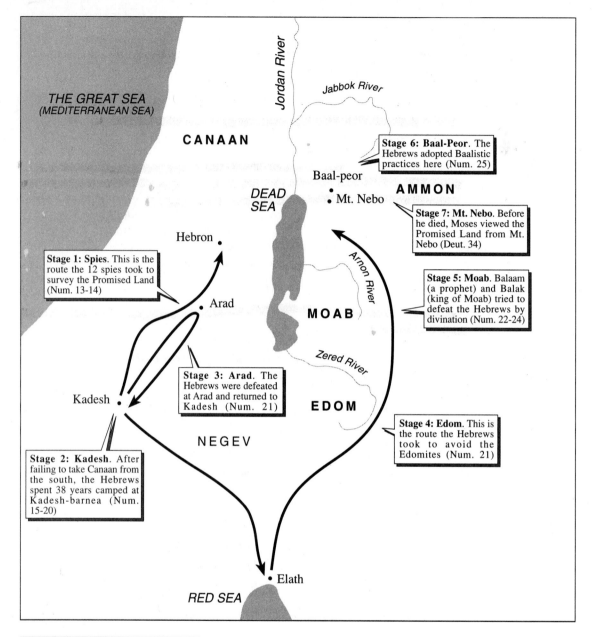

THE GREAT SEA
(MEDITERRANEAN SEA)

Jordan River

Jabbok River

CANAAN

Stage 6: Baal-Peor. The Hebrews adopted Baalistic practices here (Num. 25)

Baal-peor

DEAD SEA

• Mt. Nebo

AMMON

Stage 7: Mt. Nebo. Before he died, Moses viewed the Promised Land from Mt. Nebo (Deut. 34)

Hebron •

Arnon River

Stage 1: Spies. This is the route the 12 spies took to survey the Promised Land (Num. 13-14)

Arad •

MOAB

Stage 5: Moab. Balaam (a prophet) and Balak (king of Moab) tried to defeat the Hebrews by divination (Num. 22-24)

Stage 3: Arad. The Hebrews were defeated at Arad and returned to Kadesh (Num. 21)

Zered River

Kadesh •

EDOM

Stage 4: Edom. This is the route the Hebrews took to avoid the Edomites (Num. 21)

NEGEV

Stage 2: Kadesh. After failing to take Canaan from the south, the Hebrews spent 38 years camped at Kadesh-barnea (Num. 15-20)

• Elath

RED SEA

FIGURE 4.4 THE JOURNEY FROM KADESH TO TRANSJORDAN

Duplications. A curious feature of the story told in Numbers is that many of these episodes, all of which take place after the covenant at Sinai was given, are duplicates of experiences the Israelites had on the first leg of the wilderness journey from Egypt to Sinai. Presumably, the duplicates were retained because the independent sources each had the stories. Perhaps their retention by the editor signals that the character of the people had not changed from before Sinai to after.

Table 4.E, stages of the wilderness journey, indicates the parallels between the pre-Mount Sinai and post-Mount Sinai stages of Israel's wilderness travels.

The Numbers account of those wilderness experiences highlights the dissatisfaction of the people. They complained about the food, so God at the same time fed them and punished them (11). Aaron and Miriam complained about Moses' leadership and God vindicated him (12).

Moses sent twelve spies into Canaan from Kadesh in order to survey its fortifications. Ten spies counseled the people not to invade Canaan; only Joshua and Caleb supported the attack which Yahweh commanded. Because the people refused to follow God's leading, he punished them by decreeing that they would die in the wilderness, and only their offspring, the second generation, would gain possession of Canaan (13–14).

Following this reversal, Korah, Dathan, and Abiram complained about the leadership of Moses and Aaron, and God destroyed them; then all the tribes took exception to the special privileges of the Levites and God vindicated the Levites (16–17). When Moses reacted arrogantly to the murmuring of the people, God punished him (20). When finally the people left Kadesh to go to their invasion staging area, the entire first generation had passed away. There was certainly a lesson here for that exilic generation looking to return home after Babylonian captivity.

> **Bronze Serpent.** As the Israelites traveled toward Transjordan they were attacked by poisonous snakes. Moses made a bronze snake replica and put it on a pole. Anyone who looked at it recovered (21:4–9). A bronze serpent, called Nehushtan, was later installed in the temple and removed by Hezekiah (2 Kings 18:4). The serpent may have been adopted from the Midianites who worked the copper mines north of the Gulf of Aqabah. They are known to have used a gilded copper snake image within their cult (see Rothenberg 1972).

Chapters containing priestly regulations are interspersed among these narrative accounts of Israel's wilderness experiences. Chapter 15 prescribes offerings that atone for inadvertent sins. Chapter 18 prescribes the portions of the offerings that can rightfully be claimed by priests. The red heifer ceremony of chapter 19 provides for cleansing and the restoration of holiness.

The logic of intertwining this cultic material with the narrative is understandable. The narratives all have to do with complaints and privileges: various groups complained that other groups or individuals received preferential treatment. The priestly cultic legislation settles matters of priestly privilege, and provides the means to restore holiness after the kinds of sins that got the Israelites in trouble in the wilderness.

These same sins would plague the Israelites throughout their history. Thus, the historical material also illustrates the characteristic attitude of the Israelites, one of alternating complaint and faithfulness. It also provides the means to overcome alienation from God and restore holiness.

Events in Transjordan (22:2–36:13)

The third section contains a variety of materials all set in Transjordan. Arriving in Transjordan, the Israelites faced two significant threats. First, a Mesopotamian prophet named **Balaam** was hired by Balak, the king of the Moabites, to curse the Hebrews and thereby achieve victory for the Moabites (22–24). This is one of the most remarkable stories in the Hebrew Bible. In it, Balaam's donkey talked to him and warned him about an angry angel that was ready to stop him from completing his mission.

When Balaam finally arrived in Moab to curse the Hebrews, he ended up blessing them each time he opened his mouth. Consequently, the Hebrews prevailed. The story reinforces the destiny of these people. Nothing could stop them, neither the mighty warriors of the Transjordan, nor supernatural divination. Directed and defended by Yahweh, they would surely enter the Promised Land.

> **Deir 'Alla Balaam Texts.** A collection of text fragments mentioning Balaam son of Beor were discovered in 1967 at Tell Deir 'Alla in Jordan. They were written on plaster in Aramaic and date to the 8th century B.C.E. Balaam is called "a seer of the gods." Some of the lines of these texts are similar to the wording of Numbers 22–24. See Hackett (1984).

The second threat in Transjordan was local religion (25). A local Baal shrine located at Peor near the Hebrew camp attracted a number of Israelite worshipers. Hebrew males were found engaging in ritualized prostitution in this Baal temple. But Aaron's grandson **Phineas** stood up for Yahweh and put an end to this particularly heinous form of false worship.

Following upon these narratives the last chapters of Numbers deal with inheritance laws, practices concerning the spoils of conquest, land boundaries, and tribal allotments. Clearly attention turned to those issues the Israelites would soon face as they entered the Promised Land west of the Jordan River. This third section of Numbers thus prepares Israel to take possession of the land.

> **Zelophehad's Daughters.** Zelophehad of Manasseh died without a son. His daughters demanded they be given tribal property so their father's name would not die out. Previously, property had only been granted to males, but Yahweh declared through Moses that they should be granted property as their inheritance (27:1–11), provided they married within their own tribe so that the property would not go to another tribe (36).

NUMBERS AS A WHOLE

The book of Numbers divides into three sections on the basis of content and geographical setting (see Table 4.4). The first section is a continuation from the book of Leviticus of the Priestly Code. The second and third sections resume the narrative of Israel's experience in the wilderness of Sinai begun in the book of Exodus.

Deuteronomy follows Numbers and is both geographically and temporally continuous with it. While Deuteronomy is a completely different kind of material

TABLE 4.5 STRUCTURE OF NUMBERS

Text	Content	Location
1:1-10:10	Priestly Code Continued	Mount Sinai
10:11-22:1	The Journey Continues	Sinai to Moab
22:2-36:13	Events in Transjordan	Transjordan

from Genesis through Numbers, it smoothly picks up the story line. Numbers ends with Israel in Moab, poised to enter Palestine. In Deuteronomy Moses will exhort the Israelites (now the second generation) to remain faithful to Yahweh so that they can continue the work of conquest, enter the Promised Land, and maintain possession of it.

Table 4.E is a detailed content outline of the book of Numbers.

[handwritten annotation: 2. Everything has a set place in the divine order, & everything derives its meaning from its relationship to God. "You must be holy, for I am holy." The priestly worldview categorizes the world into clean & unclean things, & describes procedures that can move one from the state of uncleanness to cleanness.]

FOR FURTHER STUDY

Anderson (1987) is a detailed study of sacrifices and offerings, and Jenson (1992) is a structuralist interpretation of the priestly worldview.

Chapter 4 Bibliography. Also see Part 1 Torah Bibliography.

QUESTIONS FOR REVIEW

1. Who were Israel's leaders during the wilderness period? What stories deal with issues of religious leadership? *[handwritten: Moses, Aaron, Nadab, Abihu 179]*
2. Summarize the basic worldview of the Priestly Code. *[handwritten: 167, 168]*
3. What were the functions of sacrifice? *[handwritten: 171, 172]*

4. How did the organization of Israel's camp reflect the priestly worldview? *[handwritten: 176]*
5. The Israelites often complained to Moses and God about conditions in the wilderness. What stories deal with the people's murmuring and God's miraculous care for them? *[handwritten: 179]*

QUESTIONS FOR REFLECTION AND DISCUSSION

1. Reflect on offices of leadership in Israel as defined in the laws and reinforced in various stories. How did one qualify to be a religious leader in those days? How does that compare to the ways leaders are chosen today?

2. Israel's laws and rituals prescribed and prohibited behaviors in all areas of life. What does this imply about their view of religion? How do you think they would have responded to the distinction we make today between the sacred and the secular?

3. Ponder the stories which reflect negatively on the Israelites. Why were these stories told? What do they imply about the character and faith of the first generation of Israelites that left Egypt? How might these stories about the faithless first generation relate to the apparent preference (remember the first-born son stories in Genesis) for the younger son over the older?

Chapter 4 Study Guide

- *Chapter summary*
- *Key terms linked to the glossary*
- *Concept questions with answer links*
- *Progress tests: true/false, multiple choice, matching, and identification*

DEUTERONOMY: THE TORAH OF MOSES

5

Key Terms

Centralization
Covenant
Deuteronomist
Deuteronomistic History
Josiah
Shema
Suzerainty Treaty
Syncretism

FIGURE 5.1 **MOSES BY MICHELANGELO** Moses is the great lawgiver of Israel, and nothing has reinforced this perception more than the book of Deuteronomy, which is a collection of his best applications of Torah to the life of Israel.

Deuteronomy is the key that unlocks the Torah and the Prophets. So modern students of the Hebrew Bible claim. Close study of Deuteronomy inspired a revolution within biblical studies which opened new ways of understanding the theology of the Pentateuch and the narrative historical books.

Deuteronomy is unique in the Pentateuch in its consistent and uniform style. It consists almost entirely of Moses' sermons to the Israelites before they entered the Promised Land. Characterized by a certain preachiness (but do not let this put you off), it contains spiritually challenging material.

Deuteronomy gets its name from Deuteronomy 17:18, which states that the king was to receive a "copy of the Torah" to guide him. This was mistakenly translated "a second law" in the Septuagint (*deuteronomion* in Greek). Deuteronomy is not a "second law" but a retelling and reapplication of the law given at Mount Sinai. The Hebrew name for the book is *devarim*, or "words," taken from the first phrase of the book, "These are the words that Moses spoke to all Israel beyond the Jordan."

Story Line

Moses addressed the Israelites near the eastern shore of the Jordan River, recounting their experiences together during the forty years in the wilderness (Deuteronomy 1–4). He restated the Ten Commandments and urged the Israelites to both love and fear God (5–11). In a major address he laid down guidelines for Israel's worship that specified the place to worship, whom to worship, and when to worship. He gave rules for family and community life, and also defined the public offices of king, prophet, and priest (12–26). Moses solemnized the occasion with covenant renewal using curses and blessings (27–30). After authorizing Joshua as his successor (31) he recounted God's experience with Israel in song (32) and blessed the tribes (33). Then he ascended Mount Nebo and died after seeing but not entering the Promised Land (34).

WORDS OF MOSES

Deuteronomy is different from the preceding four books of the Torah in these ways. Instead of being narrative enveloping law, it consists of speeches Moses delivered to the Israelites in Transjordan as they prepared themselves to enter the Promised Land. Instead of being formed from a variety of sources, it is essentially from one source. And instead of being framed as God's words to Moses, it is Moses' words to Israel.

Deuteronomy is a series of addresses Moses gave to the Israelites in the border region just east of the Jordan River. He knew his death was imminent, so this was his last opportunity to reinforce the values of covenant existence; God denied him entry into the Promised Land because of his actions at Meribah (Numbers 20). The following texts sample the flavor of the book and introduce us to some of its main ideas.

■ THE GREAT COMMANDMENT (6:4–9)

The core of Deuteronomy is a law code contained in chapters 12–26. This law code is introduced by two speeches of Moses. The first introductory speech (1:1–4:40) reviews Israel's history from the time God spoke to them at Mount Sinai (called Horeb in Deuteronomy) to the present. Moses highlighted two features of their history. First, the wilderness generation had been unfaithful time and again. They had constantly complained, mumbled, and grumbled. Second, the Lord had demonstrated his faithfulness by giving them all they had needed, including victory over their enemies. Moses was warning the Israelites, "Do not be unfaithful, as was that first generation, or you will not reach your goal."

The second introductory speech (4:44–11:32) is a rehearsal and elaboration of the decalogue from Exodus 20, with a few changes. This generation needed to hear the commandments afresh. If they did not hear and obey them, they would be as doomed as the generation before them.

Immediately preceding the decalogue in its Deuteronomic version Moses delivers the following charge.

> *1 Moses called all Israel and said to them, "Hear, Israel, the laws and rules I speak in your hearing today! Learn them and make sure you do them. 2 YHWH our Elohim made a covenant with us on Horeb. 3 It was not with our fathers that YHWH made this covenant but with us, those of us living here today." (5:1–3)*

Notice the sense of earnestness in Moses' preaching style. This is characteristic of his addresses in Deuteronomy. There is no mistaking that he wants to impress upon the people the crucial importance of the covenant. It is not ancient history, nor did it apply just to their forbears. The covenant applies directly to them. Moses speaks in such a way that the covenant obligations fall on each generation, not just on the generation that heard the original words at Horeb.

After stating the Ten Commandments, Moses goes on to encapsulate the essence of this Torah in one of the most notable passages in the Hebrew Bible, Deuteronomy 6:4–5. The Jewish community calls it the **shema**, from this passage's first word. Along with Deuteronomy 11:13–21 and Numbers 15:37–41 it is Judaism's prime prayer, recited daily by observant Jews. Jesus identifies it as the Great Commandment (Mark 12:29–30).

> *4 "Hear, Israel: YHWH is our Elohim, only YHWH. 5 You shall love YHWH your Elohim with all your heart, and with all your soul, and with all your strength. 6 These words which I command you today—take them to heart. 7 Repeat them to your children. Say them when you are sitting in your house, when you are walking on the road, when you lie down and when you get up. 8 Tie them as a sign on your hand. Let them be headbands above your eyes. 9 Write them on the door frames of your houses." (6:4–9)*

The first few words of our text offer several possible translations, all equally allowable given the rules of the Hebrew language, yet each having a different twist.

- YHWH is our God, YHWH alone
- YHWH our God—YHWH—is one
- YHWH is our God; YHWH is one

Is the Hebrew statement affirming the oneness of God—a profession of monotheism in the face of the pantheon of gods from Canaan, Egypt, and Mesopotamia? Or is it primarily affirming that Israel's God is YHWH and that they may have no other?

It is difficult to be sure what those first words really mean. An affirmation of monotheism seems too abstractly philosophical for those times, although it is conceivable that the statement was intended to deny the many Baal and Asherah gods that the Canaanites recognized.

Yet Moses and the Deuteronomist were probably not interested in affirming the unitary nature of God so much as impressing upon Israel that there is only one God for them. His name is Yahweh. He had been faithful to them in the past, and they must be loyal to him now. There may be other so-called gods among the other nations; Yahweh is the only God that deserves and demands Israel's love. The command to love Yahweh is central to the book of Deuteronomy.

The injunction to tie these words on forehead and forearm would keep the covenant always in front of each Israelite as a guide for everyday living. This was put into practice early in the history of Judaism by binding small cases containing Torah texts (called *tefillin* or phylacteries) onto the forehead and left arm. Torah was also placed into another other holder, called a *mezuzah,* and attached to the door frames of homes and public buildings.

■ THE PLACE YHWH CHOOSES (12:2-7)

Moses promoted loyalty to Yahweh by advocating the **centralization** of worship, the policy that Yahweh could only be worshiped in one place. This would have had two purposes. One would have been to eliminate the myriad local shrines dedicated to the ancestors and to traditional Canaanite deities. The other would have been to supervise all legitimate worship practices, and not coincidentally reap the material benefits for the support of the priesthood that accrued when Israelites came to perform their duties.

> 2 *"You must completely eradicate all the places where the nations you are dispossessing used to worship their gods, places on the high mountains, on the hills, and those under lush trees. 3 Break down their altars, smash their pillars, burn their sacred poles with fire, and cut down the idols of their gods. Eradicate their name from that place. 4 Do not worship YHWH your Elohim in the same way as they did theirs. 5 Rather, you shall seek out the place that YHWH your Elohim will choose out of all your tribes to put his name, where he will dwell. You should go there. 6 Bring your burnt offerings and your sacrifices, your tithes and donations, your pledges and contributions, and the firstborn of your herds and flocks. 7 There you shall eat in the presence of YHWH your Elohim, you and your household, rejoicing in everything you undertake, in whatever YHWH your Elohim has blessed you."* (12:2–7)

The phrase "the place YHWH your God will choose" is an indefinite way of referring to Jerusalem. The exact place could not be named because the surface setting of Deuteronomy puts it at a time before Jerusalem had been founded as Israel's capital. The various types of sacrifices and offerings in this passage indicate that all forms of worship and the payment of all dues were to be made at this central sanctuary. The phrase "to put his name, where he will dwell" has been taken as an indicator of the attempt of Deuteronomy to change the common Israelite belief that God really lived in an earthly sanctuary (see von Rad 1966; challenged by Wilson 1995). By referring instead to the name of God rather than God himself as what dwells in the sanctuary, Israel was to acquire a less physical and a more transcendent understanding of the nature of God's presence.

Worship centers traditionally were located on hills or other high places, frequently in forests and groves. That goes for the Canaanites and other inhabitants of Palestine ("the nations you are dispossessing") as well as for the Israelites. Both of the places on which Israel's God revealed himself were mountains. The covenant was given on Mount Sinai, and Israel's chief sanctuary was located on Mount Zion in Jerusalem.

The Israelites were warned against using traditional Canaanite high places because of the danger of **syncretism,** blending Yahwism with Baalism, or some other foreign religious element, even in unintentional ways. The experience of the Northern Kingdom suggested that a variety of worship centers could be dangerous to the faith of the people. In the north, before its destruction, many cities contained shrines. Usually they were located in places where Baal and Asherah used to be worshiped, and aspects of Baal worship were frequently assimilated to Yahwistic worship at those places. Sometimes it was difficult to tell the difference between the two. Prophets frequently condemned such worship places (Hosea 8:11; Jeremiah 11:13). According to the prophets the attraction of such shrines was one of the major reasons why the Northern Kingdom fell.

The writer of Deuteronomy, called the **Deuteronomist,** knew all too well the price of such disloyalty. He was probably a Levite from the north, and after its destruction in 721 B.C.E. he fled south and brought a message of warning to Judah in the hope that its people might avoid Israel's fate. The centralization of worship in Jerusalem mandated in this text was initiated during the reign of Hezekiah (715–687 B.C.E.). He abolished the offering of sacrifices anywhere but in the capital. Josiah (640–609 B.C.E.) went even further by abolishing all sanctuaries and temples throughout the land, except for the Solomonic temple in Jerusalem. In this way stricter control over the religious practices of the people could be maintained.

Archaeological excavations at Arad, a Judean city in the south of Palestine, support the biblical description of these religious reforms. Arad contains the remains of a temple structure and altars dating to before the time of Hezekiah, all built according to the specifications of the Jerusalem temple and its altars (see Figure 5.2). It was destroyed during Hezekiah's reign and rebuilt during the time of Josiah, but the temple itself was not redone. These changes at Arad are consistent with Josiah's centralization efforts, as mandated in Deuteronomy.

■ A PROPHET LIKE ME (18:15–22)

One of the central themes of Deuteronomy is the exclusive relationship between Yahweh and Israel. Yahweh was their God and he demanded total loyalty. The Deuteronomist set Israel apart from the other nations in many ways, including how they would maintain contact with God. Whereas other people employed diviners, sorcerers, and soothsayers to hear a divine voice, Israel was not allowed to use such means. Instead, Israel would hear God through a prophet.

> 15 "YHWH your Elohim will raise up a prophet from among your own people, one like me. To him you shall listen, 16 just as you requested of YHWH your Elohim at Horeb in the assembly when you said, 'If I hear the voice of YHWH my Elohim and see this great fire again, I will die.' 17 So YHWH said to me, 'They are right in what they said. 18 A prophet I will raise up from among their own people, one like you. I will put my words in his mouth and he will speak to them what I command him. 19 Everyone

FIGURE 5.2 ARAD SANCTUARY The temple in Arad matches the general structure of the Jerusalem temple described in the Hebrew Bible. It proves the existence of sanctuaries outside Jerusalem during the monarchy until the time of Hezekiah.

who does not listen to my words which he speaks in my name—I will hold him responsible. 20 But, the prophet who presumes to speak a word in my name which I did not command him to speak, and which he speaks in the name of other gods, that prophet will die.' 21 You might ask yourself 'How can we recognize the word which YHWH did not speak?' 22 What the prophet speaks in the name of YHWH and which does not happen or come about is not a word YHWH spoke. Presumptuously the prophet spoke it. Do not be afraid of him." (18:15–22)

God would raise up a prophet like Moses. The need for a prophet was revealed by the fear of the people as they stood before Yahweh at Horeb. They could not stand up under the intensity of direct contact with God, but thought they would die. It is a truism of the Hebrew Bible that one cannot look upon God directly and live.

Moses mediated between God and Israel. He became the enduring Deuteronomic model for prophetic communication between God and his people. A true prophet receives his words directly from God, and is distinguished by his access to the Divine Council where he receives God's words directly from his mouth.

The criterion for true and false prophecy was the "wait-and-see" test. In Deuteronomic perspective, prophecy predicted future events. If a prophecy was genuine, it would come to pass. This was not very helpful to those who were trying to figure out at the time who was genuine; this test really only worked in hindsight, when later generations evaluated the prophetic message in terms of the events predicted. Had they taken place or not? And it only worked for past prophets (probably ones already long gone) whose words had been recorded and written down.

The Deuteronomist is really providing a test for his seventh-century contemporaries. They were able to evaluate past claimants to prophetic office—men such as Isaiah, Amos, and Hosea. Having passed the test, these men would have been authenticated as true prophets. Listen to them and learn from their writings. All others are false. As one test for canonization, this would help decide which writings would have authority within the community and which would not.

■ THE EARLIEST CREED (26:5–9)

The last chapter of the central law code mandates a ceremony of first fruits. This ceremony is one of the three big yearly festivals established in Israel according to Deuteronomy 16:16. It was called the Festival of Weeks because it occurs seven weeks after Passover. Later it was also called Pentecost, from the Greek word for fiftieth (the fiftieth day after Passover).

As proof that they had actually entered the Promised Land, and as proof that it was a good and productive place, each Israelite had to take the first produce of the wheat harvest and bring it to the sanctuary. This was authentication that Yahweh's promise to the ancestors had come true. As part of the ceremony, the one offering the harvest gift would recite the following historical summary.

> 5 "A wandering Aramean was my father. He went down into Egypt and lived there as a resident alien with only a small group. He became a great nation, strong and numerous. 6 The Egyptians treated us badly and persecuted us. They imposed hard labor on us. 7 We cried out to YHWH, the Elohim of our ancestors. He heard our voice and saw our persecution, our toil, and our oppression. 8 YHWH brought us out of Egypt with a strong hand and an outstretched arm, with awesome power, with signs and with wonders. 9 He brought us to this place and gave us this land, a land flowing with milk and honey." (26:5–9)

Three major historical moments are evoked in this sketch of Israel's early history. The first is the patriarchs, or at least one patriarch. The description "wandering Aramean" best fits Jacob, whose name was changed to Israel. He is the one who brought his family to Egypt to join Joseph. The second event is Israel's experience of slavery in Egypt, along with the plagues and the miraculous Exodus. The conquest of Canaan is the third event. The gifts of produce taken from that land are proof that they were now in the Promised Land, the "land flowing with milk and honey." This description of Canaan is found throughout the Pentateuch. It not only contrasts Canaan with the wilderness out of which Israel came, but also captures the bountifulness of the land God gave his people. The statement expresses a faith grounded in historical events where Yahweh met his people.

Credo. Von Rad (1966) proposed that these verses contain the earliest digest of Israel's faith. He suggested that the events summarized here are the core of

Israel's salvation history. He claimed the outline of events contained in this creed formed the basic historical outline of what came to be Genesis through Joshua. Carmichael (1969) has called into question the antiquity of this statement, suggesting instead that it was composed by the Deuteronomist for the first fruits festival, and is not an ancient independent creed.

■ CHOOSE LIFE! (30:15–20)

These verses form the concluding section of Moses' last address. They bring together the big covenant themes of the book: commandment, obedience, blessing and curse, promise and fulfillment. Moses demands a decision from each member of the community. "Choose life or death, but you must choose!"

> 15 "See, I have put before you today life and good, death and bad. 16 This is what I am commanding you today: to love YHWH your Elohim, to walk in his ways, and to keep his commandments, laws and rules. Then you will live and increase, and YHWH your Elohim will bless you in the land you are entering in order to possess it. 17 If your heart turns and you do not listen, but you go astray and worship other gods and serve them, 18 I tell you this very day that you will perish. You will not have a long life in the land you are crossing the Jordan to enter and possess. 19 I call as witnesses against you today heaven and earth. Life and death I set before you, blessing and curse. Choose life so that you and your offspring may live, 20 loving YHWH your Elohim, heeding his voice, clinging to him. For he is your life, your longevity, so you may settle in the land which YHWH swore to give to your ancestors, to Abraham, to Isaac, and to Jacob." (30:15–20)

This final entreaty reveals more clearly than anything else that Deuteronomy is more than just theological instruction. It is a covenant document that demands commitment from the people of God.

The choice is laid out in all its simplicity. Keeping Yahweh's covenant yields life and prosperity, breaking covenant brings death. This black and white set of options is characteristic of Deuteronomic theology generally and also finds expression in wisdom literature. The life of obedience leads to *shalom*, the Hebrew notion of complete blessing. To disregard God is foolish and leads to death. Blessing and curse are the respective outcomes of obedience and disobedience.

The focus of the Deuteronomist is transparent in passages such as this. By framing Moses' message in the second-person singular, "you," he succeeds in merging the generation that was about to enter the land with the reader/hearer of Deuteronomy in the seventh century B.C.E., when the people were threatened with the loss of their homeland by foreign invasion. It did not take great spiritual insight on the part of seventh-century Judeans see the connection between the call to faithfulness addressed to the generation of Moses (so that the people could cross the Jordan to enter the land and keep it) and the call to their own faithfulness (so that Judah would not lose the land they already possessed).

Certainly these words became even more meaningful after 587 B.C.E. when the Judeans were in fact exiled from their homeland. If the people renewed their faith-

fulness, Yahweh would bring them back to the Promised Land. Indeed, Moses'
call to faithfulness becomes timeless. His injunction to obey the covenant today
becomes a call to faithfulness in every age.

TORAH AND COVENANT

The book of Deuteronomy has attracted a great deal of scholarly discussion
about the nature of Israel's covenant in relation to extra-biblical covenants. Given
the shape of Deuteronomy as a call to covenant faithfulness it is not surprising
that major components of Deuteronomy have parallels in ancient treaty ceremonies that initiated covenant relationships between two parties. Treaty documents associated with such ceremonies were a permanent record of the conditions
of the relationship. The term *covenant* can be used for both the type of relationship between the parties and the document that defines that relationship.

Certain parallels between Deuteronomy and ancient treaty documents are so
close that some scholars have argued that Deuteronomy is explicitly a treaty document such as was used in Hittite and Assyrian covenant ceremonies (Mendenhall 1955; Kline 1963). Today this view is considered a bit of an overstatement.
Deuteronomy is not itself a treaty document, though most certainly it contains
covenant language and major elements of such ancient treaty texts. More likely,
Deuteronomy is an anthology of sermons based on the covenant concept.

Ancient treaty documents such as those known from the Hittites and Assyrians were legal texts used to administer conquered kingdoms. Using somewhat
antiquated terminology, such an administrative document is usually called a **suzerainty treaty,** a suzerain being a feudal lord who controlled a vassal state. The most
extensive body of suzerainty treaties comes from the Hittite empire of the Late
Bronze Age (c. 1400–1200 B.C.E.). Equally important and closer in time to the
Deuteronomist are legal documents from the Neo-Assyrian empire (935–612
B.C.E.) that make extensive use of the treaty form (see Figure 5.3).

Close study of these Hittite and Neo-Assyrian treaty documents has revealed
that they have a number of components in common (see Pritchard 1969: 199–206,
529–541). A complete treaty document would contain the following elements.

1. *Introduction.* Sometimes called the preamble, this section introduces and
   identifies the parties in the treaty.
2. *Historical Background.* This section details the history of the relationship
   between the parties.
3. *Conditions.* These conditions, or stipulations, are the terms of the treaty.
   Among other things, the suzerain demands the vassal's total loyalty.
4. *Publication.* This describes where the treaty document would be stored
   and when it would be recited in public.
5. *Divine Witnesses.* This specifies the gods who would be called on to witness the making of the treaty (similar to a notary public today) and enforce
   any breach of the treaty.
6. *Blessing and Curse.* This was a list of the good and bad things that would
   happen to the vassal if the treaty was kept or broken.

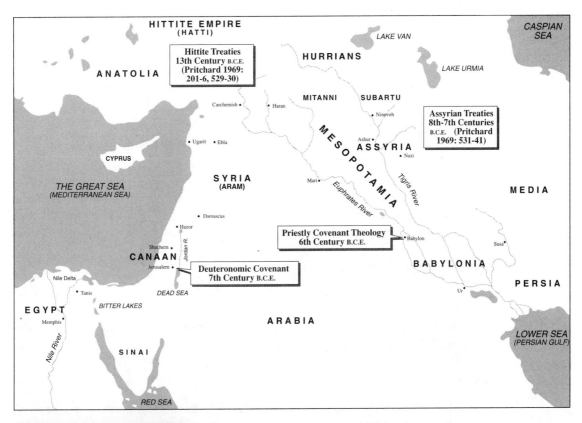

FIGURE 5.3 THE ANCIENT MIDDLE EAST, HIGHLIGHTING HITTITE AND NEO-ASSYRIAN TREATIES

The book of Deuteronomy contains remarkable parallels to the components of ancient treaty documents, as the following list suggests.

1. *Introduction.* 4:44–49. Moses speaking for Yahweh. "This is the law that Moses set before the Israelites" (4:44). This is the setting for the covenant addresses.
2. *Historical Background.* 5–11. This recollects Israel's experience at Horeb and in the wilderness, which is the occasion for Moses to warn the people to be obedient.
3. *Conditions.* 12–26. The central law code: "These are the laws and rules that you must diligently keep" (12:1).
4. *Publication.* 27:1–10. Covenant ceremony: "Write on the stones all the words of this law" (27:8). Covenant renewal every seven years with public reading is specified in 31:10–13.
5. *Divine Witnesses.* "I call as witnesses against you today heaven and earth" (30:19). Yahweh himself would guard the covenant and enforce it.
6. *Blessing and Cursing.* 28. "If you obey Yahweh your God, . . . all these blessings will come upon you" (28:1–2). Later, chapter 28 spells out the curses.

The profound similarities between Deuteronomy and the ancient treaty form suggest that the Deuteronomist intentionally framed Yahweh's relationship with Israel in treaty terms. Clearly, the Deuteronomist was influenced by broader ancient Middle Eastern legal traditions, and utilized them to shape the relationship Yahweh established with his people Israel. He used the political metaphor of treaty and covenant to conceptualize the spiritual relationship between Yahweh and Israel.

If Deuteronomy was intentionally made analogous, at least in part, to a suzerainty treaty, the theological effect may be that Yahweh stands in the role of the suzerain and Israel takes the place of his vassal. Other nations had a king as their suzerain, but Israel had Yahweh. In other words, Deuteronomy, viewed as a suzerainty treaty, presents Yahweh as the Great King of Israel. Though provision for a human king was given, that king would be subject to the Torah of the Great King (see 17:14–20).

DEUTERONOMY AS A WHOLE

The wholeness of Deuteronomy is due to its self-contained and unique character within the Pentateuch. It was not created out of a blending of different sources and traditions. Its unity of authorship finds expression in unifying themes, consistent style, and clear structure.

■ THEMES

Deuteronomy is perhaps the most deliberately theological book in the Hebrew Bible, if by theological we mean explaining in a systematic and thoughtful way what the nature of God is and what faith entails. The theological teaching of Deuteronomy can be distilled into three phrases.

1. *One God.* The Deuteronomist affirms a "practical" monotheism. "YHWH is our Elohim, only YHWH." He was not concerned with abstract theological formulations. He stated that there was only one God who was interested in Israel. God demonstrated that by his care in the past. He demands their undivided loyalty in the present. He is the one and only God for their future. The people were bound to Yahweh by means of a legal contract, called the covenant. It defined the shape of their loyalty and specified how they would remain in God's good graces.

2. *One People.* Deuteronomy is addressed to the people of God as a whole. No distinction is made between Southern and Northern Kingdoms. There are no tribal distinctions. This presumes the people of God are unified. This is affirmed in the covenant formula, "Yahweh is the God of Israel, and Israel is the people of God." The oneness of the people transcends generations. The book is addressed perpetually to the "now" generation. References to today and this day abound. The covenant is made "not with our fathers but with us alive today." The unity of the people is not based on genetic commonality but on the belief that God called them to be his people. They alone are the people of God, set apart from the rest of the nations and held together because Yah-

weh, in love, chose them. Sometimes called the "election" of Israel, this notion affirms that these people were singled out by God at his own initiative. That is what makes them special—Yahweh's "treasured possession" in Deuteronomy's language (7:6; see also Exodus 19:5, where the same term is used).

3. *One Faith*. Israel had gotten into trouble because it had lost spiritual focus. Local variations in religious practices and the tendency to drift in the direction of Baalism resulted in unorthodox worship. The Deuteronomist demanded uniformity in worship. This could only be enforced if one central sanctuary was officially designated. "The place Yahweh will choose" became the only worship center. Although left unspecified in the text, the Deuteronomist no doubt had Jerusalem in mind.

■ AUTHORSHIP

How did the study of Deuteronomy revolutionize our understanding of the Pentateuch? DeWette, a nineteenth-century scholar of the Pentateuch, was the first to recognize that Deuteronomy fits the description of Josiah's reform program in 2 Kings. He postulated that Deuteronomy was in fact the "book of the law" discovered in the temple. DeWette's insight prompted a reevaluation of the book and led eventually to the observation of its affinity with the following historical books, and its dissimilarity with the Tetrateuch.

The authorship of the book of Deuteronomy is a two-level issue, involving the surface setting of the book (what the book portrays itself to be) and the actual setting (when it was actually written).

The surface setting of Deuteronomy is evident from the book. What little action there is takes place in Transjordan (the modern Hashemite kingdom of Jordan) just before the people cross the Jordan River and enter Palestine. The best current estimate is that it would have happened around 1250 B.C.E. Moses addressed all the people of Israel, urging them to be faithful to the Lord. In so doing they would ensure prosperity and peace in the new land they were poised to enter. The speeches contain a reapplication of the Mosaic Torah to these people, updated for a settled-down life in the homeland Yahweh had promised them. Most of the book is made up of speeches by Moses, addressed directly to the Israelites. At the end of the book the manner of speaking changes to a narrative description of the death of Moses. The leadership role then shifts to Joshua, who becomes Moses' successor.

However, the compositional setting of the book, that is, when it was written down, differs from its surface setting. The core of Deuteronomy was written sometime during the Israelite monarchy, perhaps as early as the reign of Hezekiah (715–687 B.C.E.), or as late as the reign of Josiah (640–609 B.C.E.).

Deuteronomy in some form (probably only the inner core of laws) was the "book of the Torah" that was found in 622 B.C.E. during the religious revival of Josiah. The similarities between the Deuteronomic reform (told in 2 Kings 22–23) and the prescriptions of Deuteronomy are too close to be coincidental. Both involved centralizing worship in one place, celebrating Passover in a particular way, and prohibiting certain specific pagan practices. Furthermore, the phrase "book of the Torah," found in 2 Kings 22:8, is found in other places where it can only refer to Deuteronomy (for example, Deuteronomy 30:10 and Joshua 1:8 and 8:31–35).

Thus, Deuteronomy exists in two worlds, and both settings must be understood to fully appreciate the book. Set at the time of Moses, it was given its shape during the time of Josiah some five centuries later. While the core traditions may go back to the Moses of the exodus, the book as we have it today was shaped some 600 years later. Who, during the reign of Josiah, was responsible for giving the book its shape?

It is hard to pin down Deuteronomy's author. Evidence from the book suggests that he came from the Northern Kingdom and reflects its traditions. This is indicated by the terms he uses, which are consistent with other known northern traditions, for example, Horeb for Sinai and Amorites for Canaanites. Also, many of Deuteronomy's laws seem to derive from the Covenant Code (Exodus 20:22–23:33) which is from the Elohist source and embodies northern perspectives. The close connection between Deuteronomy and the religious reforms supported by Josiah might suggest that the writer was close to the royal court in Jerusalem. The description of the discovery of the law book, as described in 2 Kings 22–23, associates the find with Shaphan the royal secretary and Hilkiah the high priest. Both were trusted associates of King Josiah.

> **Who was the Deuteronomist?** The specific social background of the author is difficult to determine. The preaching style of Deuteronomy suggests that the book might have been written by northern Levites who warned and encouraged their congregations in periodic covenant renewal ceremonies at the great northern worship centers such as Shechem and Bethel (von Rad 1938). According to the Levitic priestly theory, when the Northern Kingdom was destroyed by the Assyrians in 721 B.C.E. these Levites fled south, taking with them their oral and written traditions. These then formed the foundation of their preaching in Judah. The Deuteronomist drew on this material for his book. Friedman (1987) believes the Deuteronomist was a Levitic priest from Shiloh, and he argues that Jeremiah was in fact this Deuteronomist. Another theory suggests that Deuteronomy came from administrative circles. In Israel, administrators and middle-level politicians tended to arise from scribal circles. Weinfeld (1972) studied what he felt were connections in Deuteronomy to Israel's wisdom tradition, and suggested that Deuteronomy is the product of an ancient Israelite civil service interest. Deuteronomy, he says, is the expression of a governmental group interested in shaping the structure and life of the nation. Nicholson (1967) suggests that the writer was deeply influenced by prophets and prophetic movements, especially those in Israel. The book of Deuteronomy certainly does hold a high opinion of prophets. Moses is portrayed as the model of all prophets. Thus, Deuteronomy has elements consistent with priestly, prophetic, royal, and wisdom connections. The multitude of authorship options suggests at the very least that we should be cautious about identifying Deuteronomy with any one social or political interest group in Israel.

The writer of Deuteronomy was deeply committed to revitalizing the faith and practice of Israel, and viewed himself as standing in the tradition of Moses. Indeed, virtually the entire book is framed as the very words of Moses. The writer succeeded in constructing a holistic vision of the Israelite community that accounted for all the major participants.

The critical issues of precisely when and where the book were written should not overshadow the overall impression that the book embodies a genuine testimony of Mosaic faith. Admittedly, the seventh-century writer shaped that testimony, being sensitive to the issues of faith and life in the Judah of his time. Nonetheless, he felt he was presenting the essential thrust of Moses' message. While shaping the words he put in Moses' mouth, he certainly felt he was representing the Mosaic tradition faithfully.

■ STYLE AND STRUCTURE

The content of Deuteronomy is presented as an anthology of speeches given by Moses to the Israelites just before they were to take possession of the Promised Land. He counseled and cajoled them, "Be faithful to YHWH and you will be blessed."

More obviously than any other material in the Hebrew Bible except perhaps some of the prophets, this material is sermonic, almost preachy. Deuteronomy is permeated with phrases such as "with all your heart and soul," "in order that it may go well with you," "be thankful," and "if only you obey the voice of Yahweh your God." It contains both a call to faithfulness and to social responsibility.

Deuteronomy was designed to appeal to the hearts and minds of its listeners. The bulk of the book is framed not as a narrative but as a direct address to the people. Although not noticeable in English translation (because "you" can be either singular or plural), the book vacillates, apparently indiscriminately, between address to individuals, you, and to the people as a whole, all of you. With this shotgun approach, the Deuteronomist targets each person, and—virtually at the same time—the group, suggesting that they are in this together as the one people of God.

Deuteronomy as we have it is the result of a long process of development and deliberate shaping. That should be no surprise. Almost every book of the Hebrew Bible was. The editor of Deuteronomy left us some helpful clues to the shape of the book (see Table 5.1). The main textual units are easily recognizable because a formula introduces them; the words "this is" or "these are" stand as a title at the head of all but one major section.

TABLE 5.1 TEXTUAL UNITS IN DEUTERONOMY

Text	Textural Units
1:1–4:43	"**These are** the words that Moses spoke to all Israel beyond the Jordan"
4:44–11:32	"**This is** the torah that Moses put before the Israelites"
12:1–26:19	"**These are** the laws and rules that you must diligently keep"
27:1–28:68	"Then Moses and the elders of Israel charged all the people as follows"
29:1–32:52	"**These are** the words of the covenant that the Lord commanded Moses to make with the Israelites"
33:1–34:12	"**This is** the blessing with which Moses, the man of God, blessed the Israelites before his death"

| Prologue 1-4 | Essence of Law 5-11 | Core Laws 12-26 | Curses and Blessings 27-28 | Covenant Renewal 29-32 | Epilogue 33-34 |

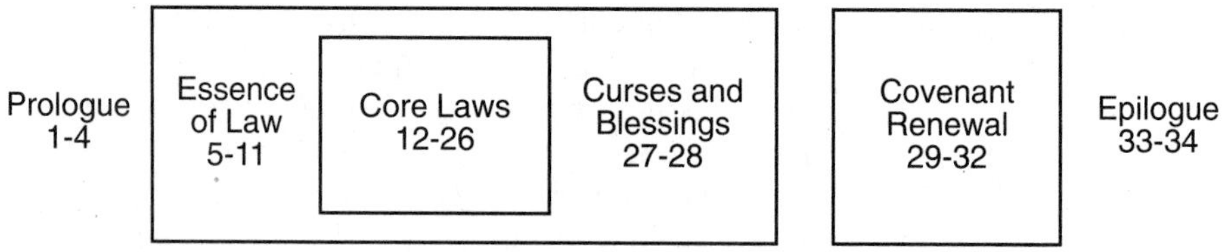

FIGURE 5.4 STRUCTURE OF DEUTERONOMY

The nucleus of Deuteronomy is the set of laws in chapters 12–26. If we visually diagram the book, we see this central set of laws surrounded by concentric sets of material (see Figure 5.4). This material reinforces those laws and gives them context. Simplifying matters somewhat, the inner circle of speeches by Moses (5–11 and 27–28) bracket the core laws (12–26), and are themselves surrounded by a prologue (1–4), and an epilogue (33–34) containing the farewell of Moses and various appendices. The covenant renewal section (29–32) is the only section which breaks the symmetry.

To a degree, the concentric structure of the book coincides with its composition history. The book was written in stages. The central law code was probably written first, no later than the reform of Josiah. The historical prologue was added to the book when Deuteronomy became the prologue to the Deuteronomistic History.

 Table 5.A is a detailed content outline of Deuteronomy.

■ DEUTERONOMISTIC HISTORY

Deuteronomy represents a theological tradition that is reflected in other books of the Hebrew Bible, including many of the prophetic books and Joshua through Kings. It is the theological lens through which Israel's greatest historian focused attention on the national epic. The history of Israel's monarchy, including the events leading up to the formation of the nation, are contained in Joshua, Judges, Samuel, and Kings. This material is not historiography in a social-scientific sense, but then it does not pretend to be. It tells the story of the nation from the theological perspective that Israel prospered or suffered in relation to how obedient or disobedient they were to the covenant. As went their faith, so went their national standard of living.

The writer of Joshua through Kings is called the Deuteronomistic historian (Dtr) because he derived his basic theology from Deuteronomy. After closely examining the book of Deuteronomy, authorities have suggested that most of the prologue, chapters 1–3, are in fact the work of the Deuteronomistic historian and not the Deuteronomist himself. Here's how the theory goes. The Deuteronomistic historian, writing at the time of Josiah, took Deuteronomy (which probably only consisted of chapters 5–26 and 28), and prefaced it with his own historical introduction (what is now chapters 1–3). He then used all that material as the first part of his magnum opus, the Deuteronomistic History (or DH for short). Many scholars think that the DH was edited later by an exilic theologian who added Deuteronomy 4:1–40, chapter 27, and chapters 29–34.

The Deuteronomistic historian really set out to answer significant questions concerning Israel's national destiny. First, by writing theological history he attempted to answer the question, "Why did Israel, the Northern Kingdom, fall to the Assyrians?" Second, he attempted to shed light on the question, "Why is Josiah trying to reform the religious practices of Judah?" We will examine his answers in Part 2.

FOR FURTHER STUDY

Mendenhall (1955) is the classic description of ancient Middle Eastern covenants in relation to the Hebrew Bible. Craigie (1976) is a commentary from a moderate Christian position, Tigay (1996) from a moderate Jewish position.

Chapter 5 Bibliography. See Part 1 Bibliography for works on the Torah generally and Part 2 Bibliography for works on the Deuteronomistic History.

QUESTIONS FOR REVIEW

1. What is unique about Deuteronomy compared to the other books of the Pentateuch? *185*
2. What are the major themes of Deuteronomy? *One God, One People, One Faith 194, 195*

3. What are the similarities between Deuteronomy and ancient Middle Eastern suzerainty treaties? *p. 192 They both contain six basic elements w/ one: intro historical*

QUESTIONS FOR REFLECTION AND DISCUSSION

1. What themes of Deuteronomy reinforce the major themes of Genesis through Numbers?
2. God used the covenant, a notion coming out of the realm of politics and international relations, to define his relationship with Israel. What is the effect and meaning of using this notion to define the divine-human relationship instead of another metaphor, such as parent-child?
3. If Deuteronomy was written in the seventh century rather than during Moses' lifetime, how does this affect your reception of the book?

Chapter 5 Study Guide
- *Chapter summary*
- *Key terms linked to the glossary*
- *Concept questions with answer links*
- *Progress tests: true/false, multiple choice, matching, and identification*

PART 2

PROPHETS

PROLOGUE TO THE PROPHETS

Key Terms

*Apocalyptic
Prophecy*

*Deuteronomistic
History*

Form Criticism

Former Prophets

Latter Prophets

Primary History

Prophecy

FIGURE 1   GREAT ISAIAH SCROLL FROM QUMRAN   was one of the first Dead Sea Scrolls discovered in 1947. The scroll dates to the 2nd century B.C.E. and is a virtually complete copy of the book of Isaiah.

The second main section of the Hebrew Bible is the Prophets (*nevi'im*, the *n* of Tanak) and follows the Torah in serial order. The basic division in the Hebrew Bible between Torah and Prophets goes back as early as the Hellenistic Period, as attested by the book of Sirach. In the Hebrew Bible the section called the Prophets includes the narrative historical books Joshua, Judges, Samuel, and Kings, as well as the books more traditionally associated with the prophetic office, namely Isaiah, Jeremiah, Ezekiel, and the twelve so-called minor prophets.

The titles Former and Latter are unfortunate because they foster the perception that the Latter Prophets are later than the historical books. In fact, the Lat-

TABLE 1   FORMER AND LATTER PROPHETS

Former Prophets	*Latter Prophets*
Joshua	Isaiah
Judges	Jeremiah
1 and 2 Samuel	Ezekiel
1 and 2 Kings	The Twelve: Hosea, Joel, Amos, Obadiah, Jonah, Micah, Nahum, Habakkuk, Zephaniah, Haggai, Zechariah, Malachi

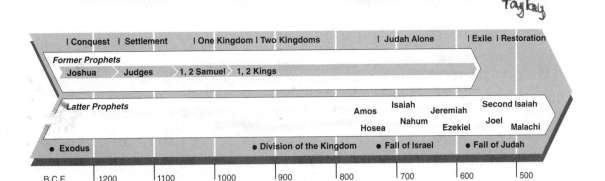

| | Conquest | Settlement | | One Kingdom | Two Kingdoms | | Judah Alone | | Exile | Restoration |

Former Prophets
Joshua → Judges → 1, 2 Samuel → 1, 2 Kings

Latter Prophets
Amos   Isaiah   Jeremiah   Second Isaiah
Hosea   Nahum   Ezekiel   Joel   Malachi

● Exodus   ● Division of the Kingdom   ● Fall of Israel   ● Fall of Judah

B.C.E.   1200   1100   1000   900   800   700   600   500

FIGURE 2 FORMER AND LATTER PROPHETS The Prophets collection of books was further subdivided into two parts (see Table 1). The narrative historical books came to be called the **Former Prophets,** and the remainder were called the **Latter Prophets.** The distinction between Former and Latter does not refer to the chronology of the books but simply their placement in the Bible, as indicated in Table 1.

ter Prophets for the most part fit within the history of the books of Kings (see Figure 2).

FORMER PROPHETS

The narrative record of the books Joshua through Kings tells the story of Israel beginning with the conquest of Canaan under the leadership of Joshua. Then it recounts the process of settling the land and defending it over against various enemies, told in Judges. The books of Samuel and Kings relate the rise of kingship in Israel and the development of Israel into two kingdoms. The story concludes with Judah's destruction at the hands of the Babylonians and the captivity of the survivors. Together the Torah and Former Prophets have been called the **Primary History,** a complete creation-to-exile account of Israel's story.

There are two main issues that we will track through the Former Prophets. One is the theological perspective of the writers and compilers of this account. Recognizing the outlook governing its composition we can better understand the intent of the story. The theological perspective of the Former Prophets is defined by Deuteronomy.

The other issue, not unrelated to the first, is the relationship between this theological literature and the history of events. The account recorded in the Former Prophets may be termed history but we must be aware of how we use that term. The writers should not be judged by our standards of scientific, objective historiography. They were believers in Yahweh, and it was their conviction that Yahweh was active in Israel's history.

It is significant that the Jewish community included the books Joshua through Kings in the section titled "The Prophets." The intent of these narrative records was not to chronicle history for its own sake, but to bear witness to the work of Yahweh in the realm of human events. In this sense they are prophetic. Among other things, prophets were spiritually attuned individuals who were able to discern God's presence and work in human affairs.

■ DEUTERONOMISTIC HISTORY

Scholars sometimes refer to the Former Prophets as the **Deuteronomistic History** (DH for short) because the books in this collection were shaped by the theological perspective of Deuteronomy. Deuteronomy is the narrative bridge between the Torah and the Prophets. It does double duty in the sense that it concludes the Torah and also sets the stage for the Prophets (see Figure 3). As the conclusion of the Torah, it wraps up the early history of Israel, and does so sounding a note of anticipation. Moses had brought the Israelites to the edge of the Promised Land, but he himself died there. The great promises of land and nationhood still awaited fulfillment. The people were not yet in their promised homeland. Concluding the Torah with the book of Deuteronomy creates a feeling of expectancy, with the promises being fulfilled, at least almost so, in the book of Joshua.

Some authorities believe that Deuteronomy was once attached to the Former Prophets, Joshua through Kings. The writer responsible for compiling this history added Deuteronomy 1:1–4:40 and chapters 29–34 to an earlier core Deuteronomy, once Deuteronomy came to be used as the preface to the entire Deuteronomistic History. According to this view, the Deuteronomistic History was completed shortly after the latest event mentioned in the book of Kings. That event was the Babylonian's release of Judah's king, Jehoiachin, from prison in 561 B.C.E.

Much research has focused on the theological perspective and integrating theme of the Deuteronomistic History. Noth (1943) was the first scholar to develop the theory of a Deuteronomistic History. He argued that the DH was composed to explain why the nation of Israel was destroyed by the Babylonians in the sixth century B.C.E. The story, he claims, focuses on the idolatry of Israel's kings and people, and explains why Yahweh allowed judgment to come upon them. Written to the Judean refugees of the Babylonian exile, the DH justified God and at least provided the assurance to the exiles that what happened, happened for a reason.

Von Rad (1962) found a more positive motivation behind the DH. In addition to the theme of judgment, which is most definitely there in the DH, von Rad suggested that grace was also present. Hope for the future was based on the covenant Yahweh had made with the house of David. That hope was still alive in the person of Jehoiachin. Von Rad argued that the release of Jehoiachin from prison, the note on which the book ends, was intended to inspire the exiles.

Wolff (1982) suggested that there is more to the purpose of the DH than justifying God's judgment or providing hope based on the Davidic covenant. He argued that the DH is essentially a call to repentance. It urges the exiles to turn from their disregard of God and repent. Only in this way would God restore his people to the covenant.

It is unrealistic to try to reduce such a complex work as the DH to one or two overarching themes. What these scholars have done is demonstrate the presence of certain significant themes that interweave the books of the DH. As you read the DH, be alert to the themes of God's judgment on apostasy, God's commitment to the house of David, and God's call to repentance.

The presence of multiple themes reflects that there was a complex history of composition to the DH. Its writers drew from many different sources and blocks of tradition. Within the books of the DH there are references to source books such

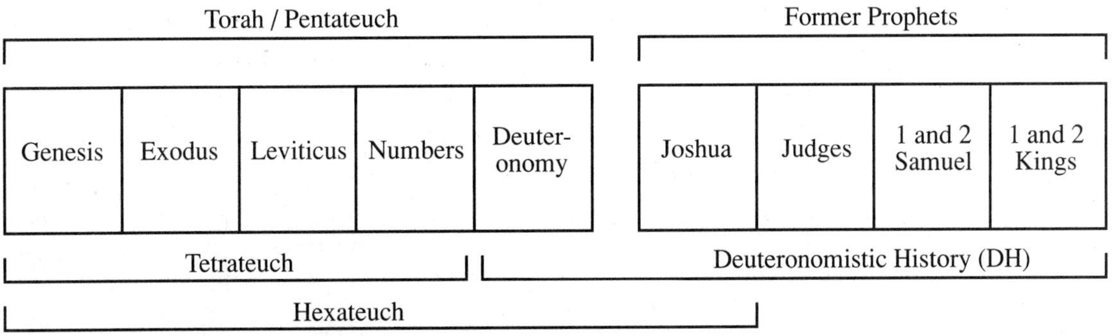

Torah / Pentateuch					Former Prophets			
Genesis	Exodus	Leviticus	Numbers	Deuter-onomy	Joshua	Judges	1 and 2 Samuel	1 and 2 Kings

Tetrateuch | Deuteronomistic History (DH)

Hexateuch

FIGURE 3 **TORAH/PROPHETS COLLECTIONS** The Primary History can be subdivided in a variety of ways. Each implies a different relationship between promise and fulfillment, as well as different composition histories.

as the "Book of the Chronicles of the Kings of Israel." The individual books vary in tone, further evidencing development. A comparison of Joshua and Judges, for example, demonstrates how different in character and outlook they are, while both still have Deuteronomic characteristics.

Cross (1973) has attempted to give account of the complexity of the editing of the DH. He has developed the theory that there were two editions of the DH. The first one was shaped by a Deuteronomistic editor (Dtr1) during the reign of Josiah (640–609 B.C.E.). Its governing themes were the effects of the sin of Jeroboam, who authorized Baal worship in the Northern Kingdom, and Yahweh's commitment to the house of David in the Southern Kingdom. It was written to be the inspiration for the reform program of Josiah.

The final edition was done during the exile around 550 B.C.E. It consisted of a modest rewriting of the first edition by a second Deuteronomistic editor (Dtr2). It reflects a more sober assessment of the future; it updated the earlier edition by adding the events that followed the reign of Josiah. The telling of the history of Israel and Judah thus becomes the occasion to enjoin the exiles to live faithfully.

While the Deuteronomistic History evidences an overall theological wholeness, each of the four books has its own literary unity, historical interest, compositional style, and theological insight.

■ ISSUES

Vast amounts of external evidence in the form of archaeological data and inscriptional documentation have prompted a reevaluation of the biblical data and have given rise to new approaches to the history and religion of Israel.

Historiography and the History of Israel

The documents of the Hebrew Bible that deal with the rise of Israel and the events of the monarchy are not first of all historiographic literature. The Deuteronomistic History and the Chronicler's History both drew upon historical sources such as

court chronicles and lists. But the DH and CH themselves are ideological literature; that is, they bring a certain perspective to bear on the telling. These works
may thus tell us a great deal about the spirit of their times as well as the events
of national history. But authorities do not take the latter for granted without independent verification. There is a strong tendency in modern studies to view the DH
as a type of literature rather than as historical chronicle.

As it just so happens, no external references to events recorded in the Deuteronomistic History exist until relatively late. No text references or artifactual remains
have been found that can confirm the accuracy or even the happenedness of biblical history from Joshua all the way until the time of Omri, the Israelite king of the
ninth century B.C.E. This does not mean that the biblical story is necessarily inac-
curate or that its players did not exist. Reasonable historians are quick to point out
that absence of evidence is not evidence of absence. Still, it is fair to say the climate
in modern biblical studies lends itself to historical skepticism given the arguably ideological nature of the texts and the ambiguous witness of external evidence.

The academic study of the ancient Middle East has divorced itself from the goal
it had in earlier times of reinforcing the accuracy of the biblical text. Today
Palestinian archaeology and textual studies are pursued largely as disciplines
independent of a biblical agenda. However, they retain a utility for those in biblical studies because they serve to build a context for Israel's story. Conditions in
Palestine from the time of Israel's entry into the land until the end of the biblical
period have been brightly illumined by the social sciences, though a great deal of
work remains to be done. Archaeology has clarified the patterns of settlement, the
movements of peoples, population densities, and material culture in all its variations. Social anthropology has defined the nature of tribal societies, patterns of
nomadism and urbanization, political processes, and the formation and organization of nation states. Historical and textual analysis of official and popular documents will clarify political, economic and social conditions. These disciplines will
continue indirectly to illumine the biblical story from the outside.

The Study of Israelite Religion

Israelite religion developed within the context of Canaan, and was strongly influenced by its religion. The high deities of Canaanite religion were El, Baal and
Asherah. El was the chief deity who had receded into the background by the Late
Bronze and Iron ages. Baal was the god responsible for agricultural productivity
and Asherah, his female counterpart, also had fertility influence. The most detailed
descriptive material comes from ancient Ugarit and dates to the Late Bronze Age,
fairly close geographically and temporally to early Israel (see Parker 1997).

Canaanite religion is portrayed as the antithesis of Israelite faith. The Hebrew
Bible is unanimously opposed to the polytheistic fertility practices of Canaan and
favors the exclusive worship of Yahweh. This, at least, is the official position strongly
argued in prophetic literature. There are hints both in external evidence and
within the Hebrew Bible itself that popular religion was a fluid blending of elements from Yahwism and Baalism.

Official Yahwism, as expressed in prophetic literature and in the Psalms,
appropriated elements of Baalism. Yahweh is described using the same phrases
that were applied to Baal. Yahweh was argued to be the one responsible for the

rains and fruitfulness, not Baal. And the motif of divine conflict between Baal and the sea is expressed in a variety of subtle ways in biblical literature (demythologized when God creates the firmament in Genesis 1; historicized as Yahweh versus hostile nations in Isaiah 51:9–11; and eschatologized as the Son of Man versus the beasts of the sea in Daniel 7).

A Hebrew inscription from Khirbet el-Kom (8th century B.C.E. Judah) writes "Blessed be Uryahu by Yahweh and by his asherah" and ones from Kuntillet Ajrud (early 8th century B.C.E. Israel) say "I bless you by Yahweh of Samaria and by his asherah" and "I bless you by Yahweh of Teiman and by his asherah" (see Freedman 1987). Evidently family and popular religion tended to blend Israelite and Canaanite religion to a degree that appalled and provoked the biblical prophets.

The disciplined study of Israelite religion from a sociological and cultural perspective contributes to a fuller picture of the conditions in which Israel's prophets found themselves as advocates of Yahwism.

LATTER PROPHETS

The subdivision called the Latter Prophets deals with certain individuals in Israel who had a recognized social and spiritual role within Israel, and who articulated a divine perspective on the events of their day. The Latter Prophets consists of Isaiah, Jeremiah, Ezekiel, and the Book of the Twelve. The Book of the Twelve consists of twelve shorter works, Hosea through Malachi, which some call the Minor Prophets. In the Hebrew Bible the Latter Prophets come between the Torah and the Writings, while in the Christian canon the Latter Prophets are, with some additions, the last division of books in the Old Testament. Note that Daniel is not included in the Latter Prophets in the Hebrew Bible but in the Writings; the Christian Old Testament places Daniel after Ezekiel.

The period that the Latter Prophets covers begins with the divided Israelite monarchy and continues into the postexilic era. Even though these books follow in canonical order the Former Prophet's account of Israelite history, most of the material must be placed chronologically within that history. It will take special effort on our part, but a necessary effort, to integrate these Latter Prophets into the time frame of the Former Prophets, especially the books of Kings.

■ PROPHETS AND PROPHETIC BOOKS

What is prophecy? The answer must be sought in the literature and culture of ancient Israel. Our present Western culture might mislead more than help us frame a response.

Definition: prophecy (prof´i sī), n. pl. -cies. 1. The foretelling or prediction of what is to come. 2. That which is declared by a prophet, esp. divinely inspired prediction, instruction, or exhortation. 3. A divinely inspired utterance or revelation: oracular prophecies. 4. The action, function, or faculty of a prophet. (*Random House Dictionary of the English Language*).

This dictionary definition encapsulates the modern notion of prophecy, but it does not accurately convey the nature of biblical prophecy. The immediate association we tend to make with the words *prophecy* and *prophet* in the modern world is predicting the future. While we do not have as many people who go by the name of prophet as in the era of Israelite history, we do have plenty of people, some more reputable than others, who traffic in the future: economists, meteorologists, marketing consultants, futures traders, and astrologers, to name a few. Only a small number of prediction peddlers, so-called psychics, baldly attempt to foresee specific events—the Cassandras and Nostradamuses of old, and the Jeane Dixons of today.

Predicting the future was not the major component of the prophetic task in the Israelite world. The most basic function of biblical **prophecy** was to analyze political and social policies in light of Yahweh's demands of justice, loyalty, and faith in him. The prophet was most concerned that these moral and religious principles govern the corporate and personal lives of God's people. The closest analogies in our modern world to the biblical prophets of old might be leaders such as Martin Luther King, Jr., and Mahatma Gandhi, who each had a keen sense of the divine requirements for social justice, freedom, and human dignity.

Biblical prophets occasionally made predictions about the future course of events, but they never did it to demonstrate how insightful or divinely inspired they were. Their predictions were basically extrapolations from the present state of affairs into the future, based on their knowledge of what God demanded. If the people would not change their errant ways, then the future would hold nothing but trouble for them. If they repented, then the grim scenario would be averted. Only in apocalyptic literature does future prediction take on a life of its own. While this literature has roots in classical prophecy, it eventually evolved into a distinct literary type.

A prophet was called a *navi'* in the Hebrew Bible. The linguistic derivation of the term suggests it could be related to the Semitic verb "to call." A prophet is then either "one who calls out" or "one who is called." The first possibility, the active meaning, is analogous to the meaning of its Greek translation equivalent *prophetes,* "to speak before," from which our English term *prophet* was derived. The second possibility, the passive meaning, may be related to the initiation call to prophetic service. In this sense, a prophet is one called by God to deliver a message. The following evidence suggests that either understanding, the active or the passive, has cogency.

A branch of biblical scholarship called **form criticism** examines the language of the Hebrew Bible in an attempt to discover the original real-life type of situation for a way of speaking. The application of form criticism to prophetic literature has been especially productive. Form critics have studied the phrase, "Thus says YHWH," which is widely used in many prophetic books. It prefaces a vast number of prophetic oracles, or divine statements communicated by the prophet. It is so frequent that it has been used to characterize the essential nature of the prophet's sense of identity, and even of the prophetic office generally speaking. In an important study, Westermann (1967) demonstrated that the background of this phrase is the procedure of sending messages long distance in the ancient world. Typically, when a king wished to communicate with a distant client he would employ a messenger to commit the message to memory. After traveling to his des-

[handwritten margin note:] 31. Disagree, because their predictions were basically extrapolations from the present state of affairs into the future, based on their knowledge of what God demanded. Whenever they were given a view of the future it was the near future. Their primary task was to analyze political and social policies in light of Yahweh's demands of justice, loyalty & faith in him. They were forthtellers rather than foretellers of the future. They spoke of mainly of judgment for sins & righteousness.

tination, the messenger would recite the message as if he were the king himself speaking in the first person ("I"), prefacing his recitation with the phrase, "Thus says the king."

That Israel's prophets used the formula "Thus says Yahweh" suggests they considered themselves divine messengers, having received the message directly from their Great King. This reconstruction of the prophet's sense of mission is supported by various prophets' descriptions of their calling to the prophetic task. Isaiah, Jeremiah, and Ezekiel each describe their experience of being in the presence of God where each felt he was commissioned. Each received a message first-hand from Yahweh. Each was then sent to the people of God to deliver that message.

The prophets typically exhibited a strong sense of vocation in connection with their calling. The prophet is one who has been called (passive) and commissioned in the divine council. Then he was sent to call out (active) the message of the divine King. Often the prophets were reluctant to follow their calling because they knew how difficult the task will be, but they inevitably accepted the challenge in faith.

We can reconstruct a viable historical context for almost every prophet. We know when he lived, where he lived, and to whom he prophesied. The same cannot be said of the editorial history of the prophetic books. These books were not necessarily finalized during the prophets' lifetime, so it is important to distinguish the human prophets from the prophetic books attached to their names.

Every one of the prophetic books of the Hebrew Bible shows signs of having been compiled and edited over a period of time. Although this oversimplifies the process a bit, we can say that the core of each book goes back to the oracles and pronouncements of the named prophet. These oracles were then written down and organized into books. Some books reworked the original prophetic core more extensively than others. But each book is the result of a composing and editing process that sometimes took centuries to complete. The final shape of prophetic books bears witness to how the words of the Hebrew prophets were heard by later communities, and how original prophetic pronouncements gave direction to later people.

The prophetic books are not autobiographies. Most were not written by the named prophet. Many times "schools" or prophetic interest groups that traced their outlook to a particular prophetic leader continued on after the death of the prophet and found their inspiration in the prophet. Many times it was they who were responsible for taking the message of the prophet and reapplying it to later circumstances. Frequently this will be reflected in the text itself.

We do not mean to scare anyone, but to be honest, reading biblical prophecy is difficult—but rewarding! The difficulty stems from many features of these books, including the largely poetic form in which they were written and the need to know the historical settings of prophetic statements, most of which are not clearly identified. The reward comes as appreciation for prophecy's wonderfully imaginative style of expression and the quality of its moral discernment.

■ ISSUES

Modern scholarship on biblical prophecy helps a great deal in clarifying the prophetic message. There are many things scholars look at when they examine the text of prophetic books, such as the following.

Forms of Prophetic Speech

The literature of the prophets contains a variety of types of speaking, including third-person narratives about the prophets, autobiographical sketches by the prophets themselves, poetically framed statements of salvation, laments, trust songs, praise songs, covenant lawsuits, and more. As we come across distinctive genres we will explain them. Form criticism has been especially effective in investigating the forms of prophetic speech and reconstructing early social settings out of which those ways of speaking make the most sense. The works of Westermann (1967, 1991) are pioneering and especially valuable in this regard. Also, the series published by Eerdmans titled *The Forms of the Old Testament Literature* has volumes covering the prophetic books.

Social Location of Prophecy

Prophets did not operate in a social vacuum but were shaped by their socio-historical situation. Each spoke out of his particular background, whether urban or agricultural, priestly or lay, wealthy or of moderate means. Each tended to be shaped by his region's theological traditions, whether northern or southern, Israelite or Judean. Readers of biblical prophecy must keep all of these factors and issues in mind in order to understand prophetic literature properly.

Much of the activity of the prophets pertained to politics, both domestic and international. Biblical and extrabiblical documents have enabled scholarship to reconstruct the national and international settings that equip us to make sense out of the prophetic books. Recent anthropological analysis of prophecy has added further sophistication by placing the prophets within the social- and class-matrices of ancient Israel (see Wilson 1980 and Gottwald 1985).

> **Mesopotamian Prophecy.** Various forms of prophetic activity are attested in the ancient Middle East, some of them analogous to features of biblical prophecy. The royal archives of Mari are an especially rich source (Pritchard 1969: 623–632). These texts from northwestern Mesopotamia of the eighteenth century B.C.E. make reference to ecstatic oracles induced by trances, divination, omen reading, and divine messenger speeches. Even closer to Israel geographically is the inscription of Zakir of Hamath, ninth century B.C.E., who prayed to Baal Shamen and was answered through seers, the same term that applied to Israel's prophets (1 Samuel 9:9; see Pritchard 1969: 655–56).

Tradition Analysis

Rather than being the mavericks of morality and spirituality earlier biblical scholars made them out to be, recent theological research has demonstrated that the prophets stand in continuity with Israel's narrative traditions. There is evidence that some prophets made extensive use of earlier traditions, and some actually quote earlier sources as the basis for their own statements. All in all, there is a considerable network of interdependence linking prophet to prophet and prophet to traditions.

Reading Guide

As you read the Latter Prophets, ask yourself the following questions:

- When did this prophet live and work? What were the political and economic conditions at the time he ministered? Where did he prophesy? (It makes a big difference whether he was from Judah or Israel.)
- What prophetic speech type (genre) did the prophet use to make his preaching more effective? Why did he use this genre?
- What historical and covenantal traditions, if any, did the prophet draw upon as the basis for his prophetic preaching and ministry? (Be especially alert to a prophet's use of the Moses-Exodus covenant, the David-Zion covenant, or any other allusions to prior historical traditions.) What message concerning God's covenant relationship with humankind did the prophet convey?

Table A is a synthesis of Israelite history and prophecy that displays prophets in relation to kings and events.

THE PROPHETS AS A WHOLE

The Former Prophets are distinct from the Latter Prophets in many obvious ways. They are different sub-collections, and the individual books within each sub-collection each has its own composition history. Yet there are notable points of commonality. The history of the monarchy as told in the Deuteronomistic History has a unity of theological expression and purpose that can also be identified in certain of the Latter Prophets. Although the character of the so-called Deuteronomic school is still being worked out by scholars, the tell-tale signs of its editorial work can be found in much of the prophetic literature. Its theological perspective became a major filter for the telling of history and for the shape of theology. Jeremiah especially is imbued with a Deuteronomic outlook and may have been edited by someone from the school of Deuteronomy.

Other prophets fall in more closely with the other pentateuchal traditions. The Yahwist source aligns with the house of David and Zion traditions. The Elohist tradition has affinities with the Elijah and Elisha prophetic stories and the book of Hosea. The Priestly source is very close to the vision of a renewed worship center in Ezekiel. It can be productive to think of Israel's narrative traditions of the Torah in relation to the Prophets, rather than as opposed.

Many of the themes of the Latter Prophets are controlling themes in the theological telling of Israel's history in the Former Prophets, and many of these themes have roots in the pentateuchal traditions.

1. *God in History.* The prophets believed implicitly that God controlled history, that he had chosen Israel as his people, formed an enduring relationship with them, and intended them to be his holy people forever. Because of this, everything that happened to Israel in history was a reflex of their relationship to God. If the people were faithful to Yahweh, they enjoyed freedom and prosperity. If they were unfaithful, God brought disaster on them in order to stir them to repentance. The Former Prophets demonstrate these biblical

principles in the history of the monarchy. The Latter Prophets contain calls to repentance for averting or overcoming disaster. After disaster occurred, the prophets brought words of hope, knowing that God would never allow his people to disappear.

2. *Covenant Traditions.* The message of the prophets was rooted in Israel's covenant traditions. The covenants of Moses and David were especially influential. These traditions defined Israel's relationship to God. On the basis of the requirements laid out in these traditions, the prophets called the people back to faith. Prophets sometimes recalled Israel's covenantal roots to reaffirm the truth of God and to ground God's faithfulness. At other times they recalled those traditions to demonstrate how God was going to do something new and even more wonderful than what he had done in the past. In any case, the prophets carry on their ministry against the background of God's covenantal relationship with Israel. Reading prophetic literature in terms of its intertextual relationships with the Torah, where the record of those covenant traditions are found, can be very exciting (see Brueggemann 1979).

3. *Faith and Worship.* The prophets tried to shape the faith of the people so that they would think and act rightly. Sometimes prophets were in conflict with institutional religion, yet they never categorically condemned religious ritual practices or formal worship but only opposed such things when they promoted religious self-satisfaction, complacency, and social injustice. In fact, some prophets were also priests, and all true prophets were informed by the best principles of Israel's priestly tradition, including the reality of sin, and the need for sacrifice, purification, and holiness.

4. *Prophetic Calling.* Many prophets conveyed their understanding of the nature of prophetic calling and the task of prophecy in call narratives: Isaiah 6, 40; Jeremiah 1; Ezekiel 1–3; Amos 7. These narratives convey the personal conviction that motivated Israel's true prophets. They believed that God revealed his word to them and that God spoke through them. Furthermore, they believed that the word of God was not just divine information, but had the power to drive and determine history. It also had the power to change personal lives and the lives of nations.

5. *The Future.* Prophecy as a practice is almost intuitively associated with the future. While this view is distorted, because prophecy is not essentially prediction, there is still a significant component of prophetic literature that is future oriented. Arguably the DH's prophetic interpretation of Israel's history was an explanation of national failure told in order to prevent a repeat of the same in the future. In its final edition the DH sought to inspire hope of a return to the Promised Land. Often when individual prophets addressed the future in their oracles they presented a preview of what Israel might expect from the hand of God if they refused to reform. Still the goal was repentance, and the future was malleable according to how the people responded. Prophecy became obsessively concerned with the future as it moved toward its late literary expression called **apocalyptic prophecy**. This form schematized history into bad and good eras, became mechanistic and deterministic, and saw the future as discontinuous with the present world of experience (see Chapter 17).

FOR FURTHER STUDY

Niditch (1997) for the history of Israelite religion, Westermann (1967) for the forms of prophetic speech, and Wilson (1980) for the sociology of prophecy.

 Part 2 Bibliography, including sections on biblical historiography, the history of Israel, and Israelite religion.

QUESTIONS FOR REVIEW

1. What are the two basic divisions of prophetic literature? Torch & Prophets
2. Why are the Former Prophets called the Deuteronomistic History in modern scholarship? 215

3. What is the basic nature of biblical prophecy? Why might some call prophecy forthtelling rather than foretelling? 210

QUESTIONS FOR REFLECTION AND DISCUSSION

1. What difference does it make if we approach the Former Prophets primarily as literature or as history? What are the arguments for viewing it as literature? What are the problems in viewing it primarily as historiography?
2. How are the traditions of the Torah reflected in the Prophets?

 Part 2 Study Guide

- *Chapter summary*
- *Key terms linked to the glossary*
- *Concept questions with answer links*
- *Progress tests: true/false, multiple choice, matching, and identification*

JOSHUA: CONQUEST OF CANAAN

Key Terms

Ai
Ark of the Covenant
Etiology
Gibeon
Gilgal
Habiru
Hazor
Holy War
Jericho
Joshua
Lots
Rahab
Shechem

FIGURE 6.1 JERICHO NEOLITHIC TOWER Jericho was a fortified city as early as the eighth millennium B.C.E., attested by this defensive tower. From the east Jericho was the gateway to Canaan and the first city Joshua and the Israelites attacked.

Palestine was the object of conquest for thousands of years. As the land bridge linking the African and Asian continents it was highly desirable for military and economic reasons. Past conquerors include the Egyptians, Hittites, Assyrians, Babylonians, Persians, Greeks, Romans, Arabs, Crusaders, and the Turks. Jews living in Palestine asserted their independence from the British in 1948 and founded the modern state of Israel.

The book of Joshua is the story of how the Israelites entered the land of Canaan in order to create a homeland. Under the leadership of Joshua, the

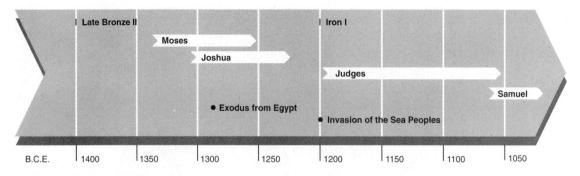

| B.C.E. | 1400 | 1350 | 1300 | 1250 | 1200 | 1150 | 1100 | 1050 |

FIGURE 6.2 BOOK OF JOSHUA

descendants of Jacob, now called the Israelites, entered Canaan and began to settle there. The book of Joshua picks up the story where Deuteronomy left off—with the death of Moses. It exhibits both historical and thematic continuity with the Torah. One of the central themes of the Pentateuch was the promise of land, and the book of Joshua details the actualization of this promise.

The book of Joshua consists of three major sections. Chapters 1–12 contain stories of military confrontations with Canaanites, resulting in victory for the Israelites. Chapters 13–21 delineate Canaanite territories that were distributed among the twelve tribes of Israel. Chapters 22–24 wrap up the book with Joshua bidding farewell to the Israelites.

Story Line

The book of Joshua begins by noting the death of Moses. God spoke to Joshua, Moses' successor, and encouraged him to lead Israel into the land of Canaan (Joshua 1). Joshua sent two spies to Jericho to provide intelligence before the battle. There they met Rahab, a Canaanite who assisted them (2). The Israelites crossed the Jordan River and went to Gilgal, where all the men were circumcised (3–5). They attacked Jericho and were victorious (6). But Achan stole some property in the process, so the Israelites lost the battle of Ai the first time; they succeeded the second (7–8). The Gibeonites became allies, but Israel attacked other cities, including Hazor (9–12). Although many territories were not taken (13), Joshua divided the conquered areas among the tribes (14–19) and designated cities of refuge (20). The Levites were given towns but no tribal lands (21). The tribes settled in their territories (22), and Joshua gathered the people to Shechem for his final address and for covenant renewal (23–24).

CAMPAIGNS OF CONQUEST (1–12)

A straightforward reading of the book of Joshua suggests that all the Israelite tribes were united in one mighty fighting force that was led by **Joshua**, and they stormed into Canaan and settled there. But be alert to hints that it may not have been quite so simple; a close reading of the books of Joshua and Judges suggests that the settlement was a long and complex process.

■ JOSHUA'S COMMISSION

After Moses died on Mount Nebo (Deuteronomy 34), Yahweh designated Joshua to take over as leader of the Israelites. Besides maintaining a connection with Deuteronomy by its references to Moses, see how the introduction to the book of Joshua in chapter 1 stresses the qualities of leadership Joshua must possess to lead the Israelites into the Promised Land.

> *1 After YHWH's servant Moses died, YHWH spoke to Joshua son of Nun, Moses' assistant, 2 "My servant Moses is dead. Get up now and cross over the Jordan, you and all this people, into the land I am giving to them, the Israelites. 3 I have granted every place on which the soles of all your feet tread, just as I told Moses I would do. 4 These will be your boundaries: from the wilderness and the Lebanon as far as the great river, the Euphrates—the land of the Hittites all the way to the Great Sea in the west. 5 No one will be able to resist you as long as you are alive. Just as I was with Moses, I will be with you. I will not fail you. I will not abandon you. 6 Be strong and courageous, for you will enable this people to inherit the land which I swore to their fathers I would give them. 7 Just be very strong and courageous. Make sure you do all the Torah which my servant Moses commanded you. Do not veer from it right or left. In that way you will succeed wherever you go. 8 Do not let this book of the Torah be missing from your mouth. Recite it day and night, so you are sure to do what is written in it. Then your way will prosper and you will succeed. 9 Have I not commanded you?—Be strong and courageous. Do not be terrified or frightened. YHWH your Elohim will be with you wherever you go." (1:1–9)*

This passage contains Yahweh's speech commissioning Joshua as the new leader of his people. Yahweh does three things here: he encourages Joshua, he defines his responsibilities, and he assures him of God's continued presence. The vocabulary and sermonic style of this passage clearly mark it as Deuteronomistic. Many of the same phrases are found, for example, in Deuteronomy 31:1–8, where Joshua received his first commissioning—phrases such as "Be strong and courageous" and "Do not be terrified or frightened." Note also the following features of this passage.

Moses is repeatedly called "YHWH's servant." This is a title of honor and reflects that Moses was dedicated to God's service. The title "Servant of YHWH" is a favorite Deuteronomistic description of holy men, and was applied primarily to kings and prophets in Deuteronomistic literature.

The death of Moses signaled the start of the occupation of Canaan. Moses was not allowed to enter the land himself because he disobeyed God at Kadesh (see Numbers 20:1–13 and Deuteronomy 32:48–52). Moses' death marks a major transition in Israel's history.

Notice the geographical markers in the text. The Jordan River is the eastern boundary of Canaan. The land lying to the east of the Jordan was called Transjordan by the Israelites. Such a term obviously presupposes a position within Canaan in order for that land to be called the "across the Jordan" land. Still, certain Israelite tribes did claim territory in Transjordan at various times, including

Reuben, Gad, and Manasseh. The reference to "the wilderness" is ambiguous. It could mean the eastern Arabian desert or the Sinai/Negev to the south.

> **Promised Land.** The boundaries of the land here laid out define the northern and western borders in an expansive way. The territory promised to the Israelites extended as far north as the Euphrates River. The Abrahamic Covenant (see Genesis 15:18) and the Mosaic Covenant (see Deuteronomy 1:7) also extended the Promised Land to the Euphrates River. Not coincidentally, the boundaries specified here in Joshua appear to align with the territorial extension of the Davidic kingdom; see 2 Samuel 8:3, which extends David's reach far into Syria, if not all the way to the Euphrates River. The point is that the eventual Davidic kingdom was viewed as a fulfillment of God's design going back to Joshua, Moses, and Abraham.

Chapter 1 ends with Joshua instructing his helpers to prepare the people to cross the Jordan River. They accepted his leadership and obeyed him, thereby demonstrating the effectiveness of his authority.

■ FIRST CAMPAIGN: JERICHO AND AI

In preparation for the invasion Joshua sent two men across the Jordan River to infiltrate **Jericho** and discover its weaknesses. The spies found an accomplice in **Rahab,** a Jericho prostitute. She hid them from the king of the city-state of Jericho and in return extracted a pledge of protection from them: When they attacked Jericho, she and her family would be spared.

Before the spies left, Rahab uttered an amazing profession of faith (2:8–13). She, a Canaanite, expressed her belief that Yahweh had providentially given the land of Canaan to the Israelites. The spies brought back an encouraging report, no doubt intentionally in contrast to the report of the ten cynical spies in the wilderness (see Numbers 13–14). Israel was ready to attack.

The priests picked up the ark and left Shittim, heading for the Jordan River. When their feet touched the waters of the Jordan, it stopped flowing and the people crossed over on dry ground. This miracle of the crossing parallels the miracle of crossing the Reed Sea (see Exodus 14), and by association with Moses and this miracle, Joshua's leadership is again validated. Furthermore, these two crossings bracket the early history of the Hebrews: Yahweh delivered them from oppression crossing the Reed Sea on dry ground, and he brought them into the Promised Land crossing the Jordan River on dry ground.

Once the entire group had crossed over, a representative from each tribe picked up a stone from the river bottom and carried it to **Gilgal.** Together they erected a twelve-stone monument to the crossing. One of the historical-theological motifs of the book of Joshua is remembering. The events to be remembered include this miraculous crossing that Yahweh engineered, the victory over Jericho, and especially the making of the covenant. As you read the book of Joshua, note how the Israelites were to remember the work of Yahweh, and how each event was marked with a physical memorial, usually a heap of stones in some distinctive formation. This twelve-stone monument is just the first of many such memorials.

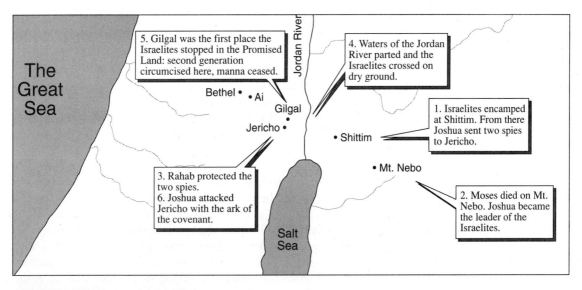

The Great Sea

Jordan River

5. Gilgal was the first place the Israelites stopped in the Promised Land: second generation circumcised here, manna ceased.

4. Waters of the Jordan River parted and the Israelites crossed on dry ground.

Bethel • • Ai
Gilgal •
Jericho •
• Shittim

1. Israelites encamped at Shittim. From there Joshua sent two spies to Jericho.

• Mt. Nebo

3. Rahab protected the two spies.
6. Joshua attacked Jericho with the ark of the covenant.

2. Moses died on Mt. Nebo. Joshua became the leader of the Israelites.

Salt Sea

FIGURE 6.3 CROSSING THE JORDAN RIVER

Also at Gilgal Joshua had all the male Israelites circumcised. The core of this circumcision story appears to be an **etiology,** that is, a story explains a phenomenon well known to the writer and his original readers. In this case, the pile of foreskins left over after the mass circumcision (notice that this is another "heap," hence a memorial) was used to explain the place name Gibeath-haaraloth (5:3), a place presumably in the vicinity of the crossing. The name literally means "Hill of Foreskins." This etiological tale was then taken up by the writer and incorporated into the narrative to make a significant point about the disposition of the Israelites. Those who were circumcised were, of course, the second generation of Israelites since the departure from Egypt. That they were uncircumcised implies that the first generation had been unfaithful in yet another way. They had failed to perpetuate the essential sign of the covenant (see Genesis 17).

Gilgal, the first stopping place in the Promised Land, had additional significance. There the Israelites kept the Passover celebration for the first time since its founding in Egypt the night of the exodus. This was supposed to be a yearly celebration, yet it was the first time it had been observed since leaving Egypt. The text again suggests that the second generation was faithful whereas the first had not been.

Finally, with an unmistakable sign, Yahweh signaled that the Israelites had finally arrived in the land of promise: the manna that had sustained them for forty years in the wilderness ceased. Why? They no longer needed miraculous feeding because the produce of the "land flowing with milk and honey" would amply provide for them.

Commander of Yahweh's Army

In a curious encounter between Joshua and a supernatural being prior to the battle for Jericho, Joshua's understanding of Yahweh's role in the conquest became clear.

13 When Joshua was near Jericho, he looked up and was surprised to see a man standing right in front of him. His sword was unsheathed in his hand. Joshua walked up to him and said to him, "Are you on our side or are you against us?" 14 He said to him, "Neither. I am the commander of the army of YHWH. Now I have come." Joshua fell face down on the ground and did obeisance. He said to him, "What does my Lord have to say to your servant?" 15 The commander of YHWH's army said, "Take off your sandal from your foot, for the place on which you are standing is holy." And Joshua did so. (5:13–15)

On first meeting this "man" Joshua thought he was just another soldier. He innocently asked him if he would be joining the Israelite cause, or was he on the Canaanite side? When his identity as a representative of Yahweh became clear, Joshua immediately humbled himself by falling spread-eagle to the ground. This "commander" is probably to be identified with the "angel of YHWH," who appears elsewhere in the Hebrew Bible, most notably in the ancestors' encounters with God. As commander he was in charge of leading the conquest of the army of Yahweh, elsewhere called "the host of heaven."

The meaning of this story is elusive and questions remain because the account is so sketchy. One possible interpretation is that this encounter would teach Joshua who was fighting for whom. This meeting clarified that Yahweh does not fight for Joshua, as if Yahweh was at Joshua's command. Yahweh's army retains its independence, with Joshua fighting for Yahweh.

The command to take off his sandals is similar to that in Moses' encounter with God at the burning bush (see Exodus 3). This experience of Joshua paralleling that of Moses further reinforces the legitimate succession of Joshua.

The statement that "this is holy ground" originally marked the site of this encounter as a holy place. Used now within the context of the Israelite movement into Canaan, it confirms that this was the "holy land," perhaps implying that Yahweh dwells here.

Cryptic though this story is, it is of signal importance, much as the other events at Gilgal were. Such a meeting with God's representative, a theophany, indicates that Yahweh is now present and accessible in the Promised Land. The fight for the holy land can now begin. The first battle is over Jericho.

Jericho's Walls Fall Down

The story of the famous fight against Jericho does not detail the military side of things. It does not describe the armor of the Israelites or any siege devices. Rather, the account describes the battle as a sacred event. Notice the centrality of the **ark of the covenant,** the sacred storage box for the covenant documents, which doubles as God's throne and marks the location of his presence.

1 Jericho was closed and inaccessible because of the Israelites. No one came out and no one went in. 2 YHWH said to Joshua, "See, I have given you control of Jericho, including its king and soldiers. 3 Have all the men of the camp walk around the city. Circle the city one time. Do this for six days. 4

Seven priests will carry seven ram's horn trumpets before the ark. On the seventh day you will circle the city seven times, and the priests will blow the trumpets. 5 When the ram's horn sounds, when you hear the sound of the trumpet, let the people shout loudly. Then the wall of the city will fall down, and each person can go straight in." (6:1–5)

Notice the repeated use of the number seven. This stamps the event as priestly and holy. The number seven is associated with the divinely ordained structure of the week. Remember the priestly account of creation in Genesis 1:1–2:3. The seventh day, the day the walls fell, would naturally be considered the Sabbath, although this is not stated in so many words. The fall of the city, taking place on the seventh day, Israel's holy day, marks the victory as the work of Yahweh. Remember that this story would have taken its final shape in the exilic community for whom circumcision and the Sabbath were central to their sense of identity.

Holy War

The army followed Yahweh's instructions and the city walls collapsed. Entering the city was now possible through breaches in the fortifications, so each soldier went straight in.

They devoted to destruction by the sword the entire city: man and woman, young and old, cow and sheep. (6:21)

avail, profit

The phrase "devoted to destruction," sometimes called "the ban," refers to the Israelite **holy war** practice of destroying the entire population of a city along with all its material goods. In the religious perspective of holy war, Yahweh alone fights the battle and achieves the victory, therefore to him alone belongs the booty. By killing and then burning the entire city, everything was given over to God. One of the implications of holy war for Israel is that making war was a not-for-profit enterprise. The Israelites were not allowed to benefit personally or materially from the spoils of victory.

The instruction to totally eliminate the Canaanite enemy was given to effect a complete separation between the incoming Israelites and the native Canaanite inhabitants. As the account of the book of Joshua goes on to describe, this instruction was not carried out to the letter. The result was that many Canaanites were left in the land, and the eventual spiritual problems of the Israelites were traced to this shortcoming. The Canaanites kept luring the Israelites to follow after foreign gods.

The notion of Israelite holy war continues to be a problem among those who hold the Hebrew Bible dear. For many modern readers it is a scandal that Israel's God should have mandated the complete destruction of a group of human beings. Can the same rationale be used in the post-biblical age to justify war against "heathens and infidels," as happened during the Crusades and at other times? How should we deal with the warfare ideology of the book of Joshua?

There is no easy answer, but certain issues should be considered. First, the biblical narrative may be an idealization; that is, perhaps the Israelites never consistently enforced the ban or completely destroyed a resident population. That they did not is in hindsight the Hebrew Bible's own theological explanation of why a pure Yahwism never took hold.

Second, we must remember that this period in Israel's history was unique. What may have been demanded at this time does not necessarily apply to later periods. Holy war was instituted only to give Israel a homeland in Canaan and cannot be generalized as a religious principle for all time.

Third, the results of archaeological investigations are inconclusive, but they do suggest that there was no complete destruction of Jericho at the time of Joshua's incursion. In other words, the archaeological record suggests that the ban was never in fact completely carried out.

> **Archaeology of Jericho.** The generally accepted date of Joshua's incursion into Canaan is late thirteenth to mid-twelfth centuries B.C.E. This puts it at the end of the Late Bronze Age or early in the Iron I period. Archaeologists have not found any remains of a fortification wall that date to this period at the only possible site of ancient Jericho, Tell es-Sultan. By the time Joshua would have arrived there, Jericho already had a venerable history of many millennia. The excavations have revealed a fortification wall and tower dating to the Neolithic period (8000–7000 B.C.E.). Walls dating to the Early Bronze Age (third millennium B.C.E.) were at one time attributed to the age of Joshua, but this correlation is now known to have been in error. Fortified walls dating to the end of the Middle Bronze Age have been identified. Wood (1990) claims the archaeological evidence of this destruction correlates well with the biblical description of the Israelite battle. But only if Joshua's battle of Jericho is dated earlier, as suggested by Bimson (1978, 1987), could Joshua be associated with this violent destruction of Jericho.

Jericho was a pile of burned rubble after the Israelites were done with it—another memorial heap. It was never to be rebuilt (though Hiel of Bethel later did it at great cost, see 1 Kings 16:34), as a reminder of the power of Yahweh and the Israelites over the Canaanites.

After the victory at Jericho the Israelites attacked **Ai.** Expecting only minimal resistance, Joshua sent a small raiding party against the city, yet the Israelite fighters were soundly defeated. This defeat was a sign that God was displeased with the Israelites. By casting **lots**—small objects made of clay, wood, or stone, like dice—an Israelite named Achan was identified as the culprit. Casting lots was the mechanical means whereby God revealed his decisions. After being thrown, their configuration provided answers. Because Achan had stolen goods from Jericho, God was displeased with all the Israelites. Only after the offender was purged from their midst would God's favor be restored.

Using a method of execution called stoning, Achan was taken outside the camp, where he and his entire family were killed. While the punishment seems severe—not just Achan himself but also his entire family were killed—it has a certain logic. The act of disobedience was considered so serious that Achan needed to be deprived of any future life in Israel. By eliminating all his offspring his family name was forever erased from among the Israelites. It is ironic that nonetheless we still remember him through the narrative. And the pile of rocks heaped over Achan and his family was a reminder to Israel of the need for strict obedience to Yahweh.

Having been purged of the sinner, the Israelites again attacked Ai. Although the community was now right with God, still Joshua was more deliberate in his plans the second time around. He set an ambush to draw the soldiers of Ai outside the city walls, surrounded them with his men, and completely burned the city and its inhabitants. The account ends with Joshua covering Ai with stones "which stand there to this day" (8:29). It seems that Joshua and the Israelites were intent on leaving stone memorials wherever they went, and they all remain "to this day." They did it at Gilgal after crossing the river, Jericho's walls fell in a heap of stones, Achan and family were buried under stones, and here is yet another stone memorial. Note where else in the following chapters of Joshua you find piles of stones, and try to determine why they are significant.

> **Archaeology of Ai.** *Ai* in Hebrew means "ruin" (today the site is called et-Tell, which in Arabic also means "ruin"). This story may be another etiological tale, along with a clever pun. The Israelites of the monarchic and exilic periods would have known this site as a ruins, and this story told them how it had happened. Ai was a massive fortified city of some twenty-seven acres through much of the Early Bronze Age (3300–2000 B.C.E.). From then until the beginning of the Iron I Age it lay in ruins. If the conquest is to be dated around 1250 B.C.E., there would have been no occupation at Ai at the time of Joshua. The Iron Age occupation began around 1125 B.C.E. covering only about two acres consisting of an unfortified village. Perhaps a later Israelite capture of Ai was credited to Joshua.

Altar at Shechem

God instructed Joshua to build an altar on Mount Ebal. Mount Ebal, along with Mount Gerizim, flanks the important site of **Shechem** in central Canaan. Here Joshua paused with the people to recall to their memory the Torah of Moses.

> *30 Then Joshua built an altar to YHWH the Elohim of Israel on Mount Ebal, 31 just as Moses, YHWH's servant, commanded the Israelites, as it is written in the book of the Torah of Moses: "an altar of untrimmed stones on which no iron tool has worked." They offered burnt offerings to YHWH on it, and sacrificed peace offerings. 32 He wrote on the stones there a copy of the Torah of Moses. He wrote it in front of the Israelites. 33 All Israel (that is, the elders, the officers, and the judges), foreigners as well as citizens, were standing on either side of the ark facing the levitical priests who carry the ark of the covenant of YHWH. Half of them were in front of Mount Gerizim and half of them were in front of Mount Ebal, just as Moses, YHWH's servant, had commanded earlier, so that the people of Israel could get blessing. 34 Then he called out the words of the Torah, blessing and curse, according to all that was written in the book of the Torah. 35 There was not one word which Moses commanded that Joshua did not call out before the congregation of Israel, including women and children and the foreigners who lived among them. (8:30–35)*

It did not take long for us to come across another rock memorial. In this passage we find yet another pile of stones, this time forming an altar to Yahweh. The altar was erected in connection with the ceremony remembering the Torah of Moses; that is, the covenant God made with Israel through Moses.

You may have noticed that this passage has strong Deuteronomic overtones. It is, in fact, a passage with many parallels to Deuteronomy 27:1–8, which calls for a time of remembering the covenant once the people reach the Promised Land. The event recorded here marks a milestone in the Joshua stories of conquest. This story seems to imply that after taking Jericho and Ai the Israelites were secure enough in the land that they could do what Moses had commanded them in Deuteronomy. Perhaps it also hints of their faithfulness.

A further note of fulfillment echoes in this passage. Although Shechem is not mentioned, every Israelite would have known that it lay between Mount Ebal and Mount Gerizim. Shechem had significant associations. It was the first stopping place of Abraham when he entered Canaan. There Abraham built an altar, and there God first promised him possession of Canaan (Genesis 12:6–7).

Shechem also has important federation associations. As we will see in Joshua 24, this was where Joshua bound the tribes together in a covenant, and was the site where the Northern Kingdom rallied under Jeroboam after it broke away from Judah.

After this Shechem interlude, the narrative returns to the business of securing the land. The first campaign in the central hill country established only a minimal Israelite presence in Palestine. New territory must now be taken—first south, then north, in two additional campaigns.

■ SECOND CAMPAIGN: FIVE SOUTHERN CITY-STATES

Most of the indigenous Canaanites viewed the presence of the Israelites in Canaan as a threat. But some isolated villages decided it would be to their advantage to make peace with the Israelites. One such village was **Gibeon**. The problem, however, was that the Gibeonites knew the Israelites were not in the practice of making peace but were under holy war orders to exterminate everyone. But the Gibeonites were clever in getting around this. Although they lived only a short distance from Gilgal where the Israelites were encamped, they disguised themselves as foreigners. They figured that if they were perceived to be foreigners, who presumably held no claim to Canaan, then the Israelites might make a treaty with them.

The Israelites were tricked by this deceit and entered into formal treaty arrangements with the Gibeonites, which included a pledge of protection. Shortly afterwards, the Israelites found out that these people lived only a short distance away. They were furious but could not dissolve the treaty and still be deemed honorable. In retaliation for their trickery the Israelites enslaved the Gibeonites, making them "hewers of wood and drawers of water," but stopped short of killing them.

When the larger Canaanite city-states of the area heard of the Gibeonites' accommodation to the Israelites they in turn were furious and attacked Gibeon. The Israelites were bound by treaty to come to their aid. In the process of rescuing the Gibeonites, Joshua and the Israelites defeated the kings of five important southern city-states: Jerusalem, Hebron, Jarmuth, Lachish, and Eglon. This secured the territory of what would become Judah for the Israelites.

Sun Stands Still. In the course of Joshua's battle against Gibeon's enemies he called upon the sun to stand still in the sky to give the Israelites enough time to defeat the Amorites. "The sun stood in the middle of the sky and delayed setting for about a full day" (10:13).

■ THIRD CAMPAIGN: HAZOR

A coalition of city-states in the region of the Sea of Galilee was organized by Jabin, king of **Hazor.** They fought against the Israelites at Merom. Joshua and the Israelites won a great victory and ended by burning Hazor to the ground.

This was a tremendous victory because Hazor was the dominant urban center in northern Canaan in the Middle Bronze Age. Yadin (1972), its principal investigator, has called it "the New York City of Canaan." It was smaller in the Late Bronze Age, yet still significant. Being able to dispose of Hazor, the Israelites must have been a considerable fighting force.

> **Archaeology of Hazor.** Hazor is a massive site that has been extensively unearthed. It was occupied during the Late Bronze Age (1550–1200 B.C.E.). The site contains unmistakable evidence of destruction by fire in the second half of the thirteenth century B.C.E. This destruction is credited to Joshua by most authorities. Hazor was resettled after this devastation and the material remains suggest it was by a less sophisticated people, usually identified as the Israelites. These people lived in tents and huts. The site was refortified and developed in the time of Solomon. See Yadin (1972).

The narrator asserts that the conquest was now complete. Note the finality of his summary statements: "Joshua left nothing undone of all that YHWH had commanded Moses" (11:15); "Joshua took all that land, just as YHWH told Moses. Joshua gave it as an inheritance to Israel. Each tribe received its allotment. The land had rest from war" (11:23).

With the wars of conquest now at an end, Joshua set about dividing up the land among the tribes.

TRIBAL TERRITORIES (13–21)

Chapters 13–21 list the tribal boundaries and settlements and, frankly, make for boring reading. Nonetheless, they provide a more nuanced picture of the occupation. In addition to tallying the territory taken by the Israelites, there are accounts of Israelite failures to expel the Canaanites.

Thematically, the narrative makes a point about possession of the land. Joshua apportioned the territories on the basis of lots, the same method used to determine Achan's guilt. Distributing the land by this means reinforced the belief that Canaan belonged ultimately to Yahweh, and God distributed it according to divine wishes.

Also notable was the establishment of cities of refuge. These were six cities to which a person could flee and find protection in case he accidentally killed another person. The intention of this provision was to call a halt to the clan feuds that would otherwise result when such accidents happened.

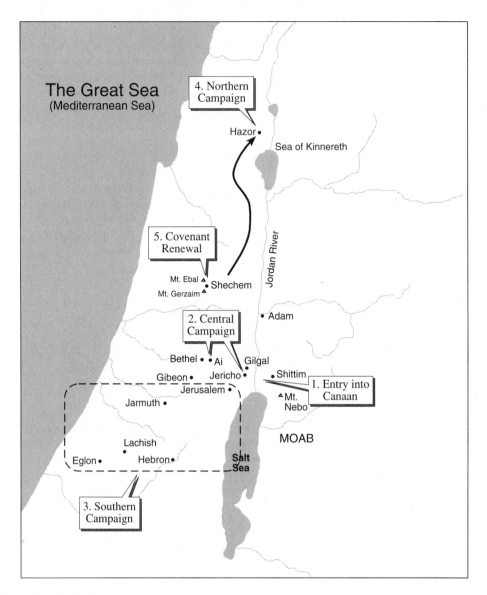

FIGURE 6.4 CAMPAIGNS OF CONQUEST

The Levites were given forty-eight cities throughout the land. The Levites did not have an extended tribal territory as such. Instead, they were scattered throughout all the other tribes and lived in these levitical cities. An examination of the cities and their histories of occupation suggests that this list better reflects a network of levitical cities in the eighth century B.C.E. rather than the twelfth century. These sites appear to have been centers for Torah instruction by the Levites. The Levites appear to be responsible for the Deuteronomistic History, so naturally they would be concerned to suggest that their special cities had authorization going back to the earliest period of the settlement, the time of Joshua.

As with the account of military occupation, so with the account of territorial allotments: the account ends with a neat summary suggesting finality and completeness.

43 So YHWH gave to Israel all the land which he had sworn to give to their fathers. They took possession of it and settled in it. 44 YHWH gave them rest on every front just as he had sworn to their fathers. Not one of their enemies remained facing them. YHWH gave them power over all their enemies. 45 Not one promise of all the good promises that YHWH spoke to the house of Israel remained unfulfilled. Everything came true. (21:43–45)

In no uncertain terms this summary reinforces the fulfillment dimension of the occupation—everything happened just as God had promised to the ancestors! God was with his people, giving them complete victory and perfect shalom. The phrase "house of Israel" (21:45) is used only here in Joshua. It encapsulates the notion of the unity of Israel and suggests that they are now a family living in a home of their own.

But how does this ideal picture compare with historical reality? The archaeological evidence from Jericho and Ai at times seems to clash with the biblical narrative. Text scholars and archaeologists have been wrestling with the historical and material evidence to reconstruct how the Israelites came to occupy Canaan. This, in turn, has implications for the question of the ethnic and sociological identity of the nation of Israel.

The stories of military conquest in Joshua 2–12 account for only a small number of Canaanite cities. Conquering Jericho, Hazor, and a handful of other places does not constitute a sweeping military subjugation of Canaan. Joshua 13 mentions certain territories that remained unconquered during Joshua's lifetime. The incompleteness of the occupation under Joshua becomes even clearer when reading the book of Judges. The first chapters contain inventories of land not taken, indicating that the Israelites were a minority in Canaan, subsisting primarily in the hill country. The cities and the plains were still controlled by Canaanites.

How, then, did the Israelites eventually come to dominate the area? All of the indications point to a complicated and gradual process of Israelite settlement and control. This issue is the subject of vigorous debate, and the issue will not be resolved for some time to come. On the basis of archaeological and socio-historical data, three basic models of the occupation have been developed.

1. *Migration Model*. Formulated by Noth (1960) and refined by Weippert (1971), this theory denies that there was any significant military action, apart perhaps from a few minor skirmishes. Instead, over a span of centuries, groups of semi-nomadic herdsmen began to settle in those regions of Canaan that were capable of sustaining a sedentary agricultural way of life. The entity called Israel took shape after such groups settled following a period of peaceful infiltration. They derived their unity not from shared ancestry but from a common socio-theological perspective. Each group took with them stories of their past, including their religious traditions. The stories were combined, unified and harmonized to suggest that from the beginning the entire history was the product of the entire group. Thus, the final story, contained in Genesis through Joshua, is a synthesis of many histories.

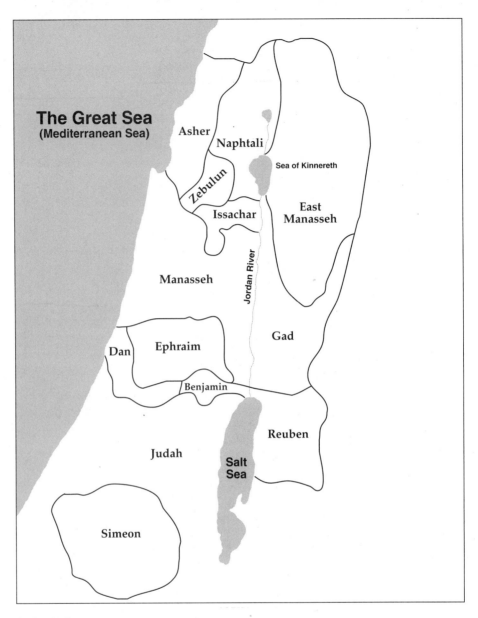

The Great Sea
(Mediterranean Sea)

Asher

Naphtali

Sea of Kinnereth

Zebulun

Issachar

East
Manasseh

Manasseh

Jordan River

Ephraim

Dan

Gad

Benjamin

Reuben

Judah

Salt
Sea

Simeon

FIGURE 6.5 **TRIBAL TERRITORIES** The ideal Israel had twelve tribes after the twelve sons of Jacob. While the number twelve was always maintained, the actual tribes that made up the twelve were somewhat fluid. In late lists Simeon disappears, Levi is omitted, and Joseph is divided into the tribes of Ephraim and Manasseh.

Amphictyony. Some authorities hypothesize that the twelve tribes were joined together as a religious league around a central sanctuary. This would be analogous to the Greek *amphictyony*, a religious confederacy best known from the Apollo league at Delphi. Shechem would have been the first shrine city, where Joshua united the twelve tribes into a covenant league (Joshua 24); later

Shiloh became the central sanctuary. For a description of the amphictyony hypothesis see Noth (1960: 85–109); for a critique see de Geus (1976).

2. *Military Conquest Model.* This approach, associated primarily with Albright (1949) and Wright (1962), tends to accept and support the essential historical accuracy of the Joshua account by relating it to modern archaeological findings. It suggests that Joshua led a core group into Transjordan and Canaan and secured their presence in the land. Evidence of a sudden violent destruction in the thirteenth century B.C.E. can be found at several city sites. Some of these cities were subsequently rebuilt, but in a manner suggesting a lower level of skill and resources. This change in technique and level of material culture correlates with the transition from a sophisticated Canaanite occupation to a less-developed Israelite takeover. One of the problems with this theory, however, is that the key sites of Jericho and Ai do not evidence destruction at the expected time.

3. *Internal Revolt Model.* First articulated by Mendenhall (1962) and now closely associated with Gottwald (1979), this theory holds that there was only a minimal incursion of foreign groups from outside of Canaan. Predominately, the birth of Israel was the result of internal political upheaval and social revolution. In the thirteenth century B.C.E. Canaan was controlled by numerous city-states, and these in turn were controlled by kings and aristocrats who oppressed the rural farmers and herdsmen. The latter became increasingly disaffected with the autocratic control of the urban establishment. These disenfranchised people banded together and wrestled control away from the oppressing upper class. Joshua and a small group of Hebrews were the catalyst for the insurrection.

Mendenhall finds support for this theory in a known group of marginalized citizens called the **habiru,** the indigenous inhabitants of inferior social status who pressured the ruling establishment of Canaan. They are attested in Canaanite-related documents called the Amarna letters. The Hebrews may have been this kind of people, living on the fringes of established Canaanite society. Other investigators, however, have discounted any connection between the *habiru* and the Hebrews, pointing out that the two words cannot be linguistically related in spite of the fact that they have similar sounds. Furthermore, the social and political conditions described in the Amarna letters do not match the Israelite situation as found in the books of Joshua and Judges.

A verifiably accurate picture of early Israel's occupation of Canaan cannot be drawn at this time. But we can say certain things about the issue. It can be granted that the story as told in the book of Joshua is to a certain extent a theological idealization intended to affirm the fulfillment of God's promise of the land. Perhaps it never intended to provide a complete historical account, choosing only a few incidents of conquest to characterize the powerful work of God.

On the other hand, history and archaeology, along with hints in the biblical text, combine to fill out our understanding of Israel at this time. Israel was certainly more diverse than authorities earlier had thought. It was a virtual melting pot of people. Certainly a core group traced their ancestry back to the patriarchs and

FIGURE 6.6

FIRST HISTORICAL MENTION
OF THE NAME *ISRAEL*
The Merneptah stele (a stone slab
bearing an inscription) dating to
the time of Pharaoh Merneptah
(1224-1211 B.C.E.) contains the
earliest historical reference to
Israel in any source. This means
that by the time of Merneptah,
Israel existed as a nation, and the
exodus must have happened
before this. The generally
accepted date of Israel's exodus
from Egypt is 1280 B.C.E. with
the conquest forty years after.

matriarchs, and the nucleus of the occupation force came to Israel via Egypt. However, other indigenous Canaanite social and ethnic groups aligned themselves with
this nucleus for religious and political reasons, the Gibeonites among them. While
the process of occupation begun under the leadership of Joshua achieved some victories that foreshadowed complete control, the occupation efforts lasted a long
time after his death and were accomplished with a combination of military confrontation and peaceful absorption. Probably none of the above models alone
explains the complex and lengthy process.

COVENANT CONSIDERATIONS (22–24)

The last three chapters of the book draw the Joshua era to a close. Joshua exhorts
the tribes to remain faithful and engages them in covenant renewal.

■ JOSHUA'S FAREWELL

Toward the end of Joshua's life a conflict arose, and the transjordanian tribes of
Reuben, Gad, and East-Manasseh fought against the Israelite tribes in Canaan

(22). The dispute was religious in nature and almost provoked a full-scale civil war. The transjordanian tribes wanted to have their own worship center, specifically an altar—yes, yet another pile of stones! The Canaan tribes believed that Yahweh could be worshiped only where the ark of the covenant was located; at this time it was Shiloh. The matter was settled only after those remote tribes agreed not to use the altar for sacrifice but only as a memorial to the work of Yahweh. These are their words of dedication: "This is a witness among us that YHWH is God" (22:34).

Although a somewhat obscure incident, it nonetheless served at least two functions. First, it affirmed the religious centrality of the worship center that housed the ark of the covenant. Here it applied to Shiloh, but the principle later applied to Jerusalem. This principle was always important to the tradition of Deuteronomy. Second, it allowed for the possibility that Yahweh could still be honored elsewhere, even in the "foreign" territory of Transjordan. Those living in exile (when these stories were finally edited) certainly took comfort knowing that just because they were distant from the "Holy City," they were not necessarily distant from God.

The first five verses of chapter 22 and all of chapter 23 are heavily Deuteronomic in style and content. Chapter 23 contains the farewell speech of Joshua. Such speeches are characteristic of the Deuteronomistic historian. The farewell speeches of Israel's great leaders clearly articulate the theology of covenant. The whole book of Deuteronomy is Moses' farewell address and it is all about covenant; likewise, Samuel's farewell (1 Samuel 12) and David's (1 Kings 2:1–9). Here in chapter 23 Joshua stresses the fulfillment of promise, and encourages the people to remain faithful to the Torah of Moses. But he also sounds a strong note of warning. The Canaanites who were left in the land would threaten Israel's loyalty to Yahweh. If Israel strayed from complete covenant loyalty and worshiped the gods of the Canaanites, it would be removed from the land of promise.

These dire words of warning portend what actually happened to Israel resulting in the Assyrian destruction of the eighth century B.C.E., and to Judah in the Babylonian exile of the sixth century. But the words are not just here as an "I told you so." They contain the theology that would enable the Israelites to make sense out of what happened to them when they were dispossessed of the land. Punishments involving removal from the land are their own fault, and restoration would come with renewed obedience.

■ Covenant Renewal at Shechem

Joshua called all the tribes to meet at Shechem. In a prophetic type of address, speaking for Yahweh in the first person, Joshua reviewed the history of Yahweh's care: I took Abraham from Mesopotamia, I gave him Isaac, I brought you out of Egypt, I gave you the land. This historical review is reminiscent of the historical prologue section of treaty documents (see Chapter 5). Indeed, Joshua seems to be holding a virtual treaty-signing session here. He got down in writing the tribes' loyalty pledge to Yahweh, their overlord.

Then Joshua challenged the people to choose Yahweh and reject both their ancestral gods and all the gods of Canaan. The people answered, "Yahweh our God we will serve. Him we will obey." Joshua recorded the covenant in the book of the

Torah of God and set up a stone as a memorial to the event. The stone monument would be a witness to the people's pledge to serve Yahweh. As throughout the book of Joshua, a monument serves as a lasting testimony to the faithfulness of Yahweh and the people's acknowledgment of God's goodness.

This covenant commitment event helps to explain how the Israelites found unity. Going back to our discussion of the nature of this early community, we recognized that early Israel was composed of many different groups. Some came from outside Palestine, descending from Abraham. Others were native to the area, such as Rahab and the Gibeonites. What did they have in common? How did they find unity? It was through a common commitment to Yahweh. This commitment was formalized in covenant and was recorded in the Deuteronomic literature. It defined the people's loyalty to Yahweh and to each other.

Concluding the book, we are told that Joshua died and the bones of Joseph, which the people had been carrying around since they left Egypt, were finally laid to rest at Shechem. Thus, the first momentous phase in the occupation of the land finds closure and fulfillment.

JOSHUA AS A WHOLE

The book of Joshua contains stories and other material from many sources; sagas of military confrontation, origin stories that explain phenomena familiar to Israelites of the monarchy (the etiological tales), lists of conquered kings, and lists of tribal territory. All of this material was organized to tell a story of lightning conquest, and it was all placed within the career of Joshua.

The book of Joshua in its final form consists of three main parts all flowing smoothly in a linear fashion: the campaigns of conquest, the distribution of tribal territories, and covenant renewal before Joshua's death. Yet the surface simplicity of the story masks an underlying literary and historical complexity, as we have seen.

Why was the conquest story told in this simplistic way? No doubt part of the reason has to do with historical memory and the creation of legends. Joshua was idealized and the sweep of victory was portrayed as absolute. The picture also has to do with the troubled times during which the story of occupation was shaped. It was crafted during the time of Babylonian domination in the sixth century B.C.E., so the writers placed emphasis on possession of the land as the fulfillment of promise. They stressed the faithfulness of Yahweh to his word, for they, too, were looking to reclaim their ancestral homeland, to recover a home of their own.

To that end, the Deuteronomistic historian framed the book with a theology of promise. Chapters 1 and 23–24 form the interpretive framework of the book. The opening address of Yahweh and the closing address of Joshua confirm that occupation of the Promised Land by the Israelites was in fulfillment of a promise made to the ancestors. On this promise, projected into the future again by the exiles who heard this story, Israel based its hope.

Turning next to the book of Judges, we find that the people's lack of faith weakened their grip on the Promised Land.

Table 6.A is a detailed content outline of the book of Joshua.

FOR FURTHER STUDY

Curtis (1994) for a general orientation to the issues of the study of Joshua, Coote (1990) for the problem of early Israel's historical identity, and Niditch (1992) for the ethical problems of Israel's holy war with the Canaanites.

 Chapter 6 Bibliography. See Part 2 Bibliography for general works on the Deuteronomistic History.

QUESTIONS FOR REVIEW

1. What were the major campaigns of the conquest? *[handwritten annotations] p. 228*

2. What is holy war and what conquest stories or parts of stories illustrate the principles of holy war?

3. What are the major scholarly models of the occupation of Canaan by the Israelites? *p. 229, 231*

4. In what ways was Joshua like his mentor, Moses? In what ways was he different?

5. Where were monuments set up in Canaan in connection with conquest events? What lesson did each monument intend to teach?

QUESTIONS FOR REFLECTION AND DISCUSSION

1. What archaeological evidence supports the narrative of the conquest? What archaeological evidence seems to contradict the narrative? Given these difficulties, what do you think the role of archaeology should be in biblical studies?

2. How is the perspective of the Deuteronomistic historian expressed in the book of Joshua? What Deuteronomic themes surface in Joshua?

3. How did the themes of the book of Joshua support the faith of later generations of Israelites?

 Chapter 6 Study Guide
- *Chapter summary*
- *Key terms linked to the glossary*
- *Concept questions with answer links*
- *Progress tests: true/false, multiple choice, matching, and identification*

[handwritten]
(#1)
1. Entry into Canaan
2. Central Campaign (Ai & Jericho)
3. Southern Campaign (Eglon, Lachish, Hebron, Jerusalem, & Jarmuth)
4. Northern Campaign (Hebron)
5. Covenant Renewal

JUDGES: SECURING THE LAND

Key Terms

Deborah
Ehud
Gideon
Jephthah
Judge
Nazirite vow
Philistine
Samson

FIGURE 7.1 **PHILISTINE WARRIOR** The Philistines were Israel's most serious rivals for the land. They arrived on the Canaanite coastal plain about the same time the Israelites crossed the Jordan River. The Philistines were Israel's most formidable foe in the period of settlement.

Adventure heroes are an unbounded source of fascination and entertainment. From comic book heroes to Rocky and Rambo, action–adventure stories reinforce the hope that good will triumph over evil, even against the greatest odds. Although they are often flawed, heroes can be empowering. They demonstrate what dedication coupled with courage can accomplish.

The judges were really heroes who single-handedly defended the Israelites from powerful, often superior, forces. And they did so in creative and courageous ways.

The book of Judges differs radically in style and character from the book of Joshua. The book of Joshua surges with excitement at the Israelite victory upon

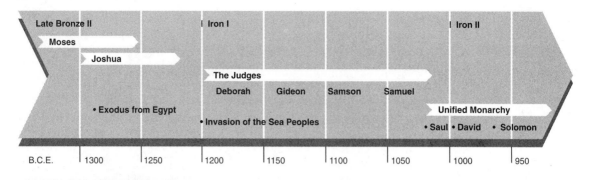

B.C.E.	1300	1250	1200	1150	1100	1050	1000	950

FIGURE 7.2 BOOK OF JUDGES

entering the Promised Land. By the end of that book Israel was secure in the land thanks to the faithful leadership of Joshua.

By the era of the judges Israel is cowering in the forests, hiding in the hills, afraid of being wiped out by Canaanites and other assorted opponents. The book of Judges finds Israel in that transitional period after the great leadership of Moses and Joshua and before the coming era of the monarchy—and things are not going well.

The age of the judges was a time of threat and danger. Internally, Israel seemed to be losing the faith of its ancestors. Externally, other peoples were threatening Israel with extinction. Significant regional political developments were afoot as groups were searching for living space. The pressures of the age forced the disparate (and desperate) groups who identified with the God Yahweh to come together in a union that transcended tribal interests. It forced them to see that Israel could exist only as a federation of tribes helping each other. It prompted them to see that they could be held together in this federation only by their common faith in Yahweh.

Story Line

After the death of Joshua the Israelites were attacked by various forces in and around Canaan (Judges 1). The narrator explains that this happened because the Israelites continued to serve Baal rather than Yahweh (2–3). A series of leaders, called judges, arose to deliver the Israelites. The more interesting ones are Ehud (3), Deborah (4–5), Gideon (6–8), Jephthah (10–12), and Samson (13–16). The remaining chapters tell of Israelite inter-tribal conflicts. Micah had a shrine and hired a Levite to be its priest, but was attacked by Danites who were migrating to the north of Canaan and took the Levite with them (17–18). The concubine of another Levite was raped and murdered in Gibeah of the tribe of Benjamin, and this provoked a devastating attack on Benjamin by the other tribes, almost wiping out the tribe of Benjamin (19–21).

NARRATIVE INTRODUCTION

The book of Judges is built around the adventures of the judges. The first three chapters establish a narrative context for their stories. The judges were needed because the Israelites had lost their spiritual direction. The problem revealed itself with the Israelites abandoning Yahweh for Baal and Canaanite religious practices. This theological explanation of historical experience is classic Deuteronomistic thinking. Faithfulness and loyalty to Yahweh is rewarded with success, forgetfulness with failure. Before this theological framework is examined, we need to clarify why the main characters of the book are called judges.

■ WHAT IS A JUDGE?

The traditional name of the book is a bit misleading. The name *Judges* was taken from references to the main figures about whom tales are told. None of the figures is actually called a **judge.** The name was applied because the text says so-and-so "judged" Israel a certain number of years.

There are twelve judges in the book, but they are not judicial figures such as the justices of the U.S. Supreme Court who sit in a courtroom behind a mahogany bench. While some of these ancient figures might have occasionally arbitrated disputes (Deborah, in particular), they possessed peculiar qualities of leadership for which they were called judges. The exact reason *judges* applies remains somewhat unclear, yet they may have gotten the title because they applied God's judgment to Israel's enemies. As in other passages of the Hebrew Bible, judging means standing up for the oppressed and delivering the afflicted, rather than judicially applying a notion of equity. The judges might better be called *saviors* or *defenders,* in keeping with their historical function.

If the traditional date of the exodus is accepted (mid-thirteenth century B.C.E.), the tales of the judges would be set in the twelfth and eleventh centuries B.C.E. From the evidence we have at our disposal, this was, to say the least, an unsettled time in Canaan. The period began with the great international powers in stalemate and then in decline. Both the Egyptians and the Hittites wished to control Canaan because of the importance of its trade routes but were unable to do so. Canaan was not dominated by either of these powers at this time, and this created a virtual free-for-all among the lesser peoples.

The most significant challenge to Israel came from a group called the Sea Peoples. They had moved into the coastal plain of Canaan as part of a larger migration of people fleeing the Aegean. One of the groups of the Sea Peoples is called the **Philistines** in the Hebrew Bible.

They sought to dominate lands eastward from the Mediterranean coast toward the Jordan River. The Israelites, assuming some form of incursion model of conquest, arrived from the east and pushed west. Meanwhile, the indigenous Canaanite population was not willing to stand for a wholesale takeover of its territory and found it had to defend itself. The book of Judges reflects the instability in the land at this time and paints a picture of various groups vying for supremacy.

■ PATTERN OF FAITH

Joshua's death was told in the book by his name. The first chapter of Judges is noteworthy for the tone it sets. While it tells of some continued successes of the Israelites after the death of Joshua, it also mentions certain failures of the Israelite conquest initiative. It seems that not all the territory of Canaan was taken or controlled by Joshua and his followers. Many Canaanites remained in the land. The

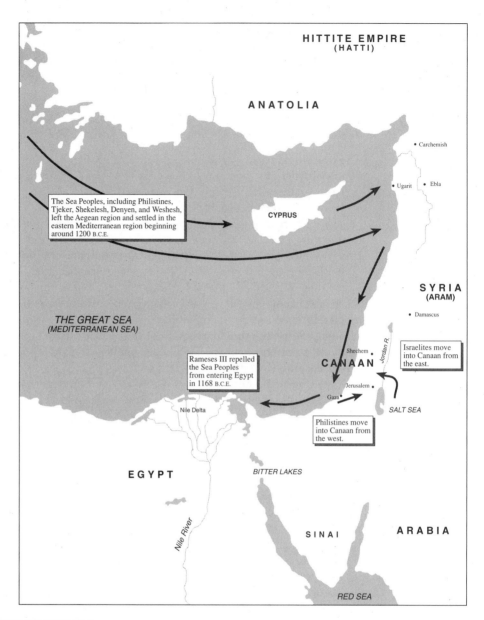

The Sea Peoples, including Philistines, Tjeker, Shekelesh, Denyen, and Weshesh, left the Aegean region and settled in the eastern Mediterranean region beginning around 1200 B.C.E.

Rameses III repelled the Sea Peoples from entering Egypt in 1168 B.C.E.

Israelites move into Canaan from the east.

Philistines move into Canaan from the west.

FIGURE 7.3 THE INVASION OF THE SEA PEOPLES

narrator, as we will see, attributes this shortcoming to a lack of faith on the part of the generation that followed Joshua.

The following passage recounts the death of Joshua as the occasion to remark on his faithfulness, that of the people, and of the elders.

6 Joshua sent the people away. Each one of the Israelites went to their inheritance to take possession of the land. 7 The people served YHWH all the days of Joshua's life, and all the days of the elders who outlived Joshua, those who had seen every great work which YHWH had done for Israel. 8 Joshua, son of Nun, the Servant of YHWH, died one hundred and ten years old. 9 They buried him within the borders of his inheritance, in Timnath-heres in the hill country of Ephraim north of Mount Gaash. 10 That entire generation was gathered to their fathers. A new generation came after them who did not know YHWH or the work he had done for Israel. (2:6–10)

This is the third time the Bible mentions Joshua's death. The book of Joshua ended with it (see Joshua 24:29–30, which has virtually the identical wording as 2:8–9) and the book of Judges began with it (see 1:1). It must have been viewed as a significant transition point for Israel. And his faithfulness sets in relief the next generation's lack of it.

The attention given to Joshua's faith can, in part, be explained because of his tribal affiliation. Joshua's burial place in Timnath indicates that he was from the tribe of Ephraim, which would become the heart of the Northern Kingdom. Thus, he comes from the home territory of the Deuteronomistic circle of theologians who were responsible for writing down this history.

The mention in the text of "the new generation who did not know Yahweh," of course, did not bode well and suggests that something had gone awry. "Did not know" means more than lack of knowledge. "To know" is typical covenant terminology, indicating that the parties in the covenant relationship acknowledge their obligation. This is what the Israelites had given up. In their unfaithfulness they were like that first generation out of Egypt, except that the first exodus generation had the advantage of knowing the work of Yahweh firsthand.

11 The Israelites acted wickedly in the eyes of YHWH. They served the Baal gods. 12 They abandoned YHWH, the Elohim of their fathers, the one who brought them out of the land of Egypt. They followed other gods, including the gods of the people living around them. They worshiped them and made YHWH angry. 13 They abandoned YHWH and served Baal and Ashtaroth. 14 The anger of YHWH erupted against Israel and he handed them over to marauders who plundered them, and he sold them to the enemies in their vicinity. They were not able to stand up against their enemies. 15 No matter what they tried to do, the power of YHWH was against them resulting in misfortune—just as YHWH had sworn to them—and they were in dire straits. (2:11–15)

Note how the text identifies Yahweh as the God of the fathers and the one who delivered them from Egypt. Both descriptions recall God's early promises and his work in history.

Baal and Ashtaroth are a male and a female god respectively. These figures and their characters are known especially from texts discovered at ancient Ugarit, where Ashtaroth was worshiped as Asherah. These gods were worshiped because it was thought they were responsible for agricultural productivity.

Baal and Ugarit. Texts from Ugarit, an ancient city discovered in 1929, contain tales of Baal and other Canaanite gods and goddesses (see Craigie 1983, Parker 1997). Though dated to the Late Bronze Age (1550–1200 B.C.E.), hence before the Hebrew Bible was written or Israel even existed, they contain important stories of gods and heroes who appear in various guises in the Hebrew Bible. The following selection from the Baal cycle provides the flavor of the texts. In this selection a divine supporter of Baal encourages him to be courageous against his enemy Yamm, the god of the sea.

"Let me tell you, Prince Baal,
let me repeat, Rider on the Clouds:
behold, your enemy, Baal,
behold, you will kill your enemy,
behold, you will annihilate your foes.
You will take your eternal kingship,
your dominion forever and ever." —Coogan (1978)

The Israelites were attracted to the gods of the indigenous Canaanites. The essential theological problem with worshiping Canaanite gods was the implied abandonment of Yahweh. The covenant that bound Yahweh and Israel together demanded absolute and unwavering loyalty between these two parties. Worshiping another god was nothing less than a breach of covenant.

For punishment Yahweh withdrew his leadership as the divine warrior. This resulted in Israel's total inability to gain the advantage over the other groups in Canaan.

> 16 YHWH raised up judges. They saved them from the power of the marauders. 17 Yet they did not even listen to their judges, but they whored after other gods and worshiped them. They quickly turned from the path on which their ancestors walked—heeding the commandments of YHWH. That is just what they did not do! 18 When YHWH raised up judges for them, YHWH was with the judge his whole life, so that he could deliver them from the power of their enemies. YHWH was moved to pity when they groaned on account of their persecutors and oppressors. 19 When the judge died, they reverted and turned out worse than their ancestors by following other gods, serving, and worshiping them. They did not abandon any of their practices or their ingrained ways. 20 So, the anger of YHWH erupted against Israel, and he thought, "Because this nation has broken the covenant to which I obligated their ancestors, and they have not obeyed my voice, 21 I will not continue to dispossess any of the nations Joshua left when he died." 22 In order to test Israel to see whether or not they would guard the path their ancestors guarded, 23 YHWH allowed to remain those nations he did not dispossess quickly, those over whom he had not given Joshua power. (2:16–23)

These verses provide the schematic outline that virtually every judge story follows. When the Israelites were in trouble, God empowered a judge to rescue them. After the judge died, the Israelites reverted to the worship of non-Yahweh gods. God again allowed a foreign group to dominate the Israelites as punishment. This cyclic pattern repeats itself each generation throughout the book of Judges: (1) Israel turns from Yahweh, (2) an enemy oppresses Israel, (3) Israel cries for help, (4) Yahweh sends a judge to deliver Israel. As you read, note how the pattern articulated in this general introduction is expressed in the tales of individual judges.

In the following paragraph from the book of Judges, the unfaithfulness of the people is also used by the theologian–writer to explain why these foreign groups were still around when they should have been completely wiped out. They were kept around to be used as Yahweh's instrument to test the people.

> *1 These are the nations YHWH allowed to remain to test Israel (all those who did not know the wars of Canaan— 2 it was only to teach the Israelite generations about war, only for those who had not experienced the wars): 3 the five Philistine lords, all the Canaanites, the Sidonians, the Hivites who live on Mount Lebanon (from Mount Baal-hermon to Mount Lebo-hamath). 4 They were for the testing of Israel, to find out whether they would heed the commandments of YHWH which he commanded their ancestors through Moses. (3:1–4)*

This note about teaching the Israelites how to fight was probably added by the exilic Deuteronomistic editor. One of his themes was teaching divine discipline through the rigors of warfare. This is also expressed in Judges 20.

THE JUDGES AT WORK

The bulk of the book of Judges is the collection of stories, as expected, about the judges themselves. Although there are twelve judges, they do not get equal treatment. Most are mentioned in only a few verses. Only a few get major treatment. Following biblical precedent, we will take an in-depth look at Ehud, Deborah, Gideon, Jephthah, and Samson.

■ EHUD (3:12–30)

The tale of Othniel follows immediately upon the theological narrative introduction. Othniel's saga (3:7–11) is very sketchy. It seems to serve as the "typical" tale, really only stating the cyclic pattern of apostasy and deliverance. It is followed by the story of **Ehud**, a left-handed judge from the tribe of Benjamin.

> **Benjamin.** Ehud is explicitly identified as left-handed. Left-handedness was considered an aberration in the ancient world and had evil or unclean connotations (compare Latin, where *sinister* means "left"). The name Benjamin is literally "son of the right hand." Perhaps this description of Ehud is the writer's way of characterizing the tribe. Judges 19–21 paints a particularly nasty picture of the tribe of Benjamin.

Ehud devised a plan to dispose of Eglon, whose name means fatted-calf. This king of Moab dominated Israel and demanded tribute.

> *16 And Ehud made a two-edged sword for himself a cubit long. He strapped it on his right thigh under his clothes. 17 Then he presented the tribute to Eglon king of Moab, a very fat man. 18 When Ehud had finished presenting the tribute, he sent away the people that had carried the tribute. 19 But he*

himself turned around at the quarry near Gilgal. He said, "I have a secret message for you, O king." And he commanded, "Silence." All his attendants left him. 20 Ehud came to him as he was sitting alone in his cool roof chamber. Ehud said, "I have a message from God for you." Eglon rose from his seat. 21 Ehud reached with his left hand, took the sword from his right thigh, and thrust it into his belly. 22 The hilt also went in after the blade, and fat closed over the blade. He did not pull the sword out of his belly, but excrement came out. (3:16–22)

Thus, Ehud's assassination of the Moabite king Eglon is described in gory detail. He was so fat that when the dagger pierced his belly it disappeared and Ehud could not retrieve it. Ehud was able to escape, and the Israelites regained their freedom.

■ DEBORAH (4-5)

The story of **Deborah** and Barak, begins with a description of the dire straits in which again the Israelites found themselves.

1 Again the Israelites acted wickedly in YHWH's eyes. Ehud was dead. 2 YHWH gave them over to the control of Jabin, the Canaanite king who ruled from Hazor, and Sisera his army general (he lived in Haroshet-hagoyim). 3 The Israelites cried out to YHWH, because Jabin had nine hundred iron chariots. He severely oppressed the Israelites for twenty years. (4:1–3)

The hard times were prompted, as always in this book, by Israel's behavior. The particular offense is not specified, but based on the theological introduction we can assume it was unfaithfulness to Yahweh.

The oppressor was Jabin from Hazor (see Figure 7.4). This places the conflict in northern Canaan. The mention of Hazor, as well as other places mentioned later in the story, position the action just to the west of the Sea of Galilee.

> **Jabin.** A problem arises with the mention of Jabin and Hazor. He was explicitly said to have been destroyed by Joshua in Joshua 11 (see Chapter 6). How can this be explained? Maybe Jabin was not originally attached to this story and was for some reason inserted later. The reference to Jabin is found only in the introduction and conclusion to the Deborah–Barak tale (verses 1–3 and 23–24) and in the mention of a treaty (verse 17). The actual fighting is against Sisera.

After the stage-setting words, Deborah is introduced as a prophet who judged Israel in Ephraim. She was obviously a respected leader. In the mode of a prophet she delivered an oracle (a message from God) to Barak commanding him to organize troops from the tribes of Naphtali and Zebulun to fight Sisera on Mount Tabor. Barak requested that Deborah accompany him. She agreed, but only after telling him that the coming victory would be credited to a woman. The story highlights the insecurity of Barak and the decisiveness and courage of Deborah.

FIGURE 7.4 **MEGIDDO IVORY**   This ivory plaque was found at Megiddo and dates to the time of the judges. The drawing depicts a Canaanite king seated on a throne in the shape of a winged sphinx. He is receiving an entourage returning from war which includes two bound captives. Jabin, a northern Canaanite king, dominated the Israelites, perhaps in like manner.

> *6 She sent for Barak son of Abinoam from Qedesh in Naphtali and said to him, "Has YHWH, the God of Israel, not commanded you?—'Go, march to Mount Tabor, and take ten thousand men from Naphtali and Zebulun with you. 7 I will march Sisera, Jabin's army commander, to you at the Kishon River, along with his chariots and his troops. I will hand them over to you.'" 8 Barak said to her, "Only if you go with me will I go. If you do not go with me, I will not go." 9 She said, "I will go with you. But you will get no glory this way. YHWH will sell out Sisera by the hand of a woman." Deborah got up and went with Barak to Qedesh. (4:6–9)*

After the battle was joined, the Canaanite army was soon outmaneuvered, and Sisera fled the battle scene on foot. He found refuge in the tent of Jael, a one-time friend. Jael greeted him warmly, gave him drink and let him rest. But after Sisera fell asleep, she sneaked back into the tent and pounded a tent stake through Sisera's temple and on into the ground. The victory was celebrated in song. The text of the victory hymn, sometimes called the Song of Deborah, is found in Judges 5. Judging by the style of its language, Hebrew linguists tell us it is one of the oldest compositions in the Old Testament and may have been written very close to the event itself.

The tale of Deborah and Barak reveals many things about the period of the judges. It illustrates how at various times, out of military necessity, individual tribes would join forces to combat a formidable enemy. But, as the Song of Deborah indicates, not all the tribes always answered the call for help. Sometimes some refused. Israel as a confederacy was still dominated by regional interests. There was no national cohesion at this time.

The story also profiles the prophetic and military role female Israelites at times played in Israel. The courage of Deborah and Jael, and the credit for victory they received, sets in relief the deplorable lack of male initiative and leadership in Israel at the time of the judges.

■ GIDEON (6–9)

The land rested for forty years after the victory over Sisera. Then the Israelites turned away from Yahweh. Again, the judge tale is framed with the editor's pattern of faith statements.

1 The Israelites acted wickedly in YHWH's eyes. YHWH gave them over to the control of Midian for seven years. (6:1)

The first stage of the pattern is thus stated. The Midianites were marauders who would descend on the more settled Israelites, foraging grain and stealing livestock.

6 Israel became very poor on account of Midian, and the Israelites cried out to YHWH. (6:6)

The Israelites realized that they did, in fact, need Yahweh. He responded by sending an angel to commission **Gideon,** who was from the tribe of Manasseh. The setting of this encounter is very revealing of the conditions in Israel generally, and of the quality of Israel's leadership specifically. The angel confronted Gideon as Gideon was threshing wheat in a winepress. A winepress is a depression carved out of rock. Normally threshing is done on a hard surface near the top of a hill, to catch the breeze. Gideon was obviously in hiding. The angel's words of address can only be heard as ironic in this context when he says, "Yahweh is with you, you mighty warrior!"

Gideon's first act in Yahweh's cause was to vandalize the local shrine of Baal. During the night he and a few of his servants sneaked up to the high place and pulled down the altar and its associated Asherah symbol. Again, the insecurity of Gideon comes to our attention. He did it at night because he was afraid otherwise someone might recognize and blame him. Only after the townspeople confronted him did he own up to his act and stand up publicly against Baal.

The Spirit of Yahweh empowered Gideon, and he mustered troops from the northern tribes to fight against the Midianites. But in another act of insecurity he asked Yahweh for a sign to signal whether or not he would find victory. He himself proposed the test of the wet sheepskin. He laid out a fleece overnight. If it were wet while the surrounding ground was dry, then he would take that as a sign of victory. It was so, but Gideon still was not convinced. He asked for just the opposite the next night, and when it happened Gideon had no choice but to acknowledge that Yahweh was signaling victory and that he would have to get on with the campaign.

Gideon then assembled a fighting force. But like Gideon, they were reluctant warriors. When the soldiers were given the opportunity to return home rather than fight, 22,000 out of 32,000 decided to leave. God told Gideon that this was still too many—he wanted to make clear that the victory would come from him. So the army experienced further attrition after Gideon observed them drinking water from a spring. Only those who brought water hand to mouth rather than by directly lapping the water from the pool were enlisted for the battle. The story seems to dwell on the timidity and even incompetence of these early "warriors," on the way to making the point that Israel's fighting men were less than valiant defenders of the Israelite federation.

Left with only three hundred men, Gideon devised a plan of attack that involved surprise and clever deception. He and his men surrounded the Midianite camp in the middle of the night. Armed with ram's horn trumpets, jars, and torches, on Gideon's signal they shocked the enemy out of sleep by smashing the jars, blowing the trumpets, and holding high the torches. Disoriented, confused, and seemingly outnumbered, the Midianites tried to flee. Gideon's three hundred gave chase and killed many of them. The chase became the occasion for the writer to illustrate the lack of cooperation, and even distrust, among the various tribes. The Ephraimites felt slighted because they had not been invited to the originating attack, and only got to be a part of the mopping up. Then the Israelites in Transjordan at Succoth and Penuel refused to help Gideon.

What happens next relates to the ideology of covenant and kingship, a major concern of the Deuteronomistic historian. After he had killed the last kings of the Midianites, the Israelites begged Gideon to be their ruler. Although he took tribute from them—a share of the booty taken from the defeated Midianites—he refused to be king, saying, "Yahweh will rule over you" (8:23).

In the following story of Gideon's son Abimelech (whose name means "my father is king"), we have the record of an individual's aborted attempt to establish a royal dynasty. Abimelech came to kingship by killing the other seventy sons of Gideon, though overlooking the youngest, Jotham. Abimelech assumed control of Shechem, and by various campaigns sought to control other villages. He died ignominiously after a defender dropped a millstone on his head. Perhaps written by an author critical of monarchy, the tale illustrates the violence-prone and typically self-important character of kings.

■ JEPHTHAH (10:6–12:7)

Jephthah delivered the Israelites of Gilead in Transjordan from the oppression of the Ammonites. He is most notable for the vow he made to Yahweh.

> *30 "If you will give me power over the Ammonites, 31 then whatever comes out of the doors of my house to meet me when I return victorious from the Ammonites will belong to YHWH, and I will sacrifice it up as a burnt offering." (11:30b–31)*

Jephthah was successful in battle, but when he returned home the first to greet him was his daughter. With grace she accepted her fate and had only one request, that she be allowed to roam the hills and weep with her friends, for she was a virgin.

After the victory of the Jephthah-led Gileadites, the Israelites of Ephraim attacked the Israelites of Gilead because they felt slighted, having been left out of the Ammonite conflict. The Gileadites took control of the ford between Gilead and Ephraim and killed any man that could not pronounce the password, *shibboleth*, as they did. Ephraimites were immediately identified because they said *sibboleth*, a dialectal variation. The term has entered the English language and means "test word."

> **Shibboleth.** "A word or sound which a person is unable to pronounce correctly; a word used as a test for detecting foreigners, or persons from another district, by their pronunciation. A peculiarity of pronunciation or accent indicative of a person's origin. A catchword or formula adopted by a party or sect, by which their adherents or followers may be discerned, or those not their followers may be excluded." (*Oxford English Dictionary*)

■ SAMSON (13-16)

Samson is one of the most colorful personalities in the Old Testament. He is a walking contradiction. Brash, bold, and impressively powerful, he is at one and the same time naive and vulnerable. He is physically massive, yet spiritually infantile. The story of Samson is the last story of the judges. As such, we may assume that the editor is telling us something special. Samson epitomizes the age. And in Samson, we have a portrait of Israel in miniature.

The Deuteronomistic editor introduces the story with an abbreviated version of his theological framework. There is no mention of the Israelites crying out for help or repenting.

> 1 The Israelites again did what was bad in YHWH's sight, and YHWH gave them into the hand of the Philistines for forty years. (13:1)

Samson was born to a woman previously unable to have children. An angel of Yahweh delivered the announcement of conception and directed her to raise Samson in a special way. Both she, during pregnancy, and he throughout his life were to refrain from alcoholic beverages, and not eat anything unclean. This implies that from the moment of conception Samson was to be devoted exclusively to Yahweh, a state or condition called the **Nazirite vow.**

By his lifestyle Samson inadvertently demonstrated that neither the Nazirite vow nor his Israelite identity meant anything to him. Against his parents wishes he chose to marry a Philistine woman. One day while going to see her, a lion attacked him. The spirit of Yahweh came upon him and he bare-handedly killed the animal. When later he was traveling the same road to his wedding, he stopped to view the carcass of the lion. A swarm of bees had made a hive there, and he scraped some honey out and ate it. By Hebrew law that honey would have been considered unclean, having been in direct contact with a dead body.

The Samson story is one long record of the love–hate relationship between Samson and the Philistines. He is drawn to them, especially to their beautiful women. Yet every meeting becomes an occasion for him to kill more Philistines. For example, at his wedding he makes a wager using a riddle about the lion and the honey, and loses. Payment of the bet was thirty sets of clothing. Samson handily killed thirty Philistines and stripped them of their garments to pay his debt.

Samson's nemesis was Delilah. Only one of many women with whom he consorted, she was ultimately his undoing. After three unsuccessful attempts, she finally got him to reveal the secret of his strength. Although Samson had enough clues to figure out that she would betray him, he unwittingly told her that if his hair was cut off, he would be vulnerable. She did just that while he was asleep. He woke up helpless and was captured by his foes. The Philistines blinded him and put him to work at hard labor. Then, in prison his hair began to grow back.

During a festival he was brought to the temple of Dagon, the high god of the Philistines, for a command performance. While waiting in the wings he found two central supporting pillars. He prayed to Yahweh for a return of his powers—then toppled those pillars and brought down the stadium. Yahweh had not abandoned him, even though he had abandoned Yahweh. In dying, he killed more Philistines than ever before.

This is the stuff of legends. A great story, full of love and lust, violence and manly challenge. Yet surely the writer is doing more than just telling a good story. He was mirroring Israel in the figure of Samson. Like Samson, Israel was powerful, even invincible when filled with the Spirit of Yahweh. But Samson, like Israel, was indifferent to his special pedigree—conceived through the special intervention of God, and dedicated to him at birth. He lusted after more enticing companions. The women in Samson's life are surely symbols of the foreign gods who continually attracted the Israelites. They were blind after having betrayed the secret of their strength, but Yahweh never totally abandoned them. The time of the judges was a time of political and religious insecurity. But the God of Israel would not leave them.

The book of Judges ends with stories describing the state of tension that existed among the tribes. The tribe of Dan migrated from the coastal plain to the far north of Israel. And some tribes tried to wipe out Benjamin.

In addition to the people's lack of faith in Yahweh, the problem was lack of leadership. The moral condition of the nation deteriorated massively after the death of Joshua. The writer repeatedly uses the statement, "In those days there was no king in Israel . . . all the people did what was right in their own eyes" to characterize the problem. This chaotic situation would soon change. Order and stability would come. The books of Samuel detail the rise of kingship in Israel.

JUDGES AS A WHOLE

The core of the book of Judges is a collection of stories told about Israel's legendary tribal leaders. The independent stories probably existed orally for a long time, transmitted from generation to generation in the vicinity where the particular judge at one time lived. Many of the stories have a setting in the north and were incorporated into the all-Israel story after the destruction of the Northern Kingdom.

Figure 7.5 locates the individual judges in the areas of their activity. Notice how no judge covered all Israel, yet when all are accounted for, they cover virtually the entire spectrum of territories.

The chronology of the book suggests that the Deuteronomistic historian artificially chained the judge stories together to create the feeling of a continuous history such that each generation after the next fell away from Yahweh. If all the time indications are added together, the book spans exactly four hundred years. This is too exact to be an accident, and much too long to fit the archaeological and historical record. A reasonable estimate for the time span of the period of the judges is one hundred fifty years. Evidently, many of the judges actually lived and ruled contemporaneously. Further suggesting a certain artificiality, many of the judges judged for twenty, forty, or eighty years—or in biblical parlance, one-half, one, or two generations respectively. Table 7.1 draws together the geographical and chronological data on the individual judges for easy reference.

The Deuteronomistic historian took up the judges' stories, gave them a theological introduction, and reshaped most of the individual stories to fit the cycle of disobedience outlined in the theological introduction. They were combined in such a way that the Israelites are pictured as continually forgetting Yahweh and falling

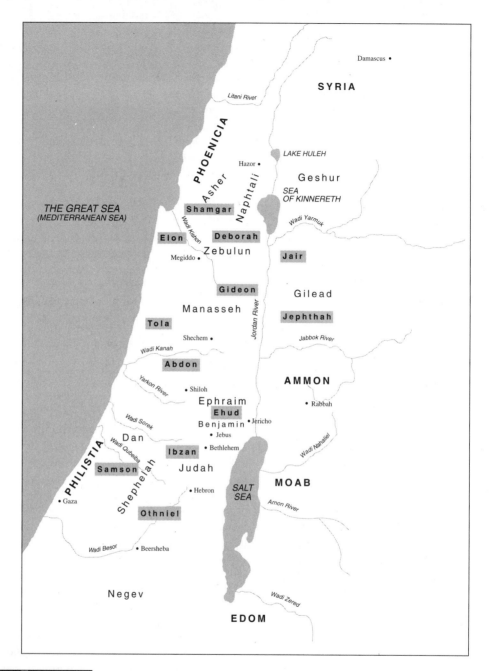

FIGURE 7.5 THE JUDGES OF ISRAEL IN THEIR LOCATIONS

into trouble. Thus, originally local stories were "universalized" into all-Israel tales and combined in linear fashion in order to say something in general about the entire nation and its faith tendencies.

Thus exposing the nation's corporate lack of faithfulness, the Deuteronomistic historian justified the need for a faithful king who would lead the people back to

TABLE 7.1 SYNOPSIS OF THE JUDGES

Judge	Text	Home Territory	Area of Activity	Foe	Years of Oppression	Years Judged
Othniel	3:7-11	Judah?		Cushan-rishathaim king of Aram	8	40
Ehud	3:12-30	Benjamin	Hill country of Ephraim and Moab	Eglon king of Moab, Ammonites, Amalekites	18	80
Shamgar	3:31		Philistia	Philistines		
Deborah	4:1-5:31	Ephraim	Mount Tabor, Naphtali, Zebulun	Sisera, Jabin king of Hazor, Canaanites	20	40
Gideon	6:1-9:57	Manasseh	Manasseh	Midianites, Amalekites, Kedemites		40
Tola	10:1-2	Issachar	Ephraim			23
Jair	10:3-5	Gilead				22
Jephthah	10:6-12:7	Gilead		Ammonites	18	6
Ibzam	12:8-10	Bethlehem				7
Elon	12:11-12	Zebulun				10
Abdon	12:13-15	Ephraim				8
Samson	13:1-16:31	Dan	Philistia	Philistines	40	20
Totals					144	256

their God. The book of Samuel picks up the story at this point, recounting the rise of kingship. Note that the book of Ruth follows the book of Judges in many English versions, but you will not find a discussion of Ruth in the next chapter of our book. Ruth is not counted among the Former Prophets in the Hebrew Bible. Rather, it is one of the Five Scrolls (see Chapter 16).

Table 7.A is a detailed content outline of the book of Joshua.

FOR FURTHER STUDY

Webb (1987) for a literary analysis of the book of Judges, Crenshaw (1978) for a study of Samson.

Chapter 7 Bibliography. See Part 2 Bibliography for general works on the Deuteronomistic history.

QUESTIONS FOR REVIEW

1. What is the theological framework of the book of Judges, and how does this shape the way the tales of individual judges are told?
2. For Ehud, Deborah, Gideon, and Samson, identify the foe and the way each judge achieved victory.

3. How is the book of Judges transitional between the era of Joshua and the rise of kingship?
4. How does the overall shape of the book of Judges, especially the people's cycle of disobedience, reflect its theology of history?

QUESTIONS FOR REFLECTION AND DISCUSSION

1. Think about the character of the major judges. What was wrong with each of them? What do their flaws say about Israel at this time in its history? Do you think the judges are heroes or anti-heroes?
2. Reflect on the writer's perspective on women in these narratives, especially in relation to the Deborah and Jephthah stories. Did the writer have a positive or a negative valuation of females in Israel?

3. The book of Judges presents clear evidence of the role of the editor in shaping the final work. What is the relationship between history-telling and history? Was the Deuteronomistic historian true or untrue to history in the way he shaped the book? What does it really mean to write history?

Chapter 7 Study Guide
- *Chapter summary*
- *Key terms linked to the glossary*
- *Concept questions with answer links*
- *Progress tests: true/false, multiple choice, matching, and identification*

8

SAMUEL: RISE OF THE MONARCHY

FIGURE 8.1 DAVID BY MICHELANGELO

Dynamic and visionary leaders create the character of nations. Especially during periods of social transition, charismatic leaders are critical in shaping the structures of government. Think of the influence of Washington and Jefferson on American democracy, and Lenin and Trotsky on the Bolshevik revolution. It is no surprise, then, that Israel had a large collection of stories about its early national leaders, most significantly, Samuel, Saul, and David.

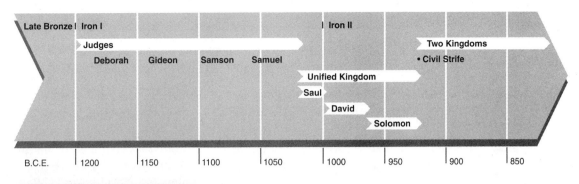

Late Bronze	Iron I					Iron II			

Judges

Deborah	Gideon	Samson	Samuel

Two Kingdoms

• Civil Strife

Unified Kingdom

Saul

David

Solomon

B.C.E.	1200	1150	1100	1050	1000	950	900	850

FIGURE 8.2   BOOKS OF SAMUEL

There is no compelling reason for these books to be called the books of Samuel. They were not written by Samuel, and they deal with Samuel only part of the time. The books might better be entitled "Kingship in Israel" or "The Rise of the Monarchy," because they deal with the development of that institution. In fact, this is very nearly what the books of Samuel and Kings are called in the Septuagint: "Kingdoms I, II, III, and IV."

Nonetheless, associating the content of these books with Samuel is not entirely inappropriate. Samuel is an important, even pivotal, figure. He guides Israel's transition to kingship and bridges the periods of the judges and the monarchy.

The Samuel material is configured as two books in English versions. Originally they were one. Ignoring the book division, the subject matter divides neatly into three main sections on the basis of the editor's transitional passages in 1 Samuel 13:1 and 2 Samuel 1:1. Each section focuses on a major historical figure: Samuel (1 Samuel 1–12), Saul (1 Samuel 13–31), and David (2 Samuel). All three figures were pivotal in the development of Israel's institution of kingship.

We were primed for a treatment of the issue of kingship by the refrain of the book of Judges, "in those days there was no king in Israel; all the people did what was right in their own eyes." As a whole the books of Samuel treat the new institution of monarchy that emerged in Israel. They consider the rocky beginnings of monarchy, its early failures, and its golden age in David.

If we place the leadership issues addressed in the books of Samuel within the context of the time the material was edited, we would have to observe that the question of leadership was especially urgent in the world of the Deuteronomistic historian. During the time of the Babylonian crisis and the exile, one of the reasons for the drastic decline of Israel was the perceived failure of political and religious leadership. If recovery was ever to happen, Israel would need strong leadership. They must have mulled over the questions long and hard—What shape should a new leadership take? Could a king extricate them from their predicament? Would God again speak through Israelite leaders? Presumably the Deuteronomistic historian thought that reexamining the period of the development of kingship might provide some answers to these pressing questions, and additionally might provide some needed instruction for any new leaders that might arise.

Story Line

Samuel's birth was a miracle and he distinguished himself early on as a prophet in Shiloh (1 Samuel 1–3). The Philistines captured the ark of the covenant, later returning it (4–6), but thereby revealed themselves as Israel's most dangerous foe. Samuel rescued Israel from the Philistines, but Israel demanded a king (7–8). Samuel anointed Saul king (9–10) and he demonstrated his leadership by rescuing Jabesh-Gilead (11). But then Saul broke holy war rules and Samuel removed Saul's divine endorsement, though Saul remained in office (12–15). Samuel anointed David king (16) and he demonstrated his character by defeating Goliath and the Philistines (17). This led to an intense rivalry between Saul and David that had Saul pursuing David to kill him, and David always eluding Saul's grasp (18–27). Saul faced the Philistines in a final battle in which he and his sons died (28–31).

David, earlier designated king, now took office in Judah and later all the tribes of Israel accepted his authority (2 Samuel 1–5). David set Jerusalem as his capital and moved the ark of the covenant there (6) and Nathan presented Yahweh's eternal endorsement of the Davidic line (7). David defeated Israel's enemies (8–10) but sinned with Bathsheba and needed to be punished (11–12). This took the form of severe infighting among his sons as they positioned themselves in line for the throne (13–14). David's son Absalom actually took the throne from his father for a time, but was killed for it (15–19). David consolidated his power and further built his empire (20–24).

SAMUEL CYCLE (1 SAMUEL 1-12)

The first part of the books of Samuel deals with its namesake. It treats the birth and career of Israel's last judge figure, **Samuel.**

Biographical Sketch of Samuel

Born to Hannah and Elkanah—1 Samuel 1, 2
Grew up in the temple at Shiloh—3
Defeated Philistines at Mizpah—7
Anointed Saul as Israel's first king—9, 10
Delivered farewell speech—12
Rejected Saul—13, 15
Anointed David to be king in place of Saul—16
Died and was buried at Ramah—25
Appeared to Saul as a spirit—28

■ THE EARLY SAMUEL (1 SAMUEL 1:1-4:1A)

The story first treats the birth of Samuel. Elkanah was a pious man who had two wives. Peninnah had children but **Hannah** had none. It was commonly thought that sterility was a sign of God's disfavor. Hannah felt low and abandoned, yet she also had faith in God. During their annual pilgrimage to the central sanctuary at

Shiloh, Hannah fervently asked Yahweh of Hosts, as he is called in these early chapters, for a son.

Eli was the high priest of the Shiloh temple. When he saw her praying, he mistakenly thought she was drunk, because he could only see her move her mouth and heard no sound; evidently, he could not recognize true piety when he saw it. Note how here and elsewhere one of the interests of the writer is to signal the ineffectiveness of Eli and his high priesthood.

God answered Hannah's prayer. She conceived, bore a son, and named him Samuel, meaning "God heard." In return for the gift of the child, Hannah later gave the child back to God by devoting him to divine service in the temple at Shiloh. Hannah prayed a prayer of thanksgiving at the dedication. A couple of the lines provide the flavor of the prayer:

1 My heart rejoices in YHWH . . . because I rejoice in your victory. 4 The bows of the mighty are broken, but the feeble gird on strength. 6 YHWH kills and gives life, he brings down to Sheol and raises up, 7 YHWH makes poor and makes rich; he humbles, he also exalts. 8 He raises the poor up from the dust, he lifts the needy from the ashes to make them sit with princes. (2:1, 4, 6–8)

The prayer has a rich poetic quality. Some scholars suggest that it once circulated as an independent poem. Maybe so, but what we notice is that it fits well here and was placed strategically to function as the theme of the books of Samuel. Often in works of literature and theology the controlling theme is stated early in the work, and later stories develop that theme. Hannah's song, as this prayer has come to be called, voices a theme that resounds through the books of Samuel. Yahweh raises up, and he pulls down. The humble are given honor and the proud are shamed. Pay special attention to the theme of the reversal of fortunes in the books of Samuel. The theme is typically worked out in an opposing pair of parties, one ascending and one descending.

> **Hannah's and Mary's Songs.** Hannah's Song, 1 Samuel 2:1–10, celebrates God's great reversal. He turns weakness to strength and death to life. Hannah's song is the model for Mary's song of thanksgiving in the New Testament, the Magnificat of Luke 1:46–55.

The first instance of this theme working out in history is the reversal of Hannah's own station in life. Hannah was vindicated over against arrogant Peninnah. Once barren, she now has a son, and a special one at that—one who now works in the holiest shrine in the land. Later, notice how Eli and his sons are contrasted with Hannah and Samuel, and how Saul and David later reverse positions. The Goliath and David pair is another instance of pride and a fall, and on the national level be alert to how the Philistines are set in contrast with the Israelites.

Immediately after Hannah's Song we get a description of the sons of Eli and their priestly practices. They appropriated the sacrifices of the people in a self-serving way, taking the best for themselves. In contrast stands Samuel. Of all things to mention, we get a description of his clothing. He wears a totally unpretentious linen garment. His humility is implicitly contrasted with the presumptuousness of Hophni and Phineas. Eli was unable to control his sons, and as a result Yahweh was about to remove them from the priestly office. The juxtaposition of futures is starkly drawn.

> *25 Yet they would not listen to their father, for it was the will of Yahweh to kill them. 26 The boy Samuel continued to grow in stature and in favor with Yahweh and with the people. (2:25b–26)*

Abiathar and Zadok. The Deuteronomistic historian was closely in touch with the prophetic tradition and frequently makes a point of how the course of history works out the prophetic word spoken by one of the prophets. An anonymous man of God came to Eli (2:27–36) and uttered the judgment word of God that Eli's family would be removed from priestly office and replaced by an unnamed "faithful priest." It would have been anachronistic for the writer to state it here, but later the Deuteronomistic historian shows whom he intended by "faithful priest"—the dynastic priesthood of Zadok, which later supported the Davidic royal line. It is likely that Eli and the Shiloh priesthood are ancestors of the Abiathar priesthood, which was dispossessed when Abiathar lost out to Zadok (see 1 Kings 2:27). This account prefigures that change in clan privileges.

Samuel grew up in Shiloh and worked in the temple there. Although "the word of Yahweh was rare in those days, and visions were infrequent" (3:1), Yahweh appeared to Samuel in the middle of the night as he slept near the **ark of the covenant.** The message he received from Yahweh was the same as that delivered by the "man of God." Eli's family would be removed from office. From then on, the word of Yahweh was revealed to Samuel and he was recognized by everyone to be a prophet.

■ TRAVELS OF THE ARK (1 SAMUEL 4:1B–7:17)

The **Philistines** surface again as the main threat to Israel's existence. Facing the Philistines in battle at Aphek, the Israelites fetched the ark of the covenant from Shiloh thinking it would automatically give them victory. The Philistines proceeded to kill many Israelites, including Hophni and Phineas, and to capture the ark. When Eli heard about these events he died.

When the Philistines took the prize home, the ark wreaked havoc within their cities. After it was placed in the temple of their chief god, Dagon, it caused his statue to topple and its head to break. Then physical illness broke out among the Philistines. They shuttled the ark among their cities until finally they decided to return it to the Israelites. It first arrived back in Israelite territory at the town of Beth-shemesh. After seventy men died there because they had peeked into the ark, the survivors sent it on to Kiriath-yearim, where it remained until David's day (see Figure 8.3 for the travels of the ark).

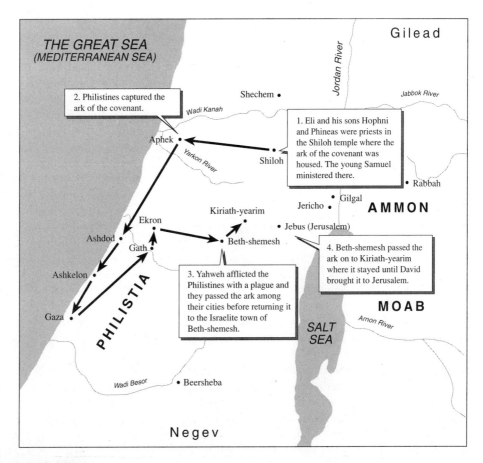

The map shows:

THE GREAT SEA
(MEDITERRANEAN SEA)

Gilead

Jordan River

Jabbok River

2. Philistines captured the ark of the covenant.

Shechem

Wadi Kanah

1. Eli and his sons Hophni and Phineas were priests in the Shiloh temple where the ark of the covenant was housed. The young Samuel ministered there.

Aphek

Yarkon River

Shiloh

Rabbah

Gilgal

Jericho

AMMON

Kiriath-yearim

Ekron

Jebus (Jerusalem)

Ashdod

Gath

Beth-shemesh

4. Beth-shemesh passed the ark on to Kiriath-yearim where it stayed until David brought it to Jerusalem.

Ashkelon

PHILISTIA

3. Yahweh afflicted the Philistines with a plague and they passed the ark among their cities before returning it to the Israelite town of Beth-shemesh.

Gaza

SALT SEA

MOAB

Arnon River

Wadi Besor

Beersheba

Negev

FIGURE 8.3 TRAVELS OF THE ARK

This account of the war with the Philistines interrupts the history of Samuel. In fact, he plays no role in it. The story appears to have been placed here to fulfill the judgment word of Eli's demise. It also demonstrates some things about the power of Israel's Yahweh. First, he refuses to be "used." He cannot be mechanically called on to perform for Israel's benefit, as they had attempted in battle at Aphek. Second, though apparently captured by the Philistines, Yahweh proves to be more powerful than their god Dagon, and Dagon even finds himself bowing down to Yahweh. Third, the Israelites had better respect him, or they will die, as did the men at Beth-shemesh.

Now Samuel returns to the story. He gathered the Israelites together at Mizpah and renewed their commitment to Yahweh. The Philistines fought them there but were defeated. In this part of the account (7:3–17) Samuel is described as Israel's great savior and judge, after the model of the earlier judge heroes. He is talked about as if he is about to pass from the scene, and yet he will be a major force behind the scenes for much of the remainder of First Samuel.

■ SEARCH FOR A KING (1 SAMUEL 8–12)

How does a society manage to move from one leader to another and still retain stability? On whose authority does the next leader take office? Can a nation peacefully change its form of government? Israel faced these challenges when Samuel, the last judge, got old. Apparently, his sons were appreciated no better than Eli's sons, and the people did not want them to take over. The nation lobbied for a fundamental change. They demanded, "Appoint a king to rule us, like the other nations" (8:5).

This was radical and unheard of in Israel! The fundamental covenantal structure that had shaped Israel's life had placed Yahweh in the position of the king, with Israel as his nation. The covenant federation founded at Shechem was based on this model. The people's demand for a human king appeared to be a rejection of that relationship. Samuel was deeply shaken by this as well as by the apparent rejection of his leadership and that of his sons. But Yahweh counseled him that it was really a rejection of himself, and not Samuel. Yahweh also instructed Samuel to go along with the people's demand.

Samuel warned them what a king would be like, drafting their sons and daughters to work for the crown, taxing them heavily, and in general making life difficult. This warning, not incidentally, is a fairly transparent prophetic critique of the monarchy as it actually came to be within Israel. Nobody could say they had not been forewarned!

Next we meet Saul. He is introduced as a tall, handsome man, the son of Kish from the tribe of Benjamin. Searching for some lost donkeys one day, he went to Samuel because of his reputation as a prophet hoping he could locate them. When Saul arrived, Samuel arranged a banquet in his honor, and afterward anointed him king. The ceremony of **anointing** involved pouring olive oil over the head of the person chosen by God. The oil may have been a symbol of the pouring out of the spirit of Yahweh. The person would need this empowerment by the spirit to carry out the responsibilities of office.

> **Anointing.** Although there is evidence that priests and prophets were anointed, the ceremony was especially used to designate kings. A person who has been authorized in this way was called an "anointed one." This is the translation of the Hebrew word *mashiach,* rendered "messiah" in English and "christos" in Greek, from which the title "Christ" was derived. Note that the designation *messiah* did not imply divinity in the Hebrew Bible. It was only a title attached to a divinely designated leader.

On his journey home Saul received proof that he was indeed Yahweh's anointed one. Passersby gave him gifts of bread and wine, presumably in recognition of his office, and he was overcome with ecstatic prophetic behavior, which was evidence that the spirit of Yahweh had in fact come upon him.

But Saul received a mixed review after Samuel formally presented him as Israel's first king. Some of the people assembled at Mizpah hailed him, while others grumbled, "How can he save us?" But shortly thereafter Saul silenced his detractors. When the transjordanian Israelite town of Jabesh-gilead was besieged by the Ammonites, "the spirit of God came upon him powerfully." He put together an army and came to their rescue. Now having seen proof of his leadership ability, the people gathered together at Gilgal and confirmed his kingship.

The time was right for Samuel to step down from national leadership and give way to Saul. Samuel took the occasion of the assembly at Gilgal to deliver a farewell speech (1 Samuel 12:6–25). He reminded the people of the nasty step they had taken—"the wickedness that you have done in the sight of Yahweh is great in demanding a king for yourselves." The farewell speech gave the writer the opportunity to encapsulate his theological perspective. So much of the theology of the Deuteronomistic historian comes out in such big speeches. This particular address expresses once again the Deuteronomistic critique of kingship.

> 14 If you will fear YHWH and serve him and heed his voice and not rebel against the commandment of YHWH, and if both you and the king who rules over you follow YHWH your Elohim, it will be well. 15 But if you do not obey the voice of YHWH, but rebel against the commandment of YHWH, then the hand of YHWH will be against you and your king. (12:14–15)

The king is not absolute. Both the king and the people must be subject to the law of God. The covenant and its demands take precedence over any rights of kingship.

Looking at it holistically, this set of stories is somewhat puzzling. On the one hand, as with this Samuel speech, the view of kingship is quite negative. A king is granted only grudgingly to the Israelites, and only with dire warnings. On the other hand, some passages reflect a positive appreciation of Saul, acknowledging that he was needed by Israel at this time. This situation has led many authorities to posit that chapters 8–12 originally contained two different sources, an anti-monarchy one and a pro-monarchy one. Scholars have termed the pro-monarchy source the A source, and the anti-monarchy source the B source. They are intertwined in an alternating way, as if to say, "we like Saul and we need a king, but we really do not want one." Table 8.1 displays the alternation between these differing viewpoints.

Samuel does not die until chapter 25. Yet the narrative focus changes at this point. Saul takes center stage as he assumes the leadership role in Israel.

TABLE 8.1   SOURCES IN SAMUEL

8:1–22	Samuel's warning against kingship	anti-monarchy
9:1–10:16	Saul and his anointing	pro-monarchy
10:17–27	Another warning by Samuel	anti-monarchy
11:1–15	Saul's victory over the Ammonites	pro-monarchy
12:1–25	Final warning by Samuel	anti-monarchy

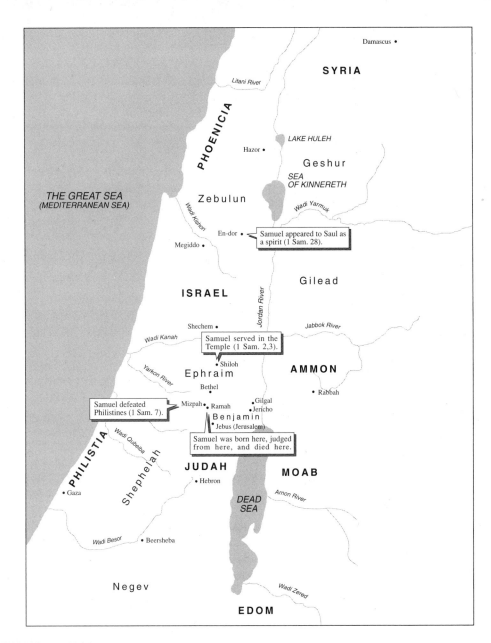

The Great Sea (Mediterranean Sea)

Damascus •

SYRIA

Litani River

PHOENICIA

LAKE HULEH

Hazor •

Geshur

SEA OF KINNERETH

Zebulun

Wadi Kishon

Wadi Yarmuk

En-dor • Samuel appeared to Saul as a spirit (1 Sam. 28).

Megiddo •

Gilead

ISRAEL

Jordan River

Shechem •

Jabbok River

Wadi Kanah

Samuel served in the Temple (1 Sam. 2,3).

• Shiloh

AMMON

Ephraim

Bethel •

• Rabbah

Yarkon River

• Gilgal

Mizpah • Ramah • • Jericho

Samuel defeated Philistines (1 Sam. 7).

Benjamin

• Jebus (Jerusalem)

Samuel was born here, judged from here, and died here.

PHILISTIA

Wadi Qubeiba

Shephelah

JUDAH

MOAB

• Hebron

• Gaza

DEAD SEA

Arnon River

Wadi Besor • Beersheba

Negev

Wadi Zered

EDOM

FIGURE 8.4 CAREER OF SAMUEL

SAUL CYCLE (1 SAMUEL 13–31)

The story of **Saul** is a tragic tale. Having risen to the position of king and having been acclaimed by the people, he fell prey to the temptations of power. Although Samuel was supportive of him early on, he later turned away from Saul. From here on we will see an increasingly frustrated and ineffective Saul, and we will see the corresponding rise of David. Remember the theme of Hannah's song—how the mighty have fallen, but Yahweh exalts the lowly. It works out in the following cycle of narratives.

Biographical Sketch of Saul

Anointed king by Samuel and presented to Israel—9, 10
Rescued Jabesh-gilead and was acclaimed king by Israel—11
Disobeyed Samuel by offering a sacrifice at Michmash—13
Battled Philistines and ordered Jonathan executed—14
Rejected as king by Samuel—15
Tried to kill David—19
Pursued but never caught David; his life spared by David—23, 24, 26
Died in battle with the Philistines on Mount Gilboa—31

■ SAUL'S DISOBEDIENCE (1 SAMUEL 13–15)

Saul gathered the troops at Gilgal to fight the Philistines. Samuel, in the role of army chaplain, was supposed to come and bless the troops. But when he did not show up on time, Saul went ahead and offered the ritual sacrifice. No sooner had the offering been ignited then Samuel appeared and condemned Saul for presuming to function as a priest. This is the first occasion Samuel indicated that Yahweh had rejected Saul and had chosen someone else to take his place as king.

Saul's tendency to make bad judgments (was it a sign that he was no longer in Yahweh's favor, or just a sign that kings tend to make bad decisions?) is seen in the next encounter with the Philistines. Saul's son **Jonathan** surprised a group of Philistines and thereby threw the entire Philistine army into a panic. The Israelites had the opportunity to completely wipe out the Philistines, except that Saul had foolishly decreed that the men should fast. This inappropriate abstention from food seems to signal a kind of misplaced religiosity on Saul's part. In any case, the Israelite warriors did not have the energy to pursue the Philistines to their death. Even worse, Jonathan had not heard about the fasting decree and unwittingly broke his father's command when he ate some wild honey. Saul would have executed Jonathan for disobedience had not Saul's own soldiers stopped him.

Later, Saul had the opportunity to eliminate Israel's oldest enemy, the Amalekites. They were the first ones ever to attack Israel, right after the Hebrews had left Egypt. But Saul did not follow the rule of holy war to completely eradicate the enemy and burn the remains. He took spoils of war and spared Agag, the Amalekite king. Samuel was furious when he found out. He summarily condemned Saul and proclaimed that Yahweh had rejected him as king. Then he himself killed Agag. Samuel completely disowned Saul and would not see him again—that is, until he came up from his grave to haunt Saul.

■ SAUL VERSUS DAVID (1 SAMUEL 16–31)

Competition for high office is often the anvil of national history. The contest is evident on many levels in the books of Samuel: Eli versus Samuel, Samuel versus Saul, and now Saul versus David.

Both having rejected Saul, Samuel and Yahweh turned elsewhere for a new king. They went to a most unlikely place to find one, the insignificant village of Bethlehem in the southern tribe of Judah. Among the sons of Jesse, Yahweh passed by the elder sons and chose the youngest boy, **David**, to be king. This peculiar choice continues the counter-cultural ancestral tradition of passing the promise to the younger son: not Cain but Abel, not Ishmael but Isaac, not Esau but Jacob, not Reuben but Judah and Joseph, not Manasseh but Ephraim.

Samuel anointed David, and immediately the spirit of Yahweh came upon him. In the Hebrew Bible the spirit of God is the power God bestows on select individuals that enables them to perform their God-given task. As if the spirit could not simultaneously be on two people at once, in the next verse we are told that the spirit of Yahweh left Saul and in its place an evil spirit (also from Yahweh) took possession of him. In hopes of calming his troubled mind, Saul hired David to be the court musician. Skilled on the lyre (a type of harp), David comforted Saul, and Saul came to love him dearly.

Again the Philistines harassed the Israelites. This time they camped in the Elah valley near an Israelite garrison. Daily their champion warrior **Goliath** taunted the Israelites, trying to goad them into a fight. None of the Israelites took up the challenge, until one day David came by. He was delivering food to his brothers in the camp when he heard Goliath's challenge. David was astounded that none of the Israelites had the courage to face him. He immediately volunteered himself. Armed with only a slingshot and stones, he faced Goliath in single combat. His first shot struck Goliath in the forehead and knocked him unconscious. David ran over to him and cut off his head. This threw the Philistines into a panic, and the Israelites drove the Philistines away.

There was great rejoicing, and women were singing in the streets, "Saul killed thousands, David killed ten thousands." Everyone, including Saul's own son Jonathan, was enamored with David—everyone except Saul himself. Saul was angered by the popularity of David. From then on he tried actively to eliminate David in one way or another. He tried to spear him in the palace, but David was too quick. He made him commander of the army, hoping he would die in battle, but David's popularity only grew as he won battle after battle.

In a plot to have the Philistines kill him, Saul offered David the honor of marrying one of his daughters and thereby officially joining the royal family. As always in the ancient world, a bride did not come freely. A bride price had to be paid to her parents. Saul stipulated the bride price to be one hundred Philistine foreskins. Saul was, of course, expecting David to get killed in the process. But David, always ready to do Saul one better, instead brought him two hundred. Saul had no choice but to give David his daughter **Michal** in marriage.

Frustrated and now obsessed with eliminating his rival, Saul planned to assassinate David. In an ironic turn, David was kept informed of Saul's plans by both Jonathan and Michal. Saul's own son and daughter betrayed him and took David's side, in effect acknowledging that he would be Israel's next king. The loyalty of Jonathan is especially remarkable, because by aiding David he was implicitly renouncing his own claim to the throne.

David found it necessary to flee. He found help and refuge wherever he could. The priest at Nob gave him provisions, and later was killed for it by Saul's men.

FIGURE 8.5 **PHILISTINE ANTROPOID COFFIN**   This Philistine pottery coffin was found at Beth-shean and dates roughly to the time of Saul (twelfth–eleventh centuries B.C.E.). The coffin is the size of an adult. The removable lid bears a face, perhaps a likeness to the one interred inside. This coffin and other material evidence prove that the Philistines occupied Beth-shean at this time, attesting how far east they had penetrated and how dire the Philistine threat really was.

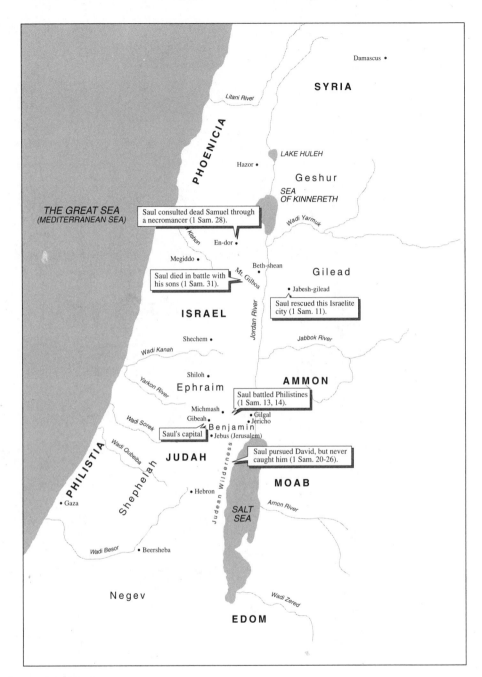

Damascus •

SYRIA

Litani River

THE GREAT SEA
(MEDITERRANEAN SEA)

PHOENICIA

LAKE HULEH

Hazor •

Geshur

SEA
OF KINNERETH

Wadi Yarmuk

Kishon

En-dor •

Saul consulted dead Samuel through
a necromancer (1 Sam. 28).

Megiddo •

Beth-shean •

Gilead

Mt. Gilboa

Saul died in battle with
his sons (1 Sam. 31).

• Jabesh-gilead

Saul rescued this Israelite
city (1 Sam. 11).

ISRAEL

Jordan River

Shechem •

Jabbok River

Wadi Kanah

Shiloh •

Yarkon River

Ephraim

AMMON

Michmash •

Saul battled Philistines
(1 Sam. 13, 14).

Gibeah •

• Gilgal
• Jericho

Wadi Sorek

Benjamin

Saul's capital

• Jebus (Jerusalem)

Saul pursued David, but never
caught him (1 Sam. 20-26).

PHILISTIA

Wadi Qubeiba

JUDAH

Judean Wilderness

MOAB

Shephelah

• Hebron

SALT
SEA

Arnon River

• Gaza

Wadi Besor

• Beersheba

Negev

Wadi Zered

EDOM

FIGURE 8.6 CAREER OF SAUL

Those who refused to help, such as Nabal, paid the price. David also stayed for
a time with the Philistines, cleverly making it look like he was on their side, while
never really injuring Israelites. Twice while he was hiding in the Judean wilderness
David had the opportunity to kill Saul, who was chasing him. Both times he held

back out of respect for Saul's office. Each time the piety of David is set in contrast to the obsessive behavior of Saul.

Meanwhile, pressure from the Philistines continued to grow, driving the Israelites back toward the Jordan River. Saul was hard pressed and tried to make a stand at Mount Gilboa. He was at his wits' end as the time for battle approached. Samuel was dead, so he had no one to give him counsel, no one to bless the troops before the fight, and no one to assure him of the presence of Yahweh. Desperate for a word from Yahweh, Saul approached a professional diviner. In a seance-like encounter the spirit of Samuel appeared before him.

> 15 *"Tell me what I should do." 16 Samuel said, "Why do you ask me? YHWH has turned from you and is now your enemy. 17 YHWH has done to you just what he spoke through me. YHWH has torn the kingdom out of your hand and has given it to your companion David, 18 because you did not obey the voice of YHWH." (28:15–18)*

Looking for help and assurance, Saul received anything but a word of comfort. Samuel only confirmed his, and Yahweh's, earlier rejection of the benighted king. Fulfilling the prophetic word of Samuel, the kingdom was taken away as Saul and his sons died in battle on Mount Gilboa. When the Philistines came upon Saul's body, they beheaded him, stripped him of his armor, and hung his corpse on the wall of Beth-shean for all to see. Hearing of Saul's demise, the citizens of Jabesh-gilead, whom Saul earlier had rescued, bravely recovered his body, along with the bodies of his sons, and gave them respectful disposal.

DAVID CYCLE (2 SAMUEL 1–24)

The second book of Samuel deals with David's consolidation of power. He subsumed under his own authority all the territory of Judah and the northern tribes. For the first time all the tribes were united in a cohesive national entity.

Biographical Sketch of David
Anointed king by Samuel—1 Samuel 16
Killed Goliath, the Philistine—17
Befriended Jonathan, Saul's son—18
Pursued by Saul, took refuge in Philistia—19–30
Mourned the deaths of Saul and Jonathan—2 Samuel 1
Anointed king over Judah—2
Anointed king over Israel—5
Captured Jebus (Jerusalem) and made it the capital—5
Brought the ark of the covenant to Jerusalem—6
Given the Davidic covenant promises by Nathan—7
Committed adultery with Bathsheba—11
Fled Jerusalem after Absalom's coup d'état—15
Built an altar on Araunah's threshing floor—24
Died and Solomon followed him as king—1 Kings 2

■ DAVID'S RISE TO POWER (2 SAMUEL 1–8)

Saul was mortally wounded and asked a soldier to finish him off. That soldier ran to David, Saul's crown in hand, with what he thought would be news well received. David was outraged that this man had finished off Saul, even though Saul realistically had had no chance for survival. What do we see here? Do we see David turning as irrational as Saul? Is this the beginning of David's decline?

Probably not. David was genuinely pained that his one-time mentor, Saul, was dead. David's emotions come out in the sensitive and touching eulogy David delivered upon the deaths of Saul and Jonathan (2 Samuel 1:19–27). This poem, not coincidentally, picks up the theme of the books of Samuel first articulated in Hannah's Song—"How the mighty have fallen!" (see especially verses 19, 25, 27). Remember, the proud are humbled and the humble exalted.

Yet in addition, David's reaction reveals his political savvy. Contrary to the expected reaction, though Saul was his rival, he did not express his approval nor would he condone in any way the death of Saul. He did nothing that might serve to alienate the loyal followers of Saul, which was virtually the entire entity of northern Israel. Even in this time of tragedy David kept the door open for the friends of Saul to join him in political union.

David went to Judah, his home tribe, to rally support now that Saul was dead. He set up his headquarters at **Hebron,** the regional capital of Judah. David ruled from Hebron for seven and a half years. Meanwhile in the north, Ishbaal had been proclaimed king by **Abner,** the commander of Saul's army. The opposing sides were now drawn, the house of David against the house of Saul. But while David's power base got stronger, Ishbaal's got weaker. Seeing that the future lay with David, Abner, Ishbaal's commander, defected. This in turn provoked **Joab,** David's commander. He and Abner had earlier had a disagreement, and in addition, perhaps Joab felt insecure in his position as David's right-hand man. Joab secretly met Abner and killed him, thus getting rid of a serious rival.

> **Shameful Name.** The Hebrew text gives Ishbaal's name as Ishbosheth, which means "man of shame." Based on 1 Chronicles 8:33 and 9:39 we know his name originally to have been Ishbaal, meaning "man of Baal." The name was changed to eliminate the divine element Baal and at the same time to disparage this pretender to the throne. The same defamation technique was applied to the name of Jonathan's son Mephibosheth, originally named Meribbaal.

David lamented Abner's death and blamed the treachery on Joab. Abner was well respected in northern Israel. Moreover, his presence in David's camp might have proven troublesome, yet none of the blame for his death fell on David. David was again sensitive to the feelings of Saul's loyalists and did not provoke their ill will.

Conditions in the north deteriorated completely. Ishbaal was attacked by two of his officers. They killed and decapitated him, carrying the head to David in Hebron as proof of their new loyalty to him. David, as we have come to expect, was not impressed; quite the opposite. He had those two traitors killed, again sending a signal that he did not condone violence done to the house of Saul.

Completely without direction or leadership, the tribes of the north asked David to become their king as well. With a covenant, David assumed kingship over both Judah and Israel, reigning over a united nation. David very wisely decided he must move his capital from Hebron. If left there it would seem he was favoring his ancestral tribe of Judah. David and his men attacked and occupied what was then called **Jebus,** to be identified with **Jerusalem.** David had it called "the city of David" to indicate it was directly under his command. Then he rid the surrounding territory of Philistines, providing greater security for his new capital city. Finally, in an act of great piety and even greater political astuteness, he fetched the ark of God from Kiriath-yearim and brought it into Jerusalem. The presence of the great symbol of the tribal federation and focus of earlier religious devotion firmly established Jerusalem as the religious center of the newly unified nation.

David had a desire to build a shrine for the ark in Jerusalem. **Nathan,** the Jerusalem royal court prophet, received word from Yahweh that David should not build Yahweh a house. With a divine double entente, Yahweh said that instead he would build a house for David, meaning a perpetual dynasty. Then, in what is termed the **Davidic Covenant,** Yahweh pledged his enduring support for the line of David:

> 16 Your house and your kingdom will be established firmly forever before me. Your throne will be established forever. (7:16)

Although Davidic kings might sin, Yahweh would never remove his support from them, as he had done with Saul. This promise is the foundation for messianic expectations in Judaism and Christianity. Yahweh promised he would never abandon the offspring of David. It implied, also, that there would be a divinely sponsored king over Israel forever.

David was at the peak of his career. Endorsed by Yahweh, loved by his people, he also managed to defeat Israel's inveterate enemies. Chapter 8 sums up his victories. He subdued the Philistines. Never again would they be a threat to Israel. He defeated the Arameans, the Moabites, and the Edomites, giving Israel peace on every side. Verse 15 concisely summarizes the era of righteous rule David inaugurated. David ushered in a time of *shalom*, and it would be remembered as the golden age of Israel.

> 15 So David ruled over all Israel. David administered justice with equity to all his people. (8:15)

David was at the height of his career. But, as you might have suspected, things were almost too good to be true. Although David had the support of Yahweh and, indeed, of the entire nation, he became complacent, presumptuous, hence ready for a fall. Remember the theme: the proud will be humbled and the humble exalted.

■ DYNASTIC SUCCESSION (2 SAMUEL 9–20)

This portion of 2 Samuel, along with 1 Kings 1–2, details the family history of David as his sons fight with each other over who would follow David on the throne, hence *dynastic succession*. The narrative reads like a short story, and may have been composed from court records. Authorities have variously termed this account the "succession narrative" and the "court history of David."

By the way the writer introduces the **Bathsheba** story, the narrator signals that something ominous had happened to David.

> *1 In the spring of the year, the time when kings normally go out to do battle, David sent Joab with his officers and all Israel. They devastated the Ammonites and besieged Rabbah. But David remained in Jerusalem. (11:1)*

David's troubles began when he neglected his royal responsibilities. Shirking his military duty—remember, it was his courage in facing Goliath that brought him national acclaim—it is no wonder that he got into trouble. David spied a beautiful woman from the roof of his house and asked her to the palace. Though married to Uriah, Bathsheba accepted David's invitation—who could refuse the king?—and David had an affair with her. Matters got complicated after it became apparent that she was pregnant, even though her husband had been at the Ammonite battlefront with David's army. David tried to cover up his responsibility for the pregnancy by recalling Uriah to Jerusalem in the hope that he would sleep with his wife. After making his report to the king, Uriah refused to enjoy the pleasures of home out of loyalty to his troops, certainly an ironic twist that sets David's sin in stark relief.

David had Uriah killed and, with a grand kingly show of caring, he wed the widow. No doubt all Israel admired their sovereign for marrying Israel's newest widow, and one with child at that. David assumed he had managed to keep his sins of adultery and murder hidden, until Nathan exposed his guilt. This would be the test of Yahweh's commitment to David. Would Yahweh abandon him, as he had abandoned Saul after Saul sinned?

On analysis, David's sins were just as serious as Saul's, if not worse. For Saul's sins, Yahweh denied dynastic succession and removed his favor from the king. But Yahweh did not react the same way to David's sins. An inquisitive reader would want to know why.

David certainly deserved to be removed from office, but Yahweh remained true to the spirit of the Davidic covenant. For the sake of the covenant promise David was allowed to remain on the throne. Yet David was not given blanket forgiveness without discipline. He was punished by the death of the baby born to Bathsheba. Furthermore, the sins of adultery and murder that he had committed in secret would be committed in public by his sons. Indeed, there is "poetic justice" here. David's own sins would be duplicated within his own family, yet in an even more heinous way. Yahweh delivered the following judgment oracle through Nathan the prophet.

> *10 "The sword will not leave your house, because you have despised me, and have taken the wife of Uriah the Hittite to be your wife." 11 Thus says YHWH, "I will raise up trouble against you from within your own house; and I will take your wives, and before your eyes give them to your neighbor. He will lie with your wives in the full light of day. 12 You did it secretly, but I will do this thing in front of all Israel, and in the full light of day." (12:10–12)*

This prophetic word of punishment becomes the literary-theological age the following narrative. This punishment works out in the family of David a sons vie for the right to follow him on the throne.

Amnon was the crown prince, the first in line for the throne. His particular sexual sin was his obsessive infatuation with his half-sister Tamar. One day, feigning illness, he deceived her, trapped her, and then raped her. Then, as the ultimate act of rejection, he refused to acknowledge her in any way. Her full brother **Absalom** took revenge on Amnon two years later and killed him.

David loved Absalom deeply, but he had no choice except to punish him. He exiled Absalom and would not allow him to appear in Jerusalem. But Absalom was a clever man, the consummate politician, much like his father. He was also very handsome. Eventually he was allowed to come near the city gate of Jerusalem, but no farther. There he endeared himself to the people. He intercepted citizens as they came looking for David's help. Instead, he offered his own services: "No need to go to the king. I will take care of you." In this way, the text says, "Absalom stole the hearts of the people of Israel."

Having won over the populace, he made a run for the crown. First, he proclaimed himself king in Hebron, the place David had first become king. Then, he gathered military support and attacked Jerusalem. Realizing he was powerless to resist, David fled into the Judean wilderness. Absalom took control of Jerusalem, and in a public display of power took David's concubines and slept with them on the roof of the palace, in full view of the citizenry. What David had done in secret, his son did in public.

Yet David was not totally without support. He had left Hushai, one of his trusted counselors, behind. Hushai feigned support for Absalom, but in fact he was loyal to David, and worked to frustrate Absalom's plans. He gave advice to Absalom that reversed the advice of Ahithophel, another royal counselor. Hushai's advice enabled David to make good his escape and eventually consolidate his strength. His advice rejected, Ahithophel went out and killed himself.

When finally Absalom mounted an attack on David in the wilderness, it was too late. Absalom's men were defeated, and he himself was killed by Joab, David's commander. Although almost incapacitated by grief, David returned to Jerusalem and resumed control.

■ DAVID'S LAST DAYS (2 SAMUEL 21–24)

These last chapters contain various materials pertaining to David and his rule but not in any clear order, and they seem to be chronologically jumbled. There is poetic material written by David in chapter 22, which finds a virtual duplicate in Psalm 18. There is a list of David's warriors. And there is an account of David's sin in taking a census of the people, read by God as a sign of his lack of faith. Instead of relying on Yahweh, he was counting the strength of his army. Yahweh punished him and the nation with a plague.

The book ends with David purchasing the property of Araunah and offering a sacrifice, which stopped the plague. The site of the altar, the threshing floor of Araunah, became the site of the Jerusalem temple. In its own way, the end of Samuel points ahead to the next momentous stage in the history of the monarchy, the reign of Solomon and the building of the temple.

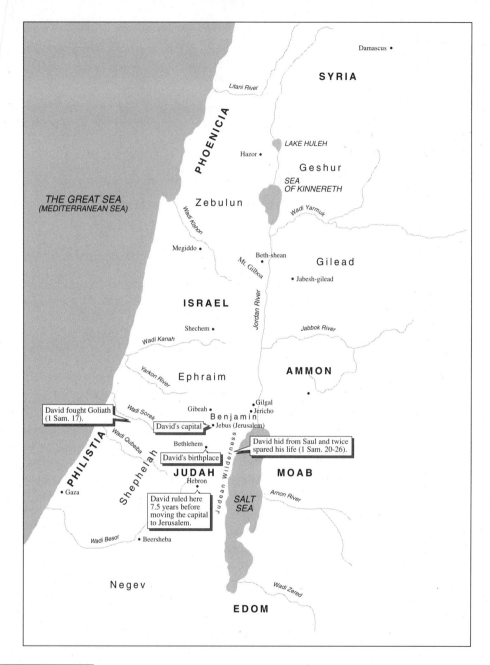

Damascus •

SYRIA

Litani River

PHOENICIA

LAKE HULEH

Hazor •

Geshur

THE GREAT SEA
(MEDITERRANEAN SEA)

Zebulun

*SEA
OF KINNERETH*

Wadi Kishon

Wadi Yarmuk

Megiddo •

Beth-shean •

Gilead

Mt. Gilboa

• Jabesh-gilead

ISRAEL

Jordan River

Shechem •

Jabbok River

Wadi Kanah

Ephraim

AMMON

Yarkon River

David fought Goliath
(1 Sam. 17).

Wadi Sorek

Gibeah • • Gilgal
• Jericho
Benjamin

David's capital → • Jebus (Jerusalem)

PHILISTIA

Wadi Qubeiba

Bethlehem •

David hid from Saul and twice
spared his life (1 Sam. 20-26).

David's birthplace

Shephelah

JUDAH

MOAB

Hebron •

• Gaza

David ruled here
7.5 years before
moving the capital
to Jerusalem.

SALT
SEA

Arnon River

Wadi Besor

• Beersheba

Negev

Wadi Zered

EDOM

FIGURE 8.7   CAREER OF DAVID

SAMUEL AS A WHOLE

The books of Samuel are a composition that went through various stages of development. They incorporate blocks of material that existed at one time separately, such as the Ark Narrative (1 Samuel 4:1–7:1), the story of Saul's rise (1 Samuel 9:1–11:15), the story of David's rise (1 Samuel 16–31), and the Succession Narrative (2 Samuel 9–20; 1 Kings 1–2).

The rise of kingship is the central agenda of the books. The retention of the two sources on the monarchy, one positive and the other negative, allows the text to give a nuanced and realistic evaluation of the new institution. Kingship was part of the plan of God to deliver the people, but it also arose out of the people's disobedience and resulted from their turning away from the theocratic ideals of the Mosaic covenant.

An editor shaped the diverse materials into a linear history that incorporated a prophetic critique of the establishment of the monarchy. Within this history, Samuel was the main figure acting on God's behalf to monitor this new institution. The rise of kingship culminated in the divine covenant established with the house of David. And the lessons of David's career reinforced the need for absolute dependence on God, along with obedience to the Torah that would hold in check a king's impulse to exalt himself above the law.

On the literary plane, the book was cogently organized into three cycles of stories, each centering on a central player in the rise of kingship. The literary-theological theme that unites these cycles and reinforces the supremacy of divine justice is the one articulated in Hannah's Song: the proud will be humbled and the humble exalted.

The final stage of Samuel's editorial development came when this prophetic history was incorporated into the larger Deuteronomistic History. This stage is marked by theological editorializing, including chapters such as 1 Samuel 8 and 1 Samuel 12, which reflect the Deuteronomistic historian's particular theological point of view.

Table 8.A is a detailed content outline of the book of Joshua.

FOR FURTHER STUDY

Brueggemann (1990) for commentary on the books of Samuel.

Chapter 8 Bibliography. See Part 2 Bibliography for general works on the Deuteronomistic History.

QUESTIONS FOR REVIEW

1. What are the three cycles of stories in the books of Samuel?

2. What major national institution developed in the books of Samuel? What theological struggle was associated with its establishment?

3. What literary-theological theme is articulated in Hannah's Song? List the many ways it works out concretely in Samuel.

4. What is the Davidic covenant? Why was it important?

5. What were the two conflicting views of kingship in Samuel?

QUESTIONS FOR REFLECTION AND DISCUSSION

1. What universal issues concerning national leadership surface in the books of Samuel? What perspectives on the issues are presented, and how may these perspectives provide guidance for today?

2. Compare the careers of Saul and David. How were they alike and how were they different? What was the effect of the Davidic covenant on the course of David's life? What was its effect on the course of the nation?

3. The books of Samuel seem almost cynically preoccupied with the rise and fall of leadership. The proud will be humbled and the humble will be exalted. Do you think the author of Samuel is here writing a treatise on human nature and the politics of power? Is it inevitable that powerful leaders become arrogantly self-important? Do you think it is unavoidable that power corrupts, and that absolute power corrupts absolutely?

Chapter 8 Study Guide

- *Chapter summary*
- *Key terms linked to the glossary*
- *Concept questions with answer links*
- *Progress tests: true/false, multiple choice, matching, and identification*

KINGS: HISTORY OF THE KINGDOMS

9

FIGURE 9.1   **SENNACHERIB'S ATTACK ON LACHISH**   This scene is from the palace reliefs of Nineveh and depicts Sennacherib's attack on Lachish, a town in Judah he captured in 701 B.C.E. Later, according to 2 Kings 19:35 and as in the Byron poem below, the angel of Yahweh decimated the Assyrian army.

The Destruction of Sennacherib
by George Gordon, Lord Byron (1815)

I
The Assyrian came down like the wolf on the fold,
And his cohorts were gleaming in purple and gold;
And the sheen of their spears was like stars on the sea,
When the blue wave rolls nightly on deep Galilee.

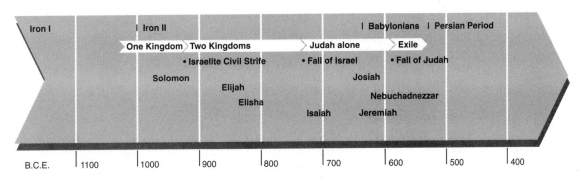

FIGURE 9.2   BOOKS OF KINGS

II
Like the leaves of the forest when Summer is green,
That host with their banners at sunset were seen:
Like the leaves of the forest when Autumn hath blown,
That host on the morrow lay withered and strown.

III
For the angel of Death spread his wings on the blast,
And breathed in the face of the foe as he passed;
And the eyes of the sleepers waxed deadly and chill,
And their hearts but once heaved—and for ever grew still!

Like the books of Samuel, the books of Kings were originally one. The story line of Kings continues the history of Israel's leadership that began in the books of Samuel. But Kings differs from Samuel in at least one feature. It does not have a small number of focal figures but instead traces the line of kings from David all the way to the exile.

Kings is a continuation of the Deuteronomistic History, which (as its name implies) traces its pedigree back to Deuteronomy. It shares a basic theological perspective with the other books of the DH. Its foundation is the covenant that united Yahweh and Israel and defined Israel's relationship to Yahweh. A concern for the quality of Israel's religious life is central to the theology of the Deuteronomistic History. If the people were faithful and loyal to Yahweh, then they would be protected and blessed by Yahweh. Otherwise, the nation would suffer.

The quality of Israel's devotion to Yahweh was measured by the exclusiveness of its religious focus. If Yahweh alone was worshiped, the people were judged faithful. If Yahweh was worshiped only in Jerusalem and in the prescribed manner, the people were judged loyal.

Note especially the theological judgments applied to the kings. It is not the king's effectiveness in domestic or international politics that the DH evaluates; it is the king's effectiveness as a religious leader and model citizen. Watch how often the writer evaluates a king by whether he (rarely) "did right" or (most often) "did evil" in the eyes of Yahweh. Kings who rejected idolatry and promoted religious reform, such as **Josiah,** were approved. Kings who encouraged or even tolerated non-Yahwistic practices were denounced.

The DH's prejudice against the Northern Kingdom is especially obvious. No ruler from the north is given approval, regardless of his accomplishments. Nothing they do can be acceptable because Israel (as the Northern Kingdom was called) was established on religiously shaky ground. Jeroboam, its first king, broke with the divinely authorized Davidic dynasty and the Jerusalem temple, and created alternate worship centers that employed golden calves as religious symbols. Because none of the following kings eliminated these centers, each is categorically condemned. Ultimately, because of the golden calves at Dan and Bethel, the Northern Kingdom was destroyed.

Story Line

Solomon gained control of the monarchy in Jerusalem by eliminating his rivals Adonijah and Joab (1 Kings 1–2). He was recognized for his wisdom (3–4) and effectively made Jerusalem the religious capital of Israel by building the temple (5–8). Solomon lost popular and divine support due to his excesses; too much public debt and too many wives (9–11). After Solomon died, the northern territories rebelled against Solomon's son Rehoboam and created their own nation, called Israel, led by Jeroboam (12–14). Israel's monarchy was less stable than Judah's until Omri took the throne (15–16). Omri's son Ahab promoted Baal practices in Israel and was challenged by the prophet Elijah and others (17–22).

The prophet Elisha followed Elijah in opposition to Omri's Israelite dynasty (2 Kings 1–8). Jehu bloodily eliminated the house of Omri and established his own dynasty; Israel and Judah coexisted (9–16). Assyria conquered and destroyed Israel (17) and attacked Judah, but Hezekiah's Judah survived (18–20). Evil king Manasseh (21) was followed by good king Josiah who reformed religion in Judah (22–23). But Judah stood helpless before Nebuchadnezzar of Babylon, who destroyed Jerusalem and deported many Judeans (24–25).

We can divide the books of Kings into three sections based on historical content. The first section deals with the kingdom of Solomon, the second with the civil conflict that led to national division and the parallel histories of Israel and Judah, and the third with the history of Judah down to the Babylonian exile.

SOLOMON AND THE UNIFIED MONARCHY (1 KINGS 1–11)

The writer of kings gives the reign of **Solomon** a great deal of attention. It is true that he ruled for a long time (961–921 B.C.E.), indeed, a "perfect" forty years. But more importantly in the mind of the Deuteronomistic historian, the reign of Solomon is the first fulfillment of one of the important parts of the Davidic covenant articulated in 2 Samuel 7. During his tenure as king the great temple to Yahweh was built in Jerusalem.

Biographical Sketch of Solomon
Became king and secured the throne—1 Kings 1–2
Received wisdom from God and demonstrated it—3–4
Built a temple in Jerusalem for Yahweh—5–8

Was visited by the Queen of Sheba—10
Married 700 wives and 300 concubines—11
Died and was buried in Jerusalem—12

■ SOLOMON VERSUS ADONIJAH (1 KINGS 1–2)

These first two chapters relate how Solomon secured the right to follow David as king of all Israel. David was now an old man. He was so frail that he needed a female companion to keep him warm at night; a beautiful young woman named Abishag was given the task. **Adonijah** was the eldest remaining son and naturally expected to inherit the throne. He had the support of Joab and the priest Abiathar. Together they held a coronation ceremony in which Adonijah was proclaimed king.

> **Succession History.** Many authorities see 1 Kings 1–2 as the conclusion of an originally independent record called the Succession History, or the Court History of David, comprising 2 Samuel 9–20 and 1 Kings 1–2. The appendixes of 2 Samuel 21–24 break the continuity. The canonical ordering of books, however, positions these first chapters of Kings as the introduction to the history of Solomon's kingdom, rather than the conclusion of a history of succession.

Nathan, the prophet who supported David, and others objected to Adonijah's kingship. They strongly promoted Solomon, a younger son, for the throne—continuing the tradition and biblical motif of the younger son supplanting the older. Apparently, the process of the dynastic succession of the eldest had not yet been firmly established.

> **Yahwist and the Younger Son.** Think of Isaac supplanting Ishmael, Jacob over Esau, Ephraim over Manasseh, and David over his older brothers when Samuel came to find a king to replace Saul. Perhaps the reason the Yahwist was so interested in stories about divine preference for the younger son over the first born was the need to justify the rise of Solomon to the throne over his older rival brothers.

Siding with Solomon were **Bathsheba,** his mother, Zadok, another priest, and Benaiah, one of David's loyal commanders. They had the support of David and held their own coronation ceremony for Solomon. Evidently Solomon also had popular support and a broader power base, so Adonijah gave up his claim to the throne and asked Solomon for forgiveness.

When he was about to die, David counseled his son Solomon to remain faithful using words reminiscent of Yahweh's charge to Joshua (Joshua 1) and recollecting the promise of the Davidic covenant, all heavily bearing the stamp of the Deuteronomistic outlook.

2 I am about to go the way of all people. Be strong and courageous 3 and keep the will of YHWH your God, by walking in his ways and keeping his statutes, commandments, ordinances and testimonies as written in the Torah

FIGURE 9.3 **HORNED ALTAR** This horned altar from Beersheba is similar to the altar of the tabernacle. Joab sought refuge by holding onto the horns of the altar, but Solomon killed him anyway (1 Kings 2:28–29).

of Moses, so that you may prosper in everything you do and wherever you go. 4 Then YHWH will affirm his word which he spoke concerning me: "If your heirs watch their way and walk before me in faithfulness, with all their heart and with all their soul, then you will not fail to have a successor on the throne of Israel." (2:2–4)

Not one to give up easily, Adonijah made a veiled play for the throne after David died. Through Bathsheba he asked Solomon for permission to marry Abishag, David's former concubine. When Solomon heard the request he read into it a challenge to his power and accused Adonijah of treason. Apparently, if one possessed the king's harem, then he was *de facto* king. We might recall how this type of move telegraphed to all Jerusalem that Absalom was king—when he slept with David's wives on the roof of the palace. Solomon took this provocation seriously and put Adonijah to death. Shortly afterward Joab, who had supported Adonijah's claim to kingship, was also executed (see Figure 9.3). Abiathar, the priest who had sided with Adonijah, was exiled to Anathoth.

Abiathar and the Deuternomist. In a Deuteronomistic editorial note we are told that this last move fulfilled the prophetic word of condemnation voiced against the house of Eli (2:27; compare 1 Samuel 2–3). Abiathar's support of Adonijah justifies the expulsion of the house of Abiathar and its exile to Anathoth in favor of the priesthood of Zadok. The rights of priesthood in

Jerusalem were jealously guarded, and this explains how the Zadokite priesthood came to power. This note may be especially enlightening if the contention of Friedman (1987) is correct that the writer of Deuteronomy was Jeremiah. We know that Jeremiah hailed from Anathoth, and authorities speculate that he came from the line of Abiathar, ultimately tracing his lineage to Eli of Shiloh.

Having neutralized all potential rivals, by either exile or execution, Solomon was secure on the throne. As the writer notes, "The kingdom was firmly in the hand of Solomon" (2:46).

■ SOLOMON'S WISDOM (1 KINGS 3–4)

Solomon's reign began auspiciously. When Yahweh came to him in a dream at Gibeon offering to grant him his wish, Solomon could have asked for anything. Instead of choosing wealth, longevity, or political security, he asked for the wisdom to discern good and evil so that he could rule God's people well. Gratified that Solomon had chosen so wisely (the wisdom of Solomon was that he was wise enough to choose wisdom), Yahweh granted him "a wise and perceptive mind" (3:12)—and provided the other options as a bonus.

As so often happens in the literature of the Hebrew Bible, the next story provides evidence of what had just been promised. In what is perhaps the most famous story involving Solomon, two women come to him looking for justice. Each had an infant, but by accident one of them had suffocated her child and had switched her dead baby with the other woman's living baby. Both now claimed the living infant was theirs. Solomon cleverly cut through the conflicting claims in this way: He ordered that a sword be brought to the court and offered to give each woman half of the disputed child. As he had hoped, the real mother revealed herself when she relinquished her claim in order to spare the child's life.

Solomon's wisdom was celebrated far and near. Even the Queen of Sheba heard of his reputation and came to bask in his wisdom. Legend has it that he was the wisest person in the world. The text also tells us that in addition to judicious decision making he was renowned for composing 3,000 proverbs and 1,005 songs, and for analyzing flora and fauna in what appears to be an early scientific endeavor. By doing the latter, Solomon follows in the venerable tradition of Adam who, according to the Yahwist account of creation (which, not by accident, was likely written during Solomon's reign), called all the animals by name.

The writer tells us that Solomon set up twelve provincial districts for the purposes of administration and taxation. The boundaries of these districts did not conform to tribal boundaries. This appears to have been Solomon's attempt to sublimate tribal loyalties and create a sense of national purpose. But in so doing he seems to have created a dissatisfaction that contributed to civil war shortly after his death. By placing the account of this change within the chapters reviewing his wisdom, the writer may have been suggesting that this administrative move was a manifestation of Solomon's wisdom. If so, his wisdom backfired. The importance of the figure of Solomon for the tradition of wisdom in Israel will be examined in Part 3.

■ BUILDING THE TEMPLE (1 KINGS 5–8)

Solomon set about building the temple in fulfillment of the terms of the covenant Yahweh had made with David. He contracted Hiram of Tyre to supply the building materials and skilled craftsmen in return for food supplies. There were cost overruns, however, and Solomon ended up paying his bill to Hiram by deeding over territory in the north of Israel. This, of course, did not sit well with the Israelites living there.

Nor did another policy. Solomon needed workers for the massive temple project, as well as for building his palace. He conscripted Israelites and constrained them to provide manual labor (a practice termed the *corvée*, or "unpaid labor force"), thereby further alienating his constituency. This reminded them of the bitter oppression of Pharaoh in Egypt before the exodus when the Hebrews were forced to work on royal building projects.

The temple was a magnificent structure (see Figure 9.4). Its walls were made of stone overlaid with wood paneling. There were two rooms within the sanctuary. The outer room housed an incense altar, lamps, and a table for ceremonial bread. The panels were decorated with carvings of flowers, trees, and cherubim. The inner room had perfectly symmetrical dimensions. It housed the ark of the covenant. The temple took seven years to build and was completed around 950 B.C.E.

The temple was the most sacred of Israel's buildings. Because it housed the ark of the covenant it was considered to be the location of Yahweh's presence among the people. This was expressed hymnically in the statement, "Yahweh sat enthroned between the cherubim" on the top of the ark. The ark was considered to be his throne and the inner sanctuary his throne room.

The configuration of the temple complex, its decorations, and its various implements suggest that the temple was intended to symbolize the world over which Yahweh rules. The outer courtyard with its bowl of water represented the waters of chaos. The outer room of the temple with its pictures of plants and animals cut into the walls and the lights of heaven represented in the lampstands depicted the physical world in microcosm. The inner sanctum was a perfect cube covered entirely with gold. It housed the ark throne flanked by cherubim and represented the perfect heaven where Yahweh dwells, enthroned among the angels of the divine council. The temple is a graphic symbol of the power and authority of Yahweh over his creation.

In addition to building the temple Solomon built an expansive (and expensive) royal palace complex. It took twice as long to build as the temple. This opulence further indebted the nation and ripened the growing dissatisfaction of the population.

■ SOLOMON'S DOWNFALL (1 KINGS 9–11)

In the evaluation of the Deuteronomistic writer, none of this was as disastrous as the trouble caused by his harem.

> *1 King Solomon loved many foreign women, including the daughter of Pharaoh, and women from Moab, Ammon, Edom, Sidon and Hatti—2 from nations about which YHWH had said to the people of Israel, "You must not marry them, neither may they marry you, for they would surely*

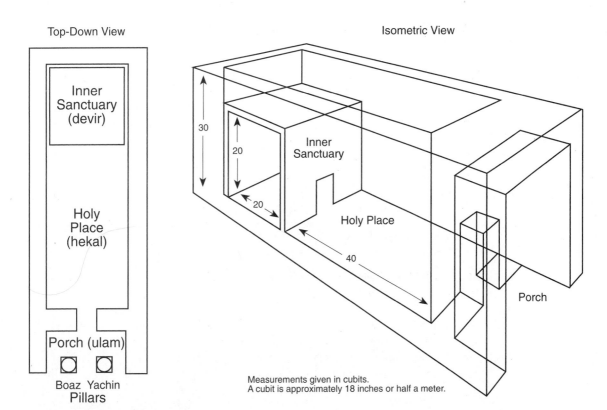

Top-Down View

Inner
Sanctuary
(devir)

Holy
Place
(hekal)

Porch (ulam)

Boaz   Yachin
Pillars

Isometric View

30

20

20

Inner
Sanctuary

Holy Place

40

Porch

Measurements given in cubits.
A cubit is approximately 18 inches or half a meter.

FIGURE 9.4   **SOLOMON'S TEMPLE**   Solomon's temple follows the basic design layout of the tabernacle (see Chapter 3). The inner sanctuary, or the Most Holy Place, has
perfectly symmetrical dimensions, befitting the dwelling place of God (see Fritz 1987).

*turn your heart away after their gods." Solomon clung to these women in
love. 3 He had seven hundred wives who were princesses, and three hundred
who were concubines. His wives turned away his heart. (11:1–3)*

What Solomon did here is not all that remarkable for his time, at least in principle. The fact that he had so many female retainers most certainly was not an
indication that he had an overly active sexual appetite. Rather, the 1,000 women
were a sign of the vast political contacts of the Solomonic administration in this
newly crafted Davidic empire. The wives of Solomon were a part of international
arrangements, marriages for political and diplomatic purpose; treaties with other
nations and city-states were contracted through political marriages.

But the Deuteronomistic writer interprets these marriages as the seeds of
Israel's disintegration. Solomon was just too tolerant. He allowed these women to
worship their native gods and goddesses right there in Jerusalem. In so doing
Solomon compromised his loyalty to Yahweh. For this, God would soon strip a
major portion of the kingdom from the control of the house of David. This sets
the stage and gives the theological rationale for dividing the kingdom into two
separate nations.

PARALLEL HISTORIES OF ISRAEL AND JUDAH (1 KINGS 12–2 KINGS 17)

The second of the three main blocks of material in the books of Kings accounts for the parallel histories of the two kingdoms that arose out of the civil conflict of 921 B.C.E.. The Deuteronomistic writer moves back and forth between Judah and Israel in his treatment of history. He introduces the kings of Judah using a standard pattern of elements, including:

1. the date the king took the throne relative to the reign of the king of Israel
2. the age at which he came to the throne
3. the name of the mother of the king (the queen mother)
4. a value judgment of the king relative to David, who was the standard of comparison

The Deuteronomistic writer introduces the kings of Israel using a different standard pattern of elements, including:

1. the date the king took the throne relative to the reign of the king of Judah
2. the location of the capital city of Israel
3. the length of the reign
4. a negative evaluation of the king (applying to all kings except Shallum, who only reigned one month)

■ DIVISION OF THE KINGDOM (1 KINGS 12–16)

Solomon was able to keep the kingdom together during his lifetime, but trouble was simmering. The seeds of dissatisfaction, primarily the cession of land in the north, high public taxation, and the use of Israelites in forced labor, prompted those in the northern districts to cast elsewhere for leadership. They found it in the figure of **Jeroboam.**

Jeroboam, the son of Nebat, had been the foreman of one of Solomon's labor crews. Being an Ephraimite, he seems to have shared in northern dissatisfaction with the Davidic administration. With the prophetic support of Ahijah from Shiloh (located in the north, it was the religious center of the tribal federation during the period of the judges), Jeroboam organized resistance to Solomon. Solomon recognized him as the ring leader and sought to kill him, but Jeroboam survived.

Ahijah is the first in a line of northern prophets mentioned in Kings; see Table 9.A for a list of northern prophets.

After Solomon died, his son **Rehoboam** ascended the throne. He met with leaders from the north at Shechem, but support from the north was not forthcoming. Led by Jeroboam, the people demanded that Rehoboam humanize his policies and lighten the burden of taxation and government service. Rehoboam refused to change royal policy; in fact, encouraged by his closest counselors, with bravado he threatened to make the load even heavier. The northern delegation declared their independence.

> *16 When all Israel saw that the king would not listen to them, the people answered the king, "What do we have to do with David? We have no inheritance in the son of Jesse! To your tents, Israel! Take care of your own house now, David!" (12:16)*

The Deuteronomistic writer framed the conflict in terms of rival administrations and national ideologies. The northern territories refused any longer to accept Davidic rulers and Zion theology. They had agreed to Davidic rule only after the house of Saul had let them down. Now they wanted out. But the Deuteronomistic writer's sympathies are clearly with the Davidic line.

Rehoboam did not have the military power or strength of will to force them to accept his rule. And the kingdom, while spared a protracted and bloody civil war, for all intents and purposes now became two nations. The northern entity, consisting of some ten tribes, kept the name Israel. As you read narratives that date to this period, note that the term *Israel* designates the Northern Kingdom rather than the entire twelve-tribe nation. The Southern Kingdom of Judah was just Judah, the sole tribe that remained loyal to the leadership of the house of David (see Figure 9.5). The twelfth tribe, Levi, did not have tribal territory, so Levites were found in both Israel and Judah.

An important order of business for Jeroboam was to consolidate his hold on Israel and give it a distinctive national identity. To that end he (re-)built Shechem and made it his capital. Attached to that site were all the associations of Israel's tribal beginnings, the good old days of the Joshua covenant.

Jeroboam had to put together a religious system that was independent of Judah's. He was especially worried that his citizens would feel compelled to make pilgrimage to Jerusalem to fulfill their religious obligations, as had become their practice under the Davidic administration. To counteract such a need, Jeroboam strategically located worship centers in his kingdom at its northern and southern boundaries, at Dan and Bethel respectively.

> **Bethel.** Bethel had a long religious history. The forebears Abraham and Jacob had special connections with Bethel (see Chapter 2). Abraham built an altar near Bethel as he made his way to the Negev (Genesis 12:8), and Jacob had his dream of the stairway to heaven at this spot (Genesis 28:10–22), thus proving that it was a point of contact between heaven and humanity—hence, a suitable place for a sanctuary.

The shape that the religious system of Israel assumed under Jeroboam called for special condemnation by the Deuteronomistic writer. Jeroboam built golden calves as the centerpieces of these shrines. The mere mention of these idols immediately recalls the fiasco at Mount Sinai that Aaron engineered (see Exodus 32). Just as heinous in the eyes of the Deuteronomistic writer, Jeroboam employed non-Levites as priests and set up a religious calendar with festivals that differed from those utilized in Jerusalem, as specified in Deuteronomic legislation. For all of these transgressions, Israel, and Jeroboam himself, could not escape God's condemnation.

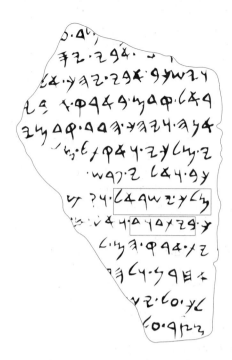

FIGURE 9.5 **HOUSE OF DAVID INSCRIPTION** An inscription found at Tell Dan in northern Israel contains the first reference outside the Hebrew Bible to the dynasty of David. This fragmentary thirteen-line inscription written in early Aramaic and dating to the middle of the ninth century B.C.E.. appears to celebrate the victory of the king of Aram in Damascus over a king in Israel. In it the phrases "king of Israel" (upper box) and "house of David" (lower box) are found. See Biran and Naveh (1993) for a full description of this text.

An unnamed "man of God from Judah," a prophetic figure of sorts (1 Kings 13), voiced Yahweh's dissatisfaction by condemning Jeroboam and the Bethel shrine. But in the end the Judean prophet was himself deceived by a Bethel holy man, resulting in his own execution by God. Clearly the message was this: Beware of the prophetic tricksters in the north, and stay away from Bethel. Although he reigned a healthy twenty-two years, Jeroboam was punished by the premature death of his son Abijah.

■ ELIJAH CYCLE (1 KINGS 17–2 KINGS 2)

The reign of **Ahab** of Israel is the setting for the prophetic activity of **Elijah.** The introduction of Ahab follows the standard Deuteronomistic pattern of encapsulating the basic facts.

29 In the thirty-eighth year of King Asa of Judah, Ahab son of Omri began to reign over Israel. Ahab son of Omri reigned over Israel from Samaria for twenty-two years. 30 Ahab son of Omri did more bad things in the sight of

YHWH than all who were before him. 31 And as if it were an insignificant thing for him just to continue committing the sins of Jeroboam, son of Nebat, additionally he took Jezebel, daughter of King Ethbaal of the Sidonians, as his wife. He continued to serve Baal, and worshiped him. (16:29–31)

Typical of such summaries, the reign of the northern king, in this case Ahab, is matched with the reign of Judah's king. The capital city is named Samaria; Ahab's father Omri moved the capital from Shechem to Samariah, where it would remain for the duration of Israel's existence. Note also the negative evaluation of Ahab, given in terms of continuing the idolatry of Jeroboam who set up the golden calves in Dan and Bethel. But Ahab went even further. He married **Jezebel,** who brazenly promoted the worship of Baal.

Like Solomon's marriages, Ahab's marriage to Jezebel was made for diplomatic reasons, to seal an alliance with the Phoenicians. But the Deuteronomistic writer sees only the religious implications of this marriage. It was yet another sign of the deterioration of Israel's loyalty to Yahweh in favor of Baal.

The core of 1 Kings 17 through 2 Kings 2 is a cycle of narratives revolving around the central figure of Elijah. Into this group of Elijah stories other material has been inserted, including the Micaiah account (22). The Elijah stories have been shaped to highlight the struggle between Yahweh's champion, Elijah, and the Israelite dynasty, which advocated the worship of Baal and Asherah.

The struggle between Yahweh and Baal was drawn up in such a way as to pit Yahweh against Baal on Baal's own turf. Baal was presumed to be the god who controlled agricultural fertility by providing the life-giving rains. In Canaanite mythic texts he is called "the Rider on the Clouds." Logically then, Elijah declared a drought on the country. What better way to find out who really does send the rain?

Elijah himself found relief from the drought and attendant famine with a widow and her son in Zarephath. The irony in the story could not be more pointed. Zarephath is in the heartland of Jezebel's homeland, the territory of her patron god, Baal Melqart. There Elijah performed life-giving miracles to demonstrate the power of Yahweh. He provided unlimited food to this poor widow, and even brought her dead son back to life.

Finally, the issue was settled by a dramatic encounter. Elijah confronted 450 prophets of Baal in a contest to determine who sends the rain. The Baal prophets, assisted by some 400 prophets devoted to Asherah, tried to get the attention of their gods with shouts and bodily mutilations, but to no avail. In contrast, Elijah called on his God, who sent lightning down from heaven, devouring a well-drenched sacrifice and proving who really manages the storm. The citizenry who witnessed the outcome of the contest sided with Elijah and Yahweh and slew the prophets of Baal. Since they had been sponsored by Jezebel, this upset her terribly, and she resolved to see Elijah dead.

Elijah fled to Horeb, a symbolic forty-day journey away. He returned to the site of Mosaic revelation, perhaps to reestablish contact with the God of the exodus. While he was there he awaited the revealing of God, expecting it to happen in storm, earthquake, or fire—the expected modes of theophany. Instead, God made his presence known in a barely audible whisper, the "still small voice" of the older

English versions. Elijah was then assured that the cause of Yahweh was not dead in Israel, and that Elijah himself would oversee the demise of the house of Ahab.

To understand the logic of the text's organization, note how the next two chapters provide a characterization of Ahab with reasons enough for his elimination. Chapter 20 has nothing to do with Elijah, though unnamed prophets are part of the action. The text at first seems flattering in the way it describes Ahab's victory over the Syrians, but then it condemns him because he failed to eliminate them totally when he had the chance. The story might remind you of Saul's similar failure to destroy the Amalekites when he had the chance. The text implies that Ahab must meet the same end as Saul.

Chapter 21 reveals the inner Ahab, the weak leader easily manipulated by his wife Jezebel. Ahab desired the property adjacent to his palace in Samaria. Its owner, Naboth, refused to sell family holdings. Jezebel arranged for Naboth to be falsely accused of a capital offense and executed. For this, Elijah condemned Ahab and declared that his dynasty would come to an end.

Ahab died in battle fighting the Ammonites, as the next chapter details. Chapter 22 is yet another chapter in which Elijah does not appear. Instead, the prophet Micaiah appears and foretells the death of Ahab. In contrast to Micaiah, about 400 prophets loyal to Ahab encouraged him to fight by predicting victory. Micaiah's voice was alone in opposition, much like Elijah's had been at Carmel. The description of Micaiah's meeting with God where he received the knowledge of Ahab's doom is especially intriguing, providing a glimpse of the divine council at work.

> 19 I saw YHWH sitting on his throne, with all the host of heaven flanking him right and left. 20 YHWH said, "Who will lure Ahab so that he will attack Ramoth-gilead and fall?" One said this and another that, 21 until a spirit came forward and stood before YHWH. "I will lure him." 22 "How?" YHWH asked. He replied, "I will go and be a lying spirit in the mouth of all his prophets." Then YHWH said, "You are to lure him, and you will succeed. Go and do it." 23 As you have seen, YHWH has put a lying spirit in the mouth of all these prophets of yours. YHWH has decreed disaster for you! (22:19–23)

In other words, the true prophet has access to the throne room of Yahweh, where he receives true knowledge and historical insight. The true prophet gets his message straight from Yahweh. False prophets claim to be speaking for Yahweh when they are not.

Obviously still loyal to Baal, the dynasty of Ahab continues to fall under the condemnation of the Deuteronomistic historian in the continuing Elijah cycle when Elijah returns in 2 Kings 1. Here we find Ahaziah following his father Ahab as king over Israel. After Ahaziah fell through the roof of his palace he tried to send messengers to Baal-zebub (a local Baal god) inquiring whether he would live or die. Elijah intercepted the messengers and told them Ahaziah would most certainly die. Ahaziah tried to retaliate by sending soldiers to assassinate Elijah, but once again Elijah marshaled fire from heaven and destroyed them.

Elijah departed from the scene in a spectacular way. While being followed by his disciple **Elisha,** he crossed the Jordan River and headed to the place in Transjordan where he would depart. While the exact location is left vague, the implication might be that he went to the Mount Nebo region to pass on (the same place where Moses had died); other experiences, including the flight to Horeb (Mount Sinai), and the miraculous crossing of the Jordan, are duplicates of Mosaic experiences. As Elisha looked on, a chariot of fire engulfed Elijah and he was whisked into heaven in a whirlwind. It appears that the theophany transported Elijah to the divine council.

> **Elijah and the Messiah.** As a result of the tradition that Elijah did not die but is with God, significant expectations of Elijah's future return developed within Judaism and Christianity. It was believed that Elijah would someday come back to earth, and his arrival would signal the dawn of the Messianic era. For texts that seem to connect Elijah with the future messiah, see Malachi 4:4–6, Sirach 48:9, and in the New Testament Mark 9:2–13. The cup of Elijah of the Jewish passover seder is another example of this expectation.

■ ELISHA CYCLE (2 KINGS 3–10)

The mantle of Elijah passed on to Elisha, his disciple, with all its attendant powers and responsibilities. Elisha was the legitimate successor to Elijah, as proven by Elisha's duplication of the Jordan River crossing miracle that got him back into Israel. The master–disciple relationship of Elijah to Elisha has more than a passing similarity to that of Moses and Joshua.

The Elisha cycle of stories has a different quality than the Elijah cycle. The Elisha cycle is much more occupied with miracles than it is with religious and political confrontation. They are listed in order of their occurrence:

1. Elisha changed undrinkable water to good
2. he directed two bears to maul some disrespectful children
3. he created an optical illusion that delivered the Moabites into the hands of Jehoshaphat of Judah
4. he multiplied a quantity of olive oil so a widow could pay off her debts (paralleling Elijah's miracle in Zarephath)
5. he resuscitated the son of the woman from Shunem (again duplicating one of Elijah's miracles)
6. he rescued some tainted stew
7. he fed 100 men with twenty loaves of bread
8. he cured Naaman of leprosy
9. he recovered an iron ax head from the Jordan River
10. he blinded the Syrian army and led them into captivity

All of these stories tend to glorify Elisha as a miracle worker and prophetic figure. Like Elijah, he was a northern prophet and represented that tradition. Elisha was also involved in Israelite and even international politics, though to a lesser degree than Elijah. He supported Hazael to be king of Syria in place of Benhadad. This was in fulfillment of Yahweh's instructions to Elijah at Horeb (1 Kings 19). It might seem strange to see this Israelite prophet encouraging Hazael,

FIGURE 9.6 **SHALMANESER III AND JEHU** Jehu is one of the few Israelite kings mentioned by name in material from outside the Hebrew Bible, and he is the only one depicted in relief. The Black Obelisk of Shalmaneser III (a ninth-century B.C.E.. king of Assyria) is a carved basalt-rock standing monument that contains pictures and Assyrian inscriptions. In this panel Shalmaneser is receiving tribute from "Jehu, son of Omri," who is on his hands and knees, though technically Jehu was the son of Jehoshaphat.

who then went on to make war against Israel. But this is the Deuteronomistic writer's way of showing how this Syrian pressure was planned by God as punishment for Israel's covenant breaking.

Elisha also supported **Jehu** in his *coup d'état* to overthrow the dynasty of Ahab. Again, this was punishment for the way Ahab and Jezebel promoted the worship of Baal and Asherah. Jehu's purge of the Ahab dynasty was swift and brutal. First, he went to Jezreel, the site of the royal retreat. He assassinated Joram, Ahab's son and king of Israel, along with his ally Ahaziah, king of Judah. Then he had Jezebel tossed out an upper-story window; landing on the pavement, she died. He continued to secure his position by assassinating the seventy sons of Ahab in Samaria, the capital; he killed anyone closely associated with or even distantly related to Ahab, and capped it off with a massacre of the royally sponsored priests, prophets, and worshipers of Baal. It is no wonder that Hosea, a later prophet, recalled those times of infighting and ruthlessness as the "bloody business of Jezreel" (Hosea 1:4). Although he acted by divine mandate according to the Deuteronomistic writer, other minds in Israel viewed this violent era with great disdain.

The house of Ahab was eliminated by divine decree and by Jehu. Jehu generally receives a good press in Kings, but he was not fully endorsed (after all, he was an Israelite king in a non-Davidic nation). He failed to eliminate the worship centers of the golden calves in Dan and Bethel. And extra-biblical evidence proves Israel was subject to Assyria in some degree during his reign (see Figure 9.6). The familiar Deuteronomistic refrain rounds out the account of Jehu: "But Jehu was not careful to observe the Torah of YHWH the God of Israel wholeheartedly; he did not turn from the sins into which Jeroboam led Israel" (10:31).

■ ASSYRIAN CRISIS (2 KINGS 11–17)

Meanwhile, the problems with the Ahab dynasty spilled over into Judah. Athaliah, of the line of Ahab, usurped the reins of government in Jerusalem and attempted to wipe out the dynasty of David. She turns out to have been the only ruling queen in Israel or Judah. The Jerusalemite priest Jehoiada succeeded in hiding Joash, the surviving heir of the Davidic line who was later restored to the throne in a bloodless coup.

Bouncing back and forth between Judah and Israel, chapters 11–15 quickly trace the careers of Joash (Judah 837–800), Jehoahaz (Israel 815–801), Jehoash (Israel 801–786), Amaziah (Judah 800–783), Jeroboam (usually termed Jeroboam II; Israel 786–746), and Uzziah, also called Azariah (Judah 783–742). Following in quick succession, the last kings of Israel, Zechariah, Shallum, Menahem, Pekahiah, and Pekah, cover only a few years (746–732), with whom Jotham of Judah (742–735) was roughly contemporaneous.

The writer occasionally pauses, usually only to detail the territory that one kingdom or the other lost to foreigners, or how a particular king broke the Mosaic covenant in some way, resulting in a typical Deuteronomistic-styled condemnation. We have nothing in the nature of a complete political history of the kingdoms, only enough on which to form a theological evaluation of the king's disposition before God.

The sins of Israel come home to roost in connection with an Assyrian movement into Canaan. First **Ahaz** (Judah 735–715) invited **Tiglath-Pileser III** of Assyria (745–727) to rescue him from a joint Syrian-Israelite venture to take Judah. The result was the Assyrian capture of Damascus in 732. Ahaz himself was forced to pay tribute to Tiglath. These events form the background to Isaiah's Immanuel prophecy (see Isaiah 7–11 and Chapter 10).

Later, Shalmaneser V (726–722) reinforced Assyrian control and made Hoshea (Israel 732–724) his vassal. Judah under Ahaz more stubbornly held out. When Hoshea attempted to get Egyptian support against Assyria, Shalmaneser laid siege to Samaria, the capital of Israel. It fell in 721 after holding out for three years. Thus, the kingdom of Israel ceased to exist. The majority of the Israelite leadership elite was deported to other Assyrian-held territories. In their place the Assyrians moved other conquered peoples. The result was a mixture of ethnic groups and religious perspectives. This mixed population lacked corporate commitment to Yahweh or his covenant. These Samaritans, as they came to be called, would forever be suspect to those in the south, who considered themselves more orthodox and obedient. Thus the old rivalry between north and south continued, albeit on slightly altered grounds.

The voice of the Deuteronomistic historian comes out especially clearly in chapter 17. Here he provides a comprehensive theological explanation for the demise of Israel. It was because they served other gods, worshiped idols, and ignored the

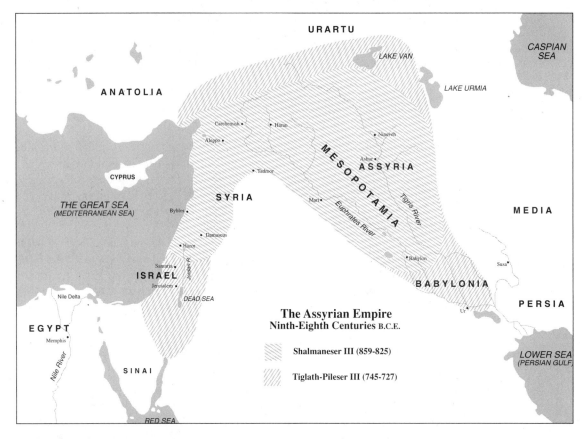

FIGURE 9.7 ASSYRIAN EMPIRE

The Assyrian Empire
Ninth-Eighth Centuries B.C.E.

Shalmaneser III (859-825)

Tiglath-Pileser III (745-727)

commandments of Yahweh. Even Judah, while spared destruction, was not immune to his criticism. The Deuteronomistic writer seems to be sending out a warning: Do not depart from the way of covenant, or you, too, will be destroyed!

TO THE BABYLONIAN EXILE (2 KINGS 18–25)

Of all the original twelve tribes, only Judah was left. The remaining chapters of Kings form a record of reigns and events down to its destruction some one hundred plus years later.

■ HEZEKIAH AND ISAIAH (2 KINGS 18–20)

Hezekiah ruled Judah well (715–687) according to the Deuteronomistic historian. Judged on the basis of his piety and religious reforms, he was one of the best kings of Judah.

During his reign, the Assyrian empire kept the pressure on Judah. **Sennacherib** attacked Jerusalem in 701 B.C.E. The account of this invasion in chapters 18–20 is closely paralleled by Isaiah 36–39. The outcome of this confrontation differed from that of the siege of Samaria. The Assyrian army departed after a disaster, attributed to the work of the angel of Yahweh, decimated the army and prompted the Assyrians to leave Canaan. According to the story, 185,000 soldiers died. The biblical text hints that problems back home might have cooperated in forcing Sennacherib and his army to return to Assyria. Shortly after his return to Nineveh, Sennacherib was assassinated by two of his sons.

> **Numbers.** These large numbers are troublesome. 185,000 men is a massive amount to lose in any campaign, dwarfing U.S. losses in the entire Vietnam War, when some 55,000 American soldiers were killed. Perhaps we should resort to the alternate understanding of the term "thousand." It can designate a company of fighting men, perhaps a squad of ten or so men; then the text may be saying 185 squads died in the camp.

But the real deliverance was attributed to the piety of Hezekiah. When surrounded by Sennacherib's army he did not react in desperation as Ahaz did under similar circumstances, looking for outside military help. Hezekiah immediately brought the matter to his God. Hezekiah took the Assyrian letter demanding surrender into the Jerusalem temple, laid it out before Yahweh, and prayed for guidance. Isaiah delivered an oracle of salvation on behalf of Yahweh in response to Hezekiah's plea for help. Hezekiah becomes the model for appropriate response in time of national crisis.

> **Assyrian Royal Annals.** Documents from Assyria provide independent witness to many biblical events. The Assyrian account of Sennacherib's invasion of Judah claims victory and boasts he shut up Hezekiah in Jerusalem "like a bird in a cage." For the Assyrian royal annals see Pritchard 1969: 274–301.

Hezekiah was followed by Manasseh (687–642), a king as bad as Hezekiah was good. Although the Deuteronomistic writer does not try, it would be difficult to explain how such a wicked king could reign so long if there is in fact a correlation between righteousness and blessing. Manasseh is spared no condemnation for rebuilding the Baal shrines that his father Hezekiah had eliminated. His breach of covenant was so serious that the ultimate blame for the destruction of Jerusalem was laid at his feet. His son Amon reigned only two years and was assassinated by opponents within his own court circle.

■ JOSIAH'S REFORM (2 KINGS 21–23)

After David, Josiah (640–609) was the best king Judah ever had. In 622 B.C.E., the eighteenth year of his reign, Josiah authorized and underwrote the restoration of the temple back to Yahwistic purposes after its disgraceful neglect under Manasseh and Amon. During the process of renovation Hilkiah the high priest, came in possession of "the book of the Torah." Hilkiah gave it to Josiah's secretary, Shaphan, who in turn read it to the king.

The king was extremely distraught when he heard words that seemed to spell doom for the nation because of their apparent departure from the covenant.

Huldah, a female prophet, interpreted the book to Josiah and the court, and comforted him with the prophecy that he himself would not see the demise of the nation because of his own faithful acts of repentance.

Josiah was inspired to make further reforms throughout Judah and the territory to the north that Judah controlled. The various religious shrines to Baal, Asherah, astral deities, and numerous other abominations to Yahweh, were all torn down. From then on, worship could take place only in Jerusalem, and the Passover was celebrated for the first time in a long time.

The description of the reforms of Josiah inspired by the "book of the Torah," especially the elimination of all worship centers except Jerusalem, and the reference to the document as "the book of the covenant," make its identification as Deuteronomy quite sure. Deuteronomy is so closely associated with the reforms of Josiah that most authorities today grant that at least the core of the book received its final shape out of that historical context (see Chapter 5).

It must have come as a terrible shock, then, given his piety and devotion to Yahweh, that Josiah was killed in a battle attempting to stop the advance of the Egyptian army. Killed near Megiddo by Pharaoh Neco in 609 B.C.E., the supremely pious Davidic king seems to have fed an accumulating mythology about that place Megiddo. Mount Megiddo is *har megiddo* in Hebrew, from which the term *Armageddon* is derived. In apocalyptic thought Armageddon will be the site of the last great battle between the forces of good and the forces of evil. But in the last days good would triumph.

■ FALL OF JERUSALEM (2 KINGS 24–25)

The Assyrian capital of Nineveh fell to the onrushing Babylonians in 612 B.C.E. Jehoahaz, the successor to Josiah, was on the throne only three months before the Egyptians removed him. The combined forces of Egypt and Assyria were unable to neutralize Babylonia at Carchemish in 605. From then on, Judah became a vassal state to Babylonia.

Jehoiakim (609–598) followed Jehoahaz. When he withheld tribute from **Nebuchadnezzar,** the great Babylonian empire builder, Jerusalem was besieged. Jehoiakim was assassinated sometime during the onslaught and **Jehoiachin** replaced him. Hapless Jehoiachin was on the throne only three months until the city fell. He was naturally held responsible and was carted off to Babylon along with other Jerusalemite notables and officials, as well as the temple treasury.

Zedekiah (598–587) was installed as king of Jerusalem on the understanding that he would promote loyalty to the Babylonian overlords. When later he rebelled, Nebuchadnezzar was compelled to return to Jerusalem to force compliance. Jerusalem was completely destroyed after an eighteen-month siege. Especially traumatic was the total destruction of the temple. The focus of Judah's religious life was now gone.

Gedaliah was appointed governor of what became the province of Judea. But Jerusalem was in such a shambles that he administered the province from Mizpah. A sorry state, or province, it was. Only the least capable elements of the population were left in Judah. All those who had not been killed in the final conflagration of Jerusalem, the priesthood, members of the royal court, tradesmen, and craftsmen, were taken to Babylon where they began a new life.

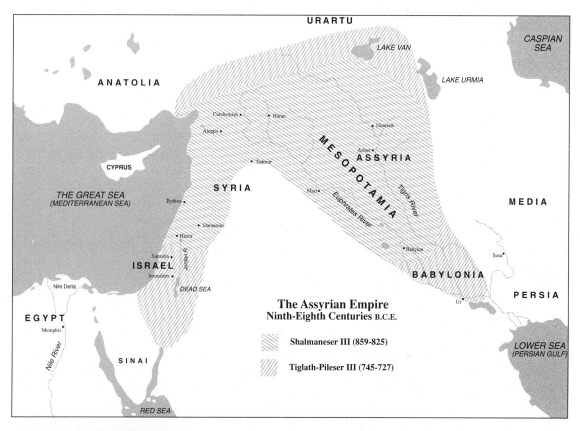

FIGURE 9.8 BABYLONIAN EMPIRE

The book ends on a note of guarded optimism. Jehoiachin, Judah's Davidic king in exile, was freed from prison around 560 B.C.E. after thirty-seven years of captivity. He was treated with respect by Evil-merodach, king of Babylon, known in Babylonian records as Amel-marduk (562–560). Babylonian historical tablets (see Pritchard 1969: 308) record the payment of oil and barley rations to Yaukin (Jehoiachin) king of Iahudu (Judah).

For the faith of God's people, the most important point was that the Davidic line of Judah had not disappeared. There was still hope for the future. Thus, the Deuteronomistic History ends negatively and positively. Judah had been destroyed, but God's community survived, implying it might one day recover greatness through the messianic line.

KINGS AS A WHOLE

The books of Kings contain clear indications that they were constructed, at least in part, using available written records and other materials. The writer drew upon a number of documents that he refers to by name, but that are no longer available to us. He mentions "the book of the acts of Solomon" (1 Kings 11:41), "the

TABLE 9.1 CHRONOLOGICAL TABLE OF KINGS AND KINGDOMS

Unified Monarchy	Israel	Judah	Mesopotamia
Saul 1020–1000			
David 1000–961			
Solomon 961–922			
	Jeroboam 922–901	**Rehoboam** 922–915	
		Abijah 915–913	
	Nadab 901–900	Asa 913–873	
	Baasha 900–877		
	Elah 877–876	Jehoshaphat 873–849	
	Zimri 876		
	Omri 876–869		
	Ahab 869–850		Shalmaneser III 859–825 (Assyria)
	Ahaziah 850–849	Jehoram 849–842	
	Jehoram 849–842	Ahaziah 842	
	Jehu 842–815	Athaliah 842–837	
	Joahaz 815–801	Joash 837–800	
	J(eh)oash 801–786	Amaziah 800–783	
	Jeroboam II 786–746	Uzziah 783–742	

book of the chronicles of the kings of Judah" (1 Kings 14:29) and "the book of the chronicles of the kings of Israel" (1 Kings 14:19). These must have been court records of some sort. In addition, the writer drew upon what were probably oral traditions of the prophets for the story cycles about Elijah and Elisha.

The books of Kings are only an outline of the history from Solomon to the destruction of Jerusalem. Not attempting to be comprehensive, the writer used a principle of selection dictated by the lessons of history he wanted to teach. The history he told ends with the loss of the Promised Land and the forced exile of the people. The writer was intent on making clear that these tragic events were the result of the people's sins and were God's judgment on those sins.

Furthermore, the working out of God's judgment on disobedience fulfilled the word of God through his servants, the prophets. The prophets of Kings, including Nathan, Ahijah, Elijah, and Elisha, warned Israel and Judah of coming disaster. But the hearts of kings and people were hard. The historical process demonstrated the power of the word of God unleashed in the world.

Table 9.1 combines kings of Judah, Israel, and relevant international players into one place for easy reference. The names in boldface held special importance

Unified Monarchy	Israel	Judah	Mesopotamia
	Zechariah 746–745	Jotham 742–735	**Tiglath-Pileser III** 745–727 (Assyria)
	Shallum 745		
	Menahem 745–738		
	Pekahiah 738–737		
	Pekah 737–732	**Ahaz** 735–715	
	Hoshea 732–724		**Shalmaneser V** 726–722 (Assyria)
			Sargon II 721–705 (Assyria)
		Hezekiah 715–687	**Sennacherib** 704–681 (Assyria)
		Manasseh 687–642	
		Amon 642–640	
		Josiah 640–609	
		Jehoahaz 609	
		Jehoiakim 609–598	**Nebuchadnezzar** 605–562 (Babylonia)
		Jehoiachin 598–597	
		Zedekiah 597–587	

in our discussion of the books of Kings and should be remembered. This chart may be a helpful reference when we read the literature of the Latter Prophets, for which keeping chronology straight can be a difficult matter.

Table 9.B is a detailed content outline of the books of Kings.

FOR FURTHER STUDY

Nelson (1987) for commentary on Kings, Brueggemann (1968) for the perspective of the Deuteronomistic historian, Hayes and Miller (1990) for the political history of Israel and Judah.

Chapter 8 Bibliography. See Part 2 Bibliography for general works on the Deuteronomistic History.

QUESTIONS FOR REVIEW

1. Briefly describe the course of Israel's history from the Unified Monarchy, through the division into two kingdoms and down to the fall of each kingdom.

2. Why did the Deuteronomistic historian criticize the Northern Kingdom of Israel more severely than the Southern Kingdom of Judah?

3. What prophetic figures appeared in the books of Kings, and what was their role within Israelite society?

4. What was the nature of the religious challenge facing Yahwism in Israel during the time of the kings?

QUESTIONS FOR REVIEW

1. Review the concept of the Davidic covenant (see Chapter 8) and explain its relevance to the history of kingship.

2. What are the parallels between the prophetic ministries of Elijah and Elisha? Between Elijah and Moses? Between Elijah and Jesus in the New Testament? What is the significance of parallels between the lives of significant biblical figures?

3. Compare and contrast the histories of Israel and Judah. What are the differing attitudes of the writer to the kingdoms? Although both kingdoms were destroyed by Mesopotamian empires, Judah survived in some form. Why did it survive? What lessons of history are to be learned from the disasters?

Chapter 9 Study Guide

- *Chapter summary*
- *Key terms linked to the glossary*
- *Concept questions with answer links*
- *Progress tests: true/false, multiple choice, matching, and identification*

10   ISAIAH

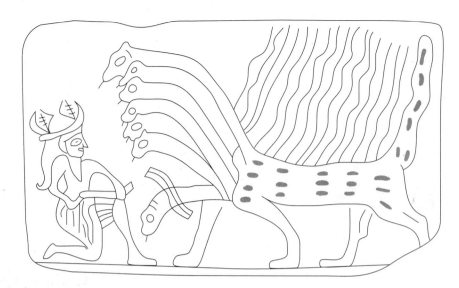

FIGURE 10.1 **SEVEN-HEADED SERPENT** The serpent Lotan (or Litan), a name akin to Leviathan, had seven heads according to Ugaritic myth (see also Psalm 74:14). This sea monster threatened life and good order but was defeated by Baal (see Day 1985).

Isaiah, one of Israel's early prophets, bolstered fragile Judah with words from Yahweh. His most famous pronouncement is the Immanuel oracle that assured God's continued protection of the house of David.

Isaiah's prophecy also included apocalyptic-style condemnations of Israel's political enemies. The arch-enemy Leviathan was the personification of the evil that God's people faced.

> *In that day YHWH will punish*
> *with his hard and great and strong sword*
> *Leviathan the sliding serpent,*
> *Leviathan the twisting serpent.*
> *He will murder the dragon in the sea.*
> *(Isaiah 27:1)*

The book of Isaiah provides a fine illustration of the growth of prophetic traditions. The entire book of Isaiah is attributed to Isaiah ben-Amoz (not to be confused with the prophet Amos) by the editorial superscription in 1:1. In fact, the book contains prophetic material spanning more than two hundred years. A nucleus of material is attributable to **Isaiah of Jerusalem**, a citizen of Jerusalem in the eighth century B.C.E. The remainder comes from a series of anonymous disciples (see 8:16, which mentions his followers) and prophets who saw themselves, or were seen by editors, as coming out of the Isaiah mold.

The book of Isaiah is widely recognized to consist of three sub-collections. Chapters 1–39 is **First Isaiah.** The core of this collection is prophecies from the namesake of the book who lived in the eighth century B.C.E. In this period Israel and Judah were threatened by the Assyrian empire. Chapters 40–55 is **Second**

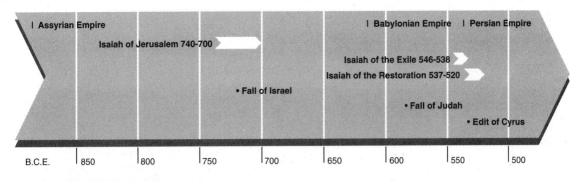

B.C.E.	850	800	750	700	650	600	550	500	

FIGURE 10.2 BOOK OF ISAIAH

Isaiah, also called Deutero-Isaiah. This collection consists largely of salvation oracles applying to the situation of exile in Babylonia dating to the mid-sixth century B.C.E. Chapters 56–66 is **Third Isaiah,** also called Trito-Isaiah, and applies to the late sixth century in Judah where a Jewish community was struggling to rebuild itself.

It would be an oversimplification to see a linear historical progression in the book of Isaiah from the pre-exilic period (chapters 1–39), to the exilic period (chapters 40–55), to the postexilic period (chapters 56–66). Later writers continued to rework earlier material and add to it, so even the first sub-collection, which is largely attributed to the eighth-century prophet Isaiah of Jerusalem, contains postexilic material. Conversely, mostly postexilic Third Isaiah took up older prophetic sayings from the pre-exilic First Temple period and incorporated them into his collection.

TABLE 10.1 THE THREE ISAIAHS

Chapters	Book	Title	Period	B.C.E
1–39	First Isaiah	Isaiah of Jerusalem	Assyrian	742–701
40–55	Second Isaiah	Isaiah of the Exile	Babylonian Exile	546–538
56–66	Third Isaiah	Isaiah of the Restoration	Restoration of Judah	538–520

FIRST ISAIAH: ISAIAH OF JERUSALEM

The first major section of the book of Isaiah, chapters 1–39, contains a core of material attributable to Isaiah of Jerusalem. Chapters 1–11 are a series of prophetic judgment statements delivered by Isaiah and autobiographical accounts by Isaiah. Chapters 13–23 are a set of oracles against foreign nations. Chapters 24–27 are the so-called Isaiah Apocalypse, a collection of sketches on apocalyptic themes such as universal judgment, the eschatological banquet, and heavenly signs. Chapters 28–32 are a set of prophetic oracles datable to 715–701 B.C.E. concerning Judah and foreign policy. Chapters 34–35 appear to be postexilic addi-

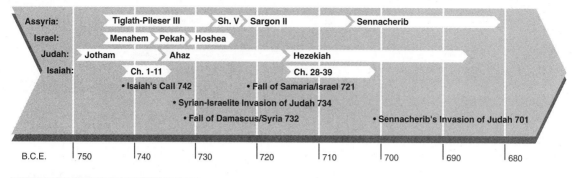

| B.C.E. | 750 | 740 | 730 | 720 | 710 | 700 | 690 | 680 |

FIGURE 10.3 ISAIAH OF JERUSALEM

tions that have affinities with chapters 40–66, and may have at one time served to bridge First and Second Isaiah. Chapters 36–39 are an historical appendix, paralleled in 2 Kings 18:13–20:19, dealing with Hezekiah and the Assyrian crisis. We will spend the most time on Isaiah 1–11 which is most securely connected with the prophet himself. These chapters apply to events surrounding the Assyrian crisis of the eighth century.

We do not know a lot of detail about the book's namesake, Isaiah, son of Amoz. We only know for sure that he began functioning as a prophet in Jerusalem in the latter half of the eighth century B.C.E. He appears to have been from Judah and generally had a high opinion of the Davidic dynasty, at least in principle. Gauging by the social circles in which he moved, he could very well have belonged to the Jerusalem aristocracy.

Isaiah has a lot in common with the other, mostly earlier, prophets of the eighth century, Amos, Hosea, and Micah. It even seems likely that he was influenced to a degree by them. In material dating to the early years of his ministry, Isaiah's critique of official religion in contrast to the demands of social justice (1:12–17) sounds a great deal like Amos. The next section, chapters 2–4, contains material also like his predecessor's, condemning the aristocracy and high society women, whose lifestyles implied disdain for the needs of the disadvantaged. Isaiah differs from Amos, of course, in targeting the ruling class of Jerusalem rather than that of Samaria.

Isaiah may also have been familiar with Hosea, judging by his description of a faithless people as a harlot. Isaiah berates Jerusalem, describing it as a prostitute (1:21–26), and later uses images from the fertility cult to denounce Jerusalem, perhaps dependent on Hosea 10:1. Again, Isaiah takes metaphors earlier applied to the north and reapplies them to Judah.

Isaiah opposed the priestly and prophetic spokespersons who stood in the service of the royal court and its policies. He frequently equated them with the "smooth talkers" of the foreign nations, the diviners, soothsayers, and necromancers. He seems to have viewed himself differently, more as a teacher of Torah (5:24; 30:9) than as a prophet (see Jensen 1973).

Unlike Amos and Hosea, Isaiah did not draw significantly from the resources of the Mosaic tradition of the exodus and settlement or the traditions of the Sinai covenant to give shape to his prophetic analysis. Isaiah's treasury was the complex of images and assurances dependent on **Zion** as the fortress of Yahweh (see the Zion poems in 2:2–4 and 4:2–6), and on the dynasty of David which administered Yahweh's rule on earth.

> **Zion.** The name *Zion* originally applied to the Jebusite fortress that David captured and made his capital (see 2 Samuel 5). Later it came to refer to the temple area and even to the entire city of Jerusalem. Zion, or Mount Zion, was considered the dwelling place of Yahweh as king.

The prophecy of First Isaiah is set within the turbulent times of the second half of the eighth century B.C.E. Assyria was a serious threat to the independence of both Israel and Judah. By the end of the century only Judah had survived, and only barely.

Life and Times of Isaiah of Jerusalem

750	Rezin became king of Damascus/Syria (750–732)
745	Tiglath-Pileser III became king of Assyria (745–727)
743–738	Tiglath-Pileser III campaigned in Syria-Palestine (he is called Pul in 2 Kings 15:19)
742	Isaiah's temple call vision inaugurated his prophecy (Isaiah 6)
738	Menahem king of Samaria/Israel paid tribute to Tiglath-Pileser III
737	Pekah assassinated Pekahiah king of Samaria/Israel, became king (737–732)
735	Ahaz became king of Jerusalem/Judah (735–715)
734–732	Syrian-Israelite War against Judah; Isaiah's war memoirs (Isaiah 7–8)
732	Hoshea assassinated Pekah of Samaria/Israel, became king (732–724)
732	Tiglath-Pileser III conquered Damascus/Syria
726	Shalmaneser V became king of Assyria (726–722), Hoshea became his vassal
725	Hoshea turned to Egypt for help
724	Shalmaneser V besieged Samaria/Israel
721	Sargon II became king of Assyria (721–705), conquered Samaria/Israel
715–701	Oracles during Hezekiah's reign (Isaiah 28–32)
704	Sennacherib became king of Assyria (704–681)
701	Sennacherib besieged Jerusalem/Judah, was unsuccessful (Isaiah 36–39)

■ COMMISSION (6)

The experience of initiation into the prophetic task can be referred to as the commission or "call" of the prophet. In a **call narrative** the prophet describes his experience of being called into divine service. While each prophet's experience is unique in the details, there are some common features. Most record the experience of having stood in the presence of God and of having been utterly frightened by the encounter. Most prophets felt ill-equipped to perform the task of voicing the divine message, but God somehow enabled them to speak.

> **Call Narrative.** Isaiah's description of the call has a lot in common with Micaiah's experience of the divine council in 1 Kings 22. The prophet Ezekiel also relates an experience of standing in the divine presence (Ezekiel 1). All these are similar to Moses' call experience at the burning bush (Exodus 3). The notion of the prophet as a messenger for God is reflected in the widely used formula that introduces prophetic oracles, "Thus says YHWH" (see Part 2; also Westermann 1967).

Out of his call experience, described in chapter 6, Isaiah became the messenger of the divine King.

> *1 In the year that King Uzziah died, I saw YHWH sitting on a throne, high and exalted. The hem of his robe filled the temple. 2 Seraphs attended him. Each had six wings: two to cover the face, two to cover the feet, and two to fly. 3 Each called to the other: "Holy, holy, holy is YHWH of hosts. The whole earth is full of his glory." 4 The hinges on the thresholds shook from the voices of those heralds, and the house filled with smoke. 5 Then I said, "Woe is me! I am doomed, because I am a person of unclean lips, and I live among a people of unclean lips. Yet, how is it my eyes have seen the King, YHWH of hosts?" 6 Then one of the seraphs flew to me, holding a live coal that had been taken from the altar with a pair of tongs. 7 The seraph touched my mouth with it and said, "Because this has touched your lips, your guilt has departed and your sin is wiped out." 8 Then I heard the voice of YHWH saying, "Whom shall I send, and who will go for us?" And I said, "Here I am, send me!" (6:1–8)*

Isaiah's vision took place in the temple, either in reality or in Isaiah's imagination. If Isaiah was really there, this might suggest he was a priest. If only imagined, we cannot draw the same conclusion. The vision took place the year Uzziah died, making it 742 B.C.E. If this call vision marks the beginning of Isaiah's formal prophetic work, then it began in that year.

In Isaiah's call experience Yahweh is envisioned as the Great King attended by the divine council. Called *seraphs* here, a word meaning "fiery ones," each member of the council had six wings. While foreign to our experience, the figures are on the analogy of the winged protector figures common in Mesopotamia (see Figure 10.4).

With two wings, these Isaian seraphs flew. With two they covered their feet. These two are an enigma until we realize that *feet* is a euphemism (here as elsewhere in the Hebrew Bible) for genitals. They were guarding their nakedness in the presence of God. With two they covered their faces. Apparently, as with humans, angels cannot look upon God and live. What is remarkable in this passage is that, while the seraphs cannot look upon God, the prophet Isaiah does, and yet he lives.

FIGURE 10.4 **WINGED PROTECTOR**   A winged figure, often called a sphinx, reflects the ancient Middle Eastern understanding of a heavenly world that included divine messengers, demons, and protectors. This carved ivory winged figure comes from ninth century B.C.E. Samaria in Israel.

But in the direct presence of God Isaiah felt his total inadequacy. He cried out in fear because he recognized his impurity. To avert disaster a seraph took holy fire and burned away the uncleanness of his mouth. The object of cleansing is the vital instrument of the prophet's messenger function. Now qualified to serve, Isaiah volunteered to represent God to the people.

Isaiah refers to God as "Yahweh of hosts" here in this passage and frequently elsewhere. This divine title almost surely originated at Shiloh in the Northern

Kingdom and is first attested during the Philistine wars. While Isaiah is clearly a Judean prophet, the use of this phrase links him, and Amos, who also uses it, with the prophetic holy war doctrine of the northern traditions. In like manner, the title "Holy One of Israel," not used here but frequently elsewhere in Isaiah, was used outside Isaiah only by the earlier northern prophet Hosea (11:9). Not too much should be inferred from this, but it does appear that Isaiah was influenced by northern prophets.

■ IMMANUEL (7)

In the final arrangement of material, the autobiographical account of Isaiah's call, dated to 742 B.C.E. , is followed by a third-person biographical narrative describing his counsel to **Ahaz** (king of Judah 735–715 B.C.E.) some eight years later in 734 B.C.E. At that time Ahaz faced a serious international problem. Judah had just been invaded by the Syrians and Israelites (in the text also called Ephraim). Ahaz was in a quandary over what to do. Should he give in and join the coalition the Syrians and Israelites were attempting to put together, or should he seek outside assistance against the Syrian-Israelite league?

Isaiah felt divinely compelled to give Ahaz advice. Meeting him in Jerusalem, Isaiah said, "Don't let your heart be afraid" (7:4). But Ahaz was not inclined to take the advice of the prophet. Apparently, Ahaz was more interested in the pressing political realities of his situation than in religious promises.

In an attempt to encourage Ahaz further, Isaiah gave him a sign or indicator of Yahweh's continued support of the Davidic dynasty. Ahaz was cavalier about this, too. He did not see the need for a sign, thereby, in the view of the writer, showing a deep callousness to the faith option. Now, the sign should not be understood as a magical act of some sort, but as an inspired interpretation of a natural happening. Isaiah's sign was this:

14 Look, the young woman is with child and will bear a son, and will name him Immanuel. 15 He will eat curds and honey by the time he knows how to refuse the evil and choose the good. (7:14–15)

What follows is at least one plausible way to understand this text. Isaiah, obviously being close to the royal court, knew that Ahaz's wife, the queen (here referred to as "the young woman"), was pregnant. Perhaps the text is suggesting Isaiah knew this even before Ahaz knew it himself. Isaiah is saying the queen would give birth to a son who would be concrete evidence of Yahweh's support of the Davidic line, evidence that the Davidic covenant was still in effect and that he was "with" them. The name **Immanuel** literally means "God is with us."

Concern for a crown prince was certainly a high priority of Judean kings, or for that matter, of any king. A son would be proof that the line would continue. A son would be evidence of God's direct intervention, as was perceived to be the case with so many births in the biblical text. We need only remember Isaac, Jacob and Esau, and Samuel to recall the role of divine intervention in conceiving a child. In the context of the present crisis, the impending birth should be interpreted by Ahaz and all Judeans as a sign of God's favor. If we continue this line of interpretation, history reveals that the son born to Ahaz was Hezekiah.

Immanuel as Isaiah's Son. The scenario above suggests that Hezekiah was the child Isaiah called Immanuel. In addition to Immanuel, two other children are mentioned in Isaiah's memoirs, and both are clearly sons of Isaiah; Shear-jashub in 7:3 and Maher-shalal-hash-baz in 8:1. Building on this, some authorities have suggested that Immanuel was Isaiah's own son, perhaps the Maher-shalal-hash-baz referred to in 8:1 (see Wolf 1972) or a third son (see Gottwald 1958).

Isaiah went on. Before this child would reach the age of puberty ("knowing how to refuse the evil and choose the good"), the threat posed by Syria and Israel would be gone.

"Curds and honey" may be an allusion to the "milk and honey" of the Promised Land, a positive allusion to security in the land derived from the conquest tradition. Hammershaimb (1949) notes parallels from Mesopotamian literature, where curds and honey are the food of royalty.

Indeed, as events worked out, Damascus of Syria was destroyed in 732 and Samaria of Israel in 721, just about the time Hezekiah, born around 734, was reaching puberty.[1]

The sign was intended to provide concrete evidence of God's continued care, so that Ahaz would trust Yahweh rather than act rashly in a political way to counter the Syrian-Israelite threat. However, contrary to Isaiah's advice to sit tight and trust Yahweh, Ahaz decided to take things into his own hands. He invited **Tiglath-Pileser III** and the Assyrians to help fend off the Syrian-Israelite league. They gladly accepted, and while Assyrian aid dissipated the immediate threat, Judah was forced to become an Assyrian client state and remained such for about a century.

You may have noticed that the autobiographical chapter 6 is separated from biographical chapter 7 by some eight years. And chapter 7 is followed by another autobiographical piece, this one foretelling the coming of the Assyrians. We might want to ask why the material is arranged this way. More specifically, why is the biographical piece about Immanuel injected here? The answer has to do with the call narrative. Isaiah's burden of prophecy, as indicated by Yahweh in that account, would be to speak to a people who would hear but not listen, who would not repent to avert disaster.

*9 "Go and say to this people: 'Keep listening, but do not comprehend. . . .'"
11 Then I said, 'How long, O YHWH?' And he said: 'Until cities lie waste without inhabitant, . . . 12 until YHWH sends everyone far away.'"*
(6:9, 11–12)

Ahaz's reaction to the counsel of Isaiah and his rejection of the Immanuel sign in chapter 7 demonstrates just the kind of callousness that Isaiah was told to expect in that inaugural vision. The result was divine judgment, which came, as chapter 8 foresaw, when the forces of Assyria swept over Judah.

---

[1] The chronology of the life of Hezekiah is difficult to pin down due to contradictions within 2 Kings 18. We follow verse 13 which places the beginning of his reign at 715 B.C.E., making him twenty-one years old when he ascended the throne, against verse 2 which puts his age at twenty-five.

From these chapters we see that Isaiah the prophet was heavily involved in Judean politics, close to the king, yet not a "yes-man." How should we understand the involvement of Isaiah in Judean political life?

■ ISAIAH AND THE DAVIDIC PROMISE (9)

Isaiah may have been a member of the loyal opposition party that opposed Ahaz's policy of accommodation to the Assyrian Empire. He also appears to have been more of a parochial Judean traditionalist than Ahaz, preferring isolationism to involvement in international affairs.

Isaiah and his party were at odds with royal policy during the reign of Ahaz. Although opposed to specific royal policies, Isaiah was still a staunch supporter in principle of the Davidic dynasty. The poems of chapters 9–11 express the hopes Isaiah attached to the Davidic heir. By their proximity to the Immanuel prophecy of chapter 7, they appear to express the profound expectations the prophet and the people had for a rebirth of national pride and status. Interpreted this way, they too probably referred to Hezekiah. Isaiah 9:2–7 could be interpreted as a coronation hymn in celebration of the crown prince Hezekiah's accession to the throne.

> 6 "For a child has been born to us, a son given to us. Authority rests on his shoulders. He will be called Wonderful Counselor, Mighty God, Everlasting Father, Prince of Peace. 7 His authority will continue to grow, and there will be everlasting peace for the throne of David and his kingdom. He will establish and sustain it with justice and with righteousness from now and into the future forever. The zeal of YHWH of hosts will do it." (9:6–7)

With these words, made especially well known by Handel's *Messiah*, Isaiah reflected the anticipation the people felt at the royal birth. Isaiah saw the ongoing tradition of Davidic kingship as the institution through which Yahweh would mediate peace and salvation to the people. Such high ideals no doubt fed popular expectations of prosperity and equity—ideals which Judah's actual kings hardly ever met. The people's disappointments, in turn, fed anticipation of yet a better Davidic king who would meet the ideal, an expectation which developed into the grand ideal of the coming Messiah.

■ ASSYRIAN INVASION (36–39)

Hezekiah succeeded his father, Ahaz, in 715 B.C.E. and inherited an independent but insecure Judah, one still threatened by Assyria. Shortly after taking the throne he instituted a policy of expansion. He sought to take Edomite territory to the south and Philistine territory to the west. He also looked to join an anti-Assyrian coalition which included Egypt. Isaiah sought to dissuade him, saying this could only lead to disaster (22:1–8, 12–14; 30:8–17).

Nonetheless, Hezekiah instituted a policy of revolt against Assyria. This fired the wrath of **Sennacherib** of Assyria, who invaded Judah in 701 B.C.E. However, by divine intervention, Yahweh demolished the Assyrian war machine and delivered Jerusalem. The text tells us that the angel of Yahweh killed 185,000 troops who were besieging Jerusalem. The crisis, told in chapters 36–37, ended favorably when Sennacherib's decimated army withdrew. This was taken as proof of the policy Isaiah promoted, and reaffirmed the power of Yahweh to protect Jerusalem and the Davidic empire.

Isaiah continued to provide counsel and support to Hezekiah. Later, Isaiah encouraged Hezekiah during a serious illness (chapter 38). Hezekiah was given added years of life as a reward for his piety. These last chapters of First Isaiah, along with 7–11, demonstrate the close connection between Isaiah and the king. Isaiah tried by various means to provide assurances, usually by means of signs, that Yahweh was protecting Jerusalem and the Davidic line.

Chapter 39, the last chapter of First Isaiah, contains Isaiah's rebuke of Hezekiah for allowing envoys of the Babylonian king Merodach-Baladan to see the royal treasury. In a bit of foreshadowing, Isaiah predicted the Babylonian exile.

5 Then Isaiah said to Hezekiah, "Hear the word of YHWH of hosts: 6 'Days are coming when everything in your house and everything your ancestors have accumulated up until today will be carried to Babylon. Nothing will remain,' says YHWH." (39:5–6)

This is a fitting, and no doubt editorially intentional, transition to Second Isaiah which is set in the time of that exile.

SECOND ISAIAH: ISAIAH OF THE EXILE

Chapters 40–55 of the book of Isaiah most likely come from the hand of a prophet who lived in Babylonian exile in the sixth century B.C.E. Dated sometime within the period 546 to 538 B.C.E., they do not come from the hand of Isaiah of Jerusalem. We know virtually nothing about this prophet, not even his name. Scholars have taken to calling him Second Isaiah, or Deutero-Isaiah (which means the same thing, but is a fancier term derived from Greek).

> **One or Two Isaiahs?** Conservative Jewish and Christian authorities tend to maintain that the entire book of Isaiah was written by Isaiah of Jerusalem, arguing that though the latter chapters apply to the situation of Babylonian exile, they were written predictively by Isaiah in the eighth century. Some of the reasons mainstream scholarship believes chapters 40–55 were written in the sixth century are references to the destruction of Jerusalem as a past event (40:1–2), Babylonia as their present setting (43:14; 48:20), and Cyrus the Persian as their coming deliverer (44:28; 45:1–4).

This prophet, though nameless, is one of the most inspiring of all time. And judging by the synthesis of traditions he was able to pull together, his originality, and his brilliant poetry, he was tremendously gifted. He drew from Israel's historic faith and reapplied it to the new setting of exile, giving the people reason for hope.

Second Isaiah consists almost entirely of poetic passages, with little of the narrative type material found in First Isaiah. Many scholars have tried to determine

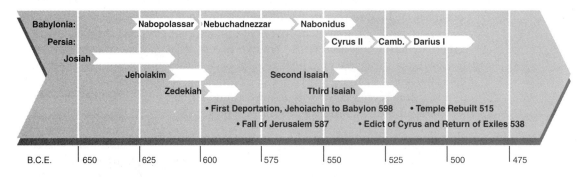

Babylonia:	Nabopolassar	Nebuchadnezzar	Nabonidus		
Persia:			Cyrus II	Camb.	Darius I
Josiah					
	Jehoiakim	Second Isaiah			
	Zedekiah	Third Isaiah			

• First Deportation, Jehoiachin to Babylon 598   • Temple Rebuilt 515

• Fall of Jerusalem 587   • Edict of Cyrus and Return of Exiles 538

| B.C.E. | 650 | 625 | 600 | 575 | 550 | 525 | 500 | 475 |

FIGURE 10.5 SECOND AND THIRD ISAIAH

the boundaries of these poems, and the logic and flow of chapters 40–55 as a whole, with varying success. The most recognizable division within the text is between chapters 40–48 and 49–55. The first subsection addresses its audience as Jacob and Israel. It deals with the fall of Babylon and the new exodus. The second subsection addresses its audience as Zion and Jerusalem, and deals with the issue of social justice. Beyond this basic division though, little else is agreed upon. Instead of trying to deal with compositional issues we will treat Second Isaiah thematically.

Table 10.A lists the various forms of speech that can be found in Second Isaiah.

■ NEW EXODUS

Second Isaiah marks a dramatic change from the prophetic tone of the monarchy era voices of the likes of Amos and Jeremiah. Their words of judgment had by now come true. God had punished Israel and Judah completely (the "double punishment" in the text below) for their sins. Now things will be different. Second Isaiah has sometimes been called "The Book of Comfort" based on passages such as the following.

> 1 *"Comfort, comfort my people!" says your God. 2 "Speak tenderly to Jerusalem and call out to her that her time of war has ended, that her sin has been pardoned, that she has received double punishment from YHWH for all her sins. . . . 6 A voice says, 'Call out!' And I said, 'What shall I call out?' This—all flesh is grass. . . . 8 The grass withers, the flower fades, but God's word will always stand." (40:1–2, 6, 8)*

The anonymous prophet called Second Isaiah, like his spiritual mentor Isaiah of Jerusalem, was conscious of his calling. Chapter 40 is a bit difficult to sort out because of the different voices that speak, most of them without explicit identification. A number of authorities have reconstructed this text as a call narrative, and this makes some sense. The divine council commissions the prophet to proclaim Judah's release from captivity. First, Yahweh issues the directive to comfort his people. Second, a member of the council ("a voice") looks for someone to go forth with the message. Then the prophet speaks up to volunteer, requests the specific message he should bring ("What shall I call out?"), and receives it ("All flesh is grass").

The divine council's summons in verses 3–5 suggests that it announces the reappearance of Yahweh, a new theophany.

> *3 A voice calls out, "In the wilderness prepare the road for YHWH, make straight in the desert a highway for our God. 4 Every valley will be lifted up, and every mountain and hill will be flattened. The irregular ground will be level and the rough areas even. 5 The glory of YHWH will be revealed so all humanity will see it. It will happen because YHWH's mouth has spoken." (40:3–5)*

The destruction of Jerusalem by the Babylonians presupposed the withdrawal of Yahweh from that city. Some Judeans may have thought he had returned to the wilderness, his original home. Second Isaiah proclaims that the God of the wilderness will reveal himself, lead his people through the wilderness, and then bring them into the Promised Land once again.

Instead of a pathway through the Reed Sea, there would be a straight and level highway right through the Arabian desert. This expressway would carry the people directly home. The exodus tradition once again becomes the basis for hope. The dynamic reuse of biblical traditions is nowhere else more apparent in Scripture than here in Second Isaiah. This prophet keeps coming back to the exodus theme to give shape to a hope for those currently in exile. He encourages them to have faith in a new exodus, this time from Babylonia rather than Egypt.

> *16 Thus says YHWH—the one who makes a path in the sea, a path through the raging water, 17 who brings down chariot and horse, army and soldier (they lie down, they cannot get up, they are snuffed out, put out like a wick) —18 Remember not earlier events. Do not dwell on the past. 19 Indeed, I am doing a new thing. It is springing up right now, do you not see it coming? I will make a path through the wilderness, rivers in the desert. (43:16–19)*

Note the details of the exodus tradition recalled in this passage: crossing the sea, the army of the enemy drowning in the sea. These recall the great salvation event at the Reed Sea of the Mosaic age. Yet, in Second Isaiah's estimation, that Egyptian event will be nothing compared to the future exodus from Babylonia. Yahweh is the redeemer of Israel. If you read other portions of Second Isaiah, be alert to the numerous allusions to Israel's earlier exodus experience, including the move from slavery to freedom, passing through the water, the miraculous providing of water and manna, and the conquest of the land. In addition to the great exodus theme, Second Isaiah develops other significant themes.

■ CREATION–REDEMPTION

The book of Genesis is by no means the only place the Hebrew Bible talks about the creation of the world.

12 "Listen to me, Jacob; Israel whom I called! I am the one: I am the begin-
ning (the first), I am also the end (the last). 13 My hand laid the foundation
of the earth, my right hand extended the heavens. When I call them they
stand at attention." (48:12–13)

The reason Second Isaiah talks about creation is to ground the redemptive
capability of Yahweh in his power. Because he is the one who created the world,
he is powerful enough to bring Israel out of captivity. In the following passage,
Second Isaiah combines the creation myth with the expectation of redemption.

9 Rouse up, rouse up, put on strength, O arm of YHWH! Rouse up, as in
the old days of past generations! Was it not you who cut Rahab to pieces?
Did you not pierce the Sea Monster? 10 Was it not you who dried up Sea,
Great Deep? Did you not make the depths of Sea a road for the redeemed
to cross? 11 Now, the redeemed of YHWH will return and come to Zion
with singing. Eternal joy is on their head. They will obtain joy and gladness.
Sorrow and sighing will leave. (51:9–11)

The terms *Rahab* (not the same as the prostitute Rahab of Jericho in Joshua
2, which is spelled differently in Hebrew), *Sea Monster, Sea,* and *Great Deep,* all
synonymous, make reference to the waters of chaos. Their use here recalls the victory of Yahweh over the waters of chaos that preceded the creation of the world
(Genesis 1). The victory was achieved by splitting Sea, similar to the way Marduk
split Tiamat in half to create the world.

This myth was used to express the cosmic significance of the act of deliverance
at the Reed Sea. The splitting of the waters of the Reed Sea (Exodus 14) became
the splitting of Sea, a victory over the waters of chaos. Second Isaiah is saying that
this type of powerful act would be repeated to return God's people to Zion.

■ SERVANT OF YAHWEH

Four poems in Second Isaiah speak of a servant figure, called the **servant of Yahweh.** They are known as the servant songs, or the songs of the suffering servant
(see Table 10.2). For a long time scholars have seen these poems as related and
have treated them together to derive a coherent identity of the servant figure.

TABLE 10.2 SERVANT SONGS

Song	Isaiah	Theme
1	42:1–6	He will bring justice to the nations
2	49:1–6	I make you a light to the nations
3	50:4–9	My back to those who beat me
4	52:13–53:12	Bruised for our iniquities

The first servant poem describes God's choice of the servant who will bring justice to the nations. The second poem describes, in the servant's own words, his experience of having been called by God to be a light to the nations. The reference in verse 3 to Israel is generally recognized as a late insertion intended to identify the servant with the nation. The third poem turns gloomy with a first-person description of how the servant was physically abused in the course of his mission. The last and longest servant poem, except for the first few verses, is a third party's observations on the suffering of the servant. What follows is a fragment of this last servant poem.

> 4 Surely he has lifted our infirmities and carried our diseases. But we reckoned him stricken, struck down by God, and afflicted. 5 But he was wounded for our transgressions, crushed for our wrongs; upon him was inflicted the punishment that made us whole, and by his wounds we are healed. (53:4–5)

On the basis especially of this last poem, the servant of Yahweh figure has also come to be called the "suffering servant". The notion is a remarkable one. It appears to represent a transference from atonement by animal sacrifice, the traditional ritual means of atonement in Israel, to atonement by a human being's suffering. By his suffering the servant of Yahweh receives God's punishment for the sins of the group.

No one knows exactly who this servant was or how to interpret the figure in the poems. Some have suggested that the servant of Yahweh is a metaphor for Judah, which suffered terribly in the Babylonian exile (remember, this is the audience Second Isaiah is directly addressing). By suffering, Judah delivered healing to other nations in the form of a witness to the saving power of Yahweh.

Others have suggested that the servant was an individual. Israel's prophetic figures were typically called "my servants, the prophets" and "servant of Yahweh." Moses is called this in Deuteronomy, and other prophets elsewhere. If the servant was a real prophetic figure, Jeremiah is a likely candidate. He was called by God (compare Jeremiah 1:5 and Isaiah 49:5). We know from Kings and the book of Jeremiah that he was socially outcast and physically abused. Besides Jeremiah, others have also been suggested, including Judah's king in exile, Jehoiachin, Second Isaiah himself (Whybray 1983), and Zerubbabel, the first governor of Judea after the exile.

Perhaps the very indefiniteness of the allusion was Second Isaiah's intention. He may have had somebody real in mind as a model; but he may have been suggesting, by keeping the identification vague, that the way of selflessness and suffering is the way salvation comes in God's plan, and not by triumphant military might. By keeping the figure indefinite, such a figure is not an historical curiosity but a model for God's chosen and redeemed people.

■ CYRUS THE MESSIAH

Second Isaiah contains, among other things, a clear example of theological interpretation of history. **Cyrus**, the Persian monarch who opposed the Babylonian empire, was viewed by the Judeans as their great deliverer. Second Isaiah even uses the term *messiah*, that is, *anointed one*, to refer to him in order to indicate the divine initiative behind his mission.

> 24 *"I am YHWH, who made all things, . . . 28 who says of Cyrus, 'He is my shepherd, he shall carry out all my plans.'" 1 Thus says YHWH to his anointed one, to Cyrus, whose right hand I have grasped to subjugate nations before him, . . . 5 'I am YHWH, there is no other. Except for me there is no god. I equip you, though you do not know me.'" (44:24, 28; 45:1, 5)*

With eyes of faith, Second Isaiah interpreted the current events of his day as ordained and directed by Yahweh, even down to the actions of their most likely political ally at that time. Second Isaiah clearly threw his support to Cyrus and promoted an anti-Babylonian policy. By 539 B.C.E. Cyrus was successful against the Babylonians.

> The references to Cyrus enable us to date Second Isaiah fairly reliably. From these Cyrus passages it is apparent that he was becoming known in Babylon for his military exploits. His first major victories were against Media in 550 B.C.E. and Lydia in 546 B.C.E. It was not until 539 that he defeated Babylon. The hope expressed by Second Isaiah, viewing Cyrus as Israel's deliverer, was no doubt framed sometime within the decade between 550 and 539 B.C.E.

And as it turned out (see Chapter 18), Cyrus was kindly disposed toward the Judeans, and even assisted the efforts of the Judeans who desired to return to Jerusalem and rebuild the temple there.

Second Isaiah's willingness to identify Cyrus as the Messiah indicates a departure from the Jerusalemite theological tradition, which attached that term to the reigning king from the line of David. Second Isaiah seems not to have put much stock in the Davidic line, nor does he look to it in hope. In fact, although there are numerous references to Zion and to Jerusalem, there are no references to David until 55:3.

> 3b *"I will make with you an eternal covenant, my faithful Davidic-type loving relationship. 4 See, I had made him a witness to the peoples, a leader and commander for the peoples. 5 See, you will call nations that you do not know, nations that you do not know will run to you." (55:3b–5)*

Second Isaiah seems to be suggesting something quite remarkable. The loving covenantal arrangement God earlier had established with David would now be transferred to his people as a whole. The dynastic covenant would become a national covenant. The people would complete the mission begun by David. In this way Second Isaiah is claiming that the Davidic covenant had not been annulled. Rather, it has been democratized.

Much more could be said about Second Isaiah's writings. They are full of images and promises of hope and restoration. However, now we turn to Third Isaiah, which was written in that period when Judah was struggling to rebuild and realize those dreams that had been fueled by Second Isaiah.

THIRD ISAIAH: ISAIAH OF THE RESTORATION

The last major component of Isaiah is called Third (or Trito-) Isaiah. It contains prophetic oracles coming from one or more of Second Isaiah's disciples. These oracles were addressed to the faithful and the not-so-faithful Judeans living in Jerusalem in the early postexilic period, that time when the people were struggling to reestablish a life in their homeland. This section of the book of Isaiah is datable to the period 538 to 520 B.C.E. Much of its message is intended to sustain the refugees who had recently returned from Babylonian captivity, especially those who were discouraged and depressed by the difficulty of life back in Jerusalem. You can sense the desperate need of the people in the following passage, which voices Third Isaiah's sense of calling.

> 1 *"The Spirit of YHWH Elohim is upon me, because YHWH has anointed me to bring good news to the afflicted; he has sent me to shore up the broken spirited, to proclaim freedom to the captives, the opening of prison to those who are bound, 2 to proclaim the year of YHWH's favor, and the day of our God's vengeance." (61:1–2)*

Table 10.B displays the unified structure of Isaiah 56–66. The anchor point of the structure is 60–62, Third Isaiah's visionary scenario of Zion as a restored Israel.

As with Isaiah of Jerusalem and Second Isaiah, this prophet expressed his awareness of prophetic calling. Third Isaiah was drawn to minister to God's people, even to fire them up. He had a formidable job to do. Jerusalem was in ruins. The community, too, was morally fragmented. There was dissension between the Judeans who had never left, the so-called people of the land, and those who had returned from exile.

Third Isaiah encouraged those struggling for faith in the absence of a temple and sacrifices. He assured them that God was present even if no building housed him.

> 1 *Thus says YHWH: "Heaven is my throne, the earth my footstool. What house would you build for me, what place for me to rest? 2 All these things my hand has made, all these things are mine," says YHWH. 3 "But this is the one to whom I will pay attention: the one that is humble and unassuming and respects my word." (66:1–3)*

Third Isaiah, as you can see, concurs with Second Isaiah in promoting the universal dimension of Yahweh's domain. Yahweh claims the entire world and desires to reveal his salvation to all people. Salvation has not yet arrived, but soon it will, and it will embrace all nations, not just Israel.

> 22 *"Just as the new heavens and the new earth which I am about to make shall stand before me, so shall your offspring and your name stand. 23 From new moon to new moon, from sabbath to sabbath, all flesh shall come to worship me," says YHWH. (66:22–23)*

Through difficult times and dreadful conditions, Third Isaiah sought to keep the faith of the people alive.

ISAIAH AS A WHOLE

The book of Isaiah has undergone a complex process of compilation, expansion, and editorializing. The history of Isaiah scholarship has tended to emphasize the separation of the book into its three main sections, assigning the different portions to different historical periods and more or less just leaving them there. Much Isaiah scholarship has delineated the individual poetic units and has tried to establish the authorship of the units, with priority frequently given to genuine Isaiah of Jerusalem sections.

There have been very few attempts to view the book as a whole, to try to construct the overall witness of the book. But we must keep in mind that somebody within the community of faith saw fit to put all this material together into one "book" under the heading "the words of Isaiah," and it was not just because they all fit conveniently onto one leather scroll. We have to ask ourselves: What gives the book its unity? What does the book as a whole have to say?

Clements (1982) argues that the destruction of Jerusalem in 587 B.C.E. is the clue to the editorial strategy that holds the book together. He argues that First Isaiah, while written primarily in reference to the Assyrian crisis of the eighth century, was edited during the Babylonian crisis and in its judgment oracles provided the prophetic explanation for the eventual fall of Jerusalem. Second and Third Isaiah were attached to First Isaiah by later scribes because they were motivated to balance prophetic judgment with prophetic promise. They wanted to say that judgment is not the last word but is followed by restoration. This basic sequence of judgment followed by renewal is echoed in the books of Jeremiah and Ezekiel, and is presented as a fundamental structure in the plan of God.

While acknowledging the critical analysis of the book into its component elements, Childs (1979) assesses the book of Isaiah from the point of view of the effect of its current shape, rather than for the purposes of a scholarly reconstruction. Childs points out that there are virtually no signals of the sixth-century authorship of Second and Third Isaiah in a plain reading of chapters 40–66. The original setting of 40–66 is effectively disguised. In its present shape, the entire book is placed in the mouth of eighth-century Isaiah of Jerusalem: "These are the words of Isaiah, son of Amoz" (1:1). In effect, this places both judgment and salvation within the eternal plan of God. For even before the destruction of Jerusalem and the Babylonian exile, as attested by 40–66, God intended to return his people to Judah. Even before destruction, he was planning ahead to their restoration.

The book, then, confirms the long-term saving word of God. Note the frequent references to the faithfulness of the word of God (40:8; 44:26; 55:10–11). God is faithful to his word and trustworthy. God plans beyond judgment to forgiveness and reacceptance. Taken as a whole, the book of Isaiah is a witness to the good will and power of Israel's God, Yahweh.

Table 10.C is a detailed content outline of the book of Isaiah.

FOR FURTHER STUDY

Writers tend to tackle one of the three Isaiahs rather than the entire book. Clements (1980) and Seitz (1993) on First Isaiah; Whybray (1983) on Second Isaiah, though he promotes a somewhat unorthodox interpretation of the Servant of Yahweh. For historical and thematic issues, the other works of Clements can also be recommended.

 Chapter 10 Bibliography. Also see Part 2, Prophets Bibliography.

QUESTIONS FOR REVIEW

1. What are the three main sections of the book of Isaiah, when was each written, and who was the audience for each section?
2. What happened at Isaiah's call to the ministry, and how does his call relate to his ministry?
3. Describe the political circumstances of the Syrian-Israelite crisis, and explain what Isaiah intended to accomplish by giving Ahaz the Immanuel sign.
4. What are the main themes of Second Isaiah, and how do they relate to the Babylonian exile?
5. Describe the "servant of Yahweh" figure of Second Isaiah, and explain his relevance to the experience of God's people in the sixth century B.C.E.

QUESTIONS FOR REFLECTION AND DISCUSSION

1. Evaluate the advice Isaiah gave to Ahaz during the Syrian-Israelite crisis. Was it politically prudent? Was it realistic? Think about the role of religious faith in political decision making today. Should national leaders make military and political decisions on the basis of divine promises of security and the advice of prophets?
2. What covenant traditions informed First, Second, and Third Isaiah respectively? Did they draw from the same traditions? Some might suggest First Isaiah drew heavily from the Davidic covenant, and Second Isaiah from the exodus traditions. Are all traditions important all of the time, or are some more appropriate than others, depending on current political and spiritual conditions?
3. Read and study the four servant of Yahweh poems. The Christian tradition has identified the figure with Jesus of Nazareth. On what basis do you think Christians make this identification? Try to discover what Jewish interpreters do with the servant. To whom do you think the servant poems refer? Could the figure be messianic?

 Chapter 10 Study Guide
- *Chapter summary*
- *Key terms linked to the glossary*
- *Concept questions with answer links*
- *Progress tests: true/false, multiple choice, matching, and identification*

11 JEREMIAH

FIGURE 11.1 JEREMIAH BY DONATELLO Jeremiah, more so than any other Hebrew prophet, emerges from the text with a personality. While the other prophets are known almost solely through their messages, Jeremiah's character and personality come out in his book through autobiography. Sometimes called "the weeping prophet," he passionately expressed his own feelings and laid bare his inner spiritual life. This feature makes the book of Jeremiah unique among the prophets.

The book of Jeremiah spans about a fifty-year period, from the end of the seventh century to the middle of the sixth century B.C.E. The general historical situation taking us up to the beginning of the book of Jeremiah is as follows.

Israel (the Northern Kingdom) had long ago disappeared as an independent entity. Judah alone remained. Assyrian power and its sphere of influence was on the decline by the middle of the seventh century. Having previously been dominated by the Assyrians, Judah toward the end of this century enjoyed a bit of independence. By 628 under Josiah, Judah was politically free and economically prosperous, and had even begun expanding northward into formerly Israelite territory.

There was no longer any external pressure on Judah to pay allegiance to Assyrian deities, as was the case under Manasseh earlier in the century. Taking the opportunity that political independence afforded, Josiah pressed for a return to indigenous Israelite religious practices and beliefs, namely Yahwism. The prophets Zephaniah (see Chapter 13) and Jeremiah supported Josiah in this move to reform worship, which began in earnest in 622.

Our approach to the book of Jeremiah will step out of our typical canonical mode and treat the material chronologically. We will not try to reconstruct the editorial history of the text to understand its present canonical shape, but rather look at texts in Jeremiah in temporal order, divided into periods based on the reigns of Judah's last kings.

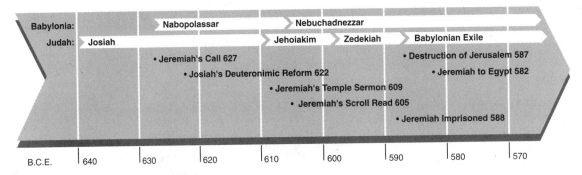

| Babylonia: | | | Nabopolassar | | Nebuchadnezzar | | | | |
| Judah: | Josiah | | | | Jehoiakim | Zedekiah | Babylonian Exile | | |

• Jeremiah's Call 627
• Josiah's Deuteronimic Reform 622
• Jeremiah's Temple Sermon 609
• Jeremiah's Scroll Read 605
• Destruction of Jerusalem 587
• Jeremiah to Egypt 582
• Jeremiah Imprisoned 588

B.C.E. 640 630 620 610 600 590 580 570

FIGURE 11.2 BOOK OF JEREMIAH

Life and Times of Jeremiah

640	Josiah began to reign as king of Judah
627	Jeremiah began his ministry
622	Josiah initiated religious and political reform (Deuteronomic Reform)
609	Josiah died at Megiddo
	Jehoahaz (Shallum) made king; lasted three months
	Jehoiakim installed king of Judah by the Egyptians
	Jeremiah delivered his Temple Sermon
605	Battle of Carchemish: Babylonia asserted its power over Egypt
	Jeremiah's scroll read before Jehoiakim, burned by Jehoiakim
598	Nebuchadnezzar laid siege to Jerusalem; First Deportation of refugees to Babylonia
	Jehoiakim died
	Jehoiachin became king, was taken to Babylon
	Zedekiah installed king of Judah by Babylonians
	Jeremiah confronted Hananiah who broke the ox yoke
588	Jeremiah imprisoned by Jehoiakim
587	Destruction of Jerusalem
	Gedaliah appointed governor of Judea
582	Gedaliah assassinated
	Jeremiah traveled to Egypt
562	Jeremiah died in Egypt

EARLY YEARS (627–622 B.C.E.)

Jeremiah began his prophetic activity during the reign of Josiah. Josiah was the king of Judah from 640 B.C.E. until 609. The early years of Josiah's reign were a time of prosperity and political independence. In the evaluation of the Deuteronomic school, represented by the books of Kings, Josiah was a fine and faithful king.

Jeremiah became a prophet in 627 and continued during those years immediately preceding Josiah's reform movement. After the reform initiative in 622, there are no words from Jeremiah for about a decade (perhaps Jeremiah felt Josiah had succeeded in doing what was necessary). He resumed his prophetic ministry after the death of Josiah.

The Jeremiah of the early years, which fall into the period from his call to 622, is represented by chapters 1–6. They have a lot in common with Amos and Micah. Like Amos, Jeremiah was concerned about social injustice and considered worship to be secondary to a lifestyle attentive to righteousness. Like Hosea, he personified Israel as an unfaithful wife (chapter 2), and longed for the days of the exodus and the wilderness experience, when Israel was thrown totally on the grace of God.

■ COMMISSION (1)

The book of Jeremiah begins with a Deuteronomic-style introduction that places Jeremiah within the context of Judah's history.

> 1 The words of Jeremiah son of Hilkiah, one of the priests in Anathoth in the land of Benjamin. 2 To him the word of YHWH came in the days of King Josiah son of Amon of Judah, beginning in the thirteenth year of his reign. 3 It also came in the days of King Jehoiakim son of Josiah of Judah until the end of the eleventh year of King Zedekiah son of Josiah of Judah, specifically until the captivity of Jerusalem in the fifth month. (1:1–3)

From this editorial introduction we learn that Jeremiah belonged to a priestly family from **Anathoth** in Benjamin. This is significant because it reveals one source of his antipathy to the Jerusalem priestly establishment. Admittedly we are dealing with a chain of evidence here, but this is how it goes.

When Solomon made his choice of priests back in the tenth century, he authorized Zadok as the legitimate family of priests and banished Abiathar to Anathoth. Zadok was chosen over Abiathar because Zadok had backed Solomon to be king, while Abiathar had backed Adonijah (see 1 Kings 2:26–27). Since Anathoth was a very small village, it is reasonable to assume that Jeremiah was part of the Abiathar lineage. Although a priest, Jeremiah would have been denied the privilege of serving at the Jerusalem temple. All of this makes some sense of the negative stand Jeremiah took against the official temple in Jerusalem and the monarchy that had exiled his family. This begins to explain why he was treated as an outsider. That he got any kind of a hearing at all in the temple and royal court is amazing.

The editorial introduction further tells us that Jeremiah prophesied during the reigns of Josiah, Jehoiakim, and Zedekiah, all kings of Judah, right up until the destruction of Jerusalem in 587 B.C.E.

The only major disputed point in this introduction is the intent of verse 2, which states that "the word of YHWH came" to Jeremiah in the thirteenth year of Josiah's reign. Does this mean that this is the year Jeremiah was called to be a prophet, the year 627 B.C.E. , or is this the year he was born? The question arises because the call narrative, which we examine next, suggests that Jeremiah was called to the prophetic ministry even before he was born.

Other prophets provide some accounting of how they concluded that God had called them to be prophets. Isaiah did it in his divine council vision account (Isaiah 6).

Amos did it in a roundabout way in dialogue with Amaziah (Amos 7). Jeremiah did it too, and it was logically placed at the beginning of the book.

> 4 *The word of YHWH came to me: 5 "Before I formed you in the womb I knew you, before you were born I set you apart— made you a prophet to the nations." 6 I replied: "But YHWH Elohim, I do not know how to speak. I am only a youngster." 7 YHWH replied: Do not say "I am only a youngster"—to all I send you, you must go, and what I command you, you must speak. 8 Do not be afraid of them. I will be with you delivering you"—says YHWH. 9 Then YHWH extended his hand and touched my mouth. YHWH said to me, "Now I have put my words in your mouth. 10 Today I have set you above nations and above kingdoms: to uproot and to break down, to destroy and to overturn, to build and to plant." (1:4–10)*

Of whom does this remind you? An alert student of the Hebrew Bible would have to say Moses. Jeremiah expressed the same reluctance as Moses to become a prophet. Jeremiah expressed the same kind of excuses as Moses, claiming a lack of qualifications. Jeremiah's hesitation concerned the same problem, his mouth, as did Moses'. And in both cases Yahweh met the "mouth" objection: in Moses' case by providing Aaron as his "mouthpiece," and in Jeremiah's by placing the words right on his lips.

Of special importance in Jeremiah's call narrative is the articulation of his mission. It is repeated throughout the book. He will break kingdoms apart, and plant kingdoms. It implies that as prophet, the authorized speaker of the word of Yahweh, he has the ability to destroy and to build. These extremes of destroying and building are another way of saying that this prophet's mission involved both judgment and renewal. In this mission he had the protection of God. As we will see, he came to depend on that protection, and at times felt disillusioned when his enemies got to him.

If we survey chapter 1 to its end we find that Yahweh gave Jeremiah two signs to confirm his calling. In somewhat the same vein as Amos' visions, there are visual puns. First, Yahweh showed Jeremiah an almond tree, in Hebrew a *shaqed*. This became the occasion for Yahweh to say to Jeremiah, "I am watching—*shoqed*—over my word to see that it happens." Then Jeremiah saw a boiling cauldron tipping away from the north toward the south. Yahweh said, "Out of the north trouble is brewing." This is a foreshadowing of the political problems that lay ahead from the north, the direction from which Mesopotamian foes reached Palestine (see Figure 11.3).

DURING THE REIGN OF JEHOIAKIM (609–598 B.C.E.)

Josiah died in battle at Megiddo fighting Pharaoh Neco. He was succeeded by his son Jehoahaz, also called Shallum. Jehoahaz lasted only three months and was deported to Egypt, where he died. **Jehoiakim** succeeded his brother Jehoahaz and ruled until 598 B.C.E.

Jeremiah was active throughout the reign of Jehoiakim. He denounced the king and the people for their idolatry and injustice. Many of the prophecies of chapters

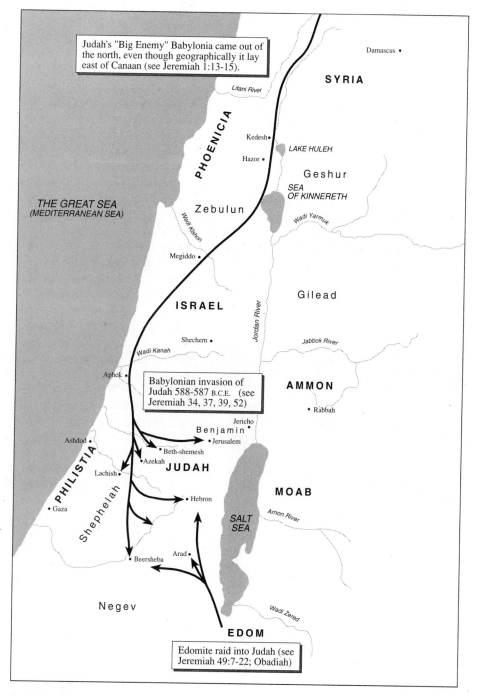

FIGURE 11.3 "OUT OF THE NORTH" Apart from Egypt, Israel's "big" enemies, Assyria and Babylonia, typically came out of the north, even though geographically they lay east of Palestine. The natural barrier of the desert forced these enemies to travel down the coastal road systems to get to Palestine.

7–19, 25–26, and 35–36 are dated to this period. Perhaps Jeremiah's most notorious denunciation speech comes in chapter 7.

■ THE TEMPLE SERMON (7)

Worship was central to Israel's religious life. A good deal of the Torah, as well as later writings, define proper worship. This includes the proper rituals, the authorized personnel, and the implements used in worship. Much of Samuel, Kings, and especially Chronicles, deals with defining and justifying notions of formal religion by illustrating them out of the life of Israel and Judah. Most of the time this meant promoting a form of worship centered in Jerusalem on Mount Zion.

Jeremiah was one of the few prophetic voices challenging the orthodoxy of Zionist theology, which defined the "right" shape of worship to the religious and political establishment. In his temple address, as recorded in chapter 7, he brought an opposing perspective to bear on the function of the temple and worship on Mount Zion. From the parallel passage in Jeremiah 26 we learn that the sermon was given in 609 B.C.E. at the beginning of Jehoiakim's reign.

Jeremiah delivered these words in the temple courtyard.

> *2 Hear the word of YHWH, all you people of Judah who enter these gates to worship YHWH. 3 Thus says YHWH of Hosts, the Elohim of Israel: "Reform your ways and your activity, and then I will let you live in this place. 4 Do not trust in these deceptive words—This is the temple of YHWH, the temple of YHWH, the temple of YHWH. 5 But if you reform your ways and your activity, genuinely act justly with each other, 6 do not oppress the resident-alien, the orphan or the widow, shed innocent blood here, or go after other gods (which can only hurt you), 7 then I will let you live in this place, here in the land that I gave your parents in perpetuity a long time ago. 8 Right now you are putting your faith in misleading words (This is the temple of YHWH!) but to no avail. 9 Would you steal, murder, commit adultery, swear falsely, burn incense to Baal, go after other gods you do not know 10 and then come and stand before me in this temple, the one called by my name, and say 'We are safe'—only to keep on doing these travesties?! 11 Has this house, the one called by my name, become a den of thieves in your opinion? Right now it appears that way to me," says YHWH. 12 "Then go now to my place that was once in Shiloh. That's where I first housed my name. See what I did to it as a result of the wickedness of my people Israel. 13 Now, because you have done these things," says YHWH (and though I spoke to you persistently you would not listen, when I called you, you would not answer) 14 "therefore I will do to the house now identified with me—the one in which you trust, the place I gave to you and to your ancestors—just what I did to Shiloh. 15 I will cast you out of my sight, just as I cast out your cousins, all the descendants of Ephraim." (7:1–15)*

It is rather easy to see why Jeremiah was not welcomed with a warm hug and a handshake after that speech. He roundly condemned the Judean people for putting their faith in the temple. But why?

Two reasons. First, Jeremiah claimed that the people were immoral, and given their immorality, nothing could save them, not even their sacred temple. Second, it seems the people viewed the temple almost superstitiously. They thought that the temple conferred automatic security. Official Jerusalemite theology claimed that Yahweh lived in the temple, and as long as he was there nothing tragic could ever affect Judah. Historical precedent backed them up in this belief. When Sennacherib surrounded Jerusalem in 701. Yahweh miraculously delivered the city, no doubt, they thought, because he lived there.

But Jeremiah brings up other historical precedent. He refers to the sanctuary city Shiloh of the judges period. Under Eli and Samuel it was the location of Yahweh's tabernacle. In spite of its unsurpassed importance at that time, it was unceremoniously destroyed—probably by the Philistines, though we do not know all the details.

Jeremiah countered that genuine security can only come from their faith in Yahweh. They must commit themselves to him, and their faith had to be actualized in moral living and undivided loyalty to him. This is none other than the Mosaic prescription. In fact, the very vocabulary of the decalogue is evident here, especially in verse 9.

As indicated by both the call narrative and the temple address, Jeremiah was thoroughly shaped by the Mosaic tradition. He has northern roots, perhaps Elohist connections—notice his reference to "the Elohim of Israel" in verse 3 and his reference to the descendants of Ephraim in verse 15. And the terminology of the sanctuary as "the place where my name dwells" sounds very Deuteronomic—the theological voice originally coming from the north.

Jeremiah was a dissenting voice in the "den of thieves," the temple courtyard, the heart of the Jerusalemite establishment. And he was pitting the Mosaic tradition against the dogma of Zionist-Davidic theology. He got quite a reaction. Although we do not hear any of it in chapter 7, we get a full report later in the book.

Jeremiah 26 provides a narrative account of the temple sermon, adding interesting contextual details and the surrounding circumstances. Jeremiah's message is given only in summary, but the reaction to it is given in rich detail. When the priests and prophets heard Jeremiah's condemnation of the Jerusalem temple, they pressed the king's government to execute him. After all, he had opposed everything they stood for. They considered it treason.

Jehoiakim's bureaucracy would have put him to death were it not for judicial precedent. In a prior age Micah (the same one as in the Book of the Twelve by that name; see Chapter 13) proclaimed destructive judgment on Jerusalem, just as Jeremiah was now doing. Back then Hezekiah declined to execute him. The people took Micah seriously and repented, and Jerusalem was delivered. More on the sober side, another case was cited, this one of a certain prophet named Uriah, who was not so lucky. He was executed by Jehoiakim. So we learn that the threat to Micah and Jeremiah was real.

This encounter between Jeremiah and the Judean establishment reveals two political and theological traditions in conflict. Both provided a way of reading God's relationship with his people and his work in history. One way, the Sinai-Mosaic track, stressed the people's covenant obligation. The other, the Zion-Davidic track, stressed Yahweh's commitment to Judah. This conflict of theologies would surface again.

The temple sermon raises two important theological questions which deserve consideration. First, Jeremiah argues that only if the people practiced personal and corporate morality would God allow them to dwell in Palestine. But is such a perspective politically realistic? What is the relationship between moral behavior, of individuals and nations, and political destiny? It would seem that international political forces, in this case the Babylonians, controlled Judah's destiny. The assertion Jeremiah and other prophets make is this: Yahweh controls the destinies of all the nations, including Babylonia.

Second, Jeremiah seems to come down hard on temple rituals and sacrificial practices. What were Jeremiah's deepest attitudes toward formal worship practices, were they entirely useless? Did he issue a blanket condemnation of religious ritual or a conditional one? If conditional, under what circumstances is worship acceptable? Both questions, the relation of morality and destiny and the role of worship, raise enduring issues in biblical theology.

■ READING THE SCROLL (36)

Not surprisingly, Jeremiah was barred from entering the temple-palace compound after that temple sermon. But there was plenty he still wanted to say to the king and his council. Jeremiah directed his companion and secretary **Baruch** to take dictation. Writing on a scroll with pen and ink, Baruch recorded Jeremiah's urging to repent and warnings of Babylonian danger. The year was 605, the same year the Babylonians bested the Egyptians in battle at Carchemish north of Palestine.

Baruch first read the scroll to a receptive audience in the temple area. They took the message seriously but advised him not to deliver it to the king personally. Fearing reprisals and persecution, Baruch and Jeremiah went into hiding while others approached Jehoiakim to read him the scroll.

Jehoiakim was in his winter palace at the time. As the scroll was read a few columns at a time, the king stripped the columns off the scroll with a knife and burned them. In this way he and his associates demonstrated their contempt for Jeremiah. They obviously were not moved to faith by the message.

After Jeremiah heard what Jehoiakim had done with the scroll, he proceeded to dictate another one and even more messages were added. But this one he did not deliver to the king. In this series of events many scholars see evidence for the construction of the book of Jeremiah and perhaps even the point of transition from an oral to a written ministry. We can assume this second scroll became the core of the book of Jeremiah as we have it today.

DURING THE REIGN OF ZEDEKIAH (598–587 B.C.E.)

Jehoiakim died just three months before Jerusalem succumbed to the Babylonian siege. In his stead, **Jehoiachin** was placed on the throne. After Nebuchadnezzar of Babylon subdued Jerusalem in 598 B.C.E. he deported many of its citizens to Babylonia, including Jehoiachin. **Zedekiah** replaced Jehoiachin and ruled with the support of Nebuchadnezzar.

Jeremiah remained in Jerusalem and continued to prophecy after the deportation of Jehoiachin and the others. The words of chapters 24, 27–34, and 37–39 come from the time of Zedekiah's reign.

■ FALSE PROPHECY (27–28)

The Babylonian kingdom of Nebuchadnezzar seemed vulnerable in 594 B.C.E. after a revolt within his army. This led many Judeans to think that their subjugation to the Babylonians might be near its end. Yahweh sent Jeremiah to Jerusalem to discourage such optimism. To reinforce his message he put an ox harness on his shoulders and declared that the yoke of Babylon would endure for a long while to come. He denounced the prophets who suggested otherwise.

> *14 "Do not listen to the talk of the prophets who say to you, 'You will not serve the king of Babylon.' For they are prophesying a lie to you. 15 I have not sent them,' says YHWH; "rather, they are prophesying falsely in my name." (27:14–15)*

Jeremiah was obviously not the only voice giving counsel in Jerusalem. There were other prophets giving advice to Zedekiah and the royal court. One of them was **Hananiah.** When he saw Jeremiah wearing the yoke bar he grabbed it off his back and cracked it in half. He prophesied that within two years Yahweh of Hosts would break the yoke of Babylon, and Jehoiachin, along with all the stolen temple implements, would return to Jerusalem. Jeremiah said he wished it would be so, but maintained that the end of Babylonian domination was not yet at hand.

While the book does not record the reaction of the witnesses to the confrontation that took place in the temple courtyard, we can assume they must have been puzzled. Both prophets spoke in the name of Yahweh of Hosts, both sounded like real prophets. We can be sure the people *wanted* to believe Hananiah; he had the more attractive message. But whom *should* they believe?

Jeremiah claimed that history favors the doomsayer, that is, himself, rather than the optimist.

> *8 The prophets who preceded you and me from ancient times prophesied war, famine, and disease against many nations and powerful kingdoms. 9 As for the prophet who prophesies peace—only if the word of that prophet comes to pass will it be clear that YHWH has sent that prophet. (28:8–9)*

Jeremiah was saying that if a prophet tells you what you want to hear, presume that he is not telling the truth. Only declare him to be a prophet if events prove him true. Otherwise, believe the worst, and you probably will not be disappointed.

■ LETTER TO THE EXILES (29)

The Judean refugees living in Babylonia were easy prey to the same false optimism as the citizenry in Jerusalem. Jeremiah was determined to debunk their illusions, as he had tried to do with the Jerusalemites. He sent a letter to the Jewish leadership in Babylonia telling them not to expect a speedy return to Judea. Instead, he said, build permanent homes in Babylonia, raise families, get on with the business of life. He even said the refugees should promote the prosperity and peace of Babylonia, the kingdom of their oppression. Outrageous! If anything was treasonous, this was. Yet he was not all gloom and doom.

> 10 "When seventy years in Babylon are finished I will come to you and fulfill my promise to bring you back to this place. 11 I know the future I have in store for you," says YHWH, "plans for prosperity and not for disaster, plans to give you a future and hope." (29:10–11)

Although the immediate future would entail the destruction of Jerusalem, there was always the "to build and to plant" of Jeremiah's message. Yet, it would not happen in the lifetime of the refugees. The seventy years Jeremiah mentions is the typical lifespan of an Israelite (compare the "three score and ten years" of Psalm 90:10). Only after a lifetime of exile, presumably the passing of a generation, might the Judeans expect to return to their homeland.

■ NEW COVENANT (30–31)

While remembered mostly for his message of doom, Jeremiah's full mission, as defined at his calling, also included restoration: "to uproot and to break down, to destroy and to overturn, *to build and to plant*." Sometimes called "The Little Book of Comfort," chapters 30–31 contain Jeremiah's message of building and planting.

During the darkest days of the siege of Jerusalem in 588 B.C.E. (see Figure 11.4), Jeremiah had the opportunity to purchase some ancestral property in his hometown of Anathoth. With the Babylonians in control of the entire area, it would have seemed foolish for anyone to lay out good shekels to buy land. Yet that is exactly what Jeremiah did. His cousin Hanamel, from whom he bought it, must have thought Jeremiah an idiot. But by this act Jeremiah was literally putting his money where his mouth was, affirming his deepest faith that Yahweh would not abandon his people or forever remove them from the Promised Land.

An additional expression of Jeremiah's faith, though this time mostly in prophetic poetry, comes in chapters 30–31. These chapters are undated, and scholars' opinions vary. Certain portions seem to echo the early chapters of Jeremiah, which date to the first years of his prophetic activity, but the overriding theme of restoration and rebuilding may suggest a setting immediately prior to the destruction of Jerusalem. Jeremiah was instructed to write down God's words as a testimony of their return.

> 3 "For see, in the coming days (YHWH's word) I will restore the restoration of my people Israel and Judah," said YHWH, "and I will bring about their restoration to the land that I gave to their fathers, and they will possess it." (30:3)

Here, and in the remainder of these chapters, Jeremiah affirms the basics of the faith, including possession of the land of Palestine and the unity of Judah and Israel.

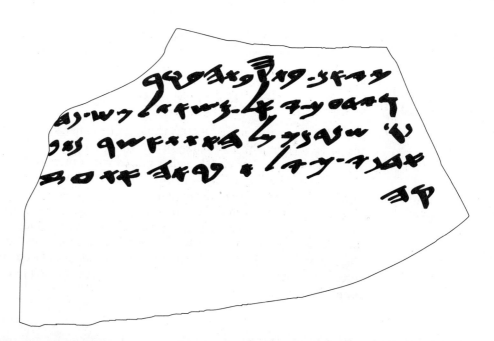

FIGURE 11.4 LACHISH LETTER   A collection of letters written on potsherds was found in a burn layer at Lachish. They date to 587 B.C.E. and contain correspondence between Lachish, a military outpost west of Jerusalem, and headquarters. According to Jeremiah 34:7, only Lachish and Azekah held out against the Babylonians.

Jeremiah is rightly famous for articulating this faith in terms of a renewed or **new covenant** with Yahweh. Jeremiah 31:31–34 builds on the old covenant and adds new features.

> *31 "See, in the coming days (YHWH's word) I will make a new covenant with the house of Israel and the house of Judah. 32 It will not be like the covenant that I made with their fathers when I took them by their hand to bring them out of the land of Egypt—my covenant which they broke, though I was their lord (YHWH's word). 33 Rather, this is the covenant I will make with the house of Israel after those days (YHWH's word): I will put my Torah inside them, I will write it on their hearts. I will be their God, and they will be my people. 34 No longer will a man teach his companion or a man his brother, 'Know YHWH!' All of them will know me, from the least to the greatest of them (YHWH's word). I will forgive their faults, and their sins I will never remember." (31:31–34)*

In this remarkable passage Jeremiah affirms the continuity of the Mosaic formulation of covenant. The allusions to the exodus are clear. The essential content of this new covenant will remain the same: the union of Yahweh and his people in a bond of unity. But the newness lies in the way the essence of the covenant will be internalized. Yahweh will put his Torah inside them. Furthermore, in the future God will overlook breaches of covenant as he did not do in the past. Jeremiah is laying the groundwork for a restoration not just of Israel's homeland and institutions, but of the Israelites' fundamental relationship to God.

AFTER THE FALL OF JERUSALEM (587–582 B.C.E.)

The fall of Jerusalem in 587 B.C.E. actualized Jeremiah's predictions of doom. On the surface Jeremiah's foretelling of Babylonian victory made it appear he was sympathetic to the victors. Though captured with others at the fall of Jerusalem, he was later released and given permission to travel wherever he wished. He was in the good graces of the Babylonians.

The story of Jeremiah's last years is told in chapters 39–44. Jeremiah remained in Judah for a time. Gedaliah was appointed governor of Judah by the Babylonians. He was betrayed by rival Judeans because he cooperated with the Babylonians and was assassinated in 582. Following the death of Gedaliah, Jeremiah was forced to travel to Egypt with a group of refugees. While there he continued to prophesy until his death.

JEREMIAH'S COMPLAINTS

A distinctive feature of the book of Jeremiah is a set of autobiographical passages which provide insight into the prophet's inner feelings about God and his calling. Called the "Confessions of Jeremiah" by some authorities, they are really laments or **complaints** that Jeremiah addressed to God. These passages have similarities to the individual complaint psalms of the Psalter (see Chapter 14). Jeremiah's complaints are found in 11:18–12:6; 15:10–21; 17:14–18; 18:18–23; 20:7–13, and 20:14–18. In them he expressed his feelings of frustration in being a prophet. He claimed that his enemies within Judean political and prophetic circles seemed always to get the upper hand. He accused God of abandoning him, even though he had been promised divine support. The complaint in 20:7–13 is especially direct in its criticism of God.

> 7 "YHWH, you have seduced me, and I fell for it, you have overpowered me, and you have won. I have become a perpetual laughable clown, everybody mocks me. 8 Whenever I speak up and cry out I feel compelled to shout, 'Bloody murder!'" (20:7–8)

The language here is quite strong. Jeremiah goes so far as to say that God "seduced" him; in effect raped him. Not only are his political opponents his enemies, even God seems so at times.

The reasons for Jeremiah's disillusionment are apparent. Jeremiah experienced mistreatment at the hands of the Jerusalem establishment. He was opposed by priests and prophets, as we saw in chapter 26. At various other times he was punished by royal officials when he seemed to be advocating the demise of the Judean monarchy. Pashur, a priest, beat Jeremiah and put him in stocks overnight after he heard Jeremiah preach the submission of Judah (20:1–6).

One especially notable incident happened right before the fall of Jerusalem, as told in chapters 37–38. When he tried to leave Jerusalem during the siege of 588 to travel to his home tribe of Benjamin on legitimate business, he was arrested and was accused of treason and inciting desertion. Court officials tried to execute him by dropping him into a cistern. Normally it was full of water. Fortunately for Jeremiah only muck was in the hole. A friend at court pleaded his case with Zedekiah, who allowed him to be lifted out of the cistern.

These incidents indicate how Jeremiah suffered the consequences for his unpopular views. Although we have these examples of rough treatment, we cannot definitively connect his complaints with any specific one of them or attach them to any identifiable period in the life of Jeremiah. They could be general reflections on his prophetic calling, or undated but specific reactions to personal experiences.

Only one of the complaints seems to be tied by editorial arrangement to a specific incident. The placement of chapter 20 implies that the complaint of 20:7–18 is a response to the physical beating that Jeremiah took from Pashur in the temple.

In spite of their general lack of context, the complaints of Jeremiah are theologically significant, even remarkable. They are amazing for the open and honest way they express Jeremiah's feelings of alienation, not only from fellow citizens, but also from God. The frankness of Jeremiah in not hiding his feeling of betrayal from God, but facing God directly, is to be appreciated for its courage.

JEREMIAH AS A WHOLE

The book of Jeremiah seems to have had a complex literary history and consists of both prose narrative and poetry. Three main types of sources underlie the book.

1. *Type A: Autobiography.* Naturally, this material is framed as Jeremiah's own speech and is found mainly in chapters 1–25 and 46–51. Much of this material is poetic and is generally assumed to be closer to Jeremiah's own utterances than the following types.

2. *Type B: Biography.* This material is third-person stories about Jeremiah, probably written by Baruch, Jeremiah's personal secretary. These biographical episodes are found in chapters 19:1–20:6; 26–29, and 36–45.

3. *Type C: Prose Sermons.* These show evidence of composition in the Deuteronomic style. That is, they contain the same vocabulary and style as the Deuteronomic school of theologians. Many have a common theme, namely, exposing the guilt of the people who have failed to heed prophetic warnings and have not repented. Included in this category are chapters: 7:1–8:3; 11:1–14; 18:1–12; 21:1–10; 22:1–5; 25:1–11; and 34:8–22. As with Type A material, these sermons are framed as the direct speech of Jeremiah.

These components were combined to create the final form of the book. Unfortunately, the book lacks a clear organization; chronology was clearly not the determining principle. The date indications in the text jump back and forth, and the book does not follow a linear chronological order. Keep this in mind if you read

TABLE 11.1 SOURCES OF THE BOOK OF JEREMIAH

Type	Form	Jeremiah Texts
A	Autobiography	1–25 including the complaints; 46–51
B	Biography	19:1–20:6; 26–29, 36–45
C	Prose Sermons	7:1–8:3; 11:1–14; 18:1–12; 21:1–10; 22:1–5; 25:1–11; 34:8–22
	Complaints	11:18–12:6; 15:10–21; 17:14–18; 18:18–23; 20:7–13; 20:14–18

the book in its entirety. It takes a special effort to orient the chapters within their historical context.

There is one obvious structural division in the book, and that comes after chapter 25. Chapters 1–25 stand out as a structural unit. It consists mostly of Jeremiah's own prophetic statements. Chapters 26–45 on the other hand mostly contain biographical narratives about Jeremiah. Chapters 46–51 are judgment statements directed against Judah's enemies. And chapter 52, the final chapter, contains an account of the fall of Jerusalem taken from 2 Kings 24:18–25:30.

It turns out that most of the Type A autobiographical material is found in chapters 1–25, as well as most of the Type C material. The introductory phrase "the word of Yahweh came to me" is characteristic of passages from these chapters. In contrast, the introductory formula "the word of Yahweh came to Jeremiah" is often used from chapter 26 to the end of the book. This has led some scholars to make the suggestion that the second half of the book (chapters 26–52), in some form at least, comes from the scribal hand of Baruch.

One of the most interesting compositional issues concerns the purpose of the completed book and its intended audience. Clearly the book in its final form was compiled after the destruction of Jerusalem in 587 B.C.E. The Babylonian invasion along with its devastating results were proof positive of the truth of Jeremiah's prophetic gift. He had been right all along! Someone, apparently someone dominated by the Deuteronomic perspective of guilt and punishment, saw the truth in Jeremiah's life and teaching, and fashioned his message into a form which could serve as preaching to the surviving refugees in exile (see Nicholson 1970). The core message was this: Yahweh had not abandoned his people. They had to be punished for their sins, but the covenant was still in effect. In fact it was a new covenant, new in the way God would relate to his people.

Table 11.A is a detailed content outline of the book of Jeremiah.

FOR FURTHER STUDY

See Holladay for commentary (1990 is a distillation of 1986 and 1989, the two more technical volumes of the Hermeneia series).

Chapter 11 Bibliography. See Part 2 Bibliography for general works on prophecy.

QUESTIONS FOR REVIEW

1. What were the main phases of Jeremiah's career in relation to the history of Judah? What was the basic thrust of Jeremiah's prophetic ministry before the destruction of Jerusalem, and what was its thrust after the destruction? In what way did his message change?

2. Jeremiah prophesied in Jerusalem but had family roots in Israel, in particular, Anathoth. How does his message reflect the regional tension that existed between north (Israel) and south (Judah and Jerusalem)?

3. What vocabulary and themes suggest that Jeremiah had a connection with the theological perspective of the Deuteronomic school?

4. How did Jeremiah both affirm the importance of the Mosaic formulation of God's covenant with his people and give it a new twist?

5. What are "Jeremiah's complaints," and what insight do they give into the personal relationship of the prophet with God?

QUESTIONS FOR REFLECTION AND DISCUSSION

1. In propounding his "new covenant," Jeremiah stresses that God would forgive the Israelites their sins and renew his relationship with them. What do you think Jeremiah means by forgiveness? Would God forget what the people had done or would he simply disregard it? What would the people have to do to get this forgiveness?

2. Jeremiah's autobiographical complaints contain frank indictments of God and the way he treated Jeremiah. Study these complaints. Do you think Jeremiah had the right to call God into question? Did God actually mislead Jeremiah at any point? Was God at fault in any way, as Jeremiah claimed? Can God be at fault? Should Jeremiah have been so frank and forthright with God?

Chapter 11 Study Guide
- *Chapter summary*
- *Key terms linked to the glossary*
- *Concept questions with answer links*
- *Progress tests: true/false, multiple choice, matching, and identification*

12

EZEKIEL

Key Terms

Ezekiel
Gog
Glory of Yahweh
Throne–Chariot
Valley of Dry Bones
Zadok

FIGURE 12.1 THE VALLEY OF DRY BONES is depicted in this third-century C.E. synagogue painting from Dura-Europos, Syria.

Ezekiel's vision of God on a throne–chariot presented the refugees in Babylon with a brand new idea. God is not stuck in a building in Jerusalem. He has wheels and can be anywhere. Even in "godless" Babylon.

God's character may be eternally the same, but the way God is apprehended changes. History has a way of forcing each generation to think of God in new ways —a process that continues to this day.

For the survivors, the trauma of Jerusalem's destruction and the Babylonian exile was as painful as the death of a loved one. Psychologists tell us that those who experience great loss go through predictable stages of grief, including denial, anger, and finally acceptance. The surviving Judeans felt all these emotions. And **Ezekiel**, as God's prophetic "pastor," supported them through this process.

But he was a curious pastor by today's standards. His way of providing moral support was to expose the people's responsibility for the disaster that afflicted them and tell them that their only hope for recovery was to change. No warm fuzzies from Ezekiel. Yet through it all Ezekiel never abandoned God's people or saw their situation as hopeless.

Ezekiel endured the Babylonian exile with the people, then emerged on the far side to present a vision of what the survivors must do to rebuild an identity. Ezekiel was a key figure in the survival of a Judean identity, and he was a major transitional figure in the move from an Israelite religion to what became the religion of Judaism.

Ezekiel was taken to Babylonia in 598 B.C.E. in the first major deportation of Judeans to the land of their conquerors. It appears that he was taken in that early deportation because he was a priest. In all, almost 5,000 Judeans were taken to Babylonia in that early displacement. Those taken were the leaders of the community, including royalty, scribes, counselors, craftsmen, and religious leaders.

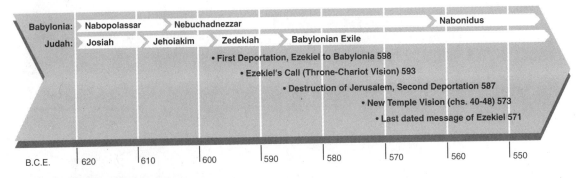

| Babylonia: | Nabopolassar | Nebuchadnezzar | | | Nabonidus | |

Babylonia: Nabopolassar › Nebuchadnezzar › Nabonidus ›

Judah: Josiah › Jehoiakim › Zedekiah › Babylonian Exile

• First Deportation, Ezekiel to Babylonia 598
• Ezekiel's Call (Throne-Chariot Vision) 593
• Destruction of Jerusalem, Second Deportation 587
• New Temple Vision (chs. 40-48) 573
• Last dated message of Ezekiel 571

B.C.E.   620   610   600   590   580   570   560   550

FIGURE 12.2 BOOK OF EZEKIEL

Ezekiel stayed in Babylonia for his entire career, being a prophet until at least 571 B.C.E. He was unable to perform the traditional priestly functions in exile, which included offering sacrifices of atonement and guarding the holiness of the community. Still, his vocation shaped his perspective on virtually everything, including religious obligations and relationships to God.

Being a priest from Jerusalem meant that he was thoroughly familiar with the rituals and procedures of temple service. This familiarity is evident in his visions, many of which center on the temple. A priestly orientation also meant he was profoundly shaped by the experience of serving in the presence of Yahweh in the temple. Priests referred to the divine presence by the phrase the **glory of Yahweh.** It was believed that Yahweh's presence in Jerusalem bestowed favor on the city and its people. Attentiveness to the divine presence dominated Ezekiel's experience.

Ezekiel was a contemporary of Jeremiah. Both were prophets immediately before and after the destruction of Jerusalem.

Life and Times of Ezekiel

598	Nebuchadnezzar laid siege to Jerusalem
	Jehoiakim died, Jehoiachin became king
	First deportation of Judean refugees to Babylonia, including Ezekiel and Jehoiachin
	Beginning of Zedekiah's reign
593	Ezekiel's commission in the throne–chariot vision
587	Destruction of Jerusalem and second deportation of Judeans to Babylonia
571	Last dated message of Ezekiel

The book of Ezekiel is much easier to follow than the book of Jeremiah because of its logical and chronological structure. It also has a certain thematic unity. There are at least three major issues which interweave the book, surfacing in various ways.

First, Ezekiel gives considerable attention to the continued presence of God among his people, along with the reasons for God's withdrawal and conditions under which he would reappear. Second, Ezekiel probes the issue of moral responsibility for the religious and political failures of Judah. Third, though getting less attention than the preceding two, Ezekiel examines the nature and legitimacy of religious and political leadership in Judah and in the restored community. Be alert to these issues as we examine the book of Ezekiel.

PROPHETIC WARNINGS (1–24)

Chapters 1–24 contain Ezekiel's visions and prophetic pronouncements dating between 593 B.C.E. (the date of his initiating experience) and the fall of Jerusalem in 587. Much of the material was written in the first person as Ezekiel's autobiographical recollections.

The pervasive tone of the entire first half of the book is divine anger.

> 13 *"My anger will find completion, and I will vent my fury on them. And they will know that I, YHWH, have spoken out of my jealousy for them, when my fury finds completion on them: 14 'I will make you a desolation and an object of derision among the nations that surround you and among those who see you as they pass by.'"* (5:13–14)

Yahweh was in a rage because his people had betrayed him.

■ THRONE-CHARIOT (1–3)

The first chapter of the book is a description of Ezekiel's visionary encounter with God in Babylonia. This vision of God functioned as Ezekiel's commission into the prophetic ministry. It occurred in 593 when Ezekiel was in Babylonia with fellow refugees who had been taken there in 598. This is the beginning of what Ezekiel saw in the vision.

> 4 *Now, as I looked I saw a stormy wind came from the north, a huge cloud with fire flashing and shining around it, and in the middle of it something like amber, in the middle of the fire. 5 And in the middle of it was the likeness of four animals. This is their appearance: they had the likeness of a human.* (1:4–5)

We note the following: The language of these verses, indeed the entire vision account, is highly descriptive, and the syntax is difficult. What is in the middle of what? How are the elements related? It's not at all clear. What we get are mostly impressions and images. Ezekiel saw a storm approaching from the north, it glowed from the inside, and strange hybrid creatures were in the middle of it.

If nothing else, what becomes clear is that Ezekiel experienced a theophany, an experience of standing in the presence of God. Although the language and the combination of images here are especially creative, it is clear that we are in the conceptual realm of the storm, cloud, and fire theophany we noticed in the divine–human encounters of Moses (Exodus 24), Elijah (1 Kings 19), Isaiah (Isaiah 6), and elsewhere (see Psalm 18).

Ezekiel's description of the theophany takes up an entire chapter. It becomes apparent that each of the four creatures had four faces (human, lion, ox, and eagle) and four wings. The creatures with their wings appear to be hybrid angels, no doubt somehow related to the divine council of Yahweh, sometimes called the cherubim. Wheels attached to these creatures gave the "storm" its means of locomotion. Stretched out over the wings of these creatures was a "dome"—the same term that designated the "expanse" created on the second day, according to the Genesis 1 Priestly account of creation. Then Ezekiel saw a figure seated above the dome.

> 26 Above the dome over their heads I saw a sapphire-colored throne-like thing. Seated on this throne-like thing was something like a human. 27 And I saw something like amber with fire in the middle of it from its midsection up. From its midsection down I saw something like fire, and it was shining all around. 28 Like a rainbow on a rainy day, so was the sheen around it. It had an appearance similar to the glory of YHWH. I saw it and fell on my face. And I heard a voice speaking. (1:26–28)

You can feel Ezekiel struggling to articulate exactly what it is he saw. He groped to describe something he had never seen before. Repeatedly he says, "I saw something like . . . " His uncertain descriptions perhaps reflect his incredulity in seeing what he finally realized he was seeing. It dawned on him that he was seeing some form of God himself on the throne.

Note that Ezekiel does not claim to see God directly but only his "glory." The glory of God is evidence of his presence, an aura of sorts, an apparition. This is priestly language (no surprise, since Ezekiel was a priest), used often to describe this presence of God. Among other things, "the glory of Yahweh" recalls the descriptions of God's appearance to the Israelites in the wilderness.

Taking the vision as a whole, Ezekiel seems to be describing a notion of great significance. In the vision Yahweh was seen traveling on a mobile throne, a version of the ark of the covenant, borne by special cherubs of the divine council. Normally thought to be permanently housed in the holiest room of the Jerusalem temple, now Yahweh on his throne was mobile. In other words, Yahweh was not restricted to the territory of Judah but could travel abroad, even so far from home that he could be with his people in exile.

Throne–Chariot. The throne–chariot vision had a mystical quality about it in a later Jewish context. A form of mysticism, called *merkavah* (after the Hebrew word for *chariot*) mysticism, developed in Medieval Judaism. The vision was considered so powerful that underage men were not allowed to read the account of it. A more radical interpretation of the vision appeared in the once widely popular (but really quite wacky) book by Erich von Däniken titled *Chariots of the Gods*. In the chapter "Was God an Astronaut?" he suggests that Ezekiel saw an extraterrestrial vehicle, an "unidentified flying object" (UFO). From out of this vehicle travelers from outer space gave Ezekiel "advice and directions for law and order, as well as hints for creating a proper civilization."

Yahweh came to Babylonia in his **throne–chariot** to commission Ezekiel to be a prophetic voice to the Judean refugees. Ezekiel was to be a watchman to the house of Israel. The metaphor used of his vocation is that of a sentinel standing on a tower, seeing the evidence of coming disaster and conveying God's warning to the people so they could prepare for trouble.

To equip him for his prophetic role, God handed Ezekiel a scroll on which were written words of woe. He ate the scroll, which curiously was sweet as honey, rather than sour as expected. Having internalized the word of God, he was sent to deliver the message—never mind whether the people heeded the warning or not (that was not Ezekiel's responsibility). The experience of commissioning and the message he was to bring were so traumatic that Ezekiel was overwhelmed, unable to speak for seven days.

Though imaginative in its handling of the details, Ezekiel's commissioning contains many of the standard elements of other prophetic call narratives. The most common elements are standing in the presence of God in his throne room, seeing God in the form of fire or brilliant light, and the equipping of the prophet's mouth to convey the word of God. A prophet was essentially a messenger who received a message directly from God and then delivered it to the target audience.

■ SYMBOLIC ACTS 1 (4–7)

The burden of Ezekiel's prophetic career from 593 B.C.E. until 587 was to convince the Babylonian refugees that God was punishing them for their wickedness through the exile, and that instead of getting better, things first were going to get worse.

Ezekiel not only spoke words of warning, he also acted them out. He made a clay model of the city of Jerusalem and played out a siege of the city. Then he lay on the ground, first on his left side for 390 days and then on his right side for 40 days, to symbolize the captivity of the two kingdoms, Israel and Judah respectively. While on the ground he ate only small amounts of food to simulate siege rations.

Then he shaved his head with a sword and disposed of the hair in ways that symbolized the fate of Jerusalem after its fall. One-third he burned, one-third he struck with the sword, and one-third he scattered to the wind. A wisp of hair he stitched up in the hem of his garment to symbolize the small remnant which would survive.

Lastly, Ezekiel faced in the direction of Palestine and announced the coming destruction of the nation of Israel and specifically its religious installations that promoted the worship of pagan fertility goddesses.

These signs have provoked considerable scholarly discussion. Some take the bizarre nature of these acts as an indication that Ezekiel was psychologically troubled, and have tried to define his psychosis. Others observe that we are not told how his audience reacted, suggesting that he never really performed these acts, and that they are merely literary in character. Still others stress the symbolic nature of these acts.

■ CORRUPT TEMPLE (8–11)

In a vision dated to 592 B.C.E., Ezekiel was transported back to the temple in Jerusalem. There he witnessed a variety of improper activities. The religious leaders of Jerusalem were secretly worshiping foreign gods in the temple compound. Women were devoted to Tammuz, the Babylonian fertility god.

These activities were an outrage to Yahweh. In consequence, he got up to leave the temple. Ezekiel's description of Yahweh's departure utilizes the throne–chariot imagery of chapter 1. The "glory of Yahweh" mounted the cherub-powered vehicle. In stages Yahweh exited the temple, stopping at certain points, including the threshold of the temple and the east gate of the courtyard, as if reluctant to leave. Hovering over Jerusalem, then over the Mount of Olives east of the city, finally Yahweh was gone.

The people had driven away Yahweh by their corrupt practices. He would no longer be there to protect them, and they would be taken into captivity. This is the message that Ezekiel brought to the exiles: Jerusalem would fall, as punishment from Yahweh.

But Ezekiel did not leave them without hope. Ezekiel assured his audience that Yahweh would not abandon them. Instead, later he would gather them from among the nations of their exile and reaffirm his covenant with them.

> 19 *"I will give them one heart, and I will put a new spirit inside them. I will remove the heart of stone from their flesh and give them a heart of flesh. 20 Then they will follow my directives, and my laws they will obey and do them. They will be my people and I will be God to them." (11:19–20)*

In Hebrew anthropology the heart was not the seat of emotions but was the center of the will and the seat of rationality. A new heart and spirit, which Ezekiel cites here and elsewhere, indicates a new willingness to abide by the covenant. In words reminiscent of Jeremiah's new covenant (31:31–34), this talk of a new spirit and a transformed heart voices the hope that the people will undergo a spiritual transformation. Although the heart of the people would change, inspiring new devotion to keeping the covenant, the original intent of the Mosaic covenant remained the same: "They will be my people and I will be their God."

As a whole, chapters 8–11 describe how false worship drove away the glory of Yahweh. The theme of this section comes full circle by the end of the book of Ezekiel in an elaborate program of restoration, chapters 40–48. Specifically in chapter 43 Ezekiel describes how true worship would bring the glory of Yahweh back to Jerusalem.

■ SYMBOLIC ACTS 2 (12–24)

Ezekiel took symbolic actions and drew numerous word pictures in an attempt to convince his compatriots that Jerusalem would fall and that they should not hold out for an early return from exile.

To symbolize the imminent fall of Jerusalem, Ezekiel packed his bags and in the middle of the night dug through a wall and hurried away as if to escape (chapter

12). In another image Jerusalem is compared to a vine that is no longer productive, and its branches can then serve only as fuel for a fire (chapter 15).

> **Vine.** The imagery of the vine is also used by Isaiah (5:1–7) and Jeremiah (2:21) to stand for Israel. It became a symbol for the New Testament church (John 15:1–11).

Chapter 16 contains an extended allegory of the history of Jerusalem. The main figure in the allegory is Jerusalem in the guise of a female who turns out to be an unfaithful wife to Yahweh. The allegory is developed in great detail. Jerusalem is first described as the daughter of an Amorite father and a Hittite mother. Abandoned by her parents she was adopted by Yahweh, who cared for her and made her beautiful. But then she used her God-given advantages to entice and seduce foreigners. God, in turn, used those foreigners to punish his wife. Ultimately he did not disown her, but restored her to full status as wife in covenant with God. The allegory of Oholah and Oholibah in chapter 23 likewise describes the unfaithfulness of Israel and Judah in terms of women wed to Yahweh.

> **Israel as Wife.** The literary comparison of Israel to a bride or wife is a common prophetic device in biblical literature. It was used by Hosea (chapters 1–3) and Jeremiah (chapter 2). The rabbis interpreted the relationship of the lovers in the Songs of Songs as an extended allegory of Yahweh's relationship to Israel. In Christian theology the church is the bride of Christ.

Ezekiel used extended images of eagles, trees, and vines to depict the uprooting of Judah and its kings in chapter 17. In chapter 18 Ezekiel addressed the issue of responsibility and blame. It seems Judeans were seeking to disown responsibility for the current state of affairs. They blamed their troubles with the Babylonians and the weakness of Judah on the sins of their fathers. The following proverb was widely quoted by the people to justify this analysis:

"The fathers have eaten sour grapes and the children's teeth are set on edge." (18:2)

Jeremiah also cited this proverb (see Jeremiah 31:27–30). Both he and Ezekiel denied the continuing validity and applicability of this proverb, and instead asserted that Yahweh knows each person individually. All people would be judged on the basis of their own actions. Each person should know that they get what they deserve. On the positive side, if they repent they can be delivered.

30 "Therefore I will judge you, house of Israel, each person according to his ways (the Lord YHWH's word). Turn and repent of all your offenses, and do not let them be a stumbling block leading to iniquity. 31 Toss away from you all your offenses by which you offend, and make for yourselves a new heart and new spirit. Why die, house of Israel?! 32 I do not relish the death of the dead (the Lord YHWH's word). Repent and live!" (18:30–32)

This passage is subject to varying applications. Many commentators argue that here in Ezekiel we have one of the first evidences of individual moral identity as opposed to a corporate concept of identity, the first glimmerings of individualism, if you will. This may be reading too much into it.

Joyce (1989) argues that Ezekiel was not affirming individual responsibility but was declaring that each *generation* makes its own moral choices and is not bound by either the sins or the merits of the preceding generation. Ezekiel in effect cuts the moral link between generations. On the one hand, the past shortcomings of the parents do not predetermine that the children must be punished. On the other hand, the current generation can no longer use the preceding generation for an excuse; it has to stand on its own moral two feet. Ezekiel told his generation to put aside their self-pity and fatalistic thinking, and take responsibility for change because then there is reason to hope.

Ezekiel continued to preach that ample opportunity for restoration would be given, if only the people would acknowledge their complicity and repent. But throughout this entire section he was invariably pessimistic about Israel's interest in repenting. Ezekiel failed to see any good in Israel at all and viewed the people as base, ungrateful, and unfaithful.

After oracles and images assuring his audience of coming disaster, this section ends with its most powerful statement yet (chapter 24). Ezekiel's dearly beloved wife died, and this understandably plunged him into deepest grief. But, by God's instructions, he did not shed a tear or give any sign of mourning. This stoicism stood as a symbol of God's own resolve, as presumably God determined not to be overcome by sentiment and forgo the punishment. Ezekiel did not speak another word, and by implication, Yahweh himself would be silent until Jerusalem had fallen.

HOPE AND RESTORATION (25–48)

The second half of the book of Ezekiel, written after the destruction of Jerusalem in 587, promotes the territorial and spiritual restoration of Israel. Ezekiel sought to rebuild the hope of the people and reassure them that Judah would be restored and that God would return to Jerusalem.

■ AGAINST FOREIGN NATIONS (25–32)

Ezekiel 25–32 is a collection of oracles of judgment against Israel's detractors. The following nations and city-states come under verbal attack and condemnation: Ammon, Moab, Edom, Philistia, Tyre, Sidon, and Egypt. These were all entities in the immediate vicinity of Judah that took advantage of Judah's woes to increase their own spheres of influence (see Figure 12.3).

> **Oracles Against Nations.** A series of oracles against the oppressors of God's people is a common feature of prophetic books (compare Isaiah 13–23, Jeremiah 46–51, and the entire books of Obadiah and Nahum). Such oracles are a projection of Yahweh's control of history.

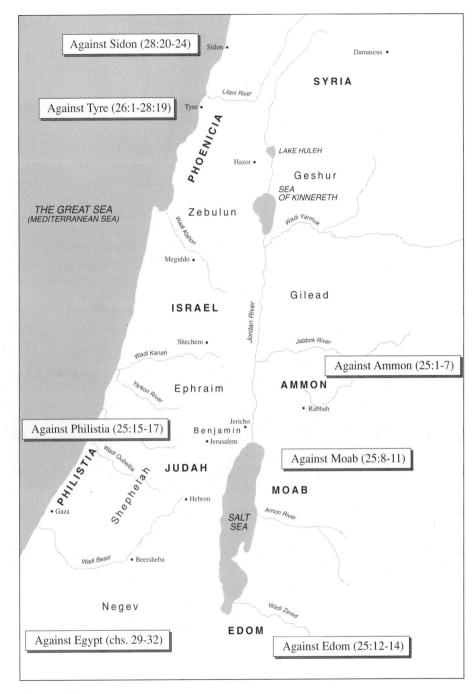

FIGURE 12.3 EZEKIEL'S ORACLES AGAINST THE NATIONS

These judgment oracles served at least two theological functions for Ezekiel's audience in exile. First, they reaffirmed God's justice. By all standards of evaluation these nations were no better than Judah; indeed they were often less humane and more ungodly. Ultimately they would have to be punished by God, even though then and there they were being used by God to punish Judah. Second, their power and influence would have to be checked in order for Judah's political restoration to take place.

Tyre and Egypt are objects of special curse in this series of oracles against the nations. Tyre is condemned in three chapters (26–28) and Egypt in four (29–32). The lamentation over the king of Tyre (28:11–19) is especially interesting for its description of the king as primeval man in the garden of Eden.

> 12 "You were a perfect seal, full of wisdom, altogether beautiful. 13 You were in Eden, the Garden of Elohim. Every precious stone covered you: carnelian, chrysolite, and amethyst . . . 14 With an anointed guardian cherub I placed you on the holy mountain of God. You walked among the shining stones. 15 You were blameless in your ways from the day I created you, until iniquity was found in you. 16 In connection with your far-reaching trading you became full of lawlessness, and you sinned. So I cast you down from the mountain of Elohim, and the guardian cherub drove you from among the shining stones." (28:12–16)

This description of beauty in the garden, expulsion, and the guardian angel, recalls features of the creation story of Genesis 2–3. Though no serpent is involved in this story, sin is the reason for the expulsion, specifically the ruthlessness of the king of Tyre. Elements additional to the Genesis version are the location of the garden of Eden on the mountain of God and the business of the fiery, shining stones. Taken with Genesis 2–3, this story is corroborating evidence that there was a widely known myth of primeval beginnings in Eden, followed by expulsion.

Ezekiel used the creation myth in order to characterize the king of Tyre as an evil man who deserved his downfall. History tells us that Tyre held out against Nebuchadnezzar and the Babylonians for thirteen years. This gave many in Judah faint hope that they too might be able to hold out against Babylonia. But Tyre ultimately fell. Ezekiel used his lament over fallen Tyre to disabuse his fellow exiles of the notion that holding out against Babylonia would be successful. The reuse of this myth in its application to Tyre is a fascinating example of the way myth could be historicized; that is, the drama of the myth was seen as a veiled account of historical events.

Hope After Defeat (33–39)

Chapters 33–39 contain oracles of restoration, written after the predicted final destruction of Jerusalem had become reality. In chapter 34 Ezekiel depicted the past rulers of Israel as negligent shepherds. In their place God would become the Good Shepherd who would rescue his sheep from disaster.[1] He would also restore the Davidic monarchy. Extending the shepherd metaphor, he says this:

[1]The use of the shepherd motif in the New Testament Gospel of John 10:1–18 has affinities with this chapter from Ezekiel.

*23 "I will establish one shepherd over them and he will shepherd them—my
servant David. He will shepherd them and he will be their shepherd. 24 And
I, YHWH, will be their God, and my servant David a prince among them."
(34:23–24)*

Ezekiel never gave up hope in the rebirth of Davidic rule. Jehoiachin was still
alive and in exile with Ezekiel. He remained the focus of the people's hope. The
Judean refugees and those back in Palestine continued to look to the line of
David for restoration of the nation. The mention of "one shepherd" expresses
Ezekiel's hope that the two kingdoms, Israel and Judah, would once again be
united. This reference to the line of David is one of the latest expressions of
Davidic messianic expectation in prophetic literature.

But the reference to the Davidic leader as "a prince" rather than as king is somewhat puzzling. The use of this term is consistent with the restoration vision of
chapters 40–48 where David is uniformly referred to as prince. The question is this:
Was this way of referring to David an expression of anti-monarchic sentiment on
Ezekiel's part, or was he just expressing the old covenant's theocratic ideal that only
Yahweh could be king?[2] The issue of leadership, its shape and legitimacy, remained
a major one throughout the exile and well into the period of restoration.

In chapter 36 Ezekiel reiterates the internal spiritual dimension of the restoration.

*26 "I will give you a new heart, and a new spirit I will put inside you. I will
remove the heart of stone from your body and give you a heart of flesh."
(36:26)*

This hope was expressed earlier in chapter 11, and now some of the implications are drawn out. The ground itself would gain from this restoration. Grain
would be abundant, fruits and vegetables would abound. There would never be
famine again. The people would be cleansed and forgiven, and even the land itself
would reap the benefits.

Ezekiel's most powerful image of restoration is the vision of the **valley of dry
bones** (chapter 37). In it Yahweh took Ezekiel out to a vast valley filled with
parched human bones (see Figure 12.1). God told him to prophesy to these
bones, to implore them to come to life. As he preached the bones began to rattle
and shake. They came together to make skeletons, then ligaments bound them
together, and skin covered them. As Ezekiel continued to preach, a spirit-wind
infused the bodies, and they became alive.

The dry bones were Israel of the exile, and Ezekiel foresaw the day when it
would be reborn as a nation and returned to its land. It can also be taken as an
affirmation of the life-giving potential of prophetic preaching. Above all, the
word of God, accompanied by the spirit-wind of Yahweh, can bring the nation
back to life.

*The famous African-American spiritual "Dry Bones" derives from Ezekiel's
vision of a valley full of bones.*

---

[2]Levenson (1976: 55–107) discusses this issue at length, and argues that the use of prince rather than
king is not a rejection of the institution of kingship.

The imagery of Ezekiel turns apocalyptic in chapters 38–39 as he describes a great battle. **Gog** of the land of Magog is evil incarnate, a caricature of all Israel's enemies combined. This enemy comes out of the north, seeking to wipe out Israel once and for all. But after a cataclysmic battle, described in great detail in these chapters, God's people are victorious. Israel will be vindicated for all time.

The exaggerated character of this account and its future setting have prompted some interpreters to read this as a prescription for an end times battle of Armageddon. More probably, it was an imaginative rendition of the expected confrontation with the Babylonians, who had long been the nemesis of Israel. The more grandiose the battle, the more impressive Yahweh's (and Israel's) victory.

■ RESTORED TEMPLE (40–48)

Ezekiel, remember, was a priest as well as a prophet. His most elaborate depiction of restoration naturally involved that most sacred of areas, the temple complex in Jerusalem. In a vision dated to 573 B.C.E. (twenty-five years after the beginning of his exile, and twenty years after his call vision) he was given a vision of the restoration of the nation. The plan for restoration placed the temple at the center of the nation both physically and spiritually. Placing the temple in the center allowed for the dwelling of Yahweh, consistently called the "glory of Yahweh" in Ezekiel, in the middle of the people.

The following are some of the important features of the restoration program as expressed in Ezekiel's vision. A rebuilt temple would be located in the geographical center of the tribes, which would be arrayed around it symmetrically, three to a side. The rights and privileges of serving in the temple itself would be given exclusively to priests from the line of **Zadok** of the family of Aaron.

The ground would be revived. A river of fresh water would flow from under the temple, and run all the way to the Dead Sea, in the process making the sea wholesome and the surrounding wilderness a paradise. Jerusalem would once again be the center of attention. Its name would be changed to *Yahweh is there* because he will again take up residence.

Overall, Ezekiel had a comprehensive vision of the need for holiness and how it would be accomplished. He had a priest's sense of the need for devotion and worship centering on the presence of Yahweh in the temple. He combined this with a prophet's attention to inward spiritual renewal and devotion. His combination of devotion, as defined by the Mosaic covenant, along with an openness to the work of the spirit of God, makes him a major figure in the emergence of Judaism.

EZEKIEL AS A WHOLE

The book of Ezekiel evidences a deliberate and well-considered overall structure. The visions of the presence of God at the beginning and end frame the book. The early visions of corruption in the Jerusalem temple are balanced by the ending vision of restoration. The book consists of two main parts. Part 1 is set before 587 and consists of warnings to Judah. Part 2 is set after 587 and holds out hope.

The oracles against the nations interrupt the flow of material applying to Judah. But there is a logic to their placement. The foreign nations come under God's judgment and must be subdued before Israel could be restored. The book as a whole also shows an intentional movement from prophecies of woe before the disaster of 587 B.C.E. (chapters 1–24) to prophecies of hope after the disaster (chapters 25–48).

Much of the critical scholarship on the book of Ezekiel concentrates on discerning the origin of individual prophetic units. Zimmerli (1979, 1983) takes great pains to separate what he judges to be texts original to Ezekiel from the commentary provided by later writers and editors. He gives priority to the former. Childs (1979) says that valuing Ezekiel's own oracles over later commentary overlooks a very important point. The so-called commentary additions were canonized along with Ezekiel's originals. The commentary is evidence of how the originals were heard and applied by the community of faith, and they, too, bear scriptural authority.

Table 12.A is a detailed content outline of the book of Ezekiel.

FOR FURTHER STUDY

See Blenkinsopp (1990) for commentary, Klein (1979) for Judah's experience of the Babylonian exile.

Chapter 12 Bibliography. See Part 2 Bibliography for general works on prophecy.

QUESTIONS FOR REVIEW

1. What are the two main sections of the book of Ezekiel, and what is the basic message of each?
2. Describe Ezekiel's throne–chariot vision and how it relates to his call to be a prophet.
3. When was Ezekiel taken to Babylonia, and how long did he stay there?

4. How did Ezekiel try to convince his companions in exile that Jerusalem was going to be destroyed? Why did he try so hard to convince them of this?
5. What visions did Ezekiel have that related to the temple in Jerusalem?
6. What does the vision of the valley of dry bones signify?

QUESTIONS FOR REFLECTION AND DISCUSSION

1. Ezekiel judged Israel to be guilty of willfully disregarding Yahweh. The first twenty-three chapters are an unmitigated declaration of Yahweh's condemnation. Clearly, Ezekiel had a demanding standard of human moral responsibility against which the people were judged. Ezekiel presumed that the people knew right from wrong but just failed to do the right thing. Is this an adequate view of the nature of human failure and sin? What other factors, other than sheer lack of will-power to do good, may be involved? Also, how does Ezekiel compare with other Hebrew prophets on the topic of sin and divine retribution?

2. The book of Ezekiel has an extended treatment of the issue of individual responsibility in chapter 18. Consider the nature of Ezekiel's argument, and the adequacy of a view that posits individual responsibility for human destiny. Do we get what we deserve? How does what we "get" relate to our past, including our family history and social context? Do you think Ezekiel really posited a theological doctrine of individual responsibility, or may there have been a rhetorical or homiletic purpose behind his way of addressing this issue?

3. Prophets such as Jeremiah and Ezekiel tried to convince the people that they spoke for God, and that disaster was inevitable unless the people changed. Why did the people not heed these prophets? Did it have to do with the message? Did it have to do with the prophets? Did it have to do with the people?

Chapter 12 Study Guide

- *Chapter summary*
- *Key terms linked to the glossary*
- *Concept questions with answer links*
- *Progress tests: true/false, multiple choice, matching, and identification*

BOOK OF THE TWELVE

ASSYRIAN PERIOD

AMOS

HOSEA

MICAH

BABYLONIAN PERIOD

ZEPHANIAH

NAHUM

HABAKKUK

OBADIAH

PERSIAN PERIOD

HAGGAI

ZECHARIAH

MALACHI

JOEL

JONAH

**BOOK OF THE
TWELVE AS A
WHOLE**

FIGURE 13.1 MARTIN LUTHER KING, JR. speaking at the Lincoln Memorial, August 28, 1963.

Words from the biblical prophets have raised human consciousness about issues of fairness and social justice through the ages. Martin Luther King, Jr., drew upon both Amos and Isaiah in his "I Have a Dream" address.

> . . . we are not satisfied, and we will not be satisfied until justice rolls down like waters and righteousness like a mighty stream. . . . I have a dream that one day every valley shall be exalted, every hill and mountain shall be made low, the rough places shall be made plain, and the crooked places shall be made straight and the glory of the Lord will be revealed and all flesh shall see it together.

The **Book of the Twelve** is a collection of twelve prophetic books. In canonical order they are: Hosea, Joel, Amos, Obadiah, Jonah, Micah, Nahum, Habakkuk, Zephaniah, Haggai, Zechariah, and Malachi.

These books have been grouped together since the earliest canonical collections. Augustine in the fourth century B.C.E. seems to have been the first to call them the "minor" prophets (*City of God* 18.29). Though it may sound pejorative, they were labeled minor only because they are shorter in length than the "major" Latter Prophets. To be called the "Minor Prophets," as is still done in some faith communities today, tends to relegate them to the shadows.

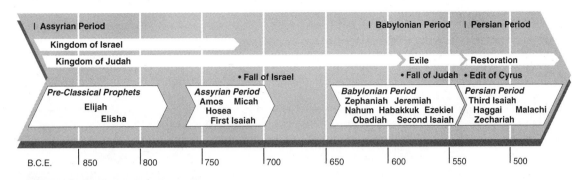

				Babylonian Period	Persian Period

Assyrian Period

Kingdom of Israel

Kingdom of Judah

Exile   Restoration

• Fall of Israel   • Fall of Judah   • Edit of Cyrus

Pre-Classical Prophets	Assyrian Period	Babylonian Period	Persian Period
Elijah	Amos Micah	Zephaniah Jeremiah	Third Isaiah
Elisha	Hosea	Nahum Habakkuk Ezekiel	Haggai Malachi
	First Isaiah	Obadiah Second Isaiah	Zechariah

B.C.E. | 850 | 800 | 750 | 700 | 650 | 600 | 550 | 500

FIGURE 13.2 HEBREW PROPHETS

Minor Prophets.
The prophets Habakkuk and Amos
Are considerably less famous
Than Isaiah or Jeremiah.
It's not that they lack fire
(The curse of any minor prophet
Can send a miscreant to Tophet).
But when they exhort,
They do keep it short.
—Jeanne Steig (1990)

As we will see, there are some gems in these books, and they are worthy of attention. The Twelve Prophets contain expressions of the highest ideals of justice and righteousness, as well as some of the most vivid pictures of the love of God. In addition, they provide insights into the nature of prophecy in Israel and Judah, and information on the history of Israel's religion.

As with the longer books of the Latter Prophets, we have to make a special effort to integrate these books into the chronology of Israel's history. These books dovetail with the historical time period covered by the books of Kings and the postexilic period of Judean restoration. Additional effort is needed to orient these twelve books because their canonical order within the Book of the Twelve is not their chronological order going from earliest to latest.

Because the individual books in the Book of the Twelve are not arranged in historical order, we will reorder them for our treatment, clustering them according to three major historical eras: the Assyrian period, the Babylonian period, and the Persian period.

ASSYRIAN PERIOD

Israelite prophecy tended to coagulate around periods of political insecurity and crisis. The eighth century B.C.E. was just that for the Israelites and Judeans, largely

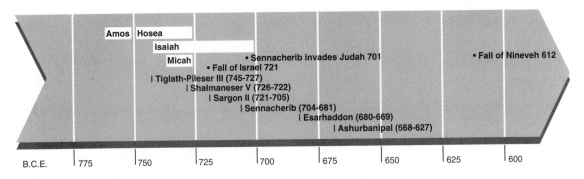

FIGURE 13.3 PROPHETS OF THE ASSYRIAN PERIOD

because of the Assyrians. The Assyrians dominated international politics from the middle of the eighth century till the end of the seventh. Important dates for the end of the Assyrian Empire are 612 B.C.E., which marks the destruction of Nineveh by the Babylonians, and the battle of Carchemish in 605 B.C.E., which definitively established Babylonia as the major power in Mesopotamia.

The earliest prophetic books of the Twelve originated at this time. Amos, Hosea, and Micah all date to the Assyrian Period. These books do not extensively deal with Assyria. Rather, they address the moral and spiritual condition of Israel and Judah in the middle of the eighth century B.C.E.

The rise of the Assyrian empire created foreign policy problems for Israel and Judah. These, in turn, had domestic ramifications. Prophecy was one response to the need for political and spiritual guidance in this period of crisis.

TABLE 13.1 KINGS AND PROPHETS OF THE ASSYRIAN PERIOD

Kings of Judah	Kings of Israel	Hebrew Prophets
Amaziah 800–783	Joash 802–786	
Uzziah 783–742	Jeroboam II 786–746	Amos c. 760–750
Jotham 742–735	Zechariah 746–745	Hosea c. 750–725
	Shallum 745	Isaiah of Jerusalem c. 740–700
	Menahem 745–737	
	Pekahiah 737–736	
Ahaz 735–715	Pekah 736–732	
Hezekiah 715–687	Hoshea 732–724	Micah c. 730

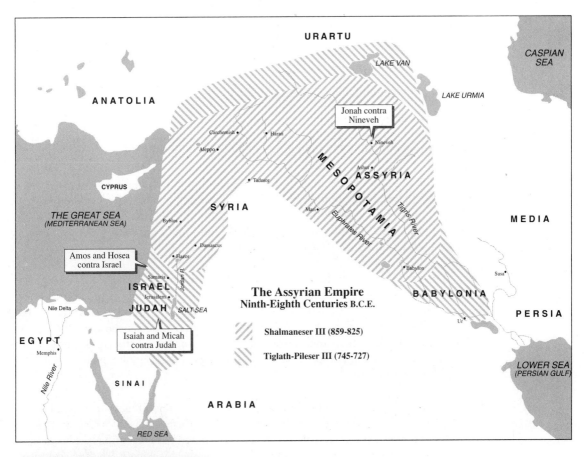

FIGURE 13.4 ASSYRIAN EMPIRE

■ AMOS

Taken in chronological rather than canonical order, Amos is the earliest of all Hebrew prophets with books named after them. **Amos** was an older contemporary of Hosea and Isaiah. He prophesied sometime during the decade 760–750 B.C.E.

The book of Amos appears at first reading to be a collection of sayings with very little organization. But a close reading looking for connections reveals that there are identifiable groupings of material. The first group of similar material is the oracles against the nations (1:3–2:16), discrete units targeting the nations of Syria-Palestine one at a time. Chapters 3–6 are a collection of various Amos sayings. Chapters 3, 4, and 5 all begin with the same phrase "Hear this word . . ." This phrase may have provided the principle of organization for this subcollection. Chapters 7–9 are largely vision reports and so have a certain commonality.

There is strong evidence that the book of Amos grew in stages. Wolff (1977) has posited six stages in the literary formation of the book, beginning with words attributed to Amos himself and ending with editorial additions in the postexilic period. Simplifying somewhat the analysis of Wolff, Coote (1981) has posited three primary editorial stages in the book. The first stage, the Amos Edition, contains Amos' words to eighth century Israel. Among the passages included in this early stage are 2:6–8, 2:13–16, 3:9–12, 4:1–3, 5:1–3, 5:18–20 and 8:4–7. In the following two stages material was added by writers who felt they were speaking with an "Amos voice" in their own age.

The first words of the book were clearly written by an editor, because they refer to Amos in the third person.

> 1 The words of Amos, one of the shepherds from Tekoa, which he saw concerning Israel during the reign of Uzziah, king of Judah, and Jeroboam son of Joash, king of Israel—two years before the earthquake. 2 He said, "Yahweh roars from Zion and thunders from Jerusalem; the shepherd's pastures dry up and the height of Carmel shrivels." (1:1–2)

The very first words are, in effect, the title of the book: "The words of Amos." The editor dates the prophet by reference to the kings ruling in Judah and Israel at the time. This places Amos in the middle of the eighth century B.C.E. Uzziah reigned 783–742 and Jeroboam 786–746. The latter king is usually referred to as Jeroboam II to distinguish him from the first king of the Northern Kingdom. This kind of introduction is typical of a number of prophetic books, including Isaiah, Jeremiah, and Hosea.

> **Earthquake.** This introduction goes further than that of most other prophetic books in making the date even more precise, specifying that the words of Amos date two years before the earthquake. The reference to the earthquake has been correlated with geological data obtained through field work. The archaeological excavation of Hazor in the Galilee region evidenced in stratum VI a particularly violent quake datable to the time of Jeroboam II (see Yadin 1964).

From this introduction we learn a few things about Amos. He was from a little town in Judea called Tekoa and he was a shepherd. This has been interpreted by some authorities to mean that he was poor, but this was not necessarily so. In addition, from 7:14 we learn that he was an agricultural worker, "a dresser of sycamore trees," and he strongly denied he was a professional prophet. Though not belonging to the prophetic guild, he was called to be a prophet directly by God.

Verse 2 contains the theme statement of the book. These, the first words of Amos in the book, describe an angry Yahweh. In roaring like a lion he laid waste the green pastures of Carmel. Note the geographical indicators, for they tell us a lot about Amos' theological and political perspective. Yahweh roars from Jerusalem, the seat of Davidic ideology, and condemns the heartland of the Northern Kingdom.

This raises an important issue concerning the perspective of Amos. It would appear, on first reading, that Amos was an advocate of Zion ideology. But this might depend on the attribution of these words. If they are Amos', then perhaps yes. If they are an editor's words, shaping the book from a Judean and Davidic slant, then per-

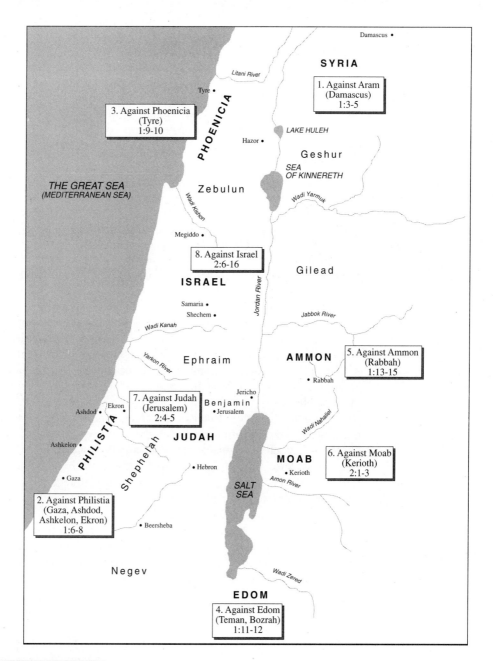

FIGURE 13.5 AMOS' ORACLES AGAINST THE NATIONS

haps no. The one other passage in the book of Amos that reflects a strong Davidic bias is the last paragraph, 9:11–15. Here is a sample, with Yahweh speaking:

> 11 "On that day I will restore David's fallen house. I will repair its gaping walls and restore its ruins. I will rebuild it as it was a long time ago." (9:11)

Clearly looking to the rebirth of the Davidic dynasty, these words are usually attributed to an editor later than Amos' day.

Turning to an examination of the book in terms of its major structural units, the first is 1:3–2:16. This section is a series of condemnatory statements aimed at the nations in Syria-Palestine in this order: Syria (Damascus), Philistia (Gaza), Phoenicia (Tyre), Edom, Ammon, Moab, Judah, and finally Israel (see Figure 13.5).

Notice how Amos jumps from one end of Syria-Palestine to the other, until finally he hits his favorite target—Israel. A sample, the oracle against Syria, gives us the flavor of Amos' language.

> 3 *"Thus says YHWH, 'For three transgressions of Damascus, and for four, I will not revoke it (the punishment) on account of their threshing Gilead with iron threshing sledges. 4 I will send fire on the house of Hazael and it will devour the fortresses of Ben-hadad. 5 I will break the gate bars of Damascus and cut off the inhabitants from the Valley of Aven and the scepter-bearer from Beth-eden. The people of Aram will go to Kir in exile,' says YHWH."* (1:3–5)

Speaking for God in the first person, Amos condemned Syria for dealing cruelly with the Israelites who lived in Gilead, that is, to the east of the Sea of Galilee. The king and his royal city would be destroyed because of their cruelty, and the population would be exiled to Kir, a place far in the east, near Elam.

The oracles continue with all of Israel's neighbors coming under God's condemnation one by one. The condemnation of Judah must have been especially sweet to the Israelites who were Amos' primary audience. They no doubt welcomed his words and urged him on. Israel's enemies deserved what they got! It was a surprise, then, when Amos continued after Judah and exposed God's anger with Israel "because they sell the righteous for silver, and the needy for a pair of sandals" (2:6).

Amos is especially to be appreciated for his sensitivity to matters of social welfare in Israel. He spared no words in condemning the royalty and aristocracy of Israel, who abused the privilege of wealth and even used their authority to get richer at the expense of the poor.

The next major unit, chapters 3–6, is another collection of oracles, but without the focus and structure of the first collection. The words from chapter 4 continue Amos' accusatory tone and strong condemnation of the Israelite ruling elite, in this case the wives of the aristocracy.

> 1 *"Hear this word, you cows of Bashan who are on Mount Samaria—you who oppress the poor, who crush the needy, who say to their husbands, 'Bring us something to drink!' 2 YHWH has sworn by his holiness: the time is definitely coming when they will take you away with hooks, even the last of you with fishhooks. 3 You will leave through breaches in the wall, each of you going straight out, and you will be tossed into Harmon."* (4:1–3)

These words of Amos are direct and announce that punishment is inevitable and close. There is no hint that it can be avoided—the culprits will not be able to dodge the coming doom. Amos does not seem to allow for repentance.

The socio-economic background for these words is an Israelite elite enjoying an indulgent lifestyle at the expense of disenfranchised peasants. Amos' announcement of punishment is so direct and certain that Coote argues Amos must have uttered these words around 745 B.C.E. when Tiglath-Pileser III, the Assyrian expansionist king, came to power and directly threatened Israel. This would account for the vividness and accuracy of the language describing Assyrian policies of capture and deportation.

In addition to castigating the rich ("you cows of Bashan") who callously oppressed the poor (4:1), Amos was critical of Israel's centers of religious worship, especially Bethel and Gilgal (4:4–5; 5:4–7).

> 21 "I hate and despise your festivals; I do not take pleasure from your pious meetings. 22 Although you offer me burnt offerings and your grain offerings I will not accept them. The peace offering of your choice animals I will not eye. 23 Away from me with the noise of your songs! The melody of your harps I will not hear. 24 Let justice roll down like water, righteousness like an eternally flowing stream." (5:21–24)

Amos' famous call for social caring, "Let justice roll down like water!" is one of his most famous statements. Amos took the religious concepts of justice and righteousness, which had primary application to the way God deals with his people, and applied them to social interaction.

In Amos' analysis, Israel was just going through the motions of worshiping God and observing proper rituals, thinking that this was the sum total of their obligation to God. In reality, God valued personal responsibility and community caring above formal worship. Amos here disparaged formal religion when its performers used it to make themselves right with God, in the absence of personal and corporate morality. His words should not be absolutized as a total prophetic condemnation of all formal worship. This is typical of Amos' unconditional language and a fine example of a sweeping condemnation, in its context appropriate, but not meant by Amos to be universalized.

The last major section is chapters 7–9 built around five visions and a prophecy of restoration (see Table 13.2). The first four visions are similarly structured. Each begins with the sentence "This is what my lord YHWH showed me." In each vision Amos saw something that indicated God was going to destroy Israel. In the first (7:1–3) he saw locusts devouring the produce of the land. In

TABLE 13.2 VISIONS OF AMOS

Vision 1	7:1–3	Locusts
Vision 2	7:4–6	Fire
Vision 3	7:7–9	Plumb line
Narrative	7:10–17	Amos vs. Amaziah
Vision 4	8:1–3	Summer fruit
Vision 5	9:1–4	Yahweh by the altar
Salvation Oracle	9:11–15	David's tent

the second (7:4–6) he saw a fire consume the land. In both of these visions, after Amos cried out with concern for Israel, God changed his mind and withdrew the punishment.

In the third vision (7:7–9) Amos saw Yahweh with a plumb line in his hand. This vision is different from the prior two. It is not an image of destruction. Rather, Amos sees God holding a measuring device against which Israel was measured.

> *8b YHWH said, "I am putting a plumb line in the middle of my people Israel. I will never again overlook them. 9 The high places of Isaac will be made barren, and the holy places of Israel will be leveled. I will come against Jeroboam with a sword." (7:8b–9)*

A plumb line is a construction worker's tool consisting of a weight attached to a string. The weighted string provides a true vertical (or plumb) standard by which other objects, such as masonry walls or door posts, can be built straight. Judged against true vertical, Israel was tilted and out of plumb. Religion was not doing it any good. Consequently, Israel's worship centers would be destroyed, especially the "high places," which had Canaanite Baalistic associations. And Jeroboam II, king of Israel, would be removed.

This, the third vision, is not followed directly by the fourth. Instead, a narrative was inserted recording a confrontation between Amos and **Amaziah,** a Bethel priest loyal to Jeroboam II. Amaziah was provoked by the preaching of Amos. In Bethel, the main Israelite worship center sponsored by the king, Amos proclaimed that Jeroboam would die and Israel would go into exile (7:11). Amaziah, in reality, told Amos to go back to Judah where he came from.

This narrative breaks up the flow of the vision accounts, but the arrangement does have a certain editorial logic. The vision accounts condemned Israel for sinning, and especially the third vision account blamed Israelite sanctuaries. The Amos–Amaziah confrontation is evidence of the perversity of Israelite sanctuaries, condemned in the third vision, and evidence of Israelite hardness of heart. Whereas after the first two visions God relented of his planned punishment, there is no relenting in the third and fourth visions. This confrontation account demonstrates that there was no repentant spirit in Israel that could warrant a removal of God's planned destruction.

The fourth vision account, 8:1–3, was built around a visual-verbal pun. Amos saw a basket of summer fruit (Hebrew qayits). Yahweh said in explanation, "the end (Hebrew qets) of my people has arrived." What follows, almost until the end of the book, is a series of disaster descriptions: famine, mourning, violence, exile, death, and despair.

The fifth vision account, 9:1–4, is structured differently from the preceding four visions. Instead of Yahweh showing Amos an object and constructing a lesson around it, here Amos sees Yahweh standing by the altar. He issues an order to "smash the pillar capitals." Either the temple was to collapse on the people and kill them, or the capitals symbolize the heads and leaders of Israel who will not escape punishment.

The last oracle, 9:11–15, contains expectation of the rebirth of the Davidic dynasty and a delightful depiction of the glorious future awaiting the land and its people. The ground will be so productive harvesters will not be able to keep pace, and the people will enjoy peace and prosperity. This last unit is so radically different from the preceding words of Amos, concerning not Israel but the rebirth of the Judean Davidic dynasty, that it is usually attributed to someone other than Amos.

Why was it attached to the book as the final unit? Perhaps because otherwise the ending would be too depressing. In the view of the compiler of Amos in its canonical form, judgment just had to be followed by salvation; it could never be the last word. It was not fitting to end on a note of despair. The final form of the book strongly suggests that judgment followed by salvation was the complete message of God.

Table 13.A is a detailed content outline of the book of Amos.

■ HOSEA

Hosea was placed first in the Book of the Twelve, but we cannot be sure why. Perhaps because it is the longest book of the twelve. Perhaps because someone at one time mistakenly thought he was the earliest prophet of the twelve. The evidence of the book itself, however, indicates that Hosea prophesied a little later than Amos. Like Amos, he prophesied in the Northern Kingdom. Unlike Amos, he was a native of the north. In fact, Hosea was the only non-Judean literary prophet besides Jeremiah.

Hosea's northern origin probably puts him in touch with the substantial northern prophetic tradition represented by Elijah, the Elohist traditions of the Pentateuch, the traditions of Deuteronomy, and probably even Jeremiah. This may account for Hosea's frequent allusions to the decalogue and the Sinai covenant traditions.

Historical indicators in the text, including the editorial framework of the first verse, suggest that Hosea prophesied from 750 to 725 B.C.E. Jeroboam II was the king of Israel at the beginning of Hosea's prophetic activity, and after he died there was virtual anarchy in the Northern Kingdom until its destruction by Assyria in 721.

The final book was compiled much after the time of Hosea the prophet. The book has a discernible structure, falling into two basic parts. The first unit, chapters 1–3, is built around Hosea's ordeal of marrying a prostitute. This marriage functions as a living parable of husband Yahweh's relationship to Israel. The second unit, chapters 4–11, begins with the phrase "Hear the word of YHWH" and consists largely of uncontextualized statements. It has no obvious thematic unity but consists of oracles of disaster and salvation. This alternation of disaster and salvation, even discernible to some extent in the first unit, provides a structuring principle to the book (see Table 13.3).

The first chapter contains a third-person narrative describing Hosea's marriage to **Gomer.**

2 The beginning of YHWH's speaking through Hosea: YHWH said to Hosea, "Go, take for yourself a promiscuous woman and children from promiscuity, because the land is promiscuous with regard to YHWH." 3 He

TABLE 13.3 STRUCTURE OF HOSEA

	Disaster	Salvation
I. Chapters 1–3	1:2–9	1:10–2:1
	2:2–13	2:14–23
	3:1–4	3:5
II. Chapters 4–14	4:1–11:7	11:8–11
	11:12–14:1	14:2–9

went and took Gomer, the daughter of Diblaim. She conceived and bore him a son. 4 YHWH said to him, "Call her name Jezreel, because in yet a little while I will avenge the blood of Jezreel on the house of Jehu, and I will put an end to the kingdom of the house of Israel. 5 In that day I will break the bow of Israel in the valley of Jezreel." 6 She conceived again and bore a daughter, and he said to him, "Call his name Lo-ruhamah, because I will no longer show mercy to the house of Israel. I will not forgive them. [7 But to the house of Judah I will show mercy, and I will save them, by YHWH Elohim, but I will not save them by bow, sword, warfare, horses, or charioteers] 8 She weaned Lo-ruhamah, conceived and bore a son. 9 He said, "Call his name Lo-ammi, because you are not my people, and I am 'Not I am' to you." (1:2–9)

Gomer had three children. The text clearly indicates the first child was fathered by Hosea himself, but the second and third might have been children of "whoredom." In any case, the children serve as prophetic signs having to do with the northern kingdom of Israel.

The first child was named Jezreel (which in Hebrew sounds very close to Israel: *Yizreel* and *Yisrael*, respectively). "The blood of Jezreel" refers to Jehu's bloody *coup d'état* and slaughter of the house of Ahab. For these acts the monarchy would be punished.

The second child's name, Lo-ruhamah, means "Without mercy." The Hebrew word *rehem* (literally "womb") to which it is related recalls descriptions of Yahweh as the merciful God of the covenant (see Exodus 33:19), the one who loves Israel with parental (a mother's?) love.

The third child's name Lo-ammi means "Not my people." This name is also related to covenant notions. The essence of God's covenant with Israel was this: "I will be your God, and you will be my people." The (anti-) covenant context is reinforced with the words "I am 'Not I am' to you." The Hebrew original of the phrase "Not I am" is *Lo-ehyeh*, and undoubtedly puns on the covenant name of God, Yahweh, whose name was revealed to Moses at the burning bush (Exodus 3) as "I am who I am," *ehyeh asher ehyeh* in Hebrew.

A major interpretive, indeed moral, issue regarding this account is whether or not Gomer was a known prostitute at the time of her marriage to Hosea. The command "Go, take for yourself a wife of whoredom and have children of whoredom," as the NEW REVISED STANDARD VERSION renders it, sounds like he was told to marry a practicing prostitute. If she was, then Yahweh was asking a very difficult thing of Hosea.

On the other hand, it is quite possible that the wording was affected by Hosea's experience and theology. The account was, of course, written after the fact of the marriage. While at the time he may not have known she was a prostitute, in retrospect it was obvious that she was. God in his providence must have known ahead of time her propensities; therefore, he had told Hosea to marry a prostitute.

Yet a third interpretive possibility is that Gomer was not unfaithful to the marriage bond as such, but that she was associated with Canaanite Baalistic bridal rites of initiation (Wolff 1965). The children were considered, metaphorically speaking, to be children of "whoredom" because conception was credited to Baal, the Canaanite god of fertility, and not Yahweh.

Hosea was the first prophet to use his family life, and in particular his children, to make a theo-political prophetic point. Prophesying shortly after him, Isaiah would do the same (see Isaiah 7–8). Hosea's marriage to Gomer was a mirror of Yahweh's experience with Israel. Marriage was equated with the covenant God had made with Israel in the wilderness.

Chapter 1 is a third-person account of Hosea's marriage. Chapter 3 is an autobiographical description of his marriage. In his own words Hosea describes "purchasing" a prostitute. Some interpreters suggest this account temporally follows the story of chapter 1, with Hosea buying back his wife after an intervening period of unfaithfulness. Other interpreters view it as the same story of chapter 1, just retold in first-person.

> *1 YHWH said to me again, "Go, love a woman who has a lover and is a prostitute, just as YHWH loves the people of Israel—even though they turn to other gods and love raisin cakes." 2 So I bought her for fifteen shekels of silver and a homer of barley and a measure of wine. 3 And I said to her, "You must stay mine in the future; you must not play the prostitute. You must not have intercourse with a man, including me with you." 4 For the Israelites shall remain many days without a king or prince, without sacrifice or pillar, without ephod or teraphim. 5 Afterward the Israelites shall return and seek YHWH their God, and David their king. They shall come in fear to YHWH and to his goodness in the days to come. (3:1–5)*

Again, the relationship of man and woman is a mirror of Yahweh's relationship to Israel. The specified purchase price consisted of silver and grain, the usual offerings to a deity. After paying the price, Hosea's expectation was that the former prostitute, now his wife, would be pure.

Originally applying to the Israel (read Northern Kingdom) of Hosea's day, the description of the relationship was reapplied by a later writer in verses 4–5 to Judah. Brought to Judah after the fall of the north, the experience of Hosea became a lesson to the Southern Kingdom.

Abstinence from sexual intercourse was appropriated as a symbol of Judah's isolation, without king or sacred paraphernalia in Babylonian exile. Mention of the return included the expectation of the return to power of the Davidic line. Although the people were wayward, days of blessing would return. Perhaps this prophetic material was shaped by Deuteronomic circles, as was so much other classical prophecy. Especially in this case it would be natural for Deuteronomic theology to have an influence, given the similar northern origin of Hosea and Deuteronomy.

As has just been suggested above, chapters 1 and 3 may be viewed as third-person and first-person renderings, respectively, of the same experience of marital betrayal and alienation. It seems, however, that the editor took chapter 3 and intended it to be an historical continuation of chapter 1. Note the use of "again" in 3:1. Perhaps his intention in repeating the scandalous affair was to suggest the patience of Yahweh, who puts up with this people even as time after time they, like Hosea's wife, go running after forbidden gods. A recurring biblical theme was this: Generation after generation of Israelites forget their genuine husband, Yahweh, and sought out the company of Baal and Asherah.

Table 13.B is a detailed content outline of the book of Hosea.

■ MICAH

Micah was a southerner, a Judean, as was Amos. Micah was a contemporary of Isaiah of Jerusalem and came from a rural background, specifically from a town called Moresheth, which lay to the west of Jerusalem. Wolff (1981) argues that Micah was, in effect, a Moresheth city councilman who served as an advocate for his people, presenting their concerns to the rich and famous in Jerusalem. Micah is cited in Jeremiah 26 as an anti-establishment prophet who, nonetheless, was respected by the king.

The book of Micah consists of three units (see Table 13.4). Each of the three main sections opens with the call: "Hear!" Each has the same basic structure, alternating disaster and salvation, such as we saw in the book of Hosea. There is scholarly agreement that most of chapters 1–3 come from Micah, with the latter chapters coming from elsewhere.

Micah prophesied in the latter part of the eighth century during the rising threat of the Assyrian Empire. Except for one oracle that includes the Northern Kingdom within its purview (1:2–7), the bulk was directed against Judah. The oracle that predicts the demise of Samaria places the earliest words of Micah before 721 B.C.E. The explicit allusion to the Babylonian exile, as well as the repatriation hinted at in 4:9–10, indicates that the book went through the hands of editors as late as the postexilic period.

TABLE 13.4 STRUCTURE OF MICAH

	Disaster	*Salvation*
1. Chapters 1–2	1:2–2:11	2:12–13
2. Chapters 3–5	3:1–12	4:1–5:15
3. Chapters 6–7	6:1–7:7	7:8–20

Micah's social criticism consists of a critique of the economic aristocrats, whose greed for homes and property had no bounds. Micah opposed the ritualistic righteousness of the pious (as did the other eighth-century prophets, especially Amos but also Hosea and Isaiah).

> 6 *"With what should I come before YHWH, and bow before God on high? Should I come before him with burnt offerings, year-old calves? 7 Would YHWH be pleased with thousands of rams, ten thousand rivers of oil? Should I give my firstborn for my sin, the produce of my own body for my very own sin?" 8 He has told you, O Mortal, what is good, what YHWH requires of you: Do justice! Love kindness! Walk humbly with your God." (6:6–8)*

This passage appears to borrow from temple liturgies through which the worshiper sought entry into the presence of God (for a similar liturgy, see Psalm 24). The prophet Micah modified this genre and applied it to one's personal relationship with God.

The earnestness with which Micah pursued a critique of the opportunistic and heartless upper class suggests that he may have been one of the farmers who was threatened by the influential aristocracy (see 3:2–3). He probably belonged to that class called "the people of the land," conservative landowners who were distrustful of royal and religious bureaucrats who sought to control their lives.

The preaching of Micah might have contributed to the Deuteronomic reform movement in Judah (Blenkinsopp 1983). It advocated land reform but at the same time was supportive of the Davidic monarchy, as long as kings remained true to Mosaic ideals (see Deuteronomy 17:14–20).

Micah wrestled with the nature of prophecy and condemned prophets who worked for wages. Perhaps he was standing in critique of cult or royal prophets who were eager to please (see 3:5–6). The prophets he criticized produced the official **Zion Theology.** Based on their belief in the divine election of the nation, the Davidic dynasty, and the city of Jerusalem, it defined a theology highly supportive of the establishment and designed to foster high morale and fierce loyalty and pride. Micah merely pointed out that a prophecy that supported this type of theology was prone to deceive the people by feeding their need for support and reassurance, and by telling them exactly what they wanted to hear. When he says "I am filled with power and justice and strength to declare to Jacob his transgression" (3:8), his challenge sounds very much like Amos'. In 3:11–12 he criticized the self-assured security of those who felt Zion and Jerusalem were impregnable.

But the book of Micah does not appear to reject Davidic ideology completely.

> 2 *You, Bethlehem of the Ephrathites, small among the tribes of Judah—you will produce for me a ruler in Israel, one whose origin is venerable, from ancient times. (5:2)*

These words, with most of chapters 4–7, are usually attributed to a writer other than Micah. They put the book more in sympathy with the mainstream of Jerusalemite views by placing hope in the Davidic dynasty. Bethlehem was venerated because "David slept there." It was his birthplace.

Table 13.C is a detailed content outline of the book of Micah.

BABYLONIAN PERIOD

The Babylonian period, technically referred to by historians as the Neo-Babylonian period, extended roughly from 630 to 539 B.C.E. Nabopolassar spread Babylonian influence westward, eclipsing the Assyrians. Babylonian power continued to grow until 605, when Nebuchadnezzar decisively established Babylonian supremacy at the battle of Carchemish. In 587 the Babylonians destroyed Judah and Jerusalem. In 539 Babylon was conquered by Cyrus of Persia, who incorporated Babylonian territory into his empire.

The prophets of the Babylonian period deal with the international crisis. The major issues surfacing in these books are the guilt of Judah, which was the reason God was punishing them, and the role of foreign powers in working out that punishment.

There is about a fifty-year gap between the prophets of the Assyrian period, Isaiah of Jerusalem being the last, and the cluster of prophecy in the Babylonian period. The dating of some of these books is uncertain, but Zephaniah may have been the first of the Babylonian era.

■ ZEPHANIAH

Zephaniah was a Judean prophet, possibly descended from the Davidic line, who was active during the reign of Josiah. His condemnation of the kinds of religious practices that were eliminated by the Josiah reformation in 622 B.C.E. suggests that he prophesied before that time, somewhere between 640 and 622.

Typical of most other Judean prophets, Zephaniah's words cover these three main topics: condemnation of Judah and Jerusalem for religious sins, condemnation of foreign nations (including Philistia, Moab, Ammon, Ethiopia, and Assyria), and promises of salvation for God's people.

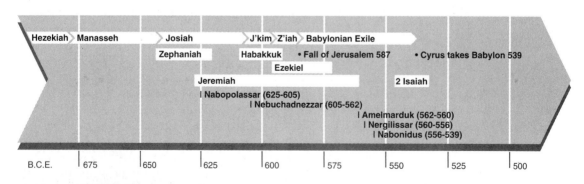

FIGURE 13.6 PROPHETS OF THE BABYLONIAN PERIOD

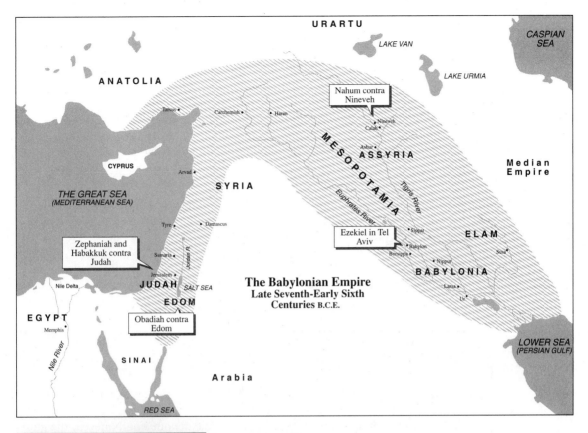

FIGURE 13.7 BABYLONIAN EMPIRE

Zephaniah follows the lead of Amos (see Amos 5:18–20) and proclaims that the **Day of Yahweh** is coming. But it will be a sad day for God's people, and not a day on which they would see victory.

> *14 The great day of YHWH is near, near and fast getting closer. The sound of the day of YHWH is harsh. On it the warrior screams. 15 A day of wrath will be that day: a day of trouble and anguish, a day of ruin and waste, a day of darkness and gloom, a day of cloud and thick darkness. (1:14–15)*

The people will see clouds and fire, effects that in the past signaled the protective presence of God, but this time God would be active to punish them.

Judgment Day. The day of Yahweh notion as found in Amos 5:18–20, Isaiah 2:6–22, and Zephaniah 1:14–2:3 is a prophetic expression signaling the impending destruction of God's own people. Authorities trace the idea back to the conquest and holy war tradition of God's appearing in victory (see von Rad 1991). At that time, of course, Israel was the recipient of the triumphs of Yahweh. The day of Yahweh is the prototype of the judgment day of apocalypticism. A final battle between good and evil will mark the end of history. The cosmic scale of this day is evident in Zechariah 14 and Joel 2.

TABLE 13.5 KINGS AND PROPHETS OF THE BABYLONIAN PERIOD

Kings of Judah	Kings of Babylon	Hebrew Prophets
Manasseh 687–642		
Amon 642–640		Zephaniah c. 640–622
Josiah 640–609	Nabopolassar 626–605	Jeremiah c. 627–562 Nahum c. 620
Jehoahaz 609	Nebuchadnezzar 605–562	Habakkuk c. 608–598
Jehoiakim 609–598		
Jehoiachin 598		
Zedekiah 597–587		Ezekiel c. 593–571
Gedaliah	Amel-Marduk 562–560	Obadiah c. 587
	Neriglissar 560–556	
	Nabonidus 556–539	Second Isaiah c. 546–538

Table 13.D is a detailed content outline of the book of Zephaniah.

■ NAHUM

The book of **Nahum** is one thing only, an oracle denouncing **Nineveh,** the glorious capital city of the Assyrian domain. The book looks forward to the destruction of this city, which epitomized everything the Judeans hated about the Assyrians. Because the city was not destroyed until 612 B.C.E., the book that places its destruction in the future must have been written before that time. Some authorities place it as early as 650, others just before the actual destruction of the city.

Nahum vividly depicts the battle of Nineveh in all its confusion and gore. The prophet seems eager to gloat—no wonder, after the decades of Assyrian tyranny and oppression under which Israel and Judah suffered. The basic theme of Nahum is this: Yahweh punishes any nation, in this case Assyria, that has exploited his people and treated them cruelly. Israel's enemies are God's enemies, and God is supreme, being even more powerful than the mightiest empire.

Table 13.E is a detailed content outline of the book of Nahum.

■ HABAKKUK

The prophet **Habakkuk** was active in Judah during the first part of the Babylonian crisis, from around 608 to 598 B.C.E. Virtually nothing is known about the prophet himself. The book essentially consists of two units. The first unit, chapters 1–2, is a dialogic give-and-take between Habakkuk and Yahweh. The second unit, chapter 3, is a hymn, much in the style of hymns in the book of Psalms, which anticipates the victory march of Yahweh who would vindicate his people.

The first unit is remarkable for the frankness of its theological inquiry. Habakkuk questions God in an attempt to understand the morality of God's actions, specifically how God could use the evil Babylonians to punish his own covenant people, who presumably are not as bad as that nasty Nebuchadnezzar. The investigation of the morality of God's actions is referred to by the theological term **theodicy.** Habakkuk put it this way:

13 Your eyes are too clean to countenance evil. You are not able to put up with wrongdoing. Why, then, do you put up with treacherous people, and are silent when the wicked devour those more righteous than they? (1:13)

Yahweh replied:

2 Write down the vision, make it legible on clay tablets so that anyone in a hurry can read it. 3 For this vision is for a time yet to come. It deals with the end and will not deceive. If it seems to be delayed, just wait for it. It will definitely come, it will not be late. 4 Now the proud, his life is not virtuous. But the righteous, by his faithfulness will he have life. (2:2–4)

Although there are translation problems in verse 4, in essence God's answer seems to be this: Be patient, Habakkuk. This is the way I planned it. The proud, that is, the Babylonians, will meet their end eventually, and in the not too distant future. The righteous, that is, the Judeans, will survive if only they remain faithful to God.

The prophecy of Habakkuk affirms the sovereignty of God, and promises that in the end the wicked would be punished and the righteous vindicated.

Table 13.F is a detailed content outline of the book of Habakkuk.

■ OBADIAH

The book of **Obadiah** is the shortest book in the Hebrew Bible. It is only one chapter long and consists of a single oracle against the country of Edom, which lay immediately to the southeast of Judah. We know virtually nothing about the prophet Obadiah, except that his name means "servant of Yahweh," a common Hebrew name.

The book of Obadiah is undated, but it is usually credited to the period immediately after the destruction of Jerusalem in 587 B.C.E. The theme of the oracle is divine condemnation of Edom because the Edomites took advantage of the Judeans after they were forced to leave Jerusalem. The Edomites even seem to have cooperated with the Babylonians in despoiling Judah at the time of the exile. Obadiah voices the words of Yahweh:

13 You should not have entered the gate of my people on the day of their tragedy. You of all people should not have gazed on their disaster on the day of their tragedy. You should not have looted their goods on the day of their tragedy. (1:13)

With nobody to stop them, Edomites encroached on Judean territory during the period of Judean exile. Obadiah makes reference to the Day of Yahweh as the time Edom would be punished by a vengeful God. He predicts a time when the exiles would return and Mount Zion would again be glorious.

There was a long-standing antagonism between Israel and Edom. The antipathy was traced in the national epic all the way back to the rivalry between Jacob and Esau, who was the ancestor of the Edomites. Obadiah stands with Amos, Jeremiah, and Ezekiel as a prophetic voice condemning Edom. In fact, Obadiah and Jeremiah stand so closely together that portions of Jeremiah's oracle of judgment against Edom in 49:7–22 are found in Obadiah 1–9.

JEREMIAH 49:14–16 (NRSV) *14 I have heard tidings from the LORD and a messenger has been sent among the nations: "Gather yourselves together and come against her, and rise up for battle!" 15 For I will make you least among the nations, despised by humankind. 16 The terror you inspire and the pride of your heart have deceived you, you who live in the clefts of the rock, who hold the height of the hill. Although you make your nest as high as the eagle's, from there I will bring you down, says the LORD.*

OBADIAH 1–4 (NRSV) *1 We have heard a report from the LORD, and a messenger has been sent among the nations: "Rise up! Let us rise against it for battle!" 2 I will surely make you least among the nations; you shall be utterly despised. 3 Your proud heart has deceived you, you that live in the clefts of the rock, whose dwelling is in the heights. You say in your heart, "Who will bring me down to the ground?" 4 Though you soar aloft like the eagle, though your nest is set among the stars, from there I will bring you down, says the LORD.*

JEREMIAH 49:9–10 (NRSV) *9 If grape-gatherers came to you, would they not leave gleanings? If thieves came by night, even they would pillage only what they wanted. 10 But as for me, I have stripped Esau bare, I have uncovered his hiding places.*

OBADIAH 5–6 (NRSV) *5 If thieves came to you, if plunderers by night—how you have been destroyed!—would they not steal only what they wanted? If grape-gatherers came to you, would they not leave gleanings? 6 How Esau has been pillaged, his treasures searched out!*

Obadiah's version is a bit wordier perhaps, but both either draw on the same tradition, or Obadiah borrowed from Jeremiah.

 Table 13.G is a detailed content outline of the book of Obadiah.

PERSIAN PERIOD

The Persian period extended from 539 to 333 B.C.E. The Persian empire was founded by Cyrus and superseded the Babylonian empire. Cyrus was kind to the Judeans, both those who had remained back in Palestine and those dispersed within his empire. He allowed any who desired it to return to Palestine, and even provided financial support.

The prophetic books dating to the Persian period are largely concerned with reconstructing Judean social and religious life after the devastation of the

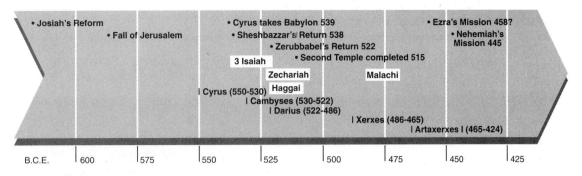

FIGURE 13.8 PROPHETS OF THE PERSIAN PERIOD

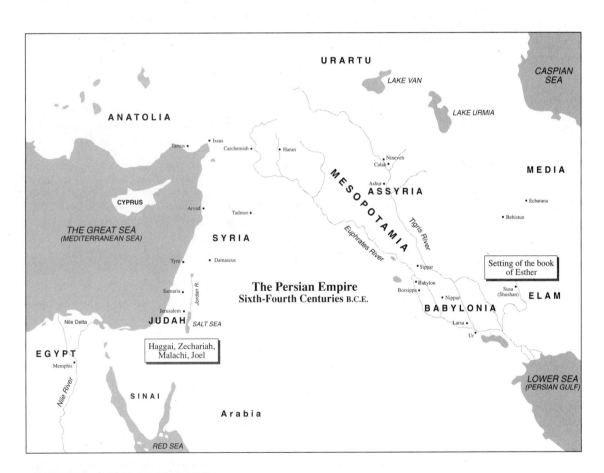

FIGURE 13.9 PERSIAN EMPIRE

TABLE 13.6 KINGS AND PROPHETS OF THE PERSIAN PERIOD

Jewish Leaders	Persian Kings	Hebrew Prophets
Sheshbazzar 538	Cyrus 550–530	
Zerubbabel c. 520	Cambyses 530–522	Third Isaiah 537–520
	Darius I 522–486	Haggai 520
		Zechariah c. 520–518
		Malachi c. 500–450
	Xerxes 486–465	Joel c. 400–350
Ezra c. 450	Artaxerxes I 465–424	Jonah c. 400 (?)
Nehemiah c. 445		Second Zechariah c. 400

Babylonian exile. Many of the prophets of this period were involved in rebuilding the Jerusalem temple and encouraging the people to support it. The prophets also helped to reshape the religious outlook of the survivors of the recent tragedy.

■ HAGGAI

Cyrus allowed the Judean refugees to return to Palestine, and he encouraged them to rebuild the temple in Jerusalem. Life was very difficult back in Judea, and the work, though begun shortly after 538, soon ground to a halt. **Haggai** was a major voice in Jerusalem encouraging the work to be completed. In 520 he gave five addresses, collected in the book of Haggai, which urged the Jewish leaders to assume responsibility for the project and finish it. The leaders at this time were **Zerubbabel**, the governor, and **Joshua**, the high priest (spelled "Jeshua" in the Chronicler's History). Addressing them and the people of Jerusalem, Haggai said,

> 2 Thus says YHWH of hosts, "These people said, 'It is not yet time to rebuild YHWH's house.'" 3 The word of YHWH came through the prophet Haggai, 4 "Is it time for you to live in your paneled homes while this house remains in ruins?" . . . 9 "You have expected much but now it has come to little. When you brought it home, I blew it away. Why?" says YHWH of hosts. "Because my house lies in ruins, while all of you are concerned about your own homes." (1:2–4, 9)

Evidently the people were busy reestablishing their own standard of living while putting off rebuilding the temple until they were satisfied. Haggai demanded that the people reverse their priorities. First, Yahweh's house must be rebuilt, and only afterwards might the people expect to prosper. In large measure due to Haggai's urging, the temple was completed in 515. This temple has come to be called the **Second Temple** to distinguish it from the first temple of Solomon.

Haggai expressed the Jerusalemite priestly perspective that the presence of Yahweh in Jerusalem was the precondition for the return of national prosperity and blessing. And Yahweh would not return until he had a dwelling place, the temple. In his last address to Zerubbabel (2:20–22) Haggai foresaw the demise of the other nations and the rise to power of Zerubbabel who would be God's "signet ring".

Table 13.H is a detailed content outline of the book of Haggai.

■ ZECHARIAH

The prophet **Zechariah** was a contemporary of Haggai, and both were contemporaries of the leaders of the early Judean restoration, Zerubbabel and Joshua. Zechariah prophesied in Jerusalem from 520 to 518 B.C.E. Whereas the style of Haggai's prophecy was hortatory, Zechariah's prophecy took the shape of visions and dialogues with God.

The book of Zechariah divides into two main parts. The first unit, chapters 1–8, is usually attributed to the prophet Zechariah of the sixth century. The second unit, chapters 9–14, are referred to as **Second Zechariah.** It was written by an unnamed prophet (a situation much like that in the book of Isaiah) in the Greek period of the fourth and third centuries B.C.E.

Zechariah was concerned about the religious purity of the people and the morale of Jerusalem's leaders. To that end he attempted to inspire them. In eight visions Zechariah glimpsed the changes ahead. In the first vision he saw four horsemen patrolling the earth in anticipation of the punishment of the foreign nations, and the return to power of Jerusalem. In the second he saw four horns representing world powers and four blacksmiths who would destroy those horns. In the third he saw a man measuring Jerusalem for the rebuilding of its walls, who was then told that the city would be huge, and Yahweh would be its protecting wall.

In the fourth vision Zechariah saw an unclean Joshua, the high priest, standing accused by Satan of being unfit for duty. Then he was confirmed by God and given the duties of the high priesthood. In the fifth he saw two olive trees, representing Zerubbabel and Joshua, who supplied a golden lamp stand that illuminated the world. In the sixth he saw a flying scroll containing the covenant laws. All wrongdoers fell under the judgment of the Torah. In the seventh he saw wickedness personified as a woman in a flying basket, which was removed to a distant land. In the eighth, forming an envelope structure with the first vision, he saw four horses patrolling the earth in anticipation of the messianic age.

The first unit closes on a highly positive note. Yahweh declared that he would return to Jerusalem, restore its greatness, and usher in a time of peace.

7 Thus says YHWH of hosts, "Now I am saving my people from the eastern territory and from the western territory. 8 I will bring them to live in Jerusalem. They will be my people and I will be their God, with faithfulness and righteousness." (8:7–8)

Here Zechariah anticipates even further repatriations of the people. Jerusalem remained the holy city of the Jews, and the ideal for the Jews of the dispersion was to return to Zion. Notice also how Zechariah uses the covenant slogan to express hope: "They will be my people and I will be their God."

We note a couple features of the prophecies of Zechariah. The book of Zechariah demonstrates a considerable awareness of past prophecy. Zechariah clearly sees himself as standing in a long line of prophetic tradition. The book begins by drawing connections.

> 4 "Do not be like your forebears, to whom earlier prophets preached, 'Thus says YHWH of hosts, return from your evil ways and from your evil deeds.' But they did not hear me, says YHWH. 5 Where are your forebears now? Do the prophets live forever? 6 But my words and my laws, which I commanded my servants the prophets, did they not overtake your forebears so that they repented and said, YHWH of hosts has dealt with us according to our ways and deeds, just as he planned to do." (1:4–6)

Zechariah attests here to the power of the word of Yahweh spoken through the prophets. The tragedy of the exile was the result of the hardness of the ancestors' hearts and happened according to God's plan. This should be a warning to the current generation. Furthermore, serving as the introduction to the visions, it reinforces the certainty of the prophetic word concerning the future.

Zechariah also shows his dependence on earlier prophecy by the way he adopts and adapts earlier prophetic images. Jeremiah's prophecy of the seventy years of captivity (Jeremiah 29) was used in the first vision to designate the length of captivity. It also became the basis of Daniel's vision of seventy weeks of years (Daniel 9). And the flying scroll of the sixth vision seems to derive from Ezekiel's scroll (Ezekiel 2–3).

The oracles found in Second Zechariah echo familiar prophetic themes: the destruction of the foreign nations, the restoration of Israel, and the coming Day of Yahweh. Second Zechariah gives special attention to messianic leadership. It describes the triumphant king who comes on a donkey (chapter 9). The evil shepherds would be removed from office (chapters 11 and 13). The evil nations would be finally destroyed, and Jerusalem would become a holy place where Yahweh the king would dwell forever.

Table 13.1 is a detailed content outline of the book of Zechariah.

■ MALACHI

Nothing is known about the prophet **Malachi.** Based on an analysis of the themes of the book, it is supposed that he lived in the period 500–450 B.C.E. He complained about abuses in the Second Temple, which was completed in 515. Concern about foreign marriages (2:10–12) was a major issue in Ezra's day (around 450).

The book of Malachi makes extensive use of the disputation literary form. That is, it frames its prophecies in a question-and-answer dialogic style. In chapters 1 and 2 Malachi examines the shortcomings of the priests using this disputation style.

> 6 "A son honors a father, and a servant his master. I am a father. Where is my honor? If I am master, where is my respect?" says YHWH of hosts to you priests who despise my name. You say, "How have we despised your

name?" 7 By offering on my altar defiled food. You say, "How have we defiled you?" By your saying that the table of YHWH is defileable. 8 "If you offer for sacrifice something blind, is that not wrong? If you offer something lame or sick, is that not wrong? Offer it to your governor! Would he take it? Would he show you favor?" says YHWH of hosts. (1:6–8)

Here the priests are exposed for dishonoring God with inferior animal sacrifices. Damaged animals were not acceptable for sacrifice. Being less valuable, they indicated less than total devotion. The priests kept the better animals for themselves.

Except for a few negative remarks about Edom, Malachi is concerned less with the foreign nations and more with the spiritual condition of the priesthood and the people. He anticipates a judgment day when the wicked would be destroyed and the righteous rewarded. The book closes with references to the two figures that epitomize the Torah and the prophets, thereby upholding the venerable covenant traditions of Israel.

4 Remember the Torah of Moses my servant, that I commanded him at Horeb for all Israel, the laws and rules. 5 Now, I am sending to you Elijah the prophet before the great and terrible Day of YHWH comes. 6 He will turn the heart of fathers to sons and the heart of sons to their fathers, so that I will not come and smite the land with utter destruction. (4:4–6)

The expectation of the return of Elijah before the judgment day is here stated clearly. This has given rise to traditions of Elijah's return within both Judaism and Christianity. Elijah has a place within the traditional Jewish celebration of the Passover yet today. And New Testament writers viewed the career of John the Baptist as the realization of this expected return of Elijah.

The book of Malachi is the last book of the Twelve. It is not necessarily the last book chronologically, given its uncertain setting and our inability to nail down the chronology of some of the other books of the Twelve. Yet it was judged to be a fitting conclusion to the Book of the Twelve, probably because of its eschatological flavor.

Table 13.J is a detailed content outline of the book of Malachi.

■ JOEL

Is it difficult to pin down the historical setting of the prophecies of **Joel**. Early readers must have thought him pre-exilic, hence his placement between Hosea and Amos. The book of Joel was placed before Amos perhaps because of the correspondence between Joel 3:16 and Amos 1:2, and Joel 3:18 and Amos 9:13. Also, Amos, like Joel, was alert to the coming Day of Yahweh.

The evidence for establishing an historical context for Joel is only inferential. Nothing is mentioned about the destruction of Jerusalem, allowing a pre-exilic date that makes him a contemporary of Jeremiah. But the absence of any reference to a king, or to the Assyrians and Babylonians, and an apparent reference to the dispersion, all suggest a postexilic date. The general consensus is that Joel is to be placed somewhere in the period 400–350 B.C.E.

The central theme of the book is this notion of the Day of Yahweh which gives the book as a whole its coherence. The book of Joel divides into two parts. The first part, chapters 1:1–2:27, centers on an elaborate vision of a locust plague, which is a way to warn of the coming judgment of God, the Day of Yahweh. The second part, chapters 2:28–3:21, describes the blessings on Judah and Jerusalem with the coming Day of Yahweh and the corresponding punishment of the surrounding nations.

Joel has sometimes been called a "cult prophet". That is, he was supportive of the priesthood and the temple, and perhaps was even a priest himself. He was concerned that offerings were not coming in as expected, in part because the land itself was not providing the produce, and in part because the people were not forthcoming. Consequently, the priests were unable to perform their duties.

9 The grain offering and the drink offering are cut off from the house of YHWH. The priests mourn, the ministers of YHWH. (1:9)

This concern for the temple and its priests is more characteristic of postexilic prophecy than pre-exilic. Compare Jeremiah, who criticized the complacency and self-servingness of the priests in the Jerusalem temple. Joel is more like Haggai and Malachi in his support of the temple.

Joel was a prophet of the judgment day. He called it the "Day of Yahweh" (1:15), as did Amos, but he broadened the concept into a comprehensive world-historical event. Presuming the postexilic dating of Joel, the book is a study in the appropriation of earlier prophetic tradition, especially that of Amos and the Day of Yahweh.

15 Watch out for THE DAY! The Day of YHWH is near. As destruction from Shaddai it comes. (1:15)

Here Joel uses the priestly designation for the God of the Ancestors, (El) Shaddai. But the God of the Ancestors has turned against Israel. The notion of the Day of Yahweh appears to come out of the conquest tradition. It was Yahweh's day, the day when he demonstrated his power by destroying Israel's enemies. Times have changed. Now his power will be unleashed against Israel. But if the people take warning and repent, disaster can be averted.

The occasion for Joel's core prophecy most likely was the devastating locust plague described in 1:4. The only way to avert disaster is though a communal fast. The coming destruction is described as a locust plague, which became a metaphor for the devastating army that would do the actual work of punishing Israel.

Joel also foresaw the coming of a new age, a time of salvation.

28 "Then afterward, I will pour out my spirit on all flesh. Your sons and your daughters will prophesy, your old men will dream dreams, and your young men will see visions. 29 I will even pour out my spirit on male and female slaves in those days." (2:28–29)

The pouring out of God's spirit seems to continue the spirit theme expressed in Jeremiah and Ezekiel. In those books, God would give the people a new heart and a new spirit. Here, if we are dealing with the same general expectation, this new spirit would have its source in God.

The pouring out of the spirit in Joel has associations with prophetic anointing. The spirit would inspire dreams and visions. The remarkable aspect of the outpouring is its democratic scope. Everyone, young and old, male and female, slave and free, would receive the prophetic gift in the latter days.

Joel's interest in the future has been read as having apocalyptic characteristics.

> 30 *"I will show portents in the heavens and on earth, blood and fire and columns of smoke. 31 The sun will be turned to darkness, and the moon to blood, before the great and terrible day of Yahweh comes."* (2:30–31)

The Day of Yahweh, in Joel's description, has cosmic associations. The fire and smoke we associate with an appearance of God, a theophany. The blood could connote many things, including the taking of life. The celestial imagery here in Joel has an apocalyptic flavor. This, combined with Joel's "end of the world," or eschatological, interest, shows he has affinities with the full-fledged apocalyptic literature which proliferates in the late postexilic period (see Chapter 17).

Table 13.K is a detailed content outline of the book of Joel.

■ JONAH

The book of **Jonah** is quite unlike any other book of the Twelve—in fact, quite unlike any other book in the Hebrew Bible. For one thing, it is a tale *about* a prophet, rather than a collection of utterances *by* him. No one really knows for sure when it was written, or where. And then, of course, there is this business of a fish swallowing the prophet, who survives and is vomited onto the shore. This is so wild, could it really have happened?

To address this and other issues we need to wrestle with the nature of the book. In particular, what is its genre, or literary type? Scholars have made many suggestions. Some authorities tend to argue for the historicity of the record, finding reasons to affirm that a fish could swallow a person live. Many others have read it as fiction, regarding it as didactic narrative, or a novella, a short story, or even a satire of Jewish piety.

The main character in the book is Jonah. He is attested as a real figure by 2 Kings 14:25, which tells us that he was from Gath-hepher and that he was a prophet during the reign of the Israelite king Jeroboam II in the eighth century B.C.E. That would have made Jonah a contemporary of Amos, probably accounting for the juxtaposition of the two books in the Twelve. The book's date of composition, however, is uncertain. Many scholars place it in the postexilic period.

This is the story line. Yahweh directed Jonah to go the Nineveh, the capital city of the Assyrian empire. Jonah went by boat in the opposite direction, so Yahweh sent a storm to stop him. The sailors determined that Jonah was the cause of the storm. After considerable moral anguish, they threw Jonah overboard and the seas calmed.

Jonah was swallowed by a large fish. From the innards of the fish he addressed God with a hymn of thanksgiving for deliverance. The fish deposited Jonah on the Mediterranean coast. From there he proceeded to Nineveh, where he declared its

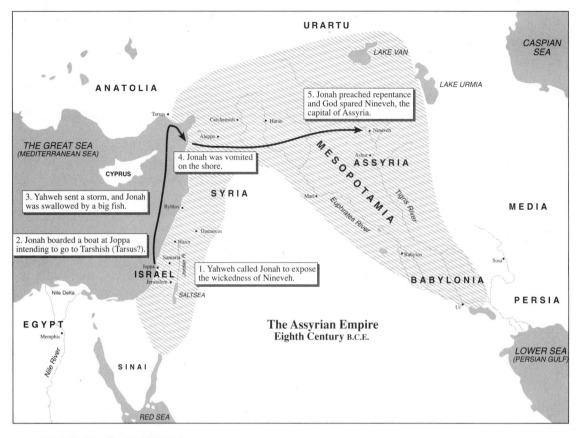

FIGURE 13.10 JONAH AND HIS TRAVELS

Within the figure:

URARTU

CASPIAN SEA

LAKE VAN

LAKE URMIA

ANATOLIA

Tarsus

THE GREAT SEA (MEDITERRANEAN SEA)

CYPRUS

Carchemish   Haran

Aleppo

5. Jonah preached repentance and God spared Nineveh, the capital of Assyria.

Nineveh

4. Jonah was vomited on the shore.

MESOPOTAMIA

ASSYRIA

Ashur

MEDIA

3. Yahweh sent a storm, and Jonah was swallowed by a big fish.

SYRIA

Mari

Euphrates River

Tigris River

Byblos

2. Jonah boarded a boat at Joppa intending to go to Tarshish (Tarsus?).

Damascus

Hazor

Samaria

Jordan R.

Joppa

ISRAEL

Jerusalem

1. Yahweh called Jonah to expose the wickedness of Nineveh.

SALTSEA

Babylon

Susa

BABYLONIA

PERSIA

Ur

The Assyrian Empire
Eighth Century B.C.E.

Nile Delta

EGYPT

Memphis

Nile River

SINAI

LOWER SEA (PERSIAN GULF)

RED SEA

---

doom. The people repented, and God withdrew the destruction he had devised for the city. Then Jonah became very angry. He resented God's mercy and left the city to pout and see if the city would really be spared.

There in the desert God created a bush for Jonah, who was overjoyed to have the shade. God removed it the next day, and Jonah was absolutely distraught that it had died. Hidden somewhere in this was a lesson about grace and mercy. Jonah should have been happy that all Nineveh's inhabitants had not been destroyed; instead he was disappointed.

The book of Jonah has been interpreted in a variety of different ways. The following are some of the interpretive angles that have been proposed.

- It is a satire with snide commentary on prophetic calling, using Jonah as a caricature to portray the reluctance of professional prophets to follow the leading of God.
- It is a criticism of Israelite prophets, exposing their insincerity at preaching repentance, without really wanting to see it, and being disappointed (and taking it as personal failure) when destructive judgment is not meted out by God.

- It is an implicit criticism of the Jewish community, which was generally unwilling to respond to prophetic calls to repentance, in contrast with the willingness of Nineveh, including king, people and even cattle, who responded immediately in faith.
- It is a criticism of an exclusionary Jewish belief in divine election, the belief that God was only concerned about his chosen people and no one else.
- It asserts God's freedom to change his mind, over against prophets and theologians who would limit that freedom.
- It explores the dilemma of true and false prophecy, showing that the words of true prophets (Jonah in this case) do not always come true.
- It is an allegory of Israel in exile, both Jonah and Judah looking to God for the destruction of an evil empire.

The point of the story is difficult to determine (if, in fact, there is only one intended point), especially in light of the indeterminate way the book ends—with a rhetorical question.

> 9 God said to Jonah, "Is it right for you to be angry about the bush?" He replied, "It is right for me to be angry, to death." 10 YHWH said, "You cared about the bush over which you did not labor or cause to grow, which between a night and a night came up and died. 11 Should I not care about the great city Nineveh, in which there are more than 120,000 people who do not know their right hand from their left, and many animals?" (4:9–11)

In light of the prophetic preoccupation with cursing foreign nations, God's concern for those notoriously nasty Assyrians is especially remarkable. Perhaps among other things, the book of Jonah is at least saying that God has the freedom to show mercy to the foreign nations if he wants to. The people of God have no right to be self-righteous or to hold on to the love of God selfishly.

Drawing on the remarkable "God is slow to anger and abounding in love" tradition of the Torah (see Numbers 14:18), Jonah angrily threw back into the face of God the divine reputation for showing compassion.

> 2 "Is this not what I said while I was still back home? That is why I fled to Tarshish in the first place. I know that you are a gracious and merciful God, slow to anger, and abounding in love, and ready to relent from punishing." (4:2)

Jonah's sarcasm exposed his own pettiness and self-absorption, in contrast to God's unbounded love and concern for all people. This lesson seems to have been needed by the Jewish community of the postexilic period, when it was natural to be resentful of its neighbors and self-absorbed. The self-criticism implicit in the book of Jonah makes its inclusion in the canon especially remarkable.

Table 13.L is a detailed content outline of the book of Jonah.

The first recorded reference to these books as the "Twelve Prophets" comes from the Wisdom of Ben Sirach in the second century B.C.E. So they have been grouped together for a long time. But why? Does the Book of the Twelve have unity in any sense? Or were these twelve rather short books placed together on one scroll of sheepskin only for convenience?

Each book has its own editorial integrity and canonical shape, and each can stand on its own. Yet the question we ask at this point is this: Do we gain anything from seeing these books as a collection? Might there have been a theological or literary reason for creating this collection and ordering it in this particular way?

Although nothing can be "proven," the answer seems to be yes. There is a rough chronological progression going from first to last in the Twelve. And there is unity encompassing diversity. The books taken as a whole address the big issues of prophecy; namely, Israel's devotion to Yahweh, the responsibility of foreign nations to respect God's people, and the expectation that God will act in the future to vindicate his people and punish wickedness. And history did demonstrate that the prophets were on target. Punishment occurred when in succession the empires of Assyria, Babylonia, and Persia were eclipsed, and vindication occurred when the people of God survived. Through it all Israel was the place where God's Torah was honored, if at times only half-heartedly.

The book of the Twelve ends on a note of anticipation. Malachi affirmed the enduring relevance of the Torah of Moses and looked forward to the return of Elijah on the Day of Yahweh. He would decisively turn the hearts of the people back to God.

Summary

The following are major emphases of the individual prophetic books of the Twelve, given in the hope that we can begin to recognize the distinctive voice of each prophet.

1. *Amos* powerfully expressed the need for social justice, and announced the coming Day of Yahweh. (eighth century)
2. *Hosea* was the only native northern prophet; he had an unfaithful wife who was a living parable of Israel's unfaithfulness to God. (eighth century)
3. *Micah* was the Judean prophet who championed the cause of the rural underclasses over against the aristocracy of Jerusalem. (eighth century)
4. *Zephaniah* preached the coming Day of Yahweh. (seventh century)
5. *Nahum* condemned Nineveh, capital of the Assyrian Empire. (seventh century)
6. *Habakkuk* asked how Babylonia, an evil nation, could be used by God to punish his own people? (seventh century)
7. *Obadiah* condemned the Edomites for taking advantage of the plight of the Judeans. (sixth century)

8. *Haggai* urged the recently returned refugees to rebuild the Jerusalem temple. (sixth century)
9. *Zechariah* provided spiritual and moral support to the returned refugees in Jerusalem through visions. (sixth century)
10. *Malachi* used the disputation style to probe the spiritual commitment of the postexilic community. (fifth century)
11. *Joel* had a vision of a locust plague, which served as a sign of the coming Day of Yahweh. (fifth century?)
12. *Jonah* tried to avoid his commission to preach repentance to the Assyrians, was swallowed by a fish, and ultimately but unhappily convinced Nineveh to repent. (fifth century?)

Each prophet of the Book of the Twelve has a table containing a content outline.

FOR FURTHER STUDY

Miller (1987) for a general introduction to prophecy that includes the Twelve; Blenkinsopp (1983) for a more critical introduction to prophecy. Interesting individual studies include Coote (1981) on Amos, Brueggemann (1968) on Hosea, and Wolff (1981) on Micah.

Chapter 13 Bibliography for bibliographies to each of the Twelve. See Part 2 Bibliography for general works on the history of prophecy.

QUESTIONS FOR REVIEW

1. Amos What was Amos' attitude to issues of social justice, and how did he perceive the relationship between religious worship and community responsibility?

2. Hosea In what way was Hosea's personal life a lesson to Israel of its relationship to God?

3. Micah What social class conflict is evident in Micah, and how does it relate to covenant theologies?

4. Zephaniah What is the Day of Yahweh theme, employed in Zephaniah and also in Amos and Malachi?

5. Nahum Why did Nahum condemn Nineveh?

6. Habakkuk What issue of God's justice did Habakkuk raise?

7. Obadiah Whom did Obadiah condemn for taking advantage of the plight of the Judeans?

8. Haggai How did Haggai explain the dismal conditions in Jerusalem after the return from Babylonian exile, and what must the people do to change this situation?

9. Zechariah How did Zechariah provide spiritual and moral support to the returned refugees in Jerusalem?

10. Malachi What did Malachi have to say about Elijah?

11. Joel What is the central theme of Joel and how is it related to locusts?

12. Jonah What are some possible interpretations of the book of Jonah, and which do you think best fits the book?

QUESTIONS FOR REFLECTION AND DISCUSSION

1. Is world history really the arena where God expresses his pleasure and displeasure with nations? Most of the twelve prophets, but especially Nahum, Habakkuk, and Obadiah, argued that Israel was "better" than this or that foreign nation. Habakkuk was upset that Judah was suffering at the hands of the Babylonians, when Judah was more righteous than the Babylonians. Is there a divine national ranking system whereby we can say one nation is better than another in God's eyes? Is there a corporate morality that is judgable and that is judged by God, independently of personal morality?

2. Reflect on the vehement prophetic condemnations of the foreign nations. A couple of the Twelve deal only with judgment on foreign nations. Then reflect on the message of the book of Jonah with regard to Nineveh. What were the options with regard to God's justice in relation to God's mercy? Did God treat the foreign nations differently than he treated his own people? Was there a different standard of judgment? For what are they held accountable?

3. The Twelve Prophets, if not the namesakes themselves, then certainly the editors and compilers, were concerned to balance judgment with salvation. Do you think God's punishment is inevitable, or will there always be salvation in the end?

Chapter 13 Study Guide

- *Chapter summary*
- *Key terms linked to the glossary*
- *Concept questions with answer links*
- *Progress tests: true/false, multiple choice, matching, and identification*

WRITINGS

PROLOGUE TO THE WRITINGS

*Apocalyptic
Literature*
Apocalypse
Chronicler's History
Eschatology
Five Scrolls
Parallelism
Stanza
Theodicy
Wisdom Literature
Writings

FIGURE 1 EGYPTIAN SCRIBE

The third major division of the Hebrew Bible is the *ketuvim* (the *k* of Tanak), otherwise called the **Writings.** The title *hagiographa* (Greek for "sacred writings") has been applied to this division by Christians. It contains a variety of materials, including songs, prayers, moral maxims, philosophical investigations, short stories, worship liturgies, and histories. Some of the individual books draw upon material going back to Israel's early history, but all the books of the Writings in their final form date to the postexilic period. The Writings was the last of the three divisions of the Hebrew Bible to take shape, sometime late in the first century C.E.

The Writings will be treated in the next five chapters. The organization of our discussion follows the traditional order of books in the Hebrew canon.

The book of Psalms contains the collection of songs and prayers that Israel used as its voice to God. Proverbs and Job are grouped together in the category

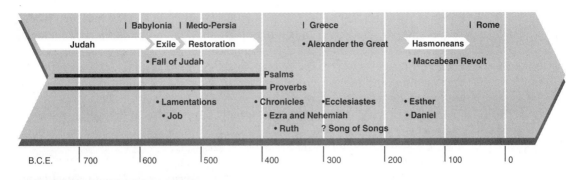

FIGURE 2 WRITINGS

wisdom literature. The Song of Songs, Ruth, Lamentations, Ecclesiastes, and Esther are grouped together and called the **Five Scrolls.** Each was read during one of Israel's major festival or fast days. Daniel is in a class by itself. Not a prophetic book in the traditional sense, it is visionary in a special way and is classed as **apocalyptic literature.** Finally, the books of Ezra, Nehemiah, and Chronicles are historical literature. Together they are called the **Chronicler's History.** It retells Israel's history from Adam to the end to the fifth century B.C.E.

While the Hebrew Bible locates these books together at the end of the canon, English translations separate the books and distribute them among the books of the Prophets, often on the basis of chronology. For example, Ruth was placed between Judges and Samuel because the events recorded in the book are set in the period of the Judges. Esther was situated after Nehemiah because both books are set in the Persian period.

Some placements were made on the basis of literary judgments. Proverbs, Ecclesiastes, and Song of Songs are clustered together because it was thought that all three were written by Solomon. Chronicles was placed after Kings because

TABLE 1 WRITINGS

Chapter	Group	Biblical Book
14	Songs and Prayers	Psalms
15	Wisdom Literature	Proverbs Job
16	Five Scrolls	Song of Songs Ruth Lamentations Ecclesiastes Esther
17	Apocalyptic Literature	Daniel
18	Chronicler's History	1 and 2 Chronicles Ezra Nehemiah

both are historical literature. Daniel was placed after Ezekiel because the prophet Daniel was considered the fourth major prophet. But some of the arrangements are based on misperceptions. For example, Daniel is quite unlike the literature of the Latter Prophets (it actually belongs to apocalyptic literature, and is much later than mainstream prophecy), and Ecclesiastes and the Song of Songs were not written by Solomon.

Three areas of study apply more broadly across biblical literature, but especially to the Writings, and so will be dealt with in this introduction: biblical poetry, wisdom literature, and apocalyptic literature.

Table A correlates the composition dates of the Writings and the history of the late biblical period.

BIBLICAL POETRY

Israel's hymns, songs, and prayers conform to the general conventions of ancient Middle Eastern poetry. Poetry is concentrated language. It compresses a maximum of thought into a minimum of words. Content and form are essential in poetry, and both need to be unpacked if poetry is to be appreciated and understood. This section explains the basic features of biblical poetry.

A significant amount of Israel's literature is poetic in form. The book of Lamentations is a set of five poetic laments over the destruction of Jerusalem. A high percentage of the Latter Prophets is poetry. Even narrative literature occasionally contains poetic inclusions, such as the Blessing of Jacob (Genesis 49), the Song of the Sea (Exodus 15), and David's dirge on the death of Saul and Jonathan (2 Samuel 1).

Defining what constitutes poetry in the Hebrew tradition is not a simple matter. A number of features taken together make for poetry. These features have to do with the nature of the language and the imaginative imagery the poet used (Caird 1980), as well as the structures and forms into which the thoughts were poured (O'Connor 1980).

■ FORMAL FEATURES

A brief treatment of biblical poetry will introduce the main levels where poetic features operate, as well as the tools and techniques available to the poet at each of these levels. Refer to Figure 2 as we discuss the levels of analysis.

Line-Level

A single line of biblical poetry, sometimes called a *stich,* might or might not be a complete sentence. If it is not a complete sentence, then it is completed by the second line, or rarely by a third line. Whether or not a single line is a sentence, there are poetic features that operate on the line level.

Alliteration is the repetition of a consonantal sound in two or more words of a line. It is a sound device that can be perceived only in the original Hebrew version, for obvious reasons. In the following line notice the repetition of the underlined consonants *y, v,* and *d,* repeated in exactly that order.

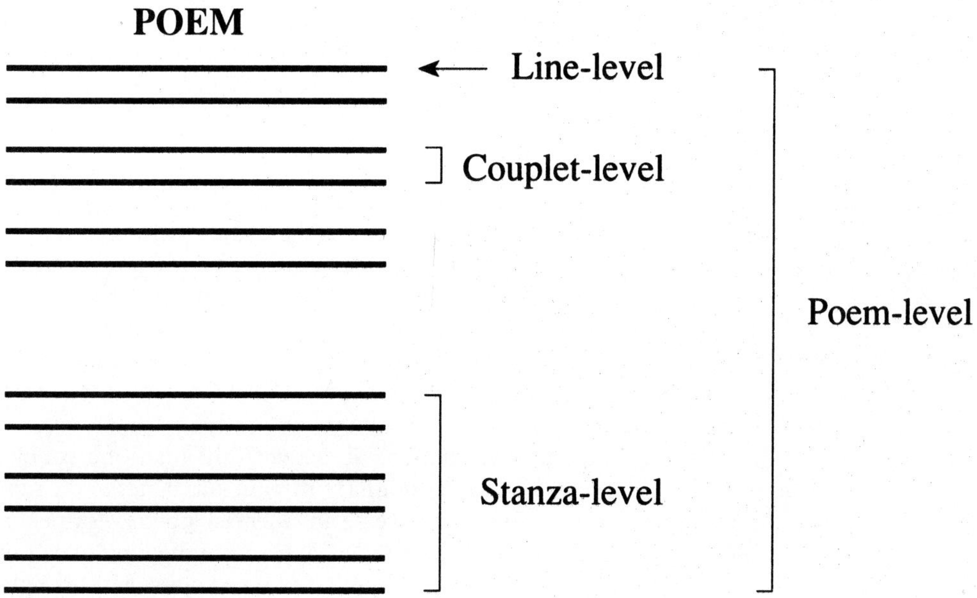

POEM

FIGURE 3   BIBLICAL POETRY FORMS AND TERMS

yovad yom ivaled bo
Perish the day on which I was born.
(Job 3:3a)

Alliteration can sometimes extend across multiple lines. In the following two couplets from Psalm 122 notice the repetition of the underlined sounds *sh* and *l*, with additional alliteration in *ayik* at the end of each couplet.

sha'alu shelom yerushalayim
yishlayu ohavayik
yehi shalom bechelek
shalvah be'armenotayik

Entreat the peace of Jerusalem,
May they prosper who love you.
May peace be within your walls,
Security within your towers.
(Psalm 122:6–7)

Paronomasia is a play on words, a verbal pun, that makes specialized use of alliteration. The poetry of prophecy contains examples of this device. Amos used it masterfully, as in the following line where *Gilgal* puns on "go into exile."

ki hagilgal galoh yigleh
For Gilgal will surely go into exile.
(Amos 5:5)

Also, when Amos saw a basket of summer fruit, *qayits,* he took this as a sign that the end, *qets,* was near (8:12). Paranomasia is used throughout the Hebrew Bible and is not restricted to poetry. For example, Genesis 2:7 says that God formed man, *adam,* out the ground, *adamah.*

Couplet-Level

The basic building block of Hebrew poetry is the couplet (also called a *distich* or *bicolon*), which consists of two contiguous lines related to each other by form and by content. Usually each verse number in English versions of the psalms is a Hebrew poetic couplet, more rarely a triplet (also called a *tristich* or *tricolon*). Poetic analysts designate the two lines of a couplet the A-line and the B-line. A fundamental feature of Hebrew poetry is **parallelism,** the matching structure of lines within a couplet.

What constitutes the formal relationship between the lines of a couplet is difficult to specify. Hebrew poetry does not have rhythm and meter in the same sense as, for example, iambic pentameter verse in Western poetry. Rather, Hebrew poetry seems to be governed by a basic balance between the lines of a couplet (or triplet) whereby each line has the same number of word units. Most couplets have three major stressed word units in each line resulting in a 3 + 3 pattern. In the following example, note that it often takes multiple English words to translate one Hebrew word.

Yahweh how-many-are my-foes						
1	+	1	+	1	= 3	A-line
Multitudes are-rising-up against-me						
1	+	1	+	1	= 3	B-line
(Psalm 3:2)						

Some couplets have unbalanced lines of 3 + 2 word units. Called lament meter (*qinah* in Hebrew), it dominates the book of Lamentations and frequently is found elsewhere. Some analysts have sought to refine the notion of Hebrew poetic meter and suggest that parallelism occurs when each line of a couplet has virtually the same number of syllables (see Stuart 1976).

O'Connor (1980) suggests that parallelism is not constituted on the formal level by rhythm, meter, or line length, but by word devices such as alliteration, verbal repetition, and syntactic dependencies that bind poetic lines together into literary sense units. The problem with analyzing biblical parallelism is that everyone recognizes *that* it exists, but agreeing on exactly *how* it exists is another matter.

A widely-used method of analysis classifies couplets by the meaning, or semantic, relationship of the two lines (Gray 1915, Geller 1979). Four basic types of relationship have been identified: synonymous, antithetic, formal, and climactic.

Synonymous parallelism is present when the notion of the A-line is repeated in the B-line.

Pay attention, my people, to my teaching,	A-line
Be attentive to the words of my mouth.	B-line
(Psalm 78:1)	

In antithetic parallelism, the notion of the A-line is stated in opposite terms in the B-line.

> YHWH *protects the way of the righteous,* A-line
> *But the way of the wicked will perish.* B-line
> *(Psalm 1:6)*

In formal parallelism, sometimes termed synthetic parallelism, the two lines have a formal relationship defined by rhythm or line length, but the A-line is semantically continued in the B-line. The couplet contains only one complete sentence, not two coordinated sentences, as in the other types of parallelism. The two lines are parallel in form but not in content.

> *Like a club, sword, or sharp arrow* A-line
> *is one who bears false witness against a neighbor.* B-line
> *(Proverbs 25:18)*

Climactic parallelism combines synonymous and formal parallelism. The B-line echoes part of the A-line, then adds a phrase that develops the meaning and completes the sense.

> *Accredit to YHWH, O Heavenly Ones,* A-line
> *Accredit to YHWH glory and strength.* B-line
> *(Psalm 29:1)*

Formal parallelism exposes a basic problem with the broad notion of parallelism. Strictly speaking, formal parallelism is semantically non-parallel parallelism, and so is not really genuine parallelism at all. Kugel (1981) challenges the traditional analysis of poetic parallelism and argues that the A- and B-lines of a poetic couplet are not typically synonymous in meaning. He claims that we should not really talk about semantic parallelism. Rather, the B-line was intended to be an expansion, elaboration, or seconding of the meaning of the A-line.

Stanza-Level

A **stanza,** sometimes called *strophe,* is a group of couplets that constitute a sense unit within a poem. It is the poetic equivalent of the paragraph. Stanzas can be recognized by features of form as well as content.

The transition from one stanza to the next can be marked by such things as changes in speaker or addressee, the use of words that signal logical or temporal transitions (such as *but* and *now*), and changes in verb-forms from imperative to past tense.

Stanza structure is obvious when a repeated refrain is used within a unit. In Psalms 42 and 43, which should be taken together as one psalm, the following refrain is found at 42:6, 42:12, and 43:5.

> *My, how downcast you are, my soul,*
> *Upset within me!*

Put your hope in God.
I will praise him yet—my savior and my God.

Parallelism can operate within stanzas to bind multiple couplets into a single thought unit. The individual couplets display their own internal parallelism and also have an external parallel relationship with each other.

A-couplet	*YHWH is my light and my salvation.*	A-line
	Of whom shall I be afraid?	B-line
B-couplet	*YHWH is the fortress of my life.*	A-line
	Of whom shall I be in fright?	B-line
	(Psalm 27:1)	

Thus, using refrains and external parallelism, literary sense units can extend beyond the limits of poetic couplets.

Poem-Level

Biblical poetry sometimes employs techniques on the level of the entire poem to bind couplets and stanzas into one composition. Some of these techniques involve alphabetic schemes in one form or another. Psalm 119 consists of twenty-two stanzas of eight couplets each. The first lines of each couplet of the first stanza begin with the Hebrew letter *aleph,* the first lines of each couplet of the second stanza begin with the letter *beth,* and so on for each of the twenty-two letters of the Hebrew alphabet.

Psalm 34 is an acrostic poem where the first verse begins with *aleph* and each succeeding verse begins with the next letter of the alphabet. Psalms 9 and 10 should be taken as a single poem by the evidence of the acrostic structure which starts in 9 and finds completion in 10.

■ LITERARY FEATURES

In addition to the formal and structural features of Hebrew poetry at its various levels, numerous stylistic features lend a high literary quality to this type of writing. One of the notable features of biblical poetry, and poetry in general, is what we could call *compression.* Poetry packs a large amount of thought into the least amount of words. This often means that a great deal is left to the reader's imagination and interpretative skill. The reader has to unpack poetic expressions to draw out their nuance and intent, and often a biblical poetic line can be rendered in many different ways. Serious study of biblical poetry (short of learning the original Hebrew), demands gathering a variety of different English versions in order to compare translations. This reveals the variety of ways the poetic text could be interpreted and opens up possibilities of understanding.

In addition, the reader must be sensitive to the use of poetic language. Poetry often communicates through the creative and evocative use of language. Imagery can help the reader visualize thoughts or feelings, as in the following verse.

Dogs surround me,
a group of evildoers encircles me.
(Psalm 22:17)

Imagery often takes the shape of simile or metaphor. *Simile* is more obvious than metaphor, because it uses *like* or *as* to introduce the comparison.

I am like a moth to Ephraim,
and like dry-rot to the house of Judah.
(Hosea 5:12)

Metaphor is less direct and more subtle, implying a comparison rather than introducing it with *like* or *as*. Psalm 18 uses metaphors to communicate the steadfastness of Yahweh to the psalmist.

YHWH is my rock and my fortress and my deliverer.
My God is my rock.
I take refuge in him.
My shield and the horn of my salvation, my stronghold.
(Psalm 18:3)

Many of the techniques found in narrative and poetry, including anthropomorphism and personification, can be classified as specialized types of metaphor.

WISDOM LITERATURE

Wisdom is such a broad notion that it might be helpful to make some distinctions. Authorities talk about wisdom literature, wisdom thinking, and the wisdom tradition. The category **wisdom literature** is a literary designation. It is not a native Hebrew category, as far as we can tell, but only a scholar's category to define a large body of literature that is present not only in the Hebrew Bible but also in the literature of Egypt and Mesopotamia. The wisdom literature of the Hebrew Bible is generally considered to be Proverbs and Job (see Chapter 15), Ecclesiastes (see Chapter 16), and the wisdom psalms (see Chapter 14). If we include deuterocanonical books, the Wisdom of Solomon and Sirach (short for the Wisdom of Jesus ben Sirach, also called Ecclesiasticus) would be added.

The books of wisdom literature share a number of characteristics, one of which is an interest in instruction, or pedagogy. This is especially evident in the book of Proverbs, and even in Ecclesiastes, though less obvious in the book of Job. We cannot be sure where and how instruction for ordinary living took place in Hebrew culture. Some authorities who discuss the setting in life of wisdom suggest wisdom may have originated in a family or clan setting, and others associate it with the royal court. Whatever the original context of instruction, the content of instruction was eventually written down. The wisdom books provide direction to those who sought to live moral and productive lives. They were textbooks of a sort to those who were looking for help in how to live life: how to think, how to cope, indeed, how to succeed.

■ THEMES AND TYPES

The notion of wisdom is difficult to define precisely. The terms *wisdom* and *wise* as used in the Hebrew Bible apply to human efforts to master the self, society, or the environment. Von Rad (1962) considered wisdom the "practical knowledge of the laws of life and of the world, based on experience." Much of the wisdom needed for a happy and successful life is gained by experience accumulated over generations. Such wisdom is gained by astute observation and the search for patterns, especially the observation of the relation between cause and effect.

Von Rad (1972) identified the program of wisdom as the search for order in creation and society. Behind the search for order is the belief that God created the world to be harmonious and consistent. The task of wisdom research is to discern this order and suggest ways human beings can align themselves with it. The wise person has the ability to discover this order and live in conformity with it. Seen in this way, wisdom has a lot in common with the modern academic disciplines of the natural and social sciences whose job, broadly conceived, is to discover the laws of the world of nature and human society.

Crenshaw (1969) says wisdom is "the quest for self-understanding in terms of relationships with things, people, and the Creator." He argues that the dynamic tension between order and chaos is a fundamental concern to Israel's faith as a whole, and was not limited just to the wisdom literature (Crenshaw 1981). In Israel's worldview, the ordered realm of God's creation is constantly being threatened by the forces of disorder and dissolution. The creation theology of wisdom literature affirms the divine order by finding it and recommending conformity to it, thereby upholding the goodness and integrity of God.

Murphy (1983) argues that wisdom literature is not so much concerned with the so-called natural order as with human conduct. In other words, he claims that it is ethical rather than philosophical in its intent. Wisdom literature is the attempt to impose order on human life rather than to discover it.

Whybray (1974) views wisdom not so much in terms of the literature that gave it expression but as an intellectual tradition or way of thinking that was not restricted to any one class of people. He says wisdom is innate intelligence and "simply a natural endowment which some people possess in greater measure than others." He argues that within Israel (and more generally throughout the ancient world) the wisdom approach to life differed from the priestly, prophetic, and legal approaches. The wisdom approach utilized logic to master life.

Wisdom literature deals with everyday life and experience. It might seem to have a secular flavor because it is based on human observation and reason, as distinct from divine revelation, as in the Torah and the Prophets. But, as the very inclusion of wisdom literature in the canon makes clear, any division between secular and sacred is foreign to the Hebrew Bible. Human rationality and the truths it discovered were no less sanctioned by God than prophetic oracles.

Crenshaw (1969) uses four different labels to classify wisdom literature. *Nature wisdom* is based on observations of the real world that enable humankind to understand and coexist in harmony with it. This is represented by the onomastica, or lists of names, of Mesopotamian wisdom literature, and is a precursor to what the physical sciences do in classifying and analyzing flora and fauna. According to 1 Kings 4:33, Solomon "spoke of trees, from the cedar that is in the Lebanon to the hyssop that grows in the wall; he spoke of animals, birds, reptiles, and fish."

Practical wisdom analyzed the social order, the modern analogs being sociology and psychology. Practical wisdom, and probably nature wisdom, originated from the everyday life of the family and clan.

Judicial wisdom sought ways to adjudicate disputes, such as when Solomon settled the matter of the two women who both laid claim to the living child (1 Kings 3:16–28). This type of wisdom originated from the royal court.

Lastly, *theological wisdom,* sometimes called speculative wisdom, sought answers to deeply puzzling issues, such as the explanation for human suffering and God's role in upholding justice among humankind. Crenshaw attributes this type of wisdom to professional scribes.

Wisdom literature cannot be easily defined by literary genre. Included within wisdom literature are proverbs, parables, discourses, songs, and poems. What unites these various materials we call wisdom literature is something bigger. An approach to reality and a theory of knowledge. The thought contained in wisdom literature approaches the world of experience through the power of human intellect, not through divine revelation, as is the case with the Torah and Prophets.

Table B lists the various literary forms of wisdom along with examples from biblical wisdom literature.

The wisdom literature of the Hebrew Bible is evidence that there was a lively community of observers and thinkers, perhaps even an intellectual class. Sages searched for the abiding principles of human behavior, sought the laws of the universe, pondered the nature of human life, and raised questions of ultimate meaning.

■ SETTING-IN-LIFE

Social and literary research has investigated the areas of Israelite life that may have given rise to wisdom thought. Was it common folk wisdom originating out of the family? If so, it would tell us about everyday life and what the common people valued. Was it something produced professionally by "academic" wise ones? Then it is more a product of sages employed by the government and religious institutions, and reinforced and encouraged the kinds of behavior they were interested in promoting. It is a question of who set the ethical agenda and determined basic social values. Was it the home or the state?

Von Rad (1962) promoted the view that the wisdom tradition was closely connected with the royal court in Jerusalem. According to his sociological reconstruction, the monarchy of David and Solomon involved an intellectual as well as political revolution. A new way of thinking developed that attended less to cultic matters and tended to view the world more humanistically. This intellectual enlightenment was centered at the royal court, where professional scribes and sages promoted the new outlook.

Crenshaw (1976) has questioned whether there was such a radical turnabout with the rise of the monarchy. He suggests that many of the sayings of Proverbs could have originated in family and clan settings. Royal wise men did not make them up but may have been the first to collect them and write them down. The connection between Solomon and wisdom, therefore, should not be understood in terms of authorship. Rather, Solomon should be considered the royal sponsor of the business of collecting and organizing family and clan wisdom. He is the one who took an official interest in it and made it the object of study and reflection.

■ WISDOM AND THE CANON

Wisdom Literature was treated as the orphan of Israelite theology when the study of theology was dominated by a salvation-history paradigm (see Childs 1970). The salvation-history approach located the central theological importance of the Hebrew Bible in the historical material of the Torah and the Prophets, which portrayed God directing historical events in order to provide salvation for his chosen people. Since wisdom literature did not directly deal with such matters and, in fact, seemed non-theological when defined in those terms, it was sidelined as being of lesser importance.

The salvation-history approach no longer dominates the study of biblical theology. One of the results is that wisdom literature is now more appreciated in its own right and as a reinforcement of other biblical traditions. In fact, many important points of contact with the Torah and the Prophets can now be recognized. Common interests are found in their creation theologies (compare Proverbs 8:22–31 and Job 28:20–28 with Genesis 1–2), and in their concern with education and the importance of instilling values in the hearts of Israel's youth (compare Proverbs 1–9 with Deuteronomy 6:20–25). Furthermore, wisdom literature's concern with faithfulness in worship activities, including offering sacrifices, making vows, and praying shows its commonality with the formal religious regulations of the Torah (see Perdue 1977).

The influence of prophetic theology is evident in wisdom literature's strong connection with the Solomonic tradition. Solomon, of course, is prominent in the book of Kings. Traditional wisdom, especially that expressed in Proverbs, correlates blessing with moral behavior. This theology of retribution has important points of contact with the Torah and the Prophets, especially with the Deuteronomic tradition.

Wisdom literature rests on a basic belief in the goodness of God's created order. This is one of its premises that gets it into certain theological binds, especially with the issue called **theodicy**. Literally, *theodicy* means "the justice of God" and is a label applied to the problem of reconciling the belief that God is a good god who controls the world he created with the facts of suffering and injustice in the natural world. In Israel's case, the issue of theodicy was occasioned most pointedly by the conflict between the Torah–Prophets worldview of a God-given order and the plight of the postexilic community, which suffered at the hands of unrighteous pagans. This issue is perhaps behind the theological discussion carried on in the book of Job.

Certainly within the various books of the wisdom literature, and then more broadly between Torah-Prophets and the wisdom literature, there is a lively theological conversation, perhaps even an argument between theologies in conflict.

APOCALYPTIC LITERATURE

The adjective *apocalyptic* is a modern label for end-time literature. Ancient writers did not tag their own material "apocalyptic." Yet the term is apt; it derives from the Greek verb *apokalyptein* which means "to reveal, disclose, uncover." From this word we get the word "apocalypse."

As we begin to study apocalyptic literature in its various dimensions it is important to define some basic concepts. Hanson (1985) criticizes scholars for mixing apocalyptic categories dealing with form, concept, and sociology. This is a good caution. **Apocalypse** designates a type of literature from the ancient world that typically contained a revelation of the future. Specifically, an apocalypse is a revelation of future events initiated by God and delivered through a mediator (typically an angel) to a holy person.

Within the Hebrew Bible, only Daniel 7–12 fits this formula; Isaiah 24–27 also has characteristics of apocalyptic literature. Other major works falling into the genre of apocalypse are the New Testament book of Revelation (its Greek title is *apokalypsis*), 1 Enoch, 4 Ezra, and 2 Baruch. The first three Gospels of the New Testament each contain an apocalyptic chapter (Matthew 24, Mark 13, Luke 24).

Table C is a list of apocalypses in Hebrew and Jewish literature.

Apocalyptic literature is more than a literary phenomenon. It is associated with identifiable religious and sociological perspectives. *Apocalypticism* applies to the thought world or worldview of the communities that gave rise to apocalyptic literature. Most of the apocalypses were written during times of political persecution. They were intended to encourage perseverance by revealing the destruction of the wicked and the glorious future that awaited the faithful.

It is now generally recognized that all literature is significantly shaped by the historical and sociological characteristics of the authoring community. Schmitals (1975) gives special attention to the developmental dimensions of what he calls the apocalyptic movement. One of the main features of an apocalyptic community is its marginal status within the larger society. In its social, political, or economic alienation the community constructs an alternate universe where eventually it will triumph. This alternate universe comes to expression in apocalyptic literature.

Another important term associated with the study of apocalyptic literature is **eschatology.** Eschatology (from *eschaton,* the Greek word for "end") refers to the complex of religious beliefs that have to do with the end times. The eschatological perspective of biblical literature views history as moving to a final culmination defined by God and brought about primarily by his initiative.

Hanson distinguishes prophetic eschatology and apocalyptic eschatology. Prophetic eschatology is more naturalistic in that it sees God using human agents and historical processes to bring about his purposes in history. This perspective on the future characterizes the classical biblical prophets. Apocalyptic eschatology is more supernatural in that God breaks into history in cataclysmic ways to realize his goal. Human agency is only secondary to divine initiative.

■ FORMAL FEATURES

Apocalyptic literature in the biblical tradition partakes of a common fund of characteristics. Not every apocalyptic literary work evidences all these characteristics, but they are representative of what you can expect to find.

Most apocalyptic literature is in the form of dreams or visions which were witnessed by a seer. The seer then describes the dream in the first-person "I". Most apocalyptic works are anonymous; that is, we do not know exactly who wrote them. The books themselves claim to be the work of certain individuals, most of whom are legendary figures. Apocalyptic books have been ascribed to Adam, Enoch (see Genesis 5), Ezra, Moses, and many others. This phenomenon of ascribed authorship is technically called *pseudonymity* or pseudonomous authorship. The practice probably was designed to facilitate the acceptance of the work.

Most apocalyptic works also employ highly imaginative symbolic imagery. Strange hybrid animals are not unusual. Numbers are also used in symbolic ways. Secret code words, presumably understood by the intended audience but unclear to the uninitiated, are also used. Many apocalypses contain a review of past history but frame it as if it were predictive prophecy. Predictive prophecy after the event (it's a lot more accurate that way) is called *vaticinia ex eventu*.

Apocalyptic literature has a more universal scope than other Hebrew literature. That is, the writers are interested in historical events beyond Israel. It might even be said that they are more concerned with the other nations than with Israel. They see the other nations as under the control of Israel's God, who is determining their history to achieve God's own ends. Almost all apocalyptic literature shares the belief that God has determined the conclusion of history from the beginning.

Apocalyptic literature is ripe with dualisms. A *dualism* is a binary or black-and-white way of looking at matters that does not allow for any gray. Apocalyptic literature's cosmic dualism construes the universe as heaven and earth, a two-storied world. The literature of Israel's monarchic period did not put much stock in a heaven, beyond referring to it as the residence of God. In apocalyptic literature heaven is the place where the most important events take place, including fierce wars between good and bad angels.

Temporal, or chronological, dualism divides the course of history into two eras. History as we know it is called "this age" and is dominated by the forces of godlessness and evil. Apocalyptic writers were very pessimistic about the prospects for improvement in their time. They believed that God would bring this age to an end and would introduce "the age to come," where goodness would prevail.

Ethical dualism is a dualism of human action and character. In apocalyptic literature humanity is divided into two groups. One group, the large one made up of everybody else, is motivated by evil and violently opposes the smaller group of God-fearing, persecuted ones. At the culmination of history God will take the side of the latter and vindicate the cause of right. But until then only the worst can be expected by the righteous remnant. The smaller group, the apocalyptic community, believes that only they are in the right. They advocate a separatist policy, no doubt in response to the domination of the majority population that has marginalized them.

■ LITERARY PARENTAGE

Only one book in the Hebrew Bible is generally classified as apocalyptic literature, and that is the book of Daniel. But that is not to say that Daniel is the only book that shows characteristics typical of apocalyptic literature. Certain motifs characteristic of apocalyptic eschatology can be found in the myths of ancient Mesopotamia. Motifs of cosmic warfare pervade mythic material, such as the battle between the high gods and the sea monsters. This divine warrior motif is also present in biblical apocalyptic literature. The royal cult of Jerusalem, where Yahweh is king, may be the source of various warrior motifs in biblical apocalyptic literature. Also, Persian dualism may have affected the development of apocalyptic ideology.

In addition to having affinities with literature that predates the Hebrew Bible, some scholars suggest that apocalyptic literature has similarities with both the wisdom and the prophetic literatures of the Hebrew Bible. Von Rad argues that it has its origins in wisdom. Hanson (1975) traces the precursors of Jewish apocalyptic literature back to biblical prophecy. He dates the movement from prophetic eschatology to apocalyptic eschatology in the early postexilic period, roughly 538–500 B.C.E. Second and Third Isaiah, dating to the sixth century, contain a good deal of apocalyptic material. This attests a move to apocalypticism, but it really achieved prominence in the second century B.C.E. during the Hellenization program of Antiochus IV.

WRITINGS AS A WHOLE

Together the books of the Writings represent an important stage in the history of Israel and the development of its religion and society. Recognizing all these books as the products of postexilic Judaism enables us better to grasp the nature of that community. Even more, it enables us to understand the theological process, that is, how a faithful community saw itself in relationship to God as it wrestled with its changed circumstances and changing identity.

As we read the individual books of the Writings be alert to the way they draw upon the literature of the Torah and the Prophets. They frequently allude to or quote passages that can be found in earlier writings. Recalling earlier traditions or prophecies became the occasion to affirm the faithfulness of God. Or it was the occasion to call the people back to faithfulness.

The Writings manifest the variety of ways the postexilic community responded to its traditions. Given the wealth of books and perspectives in the Writings, it is evident that there was no single literary response to the Torah and the Prophets. They reveal a vital, reflective community of faith that was wrestling with its theological past. The past was never of only antiquarian interest to them.

The Writings could be considered the record of a dialogue between the postexilic community and the traditions that had defined its faith to that point. In the Writings, the postexilic community wrestled with the meaning and application of the Torah and the Prophets to (what was to them) the modern world. Times change, and in order for faith to be vital and current, traditions must be activated and applied in relevant ways. The Writings are evidence of such tradition activation and application.

None of this should suggest that the Writings are a rehashing of old traditions. They embody significant new departures. For example, wisdom literature, while having roots in the period of the united monarchy, presents a new way of analyzing the world. The genre of the short story, worked out in Ruth and Esther, is a new literary form that presents heroes of the faith as models to be emulated. The Song of Songs is poetry on the theme of human sexuality and love quite unlike anything that came before it. Even the Chronicler's retelling of Israelite history does it in a distinctively new way to meet the needs of the postexilic community.

Conversation is evident within the Writings, the dialogue of old formulations of the faith with new, the dialogue of the past with the present. That dialogue is mostly implicit but sometimes explicit. We will pay special attention to this dialogue in our treatment of the individual books. The fact of the dialogue tells us at least this much about the postexilic community: Religious tradition remained central to its life, and while it responded to tradition in various ways, the "Word of God" continued to speak powerfully.

The Writings contain an almost bewildering variety of voices emanating out of the larger Jewish community. The individual books of the Writings stand as witnesses of what was deeply important to the postexilic Jewish community. The Psalter affirms the continuing centrality of prayer and worship for sustaining the community of faith. As the songbook and prayer book of God's people, it displays the full range of feelings and emotions that are proper for worshipers to bring to God. The preponderance of complaint psalms in the Psalter is testimony to the people's pain, but the complaint psalm's typical move to thanksgiving is testimony to their hope in God.

Wisdom literature supplied a set of principles and values that would sustain the postexilic community. It reaffirmed, in its own way, the principles of reward and retribution, but at the same time honestly faced the enigmas and apparent contradictions in this view of God's role in human affairs. It also provided a philosophy of life that stood as an alternative to the philosophies of the dominant cultures in which the Jews lived. Furthermore, when the demise of Davidic kingship and the absence of prophecy put the postexilic community in a crisis of authority, wisdom literature recommended new models of community leadership in the figures of the sage and the *tsaddiq,* or "righteous one," of the wisdom circles.

The Five Scrolls as a group affirm the importance of remembering formative moments in the nation's history. Some of the festivals associated with the scrolls relate to seasonal and agricultural breakpoints, such as the return of spring and the harvest. These became occasions for the community to remember foundational events in their past. The Song of Songs was read at Passover, marking the exodus from Egypt. Ruth was read at the harvest Festival of Weeks, a time of remembering the giving of the Torah at Mount Sinai.

Individually, the books of the Five Scrolls address important community issues. The Ruth and Esther short stories reveal how the Jewish community wrestled with identity and survival issues. Who can be a member of the community? Can outsiders, epitomized by Ruth the Moabite, be full-fledged members? How shall we survive within a threatening and hostile empire? Will God take care of us as he did through Esther and Mordecai?

The Song of Songs deals with the most elemental, and most essential, human virtue—love. It probes love openly and honestly and affirms that genuine love can be realized only when there is full mutuality in personal relationships. The earliest readings of the book in Jewish and Christian communities must be taken seriously. Those interpretations see the book transcending the topic of human love and view it as the most powerful literary monument in the canon to the covenantal relationship of God and his people.

Ecclesiastes represents the wisdom tradition moving to its logical conclusion. It displays a wisdom enterprise turning in on itself when it asks, What is the purpose of life under the sun? It reveals the frustration of human intellect in the absence of a piety that provides a context for life. Ecclesiastes both affirms the legitimacy of human wisdom and warns that by itself it is not enough.

Lamentations recalls the destruction of the temple in 587 B.C.E. and mourns the loss of Israel's central institution. It stands as a memorial to the importance of the human responsibility to remain faithful and the reality of God's judgment. It was Israel's unfaithfulness that occasioned the fall of Jerusalem. But the impact of the Jewish yearly commemoration of this tragedy goes well beyond breast-beating and mourning. It is a witness to the grace of God that enabled his people to emerge out of destruction and, though scarred and chastened, to flourish.

Written during a time of national crisis, the apocalyptic literature of Daniel provides the vision of a triumphant conclusion to the historical process. The great ungodly empires will one day fall and the kingdom of God will prevail. The legends of Daniel and his friends' heroism encouraged the Jews to remain courageous while their faith was being challenged.

Lastly, the historical literature of the Chronicler demonstrates the value and importance of studying the past. The postexilic community, in spite of all the changes it had undergone, still found itself in continuity with God's people of preceding eras. Seeing this continuity enabled them to affirm that they still stood in covenant with God and that the covenant endures.

The Chronicler's selective retelling of Israel's history highlights the centrality of the temple and its attendants, as well as the importance of the Davidic dynasty. In this way the Chronicler's History proposes that any hope of renewal must be centered on a divinely empowered Davidic messianic kingdom centered around God's holy temple. By tracing the origins of the Second Temple and their priestly institutions back to the time of David and Solomon, they were able with confidence to use them as the basis of community life.

Taken as a body of literature, the Writings demonstrate the persistence and adaptability of Jewish religious faith. In creative ways the community remained true to its traditions, yet found ways to adapt those traditions to meet contemporary challenges.

The forward to the book of Ecclesiasticus, written in the second century B.C.E., refers three times to "the law, the prophets, and the later authors" (or "the rest of the books"). This suggests that the Jewish community had by this time settled on a three-part division of books that together made its canon. The first two parts correspond to the books we have covered in the Torah and the Prophets. The third part, the Writings, was more fluid and open-ended, and probably remained such well into the first century C.E.

The fact that the Writings eventually did become part of the fixed Jewish and Christian canon is quite significant. As we have seen, the Writings consistently appropriate the traditions of Israel and wrestle with them in light of contemporary challenges. The canonization of the Writings is implicitly an affirmation and authorization of such theological conversation and dialogue within the community of faith. It is an acknowledgment that theological reflection is at the heart of the faith community.

God's requirements are always the same. Yet what God expects changes from age to age. God's people are always the same. Yet God's people change with changing conditions. The Writings are evidence of the continuing vitality and relevance of God's earliest and continuing revelation to humankind, and the need for God's people continually to reexamine and reapply it from generation to generation.

FOR FURTHER STUDY

Alter (1985) for biblical poetics, Murphy (1990) for wisdom literature, Hanson (1987) for biblical apocalyptic literature, and Morgan (1990) for the Writings as an appropriation and reinterpretation of tradition.

Part 3 Bibliography. Each chapter of the Writings section also has a bibliography specific to the biblical books treated in that chapter.

QUESTIONS FOR REVIEW

1. What is poetic parallelism in general, and what are the four types of parallelism that can be found in biblical poetry?
2. Name and describe one poetic feature from each analytic level of a poem.
3. Define the notion biblical wisdom and summarize the basic themes of the wisdom tradition.
4. What books constitute the biblical wisdom literature, and what is each of them about?
5. What is the difference between an apocalypse and apocalyptic literature?
6. What are the literary characteristics of apocalyptic literature?
7. What is the typical socio-political background out of which apocalyptic literature arises?
8. How do the Writings bring together Israel's traditions and their late historical experience?

QUESTIONS FOR REFLECTION AND DISCUSSION

1. Much of Israel's prophetic literature and many of the writings are in poetic form. Why would Israel's writers use this form of expression? How does the form of literature affect its reception, especially in regard to poetry?
2. The wisdom tradition represents an empirical, evidential approach to understanding reality. How is the wisdom tradition like the modern scientific approach to understanding the world? How is it different?
3. The original setting of biblical wisdom may have been either the family or the state. Does it make a difference if wisdom comes out of the home rather than the state? How does the setting of values education in the biblical world compare and contrast with the issue of where values should be taught today?
4. What books or movies deal with apocalyptic themes? How do they portray the future? Compare and contrast biblical and modern apocalyptic scenarios.

5. In what ways do we try to discern and control the future? How do our methods compare to apocalyptic methods?

6. How do the Writings affirm both the stability and the vitality of Israel's traditions?

Part 3 Study Guide
- *Chapter summary*
- *Key terms linked to the glossary*
- *Concept questions with answer links*
- *Progress tests: true/false, multiple choice, matching, and identification*

14 PSALMS

FIGURE 14.1 ANCIENT HARPIST   Music is a universal of culture. Both the iconography and the literature of the ancient Middle East reveal a rich musical heritage.

Music is a massive industry—rock concerts, musical theater, symphonies, and CDs, with a style of music for every taste and inclination, including rap, rock, reggae, jazz, classical, country, folk, and more.

Music and song have universal appeal because of their capacity to express what we feel. It is the one medium that directly and immediately resonates with each of our moods and dispositions. The book of Psalms was Israel's musical repertoire and served the same expressive purpose. The Psalms give voice to the deepest human emotions.

The book of Psalms exposes the pulsing heart of Israel. In it we find the lifeblood of the faith of God's people. In it are Israel's songs of faith, expressing joy and confidence in God and God's chosen leaders. In it are Israel's prayers out of times of despair, tragedy, and alienation. By studying the book of Psalms we put ourselves in closest touch with the ebb and flow of the people's relationship to

FIGURE 14.2 ANCIENT MUSICIANS An Assyrian soldier escorts three captive lyrists in this stone relief from the palace of Sennacherib (c. 700 B.C.E.). This scene is reminiscent of the sentiment of Psalm 137, "By the rivers of Babylon we sat down and wept when we remembered Zion. On willows there we hung up our harps. There our captors demanded we sing songs. But how could we sing Yahweh's songs in a foreign land?"

God. The book of Psalms served as the hymnbook and prayerbook of Israel from early times, and remains the voice of God's people in contemporary Judaism and Christianity.

A study of the psalms demands that we investigate both their form and content. The psalms were written as poetry. If you open any English Bible and turn to the book of Psalms this would be immediately evident. English translations use the printing conventions of poetry in their presentation of the psalms: the lines are short and there is a lot of white space on the page. Understanding biblical poetry is essential to understanding the psalms (see Part 3).

The book of Psalms, also called the **Psalter,** is an anthology of songs and prayers. It is not a book in the sense that one chapter logically follows the next. Instead, the individual psalms are like pearls on a necklace. The Psalter has less cohesion as a book than most other books of the Hebrew Bible. There is a staggering variety of psalm types. And the style of the psalms, going from one to the next, frequently changes dramatically. But this is not necessarily a weakness, and in fact may be a key to understanding the book as a whole, as we shall see.

As an anthology, the Psalter has a long history of development. Each of the 150 psalms in the collection has its own composition history. The individual psalms came from various places and times. Only after each psalm existed independently for a time were they all gathered together into the Psalter.

Many of the psalms were addressed to Israel's God. But others were about (rather than *to*) God, the king, or the Torah. Consequently, there is no uniformity across the Psalter in who is being addressed or is speaking. For the most part we do not know who wrote individual psalms. The Psalms are commonly associated with David, the king of Israel, to the point that he is viewed in the popular mind as the author of the Psalter. But this is not entirely correct. The association between David and the Psalms probably arose because he actually wrote some of the psalms, but also by general inference from the historical description of David as the star musician and poet laureate of the court of King Saul. In fact, the psalms themselves do not universally or unambiguously claim Davidic authorship.

Many psalms contain a label, called a **superscription,** that might contain musical directions, notes on how to perform the psalm, historical settings, and possibly suggestions of authorship.

> **Superscriptions.** In many English versions the psalm superscription is printed in different type from the rest of the psalm and is not given a verse number. Some versions, such as the New American Bible and the Tanakh (Jewish Publication Society), follow the Hebrew text more faithfully by giving the superscription a verse number, thereby rendering it more deliberately as part of the text. Readers of different versions should note that this quirk of the versions can result in the same verse being numbered differently in different translations. In this textbook we follow the versification of Hebrew printed editions.

The superscription *mizmor ledavid,* a Hebrew phrase sometimes rendered "A Psalm of David," is often found. While it might indicate Davidic authorship, it might otherwise indicate that the psalm was dedicated to David or belonged to a "David Collection." It remains an open question just what such a superscription means, but it is not necessarily the author's signature. It should also be observed that some superscriptions link particular psalms with the names Asaph, Korah, and Moses. Hence, if the *mizmor le-* phrase in a superscription does indicate authorship, many authors in addition to David are credited.

Table 14.A is a list of superscriptions in the psalms.

Perhaps we should not even talk about authorship in the traditional sense because it seems most of the Psalter consists of anonymous conventional poetry that developed within the community. The following discussion of speech forms and psalm types explains the conventional language of psalmic poetry.

PSALM TYPES

Gunkel (1930) set the course that modern Psalms studies would take. He pioneered a method of distinguishing and identifying the conventional speech forms found in the psalms. These were then closely examined to determine the life situations of the Israelites that made sense of these forms. This general approach is called **form criticism** (perhaps a gentler and more appropriate term would be *form critique*). Building upon the work of Gunkel form critics have refined a now widely used set of basic psalm types, called genres.

Ancient Middle Eastern Psalmody. Egypt and Mesopotamia had rich psalm traditions (see Pritchard 1969: 365–401, 573–86). The poetic forms of biblical psalmody and most of the genres can be matched in extra-biblical literature. For example, the style and theme of the Egyptian Hymn to Aton is notably similar to the creation hymn of Psalm 104. Ugaritic poetic literature is especially close in form and theme. Psalm 29 employs Ugaritic-style language and has been analyzed as in origin a Canaanite hymn to the storm-god Baal.

■ SPEECH FORMS

Speech forms are recurring ways of speaking that can be identified and traced back to typical settings within the experience of the Israelites. Gunkel traced many of the psalmic speech forms back to the worship experiences of the Israelites. Learning to recognize the conventional language of the Psalms will help us appreciate the range of the Psalter's modes of speaking to and about God.

- An **invocation** gets God's attention. It usually presupposes a problem the psalmist needs solved.

2 Give ear to my words, YHWH,
pay attention to my groaning. (5:2)

- **Complaint** language, also called **lament,** describes the psalmist's or the community's difficulty and often expresses feelings of abandonment. The language is narrative in form rather than imperative.

11 Vindictive accusers confront me,
they accuse me of things about which I know nothing.
12 The good I did them they reimburse with evil. (35:11–12)

- A **petition** calls upon God to do something, perhaps intervene and give aid, or forgive. Petition usually contains an imperative (and an exclamation point).

7 Arise, YHWH!
Deliver me, my God! (3:7)

4 Wash me completely of my crime,
and clean me of my sin! (51:4)

- **Praise** language announces the greatness of God. Praise can be generalized language affirming the character of God, or it can be thanks for some specific act for which the psalmist is grateful. As we will see, this distinction is significant.

13 Your name, YHWH, lasts forever,
your reputation, YHWH, through all generations. (135:13)

22 Blessed be YHWH,
for he has wonderfully demonstrated his steady love to me. (31:22)

- A **call to praise** enlists fellow worshipers in acclaiming the wonders of God.

1 Praise YHWH!
Praise, servants of YHWH,
praise the name of YHWH! (113:1)

- A **vow of praise** promises to credit God with the yet-to-be experienced deliverance.

26 I will give you praise in the great assembly,
my vows I will fulfill before those who fear him. (22:26)

13 I will enter your house with burnt offerings,
I will pay my vows to you,
14 what my lips spoke and mouth promised when I was in trouble. (66:13–14)

These are just some of the many modes of speech that can be found in the Psalter. Specific modes of speech combine in various ways in the psalms, often with metaphoric language, to construct larger patterns. These speech form combinations, or psalm genres, will now be identified.

Table 14.B is a table of speech forms with representative examples.

■ PSALM GENRES

Biblical research has developed a set of labels and genre classifications for the psalms. The following discussion takes these results and presents them in a simplified way using three major psalm types and a variety of minor types. Note that cataloging the psalms according to genre is not an exact science, and authorities sometimes differ among themselves on the analysis of certain psalms. Furthermore, though there is a set of ideal psalm types, many individual psalms are not "pure" but, in fact, contain features from several different psalm types. We will examine psalm samples to identify the character of each type.

Complaint

The largest number of psalms in the Psalter fall under the heading **lament.** Perhaps the term **complaint** communicates more immediately what this type of psalm expresses. The heart of a complaint psalm is a description of the suffering of the psalmist and a plea for deliverance. Many complaint psalms also contain petitions and vows of praise. Frequently there is also a statement of confidence that God will come to the rescue. There are two subcategories of this psalm type, divided on the basis of whether an individual or a group is speaking.

An individual complaint can also be called an individual psalm of lament. About one-third of the psalms in the Psalter are of this type. Often included in this category are: 3–7, 13, 17, 22, 25–28, 31, 35, 38–43, 69–71, 77, 86, 88, 102, 109, 120, 130, and 139–143.

Psalm 22 is a well-formed representative of the individual complaint psalm type, especially notable within the Christian community because it was quoted by Jesus of Nazareth as he was being crucified. The psalmist begins with a complaint addressed to God (2–11).

> *2 My God, my God, why have you abandoned me?*
> *Why are you so distant when I call for help, when I cry in pain?*
> *3 My God, I call in the day time but you do not answer;*
> *at night, but I find no relief. (22:2–3)*

Verse 12 is a petition pleading for God to make his presence known.

> *12 Do not stay far from me,*
> *for trouble is close,*
> *and there is no one else to help. (22:12)*

Next the psalmist moves to a vivid description of the trouble he experiences (13–19). Notice the highly metaphoric language he uses to describe his enemies and his own problems.

> *13 Many bulls surround me,*
> *fierce Bashan-bulls encircle me.*
> *14 They open their mouths against me,*
> *ravaging and roaring lions that they are.*
> *15 Like water my life is draining away,*
> *all my bones go soft.*
> *My heart has turned to wax,*
> *melting away inside me. (22:13–15)*

After another petition for God's help (20–22), the writer offers an expression of confidence (23–26) and looks forward to the time he will have overcome his problems through the intervention of God.

> *23 Then I will proclaim your name to the congregation,*
> *in the community I will praise you.*
> *26 I will offer praise in the great assembly,*
> *my vows I will fulfill before those who fear God. (22:23, 26)*

The psalm ends by encouraging everyone to praise God (27–32).

> *28 All the ends of the earth will worship and turn to YHWH,*
> *all the families of nations will bow down before you.*

29 For kingship belongs to YHWH,
the ruler over the nations. (22:28–29)

The psalm moves from personal complaint to anticipation of salvation. The change comes when the psalmist makes a vow to give God the credit for helping him once his problem is overcome (23). He will let everyone know that God is the one who made deliverance possible. The remarkable feature of this psalm, and ones like it, is the psalmist's firm confidence that God will come to the rescue. In expressing this confidence, the complaint psalm actually becomes a psalm of thanksgiving in advance.

A group complaint psalm follows the general outline of the individual complaint psalm but is the expression of the community as a whole. Generally included in this category are: 12, 14, 44, 53, 58, 60, 74, 79, 80, 83, 85, 89, 90, 94, 106, 123, 126, and 137. Group complaint psalms, also called community psalms of lament, expressed the needs of the community when there was a large-scale crisis, perhaps a drought, enemy attack, or national tragedy.

Psalm 80 is typical of group complaint psalms. First, the psalmist tries to get God's attention in the invocation.

2 Give ear, Shepherd of Israel,
you who lead Joseph like a flock,
you who are enthroned between the cherubim. (80:2)

Then in the petition he pleads for God to do something to help them.

4 Restore us, God.
Let your face shine,
then we will be saved. (80:4)

God is invoked as the Shepherd King who sits on his ark of the covenant throne among the divine council, here termed the cherubim. The language of holy war is used in this psalm (signaled by "God of Hosts" in 5, 8, and elsewhere) as the expression of faith in God's power of military deliverance. This is followed by the complaint proper.

5 YHWH God of Hosts,
how long will you be angry with your people's petitions . . .
8 You have let our neighbors fight over us,
and our enemies put us down. (80:5, 8)

After remembering God's past interest in them,

9 You brought us out of Egypt as if we were a vine;
you drove out the nations and planted it. (80:9)

the psalmist goes back to petition for help, and concludes with an affirmation that they would praise God for it.

19b Give us life, and we will call out your name! (80:19)

A subcategory of complaint psalms is the imprecation psalms. These psalms are distinguished by substantial curse sections, often calling down upon the enemy the most awful disasters. The most heinous curses are found in 109 and 137, with 35, 39, 69, 70, and 140 also included in this group.

8 May his days be few.
May another seize his goods.
9 May his children be fatherless,
and his wife a widow.
10 May his children wander about and beg.
May they be driven out of the ruins they inhabit.
11 May the creditor repossess all that he has
May strangers plunder the fruits of his labor. (109:8–11)

8 O daughter of Babylon, you destroyer!
Happy will he be who does to you
what you have done to us!
9 Happy he will be who takes your little ones
and dashes them against the rock! (137:8–9)

These words make obvious the anger of the psalmist. It has been difficult at times for synagogue and church to endorse such strong sentiments. And they are not necessarily to be emulated. Yet by including such raw and genuine expressions of revenge, the Psalter acknowledges the depths to which pain and suffering can drive the people of God. Thus readers of such psalms find assurance that God hears even such outrageous cries for justice, and attends to human suffering.

Thanksgiving

The psalm of **thanksgiving** is the flip-side of the psalm of complaint. Thanksgiving psalms are expressions of gratitude. Whereas the psalm of complaint anticipated God's deliverance, the psalm of thanksgiving was written after deliverance had been experienced. In it the psalmist thanks God for salvation.

The category of thanksgiving should be distinguished from the category of hymn, detailed later. A thanksgiving psalm expresses gratitude for an act of divine intervention in the life of the psalmist, whereas a hymn uses descriptive language to praise something about the character of God. Westermann (1981) calls thanksgivings "psalms of declarative praise," and calls hymns "psalms of descriptive praise." Thanksgiving psalms function to give public testimony to the caring nature of Yahweh and his will to save his people.

As with the complaint category, the thanksgiving category can be subdivided into two subgroups on the basis of who is speaking, an individual or the community. The individual thanksgiving psalm complements the individual complaint psalm. In an individual complaint psalm, the psalmist typically asks for God's help and makes a vow of praise in anticipation of its realization. In the thanksgiving psalm the psalmist makes good on his vow to praise God now that deliverance has come. Generally included in this category are: 9–10, 11, 16, 30, 32, 34, 92, 116, and 138.

Psalm 30, a typical thanksgiving psalm, begins by recalling the adversity now past and then recounts the salvation.

3 YHWH my God, I cried to you for help,
and you healed me.
4 YHWH, you have brought me up from Sheol,
you have returned me to life
as opposed to those who have gone down to the underworld. (30:3–4)

The psalmist shares his joy by calling upon the people of God to credit the turn-around to God.

5 Sing praises to YHWH, you saints,
and give thanks to his holy name! (30:5)

After recounting in more detail the story of his affliction and his rescue (7–13a), he concludes with his commitment to continue praising God.

13b YHWH my God,
I will give thanks to you forever. (30:13b)

The group thanksgiving psalm was used on occasions of regional or national celebration. Included in this category are: 65–68, 75, 107, 115, 118, 124, 125, and 129. This type of psalm arose out of Israel's experience of victory and deliverance from foreign threat.

1 If YHWH had not been on our side—
Let Israel say it!—
2 If YHWH had not been on our side
when our enemies attacked us,
3 then they would have swallowed us up alive.
6 Blessed be YHWH
who has not given us up as game to their teeth. (124:1–3, 6)

Not many psalms of this type found their way into the Psalter, perhaps because it was assembled in the postexilic period. By this time Israel no longer existed as a nation-state, so no longer experienced saving deeds of national scope. Communal psalms of thanksgiving became less relevant to their experience.

Hymn

A **hymn** is a song in praise of God or in praise of something about God. It contains generalized praise language. It is not so much praise for what God has done to save (as in psalms of thanksgiving), as praise for who God is. Often included in this category are: 33, 103, 104, 113, 117, 134–136, and 145–147.

1 Praise YHWH (Hebrew halleluyah)!
Praise, servants of YHWH,
praise the name of YHWH.
2 Blessed be the name of YHWH
from this time forward and forever!

3 From the rising of the sun to its setting
the name of YHWH should be praised!
4 YHWH is high above all nations,
and his glory above the heavens! (113:1–4)

In addition to hymns of general praise, more specific sub-types can be identified, depending on what it is about Yahweh that is deemed worthy of praise.

A *creation hymn* finds reason to praise God for the wonder and magnificence of the natural world. Usually included in this category are: 8, 19, 104, 139, and 148. Among creation hymns, Psalm 19 is notable for the way it joins the revelation of God's glory through creation with the revelation of God's will through Torah. The first half of this Psalm (1–6) deals with nature.

2 The heavens express the glory of God,
and the expanse evidences his craftsmanship.
3 Daily it speaks volumes,
nightly it declares knowledge. (19:2–3)

A *hymn of Yahweh's kingship* celebrates the rule of Yahweh. Included in this category are: 47, 93, and 96–99. Some of these psalms begin with the shout "Yahweh is king!" alternately translated, "Yahweh reigns!" Another feature held in common by this group is the affirmation that Yahweh rules over the entire world. Psalm 93 is typical of this category.

1 YHWH is king,
he is majestically robed,
YHWH is robed,
he is clothed with strength.
He has founded the world;
it will never be moved.
2 Your throne was founded in the beginning,
you are everlasting.
3 YHWH, the floods raised,
the floods raised their voice,
the floods lifted their roaring.
4 But more majestic than the thunder of powerful water,
more majestic than sea waves,
is YHWH, majestic on high. (93:1–4)

The threat to Yahweh's power is the primeval waters. Compare the mythological background to the Priestly story of creation (see Chapter 1). Yahweh triumphed at creation over the waters of chaos and demonstrated thereby his supremacy, here celebrated in hymnic praise.

New Years Festival. Mesopotamian documents attest a Babylonian new year festival when Marduk was ritually enthroned. On the basis of this evidence some authorities have attempted to reconstruct a festival of Yahweh's enthronement as king, yearly celebrated as the autumn new year observance (Mowinckel 1962). On this theory the "YHWH reigns!" psalms were used in Israel's ritual of Yahweh's enthronement. However, direct evidence within the Hebrew Bible for an Israelite festival which parallels the Babylonian new year festival does not exist.

In Jewish traditions, the kingship of Yahweh psalms are messianic and forward-looking in anticipation of the decisive historical realization of the kingdom of God. In Christian traditions, they are eschatological and prefigure the coming of the messiah.

Mount Zion was the location within Jerusalem of Yahweh's temple. As Yahweh's residence, it naturally became the object of hymnic praise in a song of Zion. Generally included in this category are 46, 48, 76, 84, 87, and 122. Psalm 48 praises Zion with obvious hyperbole.

2 Great is YHWH
and he must be praised profusely
in the city of our God.
His holy mountain,
3 beautiful in height,
is the joy of the entire earth—
Mount Zion, in the farthest north,
the city of the great King.
4 Inside its fortress God
has demonstrated he is a reliable defender. (48:2–4)

In the ancient world, mountains were the dwelling places of high gods: Zeus on Mount Olympus, Baal on Mount Zaphon, Marduk on the ziggurat, and Yahweh on Mount Sinai. As the Hebrew people moved from the Sinai to Canaan, the residence of their God moved to Mount Zion within Jerusalem. Although geographically not overwhelming, Zion took on the mythic dimensions of divine mountain dwellings. It became a symbol of the presence and power of Israel's God, and consequently Israel's absolute security.

A hymn to Israel's king, sometimes called a *royal psalm*, praises Israel's earthly king as the representative of God. Generally included in this category are 2, 18, 20, 21, 45, 72, 89, 101, and 110. Although Israel never divinized its kings, still the kings were considered to be divinely appointed and stood in a special relationship to God. The dominant theology of Israel's monarchy, the Davidic covenant, was articulated in the Deuteronomistic History. The Davidic covenant, as laid out in Nathan's oracle in 2 Samuel 7, is the object of praise in Psalm 89.

2 I proclaim that your loyalty is established for all time,
your faithfulness is as sure as the heavens.
3 You said, "I have made a covenant with my chosen one,
I have sworn to my servant David:
4 'I will establish your descendants forever,
and build your throne throughout all generations.'" (89:2–4)

As part of the hymnbook of Israel, used especially in the postexilic period, royal psalms perpetuated the messianic ideal, namely, Israel's hope in the Davidic line to provide national leadership and resurrect an independent nation.

Minor Types

The following minor psalm types do not easily fit within the three main categories of complaint, thanksgiving, and hymn.

Torah psalms, including 1, 19:7–14, and 119, are hymns in praise of God's revelation in Torah. At 176 verses, Psalm 119 is notorious for being the longest chapter in the Hebrew Bible. In this psalm, as in the other Torah psalms, the writer recommends a life of Torah-keeping as the path to wellness.

> *1 Blessed are those whose way through life is blameless,*
> *who walk in the Torah of YHWH.*
> *2 Blessed are those who keep his decrees,*
> *who genuinely seek him. (119:1–2)*

The Torah psalms, with their talk of blessing and Torah observance, have a great deal in common with Deuteronomic theology.

Generally included in the category of *wisdom psalms* are: 8, 36, 37, 49, 73, 111, 112, 127, 128, and 133. They offer practical advice for living. Also, they operate with a black-and-white contrast between the wicked and the righteous. They hold these traits in common with the wisdom tradition of the book of Proverbs (see Part 3 for wisdom literature in general and Chapter 15 for Proverbs).

> *1 Do not be intimidated by the wicked,*
> *do not envy evildoers.*
> *2 For they will quickly dry up like grass,*
> *and wither like herbs.*
> *3 Trust in YHWH and do good,*
> *so you will dwell in the land and enjoy security. (37:1–3)*

In their affirmation of God's blessing upon the righteous, they also have much in common with Torah psalms.

A liturgy is a standardized format used in public worship or in a ritual. *Liturgy psalms* have survived for entering the temple (15, 24), temple celebration (68), priestly blessing (134), covenant renewal (50, 81), and ritualized condemnation of foreign gods (82, 115). Liturgies are those psalms that most obviously involved public performance, even if the exact shape of that performance remains unknown. Psalm 15 was a liturgy used for admission to the temple. The first verse was spoken by a priest or other official, the reply given by the pilgrim seeking entry.

> *1 YHWH, who may live in your tent?*
> *Who may dwell on your holy hill?*
> *2 Those who live morally and do what is right,*
> *who sincerely speak the truth. (15:1–2)*

Songs of trust, also called songs of confidence, are found in both individual and community forms. Songs of trust are generalized expressions of faith in God, without having a specific backdrop of adversity. Generally included in this category are 11, 16, 23, 62, 63, 91, 121, and 131. Psalm 23 is the most famous song of trust.

> *1 YHWH is my shepherd,*
> *I lack nothing.*
> *2 He gives me rest in green fields,*
> *he brings me to peaceful waters.*
> *3 He refreshes me,*
> *he leads me down moral paths*
> *for the sake of his reputation. (23:1–3)*

There is an almost bewildering variety of psalms in the Psalter, and a bewildering set of terms to go along with them. But the variety and range of psalm types open a window on the spiritual life of faithful Israel. In these psalms, which range over all the possible human emotions and ways of relating to God, we see people of faith bringing all of their feelings and emotions to God. This truth may help us to grasp why the Psalter has continued to shape the voice of God's people through the ages.

Table 14.C lists the psalm types and classifies each psalm according to its type.

PSALM THEMES

The psalms are a kaleidoscope of voices and tones, forms and types. They come from many different people across the broad span of Israel's history and geography. The Psalter is far from being a system of thought. Yet a synthesis of its thoughts and themes may be able to distill an approach to life worth considering.

■ WORSHIP THE KING

The hymns of Israel sketch a picture of a world where God is king and the kingdom is glorious. The entire creation is the work of God (19) and everything in creation is well ordered to sustain life (104). His power is evident in the forces of nature which he controls (29). The king of creation maintains order against the forces of chaos and evil (93). God created humanity as the pinnacle of his creation (8).

All nations are subject to the rule of Yahweh (47). He orders the course of history to prosper his people (105, 106). His Torah word maintains justice and right order in the world (119). God rules the world from his headquarters in Zion (48, 87) and the temple is his home (11). Public ceremonies and processions keep God's beneficent rule from Zion in high awareness (24, 120–134).

God's human agents, Israel's kings, translate divine rule into community life (89) and world affairs (2). At the king's accession to the throne he is assured of divine support (110). The royal marriage becomes a national spectacle (45). And the role of Israel's kings as defenders of righteousness is celebrated (21).

Yahweh is worthy of worship for all that he has done in creation and in history to maintain justice and champion his people.

> 6 Come, let us worship and bow down,
> let us kneel before YHWH our Maker.
> 7 For he is our God,
> and we are the people of his pasture,
> and the sheep of his hand. (95:6–7)

■ LIFE AND DEATH

The psalms have a much more inclusive notion of life and death than seems to prevail in the modern world, where life and death tend to be defined in physiological terms. Physicians and ethicists, for example, agonize over when to cease life support of a brain-dead patient. The psalmist on the other hand views temporal existence as on a continuum between life and death. If the quality of life is high, then there is life; if there is sickness or poverty, then death is near. The place of greatest distance from God is *sheol* (the underworld), the pit, the miry clay.

> 3 May my prayer come before you,
> incline your ear to my cry!
> 4 For I am full of trouble,
> and my life approaches sheol.
> 5 I am reckoned among those pit-bound.
> I am a person without strength. (88:3–5)

There is no memory of God in sheol, and the dead cannot praise God, only the living. In distress the psalmist is confident he will yet see the goodness of Yahweh in the land of the living (27:13). Yahweh is the psalmist's only security. He is described as a rock, a refuge, and a fortress. The psalms of trust are expressions of confidence in his protecting power. They give reasons why the psalmist can depend on him in times of complaint.

The complaint form is by far the most common genre of psalms. Along with the thanksgiving form it reflects the two anchor points of Israel's life before God. The psalmist was either in the depths of trouble looking toward heaven for help, or in the heights of salvation reflecting on how God had saved him. The testimony of the complaint and thanksgiving psalms when seen as complementary expressions is that the person of faith is always oriented to the heights of salvation. If in the depths of disaster, by anticipation; if in the heights of wellness, by giving God thanks for it.

Brueggemann (1984) classifies the basic psalm types according to their function within the life of faith. Complaints are psalms of disorientation. They express the experience of oppression and loss. Thanksgivings are psalms of reorientation. They affirm a world of justice and order after the experience of restoration. Hymns are psalms of orientation. They direct attention away from the human experiences of loss and recovery to the secure world of blessing, wisdom, torah, and divine kingship.

Torah is revelation. Prophecy is proclamation. The Psalter is response. It is a record of Israel's faith response to the God who sustains their life. Sometimes the response is individual and personal. Other times it is communal and national. But it always comes out of a stance of faith, and no matter what the emotion, no matter how deep the alienation or exalted the praise, it is always directed to the God of their salvation.

PSALMS AS A WHOLE

The forms of the psalms indicate that they emerged out of the life of the people. The degree to which they reflect formal worship settings or just ordinary life is subject to debate. Many of the psalms are prayers of individuals and may reflect the personal piety of the psalmist.

On the other hand, some of the psalm types suggest that communal worship was their original setting in life, especially hymns with their call to praise. Liturgy psalms (15, 24) and the songs of ascent (120–34) were presumably used in formal processions to the sanctuary. Community laments would have been employed in services of prayer and fasting. Yet there is very little indication in the Psalter itself of the way the psalms were utilized in worship, apart from the superscriptions, which are themselves secondary. Perhaps the obscure word *selah* that concludes stanzas in certain psalms was a liturgical direction used in communal performance (3, 9).

While many of the individual psalms were composed in the pre-exilic period, the collection of 150 psalms called the Psalter dates to the postexilic period. The Psalter is sometimes called the "Hymnbook of the Second Temple" because the compilation and final editing of the Psalter was completed within the lifetime of the temple rebuilt by Zerubbabel, probably sometime around 325–250 B.C.E. The Psalms Scroll from Qumran is the earliest surviving manuscript that contains a collection of biblical psalms, but their serial order does not match the book of Psalms (see Sanders 1962).

Table 14.D classifies the psalms according to their possible time of composition.

On the way to compiling the Psalter from individual psalms there seem to have been stages to the collecting. Clusters of psalms can be identified having similarities of one sort or another (see Table 14.1). For example, Psalms 93–99 have to do with Yahweh as King, and 120–134 are all superscripted as Songs of Ascents. Virtual duplicates of certain psalms exist, which indicates that an independent psalm could find its way into separate subcollections of texts. For example, Psalms 14 and 53 are almost identical, the major difference being that Psalm 14 uses Yahweh as the name of God, and 53 uses Elohim. This squares with the first subcollection, 3–41, which as a whole uses Yahweh and probably originated as a collection in Judah, and 51–72, which as a whole uses Elohim and probably originated in Israel of the divided monarchy.

TABLE 14.1 PSALM SUBCOLLECTIONS

3–41	Yahwistic Psalms of David
42–49	Psalms of Korah
51–72	Elohistic Psalms of David
73–83	Psalms of Asaph
84–88	Psalms of Korah
93–99	Psalms of Yahweh's Kingship
111–118	Halleluyah Thanksgiving Psalms
120–134	Songs of Ascents
146–150	Halleluyah Thanksgiving Psalms

At some point the psalms were organized into five books (see Table 14.2). Each book ends with a benediction. Division into five books perhaps emulates the structure of the Torah of Moses, and was meant to suggest that this work contains the totality of Israel's response to God, just as the Torah contains the definitive revelation from God.

In Hebrew the Psalter is called *tehillim,* meaning "praises." On first thought this seems a bit strange, since the single largest category of psalms is the complaint. Yet something especially important is being stated through this label. Granted, there is a great deal of complaint, yet even in psalms of complaint the psalmist concludes with a vow to praise.[1] So, even though the present is a disaster, the psalmist is looking forward to the heights of salvation. Whether in the heights or the depths, the psalmist is intent on praise. At one and the same time then, the Psalter declares that complaint is authorized for the person of God, it is an allowable approach to God, and yet complaint will not, and must not, end there.

TABLE 14.2 THE PSALTER

Book	Chapters	Benediction
1	1–41	41:13
2	42–72	72:18–20
3	73–89	89:52
4	90–106	106:48
5	107–150	150 in its entirety

[1]Psalms 39 and 88 are rare exceptions to the typical movement of complaint psalms from lament to praise. These two psalms contain unmitigated complaint, with apparently no salvation in view.

An analysis of the distribution of psalm genres within the Psalter reveals an interesting pattern that may help justify *praises* as the title of the book. Individual complaint psalms dominate the first half of the book. Group genres of thanksgiving and hymn dominate the second half. Thus, there is a shift in emphasis from the lament of the individual to the praise of the community as one moves from the beginning to the end of the Psalter (see Gottwald 1985). This reinforces the movement from death to life in the theology of complaint and thanksgiving noted above.

Table 14.E displays the distribution of individual and group genres across the Psalter.

No matter where Israel happened to be on the spectrum of human experience, from adversity on the one extreme to prosperity on the other, there would be a psalm that could express its deepest fears and highest joys. The psalms taken together contain the full range of human attitudes and responses to God. Delight, appreciation of the work of God, alienation, despair, cursing, compassion. It is all here. The collection certainly is saying that all of these human feelings and emotions are permitted within the fellowship of God's people. And they can be brought before God. They do not have to be hidden.

Furthermore, these psalms constituted Israel's manual of songs and prayers used for worship. This reinforces the reality that Israel lived its life in the presence of God. Remembering, questioning, praying, and praising were all done in the context of the community's worship. Worship was not isolated from real life but was the activity where real life was sorted out, where the people sought understanding, where life was affirmed, and where credit was given to God.

Table 14.F is a detailed content outline of the Psalter.

FOR FURTHER STUDY

Gunkel (1930) for an introduction to the basic psalm types, Guthrie (1966) for the themes of the Psalter, and Brueggemann (1983) for the life of faith reflected in the Psalter.

Chapter 14 Bibliography. See Part 3 Bibliography for general works on biblical poetics.

QUESTIONS FOR REVIEW

1. What are the three basic psalm genres?
2. What are the reasons for thinking the Psalter was used in formal worship?
3. What is the basic theology of the Psalter as reflected in its most frequent genres?

4. What is the relationship between psalms and psalm superscriptions?
5. What is the evidence that there were stages in the collecting of the psalms as the Psalter took shape?

QUESTIONS FOR REFLECTION AND DISCUSSION

1. Apart from the book of Psalms, most of the Hebrew Bible is presented as God's revelation to Israel. The Torah was divine instruction mediated through Moses. Prophetic literature contained a divine perspective on history. The Psalter, on the other hand, contains the songs and prayers of Israel directed to God. Instead of "top down," they are "bottom up." In what sense, then, does the Psalter lay out the authoritative way in which God's people should approach him?

2. Why do you think Israel's songs and prayers were written in poetry? Why must we keep in mind that they are poetic? What effect does the fact that they are poetry have on the task of interpretation?

3. Considering the overall shape of the Psalter, what is the effect of having so many different types of psalms in one book? What does the variety in the psalmist's modes of speaking to God have to say about the way synagogue and church can, and perhaps should, speak to God?

Chapter 14 Study Guide

- *Chapter summary*
- *Key terms linked to the glossary*
- *Concept questions with answer links*
- *Progress tests: true/false, multiple choice, matching, and identification*

15 PROVERBS AND JOB

Life's Little Instruction Book

511 suggestions, observations, and reminders on how to live a happy and rewarding life

FIGURE 15.1 LIFE'S LITTLE INSTRUCTION BOOK by Brown (1991) is a collection of "511 suggestions, observations, and reminders on how to live a happy and rewarding life." Here are some catchy examples:

- Use your wit to amuse, not abuse.
- Think big thoughts, but relish small pleasures.
- Live your life as an exclamation, not an explanation.

The book of Proverbs was "Life's Instruction Book" for the Israelites, a treasury of short sayings for living a long life.

There is a considerable market for advice on how to be a good person and get the most out of life. Self-help volumes frequently top the best-seller lists. Seminars on self-improvement and success, such as Dale Carnegie's "How to Win Friends and Influence People," draw large crowds. Dear Abby, Ann Landers, Heloise, and other syndicated newspaper counselors dole out practical, no-nonsense advice for life's problems. And, of course, moms and dads just love to give advice . . . most frequently, it seems, when it's not wanted.

Every community finds ways to transmit its accumulated knowledge, sometimes through storytelling or through institutions of learning. In the old days, grandparents passed on wisdom seated around the campfire or the kitchen table. And parents taught their children by word and example. In the Hebrew tradition, no less than any other, parents were concerned to instruct the next generation how to cope with life and be productive citizens. Such traditions on life and success are gathered in the book of Proverbs, one of the books of Israel's wisdom literature (see Part 3).

HAGAR THE HORRIBLE

However, not everyone who adopts the tried and true habits of success will actually find success. The circumstances of life sometimes seem to frustrate every effort to achieve happiness and prosperity. How can this be so? Where is the justice of life? How should one cope with failure? The book of Job probes just such questions.

PROVERBS

Advertisers work hard to find just the right phrasing to impress their product on our minds. Sayings such as "It's the Real Thing" and "Just Do It!" have immediate associations for many of us. Likewise, insights into human behavior and prudent practice have been distilled into short memorable sayings called maxims and aphorisms. Ben Franklin's *Poor Richard's Almanac,* with sayings such as "a penny saved is a penny earned," is an American cultural artifact.

A **proverb,** much like a Ben Franklin maxim, is a short, memorable saying that encapsulates a truth about life. Proverbs are typically framed as matter of fact statements of the way things are. But really they are lessons about the way you should be. For example, the proverb "One wise-of-heart keeps commandments; a muttering fool comes to ruin" (10:8) consists of declarative statements, not commands. Nonetheless, the command is obvious: Be a wise and moral person! Although such declarative statements comprise the bulk of proverbs, there are other types of statements in the book, including riddles, allegories, taunts, and autobiographical sketches (see 24:30–32).

Just as do many English maxims, biblical proverbs frequently contain a play on words or alliteration, at least in the original Hebrew. Most biblical proverbs take the form of couplets containing parallel members, called the A- and B-lines. See, for example, Proverbs 16:1.

> *The plans of the heart belong to humans,*   A-line
> *The answer of the tongue comes from Yahweh.*   B-line

Parallelism is typical of biblical poetry generally (see Part 3). Most Israelite prophecy was written in parallel style, as were all of the psalms.

There is a clear division in the book of Proverbs between the prologue and the proverbs proper. The prologue consists of poetic discourses on wisdom topics such as the nature of wisdom and the desirability of getting it. The proverbial wisdom consists of lists of proverbs.

■ PROLOGUE (1–9)

The first collection within the book of Proverbs is chapters 1–9. It serves as an introduction or prologue to the rest of the book by developing themes in brief poetic essays. The topics of these essays include the origin of wisdom, justification for studying wisdom, the character of wisdom and folly, and the role of wisdom in creating the world.

Of all the collections the prologue contains the most variety, and, compared to the remainder of the book, it contains more references to God. This had led some authorities to date the prologue later than the rest of the book and to say it was composed to form an introduction to the proverb collections of chapters 10–31 (McKane 1965, Whybray 1965). This inference operates on the assumption that early wisdom was secular, and that wisdom was incorporated within a religious worldview only later. However, a comparison with the Egyptian wisdom tradition, which predates Israel's, calls this view into question. It uses an instructional literary form similar to that found in the prologue, and it also personifies Lady Wisdom as a goddess similar to the prologue.

Wisdom Instruction

The purposes for proverbs are stated in 1:2–6, which functions as the introduction to the book. Proverbs are

2 For learning wisdom and discipline,
for understanding insightful words;
4 for getting instruction in wise behavior,
righteousness, justice, and impartiality;
4 for giving shrewdness to the unlearned,
knowledge and discretion to the young—
5 Let the wise also hear and increase learning,
and the sophisticated improve skill;
6 for understanding proverb and puzzle,
words of the wise and their riddles. (1:2–6)

Note all the words referring to education: learning, understanding, instructing, teaching. The book of Proverbs is introduced as a textbook in wisdom. This paragraph is especially helpful because, by way of recommending the book, it provides a number of terms which are at least partially synonymous with wisdom, thus enabling us to get a sense of the scope of this foundational notion. The notion of wisdom is associated with discipline, instruction, understanding, shrewdness, knowledge, discretion, learning, and skill.

The prologue is framed as the instructions of parents to their son. Wisdom is the knowledge of the right way to live, and they look to give him guidance based on their experience.

8 Hear, my son, your father's instruction,
and do not reject your mother's teaching. (1:8)

Though perhaps self-evident, it bears mentioning: Wisdom is something that can be taught and that can be learned. The son has a choice to make. Will he choose the practice of wisdom, or will he be a fool? It is up to him. Wisdom, unlike intelligence, is neither genetically determined nor a matter of divine endowment. It can, indeed must, be acquired.

Fear of Yahweh

A fundamental theme of Israelite wisdom is that the **fear of Yahweh** is the beginning of knowledge and wisdom. This affirmation is made immediately after the purpose statement quoted above, and serves as that statement's culmination.

7 The fear of YHWH is the beginning of knowledge;
wisdom and discipline fools despise. (1:7)

The phrase "wisdom and discipline" is also found in 2a and functions as a way to bind verses 2–7 together as the thematic introduction to the proverbs. This device is called an *inclusion*. Placed before the actual instructions, the "fear of Yahweh" statement serves as the basic postulate of the book. It conditions all that follows and serves as a reminder that even though wisdom's instruction has to do with matters of personal behavior, family responsibility, business ethics, and community loyalty, it is grounded in the fear of God.

What is the intent of the phrase "fear of Yahweh"? The notion may have originated in that edge-of-death fear that Israelites felt in the presence of God, such as when they were gathered at Mount Sinai after the exodus. But in a wisdom context fear is not to be understood as terror or fright. It refers to the deep awe and reverence for God one must have in order to live properly. One must always be aware that there is a God and that he holds persons responsible for their actions. Knowing that Yahweh keeps account of behavior is a marvelous incentive to act wisely and properly.

The truth that "the fear of Yahweh is the beginning of wisdom" is well-nigh universal in biblical wisdom literature. It is found additionally in Proverbs 9:10 near the conclusion of the prologue, in Job 28:28, in Psalm 111:10 (a wisdom psalm), and in apocryphal Sirach 1:14.

Table 15.A is a key-word-in-context study of the phrases "fear of God" and "fear of YHWH" in biblical literature.

Lady Wisdom and Mistress Folly

Throughout the prologue wisdom and its opposite are made to look like real people using a literary device called **personification**. Wisdom is portrayed as a respectable and proper woman (1:20–33; 8:1–36; 9:1–6). Folly is pictured as a loose woman, ready to deceive the young man with sensuous pleasures and lead him to his death (7:6–27; 9:13–18). The description of Mistress Folly is so sexually explicit that it no doubt held fascination for the young man under instruction (see Figure 15.2). Perhaps the literary device of sensual personification was used to snare the young man's attention, just as modern advertising uses voluptuous women to sell everything from toothpaste to fast cars.

There are a couple of further observations we can make about these personifications. Wisdom is a female!—a remarkable concession for a patriarchal society (see Newsom 1989). In part this was linguistically natural because the Hebrew word for wisdom, *hochmah,* is grammatically feminine in gender. Still, this literary personification develops the notion above and beyond the demands of grammar.

The opposite of wisdom is not so much stupidity as it is willful disregard for right order. Wisdom's opposite is personified as a mistress or prostitute. This figure tries to entice its victims into abandoning honorable behavior for immediate gratification. This is wisdom literature's analogue to the personifications of prophetic literature. Hosea, Jeremiah, and Ezekiel all characterize the covenant unfaithfulness of Israel as her whoring after other divine pretenders such as Baal.

The importance of female figures in embodying wisdom notions is reinforced in the last chapter of the book where there is a return to female imagery. The concluding acrostic poem praises the ideal wife (31:10–31).

> *10 A virtuous wife, who can find?*
> *Her worth is more precious than jewels.*
> *11 The heart of her husband trusts in her.*
> *Profit he will not lack. (31:10–11)*

This passage contains perhaps the most profuse appreciation of real women in the Hebrew Bible, at least women in their role as wives. The description recalls the positive picture of wisdom, personified as a woman, in chapters 8–9. There is the hint that the industrious wife is the incarnation of Lady Wisdom. All the ideal

FIGURE 15.2 WOMAN AT THE WINDOW   "I looked out the window of my house, through the lattice I saw a young man who lacked discernment" (7:6–7). The book of Proverbs warns young men of the seductions of evil, personified as an alluring woman.

qualities of Lady Wisdom are read into the ideal wife. Or, if the prologue was in fact composed after chapters 10–31, perhaps the virtuous wife was the model for Ideal Wisdom! In either case, this poetic conclusion to the book of Proverbs concretizes the virtues of wisdom and recommends their practice.

Creation Theology

The most profound personification of wisdom occurs in 8:22–31. She describes herself as the first being Yahweh acquired or created, even before the physical world took shape. Wisdom was God's mastercrafter,[1] present with him through the entire process of world formation. The implication seems to be that wisdom was God's instrument or tool for creating his realm.

> *19 YHWH founded the earth by wisdom,*
> *he established the heavens by understanding,*
> *20 the depths broke open by his knowledge,*
> *and the clouds drop down the dew. (3:19–20)*

[1] Alternately translated "confidant" or "little child," it is not entirely clear what this term means, so we cannot base too much on it.

This association of wisdom with creation, combined with the priestly notion that God created the world by the word of his mouth ("And God said, 'Let there be...'") ascribes a powerful role to wisdom. Some have suggested that this is the closest Yahweh comes to having a consort, or female companion, in the orthodox tradition (see Lang 1986). Creation by word and wisdom was picked up by the New Testament writer John, who intentionally conjoined Jesus of Nazareth with creation, word, and wisdom when he started his gospel by saying, "In the beginning was the word, and the word was with God, and the word was God."

■ PROVERBIAL WISDOM (10–31)

Chapters 10–31 are mostly just single-sentence proverbs in linear sequence, one after another in almost random order. Hence the bulk of the book of Proverbs is sentence wisdom, short self-contained sayings in two or three parallel lines (see Part 3 for parallelism). This contrasts with the wisdom poems that typify the prologue.

The proverbs build a world of values in a binary way. Opposites are contrasted and the positive virtue is clearly identifiable. The most pervasive opposing pairs are these.

Wisdom and folly—
Wisdom is a fountain of life to him who has it,
but folly is the chastisement of fools. (16:22)

The righteous and the wicked—
The righteous will never be removed,
but the wicked will not dwell in the land. (10:30)

Rich and poor—
A rich man's wealth is his strong city,
the poverty of the poor is their ruin. (10:15)

Industry and laziness—
A slack hand causes poverty,
but the hand of the diligent makes rich. (10:4)

Humility and pride—
When pride comes, then comes disgrace,
but with the humble is wisdom. (11:2)

Proverbs are presented as observations of life based on the experience of generations of wise people. Yet they are not simply statements of the way things are. Clearly they also recommend the way things should be. The sentence wisdom of Proverbs upholds the traditional values of family, hard work, honesty, humility, and loyalty. These proverbs appear, then, to be an instrument in the socialization of Israel's youth, and probably especially its leaders, and a way to instill the time-honored values of the community.

Proverbial wisdom is also situational, or pragmatic. While proverbs are framed as universal statements, they need to be applied with discernment. Folk wisdom often sounds contradictory taken in the abstract. Put "look before you leap" alongside "he who hesitates is lost." Which is correct? Well, it depends. Sometimes caution is advisable, but other times speed is essential.

Likewise, the sage advice of the proverbs needs to be applied situationally and not automatically. The collector of the proverbs recognized this and wryly made his point.

> *4 Do not answer a fool according to his folly,*
> *or you will be like a fool yourself.*
> *5 Answer a fool according to his folly*
> *or he will be a fool in his own opinion. (26:4–5)*

Table 15.B identifies various themes in Proverbs 10–31 along with examples of each. This table would be an effective resource for studying the value system and ethics of proverbial wisdom.

Retribution Theology

The traditional wisdom of Proverbs divides humanity into two groups, the wise (equated with the righteous) and the foolish (the wicked). The characteristics and behaviors of each group are identified. But proverbs go further than just classifying two types of people. They indicate what will become of each.

> *14 Wise men store up knowledge,*
> *but the nonsense of a fool draws ruin near. (10:14)*

In this way the community values summed up in the notion of righteousness are given divine sanction. That is, righteous behavior is recognized and rewarded by God, and folly is punished. **Retribution theology** maintains that God uncompromisingly and unfailingly punishes the wicked for their evil deeds and rewards the righteous with long life and prosperity. The book of Proverbs affirms retribution theology as strongly as the Deuteronomic tradition. It maintains the strict correlation between the practice of wisdom and earthly reward, contrasted with the foolish life that leads inexorably to tragedy and ruin.

> *30 The righteous will never be removed,*
> *but the wicked will disappear from the land. (10:30)*

The book of Proverbs thus projects a vision of the world as an ordered moral universe where truth and justice rule. This basic theological perspective of the proverbial wisdom outlook will be challenged and refined in other wisdom literature, including the books of Job and Ecclesiastes.

Table 15.C is a key-word-in-context study of the word righteous *in the book of Proverbs. A study of this evidence will reveal the character of the* tsaddiq, *the righteous one.*

■ INTERNATIONAL CONNECTIONS

Israel did not exist in political, religious, or intellectual isolation from its geographical neighbors. Intellectual and even direct literary contact is nowhere more evident than in Israel's book of Proverbs.

The book of Proverbs looks a great deal like the *instruction literature* that has survived from ancient Egypt. The Maxims of Ptahhotpe and The Teaching for Merikare are major Egyptian writings that contain the advice and instruction of a father to his son (see Simpson 1972). So also the book of Proverbs is addressed to the son. This literature gives practical advice on how to behave and act in business with different classes of people and how to be a good and effective public servant. The commonality of the book of Proverbs with Egyptian instruction literature suggests that it may have been the court wisdom that was used to train the next generation of Israel's leaders for effective public service.

The Instruction of Amenemope has the most direct bearing on the book of Proverbs. Written in thirty chapters and probably dating to 1200 B.C.E., it has close parallels to many verses in Proverbs 22:17–24:22.

Bryce (1979) has done a thorough study of parallels between biblical and Egyptian wisdom literature. He notes that there are varying degrees of dependence, from direct literary borrowing to "thought" borrowing; the latter is barely

---

TABLE 15.1 PROVERBS AND THE INSTRUCTION OF AMENEMOPE

Proverbs	*Amenemope*
Direct your ear and hear wise words. Set your heart to know them. For it is pleasant if you keep them in your inmost self. (22:17–18a)	Give your ears and hear what is said, give your mind over to their interpretation. It is profitable to put them in your heart. (3, 10)
Have I not written for you thirty counsels and teachings to teach you what is right and true? (22:20)	Mark for yourself these thirty chapters: They please, they instruct, they are the foremost of all books. (27,7)
Do not make friends with people prone to anger. With the hotheaded person do not associate. (22:24)	Do not fraternize with the hot-tempered man, nor approach him to converse. (11,12)
When you sit down to eat with a ruler, observe what is before you. Put a knife to your throat if you have a big appetite. (23:1–2)	Look at the cup in front of you, and let it suffice your need. (23,16)

recognizable because it has been so seamlessly integrated. Although there are differences in wording, proverbial parallels with Egyptian Instruction sayings seem quite close here in Proverbs. This could be evidence of direct literary borrowing, or it could signal that there was a common Middle Eastern wisdom culture with universal insights of which both literatures partook.

> **Babylonian Wisdom.** Ancient Mesopotamia also had a tradition of proverbial wisdom. See Pritchard (1969: 425–27, 593–96) and Lambert (1960).

PROVERBS AS A WHOLE

The book of Proverbs is an anthology, actually a collection of seven collections. Each consists of a set of short sayings, except for the first, which consists of wisdom essays. Only the first collection (chapters 1–9) and the last (chapter 31) have longer sub-units with thematic continuity (for example, chapter 31 is the acrostic poem about the ideal wife). Each collection of sayings is identifiable because it is introduced with a title.

The second through fifth collections allude to a monarchy, suggesting a pre-exilic setting. The first, sixth, and seventh collections are generally considered post-exilic. The book as a whole does not demonstrate logical movement or plot. It was probably edited into its final form late in the fifth century B.C.E.

> **House of Wisdom.** Skehan (1971) has devised an ingenious theory that the book of Proverbs is a "house of wisdom" (9:1) designed on analogy with the Solomonic temple, with a front (1–9), nave (10:1–22:16), and inner sanctuary (22:17–31:31). The "seven pillars" of wisdom's house (9:1) are the seven columns of text into which chapters 2–7 can be divided, each having the same number of lines as letters in the alphabet.

Table 15.D is a detailed content outline of Proverbs.

TABLE 15.2 PROVERB COLLECTIONS

		Title	Collection
1.	1:1	The proverbs of Solomon son of David king of Israel	1:2–9:18
2.	10:1	The proverbs of Solomon	10:1–22:16
3.	22:17	Stretch your ears and hear the words of the wise	22:17–24:22
4.	24:23	Also these are of the wise	24:23–34
5.	25:1	Also these are proverbs of Solomon	25:1–29:27
6.	30:1	The words of Agur son of Yakeh, the oracle	30:1–33
7.	31:1	The words of King Lemuel, an oracle his mother taught him	31:1–31

The later books of wisdom literature display a growing theological sophistication. They recognize that easy answers will not suffice. The book of Job is a frontal assault on the glib retribution categories of traditional wisdom, as represented by the book of Proverbs and the Deuteronomic tradition. The book of Job probes the nature of the moral order of the universe by examining the microcosm of the man Job. There is an obvious misfit between the world of doctrine and the world of experience. Doctrine says reward follows a moral life. But reality, in the case of Job, does not uphold this doctrine.

■ STORY LINE

The basic story line is straightforward. Job was a morally upstanding individual. He had considerable wealth and a fine family. When the divine council met in heaven God expressed his pride in Job, but he was challenged by one called *the adversary,* otherwise known as **the satan.**

> *7 YHWH said to the satan, "From where have you come?" The satan answered YHWH, "From going here and there on the earth, and from walking up and down on it." 8 YHWH said to the satan, "Have you considered my servant Job? There is none like him on the earth, a blameless and upright man, one who fears Elohim and turns away from evil?" 9 Then the satan answered YHWH, "Does Job fear Elohim for nothing?" (1:7–9)*

The satan figure is the official heavenly "gadfly" whose task is to challenge Yahweh's relationship with humankind. In this case the satan is playing "devil's advocate" by giving Yahweh a counter-explanation of Job's goodness. He claims it was just a pattern of behavior calculated to get the best treatment from God.

> **Ha-satan.** Note that "the satan" does not have a capital *s* because it is not a name but a title, indicated by the definite article "the", *ha* in Hebrew. The satan figure of the book of Job is a member of the divine council, and is not the devil of later Judaism and Christianity. Satan means adversary or accuser, and this may have been an official function within the council. Satan has an interesting if only very limited history in the Hebrew Bible. The term *satan* used in reference to an individual is found in only three settings. Here in Job, in Zechariah 3:1–2 (also with the definite article), and in 1 Chronicles 21:1 (without the definite article). See Pagels (1995) for a history of Satan.

The adversary challenged God to take everything away from Job in order to see what his reaction would be. Yahweh first gave the adversary permission to remove all of Job's wealth and family and later his physical health. Job was reduced to being a suffering outcast. Three friends appeared at his side to give him counsel: Eliphaz, Bildad, and Zophar. In conversation with Job they attempted to make sense out of his plight.

But neither Job nor his friends resolved the conundrum of Job's suffering. Elihu, another counselor-friend appeared, but did not seem to further the argument. Finally, Yahweh came to Job in a terrifying theophany and commanded Job's attention. He never answered Job's questions directly. Instead, he questioned Job in a most intimidating way, seemingly belittling Job because he presumed to question the wisdom of God, who, after all, created the world. But in the end he vindicated Job. Yahweh reprimanded Job's friends and requited Job with a new family and even greater wealth. The story line is relatively simple. The theological argument is not necessarily so.

■ DIALOGUES

One way to get at the meat of the book is to survey the positions of the main players. We hesitate to do this because so much of the argument is in the telling. The following summary should not be taken as a replacement for reading the book itself. Job is a remarkable treatise and contains some of the best poetry in the Hebrew Bible. It should be savored.

Eliphaz

He observes that no one is ever completely sinless. In no uncertain terms he upholds the theology of retribution.

> 7 *Think about it. What innocent ever perished?*
> *Where were the upright destroyed?*
> 8 *I have seen that those who plow evil*
> *and sow trouble reap the same.*
> 9 *By God's blast they perish*
> *and by the heat of his anger they disappear. (4:7–9)*

Eliphaz then goes on to say that everyone can expect at least a little suffering in life. Job is relatively innocent, so he will not suffer permanently. He should be patient; his suffering will soon be over.

Bildad

He applies the theology of retribution relentlessly. He claims that Job's children must have been notable sinners to be treated so brutally by God. No doubt they died justifiably.

> 3 *Can God get justice wrong?*
> *Can Shadday distort rightness?*
> 4 *If your children sinned against him,*
> *he delivered them over to the consequences of their violation. (8:3–4)*

Since Job is still alive, claims Bildad, he must not be too bad a sinner.

Zophar

He claims that Job must be suffering for his own sin. Even though Job will not admit it publicly, he must be a sinner.

> 4 You say, 'My principles are pure,
> and I am innocent before you.'
> 5 But if God would speak
> and talk to you himself,
> 6 and tell you the secrets of wisdom—
> there are many nuances to wisdom—
> know that God is exacting less than you deserve. (11:4–6)

Job should honestly face his sin and ask God for mercy.

Elihu

Elihu speaks (32–37) after Job's other three friends have had their say. He says that suffering is the way God communicates with human beings. It is the way God reveals that we are sinners and that he considers sin a serious offense.

> 10 He opens their understanding by discipline,
> and orders them to turn away from wickedness.
> 11 If they listen and obey,
> they will end up with good days and pleasant years. (36:10–11)

All four speakers maintain the theology of retribution in some way. Their approach is very much "top down." In other words, they hold a basic belief in retribution, and they try to square Job's experience with the theological principles they hold, rather than developing a theology out of human experience.

Job

Job has no coherent response to his calamity. He argues with his friends and attacks their counter arguments. But ultimately he remains confounded. He just does not know how to handle his predicament.

Yet there are certain claims he maintains throughout, certain points he will not relinquish. He never gives in and admits personal guilt in the measure that would call forth such suffering. He often urges God to reveal himself and state why he is afflicting him so. He challenges God in what amounts to a lawsuit, much in the manner of the covenant lawsuit popular with the prophets, even though he recognizes that if God actually appears he would be powerless to respond. This sentiment is amazingly prescient of what would soon happen.

Yahweh

Yahweh does not respond to the intellectual arguments of Job and his friends, all of which had to do in some way with the theology of retribution. He quite ignores that business, neither affirming retribution nor denying it. By God's bracketing the big question of retribution, the book is saying retribution is not the real issue. God does not conduct affairs on a strictly cause-and-effect basis.

Yet God does address Job's urgent plea that he at least show himself. He appeared in a storm theophany (38–41), but instead of answering Job's questions, he put Job on trial.

> 2 *Who is this confusing the issue*
> *with nonsensical words?!*
> 3 *Brace yourself like a man.*
> *I will quiz you. You teach me!*
> 4 *Where were you when I laid the foundations of the earth?*
> *Tell me, if you really have such deep understanding! (38:2–4)*

Yahweh continues in this same vein, badgering the witness, and impressing upon Job that he really knows nothing about how God created the world and runs it. Job finally admits that he spoke presumptuously in demanding that God justify his actions.

> 1 *YHWH said to Job:*
> 2 *"Will one in need of discipline complain about Shadday?*
> *Let the one accusing God answer!"*
> 3 *Then Job answered YHWH:*
> *"I am worth nothing. How can I respond to you?*
> *I am putting my hand over my mouth.*
> *I spoke once, but have no answer for you,*
> *Twice I spoke, but I will say no more." (40:1–3)*

By now Job seems properly contrite, having been put in his place. The reader might expect Yahweh at this point to coddle Job or at least lay off him. Just the opposite happens. God launches into a second discourse designed further to impress Job with his omnipotence. He describes in great detail his creation and the harnessing of Behemoth and Leviathan. These creatures have been likened to the hippopotamus and crocodile, respectively, but the overblown language of their description suggests that God is really referring to the mythic monsters of chaos that he tamed and holds at bay (see Day 1985).

Through the whole encounter God is absolutely overpowering. One might wonder why God felt he needed to react in such an intimidating way. Yet God does give Job satisfaction of sorts, first, in the very fact of his appearing, and second, by putting the issue of suffering in perspective. The important outcome is that God ultimately affirmed Job, in fact had never abandoned him, even though it had seemed so to Job at the time.

Job wanted to know why. But God would not tell him why. This effectively marginalizes the theology of retribution. Perhaps the real issue is trust—can one, will one simply trust God and "leave the driving to him"? Job is the model of the one who suffers, with all the self-doubt, indignation, impatience, and spiritual agony typical of those in great crisis. But he is also the model of one who trusts God, even though he fails to comprehend why he is suffering.

JOB AS A WHOLE

The book of Job consists of a poetic core surrounded by a prose narrative framework. The prose framework relates the story of Job, including the tragedy that strikes him and his family. The poetic core contains the theological heart of the book, including the dialogues of Job and his friends, and the appearance of Yahweh himself. In the cycles of dialogue each of Job's friends, Eliphaz, Bildad, and Zophar, speaks in his turn, and Job responds to each.

Outline of the Book of Job
1. Narrative Prologue: Job's tragedy (1–2)
2. Job's Lament (3)
3. Cycles of Dialogue (4–31)
   A. First Cycle (4–14)
   B. Second Cycle (15–21)
   C. Third Cycle (22–31)
4. Speeches of Elihu (32–37)
5. Theophany (38–41)
6. Narrative Epilogue: Job's reversal (42)

The structure of the book raises problems for the interpreter. What is the relation of the prose framework and the dialogues? Who is Elihu? What is the function of the theophany, and how does it answer the issues raised in the book? The narrative conclusion of the book seems especially artificial and unsatisfying to many readers—though, perhaps, not to retribution theologians. In the end, Job's fortunes were restored. He was given sons and daughters to replace those he lost, and his former material wealth was doubled. Although Job was reduced to humble acceptance of the power of God, he was vindicated and was told to pray for his three friends who were in the wrong.

Yet the ending is far from satisfying. In one grand narrative stroke what we thought was the lesson of the book to this point seems to be undone. The lesson of the book seemed to be that there is no direct and necessary correlation between righteousness and material well-being. Do we now, at the last, see Job rewarded for being in the right? If so, the theology of retribution seems to be upheld after all: in the end Job is rewarded for his uprightness. It almost seems the profound lesson of the theophany (38–41) is deconstructed by the triteness of the "and they lived happily ever after" conclusion.

How can we deal with this? Literary approaches to the book abound, and many seem quite able to live with the moral ambiguity of the book. Whedbee (1977) interprets the book using categories of comedy and irony. Westermann (1977) reads it as if it were a biblical lament. Habel (1985) reads Job as an allegory of the people of Israel in the postexilic period experiencing suffering and alienation from God.

Babylonian Job. The book of Job has affinities with a number of Mesopotamian writings. The Sumerian composition "A Man and His God" counsels one to turn to God with prayer and supplication in sickness and suffering

(Pritchard 1969: 589–91). *Ludlul Bel Nemeqi,* "I will praise the Lord of wisdom," is an Akkadian composition dating to around 1000 B.C.E. It describes a man's sufferings and blames Marduk, the Lord of wisdom. Yet in the end the sufferer finds deliverance (Pritchard 1969: 434–37, 596–600). See also the *Babylonian Theodicy* (Pritchard 1969: 438–40, 601–604). The story of Ahiqar, late fifth century B.C.E., is about a scribe who suffers misfortunes and is later restored to a place of honor (Pritchard 1969: 427–30). For Babylonian Wisdom as a whole see Lambert (1960).

If Job is first of all theological literature it may be in the mold of theodicy, an attempt to cope with the impenetrable character of the governance of God. The ending may be the writer's somewhat clumsy way of affirming the ultimate justice of God. Heaven as the place where rewards and punishments will be meted out was not an option at this stage of biblical religion. Everyone, whether good or bad, went to the same underworld, called *sheol.* Thus, Job's reward had to come during his lifetime. The writer responsible for the final shape of the book was willing, it seems, to live with the resulting tension of the freedom and sovereignty of God as expressed in the theophany, the validity of the theology of retribution, and the reality of righteous suffering.

How, then, should we construe this wonder of wisdom literature? Many things could be said. For one, it represents Israel's literary and theological attempt to get behind the phenomena of reality to the underlying truth. It asks the question *why.* Wisdom literature approaches reality without dependence on divine revelation, a priesthood, or a theology of history. It uses reason, everyday experience, and the power of deduction in its attempt to discern how the power of God manifests itself in the world of human affairs.

Furthermore, Proverbs and Job represent an inner-canonical dialogue on the theology of retribution. The book of Proverbs affirms it unreflectively and somewhat naively. Not to be too hard on Proverbs, this may have been a function of its role in providing clear and unambiguous moral instruction. On the other hand, the book of Job is a frontal attack on overly-simplistic retribution theology. It shows that the principle of retribution is not the only, or even the most important, factor at work in divine-human relations.

Theological reflection on the issue of retribution continues in the book of Ecclesiastes (see Chapter 16), but indirectly. Ecclesiastes deflects attention away from retribution by deconstructing it. Since the reality of death levels all rewards and punishments anyway, retribution is not the real issue; how you live your life is.

Job in the Modern World. Modern takeoffs on Job creatively wrestle with the human condition and can be recommended for the way they suggest interpretive possibilities. These include Archibald MacLeish's *J.B.* (1956), Neil Simon's *God's Favorite* (1975), Robert A. Heinlein's *Job, A Comedy of Justice* (1984), and probably Kafka's *The Trial* (see Lasine 1992).

The body of wisdom literature attests to a lively theological tradition of dialogue and development within the Hebrew Bible. Upon examination, the wisdom literature reveals a spiritual and intellectual tradition within Israel that was not afraid to ask bold and ultimate questions, that tried to make sense out of the diversity of evidences, and that resisted dogmatism in favor of intellectual honesty. The legitimacy of such theological discussion is affirmed by the very fact that these contrary voices were all included in the canon of Scripture. This recognition should encourage continuing the conversation.

Table 15.E is a detailed content outline of the book of Job.

FOR FURTHER STUDY

Westermann (1995) on the purpose of Proverbs, Good (1990) for a translation and commentary on Job.

Chapter 15 Bibliography. See Part 3 Bibliography for general works on the wisdom literature.

QUESTIONS FOR REVIEW

1. Where do proverbial sayings come from? What is the relationship of the book of Proverbs and the historical figure Solomon?
2. What is the "fear of Yahweh," and how is it related to wisdom?
3. What was the purpose of the book of Proverbs?

4. Summarize the story line of the book of Job. Who was "the satan"? What was the basic argument of Job's three friends? What was Job's claim to their argument?

QUESTIONS FOR REFLECTION AND DISCUSSION

1. The wisdom tradition claims that the fear of Yahweh is the beginning of knowledge and wisdom. Do you think this is true? Do you think that a basic knowledge of and respect for God is essential for understanding reality?
2. Consider the ending of the book of Job. How does the ending of the book relate to the issues raised in the dialogues? Are you satisfied with the ending of the book? Does the ending of the book support or refute the argument of Job in the dialogues?

3. Compare the Job of the prologue and epilogue with the Job of the dialogues. Are they the same personality?
4. With whom is the narrator sympathetic? Job? The friends? God? Or does the writer not take sides?
5. Does retribution theology adequately account for the human situation in the real world? Consider the retribution theology of the book of Proverbs in relation to the book of Job. Do you see two theologies in conflict? Is there a way to reconcile the two?

6. Will the real Job please stand up? Evaluate the following characterizations of Job and decide which, if any, fit the picture of Job you get from the book.

He was blameless and upright, he feared God and avoided evil.

— Job 1:1

You have heard of the patience of Job.

— James 5:11 (New Testament)

Job is a good man, not a wise one.

— Maimonides (1135–1204)

Chapter 15 Study Guide

- *Chapter summary*
- *Key terms linked to the glossary*
- *Concept questions with answer links*
- *Progress tests: true/false, multiple choice, matching, and identification*

16

FIVE SCROLLS

Key Terms

Acrostic
Ahasuerus
Allegory
Bethlehem
Boaz
Esther
Five Scrolls
Haman
Mordecai
Naomi
Purim
Qohelet
Ruth

FIGURE 16.1 **LOVE AND DEATH**   Love is stronger than death, proclaims the Greatest Song. This sculpture on the lid of an Etruscan funeral monument has lovers in an eternal embrace.

We find some of Israel's most mature thinking on the deeper issues of life in the Five Scrolls. Love, loyalty, freedom, destiny, death. Some of these books are delightful, some utterly depressing. Together they reveal a tradition that framed worthy responses to the human condition.

The five books of this chapter make for strange bedfellows. They hold little form or content in common. The Song of Songs is pulsing love poetry, Ruth is a romantic short story, Lamentations is a collection of dirges, Ecclesiastes is a philosophical treatise, and Esther is a historical novella. But there are good reasons why they were gathered together into one collection called the **Five Scrolls.**

SONG OF SONGS

Now for something completely different—unlike any other literature in the Hebrew Bible. The Song of Songs, sometimes called the Song of Solomon, is the stuff of love, highly erotic human love. Readers disagree whether or not the book has a plot. It is certainly not a story on the order of Ruth or Esther. Exactly what it is—a drama, a collection of wedding songs, or something else—remains under discussion. Whatever its genre, all agree it makes for great reading.

Reader's Comments

Said Rabbi Akiba: Heaven forbid that any man in Israel ever disputed that the Song of Songs is holy. For the whole world is not worth the day on which the Song of Songs was given to Israel, for all the Writings are holy and the Song of Songs is the Holy of Holies.
—Mishnah Yadayim 3:5 (second century C.E.)

. . . the holy love that is the subject of the entire Song cannot be expressed by words or language, but only in deed and truth. Here love speaks everywhere! If anyone desires to grasp these writings, let him love! For anyone who does not love, it is vain to listen to this song of love—or to read it, for a cold heart cannot catch fire from its eloquence. The language of love will be meaningless jangle, like sounding brass or tinkling cymbal, to anyone who does not love.
—Bernard of Clairvaux (1090–1153), *Sermon 79.1*

[The Song is] not allegorical but sacramental. Human passion . . . gives us a hint of God's passion for us. We are most like God's love for us when we are aroused in the presence of our beloved. And we best experience a hint of God's love when our beloved pursues us.
—Andrew M. Greeley, *Love Song* (1989)

Three voices are distinguishable in the Song: a male lover, a female lover, and an independent group of observers called the daughters of Jerusalem. Some interpreters prefer to call the two main speakers the lover (the male) and the beloved (the female), but this implies one is active and the other passive, and the female is certainly not passive in these poems. Though less poetic, the terms "male lover" and "female lover" are more accurate.

The female lover is the first to speak.

2 May he kiss me with the kisses of his mouth—
for your love is better than wine.
3 Your anointing oils are fragrant,
your name is sweet smelling oil.
So the maidens love you. (1:2–3)

The male lover has just as rich an appreciation of his companion.

15 You are beautiful, my lover,
you are beautiful, your eyes are doves.
16 You are beautiful, my lover, really beautiful.
Our couch is rich,
17 the beams of our house are cedar,
the rafters cypress. (1:15–17)

The daughters of Jerusalem, to whom the female lover addresses herself at times, seem to be her companions, sometimes encouraging her to rush into the relationship. The female lover more than once urges them to stop pushing her.

I implore you, O daughters of Jerusalem,
by the gazelles and wild does,
not to stir up or rouse love until it is ready! (2:7 ; see also 3:5 and 8:4)

The male lover unceasingly praises her physical attributes, but appears to get a little impatient for love. Throughout the poems he calls her by the endearing term "sister."

12 A locked garden is my sister, my bride,
a locked garden, a sealed spring. (4:12)

The imagery of the garden seems to give shape to their shared experience.

Female lover
16 Awake north wind,
come on south wind,
blow on my garden
so its fragrance wafts away.
Let my lover come to his garden
and eat its luscious fruit. (4:16)

Male lover
1a I've come to my garden, my sister, my bride.
I've gathered my myrrh mixed with spices,
I've eaten my honeycomb with honey,
I've drunk my mixed wine and milk. (5:1a)

Companions
1b Eat, lovers, and drink.
Be drunk with love. (5:1b)

The book ends with a stirring affirmation of the ultimacy of love.

6 Set me as a seal on your heart,
a seal on your arm.
For love is strong as death,
passion fierce as Sheol.
Its flashes are fire flashes,
a blazing fire.
7 Mighty waters cannot quench love,
nor floods sweep it away.
If anyone would offer
all his wealth for love,
he would be laughed to scorn. (8:6–7)

Sheol is the term referring to the underworld, the residence of the dead. Nothing can compare in power to love, and love even transcends death (see Figure 16.1). Indeed, the Song itself is notable for its frank, and at times frankly erotic, love language. Many of the metaphors are at best thinly veiled allusions to human sexuality. Physical love and sensuality are the source of deep satisfaction in the Song.

The book abounds with interpretive problems. For one, is the book to be read as having dramatic movement, or are the poems simply unconnected sketches? If simply poems, were they intended to be used in wedding ceremonies or celebrations? Another issue: Is the male lover the same as the king, with *king* just being love language, or is the king in competition with a country-boy lover? However one finally decides in regard to the *dramatis personae* of the book and its dramatic movement (if any), the unmistakable message of the book is the complexity and power of human love.

Although it is one of the five scrolls, the Song of Songs has connections with the wisdom tradition of the Hebrew Bible by virtue of its connection to Solomon. English versions tend to call this book the Song of Solomon, though in Hebrew it is the Song of Songs. This phrase "song of songs" is the Hebrew way of stating the superlative, in other words, this is the greatest song. Similar biblical constructions are "lord of lords" and "king of kings." Pope (1977) translates it "the sublime song."

The book received the title Song of Solomon because the first verse appends the words *li-shlomo* to the phrase "song of songs." Depending on one's interpretation, *li-shlomo* can either be "by Solomon" or "for Solomon."[1] Perhaps the Solomonic connection was made because Solomon is mentioned in chapters 3 and 8 (though not as author), and because 1 Kings 4:32 says he composed 1,005 songs.

Various theories of the origin of the poems have been suggested. Some of the songs may go back to the early monarchic period, though this cannot be proven. The songs have their closest affinity in the ancient period with Egyptian love songs (White 1978, Fox 1985).

An Egyptian Love Song

The love of my sister is on yonder side
Of the stream in the midst of the fish.
A crocodile stands on the sandbank
Yet I go down into the water.
I venture across the current;
My courage is high upon the waters.
It is thy love which gives me strength;
For thou makest a water-spell for me.
When I see my sister coming,
Then my heart rejoices.
My arms are open wide to embrace her;
My heart is glad in its place. (Thomas 1961)

This Egyptian love song comes from the thirteenth century B.C.E. and contains the same interest in animal imagery as the love poems in the Song of

[1]The same ambiguity exists in many psalm superscriptions, where psalms are either by or for David. See Chapter 14.

Songs. Also, in both compositions, the female lover is referred to as "my sister." Nowhere outside Israel is anything like this love poetry found, except in Egypt.

Parallels with Syrian wedding songs written in Arabic have been noted for centuries. Other authorities have suggested they may be related to ancient Mesopotamian and Canaanite ceremonies uniting divinities in marriage. Pope (1977) claims that the Song of Songs was associated with funeral feasts.

Interesting from a canonical perspective is how the biblical community of faith wrestled with the book. The transparent nature of the love talk in the Song of Songs scandalized many early readers. This was so much the case that the book had some difficulty finding its way into the canon of the Hebrew Bible. The problem was heightened because, like the book of Esther, the Song of Songs never makes reference to God. The book was accepted into the canon only after rabbis viewed it as an allegory of the relationship between Yahweh and the people of Israel. An **allegory** is a story in which people, places, and things have a meaning quite different from and unrelated to their surface meaning. Later, Christian interpreters applied a similar allegorical reading, interpreting it as the love relationship between Christ and the church. This was the reigning interpretation of the Song during the Middle Ages (see Matter 1990).

The inclusion of the Song of Songs within the canon is at some level an affirmation of the essential created goodness of sex. Certainly through the history of the formation of the canon this posed problems. Perhaps the rabbinic and early Christian allegorizing of the book was really just a rationalization for including this love poetry in the canon. All along they appreciated the goodness of human love, and realized the importance of canonically affirming it.

Table 16.A is a detailed content outline of the Song of Songs.

RUTH

This book tells the story of **Ruth,** a heroine of faith. The book of Ruth is one of the best-loved works of biblical literature, notable for its simplicity and directness. The story of Ruth unfolds in four scenes, each corresponding to a chapter.

Scene 1

The Israelite family of Elimelech and **Naomi** was forced to move to Moab because of a famine (see Figure 16.2). The irony of the story is that this family from Bethlehem (the Hebrew name means "house of bread") left the supposed land of plenty to live in Moab. In this foreign land the two sons, Machlon and Kilion, married Moabite women, Ruth and Orpah.

After a time in Moab, Elimelech, the father, and his two sons died. Only Naomi, the mother, and her two daughters-in-law survived. Naomi decided to return to Bethlehem and urged her daughters-in-law to remain in Moab and find security with their families there.

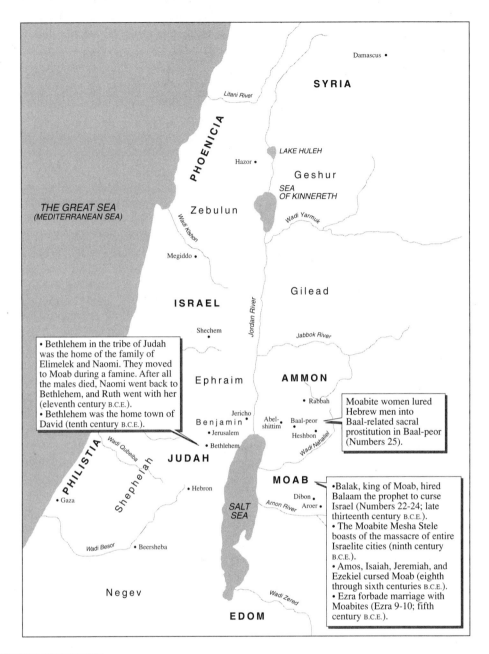

The map contains the following labels and text boxes:

Damascus

SYRIA

Litani River

PHOENICIA

LAKE HULEH

Hazor

Geshur

SEA OF KINNERETH

THE GREAT SEA (MEDITERRANEAN SEA)

Zebulun

Wadi Kishon

Wadi Yarmuk

Megiddo

Gilead

ISRAEL

Jordan River

Shechem

Jabbok River

• Bethlehem in the tribe of Judah was the home of the family of Elimelek and Naomi. They moved to Moab during a famine. After all the males died, Naomi went back to Bethlehem, and Ruth went with her (eleventh century B.C.E.).
• Bethlehem was the home town of David (tenth century B.C.E.).

Ephraim

AMMON

• Rabbah

Jericho

Benjamin

Abel-shittim

Baal-peor

Moabite women lured Hebrew men into Baal-related sacral prostitution in Baal-peor (Numbers 25).

• Jerusalem

Heshbon

Wadi Nahaliel

• Bethlehem

JUDAH

PHILISTIA

Wadi Qubeiba

Shephelah

• Hebron

MOAB

Dibon •

Aroer •

Arnon River

SALT SEA

• Gaza

•Balak, king of Moab, hired Balaam the prophet to curse Israel (Numbers 22-24; late thirteenth century B.C.E.).
• The Moabite Mesha Stele boasts of the massacre of entire Israelite cities (ninth century B.C.E.).
• Amos, Isaiah, Jeremiah, and Ezekiel cursed Moab (eighth through sixth centuries B.C.E.).
• Ezra forbade marriage with Moabites (Ezra 9-10; fifth century B.C.E.).

Wadi Besor

• Beersheba

Negev

Wadi Zered

EDOM

FIGURE 16.2 JUDAH AND MOAB

Table 16.B displays the plot of the book of Ruth in relation to the movement from emptiness to fullness that is a central theme of the story.

Orpah chose to remain, but Ruth refused to part from her mother-in-law. Ruth demonstrated dogged loyalty.

16 Ruth said, "Do not urge me to leave you or quit following you! Where you go, I will go. Where you live, I will live. Your people will become my people, and your God my God. 17 Where you die, I will die. That is where I will be buried. May YHWH do thus and so to me, and even more, if even death separates me from you!" (1:16–17)

Ruth insisted on staying with Naomi. Verse 17 contains an oath formula ("May YHWH do thus and so to me . . . if") invoking divine sanction for her pledge. Together Naomi and Ruth entered Bethlehem, with Naomi bemoaning her plight to the women of the city who came out to meet them. The first scene ends with the narrator's comment that they had come to Bethlehem at the beginning of the barley harvest. Once again there is food in Bethlehem, no doubt hinting that Naomi and Ruth might find fullness back in Naomi's homeland, perhaps in more ways than one.

Scene 2

Ruth went to glean in the field of **Boaz,** who was a relative of Elimelech, Ruth's deceased father-in-law. Gleaning is the practice of scavenging a field for stalks left behind by the hired workers (see Leviticus 19:9–10). Boaz took an interest in her, noting especially her loyalty to Naomi in her time of trouble. At mealtime he shared his food with her and arranged for the workers to leave extra stalks behind just for her. On returning home, Naomi noted Boaz's kindness, which continued through the harvest season.

Scene 3

Naomi urged Ruth to capitalize on Boaz's interest. During the harvest celebration, an overnight party held on the threshing floor near the new grain, Ruth secretly snuggled up to Boaz. She asked Boaz to spread his cloak over her, metaphorically to give her protection, but perhaps also to spend the night with her. Boaz was overwhelmed by her initiative and interpreted it as an additional sign of her loyalty to Naomi and her dead husband. Boaz promised to secure legal rights to claim her in marriage the next day and act as her dead husband's "next-of-kin." The Hebrew term used here is *go'el,* which can also be translated "redeemer."

Scene 4

Boaz went to the city gate in the morning. This is where all public business was conducted. Boaz brought the issue to a conclusion in this way. He announced that Naomi was seeking to sell the property of Elimelech. Another man stood closer in family relationship to Elimelech than Boaz, and this unnamed man initially expressed interest in purchasing the property. Then Boaz added that the one buying the property was required to marry Ruth and raise up sons to her dead husband. This other man withdrew his interest, and Boaz claimed the right to redeem.

Levirate Marriage. According to the Israelite law of levirate marriage (from Latin *levir,* "a husband's brother"), a childless dead man's brother is required

FIGURE 16.3 THRESHING FLOOR   A threshing floor is a stone patio set on a hill. Here grain is beaten out to separate the head from the husk. This threshing floor is located near Bethlehem.

to raise children to his dead brother's name by marrying the widow (see Deuteronomy 25:5–10).

The transaction was made official with a sandal-passing ceremony that transferred ownership from one party to another, and Boaz took Ruth to wife. In time Ruth had a son and Naomi was the first to rejoice. He was given the name Obed, and he became the father of Jesse, who was the father of David. Thus, Ruth, a Moabite foreigner, and Boaz became the great-grandparents of the greatest monarch of Israel.

This is a heartwarming story, as remarkable for its simplicity as for the excellence of its values. The story of Ruth is one of those rare Hebrew stories that on its most basic level was intended to be paradigmatic. That is, the characters are portrayed as models of virtue and goodness who should be emulated. Naomi is notable for the way she was concerned about the welfare of her daughter-in-law. Boaz, whose name means "strength" and was also the name of one of the pillars of the Jerusalem temple (1 Kings 7:21), went out of his way to show kindness to Ruth and provide for her protection.

Above all, Ruth displayed absolute loyalty to her mother-in-law and her adopted family, especially her dead husband. She was never motivated out of self-interest but faithfully sought to preserve the Elimelech estate. The book demonstrates that ordinary people will find peace and security when they behave unselfishly.

Additional moral lessons may have been intended. The main character of the story is Ruth, a female. She stands as yet another example of strong and influential women who shaped the course of Israelite history. Just as significantly, she was a foreigner, and a Moabite at that. The Moabites were hated by the Israelites through most of their history, but especially in the exilic and postexilic periods. Yet this story demonstrates how a Moabite could possess the qualities of loyalty and piety, and indeed could become part of the royal line of David.

The story of Ruth was set in the time of the judges, making her pre-monarchic. Because the book was set "in the days when the judges judged" (1:1) and provides background to the family of David, the early Greek version placed the book of Ruth between the books of Judges and Samuel, a practice followed by Christian versions of the Old Testament.

The actual time of the book's final composition is disputed, with Hals (1969) and Campbell (1975) advocating a date of composition in the early monarchical period. Most authorities today maintain a postexilic date. If this is the case, the book may have been intended as a counter voice to that of Ezra, who governed Jerusalem in the fifth century B.C.E. The Jewish community under Ezra took on a very nationalistic and religiously defined character. Foreigners were unwelcome, and Ezra made Jewish men divorce their Moabite wives (see Ezra 10:1–5 and Nehemiah 13:23–27).

The book of Ruth appreciates the Moabites, and perhaps foreigners in general, and demonstrates that they could be loyal to Yahweh too. Viewed in this way, the book of Ruth may be a protest against excluding all non-natives from Judaism. Ruth projects a universalistic picture of Israel that includes non-Israelites. This openness is also glimpsed occasionally in prophetic literature as, for example, in the Rahab story in Joshua, in the inclusiveness of Second and Third Isaiah, and in the book of Jonah—but nowhere more clearly than in the book of Ruth. The point is that foreigners can and sometimes do acknowledge Yahweh, and can demonstrate loyalty to the people of Israel.

The tale of Ruth is self-contained and has a remarkable wholeness to it. But the book in its final form gives evidence of canonical transformation. The tale of Ruth was taken and given another purpose beyond that of modeling ideal people of God. The original story of Ruth was repurposed and used to say something about David, even though David's line does not play any role in the body of the story.

The story in its bare form was probably not about ancestors of David. It could stand alone without the concluding Davidic notes. But the addition of 4:17b and the genealogy of 4:18–22 give the book an expanded meaning within the national epic. With these additions the book says that God was at work in the life of Naomi's family to provide for Israel's kingship needs. The genealogical additions do not add anything to the story line, but instead give the story an added context of significance as background to the royal family. Composed in the postexilic period from a pre-existing Ruth tale, and given a Davidic context of interpretation, the book of Ruth is probably evidence for an intense interest in the royal messianic line in the late biblical period.

 Table 16.C is a detailed content outline of the book of Ruth.

LAMENTATIONS

The book of Lamentations consists of five distinct poems, each in its own chapter. Each of the first four psalms is an alphabetic **acrostic** of one form or another. An acrostic utilizes the letters of the alphabet to develop a scheme. In the case of chapters 1–2, the first letter of each three-line stanza begins with the next letter of the Hebrew alphabet (twenty-two letters in all), so that the first triplet begins with *a* (*aleph* in Hebrew), the second with *b* (*beth*), and so forth. Chapter 4 consists of couplets rather than triplets in the same scheme. Chapter 3 consists of twenty-two triplets where each line of the triplet begins with the same letter of the alphabet in acrostic progression. Chapter 5 consists of twenty-two single lines without any observable alphabetic progression. Whatever the reason for these elaborate acrostic schemes, they do give evidence of the considerable poetic craftsmanship of the composer. The poems were not artlessly constructed.

Each of the five poems is a complaint psalm; this the dominant psalm type in the Psalter (see Chapter 14). Virtually all the lines of the first four lamentations were composed in the 3 + 2 *qinah* meter that typifies the lament style (see Garr 1983). Both individual and group complaint forms are found in Lamentations, with the voice changing unexpectedly from singular to plural throughout the poems. When singular voice moves into plural, the singular still stands collectively for the group. The focus of attention is on the desolation of Jerusalem.

> *How deserted sits the city, once full of people!*
> *She has become like a widow, once great among the nations!*
> *Once a princess among principalities, she has become a peasant. (1:1)*

The complaints were composed to lament the destruction of Jerusalem in 587 B.C.E. by the Babylonians). The destruction of the temple was the most devastating loss of all, for it meant the departure of Yahweh from their land. It appears from Jeremiah 41:5 that soon after the destruction of 587 people still came to the temple mount in Jerusalem to worship. Zechariah 7:1–7 and 8:19 suggest that fasts were held, perhaps as many as four a year, marking the destruction. The Lamentations were probably used on these occasions to mark the disaster. This traumatic moment in Israel's history is still observed today within the Jewish community as Tisha b'Av, the ninth day of the month of Av, falling somewhere between the end of July and the beginning of August.

Jeremiah has traditionally been identified as the author of Lamentations because of similarities to his personal complaints. For this reason the Christian canon has placed the book of Lamentations after the book of Jeremiah. In the Hebrew Bible it is included with the Writings. Jeremiah composed a lament upon the occasion of the death of Josiah (2 Chronicles 35:25), but there is no evidence he did the same thing for Jerusalem or that he composed the book of Lamentations.

> **Babylonian Lament.** The genre of city lament is also found in Babylonian literature. See the lamentation over the destruction of Ur (Pritchard 1969: 455–63) and the lamentation over the destruction of Sumer and Ur (Pritchard 1969: 611–19).

Table 16.D is a detailed content outline of the book of Lamentations.

ECCLESIASTES

Ecclesiastes is usually included in the category of wisdom literature along with Proverbs and Job (see Part 3). The style of its language, its vocabulary, and themes it holds in common with Greek philosophy suggest that it dates to the second century B.C.E.

> **Babylonian Wisdom.** Ecclesiastes has some similarity to the Dialogue of Pessimism of the Babylonian wisdom tradition, also called the Babylonian Ecclesiastes or the Babylonian Theodicy (see Pritchard 1969: 438–40, 600–601 and Lambert 1960).

The theological conversation of Proverbs and Job concerning the relationship of human behavior and divine purpose continues in the book of Ecclesiastes. Like Job, it presents a challenge to traditional theology. The book of Ecclesiastes questions the purpose of human existence. It asks, What gives lasting meaning to life? If everyone only dies in the end, what is the meaningful difference between righteousness and wickedness? The seriousness with which the book probes this basic human issue makes it one of the most accessible, almost even "modern," pieces of biblical literature.

Like Proverbs, Ecclesiastes approaches the world of experience looking for order and moral law. Using his powers of observation and reason, the writer attempts to put it all together in a meaningful way. But unlike the wisdom of Proverbs, the writer of Ecclesiastes fails to see an overall coherence or purposefulness. Sure, some things are predictable and regular.

> *1 For everything there is a season,*
> *and a time for every matter under heaven:*
> *2 a time to be born,*
> *and a time to die;*
> *a time to plant,*
> *and a time to uproot what is planted. (3:1–2)*

But ultimately, life seems to have no meaning.

> *Everything is emptiness and a chasing after wind.*
> *There is nothing to be gained under the sun. (2:11)*

The cynical wisdom of Ecclesiastes appears to challenge the neat and tidy world of proverbial wisdom. If there is no ultimate purpose to life, then why should you care whether you are wise or foolish, righteous or wicked?

The book of Ecclesiates projects itself as the work of Solomon. Solomon is the "patron saint" of wisdom and he naturally gets the credit. And the reputation of Solomon as Israel's wealthiest and wisest king (whether, in fact, true or not doesn't matter) equips the supposed author to pursue the search for ultimate wisdom, unencumbered with limitations. If anyone had the means, time, talent, and opportunity to search for wisdom and find it, that person would be Solomon. But neither the introduction nor any other verse in Ecclesiastes makes the specific claim of Solomonic authorship. The speaker is simply referred to as **qohelet** in the editorial introduction, "The words of Qohelet, the son of David, king in Jerusalem" (1:1).

> **Qohelet** is not a name but a title. Translators are not sure what it means or why the speaker of the book was called this. The word is related to the verb "to assemble," accounting for its title Ecclesiastes in the Septuagint, meaning the "churchman" (related to the Greek word *ekklesia,* "assembly, church"). The gender of the term *qohelet* is feminine, as is the gender of the Hebrew word for "wisdom"—maybe not a coincidence.

The book is royal autobiography and takes the form of personal reflections and reminiscences. It has been compared to the genre of royal journals found elsewhere (see Longman 1991). Qohelet's personal story is prefaced with a poem that clearly expresses the theme of the book as a whole and sets the mood.

> *2 Emptiness, Qohelet says, everything is emptiness. 3 What do people gain from all the work they do under the sun? 4 A generation goes and a generation comes, yet the earth remains forever. 5 The sun rises and the sun sets, and rushes back again to the place from which it rises. 6 The wind blows south, then returns to the north, round and round goes the wind, on its rounds it circulates. 7 All streams flow to the sea, yet the sea does not fill up. 8 All matters are tiring, more than anyone can express. The eye is not satisfied with seeing, nor the ear filled with hearing. 9 What is is what will be, and what has been done is what will be done. There is nothing new under the sun. 10 Is there anything of which it can be said, "See this is new!"—It has already been, in eras before us. 11 The people of ages past are no longer remembered, nor will there be any remembrance of people yet to come by those who come after them. (1:2–11)*

The central thought of Ecclesiastes is contained in that first line "Emptiness, everything is emptiness." The Hebrew term for emptiness, or vanity in older translations, is *hevel,* which means "mist" or "vapor." The assertion that all is empty is literally the beginning and the end of the book, found here in 1:2 and also in 12:8. The circularity of the system perceived by Qohelet, especially the lack of directionality and goal, is reflected in the very structure of the book, which ends where it began.

Qohelet observes the circularity of nature, the endless cycle of birth, death, and rebirth. He sees regularity and predictability. But in seeing circularity he does not sense the beauty of a self-renewing system. Rather, he senses futility and purposelessness. The wisdom enterprise up till now had prided itself in discovering and articulating the order of nature, but that has turned into something quite different, a reason for despair.

In chapters 1 and 2 Qohelet tells us how and why he arrived at this conclusion. With various experiments and investigations he sought to find the location of meaning. First he tried raw intellect. Applying his mind to know wisdom and folly, he only found that the attempt was an experiment in frustration.

Then he tried the opposite approach. He gave his life over to the pursuit of physical pleasure and personal satisfaction. He drank alcohol, built a magnificent home with palatial grounds, accumulated precious metals, possessions, and a large staff of servants. Although he found fulfillment in none of these, yet he felt there might be provisional satisfaction in these pursuits. He concluded that "there is nothing better for mortals than to eat and drink, and find enjoyment in their work." (2:24)

The cause of Qohelet's frustration is the limited vantage point available to humanity. The phrase "under the sun" occurs twenty-nine times in the book, usually in statements such as, "I saw under the sun that the race is not to the swift, nor the battle to the strong." (9:11) This may just be another way of saying "on earth," or it may serve to reinforce the limited scope of human reason and its incapacity to see the whole.

> 11 God made everything appropriate to its time. He has also done this—a
> sense of eternity he put into the heart of humankind, but without the ability
> to find out what God has done from the beginning to the end. (3:11)

The writer suspects that there is more to life than he or anyone else can figure out. God has planted in the human mind the notion of eternity, a reality that transcends human finiteness, yet he has not equipped humans to grasp it. Because we are unable to transcend our limits, Qohelet counsels us to enjoy the good things God's creation has to offer.

The book of Ecclesiastes frankly faces the limited capacity of the human spirit to create ultimate meaning. He does not deny that ultimate meaning exists, only that we can expect to find it. Yet all the while he does not come to the conclusion that there is no order. He affirms the reality and goodness of God (Elohim, never YHWH in the book). And he affirms the continuing need to fear God.

Chapters 4–11 mostly contain rather traditional wisdom observations, generally on the order of what can be found in the book of Proverbs. He gives advice for coping in a world where meaningful activity is hard to find. Granted, all may be ultimately meaningless, yet even Qohelet understands that life must be lived and might even be enjoyed for what it does have to offer.

Yet many of his observations tend to highlight the unfortunate or even tragic side of human experience. Note how Qohelet appends a cynical commentary to an otherwise commonplace proverbial statement.

> 10 The lover of money will not be satisfied with money;
> nor the lover of wealth with gain.
> This too is emptiness. (4:10)

Was Qohelet a heretic? For obvious reasons, the book of Ecclesiastes proved somewhat difficult to handle. It just does not contain the kind of upbeat, positive message that Jews wanted to hear. Yet the book was not just dismissed out of hand as the depressed (and depressing) ruminations of a tired old philosopher. There was truth in what Qohelet said, at least at some level. It probably rang true especially to Judeans who were looking to survive in a world dominated by Greek rule, where they felt at the mercy of higher political powers. They were unable to see God's larger purpose and felt unable to affect it significantly.

The Jewish community struggled to canonize Ecclesiastes. Because of its somewhat troubling observations, they perceived the need to retrieve the book from heresy and give it an orthodox patina. The editorial history of the book gives evidence of their efforts. Although there has been considerable discussion concerning the structure and editorial shape of the book (see Wright 1968), there is a general consensus that the core of the book of Ecclesiastes is 1:2 through 12:8. To this was added the introduction that "Solomonized" the book and a series of two, perhaps three, conclusions.

Verses 9–11 of chapter 12 break with the style of the rest of the book, which is aphoristic and autobiographical, and were probably written by a devoted disciple of Qohelet. They affirm the wisdom of Qohelet and his effectiveness as a thinker and teacher.

> 9 In addition to being wise, Qohelet taught the people knowledge, and how to judge, study and arrange many proverbs. 10 Qohelet looked for pleasing words and wrote truthful words plainly. 11 The sayings of the wise are like prods; like nails well set are the collected sayings of the one shepherd. (12:9–11)

Verses 13–14, on the other hand, were written by a theologian more conventional than Qohelet.

> 13 The end of the matter is this, all has been heard: Fear God, and keep his commandments. That is the whole duty of humankind. 14 For God will bring into judgment every deed, even every secret one, whether it is good or evil. (12:13–14)

The editor got the final say (see Sheppard 1980). It is as if he was worried that Qohelet's investigation would lead to nihilism or denial of God. "Lest you be tempted to abandon the faith," he says, "Fear God! Don't give up the faith, don't give up the demands of covenant! God still judges human actions. Lack of understanding is no excuse for immorality."

This concluding editorial is really quite remarkable. It attests the vitality of the faith of the postexilic community. It obviously accepted, even perhaps encouraged, the creative kinds of thinking that took Torah to the edge. It took great effort to apply Torah to their present circumstances. And the integration and synthesis were certainly not complete—yet room was made for theological thinking that stood on the verge of being unorthodox.

Table 16.E is a detailed content outline of the book of Ecclesiastes.

ESTHER

The book of Esther does not get the same unqualified reception by Jews and Christians as the book of Ruth, the other heroine tale. Not only does the book of Esther lack the standard religious features one comes to expect in Hebrew literature—reference to the God of Israel, the covenant, Torah, and Jerusalem—it appears to condone certain baser human impulses such as violence and vengeance. Yet the book is part of the Hebrew canon. We need to discover why.

The story of Esther is set in the Persian period, referred to by historians as the Achaemenid empire. The Persian monarch of the story is called **Ahasuerus,** otherwise known as Xerxes I, who ruled 486 to 465 B.C.E. The story is set in Susa, the winter palace, although Persepolis was the main capital of the empire.

The story begins with a description of a great feast. When Queen Vashti refused to be the main entertainment for the male guests, she was deposed. Ahasuerus organized a Miss Persia contest to replace her, and **Esther** won.

Esther was a Jewish orphan who had been cared for by her uncle **Mordecai.** Esther effectively concealed her Jewish identity from all at court. Mordecai, meanwhile, uncovered an assassination plot against Ahasuerus, and Esther told the king about it.

Meanwhile, the villainous prime minister **Haman** grew angry with Mordecai because Mordecai refused ever to bow down to him. Mordecai was loyal to the commandment not to bow down to anyone or anything except the God of Israel. Haman hatched a plot to kill Mordecai, as well as all Jews. An unthinking Ahasuerus went along with the plan.

When Mordecai heard about Haman's plan he asked Esther to do something about it. After all, she had access to the king and was in his good graces. At first, Esther was reluctant to intervene, citing the danger of approaching the king uninvited. Mordecai prevailed upon Esther with this argument.

13 Do you think just because you live in the king's palace you will escape the fate of all the other Jews? 14 If you keep silent at such a time as this, help and deliverance will come for the Jews from somewhere else, but you and your father's family will perish. Who knows? Maybe you have come to royal position for just such a time as this." (4:13–14)

This is the closest the book comes to expressing any kind of theological sentiment—in this case, a general suggestion of divine providence and supernatural protection.

Esther approached the king and was granted an audience. She invited the king and Haman to a banquet. When Haman heard of the invitation he was delighted, but quickly became depressed after he witnessed Mordecai's insolence in refusing to bow after he left the palace. He decided to have Mordecai hanged.

That same night, Ahasuerus was reviewing the court records and came across the entry on Mordecai's report of the assassination attempt saving the king. After inquiry he found out Mordecai had never been honored for that. Haman just happened to be around at the time, so the king called him in and asked what kinds

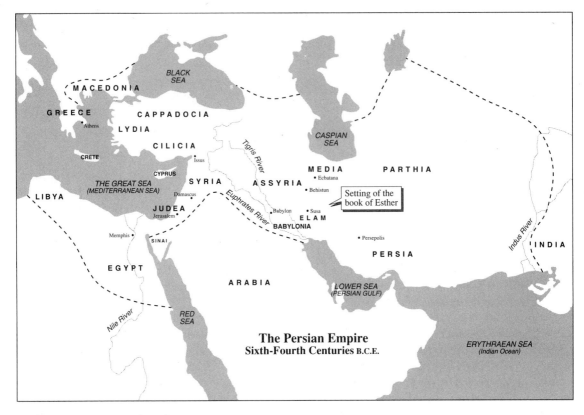

FIGURE 16.4 PERSIAN EMPIRE

of things should be done to honor a faithful citizen. Thinking that the king had him in mind, Haman devised a wonderful ceremonial procession giving public acclaim to such a man. The king told him to arrange it. He was shocked when he found out that Mordecai was the one to be honored.

Afterward at the banquet, Esther pleaded for the lives of the Jewish people. Amazingly, the king revealed little awareness of the edict he himself had authorized.

> 5 King Ahasuerus said to Queen Esther, "Who is he, and where is he—the one who has presumed to do this?" 6 Esther said, "An antagonist and an enemy, this wicked Haman!" (7:5)

Shocked (a bit dim-witted too, it seems), the king left the room. Haman fell on Esther's couch pleading for his life. When the king came back and saw Haman on top of Esther, he thought Haman was making advances on his queen. The king was even more outraged and had Haman hanged on the gallows that Haman had built for Mordecai.

Esther and Mordecai convinced the king to issue an edict reversing the intended result of Haman's plan. Official letters were drafted and sent throughout the empire authorizing the Jews to defend themselves. They killed hundreds of their enemies in Susa and thousands elsewhere. A new respect for the Jews of the Diaspora developed, and many people became converts to Judaism.

The book of Esther explains the origin of the Jewish celebration of **Purim**. This holiday came late in Jewish history and is not authorized by the Torah, so separate justification was needed. It was called Purim following the name of the divination device, the *pur* or lot (see 3:7), Haman used to determine the best day for the slaughter of the Jews.

Still celebrated by Jewish communities in February or March, it is a festival of freedom, remembering the time when Jews scattered around the world were given respect and recognition and the power to defend their own way of life. When it is observed today it can be a raucous affair. Adolescents are allowed to do things on Purim they could never get away with any other day. In celebration, the book of Esther is read in the synagogue, and whenever the name Haman is voiced, children shout, stamp their feet, and sound noise makers. Special cookies called Haman's ears are eaten in disdain of the villain. Adults are supposed to drink so much wine that they can no longer tell the difference between "Blessed Mordecai" and "Accursed Haman."

There are additional meanings to the story. The book strongly cautions the Jews not to forget their identity or think that they can somehow find safety by blending in. Mordecai pointed out to Esther that assimilating was not an option, and her position at court would not ultimately protect her. There is also the implication that the Jews must stick together, for only therein would they survive.

With Esther, we cannot fail to notice once again the importance of faithful women for the history of Israel. This story affirms the importance of a single courageous female character for the Jewish community. Indeed, its survival depended on her. The paradigmatic function of storytelling is again present, as Esther is projected as a positive role model for women of the faith.

The Hebrew Bible locates the book of Esther in the Writings as one of the Five Scrolls. The canonical tradition of the Christian Old Testament places it after Nehemiah, which makes it the last book in the collection of historical materials. This placement functions to assign a history-telling role to the book, as opposed to its storytelling role in the Hebrew Bible.

The book of Esther is a late book, obviously having been written after the reign of Ahasuerus (Xerxes I). The consensus is that it was written in the fourth or third century B.C.E. It had some trouble finding acceptance into the canon because of its lack of explicit "God talk." It has the distinction of being the only book of the Hebrew Bible not found among the Dead Sea Scrolls in at least one fragment. The old Greek version of the Hebrew Bible, known as the Septuagint, seems to have found it somewhat inadequate. It lengthened the book considerably by introducing prayers and petitions of Esther and Mordecai that refer explicitly to God.

Some scholars have suggested that the book has a pagan prehistory. For example, the name Mordecai could be derived from Marduk, the Babylonian high god, and Esther is linguistically related to Ishtar, a goddess. In this speculation, the story was originally related to the Babylonian New Year festival, and the plot was transformed along with the names to make a Jewish tale. Though unlikely, some such prehistory may at a far distant point underlie the book. But as it stands now, the book bears a recognizable historical and biblical setting.

The genealogical notes identifying Mordecai and Haman place the story within a larger biblical context. Mordecai is identified as a descendant of Kish from the tribe of Benjamin. This would make him a descendant of Saul. Haman is identified as a member of the Agag family and an Amalekite. The Amalekites were the prototypical enemies of the Israelites. They were the first to attack the Hebrews after they left Egypt in the exodus. They also harassed the Israelites during the early monarchy. Saul's failure to eliminate Agag and the Amalekites was one cause of his demise. The book of Esther implies that Mordecai finally got the job done by eliminating Haman.

The book of Esther is religiously nationalistic in focus. It has a definite "us" against "them" feel to it as it deals with Haman's planned pogrom to eliminate Jews. Esther and Mordecai proved themselves clever enough to overcome this threat to the Jews. Jewish national and religious salvation involved the execution of Haman and community self-defense. In some ways this is a violent book. What, then, is the effect of having it in the Hebrew Bible? How can such violence be justified?

Childs (1979) argues that the book itself shows evidence of wrestling with this issue. The letters of Mordecai and Esther contained in 9:20–32 appear to be additions. They change the tone of Purim considerably. They turn it from a time of slaughtering Jewish enemies to a time of celebration, gift-giving, and well-wishing. Through this canonical reinterpretation the original event became the occasion to celebrate Jewish identity and God's preservation of the Jews as a people.

> **Diaspora.** The diaspora, or dispersion, of the Jews throughout the world began with the Babylonian destruction of Jerusalem. Two Persian period archives of ancient documents provide information on the early Jewish diaspora. The Elephantine papyri from Aswan, Egypt date to the late fifth century B.C.E. They provide evidence of a large group of Jews who lived in Egypt, and may have moved there after 587 B.C.E., as Jeremiah and Baruch were forced to do (Jeremiah 43:7). The papyri intriguingly suggest that the Jews of Elephantine worshipped the Canaanite goddess Anath alongside Yahweh. The Murashu archive, also from the late fifth century B.C.E., is 730 clay tablets that were discovered at Nippur in southern Mesopotamia. The texts are business documents from the banking family of Murashu that contain many Jewish names and give evidence that Jews owned land and houses.

Overall, the book exposes the serious threats God's people face when living in an alien and hostile culture. The book of Esther reveals that God directs affairs providentially to protect and deliver his people.

Table 16.F is a detailed content outline of the book of Esther.

FIVE SCROLLS AS A WHOLE

We treat these five short books together because they were grouped together within the Writings section of the Hebrew Bible as the Five Scrolls, in Hebrew, the five *megillot*.

Why Five? This collection of five books may have been in imitation of the five books of the Torah and the five books of the Psalter. The grouping together of the Five Scrolls is attested in the earliest copies of the Hebrew Bible, upon which current editions are based. However, the earliest evidence for the order of biblical books is in the Babylonian Talmud (Baba Bathra 14b). It intersperses the Five Scrolls among other books as follows: Ruth, Psalms, Job, Proverbs, Ecclesiastes, Song of Songs, Lamentations, Daniel, Esther, Ezra–Nehemiah, Chronicles. This sequence reflects their presumed chronological order.

In spite of their lack of common style or subject, there is a logic to the collection. Each of the books was used by the Jewish community in connection with a yearly commemoration.

- The Song of Songs was read at Passover (Hebrew *pesach*), which commemorated the exodus from Egypt. It marked the growing season, and coincided with the beginning of the barley harvest.
- Ruth was read at the feast of weeks (Hebrew *shavuot*), also called Pentecost, which commemorated the giving of the law at Mount Sinai. It was observed seven weeks after Passover and marked the end of the barley harvest.
- Lamentations was read on the ninth day of the month of Av (Hebrew *tishah b'av*), marking the exact day of the destruction of the first Jerusalem temple in 587 B.C.E. It was also used later to mourn the destruction of the Second Temple, destroyed in 70 C.E.
- Ecclesiastes was read at the feast of booths, also called tabernacles (Hebrew *sukkot*), which commemorated Israel's forty years in the wilderness. Celebrated in the fall, six months after Passover, it coincided with the grape harvest.
- Esther was read at the feast of Purim in late winter and marked the time of Jewish deliverance during the Persian period.

The order of individual books within the Five Scrolls correlates with their sequence within the yearly Jewish calendar.

Table 16.G relates the Five Scrolls to the Jewish calendar.

The five books in this collection differ in many ways, including literary type and subject matter. They were grouped together primarily because they all relate to Jewish commemorative events. But we should ask if there is any further benefit, a thematic and theological bonus, in seeing them together as a collection.

If consensus reconstructions are accurate, all five of these books were compiled relatively late, in the exilic period of the sixth century B.C.E. or thereafter. These books should then be interpreted in light of the theological and sociological issues of that age, specifically the reconstruction of a Jewish community and the emergence of religious Judaism.

The book of Ruth may be viewed as a protest against a narrowly defined nationalism, implicitly arguing for a more inclusive community. The criterion for inclusion into the community should not be national affiliation but acceptance of the God of Israel. The book of Esther also addresses the issue of community, but from the opposite angle, that is, where Jews are the ones being excluded. It exposes the problems of religious intolerance and xenophobia from the perspective of the outsider. Esther portrays the ugliness of a society where Jews are systematically ostracized and abused. The book, at the same time, is empowering. The Jews of the book of Esther are not helpless or ineffectual, but are capable of defending themselves legally and physically. The story authorizes the postexilic Jewish community to affirm its identity in the face of racially and religiously based prejudice and discrimination.

The books of Ruth and Esther do not reflect the same community. They display different community attitudes especially to the non-Israelite population. They represent different challenges to pluralism. But both responses, by virtue of being included in the canon, represent legitimate responses.

The Song of Songs seems to issue a different kind of social challenge. It stands, perhaps, as a protest against a world where the free expression of love was discouraged. Remember the abuse that the lovers suffered in the book. It is critical of a society that does not value true love and would force true lovers to express their love in secret. It is also critical of a dominating patriarchal society that attempts to manipulate female love and use it self-gratifyingly. The Song is startlingly progressive in the mutuality of the male–female relationship.

Ecclesiastes continues late wisdom's challenge to retribution theology. It presses the issue of divine governance by probing for the essential meaning of existence. While it does not deny the providence of God, it does seem to give up in frustration over its inability to penetrate to the purpose of God. If the book speaks not only on the personal level but also on the communal level, it expresses Israel's frustration at not knowing what God had in store for them historically. Only a backwater province within monstrous empires, they had lost a sense of national purpose.

Lamentations continues in the vein of challenge, if not protest. The very mode of complaint that is the genre of the book could be interpreted as a challenge to God. It demands to know why God treated his people so harshly and wants to know when he would restore them. Again, the community wrestles with God.

Perhaps it is no accident that these voices gave expression through poetry and story instead of through prophetic genres. As poetry and story they might not so quickly give offense. Metaphoric poetry and heartwarming story can sometimes soften otherwise prickly lessons. In any case, they kept alive the theological discussion over the nature of the covenant community, especially the value of all members, indigenous-Israelite and non-Israelite alike, female and male alike. In all, these books were alternate voices, challenging voices, and critical voices that contested the historically dominant theologies of the Jews. Taken together, they highlight the need for foundational biblical and human values: loyalty, faithfulness, acceptance, security, freedom, and love.

FOR FURTHER STUDY

Falk (1990) and Bloch (1995) are translations of the Song of Songs. Sasson (1989) for commentary on Ruth, Fox (1991) for commentary on Esther. Short (1973) and Ellul (1991) suggest ways the book of Ecclesiastes is relevant today.

Chapter 16 Bibliography. See Part 3 Bibliography for wisdom literature generally.

QUESTIONS FOR REVIEW

1. *Song of Songs.* What are the main ways that the Song of Songs can be interpreted?
2. *Ruth.* Why is the fact that Ruth is a Moabite crucial to the story? How is this fact tied to the meaning and application of the story?
3. *Lamentations.* What is the literary type of the poems in this book, and what historical event do they commemorate?

4. *Ecclesiastes.* As speculative wisdom, with what theological issue does this book wrestle, and what are its conclusions?
5. *Esther.* How did Mordecai convince Esther to intervene to save the Jews, and what was the outcome of her intervention?

QUESTIONS FOR REFLECTION AND DISCUSSION

1. As poetry in praise of human love and sexuality, how can the Song of Songs be reconciled with the high moral tone of the rest of biblical literature?
2. How are the books of Ruth and Esther alike? How do they differ? How does each face the issues of community identity and how to deal with foreigners? Are these still relevant issues in the modern world?

3. How does Ecclesiastes address the question of the meaning of life? How does his thinking compare to the spirit of the modern age? How did the editors of Ecclesiastes try to handle the potentially disturbing effect of the book? What adjectives would you use to describe the book and your reaction to it?

 Chapter 16 Study Guide

- ■ *Chapter summary*
- ■ *Key terms linked to the glossary*
- ■ *Concept questions with answer links*
- ■ *Progress tests: true/false, multiple choice, matching, and identification*

17 DANIEL

Key Terms

Antiochus IV
Apocalypse
Belshazzar
Daniel
Hasids
Hellenism
Kingdom of God
Nebuchadnezzar
Resurrection
Son of Man

FIGURE 17.1   END OF THE WORLD?

Will the world actually end some day? If so, will that day come soon? Will it be in our lifetime? Will the world end with a bang or a with a whimper?

For decades the specter of global thermonuclear holocaust hung heavy over history. Even now, as the nuclear threat recedes, the peril of global ecological disaster provides another very scary scenario for the end of the inhabitable world. Science, technology, and industrialization provide countless ways we can kill ourselves, and take the planet with us.

Certainly, an interest in the end of civilization has fueled a great deal of speculation, not a little of which has a religious flavor.

Once By the Pacific
The shattered water made a misty din.
Great waves looked over others coming in,
And thought of doing something to the shore
That water never did to land before.
The clouds were low and hairy in the skies,
Like locks blown forward in the gleam of eyes.
You could not tell, and yet it looked as if
The shore was lucky in being backed by cliff,
The cliff in being backed by continent
It looked as if a night of dark intent
Was coming, and not only a night, an age.
Someone had better be prepared for rage.
There would be more than ocean-water broken
Before God's last Put Out the Light was spoken.
—Robert Frost (1874–1963)

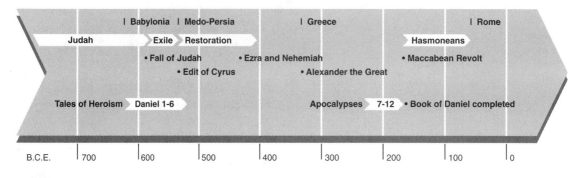

FIGURE 17.2 BOOK OF DANIEL

The book of Daniel can be divided more or less cleanly into two main parts based on content. The first part, chapters 1–6, contains six tales of Jewish heroism set in the late seventh and sixth centuries B.C.E. They are told in the third-person and concern Daniel and his three friends, or Daniel alone, or the three friends alone. The second part, chapters 7–12, contains four apocalypses which Daniel narrates in the first-person. An **apocalypse** is a dream vision of the future (see Part 3).

The book of Daniel does not claim to have been written by Daniel. The first six chapters are a narrative about Daniel (and his friends), and while the final chapters contain Daniel's first-person dream accounts, they are introduced using third-person editorial frameworks. Still, Daniel is the dominant figure of the book, absent only in chapter 3.

Who exactly was this Daniel? We get conflicting signals. The first hero tale has Daniel taken captive as a young man in 606 B.C.E. The story of Daniel in the lion's den in chapter 6 has a setting after 539, which would make Daniel an old man by this time. On the other hand, the book of Ezekiel (14:14, 20; see also 28:3), which was written around the time of the exile in 587, refers to Daniel in the same breath with Noah and Job—all exemplary righteous men. These references suggest that Daniel and the other two were already well known symbols of godliness. But how could Daniel be considered legendary to the pre-exilic Israelites if most of the stories told about him had not yet been written?

The Ugaritic texts from Syria come to the rescue. These texts, dating to the fourteenth century B.C.E. and written in a language close to Hebrew, contain an account of a Danel (close enough in spelling to the biblical Daniel that they may be considered equivalent). This Danel was a notably righteous Canaanite king who wanted to see justice done in his kingdom. This suggests that Danel/Daniel was a hero of the ancient world, and that he was the model or namesake for our hero of Israel's exilic period. Or, . . . the Daniel of Ezekiel fame has nothing to do with the Daniel of the book by that name.

The stories of Daniel are set around the time of the Babylonian exile and the tales may have originated at that time. But the apocalypses of chapters 7–12 betray a much later setting. The history they (fore-)tell culminates in the time of the Maccabees, specifically the years of Antiochus IV. The evidence strongly suggests that the apocalypses were written around 165 B.C.E. shortly before the death of Antiochus in 163, and that the entire book was edited and finalized around that time. This would make Daniel the prime candidate for latest book of the Hebrew Bible.

Additions to Daniel. The figure of Daniel became very popular in Judaism. Post-biblical stories about Daniel, called the "Additions to Daniel," were added in the Greek version of the book of Daniel. The Prayer of Azariah and the Song of the Three Young Men is found within chapter 3. The story of Susanna and the story of Bel and the Dragon follow chapter 12. The tale of Susanna is especially clever and delightful. She was a beautiful Jewish woman who was falsely accused of adultery by two Jewish elders. Daniel exposed their lies and vindicated her.

The Additions to Daniel are on disc in the Apocrypha section of the Bible.

HEROES (1–6)

The first six chapters of Daniel contain some of the most popular stories in the Hebrew Bible. Shadrach, Meshach and Abednego in the fiery furnace. Daniel in the lion's den. The handwriting on the wall. In addition to their popular appeal, the tales had moral and spiritual lessons with special application to Jews living in the diaspora.

The hero tales of Daniel send two fundamental messages. First, no matter what political and religious pressures urge you to conform to the dominant culture, do not give up your faith in Yahweh. If you are faithful God will surely deliver and prosper you. Fidelity to Mosaic torah brings divine reward. Second, ultimately the evil kingdoms of this world will crumble before the kingdom of God, for Yahweh orders history. The hero tales will be treated under these two points.

■ KEEP THE FAITH

Daniel 1 introduces the hero tales by describing Daniel and his three friends Hananiah, Mishael, and Azariah. Each was given a Babylonian name as part of the process of acculturating these young Jewish men into Babylonian society. Respectively they became Belteshazzar, Shadrach, Meshach, and Abednego. Interestingly, Daniel is referred to by his Hebrew name through most of the book, while the friends go by their Babylonian names.

These young men were handsome and intelligent and were to be trained as Babylonian counselors, presumably in the expectation that they would serve **Nebuchadnezzar,** king of Babylon, as administrators in the Judean territories. The problem for these Jewish trainees was that eating at the Babylonian court would violate their dietary laws, called the laws of kosher. They were given a special reprieve by their overseer, and in spite of eating only simple Jewish-type food, they turned out to be healthier than any other trainees. This proved that a person could observe religious laws even in a foreign land—a situation many Jews faced after 587.

Chapters 3 and 6 are similar. By now Daniel and his friends had become important government officials, and they had acquired powerful political enemies. These rivals enacted religious requirements that they knew these Jews could not obey. First the three friends (3), then Daniel (6) were found guilty of breaking the law and were to be executed. The friends were thrown into a well-stoked furnace, but were delivered by God through an angel. And Daniel was thrown into a pit full of ravenous lions. He too was protected and survived. Both incidents prove again that God cares for the faithful.

■ LORD OF HISTORY

Chapter 2 describes Nebuchadnezzar's dream experience. He woke up one time and remembered that he had had a fascinating dream, but he could not remember the details. Daniel came to the king's attention. It turned out that he was the only one who could bring the dream to Nebuchadnezzar's recollection and then interpret it. The dream's central image was of a statue with a head of gold, chest and arms of silver, mid-section and thighs of bronze, legs of iron, and feet of iron and clay. A rock pulverized the statue and it blew away. The rock grew into a mountain which dominated the earth. Daniel's interpretation associated each of the four metals with an empire. These empires were destroyed and a kingdom set up by God took over in their place. As we will see, this statue dream has important parallels to the apocalypse of chapter 7, which also has a sequence of four empires eclipsed by the **kingdom of God.**

In separate episodes chapters 4 and 5 reveal the arrogance of Babylonian power. In the first Nebuchadnezzar has a dream about a great and marvelous tree that was home to all life, but was later cut down. Daniel interpreted the tree to be Nebuchadnezzar's empire. One day after he bragged about his own kingdom and glory, Nebuchadnezzar was afflicted with madness and was removed from power for seven years, after which time he came to his senses and acknowledged the supremacy of Yahweh.

> **Prayer of Nabonidus.** Among the Dead Sea Scrolls from Qumran is a text called the Prayer of Nabonidus. It contains "the words of the prayer that Nabonidus, king of Assyria and Babylon, the great king, prayed." In the prayer the king notes how he was cut down with a dread disease by the decree of the Most High. He was set apart from men for seven years, and was later restored to his throne. The details are reminiscent of Nebuchadnezzar's seven year dementia (4:31–34). See McNamara (1970).

The second episode recounts the evening the Babylonian empire fell. **Belshazzar**, the king, was holding a raucous feast in which the sacred Jerusalem temple cups were used, clearly a sacrilege.

> *5 Immediately the fingers of a man's hand appeared and wrote on the plaster of the wall of the king's palace, opposite the lampstand; and the king saw the hand as it wrote. (5:5)*

Daniel was called in to read and interpret what turns out to be a very clever inscription, "mene, mene, tekel, parsin" (5:25). On one level the three words are terms for coins; a mina, a shekel, and a half shekel. And each of these terms is related to a verb; number, weigh, divide. Speaking to Belshazzar, Daniel spins this into an oracle of judgment. God has numbered your days, weighed your deeds, and will divide your kingdom between the Medes and Persians.

The message of both stories for diaspora Judaism is unmistakable. Yahweh will not abide profane empires forever. The words from Nebuchadnezzar's prayer articulate Daniel's theology of history.

> 35 All the inhabitants of the earth are reckoned as nothing. He does what he wants among the host of heaven and among the inhabitants of the earth. None can stay his hand or say to him, "What are you doing?" (4:35)

Yahweh is ultimately in control, and orders even the destinies of empires. The kingdom of God is coming, and Jews can partake of its glories if only they remain faithful to God and Torah.

APOCALYPSES (7-12)

To understand the setting of the final portion of the book of Daniel it is necessary to summarize the history of the Maccabean period. The Maccabean conflict is the historical setting for the apocalypses, as well as for the final compilation of the book as a whole.

Alexander the Great began his conquest of the eastern Mediterranean world beginning in 333 B.C.E. By his death in 323 B.C.E. Greek control extended as far east as the Indus Valley. After his death, control of the empire was divided among four generals, of whom only two are important for our purposes. Most of Mesopotamia went to Seleucus and became the Seleucid Empire. Syria, Palestine, and Egypt went to Ptolemy and became the Ptolemaic Empire. Palestine was roughly the dividing line between these two empires and for that reason became a matter of contention.

Palestine was under the control of the Ptolemaic Empire until around 200 B.C.E. The Greek way of life, with its attractive cultural institutions such as gymnasiums and theaters, Greek language and literature, refined manners and colorful religion, was a serious temptation to the Jewish population, and found not a few cultural converts. But during this time Judaism was still an acceptable and even thriving enterprise.

This changed when the Seleucid empire extended its area of control to include Palestine. The Seleucid ruler **Antiochus IV**, nicknamed Epiphanes, ruled his empire from 175 to 164. He faced growing opposition to his rule throughout the Seleucid empire. He interpreted the movements toward independence as being in part inspired by local religious and cultural practices. He decided to eradicate everything that smacked of provincialism and impose, by force if necessary, a uniform system of Greek cultural expression, a process called Hellenization. He outlawed such traditional Jewish practices as circumcision, dietary restrictions, and Sabbath observance, and he made ownership of a Torah scroll a capital offense.

Antiochus took visible and outrageous actions to demonstrate royal disfavor of Judaism. He forced Jews to eat pork in violation of kosher regulations, and even sacrificed a pig on the altar of burnt offering in the Jerusalem temple complex. Then he set up a statue of Zeus in the most holy place of the temple. Many Jews accommodated **Hellenism**, the culture of the Greek world, and assimilated. Others opposed any sort of compromise. They were called **Hasids**, "faithful ones." The struggle between the Seleucids and the Hasids is told in 1 and 2 Maccabees.

TABLE 17.1 FOUR APOCALYPSES OF DANIEL

Daniel	Apocalypse	Interpretation
7	Four beasts and son of man	Kingdom of the persecuted Jews
8	Ram and he-goat	Greek to Persian rule
9	Seventy weeks of years	History from exile to Maccabean war
10:1–12:4	Kings of South and North	Ptolemies and Seleucids

The text of 1 and 2 Maccabees can be found in the Apocrypha section of the Bible.

Armed Jewish resistance broke out in 167, led by a provincial Jew named Mattathias and his sons. The most famous son is Judas Maccabee, "the hammer." They successfully waged a guerrilla campaign against the Seleucids, eventually resulting in the retaking of Jerusalem. They cleansed and restored the temple and resumed ritual activity as prescribed in the Torah. The temple was rededicated in 164 B.C.E. in a celebration called Hanukkah that lasted eight days. In apocalyptic literature's typically cryptic and veiled way, the apocalypses of Daniel 7–12 relate to the history of this period.

■ SON OF MAN APOCALYPSE (7)

The apocalypses of Daniel consist of private dream visions followed by official interpretations communicated by angels. In this first apocalypse Daniel saw four beasts and the son of man (1–14) followed by the interpretation (15–27).

> *1 In the first year of King Belshazzar of Babylon, Daniel saw a dream and his mind had a vision while he was in bed. Afterwards he wrote down the dream. 2 Daniel related and said: "I saw the four winds stirring up the great sea in my nighttime vision. 3 Four great beasts came up out of the sea, each different from the others. 4 The first was like a lion and had eagle's wings. Then its wings were pulled off as I watched, and it was lifted up from the ground and made to stand on two feet like a human, and it was given a human mind." (7:1–4)*

The narrative introduction to this first apocalypse introduces the dream vision. The year is 554 B.C.E. when Belshazzar ruled over Babylonia on behalf of Nabonidus. The great sea out of which the beasts arose recalls the mythic waters of chaos associated with evil, populated with dragons and monsters (see Isaiah 51:9–10 for a similar allusion to the waters of chaos). The stormy sea is a fitting image for the tumultuous affairs of the nations that threaten God's people. The lion represents Babylonia.

Daniel goes on to describe three other beasts, a bear standing for Media, a leopard for Persia, and a beast with ten horns so terrible it was unlike any natural creature standing for Greece. As he watched:

FIGURE 17.3 ISHTAR GATE, BABYLON The gate into Babylon and the royal processional way were decorated with hybrid creatures. They may have influenced Daniel's description of the evil empire beasts.

9 thrones were put in place, and an Ancient of Days took his throne, his clothing was white as snow, and the hair of his head was like pure wool; his throne was on fire and its wheels were burning. 10 A stream of fire issued and flowed out from his presence. A thousand thousands served him, and ten thousand ten thousands stood attending him. The court sat in judgment and the books were opened. (7:9–10)

The Almighty, described as a stately elder and called the Ancient of Days, was surrounded by the divine council. He presided from atop his mobile fiery throne-chariot, recalling Ezekiel's throne-chariot vision and even Elijah's translation to heaven. Together they rendered judgment, and the terrible beast was destroyed by fire. Then another figure appeared who received command of the earth.

13 As I watched the night visions, I saw one like a son of man coming with the clouds of heaven. He went to the Ancient of Days and was presented to him. 14 To him was given dominion, glory, and kingship. All people, nations, and languages would serve him. His dominion would be an ever-lasting dominion that would not disappear. His kingship would never be destroyed. (7:13–14)

A human-like figure, "one like a **son of man**," next appeared in the vision and was given total power over the kingdoms of this world. This mysterious and intriguing figure is separate from the supreme deity yet comes from heaven. It may be the angel Michael, who appears by name in the fourth apocalypse.

> **Son of Man.** The identification of the "one like a son of man" figure in 7:13 is problematic. The phrase "son of man" is used in the book of Ezekiel when Yahweh addresses the prophet (2:1; 3:1; etc.), and seems only to mean human being. In Daniel the phrase "a human-like figure" refers to an angel (8:15 and 9:21; but a different figure is being referred to in these references than the one in 7:13). The "son of man" figure is suggestive yet open-ended. It develops into a messianic notion in post-biblical literature. According to the first book of Enoch (37–71), the Enoch of Genesis 5:24 will return to earth as "son of man" at the end of time and establish the rule of God. "Son of man" is a component of the identity of Jesus of Nazareth in the New Testament Gospels. Jesus prefers the title "son of man" over all others, perhaps just because it both affirms and veils his claim of divinity. See Borsch (1967).

One of the members of the divine council gave Daniel the interpretation of the vision. The human-like figure is a symbol for the collective people of God, just as the individual beasts each stood for an empire. The "holy ones," as they are called, come to possess the kingdom of God for all time.

The setting of this vision, as well as the detailed description of the fourth beast in verses 23–27, suggests that the term the "holy ones" stands for the righteous Jews who were persecuted by Antiochus IV. The writer of Daniel 7 wrote this apocalypse at the time of Antiochus's oppressive rule over Judea (175–164 B.C.E.). He was writing in the expectation that the Seleucid kingdom of the wicked Antiochus would come to an end, and then Israel would receive the power of the kingdom of God forever.

> **Four Ages.** Clearly the writer of the Daniel 7 apocalypse knew the tale of Nebuchadnezzar's dream in Daniel 2 and updated it to his time. The four metals of Nebuchadnezzar's dream correspond to the four beasts; the stone which becomes a mountain is the "one like a son of man," later the "holy ones." The four-age scheme of world history can be found in other ancient literature. The dynastic prophecy published by Grayson (1975: 24–37) describes the fall of Assyria and the rise of Babylonia, the fall of Babylonia and the rise of Persia, then the fall of Persia and the rise of the Hellenistic monarchies. Also, the *Works and Days* of Hesiod divides history into four ages: gold, silver, bronze, and iron.

Table 17.A displays the four-age visions of Daniel and correlates them with empire interpretations.

■ OTHER APOCALYPSES (8–12)

The other apocalypses provide additional details about the rule of the wicked kingdoms. The tale of the ram and the goat (8) allegorically relates the transition from Persian to Greek rule. It spends the most time on "the little horn," the code word throughout the book of Daniel for Antiochus IV. It tells of the desecration of the sanctuary and its reconsecration at Hanukkah.

Chapter 9 updates Jeremiah's prophecy that Israel would be in captivity to Babylonia for seventy years (25:11–12; 29:10). In Daniel's apocalypse the period of domination is extended to seventy weeks of years, or 490 years. This explains why Israel was never reestablished in power after the fall of Babylonia; restoration awaits the future.

The extended apocalypse of 10–12 relates the conflict between the Ptolemies and Seleucids for control of Palestine in great but cryptic detail. It includes a description of the great tribulation which is introduced by the military campaigns of Antiochus IV. The end times will be a period of great distress, but God's people will be delivered.

> *1 There will be a time of trouble, such as never has been since there was a nation until that time. But at that time your people will be delivered, every one whose name shall be found written in the book. 2 And many of those who sleep in the dust of the earth will wake up, some to everlasting life, and some to shame and everlasting contempt. 3 Those who are wise will shine like the brightness of the firmament; and those who turn many to righteousness (will shine) like the stars for ever and ever. 4 But you, Daniel, shut up the words, and seal the book, until the time of the end. Many will run to and fro, and knowledge will increase. (12:1–4)*

This passage contains the clearest reference in the Hebrew Bible to **resurrection,** a return to life after death, with the possible exception of Isaiah 26:19. The dead will be raised and judged, some gaining eternal life and others punishment.

> **Resurrection.** Most of the Hebrew Bible knows nothing of resurrection, and there was no developed concept of an afterlife. Only Enoch and Elijah escaped death. Ezekiel's valley of dry bones (37:1–14) is a corporate resurrection, and is essentially a symbol of national restoration. The primary mode of individual after-existence was through offspring who carried on the ancestral name. Still, death was not considered the absolute end of personal existence. After death a person descended into *sheol,* the underworld, where that person existed as a shade or shadow of the former self. This late passage in Daniel is a hint of the notion of resurrection that takes hold strongly within Judaism and Christianity after the second century B.C.E. (see Nickelsburg 1972 and Hasel 1980).

Observe that Daniel is to keep these apocalypses sealed—just the opposite of classical prophecy, which was to be broadcast. This is typical of apocalyptic literature generally. Apocalypses were to be kept secret until the end of time, that is, the time of the great conflict therein predicted. This perpetuates the literary fiction that these materials were written long before the events themselves transpired, and that their meaning would only be revealed at the end.

> **Modern Apocalyptic Literature.** Many conservative Christians lay great store in the apocalyptic material of Daniel, as well as other Old Testament and New Testament apocalyptic passages. Like pieces of a giant divine jigsaw puzzle, the biblical references are correlated with contemporary events to provide a "map" of the end of the world. Genuinely creative, apocalyptic literature could be considered the ancient equivalent of our modern genre of science fiction for the way it tries to conceptualize and visualize the shape of the future. The book of Daniel reflects a new approach to dealing with historical experience. It extrapolates from the present and tries to imagine how the future might look, heavy on the imagination. See Boyer (1992).

DANIEL AS A WHOLE

There is one feature of the book that compromises the clean division of Daniel into two parts after chapter 6. Daniel is one of two books in the Hebrew Bible that contains a substantial amount of text written in Aramaic rather than in Hebrew. The other is Ezra. The section of Daniel written in the Aramaic language, 2:4 through the end of chapter 7, spans the division based on form and content.

The book of Daniel was classed with the Writings rather than the Prophets in the Jewish canon for a variety of reasons. Daniel does not play the role of a prophet in the book but rather the roles of wise man, diviner, and counselor to kings. The latter half of the book consists of apocalypses rather than prophetic oracles of the type found in classical prophecy. And the book is much later than the prophetic body of writings, which was considered closed after around 400 B.C.E. Daniel is classed with prophetic literature in the arrangement of books in most English Bible translations. But the book of Daniel obviously differs from mainstream prophetic literature.

Childs (1979) raises an important canonical question concerning Daniel. How was Daniel heard by Jews in the post-Maccabean period? There would seem to be a problem insofar as the book of Daniel foretold the end of world history with the demise of Antiochus IV. Yet the world did not end in the way or at the time predicted. In fact, it did not end at all, as the writer expected it would. Some might judge the book to be mistaken. So how could it still speak to a later age? And how could it be canonized?

Although the future that the book of Daniel imagined did not come to pass as he had envisioned it, yet it gives powerful expression to the need for vision and the need to conceptualize the future imaginatively in order to prepare for it. The book is quite pessimistic about the ability of human structures to redeem the world. The kingdom comes by the intervention of God. Yet even this is profound testimony to the writer's abiding hope in the power of God's rule and in the ability of the faithful to cope and endure in a time of severe social and political crisis.

Table 17.B is a detailed content outline of the book of Daniel.

FOR FURTHER STUDY

Towner (1984) for commentary, Russell (1989) for Daniel and the modern world.

 Bibliography. See Part 3 Bibliography for general works on apocalyptic literature.

QUESTIONS FOR REVIEW

1. What are the two main sections of the book of Daniel, and what kind of literature is in each?
2. Who are the main heroes of the book of Daniel? What lessons did their stories teach the Jews?

3. How is the book of Daniel related to the history of the Maccabean era?
4. Compare and contrast classical biblical prophecy and apocalyptic prophecy.

QUESTIONS FOR REFLECTION AND DISCUSSION

1. Do you think the critical events of the heroes of Daniel really happened, such as the three friends surviving the furnace, or Daniel in the lion's den? Did they have to happen in order for the book to be true?

2. Should Daniel be studied to provide a road map for our future?
3. How does our vision of the culmination of history impact the way we live life in the present? What might be the message of the book of Daniel for today?

 Chapter 17 Study Guide
- *Chapter summary*
- *Key terms linked to the glossary*
- *Concept questions with answer links*
- *Progress tests: true/false, multiple choice, matching, and identification*

CHRONICLER'S HISTORY

18

FIGURE 18.1 **DARIUS ON HIS THRONE** Darius I (522–486 B.C.E.), seated on the throne, was the Persian king at the time of Zerubbabel's return. The story of the book of Esther takes place during his reign.

God cannot alter the past, but historians can.
— Samuel Butler (1835–1902)

Progress, far from consisting in change, depends on retentiveness. . . .
Those who cannot remember the past are condemned to repeat it.
— George Santayana (1863–1952)

The stars are dead. The animals will not look:
We are left alone with our day, and the time is short,
and
History to the defeated
May say Alas but cannot help nor pardon.
— W. H. Auden (1907–1973)

Who controls the past controls the future. Who controls the present
controls the past.
— George Orwell (1903–1950)

Until the lions have their historians, tales of hunting will always glorify
the hunter.
— African proverb

Modern historians assert that writing an entirely objective record of the past is impossible. All history is an interpretation of the past shaped by the present of the historian.

Furthermore, the one who has political power, which determines who gets heard, is more often than not the one who shapes written history. The priestly party, in the absence of the monarchy, emerged out of Judah's Babylonian exile firmly in control. They were the preservers and guardians of Israel's traditions and historical memory, and they shaped the period of Judean restoration. Consequently, biblical history in the postexilic period was written by the priests and Levites.

The Torah and the Former Prophets, otherwise known as the Primary History, is a comprehensive account from creation to the Babylonian exile. Chronicles is a history of equal scope, but the telling is quite different. Chronicles, along with Ezra and Nehemiah, is called the **Chronicler's History** (or CH) and extends the narrative into the Persian period.

Some authorities dispute whether Chronicles, Ezra, and Nehemiah should be considered a single unified work produced by a single author, rather than two works, Chronicles and Ezra–Nehemiah. Their main focuses are not the same. First and Second Chronicles emphasize David and the Prophets. A combined Ezra and Nehemiah emphasize Moses and the Torah.

On the other hand, they hold a number of features in common. The ending of Chronicles is the same as the beginning of Ezra, suggesting an overlap or connection of some sort. Both works abound in lists and genealogies. They also share technical vocabulary pertaining to the Levites and certain phrases that are infrequently found elsewhere, such as "house of God." Both works are preoccupied with the temple in Jerusalem, the institutions of the priesthood, and Levitical functions.

The Chronicler's History had not been all that well studied due to certain historical prejudices in biblical scholarship. Earlier scholarship was obsessed with the drive to recover the earliest sources. This was thought to provide the best chance of recovering "what really happened." The CH is a comparatively late source, so it was neglected in favor of the Former Prophets. The Chronicler used Samuel and Kings as his main sources. He did not add much to them, and what he did add was late.

Students of the biblical text are taking a new look at the Chronicler's History. A study of how the Chronicler retold the history of Israel opens up a window on the beliefs and expectations of the postexilic community of the sixth and fifth centuries B.C.E. Relatively little textual material directly relates to the culture and history of this period, and the CH turns out to be one of the most important. Also, the postexilic period is increasingly being seen as central to the development of the canon, and the writings of the postexilic period, including the CH, provide important clues as to how the canon was shaped.

Furthermore, a comparison of the Chronicler's History and the Deuteronomistic History provides an occasion to analyze how history writing is conditioned by particular historical and cultural contexts. The Deuteronomistic History reflects a sixth-century exilic perspective, while the Chronicler's History reflects a late fifth-century postexilic perspective. The Chronicler's History used the Deuteronomistic History as its main source and "repurposed" it to rebuild post-

TABLE 18.1 COMPARISON OF THE DEUTERONOMISTIC AND
CHRONICLER'S HISTORIES

	DH	CH
Authorship	Northern Levites	Postexilic Levites
Date of Composition	550 B.C.E.	400–250 B.C.E.
Audience	Exilic community	Restoration community
Theme	Reasons for God's judgment	Jerusalem temple, worship, Levites

exilic culture and religion along certain lines. Such recasting of history is sometimes called *revisionist history.*

The Chronicler's History retells the story of God's people from Adam to Ezra. It makes obvious use of pre-existing written sources. The sources include letters, lists, genealogies, and the block 1 Samuel 31–2 Kings 25 of the Deuteronomistic History. The Chronicler also drew on the Torah, Judges, Ruth, Psalms, Isaiah, Jeremiah, Lamentations, and Zechariah. As would any good historian, the Chronicler cited his sources (though certainly not all of them). Unfortunately, most of the sources cited by the Chronicler, including "the records of the seer Samuel" and "the midrash on the Book of Kings," are unknown outside the Bible. Some scholars date the composition of the Chronicler's History to the time of Ezra in the fifth century B.C.E., others to the fourth century, and still others place it in the Hellenistic period of the third century.

The Chronicler was mostly concerned with the Judean monarchy and the Jerusalem religious establishment. The Northern Kingdom of Israel is mentioned rarely and then only in passing. The Chronicler idealized the reigns of Solomon and Hezekiah and especially of David. David became the model of the godly monarch. He ruled obediently and established religious service as it was meant to be, with the temple, its priesthood, singers, prayers, rituals, and offerings.

Of course, to make such exalted claims about David, the historian had to exercise selective memory. Although the Chronicler's History of David was based on the books of Samuel, the Chronicler ignored narratives that put David in a bad light. Furthermore, he traced the establishment of important priestly and Levitic institutions back to David, although other historical evidence suggests this is unlikely. He grounded proper worship practices in the traditions of the past, mainly those of David's time, in order to give them validity.

The Chronicler's main focus in writing his history was the priesthood, the temple, and worship practices in Judea. All of history was viewed in terms of how it promoted these concerns. Kings were evaluated in terms of their disposition to temple and cult. And history moved to a climax at the time of Ezra and Nehemiah with the reestablishing of temple worship. The Chronicler was a defender of the status quo and had no vision for a better political future. As long as Yahweh could be worshiped properly, seemingly all else was acceptable.

CHRONICLES

The two books of Chronicles were originally one book. Like the books of Samuel and Kings they became two in printed editions. We will refer to combined First and Second Chronicles simply as *Chronicles.* Jewish tradition holds that most of Chronicles, along with the books of Ezra and Nehemiah, were written by **Ezra** the scribe and completed by **Nehemiah.** In Jewish tradition Ezra is venerated to a degree second only to Moses. Chronicles can be divided into two main parts on the basis of content: pre-monarchy history and the history of the Davidic monarchy.

■ PRE-MONARCHY HISTORY (1 CHRONICLES 1–10)

The first part of Chronicles retells history from Adam to Saul. Most of the story is told by means of lists of names and genealogies. Some of the genealogical lists extend all the way into the postexilic period by including individuals from that time, indicating that this material was finally edited in the postexilic period.

There is very little storytelling narrative in this first part of Chronicles. It is dominated by genealogies. Special attention was given to the names of priests and Levites. The genealogies also focus on the tribe of Judah and its line of David, the tribe of Benjamin and its line of Saul, and the tribe of Levi. These comprised the nucleus of the Persian province of Jehud (Judea) in the postexilic period.

Genealogies serve different purposes within the biblical world (see Wilson 1977). Within the family they define privilege and responsibility, as with the first-born son over against later-born children and children of concubines. Within tribes they establish political and territorial claims, especially land ownership, and might also reflect military conscription lists. Within the religious sphere they establish membership in the priestly and Levitic classes. Membership determines who can and cannot hold priestly offices, and who can acquire the privileges and responsibilities associated with them. All of these uses of genealogies are present in Chronicles.

■ HISTORY OF THE DAVIDIC MONARCHY (1 CHRONICLES 11–2 CHRONICLES 36)

This part of Chronicles covers the history of the Davidic monarchy from David to the Babylonian exile. It can be subdivided into three sections.

1. David's reign: 1 Chronicles 11–29
2. Solomon's reign: 2 Chronicles 1–9
3. Kings of Judah from Rehoboam to Cyrus's Edict of Return from Exile: 2 Chronicles 10–36

The Chronicler used the books of Samuel and Kings from the Deuteronomistic History as his main source in retelling the history of the Judean monarchy. About half of Chronicles comes from the books of Samuel and Kings.

David's Reign (1 Chronicles 11–29)

This section contains an extended account of the reign of David. In it there is no record of Saul's conflict with David. It begins with all Israel at Hebron asking David to be their king. This in itself is a recasting of the Samuel account, where first Judah acclaims David king, followed seven years later by the remainder of the tribes. Throughout his account the Chronicler uses the phrase "all Israel" to promote a perception of the unity of God's people (see Williamson 1977).

The account continues with a description of David's capture of Jerusalem and his moving the ark of the covenant into the city. A comparison of how Samuel and Chronicles tell the story of the ark's trip to Jerusalem demonstrates how the Chronicler repurposed the older account to validate the essential role of the Levites. 2 Samuel 6:1–11 is closely paralleled in 1 Chronicles 13:1–14, telling the story of the death of Uzzah when he touched the ark and the abandonment of the ark with Obed-edom. 2 Samuel moves directly to David's fetching the ark from Obed-edom and taking it to Jerusalem (2 Samuel 6:12–19). Before 1 Chronicles picks up the story at that point it inserts a lengthy account of the appointment of the Levites to carry the ark on to Jerusalem (1 Chronicles 15:1–24), including these words.

> 2 Then David said, "Carrying the ark of God is not allowed except by Levites, for YHWH chose them to carry the ark of YHWH and to minister to him forever." 3 David assembled all Israel at Jerusalem to bring up the ark of YHWH to the place he had prepared for it. 11 Then David summoned the priests Zadok and Abiathar, and the Levites Uriel, Asaiah, Joel, Shemaiah, Eliel, and Amminadab, 12 and said to them, "You are the heads of the families of the Levites. Sanctify yourselves, you and your brothers, so that you may bring up the ark of YHWH, the God of Israel, to the place I have prepared for it. 13 Because you did not carry it the first time, YHWH our God exploded in anger on us, because we did not seek out the rules for handling it." 14 So the priests and the Levites sanctified themselves to bring up the ark of YHWH, the God of Israel. 15 And the Levites carried the ark of God with the poles on their shoulders, as Moses had commanded according to the word of YHWH. (1 Chronicles 15:2–3, 11–15)

Whereas no lesson was drawn from Uzzah's death in the Deuteronomistic History's account, the Chronicler used this as the occasion to validate the special role of the Levites and to draw the lesson that only the Levites may handle the ark.

Generally speaking, the Chronicler's deviations from the Samuel–Kings account are noteworthy. The Chronicler omitted any reference to David's war against Saul and his alliance with the Philistines. He omitted the story of how David intimidated Nabal and then married Abigail. David's affair with Bathsheba was completely ignored. In one way or another all of these stories might put David in a bad light or tarnish his image, so they were conveniently left out.

On the other hand, the Chronicler added information not present in Samuel–Kings. David's extensive preparations for the building of the temple are detailed in 1 Chronicles 23–28. This effectively makes David the founder and sponsor of the Jerusalem temple. In contrast, the book of Kings attributes the entire process of temple building to Solomon.

An especially interesting retelling of history is found in the Chronicles account of David's census of the nation. Taking a census was an act of disobedience because it signaled a reliance on military forces rather than the power of God. The Samuel account implies that Yahweh incited David to take a census in order to have an occasion to punish the people.

2 Samuel 24:1	1 Chronicles 21:1
Again the anger of YHWH was inflamed against Israel, and he incited David against them, "Go, count the people of Israel and Judah."	*Satan stood up against Israel and incited David to count the people of Israel.*

In the Samuel account Yahweh is responsible for getting David into trouble. The Chronicler's account removes Yahweh and introduces Satan as the instigator. This reflects the growing interest in Satan in the late postexilic period and the Chronicler's concern to distance God as far away from evil as possible. The Chronicler probably would have chosen to omit this story altogether because of the picture it gives us of David, but retained it because the account goes on to describe how David secured the threshing floor of Araunah as the future site of the temple. Thus it still fit his overall purpose.

Solomon's Reign (2 Chronicles 1–9)

Most of this section is devoted to a description of the building and dedication of the Jerusalem temple, taken almost verbatim from the book of Kings. The Chronicler idealized Solomon just as he did David, by omitting the stories of the Deuteronomistic History that might put him in a bad light, including the following.

- The bloody political struggle between Adonijah and Solomon that ended with Solomon's triumph (1 Kings 2:13–46a)
- Solomon's adjudication of the case of the two prostitutes and their babies (1 Kings 3:16–28)
- Solomon's wealth, power, and wisdom (1 Kings 4:22–34)
- Solomon's marriages to the multitude of foreign women and the building of shrines in Jerusalem to their foreign gods (1 Kings 11:1–13)
- Solomon's enemies and the prophecy of Ahijah (1 Kings 11:14–40)

The Chronicles account of Solomon in his role as temple builder adds details not found in the Kings account. In particular, it depicts Solomon as Bezalel, who was the architect of the tabernacle at the time of Moses. Bezalel is mentioned nowhere outside the book of Exodus except in the Solomon narrative of Chronicles. In their parallel roles both Bezalel and Solomon were designated for their tasks by God, came from the tribe of Judah, received the spirit of wisdom to complete their tasks, built a bronze altar for the sanctuary, and made the sanctuary furnishings. Solomon, as the new Bezalel and great temple builder, continued in the Mosaic sanctuary tradition.

Kings of Judah (2 Chronicles 10–36)

This section is devoted almost entirely to the kings of Judah after the division of the kingdoms. Virtually no mention is made of the Northern Kingdom. The Chronicler dwells on the role of the kings of Judah in promoting worship and proper ritual. When disaster finally came by way of the Babylonians, it was because certain kings failed in their religious duties.

The Chronicler's account supplements the Deuteronomistic History on a couple of points. The reform program of Hezekiah, not detailed in Kings, is given extended attention in chapters 29–32. This includes an account of his temple cleansing and the celebration of the Passover. Also, Josiah's Passover celebration is given increased attention. All this accords with the Chronicler's interest in the right performance of religious ritual.

EZRA AND NEHEMIAH

The books of Ezra and Nehemiah are the main biblical sources for the return of the Jewish community from exile. Talmon (1987) calls Ezra and Nehemiah *biblical historiography* in the style of straightforward prose narration. They were compliled fairly close to the events they report and can be considered reliable historiography for the most part. They are generally considered to be two parts of one book.[1] The events described in Ezra–Nehemiah are the major moments in the rebuilding of a religious community after the time of Babylonian exile.

The return from Babylonian exile, the process of rebuilding Jerusalem, and the restoration of Jewish community life back in Judea took place in four stages.

1. 538 B.C.E. **Sheshbazzar** led a return after Cyrus, king of Persia (550–530), gave permission. Temple rebuilding was begun, but due to economic hardship and local opposition it was not finished at that time.

2. 522 B.C.E. **Zerubbabel** and **Joshua,** the high priest, led a second group of Jews back to Palestine during the reign of Darius I (522–486). They succeeded in completing a temple in Jerusalem in 515.

3. 458 B.C.E. Ezra led a group of Jews back to Palestine during the reign of Artaxerxes I (465–424) and reestablished adherence to Mosaic standards of law and religion.

4. 445 B.C.E. Nehemiah organized the rebuilding of the walls of Jerusalem and returned religious and civil authority to the Levites.

---

[1]The Septuagint and the Babylonian Talmud refer only to the book of Ezra when citing both Ezra and Nehemiah, indicating they were considered one book.

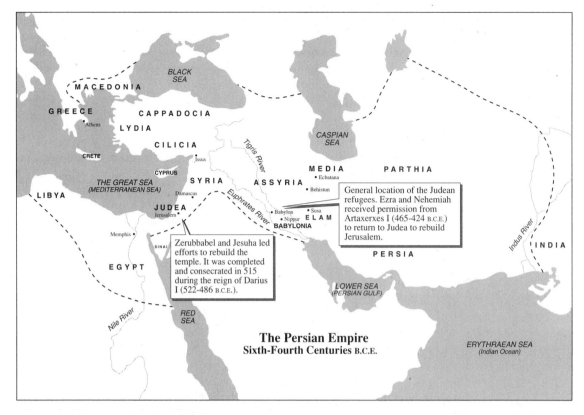

FIGURE 18.2 PERSIAN EMPIRE

The book of Ezra–Nehemiah is a single unit consisting of three identifiable sections, each centered around a significant leader of the restoration.

The editorial history of Ezra–Nehemiah is difficult to sort out, and authorities disagree about the original order of the chapters. Although opinions vary, it is reasonable to suggest that the book of Ezra–Nehemiah was completed around 400 B.C.E.

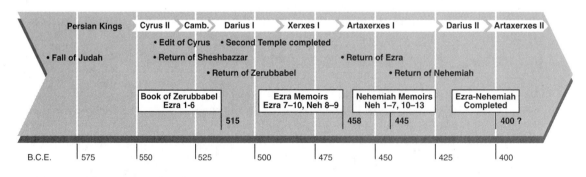

FIGURE 18.3 EZRA–NEHEMIAH

■ BOOK OF ZERUBBABEL (EZRA 1–6)

The first section of Ezra, termed the *Book of Zerubbabel,* relates the history of the early returns from Babylonian exile. It covers the period from the end of exile in 538 to the completion of the rebuilt temple in 515. The book begins with a verbatim record of the decree of **Cyrus** allowing the Judean refugees to return to Jerusalem.

> *2 Thus says King Cyrus of Persia, "YHWH the God of heaven has given me all the kingdoms of the earth. He has commanded me to build him a house in Jerusalem of Judah. 3 May God be with those of you who are his people. Go up to Jerusalem of Judah and build the house of YHWH, the God of Israel, the God who is in Jerusalem! 4 Let all who remain behind assist the people of their place with silver, gold, goods, and livestock in addition to freewill offerings for the house of God in Jerusalem. (1:2–4)*

This decree, issued in 538, authorized the rebuilding of the temple. Notice how Cyrus, a Persian, talks as if he acknowledges Yahweh, the God of Israel, and attributes to him the gift of his power. The fact that Cyrus authorized the temple rebuilding becomes important later in the book when Samaritans from the north and others opposed rebuilding activities in Jerusalem.

The first group of returned refugees was led by Sheshbazzar, who had been appointed governor of Judea. He may have been the son of Jehoiachin, Judah's king in exile. Sheshbazzar and the first group of returnees succeeded in relaying the foundations of the temple, but then the work broke off and remained unfinished until the next return.

The most productive return was led by Zerubbabel, a leader from the line of David, in 522 B.C.E. near the beginning of the reign of Darius (see Figure 18.1). The most significant event of this period was the rebuilding of the temple in Jerusalem. Authorities call this one the **Second Temple;** the one built by Solomon was the first. The Second Temple remained intact until it was destroyed by the Romans in 70 C.E. Aided by Joshua and the prophets Haggai and Zechariah (see Chapter 13), Zerubbabel motivated the people to complete the project begun by Sheshbazzar, and it was finished in 515. This section of the CH ends with an account of the dedication of the temple and the celebration of Passover.

■ EZRA MEMOIRS (EZRA 7–10, NEHEMIAH 8–9)

There is a gap of about sixty years between the events of the Book of Zerubbabel and those of the Ezra Memoirs. Chapters 7–10 of the book of Ezra, along with Nehemiah 8–9, which were misplaced, deal with Ezra the scribe.

Ezra was a priest descended from the line of Aaron through Zadok. Also called a scribe, he was a court official under the Persian king Artaxerxes I. He returned to Judea from Babylon in 458 with another group of refugees. Ezra had the full authorization of the Persian government to reestablish proper modes of Yahweh worship and adherence to the Torah of Moses.

Ezra's Mission. Authorities debate the date of Ezra's mission. The seventh year of Artaxerxes I (Ezra 7:7) would be 458 B.C.E., the date we use. The problem is this: Ezra and Nehemiah do not seem to acknowledge each other, and they seem to work independently of each other, even though the straightforward reckoning of their dates puts them in Jerusalem at the same time. Consequently, some scholars place Ezra after Nehemiah, and read <u>thirty</u>-seventh year of Artaxerxes, rather than seventh, thus placing the beginning of Ezra's mission in 428. Still others place the beginning in 398 during the reign of Artaxerxes II (404–358). Nehemiah 8:9 and 12:26, 36 place Ezra and Nehemiah in Jerusalem at the same time, though these are often judged to be late editorial insertions.

In Ezra's analysis, one of the most serious problems among the Judeans was mixed marriages. In the interim, male Judeans had married Canaanite, Hittite, Ammonite, Moabite, and Egyptian women. Ezra saw this as a breach of the injunction to remain separate from non-Israelite people. Intermarriage promoted assimilation and was a threat to Yahwistic religion. Israel's theological historians had concluded that one of the biggest reasons for Israel's downfall was intermarriage with Canaanites that led to idolatry.

Ezra required the men to divorce their non-Jewish wives and expel them, along with any children of the marriage. It was a time of great anxiety and mourning, but the priests, Levites, and ordinary people who had married foreign women carried out the directive.

Ezra also rededicated the people to keeping the Torah (see Nehemiah 8–9). He assembled all Jewish adults in Jerusalem and read the Torah to them in Hebrew. However, because Hebrew was no longer the native tongue, having been replaced by Aramaic during the exile, there were translators who interpreted the text to the people as he read. Such an Aramaic translation of a Hebrew original is called a *targum*. This is the first biblical attestation of the practice of Scripture translation from one language to another.

After the Torah was read and interpreted, the people celebrated the Festival of Booths, which is a commemoration of the wilderness wandering period of their early history. Then Ezra offered a prayer to God, recounting the history of God and his people from creation to that moment. This is not unlike other covenant renewal events, such as the ones under Moses (the entire book of Deuteronomy), Joshua (Joshua 24), and Samuel (1 Samuel 12). Such covenant renewal occasions were times of corporate reflection and rededication to the compact with Yahweh.

■ NEHEMIAH MEMOIRS (NEHEMIAH 1–7, 10–13)

Nehemiah was an official at the court of Artaxerxes I in Susa. He traveled to Jerusalem in 445 B.C.E. to be the governor of the Persian empire's province of Jehud, that is, Judea. His great accomplishment was rebuilding the enclosure walls of Jerusalem. His work was opposed by Sanballat, leader of the Samaritans, and Tobiah, leader of the Ammonites. They saw this as a threat to their power in the region. On various occasions they tried to stop the work, and they tried to assassinate Nehemiah.

Nehemiah and his crew were able to complete the rebuilding of the walls in fifty-two days in spite of the opposition. These walls gave Jerusalem the protection and security its people needed. Nehemiah served twelve years as governor of the province and then returned to Babylon in 433.

Shortly afterward he returned to Jerusalem and instituted some important religious reforms. He closed the city on the Sabbath so that no trading could take place. He guaranteed that the Levites would receive their proper support, and like Ezra, he forbade mixed marriages.

CHRONICLER'S HISTORY AS A WHOLE

In English Bibles the Chronicler's History immediately follows the Deuteronomistic History, giving the work of the Chronicler the character of a historical supplement to the Deuteronomistic History. In this ordering, Ezra and Nehemiah are separate books following Chronicles.

Ezra, Nehemiah, and Chronicles are included in the division of the Writings in the Hebrew Bible. Curiously, even though chronologically Ezra and Nehemiah follow Chronicles, within the Writings they are placed before the books of Chronicles. Chronicles' placement at the very end is deliberate and was meant to suggest that they are a summary of the entire course of history of the people of God. Chronicles does in fact go from creation to the end of exile.

The Chronicler's History essentially parallels the coverage of the combined Pentateuch and Deuteronomistic History. But why should there be two accounts of the same history in the Hebrew Bible? The fact that multiple versions of biblical history were retained affirms that each generation needs to rethink, reevaluate, and rewrite history in order to understand it in relation to present concerns. The Chronicler's History retold Israel's history with almost single-minded attention to worship institutions because at its moment in time the community needed the temple as the core of its rebuilding efforts, and the priests were the prime movers.

The Chronicler's History did not replace the Deuteronomistic History. Both are still valid. The Chronicler's History is evidence of a continuing historiographic tradition within the community of faith. In each generation the past needs to be reappropriated. The Chronicler's History is evidence of the value of studying history to understand the present. Studying the Chronicler's History enables us to see how retelling history in Israel grounded the identity of the Jews.

The tradition of retelling history continued even beyond the canon of the Hebrew Bible, some of it continuing to be connected with the figure of Ezra. The apocryphal book 1 Esdras appears to be a newer, or at least a different, edition of material from 2 Chronicles, Ezra, and Nehemiah. Later, the *Antiquities* of Josephus and the *Biblical Antiquities* of Pseudo-Philo also retold the history of the Jewish people.

Finally, the Chronicler's History, including Ezra and Nehemiah, is notable for its focus on two heroes of the faith from the Torah and the Prophets. Chronicles focuses on David in his role in the development of the temple, and Ezra–Nehemiah focuses on the importance of Moses and the Torah for community rebuilding. This is a witness for the continuing vitality of these founding fathers.

The role of Ezra in reading and reinterpreting the Torah for the fifth-century Jewish community has canonical implications. It demonstrates that the Mosaic Torah continued to provide the foundation for the faith of Israel, even though it needed reinterpretation and updating. The reappropriation of Torah demonstrates its ongoing vitality and adaptability. Ezra's role has been considered so significant for the development of the canon that he has been considered by some the final compiler of the Pentateuch, in addition to having had a role in the formation of the Chronicler's History. Still today Ezra is considered the "father of Judaism."

Table 18.A is a detailed content outline of the Chronicler's History.

FOR FURTHER STUDY

Newsome (1986) is a necessary tool for comparing the Deuteronomistic and Chronicler's histories.

Chapter 18 Bibliography

QUESTIONS FOR REVIEW

1. What books constitute the Chronicler's History? Why are they grouped together under this heading?
2. What was the Chronicler's reading of David, and why was he so prominent in the Chronicler's History?

3. What were the four stages in the Jewish return to Jerusalem and the restoration of Jewish community life there?
4. How did Ezra deal with the problem of intermarriage?
5. What did Nehemiah do to ensure the security of the Jews?

QUESTIONS FOR REFLECTION AND DISCUSSION

1. Compare the Deuteronomistic History with the Chronicler's History. For what purpose did each give an account of Israel's history? To what end might Jews today retell the history of ancient Israel? Why might Christians retell that history? Why might Muslims?
2. Why was the rebuilding of the temple so important for reestablishing a viable Jewish community in Jerusalem? Why was the restoration of the Jews at this time so dependent on religious institutions and worship?
3. Do you think it is important to study history? What does the inclusion in the Hebrew Bible of both the Deuteronomistic History and the Chronicler's History suggest about the purpose of studying history? What are the dangers of not studying history?

Chapter 18 Study Guide

- *Chapter summary*
- *Key terms linked to the glossary*
- *Concept questions with answer links*
- *Progress tests: true/false, multiple choice, matching, and identification*

CONCLUSION: AFTER THE HEBREW BIBLE

Key Terms

Apocrypha
Dead Sea Scrolls
Mishnah
New Testament
Oral Torah
Pseudepigrapha
Qumran
Talmud
Targum
Written Torah

FIGURE 1 | **JERUSALEM** This is a scale model of Jerusalem in the first century.

Jerusalem was the center of Jewish life and thought in the period of early Judaism. However, Jewish communities also existed in Egypt, Syria, and Mesopotamia. Both Palestinian Judaism and Diaspora Judaism developed a wealth of post-biblical literature. It includes wisdom, law, and apocalypse, and embodies a variety of responses and reapplications of Torah to fit the Greco-Roman context of Jewish faith.

The last book of the Hebrew Bible to take shape was probably Daniel sometime in the second century B.C.E. The Hebrew Bible eventually became a fixed body of literature, but only after much discussion and negotiation. Even so the Scriptures of Palestinian Judaism differed from those of Diaspora Judaism.

The Jewish communities of faith did not stop producing books with the end of the Hebrew Bible. They continued to generate a variety of literature, and much of it has strong theological and literary ties with the Hebrew Bible. Jewish literature demonstrates that the traditions and beliefs expressed in the Hebrew Bible retained their vitality and continued to be foundational to later communities of faith. By the creative ways they interpreted and reapplied elements of the Hebrew Bible they display a vital and continuing interest in Torah.

Chronology

B.C.E.	333	Battle of Issus; Alexander the Great (336–323) conquered the ancient Middle East; end of Persian and beginning of Greek control of Palestine (332–164)
	250	Greek translation of the Hebrew Bible, called the Septuagint
	198	Battle of Paneas; beginning of Syrian-Greek (Seleucid) rule of Palestine
	175	Antiochus IV (Epiphanes) rules Palestine (175–163) and begins aggressive policy of Hellenization
	167	Antiochus IV vandalized the temple in Jerusalem

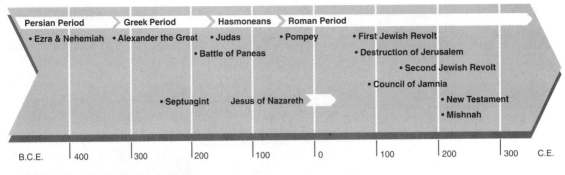

FIGURE 2   LITERATURE OF JUDAISM

164	Beginning of the Maccabean Revolt against Greek control; Hasmonean Period (164–63); Temple rededicated
63	Campaign of Pompey; beginning of Roman control of Palestine (63 B.C.E.–325 C.E.)
37	Beginning of the reign of Herod the Great (37–4 B.C.E.)
6	Birth of Jesus of Nazareth

C.E.

29	Beginning of the ministry of Jesus (29–33)
33	Death of Jesus and beginning of the Christian church
34	Beginning of Paul's missionary work (34–67)
66	Beginning of the First Jewish Revolt against Roman occupation of Palestine (66–70)
70	Destruction of Jerusalem, including the Second Temple
81	Beginning of the Roman persecution of the church (81–96)
90	Council at Jamnia which discussed the status of Hebrew Bible writings
2nd C.	New Testament completed
2nd C.	Mishnah completed

APOCRYPHA AND PSEUDEPIGRAPHA

Many Jewish books were composed between 200 B.C.E. and 100 C.E. Written in Hebrew, Aramaic, or Greek, the books include wisdom literature, history, short stories, and apocalyptic literature. Some of the books were widely used by Jews of this period, especially the Jews of the diaspora. There are two broad groups, the Apocrypha and the Pseudepigrapha. None of the books, however, became part of any official Jewish collection of scriptures.

■ APOCRYPHA

The **Apocrypha,** meaning "hidden books," are fifteen compositions included in the Greek and Latin translation traditions of the Bible. Twelve of them remain part of the canon of the Catholic church. During the Protestant Reformation these books were removed from the canon and are not now part of the official Bible of

Protestant churches. In the face of Protestant opposition to the inclusion of the apocryphal books, the Roman Catholic Council of Trent held in 1546 reaffirmed their official status and called them the "deuterocanonical" books. The following is a list of the books of the Protestant apocrypha. An asterisk marks the apocryphal books which are not canonical for Roman Catholics.

* 1 Esdras (= Roman Catholic 3 Esdras or Greek Ezra)
* 2 Esdras (= Roman Catholic 4 Esdras or Ezra Apocalypse)
Tobit
Judith
Additions to the Book of Esther
Wisdom of Solomon
Ecclesiasticus, or the Wisdom of Jesus the Son of Sirach
Baruch
Letter of Jeremiah
Prayer of Azariah and the Song of the Three Young Men
Susanna
Bel and the Dragon
* Prayer of Manasseh
1 Maccabees
2 Maccabees

The Apocrypha are included on disc.

The apocryphal books contain a wealth of evidence for the character of Judaism both in Palestine and in the Dispersion during the post–Hebrew Bible period. A small sampling of the Apocrypha should display how these books continue the literary and theological traditions of the Hebrew Bible, while at the same time adding their own twists.

The book of Ecclesiasticus stands in the tradition of Hebrew wisdom literature. It was written in Hebrew between 200 and 175 B.C.E. by a sage who lived in Jerusalem. He was thoroughly immersed in Torah, the priesthood and temple, and worshiping God. As a shrewd observer of life in Palestine, especially the pressures on Jews to become more "modern" after the model of Greek culture, he set about urging his fellows to remain true to their religious traditions. It seems he wrote his book to be a collection of wisdom and learning that could serve the Jews as a guide for living, making unnecessary a move to Greek philosophy.

10 Look to generations of long ago and see: Who believed in YHWH and came to shame? 11 Or who stood in fear of him and was abandoned? Or who called on him and he ignored him? 12 For compassionate and merciful is YHWH. He forgives sins and saves in time of trouble. (2:10–12)

Ecclesiasticus is very much like the book of Proverbs in the way it contains aphorisms and maxims and aims to give moral guidance.

21 My son, watch your time well; guard yourself from evil, and to yourself bring no shame. (4:21)

5 A sweet mouth multiplies love, and gracious lips inspire peace. (6:5)

The two books of Maccabees contain accounts of the events surrounding the attempted suppression of Judaism in Palestine in the second century B.C.E. 1 Maccabees was written around 100 B.C.E. by a Palestinian Jew who remains nameless. In describing the deliverance of the Jews through the family of Mattathias, he models his accounts of these heroes on Israel's ancient champions, the Judges, Samuel and David.

The dominating conflict at the center of 1 Maccabees is between the representatives of Greek culture, the Seleucids under the direction of their king Antiochus Epiphanes, and adherents of traditional Jewish culture. The conflict came to a head when Antiochus deliberately vandalized the temple in Jerusalem and made it a capital offense to practice Judaism.

> *54 The king set up the outrageous abomination upon the altar of burnt offerings, and in surrounding Judean cities they built pagan altars. 55 They also burnt incense at the doors of houses and in the streets. 56 Any Torah scrolls they found they tore up and burned. 57 Whoever was found in possession of a scroll of the covenant and whoever observed the torah was condemned to death by royal decree. 60 Women who had allowed the circumcision of their children were put to death, as per the decree, 61 with the babies hung from their necks. Their families and those who had done the circumcising were also killed. (1:54–56 61–62)*

The events recorded here occurred in December of 167 B.C.E. Antiochus IV Epiphanes erected a statue of Zeus in the holiest part of the temple and slaughtered pigs in sacrifice. He deliberately provoked the Jews and tried to goad them into giving up their religion. It did not work.

The family of a pious Jew named Mattathias, led especially by his zealous son Judas, who was nicknamed the Maccabee (probably meaning "the hammer"), instigated a revolt of Torah-observant Jews. The Maccabean revolt was bloody and determined, and after more than three years of struggle succeeded in displacing the Hellenizing forces from the temple mount. After ritually purifying the temple and fighting further battles, the family of Mattathias established local Jewish rule again over a Jewish-Palestinian state. This rule lasted until 63 B.C.E. when the Roman empire took control of Palestine.

■ PSEUDEPIGRAPHA

The **Pseudepigrapha** come from the same general time period as the Apocrypha. The term *pseudepigrapha* literally means "pseudonymous writings," where typically the book is falsely attributed to a character from the Hebrew Bible. The Pseudepigrapha were never part of the official scriptures of Judaism or Christianity. The following is a list of Jewish pseudepigraphic books whose core was composed before the destruction of Jerusalem in 70 C.E.

1 Enoch (or Ethiopic Enoch)
2 Enoch (or Slavonic Enoch)

2 Baruch (or Syriac Baruch)

3 Maccabees

4 Maccabees

Apocalypse of Elijah

Ascension of Isaiah

Jubilees

Letter of Aristeas

Life of Adam and Eve (or Apocalypse of Moses)

Lives of the Prophets

Psalms of Solomon

Sibylline Oracles

Testament of Job

Testament of Moses (or Assumption of Moses)

Testaments of the Twelve Patriarchs

The book of 1 Enoch was one of the most widely read and circulated books of the Pseudepigrapha. It has been found in multiple copies among the Dead Sea Scrolls. It was even quoted in the book of Jude (verses 14–15) in the New Testament. The figure of Enoch comes from Genesis 5:24, where he was said to have walked with God. Being supremely righteous in an unrighteous age, he was taken directly into heaven. Because of his peculiar position before God, so the legend goes, God transmitted to Enoch special revelations about the nature of the world and about the end times. 1 Enoch is one of the best examples of that brand of literature called apocalyptic that was wildly popular during this period.

1 Enoch contains a story about the rebellion of the angels in primeval times and their subsequent judgment. The story takes Genesis 6:1–4 as its point of departure but adds a significant amount of detail.

1 And it came to pass when the children of men had multiplied that in those days were born unto them beautiful and comely daughters. 2 And the angels, the children of the heaven, saw and lusted after them, and said to one another: 'Come, let us choose us wives from among the children of men and beget us children.' 3 And Semjaza, who was their leader, said unto them: 'I fear ye will not indeed agree to do this deed, and I alone shall have to pay the penalty of a great sin." 4 And they all answered him and said: 'Let us all swear an oath, and all bind ourselves by mutual imprecations not to abandon this plan but to do this thing.' 5 Then sware [sic] they all together and bound themselves by mutual imprecations upon it. 6 And they were in all two hundred. 1 And all the others together with them took unto themselves wives, and each chose for himself one, and they began to go in unto them and to defile themselves with them, and they taught them charms and enchantments, and the cutting of roots, and made them acquainted with plants. 2 And they became pregnant, and they bare great giants, whose height was three thousand ells: 3 Who consumed all the acquisitions of men. (6:1–7:3; Charles 1913)

Our discussion of Genesis 6:1–4 in Chapter 1 noted that the identification of the "sons of God" is not obvious from the biblical text. Some readers have interpreted "the sons of God" to have been the line of Seth. But evidence from the use of the phrase "sons of God" elsewhere in the Hebrew Bible strongly suggests that the writer had angels of the divine council in mind.

Here in 1 Enoch there is no doubt how the phrase was interpreted: it is clearly "angels, the children of the heaven." The writer understands the story to be the description of how evil angels corrupted the human race. Of special interest is how the writer elaborated on the Genesis core story. He notes how beautiful these human women were, and adds that the angels were motivated by sexual lust. The story goes on to describe how the bad angels were policed by the good angels, Michael, Uriel, Raphael, and Gabriel. The bad angels were bound, taken prisoner, and eventually destroyed.

DEAD SEA SCROLLS

The **Dead Sea Scrolls** are probably the most famous archaeological discovery of the modern world. Their fame is the product of the serendipitous nature of the find, the controversial circumstances surrounding their publication, and their potential for illuminating the texts and history of Judaism and Christianity.

The texts date roughly to the period 150 B.C.E. to 70 C.E. Most of the scrolls were found in caves in the vicinity of an ancient ruins called **Qumran.** The nature of the ruins, the identity of the people who lived there, and even the identity of the people who wrote the scrolls are still topics of hot debate. The scholarly consensus that the texts were written by a Judaic group called the Essenes who also lived at Qumran is increasingly disputed and under discussion.

The Dead Sea Scrolls manuscripts include copies of all the books of the Hebrew Bible except the book of Esther. Copies of some of the apocryphal books were found. In addition, there are numerous writings never before known.

■ BIBLICAL MANUSCRIPTS

The biblical manuscripts provide evidence for the process by which books of the Hebrew Bible were passed on by copyists. Before the Dead Sea Scrolls discovery, the earliest copies of the Hebrew Bible dated to the tenth century C.E. With the Dead Sea Scrolls we now have copies dated to the third and second centuries B.C.E.—bringing us more than 1,000 years closer to the originals.

Some of the Dead Sea Scrolls biblical manuscripts provide copies that seem more accurately to reflect the original biblical text. They have provided helpful evidence to modern translators, and some of the most recent modern-language versions of the Hebrew Bible have made use of these texts. For example, the New Revised Standard version of 1 Samuel 10 adds an entire paragraph, about seventy-one words (in the English translation) not found in the traditional Hebrew Bible.

■ ORIGINAL DOCUMENTS

Many Dead Sea Scrolls texts are original, at least never before known. The Temple Scroll, some twenty-eight feet long, deals with the structure of the temple and

FIGURE 3 **QUMRAN CAVE 4** is one of many caves near the Dead Sea where scrolls were found. Fragments of approximately 580 different ancient manuscripts were discovered in this cave in 1954.

its furniture, ritual service, and rules for sacrifices and observing the Sabbath and seasonal feasts. The Community Rule appears to contain the constitution of the Dead Sea Scrolls community. Dated to around 100 B.C.E., it contains a discourse about truth and falsehood, rules for membership, a disciplinary code, and the expectations of the leader of the group called the "teacher of righteousness."

According to a Dead Sea Scrolls belief called *dualism,* the world was governed by two forces, good and evil, described here in the Community Rule.

> *III He has created man to govern the world, and has appointed for him two spirits in which to walk until the time of His visitation: the spirits of truth and falsehood. Those born of truth spring from a fountain of light, but those born of falsehood spring from a source of darkness. All the children of right-eousness are ruled by the Prince of Light and walk in the ways of light, but all the children of falsehood are ruled by the Angel of Darkness and walk in the way of darkness." (Vermes 1987: 64–65)*

The Dead Sea Scrolls community had an "us and them" view of the world. They believed humankind is dominated by two spirits and consists of two camps, the "sons of light" and the "sons of darkness." The two will finally face off in an end-times battle, described in the War Rule. The forces of light will ultimately prevail, and God's people will be vindicated.

Most Dead Sea Scrolls texts have a close relationship to the Hebrew Bible. The various texts used in worship contain direct quotations from the Hebrew Bible. The Dead Sea Scrolls community had its own hymnbook, largely composed using phrases and lines out of the biblical Psalms. Some manuscripts are commentaries on biblical texts, mostly prophetic texts from the Hebrew Bible. Called *pesharim*, these commentaries reveal how this community read the Hebrew Bible. Their basic interpretive principles were these: Everything in the Hebrew Bible applied to their own day and, in particular, the prophetic texts predicted events in their generation. They firmly believed that the prophetic predictions of the Hebrew Bible were being fulfilled in their own experience.

The prophecy of Habakkuk of the Hebrew Bible was written out of the sixth-century B.C.E. Babylonian crisis. Essentially the prophet Habakkuk was questioning how God could use the wicked Babylonian empire to punish his more righteous covenant people of Judah. The Pesher on Habakkuk applied this directly to the conflict they faced with the Romans and the (in their view) corrupted factions of Judaism. The commentary on Habakkuk proceeds by quoting the biblical text and then expounding it.

But the righteous shall live by his faith (Habakkuk 2:4b)

Interpreted, this concerns all those who observe the Law in the House of Judah, whom God will deliver from the House of Judgment because of their suffering and because of their faith in the Teacher of Righteousness. (Vermes 1987: 287)

The original text of Habakkuk seems to be saying that the righteous Israelite would find deliverance from disaster by personal faith in God, not through membership in the community or the faith of the fathers. The Habakkuk Commentary reinterprets this and says Torah-observing Jews will be delivered through suffering and their trust in their community leader, called the Teacher of Righteousness—quite a different twist to that text.

NEW TESTAMENT

Christianity began as a Jewish movement in the first century C.E. Followers of Jesus of Nazareth became convinced after his death that he was the messiah that the Hebrew Bible had described and that Judaism awaited. The **New Testament** is a collection of writings developed by members of this messianic movement. These writings include narrations of the life of Jesus and moral instruction to his followers.

Because most of the earliest followers of Jesus were Jewish, many of the writings naturally have thematic continuity with the Hebrew Bible. Some of the writings argue that Jesus fulfills Jewish expectations, while others highlight his uniqueness. Whatever the case, the New Testament cannot be understood apart from its grounding in the Hebrew Bible. In fact, the Hebrew Bible *was* the one and only Bible of the earliest Christians. The earliest New Testament books date to the middle of the first century, years after the death of Jesus. The last New Testament books date to the late first century or early second century.

The collection of all the books which now constitute the New Testament was, for all practical purposes, closed by the end of the second century C.E. The collection took on the name New Testament, or New Covenant, to communicate both the essential continuity and the significant discontinuity with the text of the Old Covenant, the Old Testament, the Hebrew Bible.

As does the Hebrew Bible, the New Testament contains a great variety of literary types. It encompasses narratives on the career of Jesus called gospels, a history of the earliest church, letters from early leaders to congregations and individuals around the Mediterranean, and an apocalyptic-style description of an end time of tribulation. The following is a categorized list of the twenty-seven books of the New Testament in traditional order.

Gospels
  The Gospel according to Matthew
  The Gospel according to Mark
  The Gospel according to Luke
  The Gospel according to John
History
  Acts of the Apostles
Letters (also called Epistles)
  Paul's Letter to the Romans
  Paul's First and Second Letters to the Corinthians
  Paul's Letter to the Galatians
  Paul's Letter to the Ephesians
  Paul's Letter to the Philippians
  Paul's Letter to the Colossians
  Paul's First and Second Letters to the Thessalonians
  Paul's First and Second Letters to Timothy
  Paul's Letter to Titus
  Paul's Letter to Philemon
  Letter to the Hebrews
  Letter of James
  First and Second Letters of Peter
  First, Second, and Third Letters of John
  Letter of Jude
Apocalyptic Literature
  The Revelation of John

The following excerpts, one from each of the four types, are intended to display how the New Testament demonstrates continuity with the Hebrew Bible. They also show how the earliest Christian writers argued that some special act of fulfillment and consummation had occurred through the Jesus event.

A gospel, of which there are four in the New Testament, dwells on the events of the life of Jesus that evidenced his character and mission from God. The gospels as books are not biographies of the life of Jesus but are arguments for identifying him as the son of God and the messiah.

The gospel according to Mark is probably the earliest of the four gospels, quite likely written before the destruction of Jerusalem in 70 C.E. Mark 15 describes the trial, crucifixion, death, and burial of Jesus. The essential claim of the earliest Jewish Christians was that Jesus was the Jewish messiah. In fact, their very name derives from this claim: the word *christ,* from which the terms *Christian* and *Christianity* derive, comes from the Greek word *christos* which means "anointed one," the same meaning as Hebrew *meshiach,* "messiah." Throughout chapter 15 Mark ironically highlights Jesus' messiahship by recounting the non-perception and the downright denial of Jesus' kingship by Jews and Romans.

> 25 *It was nine o'clock in the morning when they crucified him. 26 The inscription of the charge against him read, "The King of the Jews." 27 And with him they crucified two bandits, one on his right and one on his left. . . . 29 Those who passed by derided him, shaking their heads and saying, "Aha! You who would destroy the temple and build it in three days, 30 save yourself, and come down from the cross!" 31 In the same way the chief priests, along with the scribes, were also mocking him among themselves and saying, "He saved others; he cannot save himself. 32 Let the Messiah, the King of Israel, come down from the cross now, so that we may see and believe."* (15:25–32, NRSV)

A messiah in the tradition of the Hebrew Bible and Judaism was a kingly figure endowed by God with power to rule over a political kingdom. Jesus did not fit this mold, yet his followers still proclaimed him messiah. They could do this only by redefining the nature of the Kingdom of God to be a spiritual and moral kingdom.

The Acts of the Apostles describes the missionary work of Jesus' followers and the founding of Christian churches. Often Luke, the writer of a gospel and this book, draws connections to the Hebrew Bible as a way to authenticate this new movement. His description of the Pentecost event and his record of Peter's sermon on that occasion are replete with connections to the Hebrew Bible. For example, his description of the distribution of the Holy Spirit recalls the storm and fire of biblical theophanies.

> 1 *When the day of Pentecost had come, they were all together in one place. 2 And suddenly from heaven there came a sound like the rush of a violent wind, and it filled the entire house where they were sitting. 3 Divided tongues, as of fire, appeared among them, and a tongue rested on each of them. 4 All of them were filled with the Holy Spirit and began to speak in other languages, as the Spirit gave them ability.* (2:1–4, NRSV)

The Jewish festival of Pentecost (also called the Feast of Weeks) marks the end of the grain harvest. It coincides with that day, seven weeks after Passover, on which according to Jewish tradition the Torah was given. The Spirit of God arrived with a wind storm and was evident in licks of fire. Storm and fire were the visible evidences of God's presence in the narratives of the Hebrew Bible, including the burning bush episode of Moses and Elijah's transfer to heaven via the fire chariot. The birth of the church, as Pentecost is usually deemed, was thus construed as the natural outgrowth of the Torah of God and its harvest.

The Letter of Paul to the Galatians, written sometime in the 50s C.E., deals with the critical question of whether or not Gentile Christians must conform to traditional Jewish laws. Essentially Paul said no. But in order to justify his position he had to reinterpret the traditional definition of Jewish identity.

> *1 You foolish Galatians! Who has bewitched you? It was before your eyes that Jesus Christ was publicly exhibited as crucified! 2 The only thing I want to learn from you is this: Did you receive the Spirit by doing the works of the law or by believing what you heard? ... 6 Just as Abraham "believed God and it was reckoned to him as righteousness," 7 so, you see, those who believe are the descendants of Abraham. 8 And the scripture, foreseeing that God would justify the Gentiles by faith, declared the gospel beforehand to Abraham, saying, "All the Gentiles shall be blessed in you." 9 For this reason, those who believe are blessed with Abraham who believed. (3:1–2, 6–9, NRSV)*

Paul quotes Genesis 15:6 to certify that inclusion in the covenant community is made possible by believing in God and not by obeying the Torah. This also warrants extending the bounds of the covenant community to non-Jews.

The Revelation of John closes the New Testament collection of books. Literally named the *Apocalypse*, it has affinities with the apocalyptic literature of the Hebrew Bible and Intertestamental period, such as the second half of Daniel and the book of 1 Enoch. The book uses a great deal of symbolism involving numbers, hybrid beasts, seals, and bowls. Due to the veiled nature of its symbolism and other factors, it is subject to widely varying interpretations.

The Revelation purports to be a vision given to John which discloses events of the end time of history. Times of warfare and conflict are described until the ultimate victory of God is achieved. Then the universe would be remade, recalling the words of Isaiah 65–66, into a "new heavens and a new earth." The last words of the Revelation also draw upon creation imagery, as if to say that the new world would be a remake of the Garden of Eden of the book of Genesis.

> *1 Then the angel showed me the river of the water of life, bright as crystal, flowing from the throne of God and of the Lamb 2 through the middle of the street of the city (i.e., the New Jerusalem). On either side of the river is the tree of life with its twelve kinds of fruit, producing its fruit each month; and the leaves of the tree are for the healing of the nations. 3 Nothing accursed will be found there any more. But the throne of God and of the Lamb will be in it, and his servants will worship him; 4 they will see his face, and his name will be on their foreheads. 5 And there will be no more night; they need no light of lamp or sun, for the Lord God will be their light, and they will reign forever and ever. (22:1–5, NRSV)*

Some clear points of contact with Hebrew Bible creation motifs are the tree of life, the river, not curse but only blessing, the light that comes from God without a sun, and perhaps even the use of the divine designation *Yahweh Elohim* (Lord

God) that was used consistently in Genesis 2–3. The Revelation provides a satisfying closure to the Christian Bible by returning the believer to the beauty of God's perfect creation.

RABBINIC LITERATURE

The specific type of Judaism associated with the Pharisees had its roots in the Maccabean period. Pharisaic Judaism became a dominant force by the first century C.E. It was the only Jewish religious group, apart from Christianity, that survived the disastrous First Jewish Revolt. It lived on in what has come to be called Rabbinic Judaism.

One valuable source of insight into the nature of Rabbinic Judaism is its translations of the Bible. As the Hebrew language receded from active use in Jewish communities and Aramaic took its place, the Hebrew Bible was translated into the common tongue. An Aramaic translation of a Hebrew Bible original was called a **targum.** Targums from various regional Jewish communities have survived, and they can tell us a great deal about how the Hebrew Bible was understood. More often paraphrases than literal translations, they reveal what the Bible meant to them.

Pharisaic Judaism was in every way closely tied to the Hebrew Bible. The Bible was the focus of religious devotion. Reading the Torah was the heart of synagogue services and thoroughly shaped Jewish liturgy. The Hebrew Bible was called the **Written Torah** in this tradition to distinguish it from the Oral Torah. The **Oral Torah** consisted of interpretations and applications of the Hebrew Bible. The Written and Oral Torahs together became the authoritative guide for life and belief within the Jewish community. The accumulation of text and interpretation came to be called *halakah,* from the Hebrew verb "to walk," because this literature provided the Torah of walking in righteousness. Judaism defined a Torah-centered nation, and the community became known as "the people of the book."

The wealth of Oral Torah that was written by generations of Jewish scholars and teachers, called rabbis, was collected and organized into tractates in the second century C.E. by Judah the Prince and is called the **Mishnah.** The process of reapplying Torah to life in the community did not stop with the finalization of the Mishnah. The **Talmud** contains an additional set of interpretations of Torah that built upon the Mishnah.

The following excerpt from the Mishnah communicates the flavor of Oral Torah. This paragraph contains a discussion of when the Shema should be recited each day. The Shema is the Jewish prayer derived from Deuteronomy 6 that became the basic creed of Judaism.

1:1 From what time in the evening may the Shema be recited? From the time when the priests enter [the Temple] to eat of their Heave-offering until the end of the first watch. So R. Eliezer. But the Sages say: Until midnight. Rabban Gamaliel says: Until the rise of dawn. His sons once returned [after midnight] from a wedding feast. They said to him, "We have not recited the Shema." He said to them, "If the dawn has not risen ye are [still] bound to recite it. Moreover, wheresoever the Sages prescribe 'Until midnight' the duty of fulfilment lasts until the rise of dawn." The duty of burning the fat pieces and the members [of the animal offerings] lasts until the rise of dawn; and for all [offerings] that must be consumed "the same day," the duty lasts until the rise of dawn. Why then have the Sages said: Until midnight? To keep man far from transgression. (Berakoth 1:1, Danby 1933)

This discussion provides an example of the Rabbinic Jewish practice of "making a hedge around Torah." That is to say, laws were often applied more strictly than was dictated by the original statement of the law in the Hebrew Bible. This was done so that a person might break the new application of the law and yet not break the original law itself.

There is a much richer body of Jewish interpretive literature from this period than this brief discussion could communicate. In addition to the translations of the Hebrew Bible and *halakah* there developed a vast collection of commentaries on biblical books and often delightful retellings of biblical stories that communicated moral lessons.

This storehouse of literature from the variety of communities which together constituted Judaism, including the Pharisees, Essenes, and Christians, reveal to us the vitality and longevity of the Hebrew Bible. It provided the foundation for life and practice in these centuries. It demonstrates how the text of Scripture provided a certain stable set of core beliefs and moral norms and yet within itself allowed for continual reinterpretation and reapplication to account for changing social and historical conditions. Stability and adaptability, continuity and change—the Hebrew Bible reveals itself to be a remarkable book that formed communities and enabled them to survive, even thrive, in a challenging world.

FOR FURTHER STUDY

Charlesworth (1983-1985) for a translation of the apocrypha and pseudepigrapha, Nickelsburg (1981) for an introduction to the literature of early Judaism, Nickelsburg and Stone (1983) for an anthology of texts from early Judaism, Vermes (1987) for a translation of the Dead Sea Scrolls, Cohen (1987) for the social history of early Judaism.

After the Hebrew Bible Bibliography

WORKS CITED

Albright, W. F. (1949; revised edition 1963). *The Biblical Period from Abraham to Ezra*. New York: Harper & Row.

Alter, R. (1981). *The Art of Biblical Narrative*. New York: Basic Books.

Alter, R. (1985). *The Art of Biblical Poetry*. New York: Basic Books.

Alter, R. (1996). *Genesis. Translation and Commentary*. New York: W. W. Norton.

Anderson, G. A. (1987). *Sacrifices and Offerings in Ancient Israel: Studies in Their Social and Political Importance*. Harvard Semitic Monographs, 41. Atlanta: Scholars.

Armstrong, K. (1996). *In the Beginning. A New Interpretation of Genesis*. New York: Knopf.

Assmann, J. (1997). *Moses the Egyptian: The Memory of Egypt in Western Monotheism*. Cambridge: Harvard University.

Bailey, L. R. (1989). *Noah: The Person and the Story in History and Tradition*. Columbia: University of South Carolina.

Barr, J. (1993). *The Garden of Eden and the Hope of Immortality*. Philadelphia: Fortress.

Barthes, R. (1974). "The Struggle with the Angel: Tetxtual Analysis of Genesis 32:23–33 21–33." In R. Barthes (Ed.), *Structural Analysis and Biblical Exegesis: Interpretational Essays*. Pittsburgh: Pickwick.

Bassett, F. W. (1971). "Noah's Nakedness and the Curse of Canaan: A Case of Incest?" *Vetus Testamentum* 21: 232–37.

Batto, B. F. (1984). "Red Sea or Reed Sea?: What Yam Sûp Really Means." *Biblical Archaeology Review* July/August. See also B.F. Batto (1983). "The Reed Sea: Requiescat in Pace." *Journal of Biblical Literature* 102: 27–35.

Batto, B. F. (1992). *Slaying the Dragon: Mythmaking in the Biblical Tradition*. Louisville: Westminster John Knox.

Beit-Arieh, I. (1988). "The Route Through Sinai—Why the Israelites Fleeing Egypt Went South." *Biblical Archaeology Review* 15/3: 28–37.

Bimson, J. J. (1978). *Redating the Exodus and Conquest*. JSOT Supplement Series, 5. Sheffield: University of Sheffield.

Bimson, J. J. (1987). "Redating the Exodus." *Biblical Archaeology Review* 14:40–52.

Biran, A. & Naveh, J. (1993). "An Aramaic Stele Fragment from Tel Dan." *Israel Exploration Journal*. 43/2–3: 81–98.

Blenkinsopp, J. (1983). *A History of Prophecy in Israel*. Philadelphia: Westminster.

Blenkinsopp, J. (1990). *Ezekiel*. Interpretation, A Commentary for Teaching and Preaching. Louisville: Westminster John Knox .

Bloch, A. & Bloch, C. (1995). *The Song of Songs*. New York: Random House.

Bloom, H. (1990). *The Book of J.* Translated from the Hebrew by David Rosenberg, interpreted by Harold Bloom New York: Grove Weidenfeld.

Bodenheimer, F. S. (1947). "The Manna of Sinai" *Biblical Archaeologist* 10: 1–6.

Borsch, F. H. (1967). *The Son of Man in Myth and History.* Philadelphia: Westminster.

Boyer, P. (1992). *When Time Shall Be No More: Prophecy Belief in Modern American Culture.* Cambridge: Harvard University.

Bright, J. (1981). *A History of Israel .* 3d ed. Philadelphia: Westminster.

Brown, H. J. (1991). *Life's Little Instruction Book.* Nashville: Rutledge Hill.

Brueggemann, W. (1968). *Tradition for Crisis. A Study of Hosea.* Atlanta: John Knox.

Brueggemann, W. (1977*). The Land: Place as Gift, Promise, and Challenge in Biblical Faith.* Overtures to Biblical Theology. Philadelphia: Fortress.

Brueggemann, W. (1979). "Trajectories in Old Testament Literature and the Sociology of Ancient Israel.*" Journal of Biblical Literature* 98.

Brueggemann, W. (1982). *Genesis.* Interpretation, a Bible Commentary for Teaching and Preaching. Atlanta: John Knox.

Brueggemann, W. (1984). *The Message of the Psalms: A Theological Commentary.* Minneapolis: Augsburg.

Brueggemann, W. (1990). *First and Second Samuel.* Interpretation Series. Louisville: John Knox.

Brueggemann, W. (1993) *Praying the Psalms.* Winona, MN: Saint Mary's. See also (1995). *The Psalms and the Life of Faith.* Minneapolis: Fortress.

Bryce, G. E. (1979) *A Legacy of Wisdom: The Egyptian Contribution to the Wisdom of Israel.* Lewisburg, PA: Bucknell University.

Caird, G. B. (1980). *The Language and Imagery of the Bible.* Philadelphia: Westminster.

Campbell, A. F. & O'Brien, M. A. (1993). *Sources of the Pentateuch. Texts, Introductions, and Annotations.* Minneapolis: Fortress.

Campbell, E. F. (1975). *Ruth.* Anchor Bible. Garden City, NY: Doubleday.

Campbell, J. (1968). *The Hero With a Thousand Faces.* 2d. Edition. Princeton: Princeton University.

Carmichael, C. M. (1969). "The Deuteronomic Credo." *Vetus Testamentum* 19: 284–9.

Charles, R. M. (1913). *The Apocrypha and Pseudepigrapha of the Old Testament in English.* Volume II. Oxford: Oxford University.

Charlesworth, J. H. (1983–1985). *The Old Testament Psesudepigrapha. Volume 1: Apocalyptic Literature and Testaments; Volume 2: Expansions of the "Old Testament" and other Legends, Wisdom and Philosophical Literature, Prayers, Psalms, and Odes, Fragments of Lost Judeo-Hellenistic Works.* Garden City, NY: Doubleday.

Childs, B. S. (1970). *Biblical Theology in Crisis.* Philadelphia: Westminster.

Childs, B. S. (1979). *Introduction to the Old Testament as Scripture.* Philadelphia: Fortress.

Clements, R. E. (1967). *Abraham and David.* Studies in Biblical Theology, 2/5. London: SCM.

Clements, R. E. (1980). *Isaiah and the Deliverance of Jerusalem: A Study of the Interpretation of Prophecy in the Old Testament.* Sheffield: Journal for the Study of the Old Testament.

Clements, R. E. (1982). "The Unity of the Book of Isaiah." *Interpretation* 36:117–129.

Clines, D. J. A. (1968). "The Image of God in Man." *Tyndale Bulletin* 19: 53–103.

Clines, D. J. A. (1978). *The Theme of the Pentateuch.* 2d. edition 1997. Supplement Series 10. Sheffield: Journal for the Study of the Old Testament.

Clines, D. J. A. (1990). *What Does Eve Do to Help? And Other Readerly Questions to the Old Testament.* Journal for the Study of the Old Testament Supplement Series, 94. Sheffield: Sheffield Academic.

Cohen, H. H. (1974). *The Drunkedness of Noah*. Alabama: University of Alabama.

Cohen, S. J. D. (1987). *From the Maccabees to the Mishnah*. Philadelphia: Westminster.

Coogan, M. D. (1978). *Stories from Ancient Canaan*. Philadelphia: Westminster.

Coote, R. B. (1981). *Amos Among the Prophets: Composition and Theology*. Philadelphia: Fortress.

Coote, R. B. (1990). *Early Israel: A New Horizon*. Minneapolis: Fortress.

Craigie, P. C. (1976). *The Book of Deuteronomy*. New International Commentary on the Old Testament. Grand Rapids: Eerdmans.

Craigie, P. C. (1983). *Ugarit and the Old Testament*. Grand Rapids: Eerdmans.

Crenshaw, J. L. (1969). "Method in Determining Wisdom Influence upon 'Historical' Literature." *Journal of Biblical Literature* 88: 129–42.

Crenshaw, J. L. (1976). "Prolegomenon," in *Studies in Ancient Israelite Wisdom*. New York: KTAV.

Crenshaw, J. L. (1978). *Samson-A Secret Betrayed*. Atlanta: John Knox.

Crenshaw, J. L. (1981). *Old Testament Wisdom: An Introduction*. Atlanta: John Knox.

Cross, F. M. (1973). *Canaanite Myth and Hebrew Epic. Essays in the History of the Religion of Israel*. Cambridge: Harvard University.

Curtis, A. H. W. (1994). *Joshua*. Old Testament Guides. Sheffield: Sheffield Academic.

Curtis, E. M. (1990). "Images in Mesopotamia and the Bible: A Comparative Study". In W. W. Hallo, et al., *The Bible in the Light of Cuneiform Literature. Scripture in Context III* (pp. 31–56). Ancient Near Eastern Texts and Studies. Lewiston: Edwin Mellen.

Danby, H. (1933). *The Mishnah*. London: Oxford University.

Day, J. (1985). *God's Conflict with the Dragon and the Sea*. Cambridge: Cambridge University.

de Geus, C. H. J. (1976). *The Tribes of Israel*. Amsterdam: Van Gorcum.

Dicou, B. (1994). *Edom, Israel's Brother and Antagonist: The Role of Edom in Biblical Prophecy and Story*. Journal for the Study of the Old Testament Supplement Series, 169. Sheffield: Journal for the Study of the Old Testament.

Douglas, M. (1966). *Purity and Danger: An Analysis of the Concepts of Pollution and Taboo*. London: Routledge & Kegan Paul.

Dozeman, T. B. (1996). *God at War: A Study of Power in the Exodus Tradition*. Oxford: Oxford University.

Edelman, D. V. (1995). *You Shall Not Abhor An Edomite For He Is Your Brother: Edom and Seir in History and Tradition*. Archaeology and Biblical Studies, 3. Atlanta: Scholars.

Ellul, J. (1991). *Reason for Being. A Meditation on Ecclesiastes*. Grand Rapids: Eerdmans.

Falk, M. (1990). *The Song of Songs: A New Translation and Interpretation*. San Francisco: Harper & Row.

Fox, E. (1995). *The Five Books of Moses. Genesis, Exodus, Leviticus, Numbers, and Deuteronomy. A New Translation with Introductions, Commentary, and Notes*. The Schocken Bible: Volume I. Dallas: Word.

Fox, M. V. (1985). *The Song of Songs and the Ancient Egyptian Love Songs*. Madison: University of Wisconsin.

Fox, M. V. (1991). *Character and Ideology in the Book of Esther*. Columbia: University of South Carolina.

Freedman, D. N. (1987). "Yahweh of Samaria and His Asherah." *Biblical Archaeologist* 50/4: 241–249.

Friedman, R. E. (1987). *Who Wrote the Bible?* Englewood Cliffs, NJ: Prentice-Hall.

Friedman, R. E. (1995). *The Disappearance of God: A Divine Mystery*. Boston: Little, Brown.

Fritz, V. (1987). "Temple Architecture: What Can Archaeology Tell Us About Solomon's Temple?" *Biblical Archaeology Review* 13/4: 38–49.

Garr, W. R. (1983). "The Qinah: A Study of Poetic Meter, Syntax and Style." *Zeitschrift für die Alttestamentliche Wissenschaft* 95: 54–74.

Geller, S. A. (1979). *Parallelism in Early Biblical Poetry*. Harvard Semitic Monographs, 20. Missoula, MT: Scholars.

Good, E. M. (1990). *In Turns of Tempest: A Rereading of Job, with a Translation*. Stanford: Stanford University.

Gorman, F. H., Jr. (1990). *Space, Time and Status in the Priestly Theology*. Journal for the Study of the Old Testament Supplement Series, 91. Sheffield: Sheffield Academic.

Gottwald, N. K. (1958). "Immanuel as the Prophet's Son." *Vetus Testamentum* 8: 36–47.

Gottwald, N. K. (1985). *The Hebrew Bible. A Socio–Literary Introduction*. Philadelphia: Fortress.

Graesser, C. F. (1972). "Standing Stones in Ancient Palestine." *Biblical Archaeologist* 35: 34–63.

Gray, G. B. (1915; 1972). *The Forms of Hebrew Poetry*. Reprint. New York: KTAV.

Grayson, A. K. (1975). *Babylonian Historical-Literary Texts*. Toronto: University of Toronto.

Greeley, A. M. (1989). *Love Song*. New York: Warner.

Greenspahn, F. E. (1994). *When Brothers Dwell Together: The Preeminence of Younger Siblings in the Hebrew Bible*. Oxford: Oxford University.

Gunkel, H. (1930; 1967). *The Psalms: A Form-Critical Introduction*. Facet Books, 19. Philadelphia: Fortress.

Guthrie, H. H. (1966). *Israel's Sacred Songs. A Study of Dominant Themes*. New York: Seabury.

Habel, N. C. (1985). *The Book of Job: A Commentary*. Old Testament Library. Philadelphia: Westminster.

Hackett, J. A. (1984). *The Balaam Text from Deir 'Alla*. Chico, CA: Scholars.

Haldar, A. (1971). *Who Were the Amorites?* Monographs on the Ancient Near East, 1. Leiden: E. J. Brill.

Hallo, W. W. & Simpson, W. K. (1971). *The Ancient Near East: A History*. New York: Harcourt, Brace, Jovanovich.

Hallo, W. W. (1977). "New Moons and Sabbaths: A Case Study in the Contrastive Approach." *Hebrew Union College Annual* 48: 1–18.

Hals, R. (1969). *The Theology of the Book of Ruth*. Facet Books, 23. Philadelphia: Fortress.

Hammershaimb, E. (1949–1951). "The Immanuel Sign." *Studia Theologica* 3: 124–142.

Hanson, P. D. (1975; revised edition, 1979). *The Dawn of Apocalyptic. The Historical and Sociological Roots of Jewish Apocalyptic Eschatology*. Philadelphia: Fortress.

Hanson, P. D. (1985). "Apocalyptic Literature." In *The Hebrew Bible and its Modern Interpreters*. Chico, CA: Scholars.

Hanson, P. D. (1987). *Old Testament Apocalyptic*. Nashville: Abingdon.

Haran, M. (1978). *Temples and Temple-Service in Ancient Israel. An Inquiry into the Character of Cult Phenomena and the Historical Setting of the Priestly School*. Oxford: Clarendon.

Harland, J. P. (1980). "Have Sodom and Gomorrah Been Found?" *Biblical Archaeology Review* 6/5: 26–36.

Harrelson, W. (1980). *The Ten Commandments and Human Rights*. Overtures to Biblical Theology. Philadelphia: Fortress.

Harris, G. M. & Beardow, A. P. (1995). "The Destruction of Sodom and Gomorrah: A Geotechnical Perspective." *The Quarterly Journal of Engineering Geology* 28/4: 349.

Hasel, G. F. (1980). "Resurrection in the Theology of the Old Testament Apocalyptic." *Zeitschrift für die alttestamentliche Wissenschaft* 92: 267–284.

Hayes, J. H. & Miller, J. M. (Eds.). (1990*). Israelite and Judaean History*. Philadelphia: Trinity Press International.

Heidel, A. (1963). *The Babylonian Genesis*. 2d. ed. Chicago: University of Chicago.

Heinlein, R. A. (1984). *Job, A Comedy of Justice*. New York: Ballentine Books.

Hillers, D. R. (1969). *Covenant: The History of a Biblical Idea*. Baltimore: Johns Hopkins.

Hoffman, L. A. (1996). *Covenant of Blood: Circumcision and Gender in Rabbinic Judaism*. Chicago: University of Chicago.

Holladay, W. L. (1986). *Jeremiah 1: A Commentary on the Book of the Prophet Jeremiah, Chapters 1–25*. Hermeneia. Philadelphia: Fortress.

Holladay, W. L. (1989). *Jeremiah 2: A Commentary on the Book of the Prophet Jeremiah, Chapters 26–52*. Hermeneia. Philadelphia: Fortress.

Holladay, W. L. (1990). *Jeremiah: A Fresh Reading*. New York: Pilgrim.

Hort, G. (1957–1958). "The Plagues of Egypt." *Zeitschrift für die alttestamentliche Wisssenschaft* 69: 84–103, 70: 48–59.

Hurowitz, V. (1985). "The Priestly Account of the Building of the Tabernacle." *Journal of the American Oriental Society* 105: 21–30.

Jeansonne, S. P. (1990). *The Women of Genesis: From Sarah to Potiphar's Wife*. Minneapolis: Fortress.

Jensen, J. (1973). *The Use of Torah by Isaiah: His Debate with the Wisdom Tradition*. Washington, DC: Catholic Biblical Association of America.

Jenson, P. P. (1992). *Graded Holiness. A Key to the Priestly Conception of the World*. Journal for the Study of the Old Testament Supplement Series, 106. Sheffield: Sheffield Academic.

Joyce, P. M. (1989). *Divine Initiative and Human Response in Ezekiel*. Journal for the Study of the Old Testament Supplement, 51. Sheffield: Journal for the Study of the Old Testament.

Kafka, F. (1925, English translation 1937). *The Trial*. New York: Knopf.

Kearney, P. J. (1977). "Creation and Liturgy: The P Redaction of Exodus 25–40." *Zeitschrift für die alttestamentliche Wissenschaft*.

Kilmer, A. D. (1987). "The Mesoopotamian Counterparts of the Biblical Nephilim." In E. W. Conrad & E. G. Newing (Eds.), *Perspectives on Language and Text* (pp. 39–43). Winona Lake, IN: Eisenbrauns.

Kirk, G. S. (1971). *Myth: Its Meaning and Functions in Ancient and Other Cultures*. Cambridge: Cambridge University.

Kitchen, K. A. (1995). "The Patriarchal Age: Myth or History?" *Biblical Archaeology Review* 21/2: 48–57, 88–95.

Klein, R. W. (1979). *Israel in Exile: A Theological Interpretation*. Philadelphia: Fortress.

Kline, M. (1963). *Treaty of the Great King. The Covenant Structure of Deuteronomy*. Grand Rapids: Eerdmans.

Krahmalkov, C. R. (1994). "Exodus Itinerary Confirmed by Egyptian Evidence." *Biblical Archaeology Review* 20/5: 54–62.

Kugel, J. L. (1981). *The Idea of Biblical Poetry. Parallelism and Its History*. New Haven: Yale University.

Lambert, W. G. (1960). *Babylonian Wisdom Literature*. Oxford: Oxford University.

Lambert, W. G., & Millard, A. R. (1969). *Atrahasis*. Oxford: Clarendon.

Lang, B. (1986). *Wisdom and the Book of Proverbs: An Israelite Goddess Redefined*. New York: Pilgrim.

Lasine, S. (1992). "Job and His Friends in the Modern World: Kafka's *The Trial*." In L.G. Perdue & W.C. Gilpin (Eds.). *The Voice from the Whirlwind: Interpreting the Book of Job*. Nashville: Abingdon.

Levenson, J. D. (1976). *Theology of the Program of Restoration of Ezekiel 40–48.* Harvard Semitic Monographs, 10. Missoula, MT: Scholars.

Levenson, J. D. (1988). *Creation and the Persistence of Evil: the Jewish Drama of Divine Omnipotence.* San Francisco: Harper & Row.

Levine, B. (1989). *Leviticus.* JPS Torah Commentary. Philadelphia: Jewish Publication Society.

Longman, T. (1991). *Fictional Akkadian Autobiography: A Generic and Comparative Study.* Winona Lake, IN: Eisenbrauns.

MacLeish, A. (1956). *J.B.* Boston: Houghton Mifflin.

Mann, T. W. (1988). *The Book of the Torah. The Narrative Integrity of the Pentateuch.* Atlanta: John Knox.

Matter, E. A. (1990). *The Voice of My Beloved: The Song of Songs in Western Medieval Christianity.* Philadelphia: University of Pennsylvania.

McCarthy, D. J. (1978). *Treaty and Covenant. A Study in Form in the Ancient Oriental Documents and in the Old Testament.* Rome: Biblical Institute.

McCurley, F. R. (1983). *Ancient Myths and Biblical Faith: Scriptural Transformations.* Philadelphia: Fortress.

McKane, William (1965). *Prophets and Wise Men.* Studies in Biblical Theology. London: SCM.

McNamara, M. (1970). "Nabonidus and the Book of Daniel." *Irish Theological Quarterly* 37: 131–149.

Mendenhall, G. E. (1955). *Law and Covenant in Israel and the Ancient Near East.* Pittsburgh: Biblical Colloquium.

Mendenhall, G. E. (1992). "The Amorite Migrations". In G. D. Young (Ed.), *Mari in Retrospect: Fifty Years of Mari and Mari Studies.* Winona Lake, IN: Eisenbrauns.

Milgrom, J. (1983). *Studies in Cultic Theology and Terminology.* Leiden: E. J. Brill.

Millard, A. R. & Wiseman, D. J. (Eds.). (1980). *Essays on the Patriarchal Narratives.* Leicester, England: Inter-Varsity; reprinted 1983, Winona Lake, IN: Eisenbrauns.

Millard, A. R. & Bordreuil, P. (1982). "A Statue from Syria with Assyrian and Aramaic Inscriptions." *Biblical Archeologist* Summer 1982: 135–41.

Miller, J. W. (1987). *Meet the Prophets. A Beginner's Guide to the Books of the Biblical Prophets.* New York/Mahwah: Paulist.

Miller, P. D., Jr. (1978). *Genesis 1–11. Studies in Structure and Theme.* Journal for the Study of the Old Testament Supplement Series, 8. Sheffield: Journal for the Study of the Old Testament.

Miller, W. T. (1984). *Mysterious Encounters at Mamre and Jabbok.* Brown Judaica Studies. Chico, CA: Scholars.

Morgan, D. F. (1990). *Between Text and Community. The "Writings" in Canonical Interpretation.* Minneapolis: Fortress.

Mowinckel, S. (1962). *The Psalms in Israel's Worship.* New York and Nashville: Abingdon.

Moyers, B. (1996). *Genesis: A Living Conversation.* New York: Bantam Doubleday.

Murphy, R. (1983). *Wisdom Literature and Psalms.* Nashville: Abingdon.

Murphy, R. E. (1990). *The Tree of Life: An Exploration of Biblical Wisdom Literature.* The Anchor Bible Reference Library. New York: Doubleday.

Na'aman, N. (1986). "Habiru and Hebrews: The Transfer of a Social Term to the Literary Sphere." *Journal of Near Eastern Studies* 45: 271–88.

Nelson, R. D. (1987). *First and Second Kings.* Interpretation, a Bible Commentary for Teaching and Preaching. Atlanta: John Knox.

Newsom, C. A. (1989). "Woman and the Discourse of Patriarchal Wisdom: A Study of Proverbs 1–9." In *Gender and Difference in Ancient Israel*, ed. Peggy L. Day. Philadelphia: Fortress.

Newsome, J. D. (1986). *A Synoptic Harmony of Samuel, Kings, and Chronicles: With Related Passages from Psalms, Isaiah, Jeremiah, and Ezra*. Grand Rapids: Baker.

Nicholson, E. W. (1970). *Preaching to the Exiles: A Study of the Prose Traditions in the Book of Jeremiah*. Oxford: Basil Blackwell.

Nicholson, E. W. (1967). *Deuteronomy and Tradition*. Philadelphia: Fortress.

Nickelsburg, G. W. E. (1972). *Resurrection, Immortality, and Eternal Life in Intertestamental Judaism*. Harvard Theological Studies 26. Cambridge: Harvard University.

Nickelsburg, G. W. E. (1981). *Jewish Literature Between the Bible and the Mishnah. A Historical and Literary Introduction*. Philadelphia: Fortress.

Nickelsburg, G. W. E. & Stone, M. E. (1983). *Faith and Piety in Early Judaism. Texts and Documents*. Philadelphia: Fortress.

Niditch, S. (1992). *War in the Hebrew Bible. A Study in the Ethics of Violence*. New York: Orbis.

Niditch, S. (1997). *Ancient Israelite Religion*. Oxford: Oxford University.

Nof, D. & Paldor, N. (1992). "Are There Oceanographic Explanations for the Israelites' Crossing of the Red Sea?" *Bulletin of the American Meteorological Society* 73/3: 305–314.

Noth, M. (1943; English edition 1981). *The Deuteronomic History*. Sheffield: Journal for the Study of the Old Testament.

Noth, M. (1960). *The History of Israel*. rev. ed. New York: Harper & Brothers.

O'Connor, M. (1980). *Hebrew Verse Structure*. Winona Lake, IN: Eisenbrauns.

Pagels, E. (1995). *The Origin of Satan*. New York: Random House.

Parker, S. B. (1997). *Ugaritic Narrative Poetry*. Society of Biblical Literature Writings from the Ancient World. Atlanta: Scholars.

Parrot, A. (1955). *The Flood and Noah's Ark*. London: SCM.

Perdue, L. G. (1977). *Wisdom and Cult*. Society of Biblical Literature Dissertation Series, 30. Missoula, MT: Scholars.

Pope, M. H. (1977). *The Song of Songs*. Anchor Bible. Garden City, NY: Doubleday.

Pritchard, J. B. (1969). *Ancient Near Eastern Texts Relating to the Old Testament*. 3d ed. with supplement. Princeton: Princeton University.

Redford, D. B. (1984). *Akhenaten: The Heretic King*. Princeton: Princeton University.

Redford, D. B. (1992). *Egypt, Canaan and Israel in Ancient Times*. Princeton: Princeton University.

Rendtorff, R. (1985). *The Old Testament. An Introduction*. London: SCM.

Rosenblatt, N. H. & Horwitz, J. (1995). *Wrestling with Angels*. New York: Delcorte.

Rothenberg, B. (1972). *Timna: Valley of the Biblical Copper Mines*. London.

Russell, D. S. (1989). *Daniel, An Active Volcano: Reflections on the Book of Daniel*. Louisville: Westminster John Knox.

Sarna, N. M. (1986). *Exploring Exodus. The Heritage of Biblical Israel*. New York: Schocken.

Sasson, J. M. (1989). *Ruth: A New Translation with a Philological Commentary and a Formalist-folklorist Interpretation*. Sheffield: Journal for the Society of the Old Testament.

Sauer, J. A. (1996). "The River Runs Dry: Biblical Story Preserves Historical Memory." *Biblical Archaeology Review* 22/4: 52–57, 64.

Schmitals, W. (1975). *The Apocalyptic Movement*. Nashville: Abingdon.

Seitz, C. R. (1993). *Isaiah 1–39*. Interpretation, a Commentary for Teaching and Preaching. Louisville: John Knox.

Shanks, H. (1981). "The Exodus and the Crossing of the Red Sea, According to Hans Goedicke". *Biblical Archaeology Review* 7/5 September/October 1981: 42–50, with responses by Krahamalkov 7/5 (1981): 51–54 and Oren 7/6 (1981): 46–53).

Sheppard, G. T. (1980). *Wisdom as a Hermeneutical Construct*. Berlin: Walter de Gruyter.

Short, R. L. (1973). *A Time to Be Born—A Time to Die*. New York: Harper & Row.

Simon, N. (1975). *God's Favorite: A New Comedy*. New York: Random House.

Simpson, W. K. (1972). *The Literature of Ancient Egypt: An Anthology of Stories, Instructions, and Poetry*. New Haven: Yale University.

Skehan, P. W. (1971). *Studies in Israelite Poetry and Wisdom*. Catholic Biblical Quarterly Monograph Series, 1. Washington, DC: Catholic Biblical Association of America.

Sproul, B. C. (1979). *Primal Myths: Creation Myths around the World*. New York: HarperCollins.

Steig, J., pictures by Steig, W. (1990). *The Old Testament Made Easy*. Michael Di Capua Books. New York: Farrar, Straus, Giroux.

Stuart, D. K. (1976). *Studies in Early Hebrew Meter*. Harvard Semitic Monographs, 13. Missoula, MT: Scholars.

Talmon, Shemaryahu (1987). "Ezra and Nehemiah." In R. Alter & F. Kermode, *The Literary Guide to the Bible*. Cambridge: Harvard University.

Thomas, D. W. (Ed.). (1961). *Documents from Old Testament Times*. New York: Harper & Row.

Thompson, T. L. (1992). *Early History of the Israelite People : from the Written and Archaeological Sources*. Studies in the History of the Ancient Near East, 4. Leiden: E. J. Brill.

Thompson, T. L. (1974). *The Historicity of the Patriarchal Narratives*. Berlin: Walter de Gruyter.

Thompson, T. L. (1987). *The Origin Tradition of Ancient Israel. Vol. 1, the Literary Formation of Genesis and Exodus 1–23*. Journal for the Study of the Old Testament Supplement, 55. Sheffield: Journal for the Study of the Old Testament.

Tigay, J. H. (1982). *The Evolution of the Gilgamesh Epic*. Philadelphia: University of Pennsylvania.

Tigay, J. H. (1996). *Deuteronomy*. JPS Torah Commentary. Philadelphia: Jewish Publication Society.

Tigay, J. H. (Ed.) (1985). *Empirical Models for Biblical Criticism*. Philadelphia: University of Pennsylvania.

Towner, W. S. (1984). *Daniel*. Interpretation, A Commentary for Teaching and Preaching. Atlanta: John Knox.

Turner, V. (1969). *The Ritual Process: Structure and Antistructure*. Ithaca and London: Cornell University.

van Hatten, W. C. (1981). "Once Again: Sodom and Gomorrah." *Biblical Archaeologist* 44: 87–92

Van Seters, J. (1975). *Abraham in History and Tradition*. New Haven: Yale University.

Vermes, G. (1987). *The Dead Sea Scrolls in English*. Third revised and augmented edition, including the Temple Scroll and other recently published manuscripts. London: Penguin.

Visotzky, B. L. (1996). *The Genesis of Ethics*. New York: Crown.

von Däniken, E. (1970). *Chariots of the Gods? Unsolved Mysteries of the Past*. New York, Putnam.

von Rad, G. (1938; English translation 1966). *The Problem of the Hexateuch and other essays*. New York: McGraw-Hill.

von Rad, G. (1962). *Old Testament Theology*. Volume 1. New York: Harper & Row.

von Rad, G. (1966). *Deuteronomy*. Old Testament Library. Philadelphia: Westminster.

von Rad, G. (1972). *Wisdom in Israel*. Nashville: Abingdon.

von Rad, G. (1991). *Holy War in Ancient Israel*. Grand Rapids: Eerdmans.

Walton, J. H. (1995). "The Mesopotamian Background of the Tower of Babel Account and Its Implications." *Bulletin of Biblical Research* 5: 155–175.

Webb, B. G. (1987). *The Book of Judges: An Integrated Reading*. Sheffield: Journal for the Study of the Old Testament.

Weinfeld, M. (1970). "The Covenant of Grant in the Old Testament." *Journal of the American Oriental Society* 90: 184–203.

Weinfeld, M. (1972). *Deuteronomy and the Deuteronomic School*. Oxford: Oxford University.

Weinfeld, M. (1993). *The Promise of the Land. The Inheritance of the Land of Canaan by the Israelites*. Berkeley: University of California.

Weippert, M. (1971). *The Settlement of the Israelite Tribes in Palestine. A Critical Survey of Recent Scholarly Debate*. Studies in Biblical Theology, 2d series, 21. London: SCM.

Wenham, G. J. (1979). *Leviticus*. New International Commentary on the Old Testament. Grand Rapids: Eerdmans.

Wenham, G. J. (1978). "The Coherence of the Flood Narrative." *Vetus Testamentum* 28: 336–348.

Westermann, C. (1967). *Basic Forms of Prophetic Speech*. Philadelphia: Fortress.

Westermann, C. (1977). *The Structure of the Book of Job*. Philadelphia: Westminster.

Westermann, C. (1981). *Praise and Lament in the Psalms*. Atlanta: John Knox.

Westermann, C. (1991). *Prophetic Oracles of Salvation in the Old Testament*. Louisville: Westminster John Knox.

Westermann, C. (1992). *Genesis: An Introduction*. Minneapolis: Fortress.

Westermann, C. (1995). *Roots of Wisdom: The Oldest Proverbs of Israel and Other Peoples*. Louisville: Westminster John Knox.

Whedbee, J. W. (1977). "The Comedy of Job." *Semeia* 7: 1–39.

White, J. B. (1978). *A Study of the Language of Love in the Song of Songs and Ancient Egyptian Poetry*. Society of Biblical Literature Dissertation Series, 38. Missoula, MT: Scholars.

Whybray, R. N. (1965). *Wisdom in Proverbs: The Concept of Wisdom in Proverbs 1–9*. Studies in Biblical Theology, 45. London: SCM.

Whybray, R. N. (1974). *The Intellectual Tradition in the Old Testament*. Berlin: Walter de Gruyter.

Whybray, R N. (1983). *The Second Isaiah*. Sheffield: Journal for the Study of the Old Testament.

Williamson, H. G. M. (1977). *Israel in the Books of Chronicles*. Cambridge: Cambridge University.

Wilson, I. (1995). *Out of the Midst of the Fire: Divine Presence in Deuteronomy*. Society of Biblical Literature Dissertation Series 151. Atlanta: Scholars.

Wilson, J. A. (1951). *The Burden of Egypt*. Chicago: University of Chicago. Republished as *The Culture of Ancient Egypt*.

Wilson, R. R. (1977). *Genealogy and History in the Biblical World*. New Haven, CT: Yale University.

Wilson, R. R. (1979). "The Hardening of Pharaoh's Heart". *Catholic Biblical Quarterly* 41: 18–36.

Wilson, R. R. (1980). *Prophecy and Society in Ancient Israel*. Philadelphia: Fortress.

Wolf, H. (1972). "A Solution to the Immanuel Prophecy in Isaiah 7:14–8:22." *Journal of Biblical Literature* 91: 449–456.

Wolff, H. W. (1965; 1974). *Hosea*. Hermeneia. Philadelphia: Fortress

Wolff, H. W. (1977). *Joel and Amos*. Hermeneia. Philadelphia: Fortress.

Wolff, H. W. (1981). *Micah the Prophet*. Philadelphia: Fortress.

Wolff, H. W. (1982). "The Kerygma of the Deuteronomic Historical Work." In W. Brueggemann & H. W. Wolff (Eds.), *The Vitality of Old Testament Traditions* (pp. 83–100). 2d ed. Atlanta: John Knox.

Wood, B. G. (1990). "Did the Israelites Conquer Jericho?" *Biblical Archaeology Review* 16: 44–59.

Wright, A. G. (1968). "The Riddle of the Sphinx: The Structure of the Book of Qohelet." *Catholic Biblical Quarterly* 30: 313–34.

Wright, G. E. (1962). *Biblical Archaeology.* Rev. ed. Philadelphia: Westminster.

Yadin, Y. (1964). "Excavations at Hazor." In . D. N. Freedman & E. F. Campbell, Jr. (Eds.), *The Biblical Archaeologist Reader 2.* Garden City, NY: Doubleday.

Yadin, Y. (1972). *Hazor.* The Schweich Lectures, 1970. London: Oxford University.

Zimmerli, W. (1979, 1983). *Ezekiel.* Two volumes. Hermeneia. Philadelphia: Fortress.

GLOSSARY OF NAMES AND TERMS

A.D. Abbreviation of *anno domini*, Latin for "year of the Lord". See C.E.

Aaron The brother of Moses, Israel's first high priest.

Abel The second son of Adam and Eve; he was murdered by his brother Cain.

Abner The commander of Saul's army; he was killed by Joab.

Abraham (Abram; adj. Abrahamic) The first father (patriarch) of Israel; first called Abram, God made a covenant with him in which God promised to make him a great nation; Isaac was his son by Sarah, and Ishmael was his son by Hagar.

Abraham cycle Genesis 12-25; a collection of stories focused on Abraham.

Abrahamic covenant The covenant Yahweh made with Abraham, sealed by circumcision.

Absalom A son of David who murdered his half-brother Amnon, took the throne from David, and was killed by Joab.

Absolute law Also called apodictic law, it is law stated in an unconditional manner without qualifying clauses; abslolute law is distinguished from case law.

Achan A contemporary of Joshua who kept spoil from the conquest of Jericho, was held responsible for Israel's defeat at Ai, and was executed by the Israelites.

Acrostic A series of poetic lines or verses whose initial letters form the alphabet, a word, or a regular pattern, as in Lamentations 1-4, Psalms 111, 112, and 119.

Adam The first male God created; he and his mate Eve disobeyed God and were expelled from the garden of Eden.

Adonijah A son of David who was executed by Solomon.

Adultery Having sexual relations with someone other than one's husband or wife.

Aetiology See Etiology.

Aggadah See Haggadah.

Ahab (869-850) King of Israel, married to Jezebel, whose Baalistic practices were opposed by the northern prophet Elijah.

Ahasuerus The king of Persia during the time of Esther, identified as Xerxes I (486-465).

Ahaz (735-715) The king of Judah at the time Isaiah was a prophet.

Ahijah An Israelite prophet who encouraged Jeroboam to rebel agains Solomon's administration.

Ai A Canaanite city conquered by Joshua and the Israelites.

Akkadian The Semitic language of Mesopotamia; Assyrian and Babylonian are dialects.

Allegory A literary device in which characters and events stand for abstract ideas, principles, or forces, so that the literal sense has or suggests a parallel, deeper symbolic sense.

Almighty (Hebrew *shaddai*) A name of God that connotes his power and strength; often found in the compound divine name El Shaddai.

Altar A raised platform, made of undressed stones, dirt, metal, or wood, on which incense or sacrifices are offered.

Am ha'aretz (pl. *ammey ha'aretz*; Hebrew for "people of the land") A term used in the Hebrew Bible for citizens, or some particular class of citizens; in rabbinic literature, for persons or groups that dissented from or were uninstructed in rabbinic halaka and rigorous purity and tithing norms; it sometimes signifies the unlearned, sometimes is used condescendingly (boor); it was also used of the broad mass of Jewish people of the first century C.E., who cannot be categorized into any of the sub-groups of the time.

Amaziah Priest of Bethel loyal to Jeroboam II, opposed Amos' preaching and presence in the Northern Kingdom.

Amnon Son of David who raped his half-sister Tamar, and was killed by Absalom.

Amoraim Jewish teachers from the period between 200 and 500 C.E., whose work culminated in the Talmud.

Amos One of the twelve prophets; eighth century prophet from Tekoa in Judah, preached to the northern kingdom emphasizing social justice and the coming Day of Yahweh.

Amphictyony Greek term for a religio-political federation with its common focus a sanctuary dedicated to God; an association of neighboring states or tribes in ancient Greece that banded together for common interest and protection; this model has sometimes been used to describe the tribal confederation in the period of the judges (prior to Saul and David) in ancient Israel.

Anathoth The hometown of Jeremiah in the tribe of Benjamin.

Ancestors In Old Testament study this refers to the forebears of the nation of Israel; the patriarchs and matriarchs of the Hebrews, usually Abraham and Sarah, Isaac and Rebekah, Jacob and Rachel and Leah, and sometimes the twelve sons of Jacob.

Ancestral story The accounts in Genesis 12-50 that pertain to the ancestors of the Israelites.

Ancient Middle East (ancient Near East) The large region of southwest Asia that includes Mesopotamia and territories bordering the Mediterranean Sea; modern nations included within this designation are Turkey, Syria, Lebanon, Israel, Jordan, Iraq, Iran, and Saudi Arabia.

Anointing To pour oil over the head; this was part of a ritual of designation by which priests and kings were initiated into office; an "anointed one" (Hebrew *meshiach*) was a divinely designated leader.

Anthropomorphism (adj. anthropomorphic) A term for the attribution of human behavior or characteristics to inanimate objects, animals, natural phenomena, or deity; with regard to deity, anthropomorphism became a point of theological discussion in Judaism, Christianity and Islam.

Antiochus IV Epiphanes (175-163) Seleucid king who persecuted the Jews of Judea during the Maccabean period.

Antithetic parallelism Type of poetic parallelism where the second line of a poetic couplet is the opposite of the first line.

Apocalypse (adj. apocalyptic; Greek for "revelation") An "unveiling" of something hidden; apocalyptic literature is a genre of literature (attested in Jewish, Christian and Muslim traditions) in which the author claims to reveal the future and to show how the divine plan will be worked out in history, often expressing it in vivid symbolism; the final book of the Christian New Testament is sometimes called (in accord with its Greek title) "the Apocalypse" (it is also known as "the book of Revelation").

Apocalyptic eschatology The view of the end times expressed in apocalyptic literature.

Apocalyptic literature Old Testament, intertestamental Jewish, and early Christian literature that consists predominantly of apocalypses; this literature is often pseudepigraphical; Daniel 7–12 is apocalyptic literature.

Apocalyptic prophecy Form of prophecy that consists mainly of apocalypses and is largely oriented to the future, as in the latter half of the book of Daniel.

Apocalypticism The thought world or world view of the community that gave rise to apocalyptic literature.

Apocrypha (adj. apocryphal; from Greek for "to hide, to uncover") It is used in a technical sense to refer to certain Jewish books written in the Hellenistic-Roman period that came to be included in the Old Greek Jewish scriptures (and thus in the Eastern Christian biblical canon) and in the Latin Vulgate Roman Catholic canon, but not in the Jewish or Protestant biblical canons; they are called deutero-canonical books in the Roman Catholic tradition.

Apodictic law See Absolute law.

Apsu The god of the fresh water ocean in the Enuma Elish, the Babylonian creation story.

Aqedah (Hebrew for "binding" [of Isaac]) The biblical account of God's command to Abraham to offer his son Isaac as a sacrifice (Genesis 22).

Aram (Aramea, Aram-naharaim, Padan-Aram) The territory north and east of Palestine where Abraham's ancestors had settled and from where the wives of Isaac and Jacob came; roughly the region of modern northern Syria and northwestern Iraq.

Aramaic A language in the same family as Hebrew, used in Daniel 2:4–7:28; Ezra 4:8–6:18 and 7:12-26; and Jeremiah 10:11; its square script replaced the Old Hebrew script in Hebrew manuscripts before the common era.

Araunah The owner of a threshing floor in Jerusalem (Jebus) where David built an altar; David bought the threshing floor and Solomon built the temple there (2 Samuel 24).

Archaeology The science of unearthing sites containing remains of ancient habitation, with the goal of learning everything such sites have to offer about culture, society, ecology, intellectual life and religion; modern archaeology employs the tools of history, anthropology, geology, and biology to recover the hidden past.

Ark of the covenant A gold-overlayed wooden chest with two cherubim on the lid which stored the tablets of the covenant; it was housed first in the tabernacle, then in the Most Holy Place room of the Jerusalem temple; it was the location of God's presence within Israel.

Armageddon Derived from Hebrew *har megiddo*, "mountain of Megiddo," it is the mythic site of the final battle between God and the forces of evil in apocalyptic thought.

Atonement (v. atone) To make right with God by satisfying the penalty for having broken a relationship; in the Old Testament this was done through offering sacrifices to God. See Yom Kippur (Day of Atonement).

Atrahasis epic A Babylonian story which recounts the creation of humankind.

Av (sometimes spelled *Ab*) A month in the Jewish calendar; the 9th of Av, or *tisha b'av*, is a day of mourning for the destruction of the Jerusalem temple in 587 B.C.E. and again in 70 C.E.

B.C.E./C.E. Abbreviations meaning "before the common era" and "common era"; theologically neutral replacements for the traditional designations B.C. ("before Christ") and A.D. ("year of the Lord").

Baal Word which means "lord, master" (in Modern Hebrew, "husband") that was applied to the chief god of Canaan; various locations in Canaan had their patron Baal gods, for example, Baal of Peor and Baal of Hermon.

Babel See Babylon and Tower of Babel.

Babylon The capital city of Babylonia in southern Mesopotamia; the Babylonians led by Nebuchadnezzar destroyed Jerusalem in 587 B.C.E. and took Judeans into Babylonian exile; called Babel in Genesis 11.

Babylonian exile. See Exile.

Balaam A thirteenth century B.C.E. Mesopotamian seer-prophet who was hired by Balak of Moab to curse the Israelites but ended up blessing them instead.

Balak King of Moab who opposed Moses and the Israelites.

Baruch Jeremiah's scribe, perhaps responsible for composing and editing the latter half of the book of Jeremiah.

Bathsheba The wife of Uriah who committed adultery with David, later became his wife and the mother of Solomon.

Belshazzar Son of Nabonidus (556-539) who ruled in his father's absence; according to Daniel 5 he was king when Babylon fell.

Belteshazzar The Babylonian name of Daniel; not to be confused with Belshazzar.

Ben (Hebrew for "son, son of"; Aramaic *bar*) Used frequently in "patronymics" (naming by identity of father); Rabbi Akiba ben Joseph means Akiba son of Joseph.

Benjamin The twelfth son of Jacob, the younger brother of Joseph; Rachel was his mother; he was the ancestor of the tribe of Benjamin.

Berakah (Hebrew for "blessing") In Judaism, an offering of thankfulness that praises God for a benefit conferred or a great event experienced.

Berit (also spelled *brit*; Hebrew for "covenant") Used in Judaism especially for the special relationship believed to exist between God and the Jewish people.

Bethel A city which became a center of Israelite worship; literally means "house of El."

Bethlehem A city in the tribe of Judah, home town of David; literally means "house of bread."

Bible (adj. biblical; from Greek *biblos*, "papyrus, paper, book" and *ta biblia*, "the books") The designation normally used for the Hebrew Bible plus the Christian New Testament; in classical Roman Catholic and Greek Orthodox Christianity it designates the Hebrew Bible plus the Apocrypha plus the New Testament .

Birthright The special inheritance rights of the first-born son giving him claim to the bulk of the ancestral property.

Blessing, bless Divine favor and approval; blessing is a mark of God's grace and evidence of his protecting and prospering presence; in return people can bless God as a display of gratitude for his goodness.

Boaz A wealthy Israelite who lived in Bethlehem; he married Ruth and became an ancestor of David.

Book of the covenant (also called the *covenant code*) Exodus 20:22–23:33; a collection of Israelite laws.

Book of the twelve (also called the *twelve prophets*) Sometimes called the minor prophets, a collection of twelve short prophetic books in the Latter Prophets.

Burning bush The bush out of which Yahweh spoke to Moses in the Sinai to reveal God's identity (Exodus 3).

C.E. "Common Era"; a non-sectarian term for the period traditionally labeled A.D. (*anno domini* or "in the year of our Lord") by Christians; thus 1999 C.E. references the same year as A.D. 1999. See also B.C.E.

Cain The first son of Adam and Eve; he murdered his brother Abel.

Caleb One of the twelve spies Joshua sent into Canaan; of the generation which left Egypt in the Exodus, only he and Joshua were allowed to enter Canaan.

Calendar Judaism follows a lunar calandar adjusted every three years or so to the solar cycle (by adding a second 12th month)—thus "lunisolar"; the oldest Jewish annual observances are Passover/pesah, Shevuot, Yom Kippur and Sukkot; other ancient celebrations include Rosh Hashanah, Simhat Torah, Hannukah and Purim; in general, Christianity operates on a "solar" calendar based on the relationship between the sun and the earth (365.25 days per year); the main Christian observances are Easter, Pentecost, and Christmas.

Call narrative An account found in some historical and prophetic books that records the prophet's experience of being called into prophetic ministry; the call was usually issued in the presence of God.

Call to praise A speech-type found in certain biblical psalms where the psalmist enjoins others to join him in praising God.

Canaan The geographical territory between the Mediterranean coast and the Jordan River that was claimed and occupied by the Hebrews; also called the Promised Land.

Canon criticism (sometimes called *canon critique*) A type of biblical study that places emphasis on the final form of the text as normative for Judaism and Christianity.

Canon The authorized collection of material constituting the sacred writings of a religious community; the material is believed to have special, usually divine, authority; the Hebrew Bible is the canon of the Jewish community; the Old and New Testaments (respectively with and without the Apocrypha) are the canon of the Roman Catholic and Protestant Christian communities.

Canonization The process whereby a religious community defined the body of texts it considered authoritative for its life and belief.

Case law Legal sayings with modifying clauses often in the *if…then* form: "If this is the situation…then this is the penalty"; also called casuistic law, this type of legal formulation contrasts with absolute law.

Casuistic law See Case law.

Catholic (from Greek for "universal, worldwide") A self designation used in early Christianity to suggest universality over against factionalism; thence it became a technical name for the western, Roman Catholic church.

Centralization (centralization of worship) A theme of the Deuteronomist whereby proper worship could only be performed in the city God designated, presumably Jerusalem.

Chaos The disordered state of unformed matter that existed before the universe was ordered; biblical and ancient Middle Eastern origin stories thought of chaos as an unruly cosmic ocean.

Charismatic Gifted, filled with the divine, with divinely given powers, or with God's spirit. This state may be linked with ecstasy or trance, which is reported to have been experienced by the early prophets and by Saul, the first king.

Cherub (Hebrew pl. *cherubim*) An angelic being, in appearance something like a human but with wings; they were mythical celestial winged creatures prominent in Temple decoration; cherubim were considered God's ruling council, also called the host of heaven.

Chiasmus (adj. chiastic) A literary device in which, for emphasis, the second part of a text is parallel to the first, but in reverse, for example, ABBA, ABCBA.

Christ (from Greek *christos*, "anointed one"; Greek translation of Hebrew *meshiach*) Applied to Jesus/Joshua of Nazareth by his followers as a title, but soon came to be treated as a sort of second name. See Messiah.

Christians/Christianity The followers of Jesus of Nazareth who believe him to be the Jewish messiah (*christos*) of God; Christianity is the collective body of Christians who believe the teachings of Jesus of Nazareth.

Christos The Greek word for "anointed one." Also see Christ.

Chronicle An annal or account of events in the order in which they occurred.

Chronicler Writer of the books of Chronicles; generally considered to be a later interpreter of the history of Judah.

Chronicler's history The books of the Writings considered to be a post-Exilic retelling of Israel's history intended to profile the role of the house of David; consists of the biblical books First and Second Chronicles, Ezra, and Nehemiah.

Church (from Greek *ekklesia*, "summoned group"; compare "ecclesiastical") The designation traditionally used for a specifically Christian assembly or body of people, and thus also the building or location in which the assembled people meet, and by extension also the specific organized sub-group within Christianity (e.g. Catholic, Protestant, Methodist, etc.); similar to synagogue and *kahal* in Judaism.

Circumcision, circumcise Cutting off the loose fold of skin at the end of the penis; circumcision was the ritual attached to the covenant God made with Abraham; in Judaism, it is ritually performed when a boy is eight days old in a ceremony called *brit milah*, which indicates that the ritual establishes a covenant between God and the individual; in Islam, it is performed at the age of puberty.

Cities of refuge Six cities designated in Mosaic law for those who accidentally killed someone.

Classical Judaism The form of Judaism that has survived as traditional throughout the centuries.

Clean animals Animals which were approved for ritual sacrifices.

Climactic parallelism The type of poetic parallelism where the second line of a poetic couplet echoes part of the first line and adds a phrase to it thereby extending and completing its sense.

Code of Hammurabi A Mesopotamian law code associated with the eighteenth century B.C.E. Old Babylonian monarch Hammurabi; it has similarities to the biblical Book of the Covenant.

Colon A single line of poetry, sometimes called a *stich* or *stichos*.

Commandments (Hebrew *mitzvot*; sing., *mitzvah*) Orders given by God; God gave Ten Commandments as the core of the covenant on Mount Sinai, and a multitude of other moral and cultic laws; according to rabbinic Jewish tradition, there are 613 religious commandments referred to in the Torah (and elaborated upon by the rabbinic sages); of these, 248 are positive commandments and 365 are negative; the numbers respectively symbolize the fact that divine service must be expressed through all one's bodily parts during all the days of the year; in general, a *mitzvah* refers to any act of religious duty or obligation; more colloquially, a *mitzvah* refers to a "good deed."

Commentary A discussion of a book of the Bible that treats linguistic, literary, historical, and theological aspects of its meaning.

Complaint (also called *lament*) A literary type that expresses the pain and alienation of the writer and asks God for help; complaints are found in psalmic and prophetic literature.

Complaints of Jeremiah A set of passages found in Jeremiah 11-20 that express his anxieties and frustrations in being a prophet.

Concordance An alphabetical listing of all the important words in a text and their textual locations; a useful tool for studying biblical themes.

Concubine A woman who belonged to a man but did not have the full rights of a wife; she was frequently acquired as spoils in war, and her main function was to bear sons for the man.

Conquest The series of initiatives and military actions of the time of Joshua that were intended to secure Israel's control of Palestine.

Consecrate (n. consecration) To set aside or dedicate to God's use.

Cosmogony A theory or model of the origin and evolution of the physical universe; ancient creation stories, such as Genesis 1–2 and the Enuma Elish are cosmogonies.

Cosmology A model of the structure of the physical universe; the Israelites viewed the world as an inhabitable region surrounded by water.

Covenant (Hebrew *berit* or *brit*) A pact or formal agreement between two parties in which there are mutual obligations and expectations; covenant is used as a metaphor of God's relationship with his people; the major covenants in the Old Testament are God's covenant with Abraham (Genesis 15), and the Sinai/Moses covenant (Exodus 19–24) between God and Israel; the Priestly writer used a succession of covenants to track the development of salvation history; in Judaism, the covenant is a major theological concept referring to the eternal bond between God and the people of Israel grounded in God's gracious and steadfast concern (Hebrew *chesed*) that calls for the nation's obedience to the divine commandments (*mitzvot*) and instruction (*torah*); for Christianity (e.g. Paul), God has made a "new covenant" (rendered as "new testament" in older English) with the followers of Jesus in the last times, superseding the "old covenant" (thus, "old testament") with Moses at Sinai (see Jeremiah 31:31–34).

Covenant code See Book of the covenant.

Creation What has been brought into being; the Hebrew Bible attributes the creation of the world to Israel's God; the classic descriptions of creation are found in Genesis 1 and 2, but there are many other allusions to creation found in Israel's Psalms and in prophetic literature. The Enuma Elish is a Babylonian account of creation.

Criticism When used in biblical scholarship in such phrases as *biblical criticism*, *higher criticism*, and *form criticism*, it means evaluating evidence to arrive at a reasoned judgment concerning the matter under investigation; it does not imply that the reader is taking a negative or "criticizing" position over against the Bible; RTOT suggests that *critique* or *analysis* may be a better term to use.

Cubit A biblical unit of measurement, the distance from elbow to fingertip—approximately 18 inches, or half a meter.

Cult The formal organization and practice of worship, usually associated with a sanctuary and involving a regular cycle of sacrifices, prayers, and hymns under the direction of priests and other leaders; when used in biblical studies the term is descriptive and does not imply anything dark, devilish, false, or unseemly, as is often the case in modern uses of the term.

Curse To ask God to bring something tragic or disastrous on someone or something else; the opposite of blessing; as a noun, it is the description of the bad thing which will happen, as in the curses and blessing of the law.

Cycle As in *Abraham cycle*, *Jacob cycle*, and *Joseph cycle*, the term refers to a collection of stories centered or "cycling" around a single individual.

Cyrus (550-530) Persian monarch, sometimes called Cyrus the Great, who founded the Medo-Persian empire in the sixth century B.C.E. and allowed the Judean refugees to return to their homeland after the Babylonian exile.

D The acronym for the Deuteronomist source of the Torah/Pentateuch, written in the seventh century B.C.E. See Deuteronomy and Deuteronomist.

Dan A son of Jacob, and one of the twelve tribes of Israel.

Daniel A Judean who was taken into Babylonian captivity by Nebuchadnezzar; a Jewish hero, he is the main character in the book of Daniel.

David The son of Jesse, anointed by Samuel to become king in place of Saul; he killed Goliath; his sons Amnon, Absalom, Adonijah, and Solomon fought to follow him on the throne; he is associated with the biblical psalms and is credited with politically and militarily uniting the ancient Israelite confederation into a centralized kingdom with Jerusalem as its capital; he created the largest empire Israel ever knew; David is said to have planned for the Temple which his son and successor Solomon built.

Davidic covenant A covenant God made with David pledging that the family of David would provide kings to rule over Israel in perpetuity (2 Samuel 7).

Day of atonement (Hebrew *yom kippur*) The one day each year when special sacrifices were made by the high priest for the sins of the people; only on this day the high priest entered the Most Holy Place of the temple to sprinkle blood on the ark of the covenant to reconcile Israel with God (Leviticus 16).

Day of Yahweh Also termed the Day of the LORD, the day God battles his enemies; derives from the holy war tradition and was cited by Amos, Joel, Obadiah, and Zephaniah.

Dead Sea Scrolls A collection of scrolls dating to the first century B.C.E. found in caves near the Dead Sea; they are generally thought to be linked with the settlement at Qumran, and with a Jewish religious group called the Essenes.

Deborah The judge of Israel who engineered victory over Canaanites (Judges 4-5).

Decalogue (Greek for "ten words") Refers to laws collected into a group of ten; *The Decalogue* is the Ten Commandments received by Moses on Mount Sinai (Exodus 20:1-17 and Deuteronomy 5:1-21); the cultic or ritual decalogue is found in Exodus 34.

Demythologize The process of interpreting a myth in non-mythic language to express its meaning without clinging to its mythic form.

Deutero-canonical Pertains to writings regarded as Scripture by some (particularly by Christian groups) but not contained in the Hebrew Bible. Also see Apocrypha and Pseudepigrapha.

Deuteronomic reform A reform of Judah's religious institutions carried out by Josiah in the seventh century B.C.E.; the book of Deuteronomy is closely associated with this initiative.

Deuteronomist (abbreviated D) The writer or school of writers responsible for the book of Deuteronomy, the fifth book of the Torah/Pentateuch.

Deuteronomistic historian The writer or editor of the Deuteronomistic history; one theory holds there were two editors, Dtr1 from the time of Josiah and Dtr2 from the time of the Babylonian exile.

Deuteronomistic history (abbreviated DH; sometimes called the Deuteronomic history) The body of material which consists of the introduction to Deuteronomy (chapters 1-4) and Joshua, Judges, Samuel and Kings; it is an extended review of Israel's history from the conquest under Joshua through the destruction of 587 B.C.E. written from the perspective of principles found in the book of Deuteronomy.

Deuteronomy The fifth book of the Torah/Pentateuch; many modern scholars consider it to be part or all of a scroll found during a reform of the temple and its institutions carried out by Josiah in 622 B.C.E.

DH (sometimes *DtrH*) The acronym for the Deuteronomistic history. See Deuteronomistic history.

Diaspora (Greek for "scattering"; also called the *dispersion*) The technical term for the dispersion of the Jewish people, a process which began after defeats in 721 and 587 B.C.E. and resulted in the growth of sizable Jewish communities outside Palestine; the terms *diasora* and *dispersion* are often used to refer to the Jewish communities living among the gentiles outside the "holy land" of Canaan/Israel/Palestine.

Dietary laws See Kosher.

Dispersion See Diaspora.

Divine council Consisted of the "sons of God," a council of angels which surrounded God and served perhaps as his deliberative assembly.

Divine warrior The notion that God is a warrior fighting on behalf of his people. Also see Holy War.

Documentary hypothesis Scholarly hypothesis suggesting that the Torah/Pentateuch was not the work one author, such as Moses, but is a composition based on four documents from different periods: J (the Yahwist) from about 950 B.C.E., E (the Elohist) from about 850, D (Deuteronomy) from about 620, and P (the Priestly document) from about 550–450. J and E were combined around 720, D was added about a century later, and P about a century after that, giving final shape to the Torah.

Dualism The belief that there are two elemental forces in the universe, Good and Evil; apocalypticism typically holds a dualistic view of the world.

E The acronym for the Elohist source. See Elohist source.

Early Judaism Also sometimes called "formative," "proto-," "middle," and even "late" Judaism; refers to Judaism in the intertestamental period (and slightly later) as a development from the religion of ancient Israel, but prior to the emergence of its classical, rabbinic form in the early centuries C.E.

Eden Also called the garden of Eden, it was the place God located the first created humans, Adam and Eve (Genesis 2–3).

Edom A territory south of Judah, the location of the Edomites, the descendants of Esau.

Ehud A judge of Israel from the book of Judges, noted for being left-handed.

El The Semitic word for God, found alone or compounded with other terms as names of God (El Shaddai, El Elyon, etc.); often found as the theophoric element in personal and place names (Elijah, Bethel, etc.).

Election A term used theologically in Judaism to indicate God's choice of Israel to receive the covenant—a choice not based on the superiority or previous accomplishments of the people, but on God's graciousness (see covenant); in Christianity, the concept of election was applied to the "new Israel" of Jesus' followers in the last times.

Eli The high priest at Shiloh with whom Samuel ministered in his early years.

Elijah An Israelite prophet during the reign of Ahab; he defeated the prophets of Baal at Mount Carmel and was taken to heaven in a fire storm.

Elisha The prophet who succeeded Elijah in the northern kingdom of Israel.

Elkanah An Ephraimite, the husband of Hannah and the father of Samuel.

Elohim A Hebrew word meaning God; Israel's most general way of referring to its deity; the Elohist portions of the Pentateuch refer to God with this term.

Elohist source (also called the *Elohist*; abbreviated E) The name given to a reconstructed source underlying certain pentateuchal narratives; it is characterized by the use of the divine name Elohim.

Enuma Elish A Babylonian story of creation, featuring Apsu, Tiamat, and Marduk.

Ephod A linen apron worn by a priest over his robe.

Ephraim One of Joseph's two sons; he became the ancestor of one of the tribes of Israel; the name Ephraim was often used as a designation of the ten northern tribes after the division of the kingdoms.

Eponym A supposed ancestor (eponymous ancestor) whose name is the same as, or related to, the name of a later group, tribe or nation.

Eretz Yisrael/Israel (Hebrew for "land of Israel") In Jewish thought, the special term for the Palestinian area believed to have been promised to the Jewish people by God in the ancient covenant.

Esau The first son of Isaac and Rebekah, the twin of Jacob; he was the ancestor of the Edomites.

Eschatology (adj. eschatological; from Greek *eschaton*, "last" or "the end-time") Refers in general to what is expected to take place in the "last times" (from the inquirer's perspective); thus the study of the ultimate destiny or purpose of humankind and the world, how and when the end will occur, what the end or last period of history or existence will be like. See also Apocalypse and Apocalyptic literature.

Essenes A Jewish group that lived in retreat in the wilderness of Judea between the first century B.C.E. and the first C.E., according to Josephus, the elder, Pliny, and Philo. See also Dead Sea Scrolls and Qumran.

Esther A Jewish heroine of the diaspora who became queen of Persia under Xerxes I, called Ahasuerus in the story; she secured the safety of the Jews when they were threatened with genocide; her story is told in the book which carries her name.

Ethical decalogue The ten commandments of Exodus 20 and Deuteronomy 5. See Decalogue.

Etiology (sometimes spelled *aetiology*; from Greek for "cause, origin") A term used to describe or label stories (etiological tales) that claim to explain the reason for something being (or being called) what it is; for example, in the old Jewish creation story (Genesis 2:23), woman (*ishshah*) is given that name because she has been taken out of (the side or rib of) "man" (*ish*).

Eve The first female God created; mated to Adam, her name means "life."

Ex nihilo A Latin phrase meaning "from nothing" that some theologians apply to the biblical story of creation; Genesis 1, as well as other Old Testament allusions to creation, suggests that God created the world out of water.

Exegesis (from Greek for "interpretation") The process of drawing out meaning from a text; interpreting a text in its literary and historical context.

Exile (also called *Babylonian exile*) The Babylonian exile was the period in the middle of the 6th century B.C.E. when Judeans were taken as captives to Babylonia and resettled there; it officially ended in 539 B.C.E., but many Judeans nonetheless remained there.

Exodus (from Greek for "to exit, go out") The term refers to the event of the Israelites leaving Egypt and to the biblical book that tells of that event, the second book of the Torah; the release from Egyptian captivity and the exodus from Egypt were led by Moses, probably in the thirteenth century B.C.E. Also see Passover.

Ezekiel A priest taken to Babylonia, he became a prophet to the community of Judean refugees living there in the sixth century B.C.E.; also, the prophetic book associated with this figure.

Ezra A priest and teacher of the Torah; he led a group of Jewish refugees back to Judea from Babylonia in the fifth century B.C.E.

Fall The disobedience and expulsion of Adam and Eve from the garden of Eden (Genesis 3).

Fear of God A deep respect and reverence of God; an important theme in the Elohist fragments and in the wisdom literature.

Fertile crescent The well-watered and fertile arc of land where early civilizations developed and prospered; it extends upward from the Nile valley in the west, through Palestine and Syria, and down the Tigris and Euphrates valleys to the Persian Gulf.

First Isaiah Chapters 1-39 of the book of Isaiah, largely attributable to Isaiah of Jerusalem of the eighth century.

Five scrolls (sometimes called the *Five Megillot*) A sub-group of books within the Writings section of the Hebrew Bible consisting of the Song of Songs, Ruth, Lamentations, Ecclesiastes, and Esther; each book or scroll is associated with a festival occasion in the life of Israel.

Flood The watery inundation during the time of Noah that destroyed all life on earth, except for Noah and the representative sample of created things that survived in the ark (Genesis 6-9).

Form criticism (also called *form analysis* or *form critique*) The examination of literary units to discover the typical formal structures and patterns behind the present text in an attempt to recover the original sociological setting or setting-in-life (German *Sitz im Leben*) of that form of literature.

Formal parallelism (sometimes called *synthetic parallelism*) The type of poetic parallelism where the second line of a poetic couplet completes the thought of the first line.

Former prophets The term designating the books of Joshua, Judges, Samuel and Kings—possibly so-called because it was assumed that prophets had written these books; *former* because they were placed in canonical order before the latter prophets.

Galilee The northern part of Palestine, specifically the territories north and west of the Sea of Galilee.

Galut (Hebrew for "exile") The term refers to the various expulsions of Jews from the ancestral homeland; over time, it came to express the broader notion of Jewish homelessness and state of being aliens; thus, colloquially, "to be in *galut*" means to live in the diaspora and also to be in a state of physical and even spiritual alienation. See Diaspora.

Gemara (Hebrew for "completion") Popularly applied to the Jewish Talmud as a whole, to discussions by rabbinic teachers on Mishnah, and to decisions reached in these discussions; in a more restricted sense, it applies to the work of the generations of the Amoraim from the third through the fifth centuries C.E. in "completing" Mishnah to produce the Talmuds.

Genealogy A list or family tree of ancestors or descendants; the Priestly history and the Chronicler's history contain extensive genealogies.

Generation A group of people born and living at about the same time, usually reckoned as forty years in the Old Testament; grandparents, parents, and children are three generations.

Genre The term used by literary critics as the equivalent of "type of literature"; the basic genres found in the Hebrew Bible are prose and poetry, with many different sub-types including song, hymn, story, saying, speech, law, genealogy, saga, history.

Gentiles (Hebrew *goyyim*) In pre-Christian times, non-Jewish peoples; thereafter, non-Jewish and non-Christian (roughly synonymous with "pagan").

Gibeon A village north of Jerusalem which tricked Joshua and the Israelites into making a treaty with them.

Gideon A judge who delivered the Israelites from the tyrany of the Midianites.

Gilgal A village near Jericho where the Israelites first stopped after they entered the Promised Land.

Gilgamesh epic A Babylonian epic centering on Gilgamesh, an ancient king of Uruk; the eleventh tablet of this epic contains a story of a flood that has parallels to the biblical story of Noah and the ark.

Glory of Yahweh The revelation of God's being, nature, and presence to humankind, often through physical or meteorological phenomena.

God The supreme divine being, called Elohim by the Israelites, who was also known as Yahweh.

Gog An eschataological figure, a personification of evil, that battled God's forces in Ezekiel 38-39.

Golden calf A statue constructed by Aaron at Mount Sinai that the Israelites worshiped; Jeroboam, first king of Israel, built golden calf shrines at Bethel and Dan.

Goliath The Philistine giant who was killed by David.

Gomer The wife of Hosea the prophet who turned out to be unfaithful to their marriage.

Goshen The territory in the eastern Nile delta of Egypt where Joseph settled the family of Jacob.

Grace An undeserved gift or favor; the undeserved attention, forgiveness, kindness and mercy that God gives.

Habakkuk One of the Twelve Prophets; a sixth century Judean prophet who sought to understand God's purpose in sending the Babylonians to punish Judah.

Habiru (sometimes spelled *hapiru* or *'apiru*) An Akkadian term denoting persons or groups who were social and political outlaws from established society; existing in the ancient Middle East in the second and first millennia B.C.E. they appear as slaves, merchants, mercenary soldiers, bandits, and outlaws; some scholars link this term to the word *Hebrew*.

Hagar The servant of Sarah and one of Abraham's wives; the mother of Ishmael, who was driven away from the family by Sarah.

Haggadah (adj. haggadic; Hebrew for "telling, narration"; sometimes spelled *aggada[h]*) Jewish term for non-halakic (nonlegal) matter, especially in Talmud and Midrash; it includes folklore, legend, theology, scriptural interpretations, biography, etc.; in a general sense, in classical Jewish literature and discussion, what is not halaka (legal subject matter) is (h)aggada; technically, "the Haggada(h)" is a liturgical manual about the exodus from Egypt in the time of Moses used in the Jewish Passover Seder.

Haggai A prophet who encouraged the Israelites to rebuild the temple after a return from the exile in Babylonia in the sixth century B.C.E.

Halakah (adj. halakic; Hebrew for "going," i.e. how we go about our daily lives) Deals with practical guidance, rules, and expectations in Judaism; any normative Jewish law, custom, practice, or rite—or the entire complex; halakah is law established or custom ratified by authoritative rabbinic jurists and teachers; colloquially, if something is deemed halakic, it is considered proper and normative behavior.

Ham One of the sons of Noah; he abused his father and Canaan, his son, was cursed for it.

Haman The wicked opponent of Mordecai and the Jews in the book of Esther.

Hananiah The Judean prophet who challenged Jeremiah over the issue of the yoke of Babylon.

Hannah The wife of Elkanah and mother of Samuel; she prayed for a son; after Samuel was born she dedicated him to God's service at Shiloh.

Hanukkah (Hebrew for "dedication") The Jewish festival of lights that commemorates the rededication of the Jerusalem temple to more traditional modes of Jewish worship by Judah the Maccabee around 164 B.C.E. after its desecration in the time of the Seleucid king Antiochus IV Epiphanes.

Hasid(s) (Hebrew for "pious one") The term may refer to Jews in various periods: (1) a group that resisted the policies of Antiochus IV Epiphanes in the second century B.C.E. at the start of the Maccabean revolt; (2) pietists in the thirteenth century C.E.; (3) followers of the movement of Hasidism founded in the eighteenth century C.E. by Baal Shem Tov.

Hasmonaean Hasmon is the family name of the Maccabees, so the Maccabaean rulers are often referred to as Hasmonaean; the Hasmoneans included the Maccabees and the high priests and kings who ruled Judea from 142 to 63 B.C.E.

Hazor A city in northern Canaan that resisted the Israelites but was conquered by Joshua.

Hebrew Bible The collection of 24 books constituting the Old Testament according to the arrangement of the Jewish canon; it can also be referred to as the Tanak; originally written in Hebrew and Aramaic, it is the written canon of Judaism and the first half of the canon of Christianity.

Hebrew The language of the Old Testament Israelites and the language in which most of the Old Testament/Hebrew Bible was written.

Hebrews Another name for Israelites, usually used in reference to them before they settled in the Promised Land.

Hebron A major city in Judah, the place from which David first ruled; Abraham and many other ancestors were buried here.

Hellenism (adj. hellenistic; Greek for "Greekish") The civilization that spread from Greece through much of the ancient world from 333 (Alexander the Great) to 63 (dominance of Rome) B.C.E.; as a result, many elements of Greek culture (names, language, philosophy, athletics, architecture, etc.) penetrated the ancient Middle East.

Hellenistic Pertaining to Greek culture as disseminated by the conquests of Alexander the Great, and the rule of his successors.

Hellenization The process of becoming enculturated by the ideals of Hellenism.

Hermeneutics (from Greek for "to interpret, translate"; hence, "science of interpretation") It denotes the strategy of interpreting texts to enable them to be applied to circumstances contemporary with the interpreter; the term is often used with reference to the study of Jewish and Christian scriptures.

Hexateuch The first six books of the Hebrew Bible; there may be an underlying assumption that these belong together historically.

Hezekiah (715-687) A king of Judah; he restored the temple, reinstituted proper worship and received God's help against the Assyrians.

High priest The chief religious official in Israel; he offered the most important sacrifices to God on behalf of the people.

Hillel Often called by the title "the Elder"; probably a Babylonian, Hillel was an important sage of the early Jewish period in Palestine around the turn of the era; his teachings convey the Pharisaic ideal, through many epigrams on humility and peace (found in *Sayings of the Fathers* 1-2); and were fundamental in shaping the Pharisaic traditions and modes of interpretation; in rabbinic lore, Hillel is famous for a negative formulation of the "golden rule" (recited to a non-Jew): "What is hateful to you do not do to your fellow man. That is the whole Torah, the rest is commentary. Go and learn it"; his style of legal reasoning is continued by his disciples, known as Beit Hillel ("House/School of Hillel"), and is typically contrasted with that of Shammai (a contemporary) and his school.

Historiography The reconstruction of the past based on a critical examination of ancient materials.

Holiness code Chapters 17-27 of Leviticus, which detail the laws for ensuring, protecting, and promoting holiness (sacredness, separateness).

Holy (adj. holiness) To set apart for God; to belong to God; to be pure.

Holy spirit (sometimes termed the "holy ghost") In the Hebrew Bible it is referred to as the spirit of God or spirit of Yahweh; in Judaism the presence of God is evidenced in the speech of the prophets and by other divine manifestations; in Christianity it is understood more generally as the active, guiding presence of God in the church and its members.

Holy war War authorized by God and led by him; Old Testament holy war called for the complete slaughter of the enemy and the dedication of all spoils to God. See Divine warrior.

Hophni He and Phineas were two sons of Eli, the high priest at Shiloh; they died in battle at Aphek–Ebenezer fighting the Philistines.

Horeb The term used in the Elohist and Deuteronomist sources to designate the location where God delivered the commandments and covenant to the Israelites through Moses, apparently the equivalent of Mount Sinai.

Hosea One of the twelve prophets; an eighth century Israelite prophet who exposed the people's lack of faith in Yahweh.

Hyksos Derived from Egyptian for "rulers of foreign countries," these Semitic rulers of Egypt from 1750-1550 B.C.E. were probably the people in control of Egypt during the sojourn of Joseph and Jacob's descendants.

Hymn A song praising God, the king, Zion, or Torah that contains a description of why the object of praise is wonderful.

Iconography The expression of religious principles or doctrines using pictorial or symbolic images or icons; icons may serve as visual metaphors; a faith which favours this type of expression is called 'iconic'.

Image of God Phrase deriving from Genesis 1:26-7; God created humankind in his own image.

Immanuel (sometimes spelled *Emmanuel*) The figure in Isaiah's prophecy (chapter 7), which means "God is with us".

Incense A component in rituals of worship; spices burned on an altar or in a censer to make a sweet smelling smoke.

Intertestamental period The period in which early Judaism developed, between about 400 B.C.E. (the traditional end date for the Old Testament/Hebrew Bible) and the first century C.E. (the composition of the Christian New Testament); the Jewish intertestamental literature includes the Apocrypha (mostly preserved in Greek) and the Pseudepigrapha (works from this period ascribed to ancient authors like Enoch, the ancestors, and Moses).

Invocation The forumla used at the beginning of many psalms that appeals to God and asks him to listen.

Isaac The son of Abraham and Sarah who inherited the ancestral promises; he married Rebekah and was the father of Esau and Jacob.

Isaiah A prophet in Jerusalem in the eighth century B.C.E., also called Isaiah of Jerusalem; also, the prophetic book which contains the words of Isaiah of Jerusalem, Second Isaiah, and Third Isaiah.

Isaiah of Jerusalem See Isaiah.

Ishmael The son of Abraham and Hagar; he was not the son of the promise; he and his mother were expelled by Sarah and Abraham.

Israel A secondary name for Jacob; the name of the ten northern tribes who formed the "kingdom of Israel" (alternatives are "Ephraim" and "Samaria"), destroyed in 721 B.C.E.; also used as the name of the twelve tribes and for the whole territory occupied by the Israelites, Canaan; historically, Jews have continued to regard themselves as the true continuation of the ancient Israelite national-religious community; in modern times, it also refers to the political state of Israel; Christians came to consider themselves to be the "true" Israel, thus also a continuation of the ancient traditions.

Israeli, Israelis Modern term designating citizens of the modern state of Israel; to be distinguished from Israelites.

Israelites (from "sons of Israel") Primarily the inhabitants of the ancient state of Israel, but also used of the Hebrews from the time of Moses to the monarchy.

J The acronym for the Yahwist source of the Pentateuch. See Yahwist narrative.

Jacob cycle The narratives of Genesis 25:19-35:29 that revolve around the ancestor Jacob.

Jacob The second son of Isaac and Rebekah; he was the twin brother of Esau; his name was changed to *Israel* after he wrestled with God at the Jabbok River; he became the recipient of the ancestral promises and his twelve sons because the tribes of Israel.

Japheth One of the sons of Noah, he was blessed because with Shem he covered his father's nakedness.

Jebus The Canaanite city conquered by David and made his capital, Jerusalem.

JEDP See Documentary hypothesis.

Jehoiachin King of Judah for only three months in 598 B.C.E., he was taken captive to Babylon.

Jehoiakim (609-598) One of the last kings of Judah.

Jehovah An early and mistaken attempt to represent the special Hebrew name for deity, YHWH; a more probable reconstruction of the divine name is Yahweh.

Jehu (843-815) King of Israel who was instrumental in engineering the demise of the house of Ahab.

Jephthah A judge of Israel from the book of Judges.

Jeremiah A prophet in Judah during the Babylonian crisis (late seventh and early sixth centuries B.C.E.); he was persecuted because of his unpopular prophetic statements, including a prediction of the fall of Jerusalem; also, the prophetic book containing his oracles and narratives about him.

Jeremiah's complaints See Complaints of Jeremiah.

Jericho The first city in Canaan conquered by Joshua and the Israelites.

Jeroboam (922-901) An administrator in Solomon's court who rebelled and became the first king of the northern kingdom of Israel; he built non-Yahwistic shrines in the cities of Dan and Bethel; a king of Israel in the eighth century B.C.E. also held this name and is sometimes referred to as Jeroboam II (786-746).

Jerusalem The political and religious capital of Israel when it was united, then of the southern kingdom of Judah; David captured Jebus and made it his capital city, the City of David; Mount Zion is the ridge in Jerusalem on which the royal palace and temple were built; Jerusalem is where Jesus/Joshua was crucified and resurrected.

Jeshua Another spelling of Joshua; Jeshua was the high priest of Judea in the sixth century B.C.E. during the time of Zerubbabel, Haggai, and Zechariah.

Jesus/Joshua ("Jesus" is the Greek attempt to transliterate the Semitic name "Joshua") The Palestinian popular figure from the first century C.E. whose death and resurrection as God's Messiah/Christ became foundational for an early Jewish sub-group known as the Nazarenes, from which Christianity ultimately developed as a separate religion.

Jethro Father of Zipporah and father-in-law of Moses, also called Reuel.

Jew The term applied to the people of God after the Babylonian exile; it is derived from the Hebrew/Aramaic term for Judeans, *jehudi*.

Jezebel The Phoenician wife of Ahab who promoted Baal worship in Israel and opposed Elijah the prophet.

Jezreel A Israelite royal city of the Omride dynasty, the place where Jehu executed Jezebel; it became a byword for Jehu's cruelty and Hosea named his son Jezreel to signal God's judgment.

Joab David's military commander.

Job A righteous man whom God tested by disaster and personal suffering; in the end God restored his wealth and family; the book of Job, considered a work of wisdom literature, contains the story.

Joel One of the twelve prophets; of uncertain date but perhaps fourth century, a prophet who preached the Day of Yahweh and the pouring out of Yahweh's spirit on everyone.

Jonah An eighth century B.C.E. Israelite prophet who was called to preach to the Assyrians in Nineveh; the book of Jonah is one of the twelve prophets.

Jonathan A son of king Saul, he had a special relationship with David; he was killed by the Philistines on Mount Gilboa.

Jordan The river which flows from the Sea of Galilee to the Dead Sea; it is the border between Canaan and Transjordan.

Joseph cycle The collection of stories centered on Joseph, son of Jacob, contained in Genesis 37-50.

Joseph Son of Jacob by Rachel; brother of Benjamin; he was sold into slavery by his brothers and became a high official within the Egyptian government; his sons Ephraim and Manasseh became tribes within Israel.

Josephus (also known as Flavius Josephus) The Jewish general and author in the latter part of the first century C.E. who wrote a massive history (*Antiquities*) of the Jews and a detailed treatment of the Jewish revolt against Rome in 66-73 C.E.

Joshua Moses' aide during the wilderness sojourn; after the death of Moses he led the Hebrews into the Promised Land; another figure was called Joshua (sometimes Jeshua), the high priest of the Jerusalem community which rebuilt the temple.

Josiah (640-609) King of Judah who reformed Judean religion and died in battle at Megiddo.

Josianic reform The religious reform of 622 B.C.E. initiated by Josiah, king of Judah, after the book of the covenant was found in the Jerusalem temple; it is sometimes called the Deuteronomic reform, because the book appears to have been an early form of Deuteronomy.

Jubilee (from Hebrew *yovel*, "ram's-horn trumpet") Every fiftieth year was a jubilee (the year following seven times seven years, or seven weeks of years); special arrangements during this year were designed to aid the poor and dispossessed.

Judah Jacob's fourth son, he was the ancestor of the tribe of Judah; Judah became the name of the southern kingdom after the northern ten tribes separated from Judah and Benjamin.

Judah the Prince (also known as Judah Hanasi) Head of the rabbinic Jewish community in Palestine around 200 C.E.; credited with publication of the Mishnah.

Judaism From the Hebrew name of the ancestor Judah, whose name also came to designate the tribe and tribal district in which Jerusalem was located; thus the inhabitants of Judah and members of the tribe of Judah come to be called "Judahites" or, in short form, "Jews"; the religious outlook, beliefs, and practices associated with these people comes to be called "Judaism," and has varying characteristics at different times and places, such as early Judaism and rabbinic Judaism.

Judas Maccabee A second century B.C.E. Judean who led the Jewish Maccabean revolt against the Hellenistic Seleucid occupation of Jerusalem and Judea.

Judge In the period of the Judges, a person who held off Israel's enemies, for example, Ehud, Deborah, Gideon, Jephthah, and Samson.

Judges The period of the Judges was between the conquest and the Davidic monarchy when Israelite tribes were settling the land of Canaan; the book of Judges contains the stories of the individual judges.

Kashrut See Kosher.

Ketuvim (Hebrew for "Writings") The last of the three main divisions of the Hebrew Bible (the *k* of Tanak), including Psalms, Proverbs, Job, the Five Megillot or Five

Scrolls (Song of Songs, Ruth, Lamentations, Ecclesiastes, Esther), Daniel, Ezra, Nehemiah and Chronicles.

Kingdom of God The realm where God rules; the state of the world in which God's will is fulfilled; expected to be brought into being at the end of time when the Messiah returns.

Kosher (Hebrew *kasher, kashrut* for "proper, ritually correct") Kosher refers to ritually correct Jewish dietary practices; traditional Jewish dietary laws are based on biblical legislation; only land animals that chew the cud and have split hooves (sheep, beef; not pigs, camels) are permitted and must be slaughtered in a special way; further, meat products may not be eaten with milk products or immediately thereafter; of sea creatures, only those (fish) having fins and scales are permitted; fowl is considered a meat food and also has to be slaughtered in a special manner.

Laban Rebekah's brother and Jacob's uncle who lived in Aram; Jacob became wealthy there and married his daughters Rachel and Leah.

Lament A cry of pain and grief; in the study of the Psalms, the lament, also called a complaint, is the literary type which expresses a cry of help, either of an individual or the community.

Latter prophets The technical name for the collection of prophetic writings comprised of the books of the three "major" prophets (Isaiah, Jeremiah, Ezekiel) and those of the twelve "minor" (or shorter) prophets, collectively called the Book of the Twelve.

Law See Commandments, Halakah, Oral torah, Ten commandments, Torah.

Leah Daughter of Laban, the first wife of Jacob who had six sons and one daughter.

Legend A general term denoting stories about heroes, usually from the distant past, whose primary intent is not historical accuracy but entertainment, illustration, and instruction; some scholars consider certain of the ancestral accounts in Genesis, some stories of Moses in Exodus, as well as some stories about Elijah and Elisha, to be legends.

Leviathan (also Litan or Lotan) The mythological sea monster of prophetic literature and the book of Job, also attested in Ugaritic literature.

Levirate marriage (from Latin *levir* for Hebrew *yabam*, "brother-in-law") A biblical system of marriage in which the *levir* marries his brother's widow (see Deuteronomy 25:5–10).

Levi A son of Jacob, one of the twelve tribes of Israel.

Levite(s) A member of the tribe of Levi; the Levites took care of the tabernacle and later the temple but generally could not serve as priests; only Levites specifically from the family of Aaron could become priests.

Literary criticism (sometimes called *literary analysis* or *literary critique*) A critical, but not necessarily criticizing or judgmental, examination of a piece of literature that seeks to determine the type of literature it is, as well as its conventions, stylistic techniques, structure, and strategies; in older scholarship, it may mean source criticism.

Liturgy (adj. liturgical). Rites of public worship, usually institutionalized in temple, synagogue, or church tradition.

Lo-ammi A child of Gomer, the wife of the prophet Hosea; the name means "not my people."

Lo-ruhamah A child of Gomer, the wife of the prophet Hosea; the name means "no mercy."

Lord (Hebrew *adonay*) This term (note the use of small capital letters) substitutes for God's Hebrew personal name Yahweh in most modern translations of the Hebrew Bible. See Yahweh.

Lord God A compound divine name; a translation of YHWH Elohim.

Lot The nephew of Abraham who accompanied him to Canaan.

Lots A mechanical means of divination, perhaps similar to dice or drawing straws, that was used to determine God's decision in certain matters; used in the phrase *to cast lots*.

LXX The abbreviation for the Septuagint, the Greek translation of the Hebrew scriptures done in the last centuries B.C.E. See Septuagint.

Maccabaean From the period of Judas Maccabaeus (Judah Maccabee) and his brothers, second century B.C.E.

Maccabean revolt The second century B.C.E. Jewish revolt against Antiochus IV led by the family of Mattathias, including his son Judas the Maccabee, described in 1 Maccabees.

Malachi One of the twelve prophets; of uncertain date but probably fifth century, a prophet who foresaw the return of Elijah.

Manna The food God provided to the Hebrews while they sojourned in the wilderness for forty years.

Marduk The chief god of the Babylonians and patron god of Babylon; he is the hero-god of the Enuma Elish.

Masoretes, Masoretic text (Hebrew for "transmitters," derived from Hebrew *masorah*, "tradition") The Masoretes were rabbis in ninth century C.E. Palestine who sought to preserve the traditional text of the Bible (hence called the Masoretic text), which is still used in contemporary synagogues; the Masoretes were scholars who encouraged Bible study and attempted to achieve uniformity by establishing rules for correcting the text in matters of spelling, grammar, and pronunciation; they introduced vowel signs, accents (pointing) and marginal notes (*masorah*).

Matriarch (from Latin for "first mother") A term used to refer to female ancestors such as Sarah, Rebecca, Rachel, and Leah.

Matzah Jewish unleavened bread used at Passover.

Megillah (pl. *megillot*; Hebrew for "scroll") Usually refers to the biblical scroll of Esther read on the festival of Purim.

Menorah The multi-armed lamp or candelabrum that was used in the tabernacle and temple; a nine-branched menorah is used at Hannukah, while the seven- branched was used in the ancient Temple.

Mesopotamia (from Greek for "between the rivers") The land defined by the Tigris and Euphrates rivers, this is the location of the birth of civilization and the origin of the Israelites; the Israelites interacted with Mesopotamian people throughout their history.

Messiah (from Hebrew *meshiach*; "anointed one"; equivalent to Greek *christos*) Ancient priests and kings (and sometimes prophets) of Israel were anointed with oil; in early Judaism, the term came to mean a royal descendant of the dynasty of David and redeemer figure who would restore the united kingdom of Israel and Judah and usher in an age of peace, justice and plenty; the messianic age was believed by some Jews to be a time of perfection of human institutions, others believed it to be a time of radical new beginnings, a new heaven and earth, after divine judgment and destruction; the title came to be applied to Jesus/Joshua of Nazareth by his followers, who were soon called *Christians* in Greek and Latin usage.

Mezuzah (pl. *mezuzot*; Hebrew for "doorpost") A parchment scroll with selected Torah verses (Deuteronomy 6:4–9; 11:13–21) placed in a container and affixed to the exteri- or doorposts (at the right side of the entrance) of observant Jewish homes (see Deuteronomy 6:1–4), and sometimes also to interior doorposts of rooms; the word *shaddai*, "Almighty," usually is inscribed on the container.

Micah One of the twelve prophets; an eighth century Judean prophet who advocated justice for all people.

Michal A daughter of Saul, given in marriage to David; she criticized David's behavior and he refused thereafter to have relations with her.

Midian Territory south of Canaan, of uncertain exact location; perhaps in the Sinai peninsula or western Arabia; Moses' father-in-law Jethro was a priest of Midian; the Midianites afflicted the Israelites during the time of the Judges.

Midrash (pl. *midrashim*; from Hebrew *darash*, "to inquire," whence it comes to mean "exposition" of scripture) The term refers to the "commentary" literature developed in classical Judaism that attempts to interpret Jewish scriptures in a thorough manner; literary Midrash may focus either on halakah, directing the Jew to specific patterns of religious practice, or on haggadah, dealing with theological ideas, ethical teachings, popular philosophy, imaginative exposition, legend, allegory, animal fables, etc.—that is, whatever is not halaka.

Midwife A nurse who helped with the birth of a baby; Shiphrah and Puah were Hebrew midwives who refused to cooperate in Pharaoh's scheme to kill male children.

Millennium (from Latin for "thousand"; adj. millenarian) A thousand year period; *millenarian* has to do with the expected millennium, or thousand-year reign of Christ prophesied in the New Testament book of Revelation ("the Apocalypse"), a time in which the world would be brought to perfection; millenarian movements often grow up around predictions that this perfect time is about to begin. See also Apocalypse and Eschatology.

Miriam The sister of Moses and Aaron; she led the Israelites in worship after the crossing of the Red Sea.

Mishnah (Hebrew for "repetition, teaching") A thematic compilation of legal material, in particular, a compilation by Rabbi Judah Hanasi ("the Prince"), of laws based ultimately on principles laid down in the Torah; produced aound 200 C.E., it became the most authoritative collection of oral torah; the code is divided into six major units and sixty-three minor ones; the work is the authoritative legal tradition of the early sages and is the basis of the legal discussions of the Talmud.

Mitzvah (pl. *mitzvot*; Hebrew for "commandment, obligation") A ritual or ethical duty or act of obedience to God's will. See also Commandments.

Moab A territory or country located in Transjordan, to the east of the land of Israel; a frequent enemy of the Israelites.

Monarchy Any state ruled or headed by a monarch; Israel and Judah were ruled by monarchies during the period of the kingdoms.

Monolatry The worship of one god while recognizing the existence of others; some scholars describe the religion of Israel as monolatry before the time of the prophets.

Monotheism The belief that there is only one God, and that no other gods even exist; it is unlikely that Israel early in her history construed reality in this way; rather, it seems that they only went so far as to claim Yahweh as their God, the god of Israel, leaving the question of the existence of other gods to later theologians and prophets.

Mordecai The uncle of Esther who looked after her and urged her to do everything in her power to effect the deliverance of the Jews throughout the Persian empire.

Mosaic covenant The covenant Yahweh mediated through Moses, including the ten commandments and rules for serving God.

Moses The leader of the Hebrews at the time of the exodus from Egypt (thirteenth century B.C.E.); he led the people of Israel out of Egyptian bondage; God revealed the Torah to him on Mount Sinai; he is also described as the first Hebrew prophet; throughout Jewish history he is the exalted man of faith and religious leader without peer.

Mount Gilboa The location south of the Sea of Galilee where Saul and his sons died while fighting the Philistines.

Mount Sinai The mountain in the Sinai peninsula where God communicated with Moses and revealed the covenant and ten commandments.

Mount Zion. See Zion.

Myth A story, theme, object, or character regarded as embodying a foundational aspect of a culture; the creation stories in Genesis 1-3 may be called myths, not in the sense that they are factually false, but because they embody core beliefs of Israelite culture.

Nadab and Abihu These two sons of Aaron offered "strange fire" to God, for which they both died.

Nahum One of the twelve prophets; a late seventh century Judean prophet who announced the coming destruction of Nineveh, the capital of the Assyrian empire.

Naomi The Israelite mother-in-law of Ruth.

Nathan David's court prophet who mediated the Davidic covenant and exposed David's transgressions.

Navi (sometimes spelled *nabi*; pl. *neviim*) Term for "prophet" in ancient Israel. See Nevi'im.

Nazirite A person dedicated by a strict vow to do special work for God; elements of the vow could include not cutting hair and refraining from alcohol; Samson lived under a Nazirite vow.

Nazirite vow A pledge to live under a special set of restrictions as an act of dedication to God, detailed in Numbers 6.

Nebuchadnezzar (605-562) Monarch of the Neo-Babylonian empire who invaded Judah and destroyed Jerusalem in 587.

Nehemiah The Jewish cupbearer of Artaxerxes of Persia in the fifth century B.C.E.; appointed governor of Judea, he rebuilt the walls of Jerusalem after the Babylonian exile.

Nevi'im (sometimes spelled *nebi'im*; Hebrew for "prophets") The second main division of the Hebrew Bible, comprising the Former and the Latter Prophets; the *n* of Tanak. See Tanak.

New covenant A theme of the prophet Jeremiah based on the Mosaic covenant; God would renew the covenant with his people and write it on their hearts.

New exodus A theme of the prophet Second Isaiah based on the exodus from Egypt led by Moses; Second Isaiah anticipated the release of Judean refugees from Babylonian exile in a new act of divine deliverance.

New Testament (abbreviated NT) The collection of Christian canonical writings that together with the Old Testament/Hebrew Bible constitute the Christian Bible. See Apocrypha.

Nineveh The capital city of the Assyrian empire, located on the Tigris river.

Noah He built a boat and survived the Flood with his family and representatives of the animal world; God made a covenant with him promising never again to destroy the world with a flood.

Noahic covenant The covenant God made with Noah promising he would never again send a flood; God signaled the covenant with the rainbow.

Obadiah One of the twelve prophets; a sixth century Judean prophet who condemned Edom for its cruel treatment of conquered Judah.

Offering Something given to God as an act of worship, often animals and grains; the offering of animals made right the relationship between God and the worshiper.

Old Testament (abbreviated OT) The name of the Hebrew Bible used in the Christian community; it presupposes that there is a New Testament; the term *testament* goes back to *testamentum*, the Latin equivalent for the Hebrew word covenant; for most Protestant Christians, the Old Testament is identical to the Hebrew Bible; for classical Roman Catholic and Greek Orthodox Christianity, the Old Testament also includes the Apocrypha.

Oracle A statement originating with God, delivered by a prophet, and directed to an audience.

Oral torah (also called *oral law*) In traditional Jewish pharisaic/rabbinic thought, God revealed instructions for living through both the written scriptures and through a parallel process of orally transmitted traditions; these oral applications of the Torah for contemporary situations later took written form in the Mishnah and other Jewish literature; the Jewish belief in both a written and an oral torah is known as "the dual Torah"; critics of this approach within Judaism include the Sadducees and the Karaites.

Oral tradition Material passed down through generations by word of mouth before taking fixed written form.

Original sin In classical Christian thought, the fundamental state of sinfulness and guilt, inherited from the first man Adam, that infects all of humanity but can be removed through depending on Christ.

Orthodox (from Greek for "correct opinion/outlook," as opposed to heterodox or heretical) The judgment that a position is "orthodox" depends on what are accepted as the operative "rules" or authorities at the time; over the course of history, the term "orthodox" has come to denote the dominant surviving forms that have proved themselves to be "traditional" or "classical" or "mainstream" (e.g. rabbinic Judaism; the Roman Catholic and Greek Orthodox Christian churches).

OT See Old Testament.

P The acronym for the Priestly source of the Torah/Pentateuch. See Priestly document.

Palestine (Greek form of "Philistine," for the seacoast population encountered by early geographers) An ancient designation for the area between Syria (to the north) and Egypt (to the south), between the Mediterranean Sea and the River Jordan; Canaan; roughly, modern Israel.

Palestinian Judaism The postbiblical form of Judaism that developed in Palestine, in distinction from Hellenistic Judaism.

Paraenesis (adj. paraenetic) A sermon or exhortation; Deuteronomy has a paraénetic style.

Parallelism The literary form pervasive in biblical poetry whereby the first line (the A–line) of a couplet is in some way mirrored or doubled in the second line (the B–line).

Passover (Hebrew *pesah*) The major Jewish spring holiday (with agricultural aspects) also known as *hag hamatzot*, "festival of unleavened bread," commemorating the exodus or deliverance of the Hebrew people from Egypt (see Exodus 12–13); the festival lasts eight days, during which Jews refrain from eating all leavened foods and products; a special ritual meal (called the Seder) is prepared, and a traditional narrative (called the Haggadah), supplemented by hymns and songs, marks the event.

Patriarch (from Latin for "first father") The father and ruler of a family; the head of a tribe.

Patriarchs A common designation for the early founding figures of ancient Semitic tradition (before Moses) such as Abraham, Isaac, Jacob, and the twelve tribal figureheads of Israel (Judah, Benjamin, etc.); the patriarchs and matriarchs together are called the forbears or *ancestors* of Israel. See Ancestors.

Pentateuch (from Greek for "five scroll jars" it comes to mean "five books/scrolls"; adj. pentateuchal) Refers to the first five books of the Hebrew Bible traditionally attributed to Moses that together comprise the Torah (the *t* of Tanak): Genesis, Exodus, Leviticus, Numbers, and Deuteronomy; known in Jewish tradition as *Torat Mosheh*, the teaching of Moses.

Pentecost (Greek for "fiftieth [day]") A Jewish feast celebrated fifty days after Passover marking the first fruits of the agricultural year. See Shavuot.

Personification The literary device of portraying an idea or non-human object as a human being.

Perushim (Hebrew for "Pharisees") See Pharisees.

Pesach (Hebrew for "passover") The festival recalling the escape from Egypt in the exodus. See Passover.

Petition A speech form used especially in biblical psalms whereby the psalmist pleads with God for help, deliverance, or forgiveness.

Pharaoh Egyptian term for "great house" that became the generic term for a king of Egypt.

Pharisees (from Hebrew *perushim*, "separatists"; adj. pharisaic). The name given to a group or movement in early Judaism, the origin and nature of which is unclear; many scholars identify them with the later sages and rabbis who taught the oral and written torah; according to Josephus and the New Testament, the Pharisees believed in the immortality of souls and resurrection of the dead, in a balance between predestination and free will, in angels as active divine agents, and in authoritative oral law; in the early Christian materials, Pharisees are often depicted as leading opponents of Jesus/Joshua and his followers, and are often linked with "scribes" but distinguished from the Sadducees.

Philistia Beginning in the twelfth century B.C.E., the territory on the southern Canaanite coastal plain where the Philistines lived.

Philistine(s) An inhabitant of Philistia; the Philistines were the most significant external threat to the Israelites during the time of the Judges and the early monarchy.

Philo Judeus "The Jew" of Alexandria; Greek speaking (and writing) prolific Jewish author in the first century C.E., he provides extensive evidence for Jewish thought in the Greco-Roman ("hellenistic") world outside of Palestine.

Phineas The grandson of Aaron who violently defended the covenant; he was granted the "covenant of priesthood" by which the line of Aaron was given the privelege of the priestly office forever. Another Phineas was a son of Eli; see Hophni.

Phylactery (pl. phylacteries; Greek for "protector") See Tefillin.

Plagues The series of divine disasters described in Exodus 5-11 that were designed to secure the release of the Hebrews out of Egypt.

Praise (Hebrew *hallelujah* means "Praise Yahweh!") A speech form used extensively in the psalms whereby the psalmist extols the greatness of God.

Priest (Hebrew *kohen*) A functionary usually associated, in antiquity, with temples and their rites; a priest offered sacrifices and prayers to God on behalf of the people; in Israel, only Aaronic Levites could be legitimate priests; in classical Christianity, the office of priest was developed in connection with celebration of the mass and eucharist, and with celibacy as an important qualification especially in Roman Catholicism.

Priestly code The body of legislation in the Pentateuch that comes from the Priestly source.

Priestly document (also called the priestly source; abbreviated P) A literary source used in the composition of the Torah/Pentateuch; it probably was composed in Babylonia in the sixth century B.C.E.

Primary history The foundation story of Israel consisting of the Pentateuch and Former Prophets.

Primeval story The account of earliest events found in Genesis 1–11.

Primogeniture The state of being the first-born or eldest child of the same parents; the right of the eldest child, especially the eldest son, to inherit the entire estate of one or both parents; this is an important theme in the Torah/Pentateuch relating to Ishmael and Isaac, Jacob and Esau, and Joseph and his brothers.

Profane To make a holy thing impure by treating it with disrespect or irreverence.

Promised Land Phrase used with a religious and covenantal connotation that designates the territory west of the Jordan River, for the most part coextensive with Canaan.

Prophecy A message from God that a prophet delivers to the people.

Prophesy The act of delivering a prophetic message of God to the people.

Prophet (from Greek for "to speak for, to speak forth") Designation given to accepted spokespersons of God (or their opposites, "false prophets"); a person who speaks in the name of God.

Prophetic eschatology The perspective on the goal and end of history held by Old Testament prophets.

Prophets A designation for the second main section of the Hebrew Bible, called the *Nevi'im*; the *n* of Tanak. See Tanak.

Prostitute A person who allowed the use of his or her body for sexual relations in exchange for compensation; Israel was metaphorically compared to a prostitute when it worshiped Baal gods.

Proto-Judaism See Early Judaism.

Proverb A short, pithy saying in frequent and widespread use that expresses a basic truth or practical precept; the book of Proverbs is one of the Writings and is classified as wisdom literature.

Psalter The book of the writings that contains 150 psalms.

Pseudepigrapha (adj. pseudepigraphical; from Greek *pseudos*, "deceit, untruth," and *epigraphe*, "writing, inscription") Intertestamental apocryphal writings purporting to be by somebody (usually a famous historical or legendary figure) who is not the author, such as Adam/Eve, Enoch, Abraham, Moses, Isaiah, Ezra, etc.; the term is sometimes used generically for deutero-canonical writings not in the Apocrypha.

Pseudonymity The practice of ascribing a work to someone, often a notable from the past, who was not the actual author.

Purim (from Hebrew for "lots") A Jewish festival commemorating the deliverance of Jews in Persia who were threated with genocide, as described in the book of Esther; held in late winter (between Hannukah and Passover), on the 14th of Adar. See Megillah.

Qohelet (Hebrew term related to the word *qahal*, "gathering, congregation"; translated *ekklesiastes* in Greek) The Hebrew name of the book of Ecclesiastes; the term used of the purported writer of the book of Ecclesiastes.

Qumran (Khirbet Qumran) The site near the northwest corner of the Dead Sea in modern Israel (west bank) where the main bulk of the Jewish "Dead Sea Scrolls" were discovered beginning in 1947; the "Qumran community" that apparently produced the scrolls seems to have flourished from the third century B.C.E. to the first century C.E., and is usually identified with the Jewish Essenes.

Rabbi (adj. rabbinic; Hebrew for "my master") An authorized teacher of the classical Jewish tradition after the fall of the second temple in 70 C.E.; traditionally, rabbis serve as the legal and spiritual guides of their congregations and communities. See Oral torah.

Rabbinic Judaism The Judaism associated with the Pharisees that survived the Jewish revolts against Rome to become the dominant shape of Judaism.

Rachel The daughter of Laban, most loved wife of Jacob, and mother of Joseph and Benjamin.

Rahab The prostitue of Jericho who harbored and assisted the Israelite spies prior to the conquest of Canaan; not to be confused with the Rahab of mythic and prophetic literture that is another name for the sea monster.

Ramses (1290-1224) According to most historians Ramses II was the king of Egypt at the time of the Hebrews' exodus (thirteenth century B.C.E.).

Rebekah (sometimes spelled Rebecca) The sister of Laban, Isaac's wife, mother of Esau and Jacob.

Red Sea See Reed Sea.

Redaction criticism (sometimes called *redaction critique*) The analysis of a book of the Hebrew Bible to determine the contribution of the editor (called the *redactor*) as he compiled and edited the book from older sources.

Redactor (n. redaction) A synonym for editor of a composite work, the one responsible for choosing and combining source materials into one coherent literary work; redaction is the editorial work of the redactor.

Redeem (Hebrew *go'el*, "redeemer"; n. redemption) To free from captivity or domination by paying a ransom; to buy back.

Reed Sea (Hebrew *yam suf*, also called the Sea of Reeds) This is the body of water the Israelites crossed on dry ground as part of the exodus from Egypt; it is termed the Red Sea in most English versions of the Old Testament.

Rehoboam (922-915 B.C.E.) The son of Solomon who became the first king of Judah after the division of the kingdoms.

Resident alien Also called a *sojourner*, a person who lives in a country but does not hold citizenship; the Old Testament specifies certain rights for resident aliens.

Resurrection The idea that dead persons who have found favor with God will ultimately (in eschatological times) be raised from the dead with restored bodily form.

Retribution Punishment for doing wrong; the theology of retribution as found in Deuteronomic theology and in wisdom literature holds that God punishes people for their bad deeds.

Reuel The name of Moses' father-in-law; in some texts he is called Jethro.

Rhetorical criticism (sometimes called *rhetorical analysis* or *rhetorical critique*) The analysis of a text on the basis of its rhetorical devices; it is very similar to literary criticism.

Righteous (n. righteousness) To be one who does what is right; to be in a right relationship with God.

Ritual decalogue The set of ten regulations found in Exodus 34 that Moses wrote on two tablets.

Rosh hashanah (Hebrew for "beginning of the year") Jewish New Year celebration in the fall of the year, the month of Tishri.

Rosh hodesh (Hebrew for "beginning of a lunar month") The New Moon Festival.

Royal grant covenant A type of covenant employed by monarchs that essentially consisted of a grant or gift to a faithful underling.

Ruth The Moabite widow who followed her mother-in-law Naomi back to Bethlehem; she married Boaz and was an ancestor of David.

Sabbath (from Hebrew *shabbat*, "to cease, rest") The seventh day of the week, a day of rest and worship; it extends from sunset Friday to sunset Saturday; it was the sign of the Mosaic covenant, and became especially important as an identifier of Jewishness beginning in the Babylonian exile.

Sackcloth A rough cloth, usually woven from goats' hair; clothing made from sackcloth was worn during mourning rituals as a sign of grief and sorrow.

Sacred Applies to holy things, things set apart for God in a special way; sacred is the opposite of profane.

Sacrifice (verb, "to offer a sacrifice"; noun, "an offering given to God to atone for the sins of the people or to establish fellowship with God") Though there are many specific types of sacrifices, typically a sacrificial animal was slaughtered and burned on an altar, and its blood was splattered on the altar.

Sadducees A group of Jewish leaders, many of them priests, who ruled during the late Second Temple period; Sadducees supported priestly authority and rejected traditions not directly grounded in the Torah/Pentateuch, such as the concept of life after death; they ceased to exist when the temple was destroyed in 70 C.E.

Saga A long, prose narrative having an episodic structure developed around stereotyped themes or object; sagas abound in the primeval and ancestral collections of Genesis.

Samaria Was built as the capital of Israel, the northern kingdom, in the ninth century B.C.E. and fell in 721 B.C.E., after which leading members were deported; exiles from elsewhere were settled here and mixed with the Israelites who remained; their descendants are known as Samaritans.

Samaritans Residents of the district of Samaria north of Judah and a sub-group in early Judaism; they are said to have recognized only the Torah/Pentateuch as Scripture and Mount Gerizim as the sacred center rather than Jerusalem; there was ongoing hostility between Samaritans and Judahites; Samaritan communities exist to the present.

Samson An Israelite judge and strong-man who harassed Philistines during the period of the Judges.

Samuel The last judge of Israel and the first prophet, he was also a priest; the son of Hannah and Elkanah, he succeeded Eli as priest, anointed first Saul and then David to be king.

Sanctify (n. sanctification) To make holy.

Sanhedrin (from Greek for "assembly" [of persons seated together]) A legislative and judicial body from the period of early Judaism and into rabbinic times, traditionally composed of 71 members. See also Synagogue, Church.

Sapiential (From Latin *sapiens*, "to be wise") Containing or exhibiting wisdom; characterized by wisdom.

Sarah (Sarai) The wife of Abraham; first called Sarai, she was barren until God enabled conception and Isaac was born in her old age.

Satan (from Hebrew for "accuser") In the Old Testament a member of the divine council who challenged God, especially in the books of Job and Zechariah.

Saul (1020-1000) The first king of Israel, he was anointed by Samuel but was later deposed because of disobedience.

Scribe (sometimes called an *amanuensis*, the Greek term for "scribe") A person trained in literacy who copied letters and books, and sometimes trained in the legal tradition; Baruch was Jeremiah's scribe; Ezra was a Jewish-Persian scribe.

Scriptures General designation for canonical or biblical writings.

Second Isaiah (sometimes called *Deutero-Isaiah*) The anonymous author of the book of Isaiah, chapters 40-55.

Second temple The Jerusalem temple rebuilt by Zerubbabel and completed in 515 B.C.E. that stood until it was destroyed by the Romans in 70 C.E.; the first temple was the one built by Solomon, which stood until 587 B.C.E.

Second Zechariah The latter portion (chapters 9-14) of the book of Zechariah datable to the Greek period.

Seder (pl. *sedarim*; Hebrew for "order") The traditional Jewish evening service and opening of the celebration of Passover, which includes special food symbols and narratives; the order of the service is highly regulated, and the traditional narrative is known as the Passover Haggadah.

Seleucid The dynasty of Seleucus, a general of Alexander the Great, that ruled Syria and Asia Minor after Alexander's death. Seleucid rule in Palestine was ended by the Maccabees in the second century B.C.E.

Semitic Pertaining to a race, language or culture linked to the line of Shem (see Genesis 10); Semitic languages include Hebrew, Aramaic, Arabic, and Akkadian.

Sennacherib (704-681) Monarch of the Neo-Assyrian empire who besieged Hezekiah's Jerusalem in 701.

Septuagint The Greek translation of the Old Testament, consisting of the books of the Hebrew Bible and some deutero-canonical books, now know as the Apocrypha; traditionally dated to the reign of Ptolemy II (285-246) it is abbreviated LXX because it supposedly was translated by some seventy Jewish scholars.

Servant of Yahweh (also called the *suffering servant*) The otherwise anonymous figure of the book of Isaiah (Second Isaiah) who delivered God's people through suffering, variously identified by interpreters as Jeremiah, Zerubbabel, Israel, and Jesus of Nazareth.

Setting-in-life (German *Sitz im Leben*) Generally referring to the context of a tradition or ritual. See Form Criticism.

Shabbat (Hebrew for "rest") See Sabbath.

Shalmaneser V (726-722) The monarch of the Neo-Assyrian empire who laid siege to Samaria, capital of Israel, thus preparing the way for Israel's destruction.

Shalom Hebrew word for "peace, wholeness, completeness."

Shavuot (sometimes spelled *shabuot*; Hebrew for "weeks"; Pentecost) Observed fifty days after Passover (*pesach*), the day the first sheaf of grain was offered to the priest; it celebrates the harvest and the giving of the Torah; also known as Festival of First Fruits.

Shechem City in central Israel that was the capital of the tribal confederacy during the time of Joshua and the Judges.

Shekel A unit of measure by weight, often used as a monetary designation.

Shem One of the three sons of Noah, he was chosen for special blessing; he was an ancestor of Abraham.

Shema (Hebrew imperative, "Hear!") Title of the Great Commandment, the fundamental, monotheistic statement of Judaism, found in Deut. 6:4 ("Hear, O Israel, the Lord is our God, the Lord is One"); this statement affirms the unity of God, and is recited daily in the liturgy (along with Deuterenomy 6:5–9, 11.13–21; Numbers 15:37–41 and other passages), and customarily before sleep at night; this proclamation also climaxes special liturgies (such as Yom Kippur), and is central to the confessional before death and the ritual of martyrdom; the Shema is inscribed on the mezuzah and the tefillin; in public services, it is recited in unison.

Sheol The shadowy underworld to which the departed spirits of the dead go.

Sheshbazzar A prince of Judah who led the first return of Judean refugees from Babylonian exile in 538 B.C.E.

Shiloh The city in central Israel that contained a sanctuary during the time of Eli and Samuel where the ark of the covenant was housed.

Shofar A ram's horn trumpet; in Jewish worship, a ram's horn sounded at Rosh Hashanah morning worship and at the conclusion of Yom Kippur, as well as other times in that period during the fall.

Sin Transgression or offense against God's laws or wishes; more generally in Christian belief, a continuing state of estrangement from God. See also Original sin.

Sinai The desert region south of Canaan and east of Egypt.

Sojourn A temporary stay, a brief period of residence; Israel's wilderness sojourn in the Sinai after the exodus lasted forty years.

Solomon (961-922) The son of David and Bathsheba who became the king of united Israel after David; he was renowned for his wisdom; he built the temple of Yahweh in Jerusalem.

Son of Man A phrase found in Daniel 7 that refers to a divine authority figure who has the appearance of a human being; it is also the phrase simply meaning "fellow" used by God throughout the book of Ezekiel to refer to the prophet.

Soul (Hebrew *nefesh*) In the Old Testament this refers to the whole person, including body, psyche and spiritual identity.

Source criticism (also called *source analysis* or *source critique*) The analysis of the Hebrew Bible to determine its underlying litlerary sources. See Documentary hypothesis.

Stanza One of the divisions of a poem, composed of two or more lines, usually characterized by a common pattern of meter, rhyme, and number of lines.

Succession narrative (also called the *court history of David*) A narrative block of material including 1 Samuel 9-20 and 1 Kings 1-2 that details the dynastic succession struggles of David's sons.

Sukkot (Hebrew for "booths, tabernacles") A seven-day Jewish fall festival beginning on Tishri 15 commemorating the *sukkot* where Israel lived in the wilderness after the exodus; also known as *hag ha'asiph*, the Festival of Ingathering (of the harvest).

Sumer (Sumerians) An ancient region in southern Mesopotamia that contained a number of cities and city-states, some of which were founded as early as 5000 B.C.E.

Superscription The psalm label that may contain musical directions, performance notes, historical setting, and an ascription of authorship.

Suzerain A master or overlord who ruled and protected his vassal clients and to whom they owed allegiance.

Suzerainty treaty (also called *suzerainty covenant*) A formal treaty drawn up to specify the terms of the relationship between a conquered and now client state and the dominating suzerain state.

Synagogue (from Greek for "gathering") A place for meeting together that arose after the Babylonian exile; the central institution of Jewish communal worship and study since antiquity, and by extension, a term used for the place of gathering; the structure of such buildings has changed, though in all cases the ark containing the Torah scrolls faces the ancient temple site in Jerusalem.

Syncretism (Greek for "draw together, combine") Synthesis of variegated religious beliefs derived from more than one religion.

Synonymous parallelism A type of poetic parallelism in which the notion of the first line of a couplet is repeated or seconded in the second line.

Syrian-Israelite crisis (also called *Syro-Ephraimite crisis*) The political crisis of 734-733 B.C.E. when Syria and Israel (also called Ephraim) attacked Jerusalem; this was the context of the Immanuel prophecy of Isaiah 7.

Tabernacle The portable tent shrine constructed at Mount Sinai that served as the residence of Yahweh.

Tabernacles, Festival/Feast of. See Sukkot.

Talmud (Hebrew for "study, learning") Rabbinic Judaism produced two Talmuds: the one known as "Babylonian" is the most famous in the western world, and was completed around the fifth century C.E.; the other, known as the "Palestinian" or "Jerusalem" Talmud, was edited perhaps in the early fourth century C.E.; both have as their common core the Mishnah collection of the Tannaim, to which were added commentary and discussion (Gemara) by the Amoraim (teachers) of the respective locales; *gemara* thus has also become a colloquial, generic term for the Talmud and its study.

Tamar The daughter-in-law of Judah (Genesis 38); the daughter of David (2 Samuel 13).

Tanak (sometimes spelled *Tanakh*) A relatively modern name for the Hebrew Bible; the acronym is composed of the first letters of the three parts of the Hebrew Bible, the Torah (Law), the Nevi'im (Prophets), and the Ketuvim (Writings).

Tanna (Hebrew for "repeater, reciter"; adj. tannaitic, pl. tannaim) A Jewish sage from the period of Hillel (around the turn of the era) to the compilation of the Mishnah (200 C.E.), distinguished from later Amoraim; Tannaim were primarily scholars and teachers; the Mishnah, Tosefta, and halakic Midrashim were among their literary achievements.

Targum (Hebrew for "translation, interpretation") Generally used to designate Aramaic translations of the Hebrew Bible; the Septuagint is, in a sense, Greek Targums.

Tefillin (Aramaic term usually translated as *phylacteries*) Box-like accessories that accompany prayer, worn by Jewish adult males at the weekday morning services; the boxes have leather thongs attached and contain scriptural excerpts; one box (with four sections) is placed on the head, the other (with one section) is placed (customarily) on the left arm, near the heart; the biblical passages emphasize the unity of God and the duty to love God and be mindful of him with "all one's heart and mind" (for example, Exodus 13:1-10, 11-16; Deuteronomy 6.4-9; 11.13-21). See also Shema.

Tell (sometimes spelled *tel*) A mound that contains the ruined remains of a human settlement; each layer or level, called a *stratum*, represents a particular historical period.

Temple A place of worship; in the ancient world, temples were the centers of outward religious life, places at which public religious observances were normally conducted by the priestly professionals; in Israel there were many temples in various locations, but the temple in Jerusalem built by Solomon eventually became the central and only authorized place to worship Yahweh; first built by king Solomon around 950 B.C.E., it was destroyed by the Babylonian king Nebuchadnezzar in 587 B.C.E., and rebuilt about 70 years later; it was destroyed by the Romans in 70 C.E.; the site of the ancient Jewish Temple is now occupied, in part, by the golden domed Mosque of Omar; in recent times, "temple" has come to be used synonymously with synagogue in some Jewish usage.

Ten Commandments Also called the decalogue, the "ten words" God delivered through Moses that became the heart of the Mosaic covenant; it is found in two versions, Exodus 20:1-17 and Deuteronomy 5: 1-21.

Tent of meeting A simple form of the tabernacle used as the place Moses met God during the period of the wilderness sojourn.

Tetragrammaton (Greek for "four lettered [name]") See YHWH.

Tetrateuch The first four books of the Hebrew Bible, Genesis through Numbers; the use of this term implies that these belong together historically as a literary unit.

Textual criticism The study of the earliest texts and early translations of the Hebrew Bible to establish the form of the text that most closely approximates the original text, called the *autograph*; no autograph of any book of the Hebrew Bible has ever been discovered.

Thanksgiving To give thanks to God for his favors; in the study of the Psalms this is a major literary type of psalm which thanks God for individual or corporate deliverance.

Theocracy (adj. theocratic; Greek for "rule of God") A constitution in which God is regarded as ruler or sovereign.

Theodicy (Greek for "justice of God") A term that denotes the issue of God's justice in relation to the problem of human suffering, used often in discussions of the book of Job relating to the attempt to justify God in the face of evil.

Theophany (Greek for "appearance of God") A manifestation or appearance of the divine; for example, when God appears in the burning bush to Moses.

Theophoric An element in a proper name which derives from a name for God; for example, Daniel contains the theophoric component *El*.

The Satan. See Satan.

Third Isaiah The third main section of the book of Isaiah (chapters 56-66), which dates to the sixth century period of the restoration of Jerusalem.

Throne-chariot The vehicle carrying Yahweh that the prophet Ezekiel saw while in Babylonia during the exile.

Tiamat The female salt-water ocean goddess who fought Marduk; out of her body were created heaven and earth; the Babylonian name "Tiamat" is related to the Hebrew word for "deep waters," *tehom*.

Tiglath-Pileser III (745-727) Monarch of the Neo-Assyrian empire at the time of Isaiah and the Syro-Ephraimite war.

Toledot (sometimes spelled *toledoth*; Hebrew for "generations") The ten "generations" used in Genesis as a way of structuring the history told in the book.

Torah (Hebrew for "teaching, instruction, direction") In general, Torah refers to study of the whole gamut of Jewish tradition or to some aspect thereof; in its special sense, "the Torah" refers to the "five books of Moses", the first main division of the Hebrew Bible; it is the *t* of Tanak. See Pentateuch and Tanak.

Tower of Babel The tower of Genesis 11 built by humans and interpreted by God as an act of defiance.

Tradition Teachings and practices that have been handed down as standard and authoritative.

Tradition criticism (sometimes called *tradition analysis, tradition critique, tradition history,* or the *traditio-historical method*) The analysis of the Hebrew Bible to uncover possible oral strands underlying the final form of the text; or, the study of the origins and development of a particular biblical theme—for example, the covenant relationship between Yahweh and Israel.

Transjordan The territory east of the Jordan River and west of the Arabian desert; the Israelite tribes Reuben, Gad and East Manasseh settled there.

Treaty An agreement between two parties; the suzerain–vassal treaties of the ancient Middle East were the model for the covenant relationship God established with the Hebrews at Mount Sinai.

Tsaddiq (Hebrew for "righteous one"; sometimes spelled *saddik* or *zaddik*) A righteous person, the ideal Israelite characterized by wisdom and piety; the spiritual leader of the modern Hasidim is the Tsaddiq, popularly known as *rebbe*.

Twelve prophets See Book of the twelve.

Twelve tribes An ideal form of social and political organization that was believed to characterize early Israel before the monarchy; each tribe was traced back to an ancestor who was one of the sons of Jacob; in fact, the various lists of the tribes in the Hebrew Bible vary—some tribes vanished or were absorbed by others, and other tribes divided into distinct sub-units.

Type-scene A typical conventionally structured story.

Typology A form of (usually biblical) interpretation wherein a person, event, or institution is viewed as foreshadowing a later one; for example, for Christian interpreters,

Abraham's intended sacrifice of Isaac (Genesis 22) is seen as a "type" of the sacrificial death of Christ.

Unified kingdom (also called *united monarchy* and *united kingdom*) The period of Israel's monarchy when all twelve tribes were united under one king; this period lasted through the reigns of Saul, David, and Solomon.

Unleavened bread (Hebrew *matzah*; pl. *matzot*) Bread baked without leaven or yeast; the festival of unleavened bread, *matzot*, was celebrated in connection with Passover.

Ur An ancient Sumerian and Babylonian city on the Euphrates river in southern Mesopotamia; the home of Abraham before he left for Canaan.

Vassal A servant or slave; an underling who is dependent on an overlord for protection; a vassal received the use of land and military protection from a lord, and in return owed the lord loyalty, obedience, and a portion of the crops as payment.

Valley of dry bones The scene from the vision of Ezekiel 37 that anticipates the restoration of Israel.

Vaticinia ex eventu A Latin phrase meaning *prophecy from the results* or *prophecy after the event*; it is used in reference to prophecy that has been composed after the events it predicts.

Vow of praise A speech form found in the Psalms where the psalmist promises to credit God with deliverance once it happens.

Vulgate The translation of the Bible into Latin done by the Christian scholar, Jerome, in the late fourth and early fifth centuries C.E.

Waters of chaos The seas conceived as monsters who challenged Yahweh's power and authority. Also see Chaos.

Wilderness wanderings (also called the *wilderness sojourn*) The forty year period after the exodus from Egypt when the Israelites lived in the Sinai peninusla before they entered the Promised Land.

Wisdom A comprehensive term used in reference to the distinctive wisdom literature and wisdom outlook of Israelite, Mesopotamian, and Egyptian cultures; suggests a perspective on understanding the world dominated by the use of reason, a search for order, and teaching moral behavior.

Wisdom literature In the Hebrew Bible, those books of a predominantly didactic (Proverbs) or philosophical (Job, Ecclesiastes) cast; in the Apocrypha, Ecclesiasticus and the Wisdom of Solomon belong to the didactic tradition of wisdom literature.

Writings The third main division of the Hebrew Bible, the *ketuvim*; it is the *k* of Tanak.

Written torah (also called *written law*) See Oral torah.

Yahwist narrative (also called *Yahwist source*; abbreviated J) A reconstructed literary source lying behind the Torah/Pentateuch, written around 950 B.C.E. in Judah.

Yahweh The hypothetical pronounciation of the divine name YHWH; by some pronounced Yahveh. See YHWH.

Yahwist The author of the narrative source in the Torah/Pentateuch that favors the use of the divine name Yahweh. See Yahwist narrative.

YHWH (Yahweh) The sacred name of God in the Hebrew Bible; also known as the *tetragrammaton*; since Hebrew was written without vowels in ancient times, the four consonants YHWH contain no clue to their original pronunciation; they are generally rendered *Yahweh* in contemporary scholarship; in traditional Judaism, the name is not pronounced, but *Adonay* ("Lord") or something similar is substituted; in most English versions of the Bible the tetragrammaton is represented by "LORD" (or less frequently, "Jehovah").

Yom Kippur (Hebrew for "Day of Atonement") Annual day of fasting, penitence, and atonement, occurring in the fall on Tishri 10 (just after Rosh Hashanah); the most solemn and important occasion of the Jewish religious year.

Zadok A descendant of Aaron, he was a priest at David's court; he supported Solomon's succession, so his descendants had rights to the chief-priestly duties in the temple.

Zealot Someone zealous for the Torah; and in particular a member of a Jewish group, founded perhaps by Judas the Galilean in 6 C.E., made up of dedicated political activists that militarily opposed Greek then Roman rule in Palestine.

Zechariah A prophet and priest who returned to Jerusalem after Babylonian exile and encouraged the Jews to rebuild the temple; the book of Zechariah contains post-exilic visions and divine oracles.

Zedekiah (597-587) The last king of Judah.

Zephaniah One of the twelve prophets; a seventh century Judean prophet who proclaimed the coming Day of Yahweh.

Zerubbabel A member of the royal Davidic line, an heir to the throne of Judah, who led a return from Babylonian captivity in the sixth century B.C.E.; he was appointed governor of Judea by Cyrus, king of Persia.

Ziggurat (from Akkadian *ziqquratu*, "pinnacle, mountain top") Of Sumerian origin, a Mesopotamian pyramidal staged-temple tower of which the tower of Babel was one.

Zion (also called Mount Zion) The hill on which the city of Jerusalem first stood; David's royal palace and the temple of Yahweh were both located on Mount Zion; later Zion was used to refer to the entire city of Jerusalem; already in biblical times it began to symbolize the national homeland (see, for example, Psalm 137:1–6); in this latter sense it served as a focus for Jewish national-religious hopes of renewal over the centuries.

Zion theology The ideology in Israel that affirmed the divine promises to the house of David and the invulnerability of the city of Jerusalem.

Zipporah Wife of Moses, mother of Gershom, dauther of Jethro/Reuel.

INDEXES

INDEX OF SUBJECTS

Biblical poetry, 386-391
Biblical story, 17-29
bicolon, 388
Bildad, 433
Bilhah, 116, 127
Birthright, 113-114
Blessing, 58, 95, 111-120,
114, 117-119, 124,
133, 180, 192
Blood, 156, 172
Boaz, 447-448
Book of comfort, 328
Book of the covenant,
151-152, 156, 161, 294
Book of the torah, 195,
293-294
Book of the twelve, 209,
349-380
as a whole, 378
Assyrian period,
351-364
Babylonian period,
364-368
Persian period, 368-377
summary, 378-379
Book of Zerubbabel, 483
Bronze age, 95
Bronze serpent, 179
Burning bush, 132, 136,
222, 360, 498

C.E., 13
Cain, 72, 74
Caleb, 179
Call narrative, 214,
303-306, 310
Call to praise, 407
Campaigns of conquest,
218-227
Canaan, 14, 219
Canaanite religion, 208-209
Canon, 10
Carchemish, 352, 364
Carmel, Mount, 287-288
Case law, 152
Cassandra, 210
Casuistic law, 152
Centralization, 195
CH, 476
Chalcolithic period, 19
Chaldean, 93
Chaos, waters of 53-54,
282, 312
Charter covenant, 97
Cherubim, 68, 161, 282,
338
Child sacrifice, 109
Christian, 498
Christianity, 498
christos, 260, 498
Chronicler's history, 207,
385, 398-399, 474-487
as a whole, 485-486

Chronicles, 175, 478-481
Chronological dualism, 396
Chronology, 13, 45
Circumcision, 94, 99-102
City of David, 269
Clean and unclean,
167-168
Climactic parallelism,
388-89
Code of Eshnunna, 153
Code of Hammurabi,
153-154
Code of Lipit-Ishtar, 153
Code of Ur-Nammu, 153
Community rule, 495
Complaint psalms, 407-410
Complaint, 406
Complaints of Jeremiah,
330-331
Confessions of Jeremiah,
330-331
Conquest and settlement,
21-22
Conquest of Canaan,
216-235
internal revolt model,
231
migration model,
229-231
military model, 231
corvée, 282
Cosmic dualism, 396
Cosmology, 55, 149
Council of Trent, 491
couplet, 388
Covenant, 43, 80, 97, 116,
127, 131, 191-194,
214, 232-234
ancestral, 43
ark of, 222
charter, 97
creation, 43
cut a, 99
Davidic, 413
of circumcision, 99-102
parity, 97
royal grant, 97
Sinai, 44
structure, 192-193
suzerain-vassal, 97
Covenant banquet, 155
Covenant breaking,
157-158
Covenant code, 151, 196
Covenant confirmation,
154-156
Covenant remaking,
158-159
Covenant renewal, 198,
233-234
creatio ex nihilo, 54
Creation, 51-71, 160, 282,
311-312, 427-428

Creation-redemption,
311-312
Creation stories, ancient
middle eastern, 69-71
Creation theology, 427-428
Credo, 190-191
Creed, earliest, 190-191
Curse, 67, 192
Cycle, 92
Cyrus, 309, 313-314, 364,
368, 370, 481, 483

D, 40
Dagon, 248, 258-259
Damascus, 291
Dan, 157, 285, 287
Danel, 464
Daniel, 209, 397, 399,
463-473, 499
additions to, 465
apocalypses, 467-472
as a whole, 472
heroes, 465-467
Darius, 475, 481
Dathan, 176, 179
David, 122, 233, 254, 264,
314, 345, 358-359,
363, 405, 448-449,
477-480, 485
biographical sketch,
267
court history of, 270
covenant, 213-214
last days, 271
rise to power, 268-269,
273
David by Donatello, 4
David cycle, 267-272
Davidic covenant, 269
Davidic theology, 325
Day of atonement, 173-175
Day of Yahweh, 365,
373-375
Dead Sea Scrolls, 203, 457,
466, 494-496
Death, 67, 416-417
Deborah, 244-245
Decalogue, 359
ethical, 148-151
ritual, 159
Deir 'Alla, 180
Delilah, 248
Delphi, 230
Deluge tablet, 76
Destruction of Sennacherib,
276-277
Deuternomy, 294
Deutero-Isaiah, 301
Deuterocanonical, 491
deuteronomion, 184
Deuteronomist, 188, 196
Deuteronomistic historian,
198

Deuteronomistic history,
45, 198-199, 206-207,
277, 476, 485
Deuteronomy, 36, 40-41,
181, 206, 359, 484
authorship, 195-197
story line, 185
structure, 198
style and structure,
197-198
textual units, 197
devarim
DH, 198, 206
Diaspora Judaism, 26, 489
Diaspora, 10, 26, 458, 490
Dilmun, 63
Dispersion, 10, 371, 458,
491
distich, 388
Divine council, 58, 74, 76,
83, 161, 282, 304,
310-311, 338, 469-470
Divine kingship, 415-416
Divine name, 83, 138
Divine warrior, 143, 242,
397
Divine witnesses, 193
Divine-human
intermarriage, 73-74
Division of the kingdom,
284-286
Documentary hypothesis,
36
Dome, 55
Dreams, 120-121
Dtr, 198, 207
Dualism, 396-397, 495
Dumuzi and Enkimdu, 72
Dynastic succession,
269-271

E, 39
Ea, 50, 70
Early bronze age, 19
Early Israel, 21-22
Early Judaism, 26-29
Easter, 131
Ebal, Mount, 225-226
Ecclesiastes, 174, 391, 399,
429, 437, 451-454, 460
Ecclesiasticus, 391, 399,
491
Eden, 62-63, 344
edinu, 62
Edom, 112, 367-368, 373
Eglon, 226, 243
Egypt, 128, 406
creation theology,
69-70
Egyptian literature, 123
Egyptian wisdom literature,
430

Ehud, 243-244
ehyeh asher ehyeh, 360
ehyeh, 138
ekklesia, 452
El Elyon, 16, 96
El Shaddai, 16, 100
El, 96, 115, 208
Eldad, 177
Elders, 177
Elephantine papyri, 458
Eli, 257-258, 280, 281
Eliezer, 98
Elihu, 434
Elijah cycle, 286-289
Elijah, 148, 213, 286, 296, 338, 359, 373, 469, 471, 498
Elimelech, 445, 447
Eliphaz, 433
Elisha, 213, 288, 296
Elisha cycle, 289-291
Elkanah, 256
Elohim, 16, 36, 53, 100
elohim, 65
Elohist source, 36, 39-40, 87, 103-109
    and Aaron, 158
    covenant traditions, 148
    tradition, 213
Elyon, 96
Enki and Ninhursag, 63
Enki, 70
Enlil, 70
Enmeduranki, 73
Enoch, 72, 396, 470-471, 493
Enuma Elish, 66, 70-71
Ephraim, 120, 124
Ephron, 109
Eponym, 91
Esagila, 71
Esau toledot, 120
Esau, 111-113, 117-120, 128, 368
Eschatology, 395
eschaton, 395
Essenes, 494
Esther, 173, 398, 454-458, 460, 494
et-Tell, 225
Etemenanki, 84
Ethical decalogue, 148-152, 156
Ethical dualism, 396
Etiology, 221, 234
Europa, 74
Eve, 64
Evil-merodoch, 295
Exile, 18, 41, 44
Exodus from Egypt, 131, 141-143
Exodus, 18, 130-163, 213
    as a whole, 161-162
    chronology, 134

deliverance traditions, 132-144
    route of, 142
    story line, 132
    traditions, 161
Ezekiel, 169, 213, 316, 334-348, 368, 469-471
    as a whole, 346-347
    life and times, 336
    prophetic warnings, 337-342
Ezra memoirs, 483-484
Ezra, 175, 396, 449, 481-485

Faith, 195, 214
Fall of Jerusalem, 330
Fall, 65-66
Fallen ones, 74
Fear of God, 40, 104, 147, 151, 454
Fear of Yahweh, 425
Feast of booths, 174, 459, 484
Feast of tabernacles, 459
Feast of weeks, 190, 398, 459, 498
Fertile crescent, 16
Firmament, 55
First fruits, 190
First Isaiah, 300-309
First Isaiah, commission, 303-306
Firstborn, 113, 127, 140, 176, 279
Five scrolls, 251, 385, 398, 440-461
    as a whole, 458-460
Flood, 74-77
Flood archaeology, 76
Foreign nations, 342-344
Form criticism, 210, 405
Formal parallelism, 388-89
Former prophets, 203, 205-209
Four ages, 470

Gabriel, 494
Galatians, 499
Gandhi, Mahatma, 210
Garden of Eden, 61, 344, 499
Gath-hepher, 375
Gedaliah, 294, 330
Genealogy, 71
Generations, 60
Generations to Abram, 85
Genesis, 49-129
    themes, 126-128
Genesis 1-11, 49-89
    as a whole, 85-88
    story line, 51
Genesis 12-50, 90-129
    as a whole, 125-128

Genre, 405, 407
Gerizim, Mount, 225-226
Gezer, 115
Gibeath-haaraloth, 221
Gibeon, 218, 226-227, 232, 234
Gideon, 245-247
Gilboa, Mount, 267
Gilead, 356
Gilgal, 220-221, 261, 263
Gilgamesh, 76
Gilgamesh epic, 76-77
Glory of Yahweh, 336, 338, 340, 346
go'el, 447
God of the fathers, 127, 137
God, name of, 149
Gog, 346
Golden calf, 157-158
Golden calves, 285, 287
Goliath, 264
Gomer, 359-360
Goring ox, law of, 152
Goshen, 120, 124
Gospel, 497
Grain offering, 171-172
Great commandment, 185-187
Greek philosophy, 491

Ha-satan, 432
Habakkuk, 366-367, 496
Habakkuk pesher, 496-497
habiru, 135, 231
Hagar, 99, 116, 127
Haggai, 370-371, 374, 483
hagiographa, 384
halakah, 500-501
Ham, 80-81
Haman, 455-457
Hammurabi, 153-154
Hammurabi monument, 153
Hanamel, 328
Hananiah, 327, 465
Hannah, 256-257
Hannah's song, 257, 273
Hanukkah, 173, 471
har megiddo, 294
Haran, 85, 116, 128
Hasids, 467
Hazael, 289
Hazor, 218, 227, 229, 244
    archaeology of, 227
Heavenly lights, 57
Hebrew Bible, 9
Hebrew Scriptures, 9
Hebrew, 14, 134-135
Hebron, 128, 226, 268
Hellenism, 467
Hellenization, 467
Hesiod, 470
hevel, 452

Hezekiah, 179, 188-189, 195, 292-293, 306, 308-309, 481
Hiel, 224
High priest, 170
Hilkiah, 196, 293
Hiram, 282
Historical analysis, 12
Historical minimalism, 46
Historiography, 205, 207-208, 481
History, 213
Hittite laws, 154
Hittite treaties, 192
hochmah, 426
Holiness, 167
    cultic theory, 167
    hygiene theory, 167
Holiness code, 167, 175
Holiness laws, 167
Holiness spectrum, 169
Holy people, 170
Holy places, 169
Holy times, 172-174
Holy Trinity, 58
Holy war, 223-225, 263, 305
Holy, 167
Hophni, 258
Horeb, 136, 147, 185, 287, 289
Hosea, 190, 213, 290, 359-362
Hoshea, 291
House of David, 207, 286
Huldah, 294
Hur, 156
Hushai, 271
Hyksos, 133
Hymns, 410-414
    of creation, 412
    of Yahweh's kingship, 412

Iahudu, 295
Image of God, 58-60
Images, 149
Immanuel, 291, 306-308
Imprecation psalms, 410
In Egypt and the exodus, 21
Inclusion, 144, 425
Instruction literature, 430
Instruction of Amenemope, 430
Instructions for Merikare', 70
Invocation, 406
Io, 74
Isaac, 102-109
    birth announcement, 102-103
Isaiah, 190, 292, 299-317, 338
    as a whole, 316

Index of Text References

INDEX OF MODERN AUTHORS

INDEX OF FIGURES

INDEX OF TABLES

ABBREVIATIONS

B.C.E.	Before the Common Era
c.	circa, "about," used to indicate an approximate date
C.E.	Common Era
NRSV	New Revised Standard Version

CREDITS

Cover Cult mask from Hazor, 14-13th century B.C.E. Israel Museum IDAM 67-1195. See *Treasures of the Holy Land: Ancient Art from the Israel Museum*. New York: Metropolitan Museum of Art, 1986. Courtesy of the Israel Antiquities Authority. Photo © Israel Antiquities Authority, Jerusalem.

Page 4, Figure 1 David by Donatello, 1440. Museo Nazionale del Bargello, Florence, Italy. Photo by Barry Bandstra, July 1998.

Page 18, Figure 1 Ishtar Gate, Babylon. Istanbul Archaeological Museum, Istanbul. Photo by Barry Bandstra, April 1998.

Page 34, Figure 1 Studying Torah. Western wall, Jerusalem. Photo by Barry Bandstra, May 1996.

Page 50, Figure 1.1 Ea in the Apsu. Line drawing by Barry Bandstra, after a cylinder seal of the Akkadian period found at Ur. See Jeremy Black and Anthony Green, *Gods, Demons and Symbols of Ancient Mesopotamia. An Illustrated Dictionary*. London: British Museum, 1992; page 27, no. 19.

Page 84, Figure 1.4 The Ziggurat of Ur-Nammu. From Leonard Woolley, *Ur Excavations, Volume V: The Ziggurat and its Surroundings*. New York, 1939; plate 86.

Page 91, Figure 2.1 Asiatic Semites Arrive in Egypt. From C. R. Lepsius, *Denkmäler aus Ägypten und Äthiopien*. Berlin, 1849-1859; volume 2, plate 133.

Page 100, Figure 2.4 Circumcision. Line drawing by Barry Bandstra, after a Saqqara tomb painting from the Sixth Dynasty (2350-2000 B.C.E.).

Page 101 Ann Landers column, February 21, 1993, "Experts Divided over Circumcision." Courtesy of Ann Landers and Creators Syndicate.

Page 131, Figure 3.1 Photo of the Sinai peninsula from the Gemini II spacecraft, 1966. Courtesy of the National Aeronautics and Space Administration.

Page 135, Figure 3.3 Brickmaking in Egypt. Line drawing by Barry Bandstra after Norman de Garis Davies, *The Tomb of Rekh-mi-Rê at Thebes*. New York: Metropolitan Museum of Art Egyptian Expedition, 1943; plate 58.

Page 153, Figure 3.5 Stele of Hammurabi. The Louvre, Paris. Courtesy of Gianni Dagli Orti/Corbis.

Page 165, Figure 4.1 Mount Sinai Range. View from the top of Jebel Musa, Sinai, Egypt. Photo by Barry Bandstra, May 1996.

Page 184, Figure 5.1 Moses by Michelangelo, 1515. San Pietro in Vincoli, Rome, Italy. Photo by Barry Bandstra, July 1998.

Page 189, Figure 5.2 Arad Sanctuary, Arad, Israel. Photo by Barry Bandstra, May 1996.

Page 204, Figure 1 Isaiah Scroll from Qumran. See John C. Trever, *Scrolls from Qumran Cave I*. Jerusalem: Albright Institute of Archaeological Research, 1972. Courtesy of John C. Trever.

Page 217, Figure 6.1 Jericho Neolithic Tower, Jericho, West Bank. Photo by Barry Bandstra, May 1987.

Page 232, Figure 6.6 Merneptah Stele, First Historical Mention of the Name Israel. The Egyptian Museum, Cairo, Egypt. Photo by Barry Bandstra, May 1987.

Page 237, Figure 7.1 Portrait of a Captured Philistine. Relief from the main temple of Ramses III (1193-1162 B.C.E.), south tower, 2nd pylon, 20th Dynasty (1196-1080 B.C.E.), New Kingdom. Medinet Habu, West Thebes, Thebes, Egypt. Courtesy of Art Resource, New York.

Page 245, Figure 7.4 Megiddo Ivory. Line drawing by Barry Bandstra after G. Loud, *The Megiddo Ivories*. Oriental Institute Publications, 52. Chicago: University of Chicago, 1939; page 13, plate 4. Also see *Treasures of the Holy Land: Ancient Art from the Israel Museum*. New York: Metropolitan Museum of Art, 1986; pages 148-149, no. 69. Israel Museum, IDAM 38.780.

Page 254, Figure 8.1 David by Michelangelo, 1501-1504. Galleria dell'Accademia, Florence, Italy. Photo by Barry Bandstra, July 1998.

Page 265, Figure 8.5 Philistine Anthropoid Coffin, Rockefeller Museum, Jerusalem, Israel. Photo by Barry Bandstra, June 1979.

Page 276, Figure 9.1 Assyrian Relief of the Siege of Lachish. ©Werner Forman/Corbis. Courtesy of Corbis.

Page 280, Figure 9.3 Horned Altar, Beersheba, Israel. Photo by Barry Bandstra, May 1996.

Page 283, Figure 9.4 Solomon's Temple. Line drawing by Barry Bandstra after Volkmar Fritz, "Temple Architecture: What Can Archaeology Tell Us About Solomon's Temple?" Biblical Archaeology Review July/August 1987, p. 41.

Page 286, Figure 9.5 House of David Inscription. Line drawing by Barry Bandstra after Avraham Biran and Joseph Naveh, "An Aramaic Stele Fragment from Tel Dan." *Israel Exploration Journal* 43/2-3 (1993): 81-98.

Page 290, Figure 9.6 Shalmaneser III and Jehu, Black Obelisk of Shalmaneser, British Museum, London, Great Britain. Photo by Barry Bandstra, March 1998.

Page 300, Figure 10.1 Seven-headed Serpent. Line drawing by Barry Bandstra after Rivka Merhav (ed.), *Treasures of Bible Lands.* Tel Aviv: Tel Aviv Museum, Modan Publishers; no. 16.

Page 305, Figure 10.4 Ivory Plaque of a Winged Protector, from Samaria. Israel Museum IDAM 33.2572. Courtesy of the Israel Antiquities Authority. See *Treasures of the Holy Land: Ancient Art from the Israel Museum.* New York: Metropolitan Museum of Art, 1986; pages 166-168, no. 82.

Page 319, Figure11.1 Jeremiah by Donatello, 1423-1425. Museo dell'Opera del Duomo, Florence, Italy. Photo by Barry Bandstra, July 1998.

Page 329, Figure 11.4 Lachish Letter III. Line drawing by Barry Bandstra after Harry Torczyner, *Lachish I (Tell ed Duweir): The Lachish Letters.* Oxford: Oxford University Press, 1938.

Page 335, Figure 12.1 Valley of Dry Bones, Dura-Europos Synagogue. C. H. Kraeling, ed., *The Excavations at Dura-Europos,* Final Report VIII, Part 1. New Haven: Yale University Press, 1956. Plate LXIX. Panel NC1, Ezekiel, the Destruction and Restoration of National Life, Section A. Courtesy of Yale University Press.

Page 350, Figure 1 Martin Luther King, Jr. Speaking from Lincoln Memorial, August 28, 1963. Courtesy of Flip Schulke/Corbis.

Page 384, Figure 1 Nespekasuti, Scribe of Karnak. Courtesy of Archivo Iconografico, S.A./Corbis.

Page 403, Figure 14.1 Plaque of a musician, Old Babylonian period from Ischali, Iraq. Courtesy of the Oriental Institute of the University of Chicago. See H. Frankfort, *The Art and Architecture of the Ancient Orient.* London: Penguin, 1954. Plate 59b.

Page 404, Figure 14.2 Three captive lyrists. Assyrian relief. British Museum, London, Great Britain. Courtesy of Art Resource, New York.

Page 422, Figure 15.1 Cover of *Life's Little Instruction Book* by H. Jackson Brown reprinted by permission of the publisher, Rutledge Hill Press, Inc.

Page 423, Hagar the Horrible, 12/13/83. Courtesy of King Features Syndicate.

Page 427, Figure 15.2 Woman at the Window. From *A Guide to the Babylonian and Assyrian Antiquities.* London: British Museum, 1922; plate 41, no. 13.

Page 441, Figure 16.1 Love and Death. Line drawing by Barry Bandstra after the sculpture of a wedded couple on the lid of an Etruscan sarcophagus. See Axel Boëthius, et al. (eds.), *Etruscan Culture, Land, and People.* New York: Columbia University Press, 1963; figure 476.

Page 448, Figure 16.3 Threshing Floor, on the road between Bethlehem and Beit-Sahur, West Bank. Photo by Barry Bandstra, May 1996.

Page 463, Figure 17.1 Atomic Cloud. Courtesy of The National Archives/Corbis.

Page 463, "Once By the Pacific" by Robert Frost. From *The Poetry of Robert Frost.* Copyright © 1956 by Robert Frost. Copyright © 1928, 1969 by Henry Holt & Co., Inc. Reprinted by permission of Henry Holt & Co., Inc.

Page 469, Figure 17.3 Ishtar Gate, Babylon. From Eckhard Unger, *Babylon: Die Heilige Stadt nach der Beschreibung der Babylonier.* Berlin: deGruyter, 1931; plate opposite title page.

Page 475, Figure 18.1 A Mede Officer and Two Persian Guards before Darius the Great, Persepolis. Courtesy of Gianni Dagli Orti/Corbis.

Page 489, Figure 1 Model of Jerusalem in the first century C.E., including the Herodian Temple. Holy-land Hotel, Jerusalem, Israel. Photo by Barry Bandstra, July 1987.

Page 495, Figure 3 Qumran Cave 4, Qumran, West Bank. Photo by Barry Bandstra, May 1984.

Note: all time lines, maps, and other diagrams are by Barry Bandstra.

Archaeology

| Early Bronze | Middle Bronze | Late Bronze | Iron | Persian | Greek | Roman |

Biblical History

- Ancestors
  - Abraham
  - Isaac
  - Jacob
- In Egypt
  - Moses
  - Exodus from Egypt
- Judges
  - Conquest of Canaan
  - Joshua
  - Invasion of the Sea Peoples
  - Yahwist
  - Elohist
- Israelite Kingdoms
  - David and Solomon
  - Fall of Israel/Samaria
  - Deuteronomist
  - Priestly
- Exile to Babylonia
- Fall of Judah/Jerusalem
- Maccabean revolt
- Pentateuch completed
- Prophets completed
- Writings completed
- Jesus of Nazareth
- 1st Jewish Revolt
- Destr. of Jerusalem
- Tanak completed
- Mishnah completed

Mesopotamian History

- Ur III
- 1st Babylonian Dyn.
  - Hammurabi
- Old Hittite Empire
- Kingdom of Mitanni
- Assyrian Empire
- New Assyria
  - Tiglath-Pileser III
  - Sennacherib
- New Babylonian Empire
  - Nebuchadnezzar
  - Cyrus the Great (Medo-Persia)
  - Alexander the Great (Greece)

Egyptian History

- Middle Kingdom
- 2d Intermed.
  - Hyksos invasion of Egypt
  - Expulsion of Hyksos
- New Kingdom
  - Amarna age
  - Rameses II
  - Sea Peoples defeated by Rameses III
- Persian conquest
- Ptolemaic rule
- Roman rule

B.C.E. 2100 1800 1500 1200 900 600 300 0 300 C.E.